★

THE U.S. MARINES
AND
AMPHIBIOUS WAR

★

EDITORIAL BOARD OF
THE PRINCETON UNIVERSITY MARINE CORPS
HISTORY PROJECT

~~~~~

GORDON A. CRAIG, *CHAIRMAN*
JOSEPH R. STRAYER
ROBERT G. ALBION
FRANCIS R. B. GODOLPHIN

THE U.S. MARINES AND AMPHIBIOUS WAR

Its Theory, and Its Practice in the Pacific

★

*BY JETER A. ISELY
AND PHILIP A. CROWL*

★

PRINCETON, NEW JERSEY
PRINCETON UNIVERSITY PRESS
1951

*Reprinted with permission of the
Princeton University Press
By
The Marine Corps Association
Quantico, Virginia
December 1979*

*Copyright, 1951, Princeton University Press
London: Geoffrey Cumberlege, Oxford University Press*

PREFACE AND ACKNOWLEDGMENTS

SINCE the end of the war, the American public has been deluged with operational accounts of battles and campaigns, memoirs of generals and admirals, and résumés by front-line correspondents. So many volumes have rolled from the presses that it might appear reasonable to suppose there is nothing left to write about the recent conflict. Closer examination of the mass of war literature, however, will reveal that there has yet been little attempt at scientific analysis of the doctrines and techniques employed in World War II, and this is certainly true of the Pacific campaigns as a whole.

This volume is an attempt partially to correct the existing situation. It was planned not as another history of operations but as a study of the Marine Corps' development of a doctrine of amphibious fighting in the period between the two World Wars and of the application of that doctrine in the Pacific. While the actual events of the amphibious attacks are described in some detail, the emphasis is always focussed on the theory of amphibious war as exemplified and developed in practice. This centers the study on the marines and an analysis of their tactical and logistical problems in the Pacific, but effort has been made to round out the picture with strategical considerations when pertinent, and in so far as is possible with Japanese documents existing in this country, to sketch in the background of military decisions made by the enemy.

The people of the United States have generally overlooked the place of amphibious war in the security of the nation. Perhaps the oversight is a reflection of the country's earlier isolationist feeling, fortified by the fact that when America entered World War I her troops debarked through friendly ports, were taken to the front by road and rail, and there with relative ease deployed on dry land for combat. The leisurely procedure of 1917–1918 was denied the United States in World War II, and possibly will never again occur—in any event national security demands that recurrence not be relied upon.

Unless America plans to fight defensively, and unless and until friendly powers are well secured on the strategic islands of the Seven Seas and on the important littoral of the Eurasian land mass, the United States must be prepared to deploy tactically on water and to land on shores held by hostile powers. Certainly such was the case in

World War II, and to the United States Navy and the Marine Corps goes the bulk of the credit that an up-to-date doctrine for such fighting was at hand in December 1941. Airborne troops and supplies were valuable during the Second World War, and further developments in that direction are under way. But whether or not airborne tactics and techniques supplant those of deployment on the sea as used from 1942 through 1945 in the Pacific and elsewhere, the problem of landing on shores held by an enemy remains. History is of value only if it helps to solve pending and future problems. There is always a tendency in some military quarters to fight the next war with the weapons and tactics of the last, and the Editorial Board and authors will consider their mission accomplished only if this volume stimulates and helps toward further tactical developments.

The Marine Corps and the Navy have cooperated in the preparation of this work, making available all sources save those which might jeopardize current security; this means that nearly all sources dated up to the end of World War II were available. The volume was sponsored by the Marine Corps, but is in no way an official history. At the outset, the Commandant of the Marine Corps stated that any alteration of the final manuscript by officers of the Corps would be "restricted to the correction of factual data and the deletion of matter which may be in violation of then existing security regulations." It was further said that the Commandant "will have no competence to alter or modify the findings of the authors or the conclusions reached in the study." *

This agreement has been carried out in full by the Commandant and by his representatives. Deletions from the original and final manuscripts made for security reasons are so few and so insignificant as to be negligible. The authors have been free to reach their own interpretations, and those expressed in this study must be attributed to the authors alone, and are not in any way the official views of the Marine Corps, the Department of the Navy, or the Department of Defense.

Army, navy, and marine officers as well as military historians both in official and unofficial capacities have kindly lent their advice and criticism when called upon. A number of seminars on various aspects of the subject were held at Princeton during the years 1947-1949, attended by officers who had participated in the events under study. Both the authors and the Editorial Board found these sessions inspiring, and in each case they brought to light forgotten documents or pointed up new areas for research. In addition, early drafts of

* Agreement between Princeton University and the Commandant of the Marine Corps, approved by James V. Forrestal, Secretary of the Navy, 28 April 1947, Princeton University Library.

chapters were mimeographed and circulated, resulting in a large collection of criticisms, and these letters are now deposited in the Princeton University Library. Those readers who follow references will find acknowledgment to such assistance, but since the individuals involved are in no way responsible for the interpretations contained in this volume and since they did not speak in an official capacity, they are referred to without notation of rank or position.

A listing of all who have helped in writing this history is impossible, but those to whom the Editorial Board and authors feel most indebted are accorded our warmest appreciation here: Hanson W. Baldwin, William H. P. Blandy, Charles W. Boggs, Jr., Bernard M. Brodie, William W. Buchanan, Clifton B. Cates, Richard L. Conolly, Charles H. Corlett, Edward A. Craig, W. Frank Craven, Robert E. Cushman, Jr., Morton L. Deyo, Edward M. Earle, Merrit A. Edson, Gordon D. Gayle, Wallace M. Greene, Jr., Kent Roberts Greenfield, Franklin A. Hart, Field Harris, Robert D. Heinl, Jr., Harry W. Hill, James D. Hittle, Carl D. Hoffman, Robert E. Hogaboom, Frank O. Hough, Leroy P. Hunt, Clayton C. Jerome, Horace E. Knapp, Jr., Ernest J. King, Victor H. Krulak, John S. Letcher, Eugenia Lejeune, Harry B. Liversedge, Francis B. Loomis, Arthur T. Mason, Vernon E. Megee, Frank D. Merrill, John Miller, Jr., Ralph J. Mitchell, Samuel E. Morison, Louis Morton, David R. Nimmer, Arthur S. Nevins, Chester W. Nimitz, Grace S. Person, Edwin A. Pollock, John N. Rentz, Frederick G. Richards, William E. Riley, James P. Riseley, Presley M. Rixey, Keller E. Rockey, William W. Rogers, Harry Schmidt, John T. Selden, Lemuel C. Shepherd, Jr., Robert Sherrod, Merwin H. Silverthorn, Albert F. Simpson, Julian C. Smith, Oliver P. Smith, Robert R. Smith, Edward W. Snedeker, Raymond A. Spruance, James R. Stockman, Leland S. Swindler, Gerald C. Thomas, Merrill B. Twining, Pedro A. del Valle, Alexander A. Vandegrift, Donald M. Weller, Walter W. Wensinger, Louis E. Woods, Thomas A. Wornham, and John L. Zimmerman.

Finally, the working staff of this project has been of incalculable help. The research assistants were Gordon B. Turner, Kenneth W. Condit, Eve S. Martin, Thomas B. Hartmann, and Barbara Britten. The maps were drawn by Harry M. McCully. Rose F. Greenberg typed the manuscript.

J.A.I. and P.A.C.

Princeton, N.J., and
Washington, D.C.
August, 1950

CONTENTS

PREFACE AND ACKNOWLEDGMENTS		v
I.	MISSION OF THE U.S. MARINES, THE AMPHIBIOUS ASSAULT	3
II.	EVOLUTION OF AN AMPHIBIOUS DOCTRINE, 1901–1934	14
III.	TRAINING FOR AMPHIBIOUS WAR, 1934–1942	45
IV.	BACKGROUND FOR GUADALCANAL, THE DECISION TO ATTACK	72
V.	INITIAL OFFENSIVES, SOLOMONS–NEW BRITAIN–NEW GUINEA	99
VI.	THE FIRST MAJOR ASSAULT, TARAWA	192
VII.	THE MARSHALLS, GAINING MOMENTUM	253
VIII.	THE MARIANAS, BASES FOR THE A.A.F.	310
IX.	PALAU AND THE PHILIPPINES: MARINES IN SUPPORT OF MACARTHUR	392
X.	THE SUPREME TEST, IWO JIMA	432
XI.	OKINAWA, SPRINGBOARD TO JAPAN	531
XII.	AMPHIBIOUS PROGRESS, 1941–1945	580
REFERENCES		591
INDEX		627

LIST OF MAPS

1.	The Central and Western Pacific	75
2.	Theater boundaries, showing change made by the July 1942 directive	91
3.	The Solomons–New Britain–New Guinea region	100
4.	Guadalcanal	102
5.	The Ichicki attack on Henderson Field, August 1942	141
6.	The Kawaguchi attack, September 1942	144
7.	The attack of the Sendai, October 1942	147
8.	Landings, Central and Northern Solomons, June 1943 to February 1944	169
9.	Marines clear Dampier Strait, December 1944	187
10.	The Gilberts and Marshalls	195
11.	Betio Islet with insert of Tarawa Atoll	209
12.	Kwajalein Islet with insert of Kwajalein Atoll	259
13.	The islets of Roi-Namur	279
14.	Principal landings on Eniwetok Atoll, February 1944	295
15.	Japan and the islands to the south	313
16.	The struggle for Saipan, June–July 1944	321
17.	Tinian	353
18.	Guam	375
19.	Peleliu and adjacent islands	405
20.	The Philippines	425
21.	Capture of Iwo Jima, February–March 1945	477
22.	Okinawa and nearby islands	537
23.	Southern Okinawa	545

★

THE U.S. MARINES
AND
AMPHIBIOUS WAR

★

CHAPTER I

MISSION OF THE U.S. MARINES, THE AMPHIBIOUS ASSAULT

"My military education and experience in the First World War has all been based on roads, rivers, and railroads," said General George C. Marshall late in 1943. "During the last two years, however, I have been acquiring an education based on oceans and I've had to learn all over again. Prior to the present war I never heard of any landing-craft except a rubber boat. Now I think about little else." [1]

Marshall was not alone in being unprepared for the amphibious operations that were a great part of America's effort in World War II. The United States Army as a whole suffered from this deficiency, and the oversight was understandable. The lack of funds was such that, until a crisis arose in Europe, few army garrisons larger than an understrength regiment existed, and once the army began to expand, emphasis was necessarily placed on land tactics. Nor had the army's ranking commanders clearly seen the need for amphibious training. In the period after the Versailles Treaty, the War Department had premised its reorganization on the recurrence of a one-front war of position, and until the Nazis overran France, army planners continued to think in terms of such dock facilities as those of Cherbourg and Le Havre for the easy transfer of America's land power onto the European continent. Hitler's success in the spring and summer of 1940 shattered these illusions. "On 26 June 1940," laconically remarks an official army historian, "the 1st and 3d Divisions were directed to practice landing operations." [2]

That the United States Army was able so quickly to train troops for crossing beaches held by hostile nations is attributable to its own flexibility and leadership and, equally important, to the availability for its guidance of a sound body of amphibious doctrine previously drawn up by the United States Navy and the Marine Corps. For about two decades before the outbreak of the Second World War the marines had been establishing themselves as specialists in amphibious warfare. Thus they were ready in 1940 with a cadre of officers who began indoctrinating army troops in amphibious matters; and, more significantly, they provided a doctrine for amphibious operations which was drawn from Navy and Marine Corps publications and circularized as a United States Army field manual.

Military doctrine, the working principles of war, is distinct from military techniques, the manner and means of implementing those principles. In the field of amphibious techniques, largely because of budgetary restrictions, the marines still had a long way to go at the time of the attack on Pearl Harbor, and improved techniques throughout the course of the struggle were made by all the armed services of the United States, assisted by the British. The amphibious doctrine of the United States Marines, however, underwent no basic change during World War II. It was used repeatedly by all the principal Allied powers, except Russia. The Germans also were unprepared for amphibious warfare, and for this reason, partly, were unable to cross the narrow English Channel. In fact, both the Germans and the Russians, being land-minded, failed to exploit vigorously their possession of the littoral of the Black and Baltic Seas to turn the flanks of their opponent; but the Western powers missed fewer such opportunities. As General Alexander A. Vandegrift observed after the defeat of the Axis nations: "Despite its outstanding record as a combat force in the past war, the Marine Corps' far greater contribution to victory was doctrinal: that is, the fact that the basic amphibious doctrines which carried Allied troops over every beachhead of World War II had been largely shaped—often in the face of uninterested or doubting military orthodoxy—by U.S. Marines, and mainly between 1922 and 1935." [3]

It was not difficult to master such a doctrine once it had been developed. There is nothing occult about amphibious fighting. Man has conducted landing operations since the beginnings of naval history. The British have always been interested in amphibious strategy, and are continuing to make notable contributions to its study. Over a century ago, moreover, a keen continental student of military history, Antoine Henri Jomini, enumerated the broad precepts on which all of the purely amphibious phases of war have been based. These were to deceive the enemy as to the point of debarkation, to select a beach with hydrographic and terrain conditions favorable to the attacker, to employ naval guns in preparing the way for the troops, to land artillery at the earliest practicable moment, and strenuously to push the invasion by seizing the high ground commanding the landing area, thus securing the beachhead from enemy guns, allowing a quick build up of supplies ashore, and permitting the transfer of the conflict from amphibious to land warfare.[4]

Technological developments, especially those of the present century, have complicated amphibious warfare. The component parts of the amphibious attack force charged with the mission of effecting a landing from the sea have increased, and this in turn has made more difficult that careful integration of all arms and troop movements needed to gain success. In the first years of this century, technological improvements apparently strengthened the defender more than the attacker; this was most strongly felt in the fields of gunnery and airpower. It was believed that offshore mines, torpedoes, and land-based weapons would prevent naval gunfire support for the troops engaged in getting ashore. The British fiasco at Gallipoli in 1915 seemed to confirm such fears, and many military writers concluded that crossing a hostile beach was no longer feasible. Alexander Kiralfy contended that the industrial revolution had given any guardian of the continent of Europe both superior defensive weapons and a high land mobility. These would prevent operations against the coasts of Europe, and therefore that continent could best be entered by striking through the relatively backward areas of Asia. Liddell Hart was convinced that the great mobility and flexibility of airpower had weighted the scales heavily in favor of the defender. "A landing on a foreign coast in face of hostile troops," he said, "has always been one of the most difficult operations of war. It has now become much more difficult, indeed almost impossible, because of the vulnerable target which a convoy of transports offers to the defender's air force as it approaches the shore. Even more vulnerable to air attack is the process of disembarkation in open boats." [5]

But the United States Marine Corps, despite improvements in aircraft, remained confident that such beaches as those at Gallipoli could be seized and secured. The British had failed to take the Dardanelles because of faulty doctrine, ineffective techniques, poor leadership, and an utter lack of coordination between the services. Fortified by this surmise the United States Marines, in collaboration with the navy, and acting to fulfill the mission assigned by the Joint Board of the Army and Navy, the predecessor of the Joint Chiefs of Staff, began stressing the study of amphibious warfare in their schools and putting their ideas to practice in amphibious exercises. They tailored their weapons and tactical units to fit on shipboard, and started compiling data for "combat-loading," which is planned stowage of equipment and supplies in accordance with the anticipated situation ashore, so that these may be rapidly unloaded in the sequence needed. Other and equally important aspects of deploying land strength from out of the sea into combat at the water's edge were analyzed and tested. These included designing new craft for the ship-to-shore movement, utilizing aircraft and submarine reconnaissance for improved intelligence, forming shore parties (called pioneers) to handle supplies, installing radio communications in order to assure a continuing high degree of coordination, and experimenting with the specialist groups needed to control naval gunfire and close air strikes accurately. Although hampered by inadequate

Congressional appropriations before the outbreak of World War II in Europe, the navy and marines led the way in developing close air support for the troops below. Such a concept came easily for the marines, since they had employed close air support in Nicaragua as early as the 1920's and since striking power from the air is similar to supporting naval gunfire, so far as amphibious doctrine is concerned.[6]

Thus the marines in 1940 had a sound amphibious doctrine based in part on experimentation and in principle fully abreast of all the technological advances which might help the attacker. Although the up-to-date doctrine formulated by the marines was not difficult of comprehension, the training of army troops and recently enlisted marines and the mass production of equipment were manifold and complex problems. Here both the navy and the marines were of assistance to the army. The navy had worked the doctrine out in conjunction with the marines, and was after all principally responsible for setting the troops ashore with proper protection. General Dwight D. Eisenhower in an interview after the war succinctly stated the navy's responsibility, but he seems largely to have forgotten the amphibious training and experience his troops needed before setting foot on the coast of Normandy. "You know an amphibious landing is not a particularly difficult thing," he said, "but it's a touchy and delicate thing, and anything can go wrong. In some ways, from the land fellow's viewpoint, it is one of the simplest operations. You put your men in boats and as long as you get well-trained crews to take the boats in, it is the simplest deployment in the world—the men can go nowhere else except to the beach."[7]

Eisenhower's words bear eloquent tribute not only to the navy, but to the fact that the landing phase of the Normandy campaign was relatively easy. Had he served in the Central Pacific where heavy opposition at the water's edge was the rule rather than the exception, his reaction might have been different. The most important contribution of the United States Marines to the history of modern warfare rests in their having perfected the doctrine and techniques of amphibious warfare to such a degree as to be able to cross and secure a very energetically defended beach. It was this aspect of amphibious development which led the brilliant and iconoclastic contemporary British student of military history, Major-General John F. C. Fuller, to conclude that amphibious warfare had been "revolutionized" by what was, "in all probability . . . the most far-reaching tactical innovation of the war."[8]

There are two prerequisites to a successful amphibious operation. These are secure lines of communications from rear bases into the zone of conflict, and command of the sea and air around the objective.

Lines of communication may be rather widespread, but the commander on the offensive must be reasonably assured of the safety of his convoys and shipping moving toward the objective before undertaking an amphibious operation. This applies not only to troop and cargo transports accompanying the attack force, but also to the shipping required for the later build up, on which in turn depends the strengthening of the newly acquired position and its subsequent use in the war. Likewise, the target itself must be isolated if the amphibious operation is to be successful. If the objective is a small island, command of the sea and air alone will bottle up the enemy; but if the lodgment is being made on a larger land mass, it is decidedly advantageous to have many of the defender's forces contained elsewhere, as along the Eastern front during the Normandy operation. In any case, the defensive positions along the selected beaches must be, in so far as is possible, destroyed or neutralized, and the tactical mobility of the forces available to the enemy must be curtailed by air strikes, paratroopers, naval guns, and if within range, by artillery firing from friendly shores. Otherwise, as is sometimes the case in non-industrialized regions of the globe, the attacker can rely on geographical obstacles such as a desert, a deep river, or a mountain range to keep the defender from concentrating for a counterblow against the beachhead during the critical juncture of the landing.[9]

Holding lines of communications and isolating the objective for an amphibious attack are among the missions of the United States Navy and the Air Forces, and involve a complicated employment of all aspects of sea-air power. These two services carried out their missions in a commendable fashion during World War II, but this volume treats in detail only those aspects of naval warfare which mainly engaged the marines, namely the seizure of advanced bases in the Pacific. Here the mission of gaining and holding command of the sea and air was borne principally by the navy with its aircraft carriers, while land-based air played an important role under General Douglas MacArthur in the Southwest Pacific, but a decidedly secondary role in the landings on Guadalcanal and Tulagi and in the drive across the Central Pacific. The part played by carriers was generally dependent upon geography. Land-based air was usually available to the attack force commander operating adjacent to large land masses, although it should be noted that on three important occasions MacArthur relied on the greater mobility of carrier air to increase the range of his advances. These were the invasions of Hollandia in Dutch New Guinea, and of Leyte and Luzon Islands in the Philippines.

Without exception, each of the campaigns in the Central Pacific saw the navy and its carrier-based air arm support the greater part of the burden of securing the lines of communication and of isolating the area of the objective. Once a target was seized, it was immediately exploited as a forward base for bombers and reconnaissance planes, and as an air, and, sometimes, a naval base to assist in holding the lines of communication into the forward area.

Given secure lines of communications, there are but two methods of projecting land power overseas. The first requires no isolation of a target. It is the simple task of ferrying men and commercially loaded supplies across the oceans and docking them in friendly ports for subsequent deployment against the enemy, such as the transport of United States troops to France in the First World War.

The other is the amphibious operation. It involves a tactical deployment on the sea (recently, sometimes supplemented by airborne troops and supplies) and movement against a hostile shore with the immediate objective of securing a beachhead and the ultimate objective of shifting from amphibious to land warfare in order to bring defeat to the enemy. Of course amphibious operations are not all alike. The movement may be either ship-to-shore or shore-to-shore, or a combination of both, depending upon the distance to the target from the staging base; but this makes relatively little difference in the nature of the operation. The degree of opposition encountered at the beach is the important criterion. The amphibious operation that meets no resistance or only light and perhaps in places sporadic or moderate resistance at the beach is relatively simple in execution. Such, in general, were the landings in Europe and in the South and Southwest Pacific. The amphibious operation characterized by heavy and unavoidable resistance at the water's edge is so different that it warrants a distinctive subclassification; this is the type of landing the marines frequently encountered in crossing the Central Pacific, and in this study it is called the *amphibious assault*.

The defender may or may not choose to resist along a particular beach. There was not, in truth, anywhere else that he could defend on many of the small islands of the Central Pacific. Also, previous to and throughout most of the Pacific War, it was correctly assumed by the Japanese that the invader was most vulnerable just as he tried to set foot on shore. In this connection, however, the striking power of America's naval gunfire and close air support became so formidable and so feared by the Japanese that late in the war, at Okinawa, they evacuated their beach defenses before final preparations for the attack began. Furthermore, unless the target is a small island, it is probable that, should the defender enjoy great tactical mobility, inland concentrations at vital communications centers are preferable to committing men and material to widely dispersed perimeter positions. Whether or not the defender selects to resist along a specific beach, the right of such choice should be, if possible, taken from him by the attacking commander who, after all, picks the point of debarkation. For these reasons, the unopposed or lightly opposed amphibious operation is usually realized against a large land mass or amid a group of many islands where the attacking commander has the opportunity to employ strategic maneuver in selecting one of a number of feasible landing areas and to make tactical feints in order to throw his enemy off balance and gain surprise. In other words, only when operating against a large land mass or when threatening one of many adjacent islands, can the commander on the offensive fully exploit the initiative that is his and bend the enemy to his will. Under such circumstances the attacker should always fulfill Jomini's first precept for amphibious warfare; that is, he should deceive the enemy. In short, the commander implementing the landing should take advantage of the fact that if his opponent is compelled to guard an extensive coast line, then the opponent cannot be strong at every point.

Securing a beachhead at a place where enemy resistance is weak or altogether absent is but the application of common sense to amphibious strategy. Vandegrift, in reporting on the Guadalcanal-Tulagi campaign, phrased it neatly: "A comparison of the several landings leads to the inescapable conclusion that landings should not be attempted in the face of organized resistance if, by any combination of march or maneuver, it is possible to land unopposed and undetected at a point within striking distance of the objective." [10]

Almost all the beachheads won by the Allies in the Solomons during the Pacific War resulted from unopposed or lightly opposed landings. The same was true of most if not all of those in the Southwest Pacific Area. Robert Sherwood characterizes MacArthur's strategy against the Japanese as one of "Hit 'em where they ain't!" [11] This was made possible by a combination of geography and good leadership. MacArthur, always advancing along relatively large land masses or through a multitude of possible island objectives, turned in a brilliant strategical and tactical performance of avoiding heavily contested beaches. Likewise Eisenhower's operation against Normandy in June 1944 was a superbly executed landing. Ruse and deception plus the employment of tactical air power curtailed the enemy's land mobility, so that there was relatively little resistance along most of the Allied beaches.

But since the commander of the amphibious operation can never be sure that he will be able to strike at a lightly held coast, he should always plan for a beach assault. Unless intelligence can insure an uncontested beach, the unopposed or lightly opposed amphibious operation should never differ from the amphibious assault in the planning phase, and should change only when in the course of execution the resistance encountered so permits. Here again, Eisenhower's Normandy operation affords an excellent example. He was compelled for logistical reasons to establish as short a line of communications to his bases in England as was feasible within the given strategical picture. Similarly, he needed harbors in order rapidly to build up a reserve of men, supplies, and equipment and to shift from amphibious to land warfare; the beaches he selected at the northern base of the Cotentin Peninsula were excellent for these purposes. The Germans were led to believe the main effort would come on to the northeastward, across the Calais coast, and the enemy was caught unawares. Properly, however, the employment of tactical land-based air and naval gunfire support, as well as beach logistics, had been planned just as if an amphibious assault were inevitable. This was necessitated by the threatening nature of the German defensive installations at the base of the Cotentin Peninsula, should the enemy choose to man them heavily with first-class troops. Moreover, although the Germans were caught off balance strategically, they happened to have a division on maneuvers along one set of the Allied beaches (code name, "Omaha"), where considerable opposition was encountered. Taken as a whole, however, lodgment on Normandy was relatively easy, thanks to Eisenhower's skill as a strategist and to the excellent plans and support of his staff and his air and naval arms.[12] Or, to state it another way, the assault began, not along the coast, but after the beachhead had been secured, in the breakthrough at St. Lô. As Eisenhower himself was able to recall five and one-half years later, "a landing" on "a continental land mass . . . is nothing but a prelude to a campaign." [13]

Only in the Central Pacific was the amphibious assault almost always inevitable. It was, in fact, the apparent necessity of driving across the Central Pacific in the event of a war with Japan that caused the marines to devote virtually all of their attention to amphibious warfare during the period of armistice between the two world conflicts. After the Washington Conference of 1921–1922 went far in making possible later Japanese dominance of Far Eastern waters, the basic war plans of the United States Navy directed the seizure of small islands or atolls in the Central Pacific as advanced naval bases essential to the projection of America's military strength against the Japanese. Normally these plans were premised on the assumption that the United States would fight offensively and alone, without allies; [14] and the main drive against the Japanese was, in accordance with these plans, across the Central Pacific, despite the fact that when the struggle came the United States already had bases in the South and Southwest Pacific and assistance throughout the war from the

British Commonwealth. Only by controlling the mid-Pacific could the United States Navy economically and quickly strangle Japan. It should be further emphasized that the marines became just as important an adjunct of the Army Air Forces in the Pacific as of the navy; for without those amphibious assaults which captured airfields for army pilots, intensive bombing of Japan would have been greatly delayed, and would have been far more expensive in men and planes.

From Tarawa through Okinawa, the navy and marines, normally with some assistance from Army Ground and Air Forces, planned for amphibious operations knowing it was virtually certain that an amphibious assault would ensue in the execution phase. Here was the acid test of amphibious warfare. Beaches were so few and so narrow that the Japanese could hardly avoid being there, dug in, and patiently waiting to shoot the men who must move up out of the sea. Under such circumstances well-trained amphibian specialists were essential to the job at hand—men who, supported by all the naval gunfire and close air strikes they could muster, were able to integrate their sea borne deployment with the aim of achieving utmost momentum across the beach.

Admiral Chester W. Nimitz clearly recognized the difference between an unopposed or lightly opposed landing and the amphibious assault. The "small size" of Iwo Jima, he said, "far from implying weakness, was a source of strength. It had no extensive coast line affording to the attackers a choice of numerous landing points, where the invading troops would meet little opposition. . . ." Vandegrift put the matter even more clearly when in referring to the march across the mid-Pacific he concluded, "the invasion . . . generates into what is purely and simply assault. By assault we mean the last stages of an attack. The operation becomes assault from beginning to end." [15]

The war in the mid-Pacific showed that an efficient combat team is required to deliver the amphibious assault. Movements were mainly ship-to-shore, across wide expanses of water, and were necessarily conducted in close coordination with carrier-based air and naval guns aboard men-of-war. Ordinarily, the landing force spent weeks in reaching the target. These operations were, in short, naval assaults, highly intricate in organization and exceedingly complex in tactical execution. The Fleet Marine Force, by tradition and through indoctrination a part of the navy, was the logical arm to land in assault. Marines were prepared to push through to a rapid victory thus satisfying another cardinal principle of amphibious warfare—to finish the fighting ashore with the greatest speed possible—and this expedited the unloading of amphibious shipping, permitting it to turn around quickly, leave the danger zone, and reload for the next operation. A study of the Pacific War reveals, further, the readiness and flexibility of the Marine Corps. Not only were the marines able to expand air and naval power by seizing small islands in spite of determined opposition at the beach, but also they proved themselves highly competent in fighting on large land masses. They were ready as early as the offensive against Guadalcanal to take and hold against great odds a tactical and stratcgical air base while their companions in the navy contested command of adjacent waters with the Japanese. Finally, as the struggle in the Pacific closed, six marine divisions were preparing to help wrest the beaches from the enemy on the Japanese home islands of Kyushu and Honshu, and thus to clear the way for land warfare.

Such was and is the chief mission of the United States Marines: constantly to study and perfect amphibious warfare so that, irrespective of technological changes, the amphibious assault is always feasible. Fulfillment of such a mission was essential during the Pacific War for securing advanced bases for the Navy and Army Air Forces; and it supplied the Army Ground Forces with effective principles for invading large land masses. If an assault against a very heavily defended beach can be made, then the use of the same doctrine and techniques assures the success of a landing on a large land mass, which usually is the task of the army.

America, unless she becomes reconciled to an invasion, must always fight offensively, and for reasons of geography this means that she must fight overseas. It would certainly be dangerous to rely on a repetition of the ferrying technique used in World War I; therefore it is imperative that the United States have a branch of the services which devotes full time to devising ways of projecting land power overseas against targets held by hostile forces. Nothing better illustrates that need than a study of World War II.

Nor is there at this moment a complete substitute for amphibious assault. Important as are airborne troops and supplies to modern war, best illustrated in the recent past by the German seizure of Crete, they remain auxiliary to ocean shipments. Present technological developments are rapid, and the time may come when sea transport will be auxiliary to air, but even so, the problem of seizing and holding enemy targets overseas will remain. Under present conditions, such operations demand a tremendous tonnage of men, supplies, and weapons that surpass the possibilities of any foreseeable air lift.[16] For example, the Okinawa campaign, which was certainly a small task when compared with the invasion and subsequent build up in France in 1944, required the shipment of more than 2,000,000 measurement tons * from the Western Hemisphere to the Far East.[17]

The Marine Corps has a long and admirable history, but only

* A measurement ton is usually reckoned at forty cubic feet.

in the course of the past generation has the fulfillment of its mission been essential in the utmost degree to the security of the United States. From its inception in 1775, the Corps has been on hand to fight at a moment's notice. Marines down to 1940 functioned either as landing troops for navy operations, as a small reinforcement for the army, or independently. During times of peace and war, marines served as boarding troops, gunners, and the nucleus for small landing parties on men-of-war, and as troops for guarding naval stations ashore, for employment in overseas diplomatic missions, and for carrying out State Department policies in Asiatic, West Indian, and Central American countries in such a fashion as to remain "short of war." The small size and compact leadership of the Corps, along with other factors, permitted the establishment of a high morale, and this in turn has contributed to a state of constant and instantaneous readiness to perform any given task within its power.[18] These qualities of morale and readiness were of great assistance to the Corps as it took on its more formidable job of developing an up-to-date doctrine of amphibious warfare shortly after the close of World War I, and as it helped to perfect amphibious techniques before and during World War II.

CHAPTER II

EVOLUTION OF AN AMPHIBIOUS DOCTRINE, 1901–1934

THE first of April 1945 was celebrated in the Western world as Easter Sunday, dedicated to the worship of the Prince of Peace. In English speaking countries, coincidentally, it was All Fool's Day which is customarily given over to practical jokes and harmless deceits. On the island of Okinawa in the Nansei Shoto (Ryukyu Archipelago) in the Japanese Empire, however, there was neither peace nor jocularity. For on that day the shores of this remote island, only some 500 miles * from the Japanese homeland were struck and overrun by the largest and most potent American amphibious force assembled in the Pacific during World War II.

It was the culmination of three and a half years of bloody island fighting and of three decades of painstaking research, experimentation, and practice in the once little-known art of amphibious warfare. That the attack was a success and a brilliant success was due in part to the courage and combat efficiency of the Navy, Army, and Marine Corps personnel who launched it, and in part to the superior quantity and quality of the ships, guns, and other fighting equipment which American wealth and industry had made possible. But no small measure of the victory can be credited to the ingenuity and dogged labor of a little group of military and naval pioneers who during the years of peace realized the possibilities of amphibious warfare, took hold of a neglected and discredited theory, and reduced it to a practical science. In the vanguard of this group was the United States Marine Corps.

1. Success at Okinawa—Failure at Gallipoli

The attack on Okinawa will be discussed in detail in Chapter XI, but a brief description of it here is in point to illustrate the enormous size and complexity which amphibious operations had achieved by the close of World War II. The first step was to soften up the target by aerial bombing. As early as October 10, 1944, a fast carrier task force unleashed heavy air strikes against the island, leaving its principal city in flames and sinking much of the shipping in its harbors.

* All distances, unless otherwise noted in the text, are nautical miles.

(See map 22.) The same task force returned in January and again in March of the following year to repeat the performance. During February and March, army and navy planes based in the Southwest Pacific and in the Marianas made almost daily runs over the area, bombing it incessantly and taking detailed photographs for intelligence studies.

Six days before the attack on the main objective, an army division landed on a cluster of rocky islets known as the Kerama group some fifteen miles to the west of Okinawa and speedily occupied the most important of these with the help of navy guns, rockets, and mortars. The purpose of this preinvasion attack was to secure a safe seaplane base and fleet anchorage. It was followed by seizure of Keise Shima (Island) a few miles eastward, from which heavy guns could sweep the southern portion of the main island.

Meanwhile, battleships, cruisers, and destroyers of the amphibious support force, charged with the mission of softening the main target and preparing for the landing, stood well off the western coast of Okinawa lobbing in heavy shells high over the mastheads of the little minesweeps as they cautiously probed the offshore waters for enemy mines. As these were gradually cleared the warships moved in close to deliver pinpoint fire against the defenders' guns and ammunition dumps. At the same time carrier planes concentrated on inland targets protected by terrain configurations, that is defiladed, from naval gunfire. The pilots struck at artillery emplacements, bridges, airfields, and any other military objectives that fell to their province. Finally, the day before the scheduled landing, navy underwater demolition teams sent their hardy swimmers into the beaches' edge to search the shallows for mines and traps and other obstacles that might impede the water borne troops as they approached the shore. The stage was set at last for the big show, and it was to be a spectacle to awe even the most seasoned fighters who witnessed it the next day.

At dawn on April first some 1,300 naval vessels stood off the western coast of Okinawa. It was a weird assemblage. Battleships, cruisers, and destroyers were stepping up their fire to fever pitch. Before the first troops touched the shore the navy had let loose a total of almost 45,000 rounds of shells, 33,000 rockets, and 22,500 mortars. Through this din and smoke, vessels carrying the first waves of landing troops slowly felt their way to their assigned positions, dropped their stern anchors, and came to rest fronting a shore line more than seven miles in length. These were strange craft that would have shocked any honest sailor ten years before—ungainly, flat-bottomed, scrofulous with varicolored camouflage paint. They were the tank landing ships (LSTs) and their smaller sisters the medium landing ships (LSMs), both with double doors fitted into their bows almost flush with the water line. As the doors swung open, out swarmed hordes of another singular craft, if such it can be called. This was the tracked landing vehicle (LVT), frequently called the amphibian tractor, one of the few truly amphibian vehicles of the war. Hull well down in the water, it could propel itself at something better than four knots and, what was more important, its treaded tracks like those of any ordinary tractor allowed it to crawl through shallow water or over coral heads that would have grounded a more orthodox landing boat.

Once disgorged from their mother ships, the amphibian tractors, each carrying about thirty troops, circled sluggishly until the signal came to move off to the line-of-departure about a mile offshore where they formed in line abreast to wait the final order to attack. (See Plates 1, 2, 11, and 14.)

Navy pilots were now flying low along the beaches, saturating them with last-minute bombs and rocket fire. Fifteen minutes before the scheduled landing hour, control boats stationed along the line-of-departure gave the signal to advance and the deadly procession almost eight miles in depth commenced to move slowly forward. First in rank went gunboats to pound the beaches with a last-minute barrage of rockets, mortars, and 40-millimeter shells. A hundred yards astern came a wave of armed and armored amphibian tractors (LVTAs), their howitzers ready to take up the chorus when the gunboats reached the abutting reefs and had to turn back. And last came the five to seven waves of amphibian tractors bearing the troops in whose hands lay the issue of the landing. They were the battalion landing teams of the First and Sixth Marine Divisions and the 7th and 96th Army Infantry Divisions. The first wave touched the shore within seconds of the scheduled time. To the great surprise of these troops though not to their sorrow there was virtually no opposition. What had been planned as the largest amphibious assault of the Pacific War turned out to be a virtually unresisted landing. The first waves moved rapidly inland with little or no hindrance. Within an hour over 16,000 men were ashore. They were followed quickly with tanks and artillery carried in assorted types of landing craft. By the day's end a beachhead of about 15,000 yards in depth was secured. Over 60,000 troops were ashore with tanks and artillery. Artillery weapons and ammunition were brought ashore in Dukws,* 2½-ton amphibian trucks which were also capable of crossing reefs. Development of the Dukw had been pioneered by the United States Army and was one of the army's important contributions to amphibian techniques. From the time of the Marshalls invasions early

---

* Research has failed to reveal the origin of the term "Dukw," but the best explanation offered is that it is a code designation assigned by its commercial manufacturers.

in 1944, the Dukw had served as the chief logistical work horse of the Central Pacific.

Meanwhile on the beachhead, navy personnel in beach parties and army engineers and marine pioneers in shore parties were directing traffic, guiding the assorted trucks and tanks and tractors and Dukws to their appointed destinations as they landed, and dispatching the landing craft to new duties as soon as their loads of men and supplies were deposited. Communications teams were in full operation, channelling messages from ships and planes to troop units and back again. Engineers were preparing to lay roads inland and already were commencing to undo the tremendous damage done by naval bombardment and aerial bombing. Of course the operation was far from finished. Almost three months of rugged fighting lay ahead before the island could be declared secured. But a critical phase—the ship-to-shore movement and the establishment of a solid beachhead—had been accomplished with clockwork precision and amazing ease.

This was in April of 1945. Thirty years earlier in another April and on another shore a similar amphibious venture had not met with such success. The tragedy of the Dardanelles-Gallipoli campaign of the First World War serves to highlight the brilliant success of Okinawa and to indicate the phenomenal progress made in the doctrine and techniques of amphibious warfare in only three decades.

Early in the year 1915 at the request of the Russian government, whose troops were being sorely pressed in the Caucasus, the British War Cabinet gave its consent to a project sponsored chiefly by Winston Churchill, First Lord of the Admiralty, to force the Dardanelles. The object was to drive Turkey out of the war; the execution was originally put into the hands of the Royal Navy alone, with assistance from French men-of-war. A number of old battleships and cruisers was assembled under the command of Vice-Admiral Sir Sackville Carden, and in late February he commenced to bombard the Turkish fortresses guarding the Mediterranean entrance to the Straits. These efforts met with considerable success; the southernmost forts were silenced by naval gunfire and their guns destroyed by landing parties of bluejackets and Royal Marines. March 18 was then set as the day for a full-scale drive through the Straits and into the Sea of Marmora. Minesweepers had previously reported the channel to be free and four French and five British battleships plus one battle cruiser steamed in to engage the remaining forts. As they headed toward the narrows, outshooting the shore artillery as they went, the whole expedition was brought to a sudden halt when four of the battleships were struck by mines, one of them sinking with almost all hands aboard. The Allied naval force withdrew in haste and it was subsequently decided not to risk another encounter without aid from the army. Thus was launched the greatest and most unfortunate combined operation of modern military history up to that time.

The troops selected for this enterprise, about 78,000 English, Anzac (Australian and New Zealand), and French, were put under the command of General Sir Ian Hamilton. Those embarked from England were hastily assembled, poorly equipped, and ill-trained for such operations. They were loaded aboard transports in hopeless confusion. Their first stop was the harbor of Mudros on the island of Lemnos, which was quite inadequately equipped to handle a force of this size, especially since all the equipment had to be unloaded and restowed so that the landing troops could get at what they needed when they wanted it. No attempt at what later became known as combat-loading had been made at all, and total confusion resulted. This necessitated retiring with the whole force to Alexandria where some order was brought out of the chaos. It was a costly three weeks, however, since it gave the Turks and Germans, who were clearly cognizant by this time of their enemy's intentions, time to reinforce Gallipoli Peninsula on the European side of the Straits, which was the object of the attack.

Finally the 300-odd ships and craft of the attacking flotilla were assembled and dispatched and at dawn of April 25 stood off the southern tip of Gallipoli. The plan called for a landing at points over a sixty mile front, with the main landings at the tip of the peninsula. There were three sets of landing beaches. The beaches in the first set were extremely shallow, separated by thousands of yards from each other, and surrounded by high rugged ridges. In short they lacked all features favorable to an easy landing, although their choice was probably justified for other tactical reasons. Ten miles to the northeast lay the second set landing area, a single beach assigned to the Anzacs. Its terrain features were much more promising. The third beach on the Asiatic side of the Straits was merely the scene of a temporary landing and demonstration by the French.

Allied commanders had some knowledge of the terrain they were facing but very little of the disposition of the enemy forces. There had been little aerial reconnaissance and no aerial bombing. No attempt had been made before the target date to bombard the shore line with naval fire, and indeed any such effort would have been out of the question since all available warships were deemed essential to escort the troop-laden transports and to screen them from hostile submarines.

For the movement from ship-to-shore, troops were loaded in standard open ships' boats and towed close in to the beaches by tugs or lighters. At the northern (Anzac) beach the plan called for a surprise landing at dawn which meant there could be no preliminary naval bombardment. It also meant that the tows had only a vague idea of where they were heading. The surprise came off as scheduled, but the Anzacs were almost as startled as the Turks when at daylight they discovered that an unexpected current had set them ashore about a mile above their destined beach. The landing was carried out expeditiously; in three hours some 8,000 men were put ashore with very little resistance, and another 8,000 got there by nightfall. Once ashore however they made comparatively little progress against determined Turkish opposition, chiefly because of the error in landing. The troops were set ashore on ground not covered by their maps, which would have been inadequate even under ideal circumstances, and the resultant confusion made them easy prey to hard-pushed counterattacks.

To the south, matters went even worse. On the tip of the peninsula, five separate beaches had been designated for the landing. On the northernmost beach, two battalions backed by reasonably adequate fire from the guns of escorting battleships were landed at dawn without opposition and without loss. However their orders were vague, and instead of pressing the attack forward they waited to be met by troops from adjoining beachheads. In the end they allowed themselves to be caught unawares by a night counterattack of a force grossly inferior in number and had to be evacuated the next day. Similarly a small force put ashore at the southernmost beach sat on its hands and accomplished nothing for want of either reinforcements or orders.

On the beaches just to the northward of these idle troops, the landing was preceded by comparatively heavy naval fire though with questionable results. No attempt was made at surprise and the boats moved forward in full daylight. This was also the scene of an interesting experiment in improvised landing craft. An old collier, *River Clyde*, had been converted into a sort of primitive tank landing ship. Doors were cut into her sides to permit egress down gangplanks fastened to her hull. She towed lighters alongside to act as piers from which the attacking troops could presumably walk easily to shore. This made her extremely unwieldy, especially when lateral currents hit the lighters and forced the ship broadside to the shore where she almost broached. The troops who attempted to disembark from this awkward position were met with fierce rifle fire and almost none who tried to get ashore during the day made it alive. Those who approached in the more orthodox manner in small boats suffered almost equal casualties. The other beaches were also well defended, not only by enemy marksmen, but also by well-emplaced underwater obstacles and barbed wire along the beach. Losses there too were extremely heavy.

Thus by the end of the day the hold of the British on the beaches was tenuous, and although their lines were gradually consolidated no significant progress inland was ever made. There were, of course, other factors responsible besides the failure to secure an adequate beachhead in a short time and the casualties suffered in the attempt to do so. There were no reinforcements and none were sent for almost three months. Living conditions on shore were miserable; dysentery broke out in epidemic proportions and medical supplies and care were inadequate to meet the situation. There was insufficient artillery and insufficient aerial support. After May, when German submarines began to infest the area, the bulk of the fleet was removed to safer quarters, leaving the troops ashore without benefit of naval gunfire. Logistics were in a hopeless muddle; there were no well-equipped advanced bases close to the scene of operations, and the distance to home bases was too great to meet the situation even if the Royal Navy in English waters had been prepared to do so.

Finally in August the long-awaited reinforcements came in the form of an amphibious landing of a whole army corps in Suvla Bay just north of the positions held by the Anzacs. As an amphibious exercise it was far more successful than those of the previous April. Aerial reconnaissance and ground intelligence work afforded the attackers a much clearer idea of the nature of their objectives than their predecessors had enjoyed. To carry the troops ashore the British had devised a novel landing craft called the "beetle." It was a long barge-like craft, armored, motor-powered, and capable of five knots speed. It could carry 500 men and had a swinging platform projecting from the bow which could be lowered to form a broad ramp to shore when the craft was beached. Troops were loaded aboard and towed astern of destroyers from a nearby island, and then sent in under their own power before daybreak of August 7. As a landing operation it was a success.

But once ashore the attack bogged down chiefly because of inept and indecisive command. At home the British and French cabinets, whose members had never been entirely convinced of the wisdom of the campaign in the first place, gave up all hope and ordered a general evacuation. By January all Allied troops were withdrawn and Gallipoli was written off as a total failure.[1]

This dismal experience made a profound impression on military thinking throughout the world. Although there were almost as many opinions as to the fundamental causes of the failure as there were "experts" who wrote about it, the general conclusion was that large scale amphibious operations against a defended shore, especially if conducted in daylight, were almost certain to be suicidal. Even Commodore Roger Keyes, second-in-command of the naval force present at the time and who became the most insistent apologist for the soundness of the basic plan of operations, remained convinced that only surprise night landings were practicable. As late as 1943 he stated: "Among the most valuable lessons we learnt from the original landings was the folly of attempting to storm a defended beach in daylight." [2]

Other students of the campaign were even less sanguine. One of them, an American writing in 1927, concluded a phase of his study with the interesting observation that even if Great Britain could survive another war it was doubtful that she could survive another Churchill, the author of the fateful Dardanelles expedition.[3]

Yet in spite of the Gallipoli disaster and the general gloom and pessimism it engendered, in less than thirty years amphibious warfare was elevated to an eminent position as a highly respectable and very significant branch of military and naval science. Indeed, excepting possibly in the field of aviation, no other technique of war underwent such a complete and rapid metamorphosis; and unlike aviation, it did so without the benefit of glamor, publicity, or widespread civilian interest.

There are several reasons for this phenomenon. The strategical necessities of World War II as it developed would inevitably have demanded the evolution of amphibious skills sooner or later. Technological developments especially in the field of naval gunfire and small craft construction contributed to its growth. But the fact that the United States and her allies were prepared by 1942 and 1943 to launch full-scale amphibious assaults against powerful enemies in either ocean was primarily due to the foresight and planning of the United States Navy and more particularly the United States Marine Corps.

2. *Advance-Base Force and Early Study of Amphibious Warfare*

The Marine Corps' preoccupation with the manifold problems of landing water borne troops against hostile shores was not born full grown nor did it date only from World War I. Shortly after the conclusion of the Spanish-American War the attention of high naval planners was turned toward the problem of building a permanent force capable of seizing and holding advanced bases to be employed by the fleet in the prosecution of naval war in distant waters. Up to that time the duties of the Marine Corps had been limited largely to supplying marine detachments to vessels of the fleet and furnishing guards for navy yards, except during wartime when units of the Corps had actually participated in minor landings.[4] The relatively easy victory over Spain did not conceal the fact that the fleet was incapable of sustained operations even in waters as close as those of Cuba, and the projection of American power far into the Pacific as a result of

Commodore George Dewey's victory at Manila Bay made the problem of acquiring bases even more acute. Dewey himself remarked afterward that had he had under his command a force of 2,000 marines he could have forced the surrender of the Spanish army and occupied the city of Manila with comparative ease. This he claimed would have cleared the way for subsequent occupation of the islands by the United States Army and would probably have prevented the native insurrection which took so many years to quell.[5]

At any rate, shortly after the war the General Board of the Navy, impressed by recent events and under the spell of Captain Alfred T. Mahan's persuasive doctrines, determined to set up a permanent advance-base force within the naval establishment. It was axiomatic that warships powered by steam were tied to their bases by the distance of their steaming radii and, since it was impracticable to maintain permanent bases in all parts of the world where the fleet might conceivably engage in action, it would be inevitably necessary in wartime to seize temporary bases against opposition if necessary. Defense of such bases once seized was an inseparable problem. The Marine Corps, an organization consisting of ground troops but with naval experience and under naval authority, was the obvious solution to the difficulty. Immediately tentative steps were taken to prepare the Corps for this new line of activity.[6]

In 1901, guns were taken from battleships and mounted on shore by marines, and a class of officers and enlisted men was formed at Newport, Rhode Island, for instruction in the preliminaries of advance-base work. In the winter of 1902–1903 a battalion of marines sailed to the island of Culebra, off the coast of Puerto Rico, to engage in base-defense exercises in conjunction with the annual maneuvers of the fleet. In a sense unsuspected at the time, this was an occasion of considerable historic significance, for this little island was to become the scene of all the important marine amphibious training exercises until the acquisition of a better site at New River, North Carolina, in 1940. Indeed there is some truth in the statement of General Holland M. Smith USMC years later that if Waterloo was won on the playing fields of Eton, the Japanese bases in the Pacific in World War II were captured on the beaches of Culebra.[7]

Duties in Panama and Cuba kept the marines diverted for the next few years, but in 1910 the first formal school for instruction in advance-base work was set up in New London. It was removed next year to Philadelphia where it remained in operation until 1920, when it was transferred to the newly acquired marine base at Quantico, Virginia. Even during the years of World War I when the drain on Marine Corps personnel for service in France was extremely heavy, the advance-base force was maintained at full strength.[8]

In 1912 the Commandant of the Marine Corps outlined the main objectives of the school's training program and set up a curriculum. It was directed along three main lines: to train officers and men in the handling, installation, and use of advance-base material; to investigate what types of guns, gun platforms, mines, torpedo defenses, and other equipment was best suited to advance-base work; and to study "such military and naval subjects as pertain to the selection, occupation, and attack and defense of advanced-base positions, or to the expeditionary service in general. . . ." [9]

Two years later, over 1,700 officers and men had been trained, and they gave a practical demonstration of their work in an exercise held at Culebra. Two naval ships participated, but the Commandant seemed to suspect a widespread indifference to advance-base work among navy circles in general; he remarked "that the impression seems to prevail that advance-base work is purely a Marine Corps matter. This," he stated, "is an error, as there can be no doubt but that advance-base work is essentially a naval matter in which the entire service is deeply interested, and while the execution of the work is placed in the hands of the Marine Corps, it is nevertheless necessary for successful results that it be given earnest cooperation by and coordination with the various branches of the naval service." [10] This was not the last time that a marine officer was to complain that the navy showed something less than enthusiasm or proper appreciation for the Corps' own specialty.

Although the germs of later amphibious training may be found in this early advance-base activity, it is clear that the great weight of the emphasis was not on offensive landing operations. In fact there is little resemblance between this early concept of the main function of the Marine Corps and its subsequent role as a military organization specially trained for amphibious assaults against enemy shores. Although in theory the advance-base force was supposed to be prepared to seize as well as to defend bases, in practice all of the training concentrated on the defense. This becomes obvious on an inspection of the 1912 instructions by the Commandant mentioned above. The main objective of the Advanced Base School was to educate officers and men in the handling of equipment suited for the *defense* of a base against possible attack from the sea. This is even more clearly borne out by examining a lecture to the Naval War College delivered in 1915 by Major Dion Williams USMC, who was intimately connected with advance-base work from its inception. He explained in detail to the assembled naval officers the necessity for establishing an advance-base force of at least brigade strength, and then continued: "The object in view [is] the rapid defense of a temporary base for the battle fleet against a raiding force of the enemy, which may be presumed to consist of a squadron of cruisers and a landing force of one brigade at the most. . . ." Instruction, he added, should concentrate on the use of heavy artillery, mines, searchlights, wireless telegraphy, dynamos, and other equipment.[11]

It is obvious then that before 1920 there was no indication that the Marine Corps considered itself to be a special amphibious branch, at least in the World War II sense of that term. Some spade work had been done in the field of advance-base work, but it is clear that this did not imply landings against defended shores. It was apparently assumed that whenever any offensive action was taken to seize a base it would be against no or at most nominal opposition. The advance-base force was in actuality little more than an embryo coastal artillery unit.[12]

Nor is there any indication that there was any widespread interest in the work even in its defensive aspects among the personnel of the Marine Corps immediately after the conclusion of World War I. During that war, units of the Corps fought alongside army troops and under army command, and there was no noticeable distinction between the two branches either in services performed or in their respective concepts of their special functions. In 1920 the old Marine Infantry School and the Training School were combined under the single administration of the Marine Corps Schools located at Quantico. As the Commandant reported: "The course to be pursued is being prepared to follow similar lines to the one in the Army School of the Line at Fort Leavenworth, and is based somewhat on the course given in the Marine Officers' Infantry School for 1920. This course is not as extensive nor as advanced as that at Leavenworth, but it is exceedingly well adapted to meet the needs of the field officers of the Marine Corps. . . ." [13] It is clear that as of this date the Corps was not organizing itself for any special offensive amphibious functions.

Nevertheless, interest in all phases of advance-base work continued to grow, and during the 1920's more and more marine officers of high rank became convinced that this was a military specialty to which the Corps was particularly suited and to which it should devote most of its attention. Gradually it became apparent that no branch of the service was even remotely prepared to undertake the highly complex task of seizing distant island bases held by an enemy power, and even less, that of landing an expeditionary force of any size on a hostile shore preparatory to large-scale land operations. The almost total debility of the United States in this respect became more serious after the Treaty of Versailles and the establishment of the League of Nations. Under that settlement many of the Western Pacific islands formerly belonging to the German Empire were mandated to Japan, whose imperial ambitions were already becoming evident. Strategic bases in the Marianas, Carolines, and Marshalls were now in Japanese hands, and although by the terms of the treaty they could not lawfully be fortified, treaties, as recent history had shown, could be mere "scraps of paper."

Thus it was that the United States emerged from a victorious war only to discover that her military and naval position in the Pacific was, if anything, worse than it had been before the war. Committed still to the Open Door policy in China, America had few visible means of enforcing that policy against any Asiatic power that might in the future see fit to dispute it. True, the United States still retained the strategic islands of Guam and the Philippines, but flanking the overseas route to both of these were the mandated islands which, if converted to naval and air bases, would seriously jeopardize American naval superiority in the Western Pacific.

The danger was not immediately apparent to many Americans, and indeed it would have been a bold prophet who would have predicted in 1921 the rapid rise of Japanese power or of a war between the Empire and the United States within two decades. Yet it is the duty of military planners to prepare for even the remotest contingencies, and there was at least one such within the Marine Corps. This was Major Earl H. Ellis, whose untimely and mysterious death in 1923 on Japanese-held Palau deprived the Corps of one of its most brilliant minds.

Even before Japan had reaped her share of spoils from World War I in the form of the German islands, Ellis was directing his attention to the problem of a future Pacific War and was sketching an outline plan of naval strategy with particular reference to the Marine Corps' role in its execution. He presented this first scheme in a detailed lecture delivered some time before 1919. Starting with the assumption that Japan, because of her imperialist pretensions, was the only possible rival to challenge American interests and power in the Pacific, he proceeded to present in some detail a plan for setting up a system of outlying bases essential to support United States fleet action in the Western Pacific. The burden of this work, he maintained, would fall naturally on the Marine Corps as the Advanced Base Force of the Navy.[14]

The bases which Ellis proposed fell into two categories: first, those located on islands already in American possession, and second, those that were owned by the Japanese. In the former category were Pearl Harbor, Apra Harbor on Guam, and Pelelle Harbor on the island of Luzon in the Philippines. These, he maintained, should be strongly fortified against possible enemy naval or military attack and well stocked with fuel and other supplies essential to the fleet. In addition, other smaller bases closer to the heart of Japan itself would have to be seized and occupied. Specifically he recommended for consideration one island in the Nanpo Shoto (group) and several others in the Ryukyu Islands, all of which lay within striking distances of the Japanese homeland. Both the construction and defense of bases already held by the United States as well as the seizure of new bases in enemy hands would fall to the Marine Corps, and Ellis exhorted his colleagues to make plans for the event.

By 1921 the situation in the Pacific had changed and the United States was in an even less favorable position than when Ellis' first plans were submitted. He therefore revised some of his original ideas and submitted a plan of operation which was officially approved by the Commandant on July 23, 1921, and therefore became the keystone of Marine Corps strategic plans for a Pacific War, in so far as the Corps was concerned with strategy. His predictions as to the general course of a future war against Japan and his recommendations for the prosecution of that war reveal rare insight, not to say prophetic genius.

"In order to impose our will upon Japan," he began, "it will be necessary for us to project our fleet and land forces across the Pacific and wage war in Japanese waters." To do this, it would be necessary to "have sufficient bases to support the fleet, both during its projection and afterwards. As the matter stands at present, we cannot count upon the use of any bases west of Hawaii except those which we may seize from the enemy after the opening of hostilities. Moreover, the continued occupation of the Marshall, Caroline, and Pelew [Palau] Islands by the Japanese (now holding them under mandate from the League of Nations) invests them with a series of emergency bases flanking any line of communications across the Pacific throughout a distance of 2,300 miles. The reduction and occupation of these islands," he concluded, "and the establishment of the necessary bases therein, as a preliminary phase of the hostilities, is practically imperative."

The first phase of this strategy was the capture of the Marshall Islands with Eniwetok, Wotje, and Jaluit as the first objectives. Next the Carolines were to be occupied as far west as the Lamustrek group, and finally the third phase involved the reduction of the remainder of the Carolines, including Yap and the Palau Islands. Tactical planning for these operations was worked out in some detail. Night landings, except possibly for small reconnaissance parties going ashore prior to the main attack, were discouraged as too dangerous. Transports carrying the assault troops should approach the transport area under cover of darkness, but the landing should ordinarily be made during the early morning so as to permit the fullest use of all weapons and to afford the landing force ample daylight in which to secure a beachhead. Naval vessels should take position on the flanks of the landing troops and sweep the beaches during the ship-to-shore movement. Aircraft should be employed in full measure not only for reconnaissance but also for strafing after the troops were landed. Smoke screens over the transport area or over the landing boats during their approach to the shore should be used cautiously and only when there was no danger of masking enemy defensive installations from the fire of men-of-war. Troops should be landed in ships' boats towed to the beach by power craft equipped with bow guns. At least two waves of tows should be sent in, each tow composed of not more than three boats, properly dispersed to avoid concentrated fire from the beach. In addition to the regular infantry, machine gunners, signal troops, and field artillery, Ellis proposed that demolition specialists equipped with wire cutters and explosives for breaking up obstacles on the beach and in the water constitute a part of the first wave.

Some of these suggestions appear obsolete today, but they contain the seeds of what was to flower into the refined amphibious art of World War II. Even more prophetic was Ellis's estimate of the number of troops required to make a successful landing against the opposition which the enemy would probably put up. Of the three islands (Eniwetok, Wotje, and Jaluit) for which he gives such estimates, only Eniwetok was actually assaulted by American forces during World War II. For this operation Ellis recommended the employment of two reinforced regiments totalling about 4,000 officers and men. In fact this was very close to the number actually used when army and marine troops captured the atoll in February of 1944.

The lesson of all this was clear. The Marine Corps was peculiarly suited to this kind of warfare and it should prepare accordingly. "To effect such a landing under the sea and shore conditions obtaining and in the face of enemy resistance," Ellis concluded, "requires careful training and preparation, to say the least; and this along Marine Corps lines. It is not enough that the troops be skilled infantry men and jungle men or artillery men of high morale; they must be skilled water men and jungle men who know it can be done—Marines with Marine training." [15]

Other marine officers, higher stationed and more influential than Earl Ellis, agreed that the Corps should concentrate on advanced base work and prepare to spearhead the navy's drive against a future enemy by seizing and holding distant islands. Brigadier General Rufus H. Lane, Adjutant and Inspector General of the Marine Corps, wrote in 1923 that ships' crews could not be spared to perform these essential duties and the army was not suited, first, because no units were trained with the navy and, second, because it would raise questions of divided command and "history is full of the failure of combined operations due to the lack of understanding between the two branches of the service. . . ." The only solution, he concluded, was to employ the Marine Corps.[16]

John A. Lejeune, Major General Commandant, repeatedly dwelt on the same theme. Speaking before the Naval War College in 1923, he said: "The seizure and occupation or destruction of enemy bases is another important function of the expeditionary force of the Marine Corps. On both flanks of a fleet crossing the Pacific are numerous islands suitable for utilization by an enemy for radio stations, aviation, submarine, or destroyer bases." All these bases should be mopped up as United States forces advanced. Lejeune felt that preparedness for amphibious war was of primary concern to the Corps. "The maintenance, equipping and training of its expeditionary force so that it will be in instant readiness to support the Fleet in the event of war," he concluded, "I deem to be the most important Marine Corps duty in time of peace. . . ." [17]

Major General Eli K. Cole USMC repeated the same idea. "The major war mission of the Marine Corps," he wrote in 1929, "is to support the fleet by supplying it with a highly trained, fully equipped expeditionary force for the minor shore operations which are necessary for the effective prosecution by the fleet of its major mission, which is to gain control of the seas and thereby open the sea lanes for the Army overseas. . . ." [18]

By this time the contention that such was "the major war mission of the Marine Corps" had been recognized by both the army and navy. In 1927, in order to correct or eliminate disharmony among the services, the War Department and the Navy Department adopted a policy to govern joint operations in which the two services were involved. This directive was issued by the Joint Board of the Army and Navy, forerunner of the Joint Chiefs of Staff. It was entitled "Army-Navy Joint Action," and stated in detail the duties of each branch, as well as defining their respective spheres of authority. The duties of the army in landing attacks against shore objectives included the deployment into boats provided by the navy, firing at shore targets from landing boats, deployment from landing boats, gaining a foothold on shore, organization of defensive beachhead, and the conduct of operations beyond the beachhead. To the Marine Corps were assigned the same duties as to the United States Army, and in addition, it was stated that "Marines . . . because of their constant association with Navy units, will be given special preparation in the conduct of landing operations." [19] Thus by 1929 it was well established both in the minds of highest ranking officers of the Corps and in the official policy promulgated by War and Navy Departments that the special role of the Marine Corps within the military establishment was to provide a small well-trained amphibious assault force to seize and occupy overseas bases for fleet operations.

Unfortunately, as is often the case, actual achievement fell far short of aspiration, and facts corresponded only slightly with theories. The truth is that although halting steps were taken in the direction of building in the Marine Corps a truly efficient amphibious force, the goal was still far distant in 1929.

There are several reasons for this failure. One was the lack of unanimity within the Corps itself as to what should be its paramount function. The memory of World War I died hard, and there were many who persisted in the belief that preparation for large-scale ground maneuvers in the army style was still the main duty of the Marine Corps in peacetime. As late as 1926 the staff of the Marine Corps Schools was still in the thrall of "outmoded military thought" and still "floundered among the outdated doctrines of World War I," according to Holland M. Smith who went through the field officers' course in that year.[20]

Even without this military conservatism, however, it is doubtful that great progress could have been made toward the development of a well-rounded training program. In the first place the navy was too preoccupied with preparing its ships and personnel for the traditional type of surface fleet actions to give more than sporadic attention to the problem of landing operations. In the second place the Marine Corps was always short of funds. Finally and most important, it had other more pressing duties to perform. From 1924 until January of 1932, the marines were busy fighting and patrolling in China and Nicaragua, and it was impossible to set up any organized continuous training program in amphibious tactics.[21]

Yet some progress was made in spite of these handicaps. The advance-base force which had been moved to Quantico in 1920 was reorganized in 1921 under the new name of Expeditionary Force. As of 1925 it consisted of infantry, artillery, auxiliary troops such as engineers, signal, gas, tank and aviation units, all of them equipped and trained for service with the fleet. In the same year a similar though smaller force was organized for the west coast and stationed at San Diego.[22]

For the first few years practical training of these troops alternated between standard infantry ground maneuvers and landing exercises, with emphasis on the former. This first type consisted mostly of mock battles "fought" on Civil War sites, and these seem to have been designated almost as much for publicity as for practical reasons. In 1921 Brigadier General Smedley D. Butler USMC conducted extensive field maneuvers in the vicinity of the Civil War battlefield at Wilderness Run. The following year Gettysburg was the scene of these exercises which included a historic reproduction of Pickett's last charge for the special benefit of President Warren G. Harding and his party. In the autumn of 1923 the expeditionary brigade marched from Quantico to

Newmarket, Virginia, where the battle of Newmarket was reenacted, with the cadet corps of the Virginia Military Institute participating in the demonstration. This was to commemorate the historic occasion when the cadets of V.M.I. volunteered to a man to join the Confederate Army and halt the Yankees' drive up the Shenandoah Valley in June of 1864. The next year field exercises were held near Sharpsburg, culminating on national defense day (September 12) in a demonstration of attack under modern battle conditions on the battlefield of Antietam. Forty thousand spectators and a host of official visitors witnessed this event, and at its close the troops marched back to Quantico via Washington where they were reviewed by the President.[23]

On the more practical side, one battalion of the expeditionary force was sent to Culebra in the winter of 1922 where exercises were held in embarkation and debarkation of troops in conjunction with elements of the Atlantic Fleet. In January 1924, marines participated for the first time in a large-scale landing exercise, and the negative results should have been impressive enough to convince the Navy Department of the dire necessity for repeated practice maneuvers of the same sort. The Fifth Marine Regiment sailed to Panama to take part in Fleet Problem Number 3 in which an attempt was made by one naval force to pass through the Canal from the Pacific to the Atlantic while opposed by another naval force. The marine unit, acting with the defense force, made a successful landing on the Atlantic side and constructively captured positions (from army detachments) which would have enabled it to destroy the locks before the attacking fleet arrived. Meanwhile the balance of the Expeditionary Force (about 1,600 men in all) had landed at Culebra and had prepared the defenses of the island as for an advanced base. They mined the entrance to the main harbor, set up artillery positions, built roads, and established booms and wire entanglements across the most likely landing beaches.[24]

After the termination of the Panamanian exercise the Fifth Regiment reembarked to participate in Fleet Problem Number 4, a simulated landing on Culebra. The total strength of this unit was about 1,700 troops. Battleships simulated bombardment of the shore for about an hour at a range of three miles. In the early morning of February 1 troops were embarked in small boats which landed them in two waves of about twenty boats each.

The results were far from satisfactory. Brigadier General Eli K. Cole, commanding general of the Marine Corps Expeditionary Force, was thoroughly displeased with the whole exhibition. The attack force was too small. It should have outnumbered the defenders by at least three to one. It was a mistake to attempt a landing in force before dawn, and there were insufficient boats to do the job. In general, he concluded, "chaos reigned. The boat officers had not been informed of the designated landing beaches. There was no order maintained among the boats carrying the landing party . . . to the landing beaches. Certain boats became lost for a time and landings were made on beaches which had not been designated for certain units. . . . The Navy 'fell down' in landing the troops on the beach. This is the most important situation which should be corrected."

Other observers were equally discouraged. The simulated naval bombardment would have done practically no damage to artillery positions or personnel located on reverse slopes of the hills fronting the beaches. During the approach to the beach the small boats were under active and effective shrapnel fire which would have made a successful landing impossible under actual wartime conditions. To complicate matters the single troop transport had been badly loaded. No food came ashore the first night, although a post exchange was set up within a few hours after the landing. Medical stores had been stowed at the bottom of one of the holds and were almost completely inaccessible at the time they were needed. It took nine days for the medical department to get all of its supplies.

In short, almost all the mistakes conceivable in a landing operation were made. Rear Admiral Montgomery M. Taylor, who commanded the naval attack force, emerged from this experience a wiser man by two lessons he had learned; "(a) the Navy should develop a doctrine on the seizure, defense and attack of naval advanced bases. (b) the Navy should undertake training for the solution of such problems. . . ." [25]

Unhappily this sound advice went practically unheeded for almost ten years.

The exercise was significant however, not only for the glaring defects in amphibious training it revealed, but also because it marked the beginning of serious experimentation with landing craft more suitable than the old-fashioned standard ships' boats. Two new experimental types were tested with what the Commandant cryptically defined as "interesting, though not decisive, results." [26] One of these was a twin-motor fifty-foot troop-carrying boat, with armor protection and a bow ramp for the discharge of wheeled equipment. It was designated "Troop Barge A" and had been developed under the supervision of Eli Cole.[27]

Another interesting innovation introduced that winter at Culebra was an amphibian tank invented by J. Walter Christie. Models of this vehicle had been tested earlier with some success in the Hudson and Potomac Rivers, but on the ocean it proved unseaworthy. Even though never perfected, it was the earliest forerunner of the amphibian tractor (LVT) which was to make such a remarkable record in World War II.[28]

This 1924 exercise was the high point in practical training in amphibious tactics during the decade of the twenties. In the next year about 1,500 marines participated in a joint army-navy exercise on Oahu, and although the landing ran somewhat more smoothly than on the previous occasion, it was still handicapped, chiefly for want of adequate landing craft. This was the last time any marine detachment attended fleet maneuvers until the winter of 1931–1932, when a reinforced battalion underwent a period of intense training aboard two battleships operating in the Atlantic, Caribbean, and Pacific, and another force of 700 marines took part in a joint army and navy exercise in Hawaiian waters. Meanwhile, only slight progress was made in the theoretical education of Marine Corps personnel in the art of amphibious warfare. An "expeditionary force" course was added to the curriculum of the Field Officer's School at Quantico in 1926, but no radical revision of the general training program ensued.[29]

During this same period Marines were acquiring some experience and skill in aviation and particularly in those branches of it that were especially adapted to amphibious warfare, namely aerial observation and attack aviation, or low-level bombing and strafing in support of ground troops.

Aerial observation was important enough as the "eyes of the artillery" in ordinary land fighting, but it achieved an even greater usefulness in landing operations where observation planes were absolutely essential to the proper direction of naval gunfire against masked targets on the shore. This was the first activity of marine aviation, and duties of attack aviation were to be expanded to include the highly essential function of delivering the last-minute blow to the beaches before assault troops were landed as well as providing firepower in close support of ground troops.

As early as 1916 a Marine Corps aviation company of ten officers and forty enlisted men was organized for duty with the advance-base force. After the location of the advance-base (now the "Expeditionary") force at Quantico, this unit was expanded into the First Aviation Group consisting of a fighter squadron, an observation squadron, and a kite balloon squadron. In addition the Corps had two other observation squadrons located in the Caribbean, and a scouting squadron on Guam. By 1932 Marine Corps aviation had been enlarged to include two observation and one fighting squadrons operating with the east coast expeditionary force at Quantico, one of each attached to the west coast expeditionary force at San Diego, an observation squadron on Haiti, another on the fleet aircraft carrier *Saratoga,* and finally a scouting squadron on the fast carrier *Lexington.*[30]

Throughout these years marine pilots were trained in the standard aviation techniques of aerial combat, bombing, strafing, artillery observation, reconnaissance, aerial photography, and scouting. They participated in the joint army-navy exercises on Oahu in 1925. During the troubles in Nicaragua they flew supplies, dropped messages, evacuated the wounded, made reconnaissance and observations sorties and, more important, flew many attack missions in close support of ground troops against the insurrectionists.[31] What is most significant about this early training is that in the Marine Corps aviation was closely integrated with the ground troops. The connection between the pilot and the infantryman was intimate and constant. All marine pilots were previously trained in ground tactics and consequently had an understanding and appreciation of infantry problems that a mere airman could not possibly acquire. This tended to breed a mutual confidence between the two branches which is the essential ingredient of close air support.[32]

3. The Turning Point—Fleet Marine Force Established

The year 1933 marked the most crucial turning point in Marine Corps history. With the final evacuation of the last marine detachment from Nicaragua in January of 1932 the way was at last open for a continuous program of training and indoctrination in advance-base or expeditionary work with the fleet. Before any such scheme could be practically realized however, one preliminary step was essential— a sizeable body of marines would have to be permanently attached to the fleet for this purpose. Otherwise, as in the past, training in this sort of work would be continually interrupted by the detachment of one unit after another for petty jungle wars, or for guarding shore stations at home.

The critical nature of the problem was realized by many in the Marine Corps and Navy, but it was Major General John H. Russell, Assistant Commandant, who took the initial steps toward a solution. Russell set up a staff at Quantico to work out plans for organizing a striking force which could be mobilized rapidly for service with the fleet. Then in August 1933 he wrote to the Commandant suggesting the discontinuance of the old "Expeditionary Force" and the substitution of a new body to be called either the "Fleet Base Defense Force" or the "Fleet Marine Force." This force, he insisted, should "be included in the fleet organization as an integral part thereof, subject to the orders, for tactical employment, of the Commander-in-Chief, U.S. Fleet." Within less than a month these recommendations were accepted by the Commandant, the Director of War Plans Division of the Navy Department, the Chief of Naval Operations, and the Commander-in-Chief, U.S. Fleet. The Commandant was ordered to prepare a set of instructions for establishing appropriate command

and administrative relations between the new Fleet Marine Force and its parent body the United States Fleet. This was accomplished forthwith, and Major General Russell, acting for the Commandant, drew up a set of general rules governing the newly established Fleet Marine Force; these rules were subsequently embodied verbatim in Navy Department General Order No. 241 issued on December 8, 1933, which gave official birth to the new organization.[33]

For the first year of its life the Fleet Marine Force was a badly undernourished baby. Only one full regiment of infantry (plus a skeleton regiment of ten per cent strength), two batteries of 75-millimeter pack howitzers, one battery of .50-caliber antiaircraft machine guns, and two aircraft groups were activated. This left completely unorganized the remaining components of the brigade strength which had been authorized, namely two infantry regiments, three battalions of light artillery, two battalions of 6-inch guns, and four battalions of antiaircraft guns.[34] These shortages in personnel were hard to remedy in the lean years of the early thirties, but at least a start had been made.

What is more important is that with the creation of the Fleet Marine Force the Marine Corps had finally and unequivocally committed itself to the doctrine that its paramount mission in wartime was to serve the fleet by seizing bases for naval operations and in peacetime to prepare for the successful execution of that function. One of the first steps taken in this direction was a general overhauling of theoretical instruction at the Marine Corps Schools in Quantico. This was accomplished by 1934 when three separate classes were set up for officers' training. The course for the first-year class, according to school regulations, included "tactical and strategical operations, with command and staff functions of all units up to and including the brigade as an independent unit, *and as part of a force in naval landing operations, including the seizure of naval bases, the occupation and defense of naval bases,* small wars, and emergency operations such as Marines are frequently called on to perform. . . ." The course for the second-year class was to include "the entire field of naval landing operations with special emphasis on the Marine Brigade, the Fleet Marine Force, both when acting independently and when part of the Fleet. . . ." [35] The third course, entitled the "Base Defense Weapons Class," was designed primarily to prepare officers for service within the Fleet Marine Force and consisted primarily of technical and practical instruction in base defense weapons.

The next step was to prepare a manual of landing operations which would set forth in as much detail as possible the known facts about this difficult and still mysterious type of operation, and to include in addition a theoretical doctrine to be tested later by practical exercises. It is true that as early as 1920 the navy had prepared a manual for ships' landing forces, to instruct naval personnel on the conduct of shore operations. But only a very small part (7 out of 760 pages) was devoted to a discussion of actual landing, and the treatment was too brief and elementary to be of any use. The same manual reissued in 1927 contained only five pages pertaining to landing operations.[36] Also, the Joint Board had already prepared a general doctrine covering joint army-navy overseas expeditions. Issued in January 1933, this constituted a useful statement of many of the problems and some of the solutions in amphibious warfare with which future planners would have to deal. It defined an amphibious landing as "in effect the assault of an organized defense position modified by substituting naval gunfire support for divisional, corps, and army artillery, and generally navy aircraft support for, the army aircraft support." It set forth a procedure for preparing plans for this type of operation and gave many practical and well-considered suggestions on such matters as combat-loading, selecting the beaches to assault, aerial and naval gunfire support, debarking the troops, the ship-to-shore movement, organizing traffic on the beaches, and many other technical matters of importance for planning and executing successful amphibious landings.[37] In fact, many of the definitions and solutions presented in this document became permanently incorporated in standard American amphibious doctrine and recur frequently in the subsequent handbooks and manuals on the subject issued both before and during World War II. This statement of 1933 is noteworthy as evidence that the Marine Corps was not alone in giving early consideration to the study of amphibious tactics. Army and navy personnel on the Joint Board were also devoting careful attention to the problem well before the formation of the Fleet Marine Force, even though they subsequently delegated to the Marine Corps most of the practical work of preparing detailed plans.

The chief defect of the Joint Board publication was its brevity, and it was left to members of the Marine Corps, especially those stationed at Quantico, to sketch the details into the broad pattern set down. By order of the Commandant, classes at the schools were discontinued as of November 14, 1933, and the staff, assisted by resident students, began to assemble a manual for landing operations. The Joint Board pamphlet of January 1933 was to be accepted as the basis for any instructions, and the staff was ordered to deviate from the principles and doctrine prescribed therein "only after due deliberation and a firm belief that the Marine Corps Schools in collaboration with the Fleet Marine Force are right, and the Joint Board is wrong. . . ." Each officer involved in the study was required to write out his idea of a chronological itemized list of things to be done from the beginning to the end of a Fleet Marine Force landing. Then a committee of nine was appointed to consider these papers and each member on conclusion submitted his own list based on the result of his studies of all papers submitted. These nine papers were finally submitted to a committee of five who recommended a general outline for the manual, and all staff and students were then divided into groups for working out the details.[38]

It was pioneer work of the most daring and imaginative sort. Except for one brief directive manual, a few historical studies of past amphibious operations, and a somewhat sketchy experience in landing practices, the men who prepared this new document had almost nothing to go on but their own intuition and common sense. The marine captain who headed the aviation committee frankly reported that his group "approached its subject . . . about the same as every other committee, with a lantern in one hand and a candle in the other—but neither of these seemed to throw much light on the subject, so we wound up by hiding our lights under a bushel and using the imagination that God gave us to use for this particular purpose. . . . We approached it with fear and trembling . . . fear for the aviators who put these operations into execution after we wrote them, and trembling for the troops if we fail to provide adequate air support for their protection." [39]

The result was in every way a remarkable document. It was immediately put to use as the basis for all theoretical instruction in amphibious warfare in the Marine Corps Schools. It served as the guidebook for all the early landing exercises which Navy and Marine Corps thereafter held each year until World War II. It was adopted with revisions by the navy in 1938 under the title *Fleet Training Publication 167* and became official doctrine for landing operations. This navy manual was in turn copied in large part verbatim by the army when it issued its first basic field manual for landing operations on hostile shores, in 1941.[40] If these and later publications by all the services during and before World War II can be considered the Holy Writ of modern amphibious warfare, then the *Tentative Manual for Landing Operations* published by the Marine Corps Schools in 1934 deserves to be thought of as a sort of combination of the Pentateuch and the Four Gospels. It warrants detailed attention not only as a historic document, but also because a careful examination of this manual will serve as an introduction to what were the main problems in modern amphibious operations and to the lines along which those problems were to be solved.

4. The Tentative Manual for Landing Operations

Amphibious warfare has many features in common with ordinary ground fighting, and many of the tactical rules that govern the latter hold good with modification for the former. The main difference between the two, in the simplest terms, is that in amphibious fighting, troops must be embarked on ships, carried considerable distances over the seas, disembarked into some kind of landing boats and put ashore on enemy territory with only light equipment and without benefit of immediate artillery assistance—all before they can even commence the actual seizure and occupation of the objective. Or to use the official definition stated in the *Tentative Landing Manual*, "A landing operation against opposition is, in effect, an assault on an organized or unorganized defensive position modified by substituting initially ships' gunfire for that of light, medium, and heavy field artillery, and frequently, carrier-based aviation for land-based air units until the latter can be operated from ashore." [41] This task, even when reduced to this lowest common denominator, is on the face of it a highly complex one. It raises certain special problems unknown to land warfare. The main purpose of the men who prepared the *Tentative Landing Manual* of 1934 was to isolate these problems and suggest practical solutions.

For purposes of analysis, amphibious warfare can be broken down into six component parts, each representing a peculiar feature of this type of combat. These are (a) command relations, (b) naval gunfire support, (c) aerial support, (d) the ship-to-shore movement, (e) securing the beachhead, and (f) logistics, including loading, unloading and distribution of supplies and equipment. To understand some of the niceties of these problems it will be well to examine in some detail how they were treated in the 1934 manual.

Command Relationships. It is easy for a landing operation to founder at the very outset on the shoals of jurisdictional controversy between naval and land forces. This was demonstrated at Gallipoli, when only rarely was there complete accord between naval and army commanders as to their respective duties and powers. When the two senior services, army and navy, are involved, there can be all kinds of nice questions as to who is in command over whom, and when, and where. These are intensified by traditional interservice rivalries and by the apparently congenital inability of many naval officers to appreciate the needs and problems of army troops and vice versa. But since the Fleet Marine Force was by definition under the administrative command of the navy, many of these latent difficulties were theoretically eliminated. Consequently the *Tentative Landing Manual* devotes comparatively little space to the question.

According to the manual, naval overseas expeditions will be initiated as a part of a naval campaign. The expedition assigned to a specific landing operation will be organized as a task force of the fleet under the immediate command of a flag officer of the navy who will direct the employment of all forces participating in the landing operation. This task force is designated as the naval attack force and is made up of two parts, both under command of the naval attack force commander. These are, first, the landing force consisting of the troops to be landed, in this case the Fleet Marine Force or units thereof, and second, naval supporting groups. The latter consist of a fire-support group including all vessels assigned to gunfire support, an air group, a mine group, an antisubmarine group, a transport group, a screening group employed to locate and warn the attack force against enemy vessels, and a salvage group to rescue personnel and haul off grounded ships.[42]

The chain of command in this organization is comparatively simple. The naval attack force commander would have ultimate authority to make decisions affecting either the landing force or the various naval support groups, all of which would enjoy parallel command functions. This later proved to be an oversimplified solution to some of the complexities of command relations that were to evolve during the war years, and had to be considerably modified. But it was a start, and at least it avoided some of the confusion inherent in joint operations.

Naval Gunfire. Obviously the most vulnerable feature of landing operations is the absence of artillery support at the time it is most needed, namely just before and during the ship-to-shore movement. This was the main stumbling block upon which many previous planners of amphibious operations faltered and fell. Nelson's ancient adage that "a ship's a fool to fight a fort" was typical of most orthodox thought of the navy on the subject, at least up to World War II, and with some reason. The inherent limitations of naval gunfire were well recognized by Marine Corps planners in 1934, but their general conclusion was that many of these handicaps could be at least partially overcome with practice and experimentation, and that effective employment of ships' guns in lieu of artillery was well within the realm of practical possibility. The first of these limitations was that naval guns in general had far flatter trajectories than land-based artillery of the same caliber, for the obvious reason that naval guns were designed to fire against ships on the surface of the ocean and not over hills and other obstructions. This meant that their usefulness against land targets located on the reverse side of slopes or masked by other obstructions was severely restricted. Also, ships' fire is generally less accurate, at least in range, than land-based artillery, and there is great danger of some shells falling within the lines of friendly troops. Finally, the effectiveness of naval gunfire is limited by the amount of ammunition a ship can carry in its magazines, and ordinary naval ammunition is unsuited for destruction of most land targets. The delayed action fuse of the ordinary navy service projectile permits the shell to bury itself in the ground before bursting and is consequently quite ineffective against open ground and troops as compared with corresponding types of army projectiles.

To overcome all these limitations the promulgators of the Marine Corps *Manual* made certain specific proposals. Even if ships' guns cannot search out and destroy all enemy artillery and machine gun installations, it will usually be possible to neutralize these weapons during the most critical stages of the ship-to-shore movement; that is, the defenders can be forced to take cover and abandon their positions temporarily. Concentration of naval gunfire against the landing beaches in well-timed surprise bursts of fire of maximum intensity is well adapted to ships' guns and may be very effectively employed against the sort of opposition to be expected. If it is hard to deliver naval fire against reverse slopes from the front, ships do have the advantage of mobility and can possibly take positions behind or parallel to the hills and do considerable damage in that fashion. The problem of firing shorts into friendly troops can be partly solved by delivering fire only on their flanks or by moving to positions parallel to the infantry advance, in which case more accurate fire will be possible since errors in deflection are much less common than those in range.

Heavy ships might accompany the assault waves close to the beaches and blast away at machine gun defenses, or the same function could be performed by light vessels. If present naval ammunition is inadequate to do the job against land targets, new special types will have to be developed. A system of communications between ship and shore must be worked out. Fire-control parties consisting of regular ships' fire-control parties assisted by artillery or infantry personnel must be organized to coordinate naval gunfire with artillery fire and infantry movements. It might be practicable to beach merchant vessels or transports and use them as stationary platforms employing naval guns instead of artillery.[43]

In short, the job must be done, and the Navy and Marine Corps must find ways of doing it. This very recognition of the possibilities inherent in naval gunfire in support of landing operations was a considerable step forward from the general counsel of despair that typified most contemporary naval thinking on the subject. If some of these suggestions were to prove impractical and others naïve, at least the issue was faced squarely, and the main lines for further experimentation and development were clearly laid down.

Aerial Support. One of the fundamental prerequisites to successful landing operations is the maintenance of air superiority of at least three to one. The first job that falls to aviation is reconnaissance. Although this is important enough in land operations, it is even more vital in amphibious operations, since the chances are that the attacking force will have comparatively little previous information about the terrain, defense installations, and troop dispositions of the target area. This is particularly the case in operations against remote island bases about which there is very little intelligence. But effective aerial reconnaissance is not an unmixed blessing. Air and surface scouting carried long distances to seaward will in all probability result in the early discovery by the enemy of an approaching expedition. Therefore it is recognized that strategic surprise must probably be sacrificed. The same is true if carrier planes are used to bombard hostile defenses before the actual landing takes place. In either case, the manual concludes, the loss of surprise is a necessary and justifiable price to pay since the gains will ordinarily far outweigh the losses.

A second duty of air support during a landing attack is to provide fighter protection over the transport area during the period of debarkation from transports to landing craft. At the same time scout planes must initiate intensive reconnaissance of the hostile defenses and enemy installations, particularly those located on or near the beach, and relay this information immediately to appropriate commands. Finally, while the troops are still being loaded into their landing boats, bombers must commence attacks against hostile aircraft on the ground and against long-range guns located inland.

During the ship-to-shore movement aviation will play a vital function. Fighters will operate to destroy enemy aircraft which might harass the landing troops. If smoke screens are desirable to protect the leading waves from machine-gun fire from the beach, planes will be the most practicable method of laying them. Also, guide planes may be used to direct the first boat waves to the proper beaches. Finally, and most important, as the troops approach the shore and naval gunfire lifts inland, dive bombers and attack planes must take over the job of neutralizing strong points in the beach defenses.

Meanwhile observation planes must be employed to spot targets for naval gunfire. This job becomes even more important after the troops have landed and ships' fire lifts from the beach inland, since accurate spotting becomes essential to prevent naval gunners from firing into their own troops. After the seizure and organization of the beachhead, aviation will revert to normal practices of land warfare except that lines of communications between ship and shore present novel problems. Attack planes, however, will normally concentrate on destroying or immobilizing hostile reserves and reinforcements, striking aircraft on the ground, neutralizing antiaircraft guns, and supporting the infantry in their advance.

It is recognized that one of the chief difficulties of employing aircraft in amphibious operations is that of proper coordination of air with naval gunfire, artillery, and troop movements. This is essentially a problem of communications. In ordinary land fighting it is *relatively* simple to maintain contact between different troop units, or between front line infantry and rear command posts or between infantry and artillery by means of radio, telephone, or runners. The introduction of aerial and naval support complicates the matter tremendously, and the planners of the *Tentative Landing Manual* had to address themselves to the problem of overcoming these new difficulties.

All aircraft, they concluded, should be individually equipped with radio capable of being used in two-way telephonic and telegraphic air-ground, air-ship, and inter-plane communication. Since mechanical failures in radio equipment are always possible, alternate means of contact must always be available. One of these would be the use of searchlight code signals between ships and planes in flight. For communication with troops, ground panels (usually cut strips of cloth in various colors) using prearranged codes could be employed for sending messages and marking front lines. Wing and engine signals, firing of rockets, and dropping and pick up of written messages were other possibilities suggested.[44]

As to the question of assignment of responsibility for these sundry duties, the manual concludes that during the initial phase of the attack naval carrier-based planes will probably have to assume the burden of the job, at least until airfields can be established for the use of land-based planes. In the meantime, Marine Corps pilots and observers may be utilized in navy planes which are engaged in reconnaissance, artillery spotting, and attack missions in support of ground operations. Finally, it is concluded, if at all possible "every effort should be made to provide for the participation of landing force [Marine Corps] aircraft in the initial operations. The ideal arrangement involves the assignment of a carrier or carriers solely for the use of these units. . . ."[45]

This plea for the allocation of separate carriers to Marine Corps use was one which Marine Corps spokesmen were to keep repeating for more than a decade—and with no success.

Ship-to-shore Movement. This is the beginning of the actual attack, comparable to an infantry attack in land warfare. This ship-to-shore movement has to be considered as more than a mere ferrying operation, since it is a tactical movement in its own right. An attack on land opens with preparatory gunfire laid on enemy positions, increasing in severity until masked by the assaulting infantry. Usually the troops commence their approach in long columns and as they close on the target they deploy into small units to minimize the danger of enemy fire. Then at the right moment artillery fire lifts, and the infantry rushes the enemy positions. The ship-to-shore movement is similar in every respect except that the troops are water borne. Naval gunfire rather than artillery precedes the attack. The troop-laden boats must deploy in much the same manner as infantry to avoid enemy fire. As they approach the beach they add their own automatic or machine-gun fire to that of the heavier guns. Finally, at the last moment, ships' fire lifts and the small craft carry the attack across the beach's edge.

Therefore the main problem in planning a ship-to-shore movement is to get troops disembarked into their boats rapidly and in the right order, and to dispatch the landing craft to the beach as quickly as possible in formations that will reduce the danger of being hit. In the first place it is axiomatic that the plan of debarkation must be based on the planned scheme of maneuver ashore. This means that individual transports should carry aboard the entire troop unit or units assigned to a particular beach area. If possible, transports should also carry the boats allocated to the troops they have aboard, so that there will be no crossing of boats. They must anchor in a position immediately seaward of the beach or beaches assigned to their own troops. Troops must be disembarked expeditiously according to prearranged plan and so as to avoid breaking up the integrity of smaller troop units. Boats will be organized into flotillas under command of a naval officer. After receiving assigned troops, boats will be towed in strings of about three to a line-of-departure which is a coordinating line parallel to the beach, from 2,500 to 4,000 yards from shore and marked by buoys or by anchored small craft. Thence they proceed under their own power to the beach on a prearranged signal, either in line abreast, in separate waves deployed, or in V formation. If the occasion permits, troop-carrying minesweeps or tugs might follow the first wave into the beach and disembark their troops into small boats just offshore.

The equipment of the personnel of the assault battalions must be light. During the early phases of the landing they will have to be reinforced with pack howitzers and possibly even tanks.[46]

Securing the Beachhead. "Beachhead" is defined as "a zone contiguous to the beach the possession of which permits the continuous landing of troops, equipment and supplies without serious interference from the enemy, and ensures the maneuver space and the terrain features requisite for a further advance." The techniques necessary for securing this area are somewhat different from those employed in ordinary ground warfare. In the first place, at least in the early stages, only light artillery and light tanks can be employed. The landing of both requires special types of lighters, and in the case of the latter it would be desirable to develop an amphibian tank.

One of the chief problems rising out of landing attacks is congestion on the beach. This requires the establishment of beach and shore regulating parties which will consist of both navy and marine corps personnel and to which are assigned a heterogeneous assortment of duties. The men must be landed in the first wave or subwave. They then mark the beaches clearly so as to avoid confusion among later waves. They are responsible for emergency repairs to boats. They must set up a central communications center, maintain continuous contact with the flagship, with firing ships, and with naval fire-control parties as the latter move inland. It is the job of the beach and shore parties to expedite movement of troops and supplies inland and to control all labor gangs on the beach, and they are charged with the responsibility of evacuating the wounded.[47] Navy officers in consultation with marine liaison personnel aboard vessels at the line-of-departure control the dispatch of men and supplies to the coast, and their transit to and from the line-of-departure to the water's edge falls under the purview of navy personnel (the beach party) headed by a beachmaster. Thereupon the marine shore party takes charge to move supplies from the beach to the fighting troops.

Logistics. As the Gallipoli experience indicated, one of the most essential conditions for successful landing operations is the proper loading of the vessels carrying troops and their supplies and equipment. For most landings, at least if opposition is expected, this calls for "combat unit loading" which means that "certain units, selected because of their probable employment to meet tactical situations, are completely loaded in one transport with at least their essential combat equipment, transportations and supplies immediately available for debarkation with the troops." This means in effect that supplies and equipment have to be stowed aboard ship in such a manner that they can be located promptly and handed over to the troops at the precise time they are needed. Certain basic rules must therefore be observed in allocating materiel into the various ships' holds and cargo spaces. All equipment and supplies must be so allotted as to permit debarkation in the order required. If possible, the materiel belonging to each organization should be loaded in the same part of the ship. Combat equipment and supplies which are required early in a landing should be assigned to accessible spaces near the unit concerned. Materiel not needed until later in the operation should be stowed near the bottom of ships' holds and outward from the hatch openings. The higher the priority the closer it should be stowed toward the top and center of the particular hold in question. The most essential materiel should be located immediately under the hatch cover. At the same time consideration must be given to the effect of loading on ship stability, and a compromise must be reached between the combat requirements of the troops and the minimum safety standards of the vessel carrying them.

To supervise this complicated job a transport quartermaster should be assigned to each transport, under the commanding officer of the troops aboard. He must acquaint himself with the blueprints of the ship to which he is assigned, and know the exact location of all holds and storage spaces and the deck space and cubic footage of each. With this data he must compute the cubic footage, the dimensions, and the weight of every item of Marine Corps equipment and supplies that will be carried aboard. With all this information in hand he can then assign each item to its proper stowage place, keeping in mind all the considerations stated above. It is a job which requires the most meticulous attention to detail; and the *Manual,* by outlining the sequence of the particular steps to be followed and by establishing standard forms and procedure, made a significant contribution to the development of scientific combat-loading.[48]

Thus *The Tentative Landing Manual* prepared at Marine Corps Schools was the first attempt to set forth in a systematic fashion a detailed treatise on modern amphibious warfare. It was a pioneering effort, and by no means the last word. From the vantage point of fifteen years of experience, four of which were spent in the supreme test of war, some of its solutions seem primitive. But the changes which years of training exercises, "war games," and war itself have wrought in the original doctrine are less fundamental than is the persistency with which the doctrine has endured under the most critical conditions. The foundation laid in 1934 was an enduring one.

CHAPTER III

TRAINING FOR AMPHIBIOUS WAR, 1934–1942

WITH the main outlines of the possibilities and problems of amphibious warfare sketched in broad detail, the next steps were to make empirical tests of the theories set forth, to perfect techniques by experimental study, to train large numbers of military personnel in the applied art of amphibious warfare, and to encourage technological improvements in landing craft, guns, communications, and other equipment. Only thus could the hypotheses which had been formulated largely through historical study and intuitive reasoning be translated into practical rules of warfare. With the groundwork laid down in 1934, further progress to the beginning of World War II followed three parallel but closely connected lines: an increasingly heavy stress on historical and theoretical study of amphibious operations in the Marine Corps Schools; annual landing exercises with elements of the fleet; and a continuous program of technological development especially in the field of landing craft.

In the Marine Corps Schools at Quantico the scope of activities was gradually expanded after 1934, and in all courses emphasis was placed more and more on the tactics and technique of landing operations. By 1936 the curriculum had been expanded to four resident courses: a senior course, a junior course, a base-defense weapons course, and a basic course.[1] Every year from 1932 to 1941 the senior course culminated in practical projects in which student officers and staff members jointly worked out the details of a particular "problem" involving either the attack or defense of an advance base. In addition the schools submitted solutions of similar amphibious problems to the Naval War College every year from 1935 to 1943. These involved working out detailed plans for the capture of various advanced bases including Truk (in 1935), Palau (1936), Guam (1939), Saipan (1940–43), and a number of islands in the West Indies.[2] Although amphibious techniques changed so rapidly during the intervening years as to render these earlier plans somewhat obsolete, they were nevertheless of great value in acquainting marine and navy officers with the exact nature of the operations which would have to be waged in the Pacific and with the special amphibious tactics that were adaptable to each of the particular islands chosen for study.

1. *Applying the Theory—Early Fleet Training Exercises*

The main training ground for future amphibious warriors was not, however, the class room, but rather the practical training exercises that were conducted yearly either at Culebra or on the island of San Clemente off San Diego. These "Fleet Landing Exercises" were held each winter in conjunction with elements of the fleet, and it was here that the marines got their first really continuous practical training in landing operations and that the full details of a workable amphibious doctrine were hammered out.

The first of these exercises was conducted early in 1935. One cruiser and three destroyers of the Special Service Squadron, two battleships of the Training Squadron, Scouting Force, and a single transport were assigned to the troop elements participating. These consisted of the Fifth Marines (less one battalion); the Tenth Marines, an artillery regiment; and an observation squadron of twelve planes from the First Marine Air Group. Five army observers were also present.[3]

For the infantry the exercises consisted of daily debarkation (from gangways) into standard navy boats and movement into the beach where various types of ordinary maneuvers and firing practices were held. One full-scale two-battalion landing was made, but without accompanying naval gunfire, so its value as a rehearsal was limited.

The most significant exercises were those involving naval gunfire support and aerial bombardment. Naval fire-control officers from each of the firing ships went ashore well beforehand to acquaint themselves with the terrain, and the ships' officers had ample previous opportunity to explore the shore line and pick out the best positions from which to deliver their fire. Since there was little or no reliable data available as to the efficacy of naval gunfire against beach targets, the primary purpose of these exercises was to test the ability of naval guns to train on various types of targets on land and to discover which varieties of naval shells were the most useful. A great many artificialities were introduced, however, and there was no real effort made to simulate wartime conditions. The targets were wooden panels, so there was no opportunity for naval gunners to identify various types of military objects that would be their normal targets in wartime.

Nevertheless the 1935 exercises had some practical value in spite of the artificialities. Among other things, they proved that naval fire could be accurate against ground targets (at least under ideal conditions). More important, they established definitely what types of naval shells were and were not suited for shore bombardment. As had been predicted in the *Tentative Landing Manual,* the standard large (12-inch) armor-piercing shells were totally useless for this type of work, and flat nose high-capacity projectiles were the best adapted of all existing naval ammunition to counterbattery, neutralization, and interdiction work which would be required of naval support ships in wartime.[4] It was not yet realized that some of the defensive emplacements encountered on the beaches in World War II would be so strongly built as to require armor-piercing shells.

Equally important was the experience gained in the use of observation planes in spotting naval gunfire and in radio communications between ships and aircraft. Pilots discovered that the best technique for observation was to fly at an altitude of three to six thousand feet in a semi-circle about one-third of the distance between ship and target. Of course the value of this discovery was somewhat vitiated by the fact that there was no enemy firing at them from below.

These same planes also went through numerous practice runs against beach targets, flying at low altitudes and alternately bombing and strafing. Surprisingly, low-altitude bombing proved more effective than dive bombing.[5]

As to the small boats employed in the 1935 landing exercises, the main conclusions were that there were not enough of them, that standard navy boats were unsuitable for the purpose of landing operations, that experiments in the development of special boats should be revived, and that a number of such boats should be employed for experiment and standardization during the next annual exercises.

Two interesting but inconclusive experiments were made with special landing craft. A new type of artillery lighter (Type B) was used to get 155-millimeter guns ashore. It was equipped with ramps at the bow, which was a novelty, but on the whole, though it seemed satisfactory at the time, it was a clumsy craft. It was not self-propelled, but had to be towed and shoved into position by motor launches; its ramps were operated by hand, and it was too deep-drafted to beach properly, so that a log corduroy matting had to be laid down between the bow of the lighter and dry land before the guns could be hauled ashore.

An effort was also made to attach a ramp to a standard fifty-foot motor launch equipped with a special contraption known as "Boat Rig A" for lowering the ramp to permit debarkation of light trucks. Boat Rig A was designed by the navy for use on standard motor launches. It consisted of an improvised deck above the gunwhales, on top of which was a ramp with rollers. With this device a small piece of equipment up to the size of a 75-millimeter gun could be put ashore from a motor launch. It proved too top-heavy to be practicable. Although this gadget worked reasonably well in sheltered water, the boat was unseaworthy in even a moderate swell, and after one harrowing experience when it almost capsized in the trough of a small wave, the experiment was abandoned.[6]

Viewed against the total picture of amphibious development, the net results of the 1935 exercises seem rather trifling. Less than a half dozen naval ships fired a few days on land-based artificial targets under extremely unrealistic conditions. The results merely confirmed the obvious—that heavy slow-fused armor-piercing shells buried themselves in the ground before detonating and did relatively little damage to exposed targets. Some 1,500 marines learned, if they did not already know, what it was to ride the sea in open boats and get wet up to their waists in a surf. A single observation squadron got some practical experience in air spotting and beach attack. A converted naval motor launch was found to be useless to ferry vehicles. A clumsy tank lighter was tested with dubious results.

Still, it was a beginning. The Navy and Marine Corps personnel who took part were convinced that the road ahead to genuine amphibious efficiency was long and rough and that much more practice was needed.

The next year's exercises (Fleet Exercise Number Two) were on a somewhat more elaborate scale.[7] The understrength First Marine Brigade consisting of the Fifth Marines * less one battalion, the Tenth Marines, chemical and engineering companies, and all of the First Marine Air Group participated. Five ships which had been in the last exercise, two battleships, two destroyers, and one troop transport, were on hand this time as well as three new arrivals, a cruiser and two destroyers.

The period of training was considerably longer than on the previous occasion (lasting from January 4 to February 24, 1936), and although much of the time was still spent in standard combat training ashore, a far more comprehensive program in actual landing operations was devised. Eight separate landing exercises were held, the troops debarking over the sides of battleships or destroyers and running into shore in motor whaleboats or standard navy motor launches. This time, in place of the old-style gangways, cargo nets were used on some occasions to get the troops off the ships, an innovation which was used consistently throughout World War II. Both battalions of the Fifth Marines underwent three types of landings: a daylight landing, a daylight landing screened by smoke, and a night landing attack. Then came a full-scale regimental assault at daybreak, and finally a full-scale brigade landing calculated to approximate actual battle conditions as nearly as possible.

The two battalion daylight exercises proceeded without hitch and were conducted more expeditiously than in the previous year. Experiments were also made in landing waves of boats under cover of smoke. A single plane laid down a screen when the first wave reached

---

* Marine Corps terminology, meaning the Fifth Marine Regiment reinforced with ground support and service troops.

a point about 1,400 yards offshore, and another screen was laid on the beach as the troops came within 600 yards of the coast. Neither screen proved to be of any value, and in fact the first tended only to delay the boats as the coxswains were afraid to risk collision or grounding.

The night landings were even less satisfactory, although there was some difference of opinion as to their feasibility for future operations. The Second Battalion, Fifth Marines, made the first try with unfortunate results. Boats failed to show up in their proper order and got lost in the dark even before their troops were aboard. After some delay most of the marines were loaded on some boat or another and thereafter complete confusion reigned. Coxswains had little notion of where they were, circled uselessly looking for their proper station, and landed considerable distances from their assigned beaches. Yet each boat carried a strong blue stern light visible two miles offshore, and the control boat circulated throughout the milling mass with glowing running lights in a futile effort to bring some order out of chaos. Had normal battle conditions of absolute darkness been observed it is doubtful if the troops would ever have reached shore before daylight. The next attempt by the First Battalion was somewhat more successful, perhaps as a result of an intervening conference held between the battalion commander and all the navy boat commanders.

During the regimental landing, scheduled for daybreak, the same trouble was experienced as before—boats got lost in the minutes before dawn, failed to leave the line-of-departure simultaneously, and moved to the wrong beaches.

The final exercise involved the entire brigade (which was actually a reinforced regiment, less one of its three battalions). It was a daylight exercise and on the whole went well, except for some confusion on the beach. This was also the first occasion when a shore party was present. It did not operate as a message center, however, and although units ashore were in contact with a navy beachmaster, the shore party was by-passed in calling for supplies, thus negating one of its essential functions.

The main shortcoming of all these exercises, valuable as they were for the participants, was again the artificialities introduced. Only the ideal beaches were chosen, both ships and boats were brightly lighted during the night operations, and even shore lights were kept on. The reason for this was the navy's reluctance to risk boats to loss or damage, a reluctance which almost reached the point of fixation with any well-indoctrinated navy coxswain. Of course, as the chief army observer present admitted, this attitude could be appreciated since the cost of each motor launch was about $10,000 and even the whaleboats came to $2,000. But it did detract from the training value of the exercises.

The naval gunfire practices took up where they had left off in 1935. They were designed to investigate different combinations of range, muzzle velocities, and types of shells for hitting small targets on reverse slopes, to test the ability of air spotters to identify ground targets selected from a gridded map and to designate the targets to the ship, to test the ability of a battleship to hit targets concealed by smoke, and to discover the effectiveness of destroyer guns in direct support of ground troops. The results were pleasing and somewhat more useful than those of the previous year. Spotting by the use of gridded maps was an important innovation, and the experiment was a success. Observation planes were also used to direct fire on beach targets under cover of smoke simply by flying above the smoke along the axis of the gun toward the target. This was a rather primitive system for avoiding errors in deflection, however, and quite impractical for wartime, as the planes might easily be driven off course by enemy fire. What was considered to be the impracticability of navy armor-piercing shells against shore targets was again demonstrated. Finally, naval vessels got their first experience in delivering a prolonged bombardment, all ships present participating. For two hours and ten minutes they kept the target area under constant fire of all sorts. Even so, there was some doubt as to the feasibility of close naval gunfire support from directly behind the attacking troops. Errors in range were still uncontrollable, and the general conclusion was that ships had better confine their close support missions to firing at right angles to the direction of the line of advance, in which case they could drop their shells within 250 yards of the first boat wave.[8]

As for aviation, the 1936 exercises proved far more useful than those of the previous year. The full strength of the First Marine Air Group (less one service squadron), including more than fifty land-based planes, participated. For a month they made live machine gun and bombing runs against beach targets, laid smoke, spotted for ships' fire, flew reconnaissance and photographic sorties, and performed sundry other services for the ground troops. One observation in connection with these maneuvers deserves special comment. The Marine Corps as yet had no planes specially designed for attack missions. Observation and fighter planes were all that were available for bombing.[9] This, as the commanding officer of one fighter squadron noted, "interferes materially with the normal missions of these types, and is at best a makeshift expedient." He concluded with a plea that the Corps seriously consider procuring modern attack planes for specially trained squadrons for future landing operations. "The importance of ground strafing as an aid to landing troops against opposition would seem to require the most effective tools available for that purpose."[10]

In addition to the regular landing exercises, two special tests were made in running motor launches over coral reefs and through mangroves, such as might be encountered in a Pacific war. The latter exercise was a success, but not the former. A forty-foot motor launch carrying two rifle platoons tried to ground on a coral reef abutting about fifty yards from the beach. A hundred yards off, the stern anchor was dropped; at fifty yards a swell caught the boat by surprise and almost broached it on the reef. With much backing of engines and hauling in on the anchor, the launch worked itself free, much to the relief of the attendant navy boat officer who later reported with restrained horror: "What could have happened [to] the boat . . . is left to conjecture, except that, unless the swells were very slight, the boat would probably be damaged so as to make its seaworthiness extremely doubtful!" [11]

As in the previous landing exercise, tests were again made with the Artillery Lighter and Boat Rig A. The former proved to be about as useful as it had in the earlier experiment, but it was discovered that a motor launch carrying the boat rig, if ballasted with four and a half tons of concrete, was reasonably seaworthy and could be used to haul trucks and tractors ashore.[12]

As for logistics, no effort was made to combat-load the single transport that accompanied the expedition. But by this time the Marine Corps had made some progress in preparing the way for efficient loading. Two pamphlets had been compiled containing most of the basic information required for planning the loading of equipment and material. These were the "Marine Corps Organization and Tonnage Tables" and "Reference Data for Loading and Stowing Marine Corps Material." From these tables the space and tonnage required for any desired organization could readily be obtained. Knowing this and the available cargo capacity of any ship, a workable plan of loading could then be prepared in advance.[13] As it turned out, however, these precautions were of little use in loading the transport *Antares* either in the 1935 or 1936 exercises, since the data available for the ship's own characteristics were inaccurate. The figures as to deck space were wrong, and changes in the ship's holds since the original design had not been recorded. Also, not all the cargo was ready when loading began, and additions were made to the cargo list just before departure, so that proper loading was impossible.[14] It was no doubt fortunate that combat-loading had not been attempted.

In spite of all these disappointments and defects, the Second Fleet Landing Exercise can still be regarded as a success. The discovery of error is the first step to truth, and the empirical method presupposes many false steps. Certainly the leading army observer present was highly impressed with the show put on by Navy and Marine Corps. At any rate he concluded "that the *Tentative Landing Operations Manual,* published by the Navy Department under date of May 25,

1935, [the Marine Corps Schools manual with slight changes, chiefly in nomenclature] furnished a sound and comprehensive guide for the planning and execution of a landing operation. It should be available to any army unit engaged in such an operation." [15]

The Third Fleet Landing Exercise held between January 27 and March 10, 1937, differed in three important respects from the previous ones. In the first place, the locale was changed to the island of San Clemente off the Pacific coast near San Diego. Secondly, a far larger number of naval vessels participated, and for the first time the Second Marine Brigade stationed on the west coast was given a chance to share in the training. Finally, also for the first time, an army unit took an active part in the landing exercises.[16]

Both marine and army units had undergone considerable preliminary training before the exercise itself was carried off. For three months, from October 1 to December 31, the First Marine Brigade carried out an extensive training program combining field exercises and landings in the Potomac area.[17] Meanwhile on the west coast an army unit, the First Expeditionary Brigade, consisting of the 30th Infantry Regiment plus attached artillery and engineer elements, was being assembled. During December and January the army officers were given a quick introductory course in subjects pertaining to landing operations, using the *Tentative Landing Operations Manual* as the basis for instruction. This was followed by an intensive practical training course for both officers and enlisted men under the supervision of Lieutenant Colonel Thomas E. Watson USMC and other marines; this course consisted chiefly of indoctrinating army personnel in the special problems of climbing down cargo nets into small boats, landing on beaches both by day and night, and in general initiating them to some of the mysteries of amphibious warfare.[18] On the whole the training was successful, and the commanding general of the Fourth Army was sufficiently impressed by the amphibious skills demonstrated by Navy and Marine Corps during the preliminary as well as the final exercise to recommend strongly continued army training in the subject, using the *Tentative Manual* as the basic text. He also recommended army participation in future fleet landing exercises, but his advice was not followed.

On San Clemente the landings themselves were carried out in the usual fashion so as to give all units experience in landing in daytime, at night, and under smoke screen. Finally on February 17 a joint landing exercise was held employing all units of the two marine brigades plus the army regiment, but in no case did these maneuvers go as smoothly as they had the previous year at Culebra, chiefly because of the heavy surf encountered. As usual, various types of standard ships' boats were employed, although for the first time three navy experimental boats were also tested. These landings in rough water demonstrated conclusively the complete inadequacy of ordinary boats for the job, if it needed to be demonstrated. In one landing conducted on February 15 by the First Marine Brigade in a surf of about four feet, five of the boats foundered, and so much time and manpower was expended trying to rescue the personnel and haul the boats to safety that the umpire had to rule that the attacking force would have suffered sixty-five per cent casualties, and the landing was judged a complete failure. Subsequent maneuvers over somewhat less heavy surf had only slightly better results. As the commanding officer of the Fifth Marines concluded, "Navy standard boats are totally unsuited for landing troops of the leading waves, even under moderate surf conditions. They are in no sense tactical vehicles, for they are lacking in speed and maneuverability and are extremely difficult to handle in the surf. They do not permit the rapid debarkation of troops at the water's edge. To armor these boats will still further augment their present disadvantages." [19] If additional evidence were needed to convince the navy of the absolute necessity for further experimentation in and rapid development of useable landing craft, the Third Fleet Landing Exercise certainly supplied it in quantity.

Naval gunfire proceeded as usual except that a larger number of ships participated, including six battleships, five cruisers, and a destroyer division. The conclusions were that long-range counterbattery fire against targets on reverse slopes was feasible, that effective close and deep supporting missions could be delivered by any type of naval vessel, that the best ammunition for use against shore targets were high-explosive bombardment type projectiles for major caliber guns and flat-nose projectiles for those of medium caliber.[20] Originally it had been planned to conduct a full-scale landing of all troop units with actual instead of simulated gun support. But on the day it was scheduled the sea was so heavy that it was decided not to risk the men in small boats, so the troops were kept on board while the ships fired.[21]

Like naval gunfire, air support was conducted on a far larger scale than previously. Both the First Marine Air Group from Quantico and the Second Marine Air Group at San Diego took part. The two units were combined into a Force Aircraft containing a total of eighty-three land-based Marine Corps planes. In this instance all aerial spotting for naval gunfire was conducted by navy planes, so the marine aircraft confined their training to reconnaissance, laying smoke, general observation, and attack missions in support of the several troop landings.[22] Again the recommendation was made, and from almost all quarters involved, that the Marine Corps needed modern attack planes and that attack aviation should become an integral component of

Marine Corps aviation if it was to carry out one of its primary missions of destruction and neutralization of beach defenses.

One of the salient weak spots that previous exercises had brought to light was the inadequacy of standard Marine Corps radio equipment, particularly for use in the ship-to-shore movement. In 1937 the Second Marine Brigade used for the first time two army-type high-frequency radios which produced such excellent results that it was suggested that this type be adopted by the Corps as permanent equipment.[23] As far as progress in communication is concerned, perhaps the most important lesson derived from this exercise was a very practical and dramatic demonstration of how badly fouled a landing operation can become in the absence of perfect communications between all units. During the joint Army-Marine Corps landing maneuver on February 17, after all troops had been embarked in small boats, a last-minute change of orders was issued directing the army to land on a different beach from that originally assigned. This order was not transmitted in full to all units, and as a result the army boats continued into the beach originally assigned, several of them broached in the surf, and the whole plan of execution went awry.[24] Such confusion in an actual operation would have been disastrous.

As in the past no effort was made to approximate wartime conditions of combat-loading. This was due in part to the lack of naval transportation from the east coast, which meant that units of the First Marine Brigade had to be brought westward in a piecemeal fashion. Also the last minute breakdown of the battleship *Arkansas* in which some troops were scheduled to be transported made it necessary to assign units to vessels not prepared to carry either the men or their equipment. Nor was any real effort made to attack the basic problems of amphibious ship-to-shore supply. The forces participating carried only very limited supplies and expended little of what they had, but rather relied heavily on supplies and motor transport already ashore which would not normally be available during the first days of an actual landing against a hostile coast. As the commanding general of the Fleet Marine Force observed, "there is grave danger that those participating in such exercises may get the impression that the service of supply is of little significance, and may minimize its importance. Little of importance relative to the methods of supply that will be necessary in actual operations, or to the difficulties of supply in landing operations is gained by these exercises." [25]

There were other defects in amphibious preparation observed by marine officers as a result of these 1937 exercises. One was the impracticality of relying on old transports or on warships as troop carriers. The former were inadequately armed, and the latter had other duties of naval gunfire and of covering the landing area against possible hostile fleet actions. The only solution, as was suggested by the commanding general of the First Marine Brigade, Brigadier General James J. Meade, was to equip destroyers as attack transports from which troops could move quickly close into shore and disembark under protection of the ships' guns.[26]

More general criticisms of the entire program of amphibious training to date were voiced by the same officer during the critique held after the third landing exercise was completed. He observed that except for the fact that the personnel involved undoubtedly profited greatly in the technical training of landing operations and thereby increased their fighting value, "there has been no material gain in the tactical knowledge of amphibian operations resulting from Fleet Landing Exercise Number 3, over exercises conducted in past years." He further maintained that the mere landing of troops at the water's edge in standard navy boats had been overemphasized to the exclusion of more important tactical aspects of a landing attack. "There seems to be a tendency," he continued, "to confine ourselves too much to the technical features of the landing attack and at the same time to accept unequivocally the contents of the *Tentative Landing Operations Manual*, which is a peacetime compilation of methods, based largely on the study of a conclusion drawn from historical examples of past amphibian wars."

Insufficient attention, he felt, was devoted to terrain, to the problem of searching out and destroying well-concealed gun positions either by ships' fire or aviation, and to the solution of the hundred other difficulties that would face attacking forces in a genuine amphibious assault against strong opposition. The chief shortcoming of all amphibious planning, he claimed, was the failure to recognize the applicability of lessons learned during World War I as to the effectiveness of machine-gun fire located behind barbed wire obstacles against attacking troops even with the best artillery support. Artillery alone never satisfactorily solved the problem of the machine gun and barbed wire; and naval gunfire support, he argued, no matter how efficient, would be no better against similar defenses on the beaches. Furthermore, the infantry in a landing is worse off than in ground fighting because of their exposure during the ship-to-shore movement. In World War I, he continued, it was only with the advent of the tank that infantry began to find its way opened to the defender's position and could then cope with local resistance. The lesson for amphibious planners was clear. It was essential, absolutely essential, that amphibian tanks and efficient tank lighters be developed and developed fast. Although some marines might have disagreed with this criticism of the usefulness of Fleet Landing Exercise Number Three, none would have dissented from the final conclusion.[27]

During the next four years the major annual fleet landing exercises were held again at Culebra, and at the same time training in landing operations was stepped up both at Quantico and at San Diego. Until January of 1941 the marine elements engaged consisted as usual of the First Marine Brigade, made up of Brigade Headquarters, the Fifth Marine Regiment less one battalion, a battalion of the Tenth Marines (artillery), and attached engineer, tank, and chemical companies, plus the First Marine Air Group, all stationed at Quantico. In 1938, during the Fourth Fleet Landing Exercise, the Second Provisional United States Army Brigade, consisting of the 18th Infantry Regiment and a battalion of the 7th Field Artillery, also took part. This, however, was the last time until January 1941 that any army unit attended the exercises. In 1939 the army was invited to join Fleet Landing Exercise Six, to be held in January of 1940, but the Chief of Staff declined on the grounds that it would be "impracticable." So it was that in these critical few years during which the boiling pot of European diplomacy finally erupted into armed warfare, only the Navy and the Marine Corps continued to train and prepare for the landing operations that would probably come if the United States became involved.[28]

For the most part the training programs at Culebra followed the usual pattern of practice landings under various conditions, experimentation with new types of landing craft, naval gunfire support exercises in which an ever increasing number of vessels participated, and aircraft exercises in such missions as bombing, strafing, spotting, observation, and reconnaissance.

In 1938 experiments in night landings were again conducted. During the first of these, two companies were transferred at sea from transports to destroyers and preceded the rest of the approaching naval attack force to Culebra by about six hours. The troops then disembarked from the destroyers, which lay close to the beach under cover of darkness, and in less than an hour had landed and had simulated a seizure of the beachhead. Later a night landing was executed against the southern coast of Puerto Rico by the Fifth Marines, although, since it was an attack in force, with somewhat less than satisfactory results. On one beach the inherent difficulties of night landings were demonstrated fully. Boats struck unexpected reefs and shoals, landed on the wrong beaches, and troop units became hopelessly entangled once they reached the shore. The terrain was swampy and covered by heavy brush which resulted in parts of four companies intermingling in the same defile. All units reached their objectives late, and until well after daylight all contact between units was lost.[29] This was the beginning of continuous training in the type of night landings which attracted some public attention. Actually, marines seldom resorted to these tactics in World War II, one exception being the First Parachute Battalion against Tanambogo in the Southeastern Solomons.

Night landings were made during the 1939 and 1940 exercises, but serious difficulties were again encountered. Also in 1940 the first night patrols were landed, either from submarines or destroyers, for reconnaissance purposes.[30]

During these same three years 1938–1940 some progress was made in the construction and testing of various types of experimental landing craft and lighters. In 1938 for the first time a self-propelled tank lighter capable of carrying a single light tank was employed, and with great success. Although still somewhat too heavy, it was efficient enough to permit its tank to get ashore within nineteen seconds after it beached, which was a noted improvement over the old tow-type lighter that had been employed in earlier exercises. At the same time three experimental landing boats were employed, and again their superiority over standard navy boats was clearly demonstrated. These craft (*Freeport, Red Bank* and *Bay Head*, boats adapted after commercial fishing craft) were always capable of making two to three trips from ship-to-shore while the navy boats were making one. In the following year the first boat manufactured by Andrew J. Higgins was introduced and immediately proved itself superior to all previously-tested landing craft. It was of shallow draft, and beached and retracted easily. During Fleet Landing Exercise Number Six, in 1940, a large number of assorted experimental types were available. These included two tank lighters, two self-propelled artillery lighters, twenty-five special landing boats of which twelve had been constructed by the Bureau of Ships, eight special landing skiffs, and two types of rubber boats. Again it was clear from the tests that the Higgins boat was the most suitable.[31]

One long-awaited and ardently prayed for innovation finally made its appearance in 1936. This was the debut of the first destroyer converted to transport duties, the forerunner of the World War II attack destroyer transport (APD), for which marines had long been agitating. The first one was an old destroyer, the *Manley*, renovated to provide accommodations for 120 marines, and more such conversions were soon to follow.[32]

Naval gunfire practices during these years were carried out with little deviation from the norm and with little further progress except that a larger number of ships and naval personnel at least got a taste of firing at shore targets. The chief trouble was the inadequacy of the range at Culebra, which was too small to permit well-rounded practices. One of the worst defects in naval gunfire doctrine was that very little or no theoretical training in shore observation work had been held prior to Fleet Landing Exercise Number Six, except during actual firings. During this exercise held in 1940, for the first time the artillery officer of the First Marine Brigade was made available to train navy officers in the subject. Later in the year, during special exercises held in November, this same officer undertook to conduct a thorough course of instruction for personnel of the battleship *Texas* and of the cruisers *Vincennes, Chester, Omaha,* and *Memphis*.[33]

2. Amphibious Preparedness on the Eve of War

By the close of 1940 most of the major problems of amphibious warfare had been worked out in theory, and valuable practice and experimentation had gone far to refine the doctrine, provide training for a sizeable number of Marine Corps and Navy personnel, and eliminate some of the more critical "bugs" in procedure. Progress was at last beginning to be made in the evolution of efficient landing craft and lighters, in the construction of attack transports, and in the perfection of communications procedures and equipment. Little actual training in combat-loading had taken place, although the techniques were fairly well developed. Marine pilots had received useful training in the large variety of jobs to which they might be assigned, although no clear decision had yet been reached as to whether their main function was or was not to be the close support of troops during and after the landing attack.

In this connection, Marine Corps doctrine revealed a curious ambiguity. Close air support was officially defined (after the war) as "attack by aircraft of hostile ground targets which are at such close range to friendly front lines as to require detailed integration of each air mission with the fire and movement of the ground forces in order to insure safety, prevent interference with other elements of the combined arms, and permit prompt exploitation of the shock, casualty, and neutralization effect of the air attack. It does not include missions executed off the battlefield or at such range from the ground forces as to require no specific coordination of air and ground action beyond the general delineation of a zone in which air action is restricted."[34] Perhaps a more meaningful definition is that attributed to a soldier on Mindanao who is quoted as remarking: "Close air support means that those bombs are so close that if you don't get in a hole or down as flat on your belly as you can, you're mighty likely to get your backside full of arrows."[35]

By the end of the war a doctrine had been evolved which contemplated using aircraft in support of ground troops, not only in the absence of artillery or naval gunfire or against targets which neither artillery nor naval gunfire could reach, but as a supplementing arm to be employed in coordination with artillery and naval gunfire against troops and installations in the immediate vicinity of the advancing infantry. In spite of the fact that Colonel Roy S. Geiger USMC (and others) could say as early as 1939 that "the primary reason for the Marine Corps' having airplanes is their use in close support of ground units," [36] there seems to have been some difference of opinion within the Corps as to how close to troops close air support could safely be used. At any rate, in setting forth a written doctrine on the subject in 1940, Marine Corps Schools aviation section were quite modest in their claims. "When aviation is acting in close support of the ground forces, its striking power should be used against [only] those targets which cannot be reached by the weapons of ground arms, or on targets for which ground weapons are not suitable or available. In almost all ground situations there are vital targets beyond the range of weapons of ground arms which can be powerfully dealt with by attack aviation. Therefore, the use of attack aviation to supplement the fire power of ground arms is generally discouraged as it may result in the neglect of more distant, and perhaps more vital objectives. As a general rule, attack aviation should be used in lieu of artillery only when the time limit precludes the assembly of sufficient artillery units to provide the necessary preparation, and when such absence of artillery may involve failure of the campaign as a whole." [37] In short, doctrine of genuine close air support as it later came to be understood was yet to be evolved.

The chief factor that militated against one hundred per cent amphibious preparedness in 1940 was that, in spite of some effort to approach realism in the training exercises, many artificialities still persisted. Some of these were unavoidable, since the only really first-rate school of warfare is war, and that had not yet opened its doors. But other deficiencies might still be corrected in peacetime. Of these, according to Brigadier General Holland M. Smith, who commanded the First Marine Brigade, the most glaring was the lack of sufficient transports or the unwillingness of the navy to assign transports to the marines for use in their exercises. The system of loading troops aboard warships was obviously unrealistic and afforded little opportunity for the men to engage in practice landings under conditions comparable to those they would meet in wartime.[38]

In the early winter of 1941 this defect was remedied, but only in part, during Fleet Landing Exercise Number Seven, the last exercise so designated. Three navy transports, *McCawley, Wharton,* and *Harry Lee;* two army transports, *Hunter Liggett* and *Chateau Thierry;* and three new destroyer transports, *Colhoun, Gregory,* and *Little,* were provided for this operation. Even these left much to be desired. Speaking of all but the three new destroyer transports, Rear Admiral Ernest J. King USN, Commander, Atlantic Fleet, noted that "none can service their own landing boats; none has adequate water-making facilities; the motive power of the *McCawley* is in doubtful state; the *Harry Lee*

... cannot hoist tank lighters and her bureau boats make about 6 knots. . . ." This was concurred in by Holland Smith and by Captain Robert M. Emmet USN, Commander of Transports, Atlantic Fleet, who added that the "material condition of the *Harry Lee* and the *Wharton* was so bad as to be grotesque. Their crews are untrained. . . . They had to struggle continuously to keep their ships going."[39]

This last fleet landing exercise was conducted on larger scale than any of those held before. The naval attack force contained all the available ships of the Atlantic Fleet, including three battleships, two cruiser divisions, and a destroyer squadron. The air attack group consisted of two carriers plus the First Marine Air Group. The First Marine Brigade had just been redesignated the First Marine Division. A reinforced marine division, using the terminology later employed, was lifted to the objective by a transport squadron. The division consisted of five regiments, three infantry (each of three battalions), one artillery (normally four battalions), and one engineer (a pioneer or shore party battalion, an engineer battalion, and in the middle portion of the war a Naval Construction or Seabee Battalion), plus other elements such as a tank unit attached. The term "triangular strength reinforced" arose from the assignment of artillery, engineering, and other strength to each of the three infantry regiments for beach landings. Each of these regiments thereupon became a regimental combat team, and each was lifted to the target by a transport division usually consisting of three attack transports (one for each battalion landing team in the infantry regiment) and one attack cargo vessel. When organized in 1941, the First Marine Division mustered two regimental combat teams, and thus in actuality was only brigade strength.[40]

The 1941 exercises went fairly well in spite of the rawness of some of the troops. Still there were not enough boats on hand. Even with the employment of standard navy boats borrowed from the combat ships of the fleet there were scarcely enough boats available for the initial landing of troops of even two battalion combat teams, whereas five whole teams plus three reinforced companies on destroyer transports were at all times available for operations. Tank lighters of varying sizes were available for the maneuver but not in sufficient numbers, and these so slow as to require from two to three hours to make the round trip from transport to beach and back.[41]

Another serious mechanical deficiency which quickly revealed itself was the inadequacy of naval ordnance to meet the requirements of shore bombardment. To do this effectively ships ought to have had the most modern fire control equipment, since the majority of calls for fire were normally on targets not visible from seaward. They should have carried an adequate supply of quick-acting fuse and high-fragmentation projectiles. Finally the ideal gun was one with relatively low muzzle velocity and resultant high angle of fall, capable of reaching reverse slopes, valleys, and ravines. The only ships in the entire Atlantic Fleet reported possessing all these characteristics were those of the heavy cruiser class. The rest were deficient in one respect or another.[42]

Also, communication between ships and shore observation parties was demonstrated to be faulty. Radio personnel were unfamiliar with their equipment and too often did not understand proper radio procedure. In the event of radio failure the only way an observation party could contact its firing ship was by indirect route via the navy's beachmaster, obviously a slow and clumsy system. Even worse was the condition of communications between transports and the shore, due chiefly to obsolete and insufficient radios carried aboard these vessels.[43]

It was apparent that no matter how sound the basic amphibious doctrine, or how well-prepared individual troops had become, the United States would not be ready to conduct successful landing operations unless a rapid acceleration in the production of essential amphibious materiel took place immediately.

As the threats of American involvement in the European war became daily more acute in 1941, the pressure for intensive and widespread amphibious training became proportionately more urgent. The old site of Culebra was no longer satisfactory, not only because of its size and other limitations but because the Caribbean was no longer an American lake where United States naval forces might wander at will without fear of German submarines. Late in 1940 the Marine Corps succeeded in obtaining appropriations for the purchase of a new and better site at New River, North Carolina, and in June 1941 plans were prepared to hold there the largest amphibious exercise yet conducted.[44]

3. Reorganization and Expanded Training

Meanwhile, important organizational changes had been going on within the Corps and within the Atlantic Fleet. The new marine division authorized the previous year contained two infantry regiments (Fifth and Seventh, with a third yet unactivated), an artillery regiment (Eleventh) consisting of three battalions of 75-millimeter pack howitzers and one battalion of 105-millimeter howitzers, an engineer battalion, a light tank battalion, a special weapons battalion, a scout company, a signal company, an amphibian tractor battalion, a medical battalion, a service battalion, a guard company, and the division headquarters company.[45]

For purposes of joint training of Army, Navy, and Marine Corps a new organization was set up within the Atlantic Fleet and designated the First Joint Training Force. Later this title was altered successively to Atlantic Amphibious Force; Amphibious Corps, Atlantic Fleet; and Amphibious Training Staff. Under whatever designation, command rested in the competent hands of Major General Holland M. Smith, formerly commanding general of the First Marine Brigade and subsequently the First Marine Division. This tough, egocentric, cantankerous, exacting little marine general, who became one of the most controversial figures in World War II, provided the main power drive to all amphibious training on the east coast in the crucial year of 1941. Whatever may be the judgment of his contemporaries or of history concerning his role in the Pacific War, there can be little doubt that he played the leading part in forging a fighting amphibious team that made possible the eventual successful landings in both the Atlantic and the Pacific.

General Smith's primary qualifications for the particular job at hand were that he was a driver and a perfectionist. Never did he allow himself the comfortable satisfaction of believing that the training exercises under his direction came off as well as might have been expected under the circumstances and therefore could pass muster. Never did he allow his subordinates in the Navy and Marine Corps or his equals and superiors in the Navy to relax in the drive for perfect planning and execution of all phases of landing operations.

In a conference held in January of 1942, following a poorly executed landing exercise, Smith was especially critical of the apparent lack of interest demonstrated by the navy as evidenced by the small number of ships and planes they had allotted to the maneuver. He pointed out in stern tones to the ranking navy officers present the inadequacy of their forces and the absolute necessity for backing landing troops with overwhelming naval and aerial power. He added that "he would not be a party to any operation which was founded on an inadequate basis; that he would be relieved before acquiescing to any such scheme." The admiral in command of the naval attack force present, answered that he believed this principle to be generally admitted by all hands. Smith retired, muttering, "I am not certain!" [46] He was never certain that his colleagues were applying themselves with the proper zeal or had a full appreciation of the enormous problems of amphibious assault. His was an altogether healthy attitude in 1942.

Under his command not only did the First Marine Division continue to perfect its landing techniques, but both the 1st and 9th Army Divisions received their initial training in amphibious warfare. At the same time, a second training command was established at San Diego under Major General Clayton B. Vogel USMC, who carried on a similar program with the Second Marine Division and the 3rd Army Division. When Vogel left in August 1942 for overseas duty as commanding general of the First Marine Amphibious Corps, Smith relieved him and continued the indoctrination of the Second Marine Division as well as the 7th Army Division. Fleet Marine Force doctrine was thus spread widely through all the services and through all combat areas where landing operations took place.[47]

The New River exercises of 1941 were held in two phases. June and July were spent by both army and marine units in small unit training ashore and in regimental and battalion landing exercises. This was climaxed by a full-dress two-divisional landing on August 4. The ship-to-shore movement was in general successful, considering that this was the first time such a large scale operation had been conducted. Other features of the exercise, however, were reported to show serious defects, revealing not only the inexperience of many of the personnel concerned but also the ever-growing sense of urgency of those who reported them.

The rifle regiments of the 1st Infantry Division suffered the most because of their relative newness at the game. When theoretical training for these regiments commenced at Fort Devens, Massachusetts, it was discovered that there was no instructional material for landing operations available, and a hurried call went out for copies of *Fleet Training Publication 167* and the army manual copied from it (Field Manual 31–5). These plus an army observer's report of Fleet Landing Exercise Number Seven and a Marine Corps training film were the sole library from which instruction could be given.

Embarkation of the troops also presented a serious problem in the absence of adequate doctrine or data for proper loading. Ships' diagrams failed to arrive on time, and the ignorance on the part of officers in charge of loading cargo as to weight, volume, and classification meant that everything had to be reloaded when the transports lifting the army troops put into New York en route to New River.[48]

Nor was the embarkation of the First Marine Division conducted expeditiously. Although some attention was paid to proper combat-loading procedure as far as equipment and supplies were concerned, the troops themselves were scattered over three separate areas on the east coast, and embarkation was a piecemeal proposition extending over a period of five weeks with some 1,700 officers and men, in the end, left out entirely because of lack of transports.

The ground forces were unanimous in condemning the navy transports, and although some of the criticisms can perhaps be discounted as the normal gripings of troops against shipboard conditions, most of the complaint was justified. One regimental commander reported of *McCawley* that not only was she overcrowded, but that troop spaces, washroom, and toilet facilities were in such a deplorable condition as to cause a general depressing effect on the troops and raise the absentee list to unheard of heights when "the relatively small percentage of weaker spirits who felt that they could not 'take it' on board a transport for an indefinite period began to absent themselves." He failed to see any hope for a general change for the better until the navy altered its point of view toward transports and commenced to consider them "to be combatant and not train ships and that the combatant elements on board being the embarked troops, everything must be pointed toward their welfare and efficient performance of assigned tasks. This is admittedly a difficult change in point of view for officers who have spent a lifetime being indoctrinated to believe that the ship always takes precedence. . . ."[49]

Another more serious drawback was that some of the transports of the smaller type simply were not large enough to accommodate properly a balanced, reinforced rifle battalion. If units of this sort were to be broken up among various ships one of the most fundamental tenets of sound amphibious doctrine would be flaunted. Since the early twenties marines had realized that the infantry battalion, to be effective in beach assault, should have the necessary supporting arms and service units attached to it. The authors of the *Tentative Landing Manual* expressed the idea that each of these reinforced units should be combat-loaded on one ship. In all of the Fleet Landing Exercises an effort was made to observe this doctrine within the limitations imposed by available shipping.

Tests were again conducted with small boats, and again it was discovered that the Higgins craft were superior to all others. A new Higgins boat with bow ramp worked successfully, and the recently constructed Higgins tank lighters retracted from the beach rapidly and were equipped with reliable engines. By contrast the tank lighters designed by the Navy Bureau of Ships were heavy, slow, difficult to control, difficult to retract, and equipped with unpredictable power plants.[50]

One of the worst aspects of the landing proved to be the very faulty shore party organization. No separate shore party units (pioneers) had yet been set up within the marine divisions, so all personnel had to be drawn out of combat units, thereby reducing the latter's effective strength. There was no clear division of authority between the marine shore parties and the navy beach parties, and the former complained that they found themselves too frequently doing the latter's work. Up to that time there had been no separate specialized training for permanent shore parties, and the result showed itself during this exercise. One battalion of the Seventh Marines had to be withdrawn entirely from combat practice and put to this sort of work even though completely untrained for it. On the beach assigned to this regiment boats arrived in such numbers and so fast that unloading them with any speed was impossible. There were insufficient men available, no clear-cut doctrine as to who was responsible for what, and the result was general confusion at the beach.[51]

Since all naval gunfire support was simulated, no concrete conclusions could be drawn about its probable effectiveness. However it did develop that the naval shore observation parties off the attendant transports were too inexperienced to be any good and lacked adequate communications equipment. Only two out of eight parties were ever able to establish contact with their parent ships. Another serious shortcoming in communications was that army officers proved to be generally unfamiliar with standard naval signal procedure.[52]

At New River for the first time the newly organized raider battalion had a chance to operate. This was not yet a separate unit. In May of 1941, the First Battalion, Fifth Marines, had been reorganized into six reinforced rifle components for training as mobile landing units in rubber boats from destroyer transports. As reorganized, each of these rifle units came to a total strength of over a hundred men, and the mission of the battalion was to include reconnaissance, feints, raids, secondary landings or diversions, and night landings for any of these purposes, or to act as a covering force for the entire division in delivering flank attacks aimed at hostile communications or at reserves in the rear of the main beach defenses, and in other similar activities.

According to Lieutenant Colonel Merritt A. Edson USMC, the commanding officer of this multi-purpose battalion, the concept was a mistake, and the operations at New River and elsewhere proved it. Since the battalion would probably be used only on detached missions it should not have been incorporated as part of a regular infantry regiment. This not only deprived the regiment of its full strength when the battalion was off on separate missions, but also deprived the battalion (which had special weapons and equipment) of its proper equipment and supplies whenever it reverted to the status of a regular infantry battalion. Hence, being neither fish nor fowl, it could not do either job well, and it was strongly recommended that the battalion be given separate and independent status.[53] This was done, but questions as to its proper place and functions were answered only after the Pacific War had begun.

The next exercise conducted under Holland Smith's command was held in January 1942 at Lynhaven Roads off Cape Henry at the mouth of the Chesapeake, chiefly because war had finally come to the United States, and it was too dangerous to carry troops out into the North Atlantic to New River without sufficient combat escort.

No naval gunfire or air support groups were present, so the exercise was more of a ship-to-shore practice than a full-scale amphibious exercise. Both marine and army personnel took part, but in much smaller numbers than at New River. The only marine units involved were the raider battalion (now designated First Separate Battalion), the First Marine Parachute Battalion, which had been activated the year before, and a battalion of the Eleventh Marines (artillery). Four battalions of the 1st Infantry Division constituted the main element of the training force. Although there were noticeable improvements both in combat-loading and in the promulgation of intelligence plans, the ship-to-shore movement was a total failure. The initial marine battalion landed at the correct time and place, but thereafter nothing went right. Not a single army battalion was landed with all troops on the proper beach. One battalion was scattered over a two-mile front and lost all contact, and another landed in an off-limits area. The main trouble was lack of coordination or previous planning between army and navy commanders.

Shore fire-control parties (the new designation for "shore observation parties") failed to keep continuous contact with their ships. Signal communications were still unsatisfactory because of lack of coordinated training in procedures between the navy and ground troops. About the only real improvement over the New River exercise was in shore party organization. Following the August 1941 fiasco all echelons had strongly recommended the establishment of a shore party (pioneer battalion) under command of the Landing Force. This was approved tentatively by Commander, Atlantic Fleet and put into operation at Lynhaven. Although, because of lack of training, it failed to function as well as expected, and shore parties on some occasions landed on the wrong beaches and were scattered over about two miles of beach front, it was still an improvement over the earlier organization.[54] The problem of the shore party, however, remained to plague the landing on Guadalcanal.

After the completion of this exercise, the center of most practical amphibious training on the east coast was shifted to the naval amphibious base at Solomon's Island, Maryland, where battalion and regimental exercises were conducted during the spring and summer of 1942. In each case, following ten days of preliminary battalion training, the regiment conducted a communication exercise in which all communication elements of the regiment and escorting naval vessels were employed, a day landing of the reinforced regiment including debarkation of vehicles and supplies for five days, and a night landing. In each case shore party functioning and other logistical aspects of the exercises were stressed. The troops involved were the Fifth Marines, the newly organized First Battalion, First Marines, the First Separate Battalion (redesignated the First Raider Battalion), and all three regiments of the 9th Infantry Division.

Concurrently the Amphibious Corps, Atlantic Fleet, set up a variety of training programs for specialized aspects of amphibious warfare. At Quantico and Parris Island, South Carolina, special schools were established to train navy, army, and marine officers in the duties of shore fire-control parties. This instruction covered the characteristics and capabilities of naval batteries, the technique of naval gunfire on shore targets, and the spotting of actual artillery fire using naval technique. At Quantico and Norfolk transport-loading schools were formed, and officers from the 1st and 9th Infantry Divisions and the First Marine Division were instructed in the fundamentals of combat-loading. Instruction was given in the preparation of embarkation plans, followed by practical exercises in the actual loading of transports for training exercises. At Quantico and Fort Bragg, staff personnel from Corps headquarters and from the 9th Infantry Division were given theoretical and practical instruction in radio code reception, message center operation, and the fundamentals of joint army-navy communications procedure.[55]

The ultimate effects of these various training programs plus similar ones conducted on the west coast are impossible to trace, their ramifications were so widespread. The 1st Infantry Division, which received its initial amphibious indoctrination under Marine Corps auspices, participated in the invasions of Oran, Sicily, and Omaha Beach, Normandy. The 3rd Infantry Division, similarly trained on the west coast, spearheaded the landing at Casablanca, captured Palermo, Sicily, and landed at Anzio. The 7th took Attu, Kiska, and Kwajalein Islet, and was among the troops landing on Leyte and Okinawa. The 9th Division seized the beaches at Port Lyautey and Sojro in Algiers, and landed at Palermo and at Normandy. Members of the original First and Second Marine Divisions not only fought with their own organizations on Guadalcanal, Cape Gloucester, Tarawa, Saipan, Tinian, Peleliu, and Okinawa, but were eventually scattered throughout the other four marine divisions formed during the war, and played a large part in the defeat of Japan. Officers and men of the Navy, Army, and Marine Corps, trained in these exercises, ultimately found their way into every theater of war where amphibious operations were conducted. Like concentric circles from a stone dropped in still water, Fleet Marine Force amphibious doctrine and training spread out into every area of the war and permeated all the services.[56]

4. New Landing Craft and Naval Gunfire Techniques

In the field of technological improvements, significant developments were taking place. Of these, the most important were the gradual evolution of a small landing craft suitable for transporting assault troops from ship-to-shore, and of an amphibian tractor which could be used not only as a cargo and troop carrier but as an armored amphibian tank. Although in both instances these needs were ultimately filled by private industry, the inspiration and impetus came from the Marine Corps.

The leading industrial pioneer in the field of landing craft in the period before and during World War II was Andrew J. Higgins of New Orleans. In the mid-twenties, for the use of fur trappers and oil drillers in the bayous of Louisiana, Higgins developed a small boat which was designed for running through shallow waters and beaching and retracting easily. The chief characteristics of this boat, named "Eureka," were its shallow draft and protected propeller. This construction permitted navigation through weed and root-infested waters without too much danger of fouling the propeller. Also, it beached by the bow, and possessed a small turning circle which enabled it to leave a beach quickly without excessive danger of broaching from heavy surf.

In 1934 Higgins visited Quantico for the purpose of interesting the Marine Corps in adapting his craft to military purposes. He received encouragement but no money, since none was available. Nevertheless, from that time forward he worked in close conjunction with various officers of the Corps who encouraged him and bolstered his spirits in a protracted battle with the Bureau of Ships to get the Eureka and other Higgins craft officially accepted.[57]

From 1939 to 1941, Higgins boats were tested in the annual fleet landing exercises and invariably proved superior to other types. The only serious defect in their construction was the lack of easy means for troops to debark, except by the rather clumsy method of going over the sides. In April 1941 Higgins again visited Quantico and agreed to remedy this defect by changing the design of the bow to a ramp form that could be lowered as soon as the craft hit the beach, thereby permitting troops to debark quickly and at the same time allowing the boat to be used to carry trucks and small tanks. This new design was worked out by Higgins himself in consultation with Brigadier General Emile P. Moses USMC, head of the Marine Corps Equipment Board.

Also in 1941, after the Culebra exercise had proved forty-five foot tank lighters designed by the Bureau of Ships to be impractical, Higgins set out to design a better one. Again working in close cooperation with marine officers, he perfected a new design, which, after much opposition from the Bureau of Ships, became the standard medium landing craft (LCM) used by United States forces throughout the war.[58]

As in the case of the Higgins boats, the first experiments in construction of amphibian tractors were conducted by private manufacturers. The old Christie amphibian tank had been discarded, but in 1933 Donald Roebling, a retired manufacturer, invented an amphibian tractor devised for rescue work in the Everglades of Florida. In 1937 the attention of several marine officers at Quantico was brought to this device, and an officer (Major John Kaluf) was dispatched to Florida to investigate it. His report was favorable, and the Marine Equipment Board decided to accept the design. Three experimental craft were purchased in 1939, and in November of 1940 the first of the Roebling "Alligators" was demonstrated at Quantico. That same year, under Marine Corps pressure, the Navy Department set aside funds for further development and let the first navy contract to Roebling to produce his tractor in large quantities. This was the origin of the first tracked landing vehicle (LVT).[59]

Meanwhile the executive officer of the Marine Corps Equipment Board, Major Ernest E. Linsert, was working out plans for an armored amphibian adapted from the basic design of the Roebling Alligator. His original plans called for a vehicle of over twenty feet in length, twelve feet wide, and six and one half feet high. The hull was to be composed of structural steel, turrets were to be of $\frac{3}{8}$-inch steel castings and would be operable by hand. Each such vehicle was to be armed with a 37-millimeter gun and one .30-caliber machine gun in the center turret, one .50-caliber machine gun in each side turret, and two fixed .50-caliber machine guns fired by the driver by means of buttons at the top of the two steering levers. Propulsion would be obtained from 4-inch T-shaped curved cleats bolted to roller chains. Roebling accepted the idea with modifications. By November 1940, Marine Corps Headquarters had given approval, and production of the first model armored amphibian (LVTA) was begun.[60]

Meanwhile the Bureau of Ships was working independently on an armored amphibian, resulting in another model made by the Borg-Warner Corporation. By June 1942 these were being produced on an assembly-line basis, although not yet in sufficient quantities to be ready for the forthcoming Guadalcanal operation.[61]

Another important development in 1941–1942 was the rapid improvement in the training of navy vessels for effective gunfire support. With the formation of the First Joint Training Force in May 1941, definite ideas for the improvement of shore fire-control party organization had crystallized. Accordingly, at a conference attended by Ernest J. King and Holland Smith, among others, a general reorganization of the shore fire-control party was approved. It was decided to substitute a marine (or army) artillery officer for the navy officer who had, up to that time, acted as naval gunfire spotter. The naval gunfire liaison officer of the shore fire-control party, who had been provided by the supporting ship without much attention to his special qualifications for the job, was to be replaced by a navy officer with special training for the assignment. Radio personnel for the spotter was to be furnished by the marine (or army) regiment.

Following this conference, twelve young navy officers (ensigns) were assigned to duty as naval gunfire liaison officers and ordered to Parris Island for training under the Naval Gunfire Officer of the First Joint Training Force. They received instruction in spotting on land targets, using the artillery of the First Marine Division to simulate the firing ship. After completing this course in July 1941, they joined their assigned attack transports and participated in the New River landing exercise of August. As a result of these maneuvers it was concluded that the assignment of these officers to transports was a mistake, since they became involved in extraneous duties aboard ship which prevented their concentration on the peculiar problems of naval gunfire support. Accordingly they were transferred to Headquarters, Amphibious Corps, Atlantic Fleet, for further training and for subsequent assignment to combat units as required. Marine artillery officers and naval gunfire liaison officers received joint training at Quantico and Parris Island from September 1941 to March 1942, and artillery officers of the First Marine Division and the 9th Infantry Division took a similar course in concentrated form at Fort Bragg, North Carolina. Beginning on June 22, 1942, eighteen additional navy officers were similarly trained in their duties as naval gunfire liaison officers for assignment to combat elements of the Marine Corps.

Although no great numbers were involved in this training program, it did result in the formation of an important nucleus of navy officers who were well indoctrinated in the problems of naval gunfire support and could carry the gospel into the various theaters of operations. Of the original twelve, three participated in the landings in North Africa, Sicily, and Normandy as assistant staff gunnery officers of the various naval amphibious commands. Two others ended up in the Southwest Pacific with General Douglas MacArthur USA, and played an important role in training for gunfire support in that area. Still others played the same role in the South and Central Pacific Areas. On their return to the United States, some of these officers staffed Naval Gunfire Liaison Officers' schools on each coast. Thus, these twelve young men had considerable influence on the development of naval gunfire support doctrine—far beyond what their number and rank might indicate.

Another important step in the development of gunfire support doctrine was the training of navy observation pilots in the duties of spotting shore targets. Pilots from the battleship *Arkansas,* and the cruisers *Quincy, Savannah, Philadelphia,* and *Cincinnati* were put through an accelerated course in spotting land targets at Quantico and Fort Bragg in the spring of 1942. Again, it was not the number that was important but rather that a nucleus of experienced navy aerial spotters had been formed to carry the word to other commands through the medium of their positions on staffs of amphibious forces.

Finally, steps were at last taken in 1942 to obtain an adequate firing range for naval bombardment. Culebra was too far away and too exposed to German submarines to be used as a site for sustained gunnery exercises in which any large number of ships and personnel could practice firing. At the instigation of Holland Smith's naval gunfire officer, Major Donald M. Weller USMC, Admiral King consented to purchase Bloodsworth Island off the eastern shore of Maryland in Chesapeake Bay. This was the first amphibious gunnery range ever to be established for that sole purpose, and its procurement opened a new chapter in the history of naval gunfire training. Under a program established by the Marine Corps, naval warships of all types at last received continuous and coordinated training in the type of fire support missions which they would so often be called on to perform in the coming combat operations.[62]

5. Conclusion

It cannot be said that the Marine Corps or any other branch of the armed services was fully prepared by the summer of 1942 to conduct landing operations against hostile shores. The many errors in execution which the recent landing exercises had disclosed proved without doubt that there was still a long way to go before near perfection could be claimed. But the very fact that the errors had been demonstrated empirically and that cognizance had been taken of them was in itself an immense stride in the right direction. More than that, a detailed doctrine of amphibious warfare had been evolved, tested, improved, and found to be sound in its main principles. Large numbers of marines as well as army and navy personnel had been trained in the fundamentals of amphibious fighting, which requires technical and physical skills by no means easy to acquire. The remaining test was the ultimate one of battle.

CHAPTER IV

BACKGROUND FOR GUADALCANAL, THE DECISION TO ATTACK

AMERICAN arms in the Pacific seemed consigned to the doldrums of defeat during the bleak winter of 1941–1942, but the following spring brought freshening signs that the Japanese could be contained and crushed. An opportunity for a limited offensive against the enemy appeared, and on July 2, 1942, the highest military leaders of the United States, despite the calculated risks involved, directed the navy and the marines to undertake the first Allied amphibious operation in the Pacific.

The ability of the United States to attack at this early date stemmed from two important facts. Her carrier air strength was left unscathed by the raid against Pearl Harbor, and compared to the Japanese had sustained few losses by mid-1942. Equally significant, a marine division in keeping with the long tradition of the Corps, was in the Pacific and was trained for amphibious war. The Japanese, on the other hand, failed at Pearl Harbor and later to gain undisputed command of the Pacific Ocean. The geography of that sector of the globe posed both tactical and strategical problems which they were unable to solve. They could effect amphibious operations in the waters of the Far East when these were unopposed or lightly opposed, but they had perfected neither the doctrine nor the techniques of amphibious warfare to the degree necessary for delivering an amphibious assault. Even more pertinent as background to the Guadalcanal campaign was the inability of the Japanese to gain mastery of the sea and air and thus to isolate the targets of two amphibious operations undertaken in the late spring of 1942. In making efforts in this direction, the Japanese suffered heavy losses in carriers and pilots, and their amphibious attack forces were turned back.

These factors, therefore, enabled the United States to seize the offensive in the Pacific, in spite of a global decision to give first priority to crushing Germany. This decision had been tentatively reached by Anglo-American staff conferences before Pearl Harbor, and shortly thereafter was formally approved by President Franklin D. Roosevelt and Prime Minister Winston Churchill acting in his capacity as Minister for Defence. It called for defensive action against the Japanese, since Germany's military power, actual and potential, was judged the more formidable. The Guadalcanal campaign was in harmony with this overall decision. The immediate strategic objective of the first Allied advance in the Pacific was to hold the line of communication between the west coast of the United States and Australia.

1. Geography and the End of Japan's Offensive

The directive that resulted in the Guadalcanal campaign was issued after a combination of geography and the air arm of the United States Pacific Fleet had defeated the Japanese at the Battle of Midway.

The Pacific basin is so large that its rim almost encircles the globe; its area includes almost half the world. (See map 1.) The edges of the basin outline the principal region of shrinkage on this planet, as through the course of the years the world has lost much of its internal heat to the surrounding space. Subsequently, however, earthquakes and volcanic actions have tossed the ocean floor about, and this along with reef formations has resulted in the present island growth in the Pacific.

Newly formed islands border the ocean on nearly all sides. These are in reality high mountains arranged in long sweeping arcs. Northward of the equator the outermost series includes the Aleutian, Kurile, Japanese, Bonin, Volcano, Mariana, Yap, and Palau arcs. It then drops southward and eastward to encompass the Admiralties, the Bismarcks, the Solomons, the New Hebrides, the Fijis, and New Zealand, where the chain stops.

The island-continental empire which Japan sought to consolidate by war lay to the westward of this huge crescent of newly formed islands, and comprised the Philippines, the Netherland East Indies, New Guinea, New Britain, China, and Southeast Asia. Here was the wealth of natural resources and exploitable labor which Japan sought to control, but strategical considerations dictated that she protect this empire by occupying those of the newly formed islands not already in her possession; and since the United States Navy constituted the greatest threat to the holdings of the Nipponese, it was necessary for them to dominate the islands of the Central Pacific.

These are volcanic peaks thrust upward from the floor of the Pacific as small, solid land masses, or else reef-fringed atolls representing all that remains of mountains that have sunk beneath the waves. They straddle the equator, and, beginning with the Hawaiian and Tuamotu groups in the east, run westward through Johnston, Wake, the Gilberts, the Marshalls, and the Carolines, to mention but a few. Even before the outbreak of World War II, the Japanese had gained the Carolines and Marshalls as mandates from the League of Nations.[1]

Japan began the Pacific War with a carefully planned timetable of acquisitions. She was moving, so to speak, into a military vacuum. Fortunately for her enemies, she was overcautious. Her first step was unnecessary for strategical reasons, and turned out to be a political mistake of the first magnitude. At the time the United States Pacific Fleet was not planning to move into Far Eastern waters unless and until reinforced; but by raiding Pearl Harbor on December 7, 1941,* Japan hoped to remove all possible threats to her unfolding empire. The attack succeeded in drastically weakening the battle line of the United States Navy. But since American carrier strength was not touched, the military advantages accruing to the enemy were not decisive; and they were offset by the political consequences of the attack. With dramatic suddenness the news of Pearl Harbor united the American people and created a burning determination to destroy Japan.

For the caution which prompted the Pearl Harbor raid, Americans may censure, or thank, the influence of Alfred T. Mahan on the mind of the Japanese. Their naval planners were seemingly unaware of the basic contradiction in their strategy. They recognized that theirs was a limited war with limited objectives, and yet with one stroke they sought to seize command of the entire Pacific Ocean. Not until the time of Midway, and then apparently as an afterthought, did they attempt to test their strategical control of the Central Pacific. When they did so, they discovered that the raid against Pearl Harbor was a hollow victory which had plunged Japan into the vortex of war with a powerful and implacable adversary.

The conquests of the Nipponese from December 8, 1941, through the spring of the following year were all launched amphibiously. Overrunning the Netherlands East Indies, Southeast Asia, New Britain, the Admiralties, New Ireland, the Solomons, the Gilberts, all of New Guinea except the Papuan Peninsula, and most of the Philippines was a simple task because resistance was at best sporadic. Seizing the island of Guam was equally easy. Guam was an American possession in the Marianas, and the only part of that group which had not been mandated to Japan after World War I. It was defended by a few hundred United States Marines and some native troops, all lightly armed. Hopelessly isolated and invaded in overwhelming strength, Guam surrendered after a brief fight. But American army troops on the Bataan Peninsula, soldiers and marines on Corregidor, and marines on Wake and Midway gave a different account of themselves.[2]

Wake and Midway, pinpoints in the center of the broad expanse of the Pacific basin, were garrisoned by elements of marine defense battalions. These units were heavily equipped, sacrificing tactical maneu-

* All dates and times are local at the place involved.

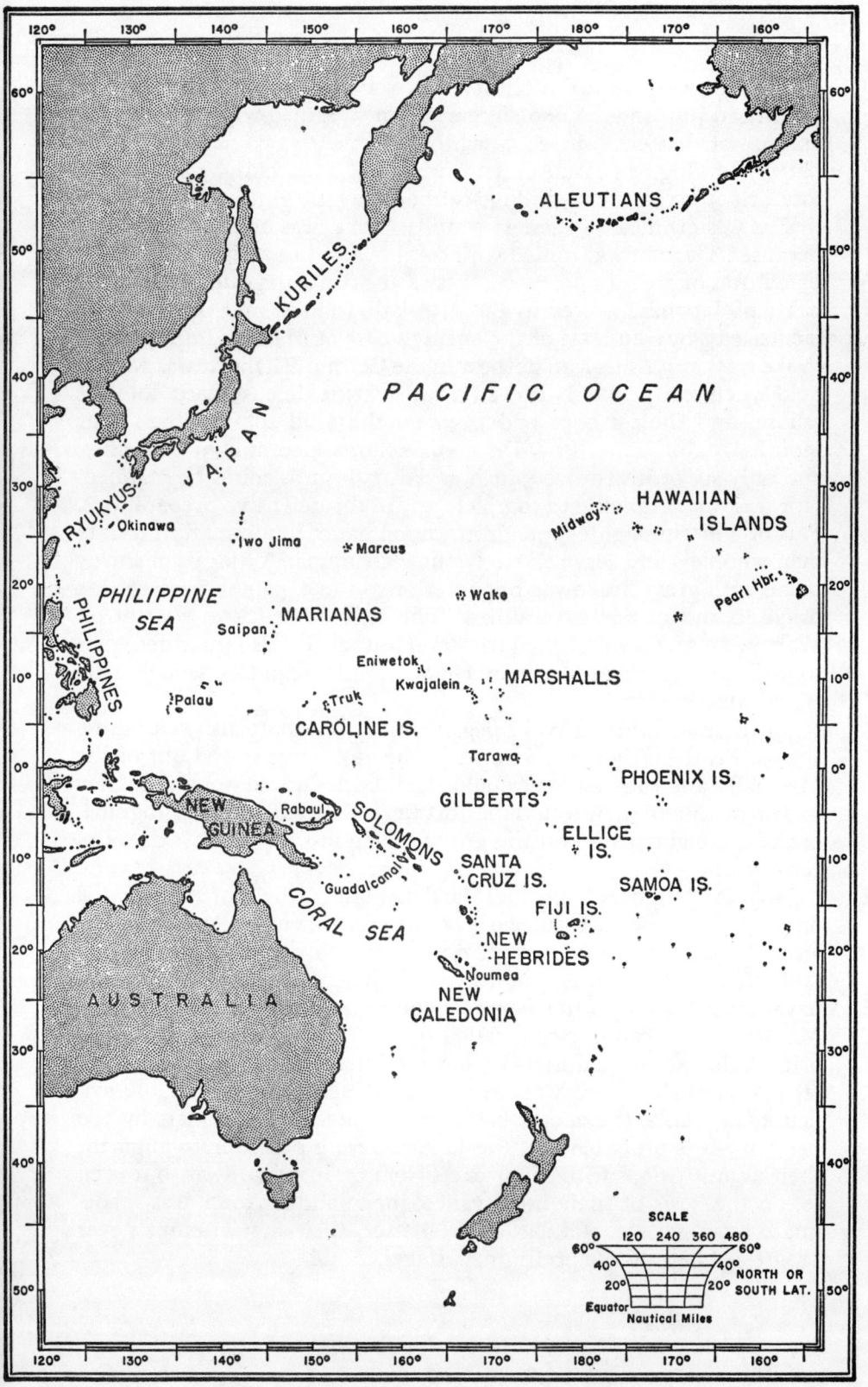

MAP 1. The Central and Western Pacific.

verability for strategical mobility. In 1941 a typical defense battalion comprised just under 1,000 officers and men, armed with three 3-inch antiaircraft batteries, three 5-inch batteries with two naval guns per battery serving as coastal defense weapons, a searchlight and sound locator battery, and .50- and .30-caliber machine gun batteries.

The westernmost of these two atolls, Wake, was useless as a harbor because its lagoon was fouled with coral heads; but as an advanced air base it was of great importance. It lay some 600 miles due north of the heart of Japanese power in the Marshall Islands, and only slightly farther east by southeast of the enemy's base at Marcus. Important as Wake was as an American outpost in the Central Pacific, it was weakly held when war broke. Not even a full marine defense battalion was ashore, and these troops had been on the atoll for less than four months. Major James P. S. Devereux commanded only 388 marines, and only six of his twelve 3-inch antiaircraft guns could be manned. Nor was time available to complete any of the defensive preparations. Part of a marine fighter squadron was on hand, totaling around sixty men who flew and serviced twelve new Grumman Wildcats, a sturdy plane with great firepower but inferior to the Japanese Zero in rate of climb and in maneuverability. The only other forces present on Wake were seventy unarmed navy and four army (also unarmed) personnel under Commander Winfield S. Cunningham USN, who was the island commander.

Japanese air raids on Wake began almost simultaneously with those against Pearl Harbor. Those against the atoll were staged out of the Marshalls, and the first one caught the marines unaware because they had no radar and their sound locators were useless beside a raging surf. Six of the eight planes on the ground were lost on the first day, December 8.

Japanese bombers from the Marshalls lashed the marines isolated on Wake for three days, and early on the morning of December 11, the enemy's attack force arrived. It was abominably commanded; its assault element was contemptuously weak. There were only 450 special naval landing troops, the Japanese counterpart of the United States Marines. American doctrine called for at least a three-to-one superiority under such circumstances, but the Japanese must have believed all Americans either cowards or inept fighters; for if available evidence is reliable, the enemy had overestimated the defenders by 100 per cent. It is probable that the Japanese were planning to augment their assault troops with bluejackets from their men-of-war, but even so, on the basis of their intelligence, their landing force was inadequate by American standards. No matter, their first attempt never progressed beyond the preliminary stages.

The Nipponese correctly calculated that no covering force was needed, and none was on hand. Their special landing troops were lifted in two old destroyers converted to transports, while their garrison components were embarked in medium-sized transports. Six destroyers, two obsolete light cruisers, and the new light cruiser *Yubari* screened the transports and attempted to deliver effective gunfire support.

The enemy's attack force commander, apparently serene in the belief that earlier air strikes had knocked out the coastal batteries on Wake, violated a basic principle of amphibious warfare. Rather than beginning to fire his heavier weapons while beyond the range of the coastal guns, he boldly sailed up to within four miles of Wake and, just at dawn, started gunfire preparation. Some hits were scored, but Devereux astutely held fire while the Japanese ran in ever closer to the muzzles of his 5-inch guns. Then the marines opened up with salvos that holed *Yubari,* damaged an old light cruiser, a destroyer transport, a medium transport, and three destroyers, and sank a fourth destroyer. Such accuracy must have surprised the Japanese, and they would have been more than a little upset had they known at the time that the marines were not fully equipped with fire-control mechanisms and that those they had were obsolete. The Japanese were for the moment beaten. They retired behind a smoke screen, but one of the remaining marine fighters took the air and with a single bomb exploded a destroyer which apparently was carrying a deck-load of depth charges.

When the Japanese made their second effort against Wake on December 23, they knew the United States had fleet carriers operating in the Pacific and they could no longer rely on the disruptive impact of an attack against Pearl Harbor. They sensibly called in two covering forces, but these were poorly deployed. Six heavy cruisers and six destroyers sailed to the eastward of Wake in close cover of their attack force, while several hundred miles to the northwest of that atoll they disposed a carrier force in strategic cover. Japanese carrier planes could strike Wake, but would have been unable to reach any American carrier which launched planes against the close covering and attack forces. America's top navy commander in the Pacific was simultaneously attempting to send a relief expedition to Wake, covered by a fast carrier; but delay and indecision on both the implementing level of command and at Pearl Harbor caused the United States Navy to miss an opportunity so rare that it would be paralleled only twice in the course of the Pacific War. At the Battle of Savo Island in the Southeastern Solomons and the Battle for Leyte Gulf in the Philippines, the fates of war favored the Japanese, and they fumbled rather than missed their golden opportunities. As for Wake, the United States relief expedition for that atoll was recalled at the critical juncture.

Preliminary to the second attempt to capture Wake, the Japanese laced the atoll with both land- and carrier-based air strikes, and then turned up with a greatly strengthened attack force. Earlier ship losses had been more than replaced, and the number of special naval landing troops had been more than doubled. Even so, the Japanese were so fearful of an amphibious assault that they refused to risk it. They failed to utilize their vastly superior ship batteries for preliminary naval gunfire support. Rather in the dark of night they beached their landing craft, including two destroyer transports, and took Wake by beach infiltration. Against defenses normal to similar targets in the Central Pacific throughout the remainder of the war, such tactics would have been quickly fatal to the attacker; but against Devereux's tiny force, poorly equipped, without a functional searchlight, and battered by more than two weeks of continuous air strikes, these tactics, although at substantial loss in Japanese lives, were successful. Wake proves that the Japanese were unprepared to deliver the amphibious assault.[3]

Circumstances surrounding the capture of Corregidor by the Japanese differed greatly from those at Wake. Corregidor is adjacent to land masses, and was pulverized by shore-based Japanese artillery as well as by enemy air strikes before an assault was attempted. When it came, the marines and the army and navy troops defending the island were underfed and haggard after a five months' siege, and they had always been deficient in equipment.

Defense of a large sector of Corregidor's beaches was assigned to the Fourth Marine Regiment, commanded by Colonel Samuel L. Howard. His troops were evacuated from Shanghai very late in November 1941, and arrived in Lingayen Gulf just before the Japanese began the Pacific War. Their commander urged General Douglas MacArthur's chief of staff to let them fight on Bataan, but this request was turned down. In China, the regiment had been under strength, but as it moved onto Corregidor it was augmented with the marines previously stationed at Cavite naval base, and subsequently it absorbed bluejackets and miscellaneous army troops until the total strength was more than 4,000 men. The majority of these, however, were marines, and to them should go much of the credit for the fact that the island they helped to defend held out longer than any other position inundated by the first Japanese offensive.

Aerial bombing rocked Corregidor from the outset of the Pacific War. The real siege began on April 9 when Bataan, after a heroic defense by United States Army and Filipino troops, fell to the enemy who quickly placed batteries on that peninsula to join voices against Corregidor with those guns already firing from the vicinity of Cavite on the southern shore of Manila Bay. Air attacks never lessened, and these along with the shore-based Japanese weapons took out the defensive installations on Corregidor one by one.

Again the Japanese began their amphibious attack at night, an hour before the moon rose during the evening of May 5. They operated against some of the beaches held by the Fourth Marine Regiment. Their preparation was thorough, and their plans were good, but the shore-to-shore movement was disorderly and lacked momentum. Although the marines and their army-navy comrades had little more than small arms with which to beat back the onslaught, for a time its success quivered in the balance. Lieutenant General Masaharu Homma, commanding the Japanese Fourteenth Army from his headquarters on Bataan, is said to have groaned as he listened to reports of the fighting, "My God, I have failed in the assault."

Already, however, the sun had dawned on May 6, the marines had committed their last reserves, and finally the Japanese managed to get tanks ashore. That ended the contest. The marines had no antitank guns. Major General Jonathan Wainwright USA, faced reality and ordered capitulation. Howard of the Fourth Marines echoed Homma. "My God," he said, "and I had to be the first Marine officer ever to surrender a regiment." [4]

Guam, Wake, and Corregidor, like other Japanese victories in the first phase of the Pacific War, were obtained after gaining complete mastery of the sea and air in the target area. Failure to repeat this performance in two similar efforts during the late spring of 1942 resulted in reverses for the Imperial Japanese Navy, and made feasible an Allied amphibious operation against the Southeastern Solomons.

Just as Corregidor fell, a United States carrier task force turned the Japanese back from an attempt to land in the vicinity of Port Moresby, close to the southeastern tip of the Papuan Peninsula, British New Guinea. Despite the delay encountered in the Philippines, the enemy was ahead of his schedule of conquests, and in May and June of 1942 was embarking on a new series of expansions in an effort to secure even stronger bases for the protection of his newly won empire. These new movements, ranging from the Aleutians southward through Midway to the Coral Sea, were only tentative parts of the enemy's original war plan. Having begun cautiously and having met with great success, the Japanese were now overconfident. Their top naval commanders insisted on further aggrandizement, and at the critical juncture the navy's hand was strengthened by Lieutenant Colonel James H. Doolittle's Army Air Force raid from the fleet carrier *Hornet* against Tokyo.[5]

The first of these new moves chronologically was against Allied positions adjacent to and south of the Solomon Sea. The strategic objective was to isolate Australia from the United States, and eventually to place New Zealand in the same weakened position. Early steps toward such setbacks for the Allies had already been taken. The Japanese in January 1942 had captured Rabaul, an excellent harbor at the northeastern tip of New Britain, and were building it up as a pivotal base in guarding the southeastern corner of their empire. In order to consolidate their hold on Rabaul, and to isolate if not to invade Australia, they were forced to encircle the Solomon Sea. (See Map 2.) Nor would the process end there. They must burst loose from the Solomon Sea southward into the Coral Sea before capturing Port Moresby and destroying Allied strength in the New Hebrides and New Caledonia.

Tulagi, key harbor in the southeastern portion of the Solomon Islands, fell to the Japanese without resistance on May 3, but the amphibious expedition headed for Port Moresby was forced to turn tail because of a strategical defeat which the Japanese navy suffered at the hands of the United States Pacific Fleet in the Battle of the Coral Sea, May 7-8. It was here that Japan's carrier air strength, with the loss of a light carrier and major damage to a heavy carrier, began to dwindle.[6]

From the Coral Sea the scene shifted to the Central and Northern Pacific where in early June the Japanese landed on Attu and Kiska, and attempted to seize Midway. The atoll at Midway is the most important military position in the northwestern sector of the Hawaiian chain. In the words of the Japanese, "Midway acts as a sentry for Hawaii."[7]

The Japanese, sailing under the flag of their highest ranking admiral afloat, Isoroku Yamamoto, showed at Midway that they understood the prerequisites which make amphibious warfare possible, but, unlike Wake, they never had an opportunity at Midway to exhibit whether or not they could assault a heavily defended beach. They advanced on Midway with the same intent and essentially the same command and task organizations that would later guide the United States under similar circumstances. Yamamoto sought a fleet engagement which would complete the job begun at Pearl Harbor by sinking America's fast carriers in the Pacific and would give the Japanese unquestioned command of the sea and air. For this reason fast carriers were in the vanguard of their approach, but the Americans were waiting. The commander of the Japanese carriers, concluding that he had achieved strategical surprise, launched his planes for a strike against Midway early on the morning of June 4, and was virtually defenseless against United States carrier planes when these began swarming over his task force a few hours later. On that day and the next, the Nipponese lost four fleet carriers, all they had on hand at the time. The amphibious attack force steaming for Midway, now without air cover, reversed course.

Midway has been interpreted as a victory of land-based against carrier-based air. This view was given credence at the time because of the exorbitant claims of the Army Air Forces. The air general on the scene stated that the battle was principally won "in the blasting by the Flying Fortresses of the Japanese Naval Task Force, including carriers," and even the cautious New York *Times* concurred editorially. Lieutenant General Henry H. Arnold USA was even more expansive, stating that during the first six months of the Pacific conflict, army planes had sunk thirty-three warships and forty-four transports, freighters, and tankers.[8]

Had such an interpretation been widely accepted in responsible military quarters, it would have altered the future course of the Pacific War. The conclusion would have been that carriers could not operate against land-based planes, and as a result there would have been no means by which targets in the Central Pacific could be isolated and prepared for the amphibious assault.

Facts brought to light after the war show conclusively that naval airmen were correct in their analysis of the Midway encounter, that it was a victory of carrier air against carrier air. The Joint Army-Navy Assessment Committee carefully checked all Japanese navy and merchant shipping losses and credited the United States Army Air Forces during the first six months of the war with sinking only two small Japanese minesweepers, and, assisted at times by other arms, with demolishing eight transport and cargo vessels displacing 500 tons and over. The accurate study of the Joint Army-Navy Assessment Committee goes further. It reveals that not only before and during the Battle of Midway, but for the remainder of the Pacific War, the majority of Army Air Force pilots were untrained and unequipped to hit ship targets. They insisted on releasing their bombs at fantastic altitudes, while airmen flying carrier-type planes were drilled in the necessity for coming in low. There was one blanket exception to this statement. The army flyers under Major General George C. Kenney USA, MacArthur's air commander, were given special training and equipment, and beginning early in 1944 they achieved notable successes at low altitudes in antishipping strikes.

As for the Battle of Midway, official Air Force historians have pointed out that the twenty land-based heavy and medium bombers participating flew a total of fifty-nine sorties, but failed to touch a single Japanese carrier while it was operational and maneuvering at high speeds. The army pilots probably inflicted slight damage on a transport, and late in the battle, by descending to the altitude of 3,600 feet, possibly damaged a destroyer, and bombed, strafed, and helped to sink a carrier that had already been chewed up by United States Pacific Fleet planes. In extenuation of the army airmen, they were inexperienced in the type of warfare involved, were near exhaustion from having flown extensive reconnaissance sorties and from having helped hand-service their own planes, which were too few in numbers to expect to obtain a hit accidentally through their own doctrine of mass drops.

Marine pilots flying from Midway Atoll also participated in the battle; their craft were carrier types and they were indoctrinated in low altitude attack tactics. Their performance was superior to that of the army flyers, but even so it left much to be desired. Most of these marines, like the army airmen, were inexperienced and some were not fully trained. They too had to help service their own craft, and three-quarters of their twenty-eight fighters plus almost one-half of their thirty-six dive bombers were obsolete. A marine pilot testified that the antique Brewster fighters seemed tied to a string when Japanese Zeros made passes at them. Nevertheless, the greatest contribution made by the marine airmen at Midway was in shooting down enemy aircraft.

Damaging or sinking Japanese warships was a different story. If the postwar testimony of one of the captains of an enemy carrier lost at Midway is to be believed—testimony refuted by other evidence—a marine dive bomber attack came down to from 500 to 200 feet altitude and damaged an enemy carrier very early in the battle, but this injury, if inflicted, was minor and repairs were quickly made. It is possible that a battleship was also lightly shaken up by other marine airmen at about the same time. Late in the engagement, marine dive bombers jumped two Japanese heavy cruisers which were limping away from Midway after colliding with one another. One of these cruisers was sunk, and additional misery was dealt out to the second.[9]

Unquestionably it was carrier-based American pilots who denied the enemy command of the sea and air at Midway, although the claims of the Army Air Forces were used in an effort to influence subsequent operational planning of the United States in the Pacific.

Since the Japanese were unable to localize the target at Midway, what would have developed into an amphibious assault never took place. The atoll was well guarded by marine defense battalions. Whether or not the enemy's tactics would have shown improvement because of his experiences at Wake will forever remain a mystery.

The principal lesson of Midway is the fact that this battle, along with the earlier raid on Pearl Harbor, clearly reveals the concern of the Japanese for the Central Pacific, control of which was essential in protecting their co-prosperity life line, running from their home islands south into the Netherlands East Indies and Southeast Asia. It was in the Central Pacific that their navy made its final all-out effort to advance amphibiously; here they established key defensive positions; and when the tables were turned and the United States assumed the offensive, the Japanese ultimately capitulated, in large part under the pressure exerted in the Central Pacific. Unlike the Japanese, the United States Navy and its marine arm, assisted by Army Air and Ground Forces, were able to seize control of the sea and air and to deliver the amphibious assault.

2. *Command Relations and America's First Offensive*

The drive across the Central Pacific was launched only after a dispute between the United States Army and Navy in another quarter of the Pacific had been resolved. America's high command was anxious to capitalize on Japan's reversals in the Coral Sea and at Midway, and this could best be done by taking the offensive immediately. The discussion was couched in terms of the precise geographical point to be seized by America's first amphibious operation in World War II, which in turn involved the designation of the implementing commander, army or navy. The compromise reached was, under the supervision of the navy, to secure a lodgement in the Southeastern Solomons.

At the time this controversy occurred, which was in the early summer of 1942, the connection between it and any march across the Central Pacific was, on the surface, remote; but it is safe to conclude that the participants were fully aware of the implications of their decision, which helped lead directly to Tarawa and beyond. The basic issue was whether the naval or the army forces in the Pacific would spearhead the attack against Japan. Suspicions arose that each service, army and navy, was trying to make the other subservient in the Pacific. The basic issue, however, was fought out in terms of geography, and this brought up the problem of command. It is thus necessary to discuss command relationships from the highest echelon down to the implementing level. The focal point of interest is the officer in command of a joint task force comprising army, navy, and air force components.

The command hastily established under General Sir Archibald Wavell by the Americans, British, Dutch, and the Anzac commonwealths never had an opportunity to function well and disintegrated as the Japanese engulfed the Malay barrier and the Netherlands East Indies. Shortly thereafter, in February and March 1942, command arrangements were made for the Pacific which lasted throughout the war.[10]

The United States was, through agreement with the other Allied powers at war with Japan, given full strategic responsibility for the entire Pacific basin, except for the Malay barrier. This was done by the Combined Chiefs of Staff, who were the principal military advisers to President Roosevelt and Minister for Defence Churchill. Early in 1942 the Combined Chiefs of Staff agreed that Germany should be defeated first, but the Japanese had to be stopped and the United States Navy was anxious as early as possible to begin placing unremitting pressure on them.[11] Thus the Combined Chiefs of Staff, by controlling the allocation of men and materiel, retained technical supervision over the Pacific War; but since the strategical use to which these troops, weapons, and supplies were put was solely up to Roosevelt's ranking military advisers, these men are of principal interest in a study of the conflict in the Pacific.

These officers began calling themselves the Joint Chiefs of Staff in February 1942. The composition of the body varied slightly early in the war, but soon settled down to four men: Admiral William D. Leahy, Chief of Staff to the President; General George C. Marshall, Chief of Staff, United States Army; Admiral Ernest J. King, Commander in Chief of the United States Fleet and Chief of Naval Operations; and General Henry H. Arnold, Commanding General, Army Air Forces.

The United States has always, in theory at least, enjoyed unity of command. During World War II the Joint Chiefs of Staff served as the agency for gaining unity of command in practice. The President is, according to the Constitution, "Commander in Chief of the Army and Navy . . . ," and Roosevelt retained the right to decide the political issues involved, but delegated the purely military duties to the Joint Chiefs of Staff, who carried them out superbly. It is becoming increasingly popular to condemn the concept of the Joint Chiefs of Staff as unwieldy and as "war by committee." But the President is not a committee. If the attack against the Joint Chiefs of Staff is successful, it will probably place final military control in hands other than those of the President.

The Pacific is frequently pointed to as an example of divided command, in that the ocean was split into two important theaters and placed under two different commanders. The truth of the matter is that the Joint Chiefs (acting on authority of the President) actually commanded in the Pacific. Under the circumstances, there was no acceptable alternative. The problems were so complex that they could never have been settled properly and with due regard for the interests of all the services simply by naming a single Pacific commander. The difference of military opinion between the army and the navy in the Pacific as represented by Admiral Chester W. Nimitz and General

Douglas MacArthur was so wide that Air Force historians have described it as an "abyss." The Joint Chiefs of Staff was the agency which harmonized these views and set overall strategy for the Pacific. Their decisions had to be unanimous, and any one of the four had direct access to Roosevelt in the event of a deadlock.[12] Concerning the Pacific War, an independent appeal to the President was seldom necessary, since controversies were resolved among the officers themselves.

The antecedent of the Joint Chiefs of Staff, the Joint Board, had agreed in 1935 to the doctrine of command relationships set forth in a revised edition of *The Joint Action of the Army and Navy*. The principles enunciated in this publication set the pattern by which the unity of command given to the President by the Constitution was transferred through the Joint Chiefs of Staff to the theater commanders, and from these to the implementing commanders of task forces jointly comprising army, naval, and air force components. Indeed, the same principles were absorbed by the Combined Chiefs of Staff and were applied to the commanders of task forces combining elements of the different services of the United States and of the British Commonwealth, both in the Pacific and elsewhere.

That the pattern for unity of command was set several years before the United States entered World War II was fortunate in view of the intricate nature of joint operations, especially amphibious operations. It must be added that the disaster at Pearl Harbor was aggravated, not because the doctrine for unity of command did not exist, but because it had not been placed in effect in Hawaii before December 7, 1941.

The 1935 publication declared that in order to achieve unity of command, one man would have delegated to him both the responsibility and the authority to join elements of all services into a task force, to assign missions and designate objectives for each of the component elements involved, to provide for logistical support, and to exercise such coordinating control as he might deem necessary to insure the success of any given operation. Negatively, unity of command was never to be construed as authorizing the single commander to infringe upon the administrative or disciplinary functions of any component service other than his own; nor was the single commander to direct an officer of another service how his mission was to be carried out. This last restriction is highly important. The unifying commander was empowered to assign missions, that is to tell his subordinates from the other services what to do and when to do it, but he was instructed to refrain from spelling out the tactical details of how that mission was to be accomplished. In this connection the integration of the Fleet Marine Force within the Pacific Fleet was to lead to some confusion in command relations, especially in the early stages of the war. Traditionally, the marines had been outranked by navy officers, and the sudden expansion of the Marine Corps both in size and importance ran afoul of the preconceived ideas of some navy officers who continued, in effect, to consider the marines as small landing units aboard a man-of-war. The question was how far it was advisable to permit a navy officer to interfere with the tactics of the marines ashore. While recognizing that the navy officer commanding the amphibious attack force is responsible for setting the troops ashore and for continued logistical support, and must therefore at least indirectly influence the fighting on the beach and inland, there is a limit beyond which he should not go. In the early phases of the struggle in the Solomons, it is evident that ranking navy officers intervened too much in marine tactics ashore. King himself took cognizance of this fact and in mid-1943 categorically reaffirmed the command relationship established in 1935. Further, he clarified the doctrine as regards the marines by listing them specifically alongside army forces and by reaffirming his order to navy officers to refrain from interfering with the details of how either a marine or army commander fulfilled his assigned mission.[13]

A final aspect of the command relations established in 1935 must be examined. The appointment of one unifying commander carried with it the power further to delegate the responsibility and authority involved, and directed the higher echelon officer in so doing to select as the implementing commander of any given joint task force an officer from that service which held a paramount interest in the common mission involved.[14]

This doctrine as applied by the United States in World War II permitted each member of the Joint Chiefs of Staff, acting for the President, to command in that broad area of dominant interest to his service. Also, it authorized the Joint Chiefs of Staff, functioning as a composite body, to transfer any given component of joint forces from theater to theater as the strategical situation might necessitate. Likewise, through international agreement, combined forces in the Pacific were similarly under the control of the Joint Chiefs of Staff.

The Joint Chiefs applied the principles of *The Joint Action of the Army and Navy* to the Pacific during the early spring of 1942 by creating in that half of the globe three theater commanders, two navy and the other army, as the geographic situation and service interests dictated.

The Southeastern Pacific Theater, of little importance during the war since the Japanese offensive was stopped beyond its limits, included a long stretch of water west of the Panama Canal and South America to 110° west longitude.

The two theaters in which the Pacific War was fought were assigned to Admiral Nimitz and General MacArthur. Nimitz, Commander in Chief of the Pacific Fleet, was placed in charge of a vast expanse of ocean and islands reaching from the coast of Asia north and east of the Philippines, then south to the equator, then east to 165° east longitude, then south to 10° south latitude, thence southwesterly to the point formed by 17° south latitude and 160° east longitude, and finally south along that meridian to the Antarctic. (See map 2.) King, as the Commander in Chief of the United States Fleet, was named the executive agent through whom the directives of the Joint Chiefs of Staff would be passed along to Nimitz. Also, by international accord, Nimitz was given command of all Allied (combined as well as joint) forces then present or later sent into his theater. As such Nimitz became Commander in Chief of the Pacific Ocean Areas, but in this capacity likewise he remained subordinate to King and the Joint Chiefs of Staff.

Nimitz's theater was so huge, and the importance of protecting the lines of communications between the United States and the Anzac region so great, that he was ordered to establish a separate command, under his overall supervision, including the area under his command south of the equator. This became the South Pacific Area, and its first commander was Vice Admiral Robert L. Ghormley USN.

That portion of the Western Pacific not under Nimitz went to MacArthur, Commanding General of the United States Army Forces in the Far East. Marshall became his executive superior for the transmission of directives from the Joint Chiefs of Staff. Similarly, MacArthur was given an Allied post as Commander in Chief of the Southwest Pacific Area, but here also he remained under the orders of Marshall and the Joint Chiefs of Staff.[15]

Command relations in the Pacific were thus established before the Battle of Midway abruptly shifted the strategic situation in that ocean to the advantage of the Allied powers. The most serious remaining menace of the Japanese was their advance down the Solomons. Occupation of the central and southeastern portions of that group jeopardized the shipment of men and supplies from the United States into the South and Southwest Pacific Areas, and covered Japanese operations along the northeastern coast of the Papuan Peninsula. How best to stop the Solomons thrust and capitalize upon the strategic victories in the Coral Sea and at Midway demanded the attention of the Joint Chiefs of Staff and their theater commanders in the Pacific.

At this stage of the war, an Allied offensive mounted from any quarter of the Pacific would have required improvisation as to means. Since the conflict in and across the Atlantic had been given top priority, the plan was to remain on the defensive in the Pacific until at least January 1943, but King personally was straining in anxiety to get an offensive from the South Pacific Area under way. The Battle of the Coral Sea allowed him to bring his ideas before the Joint Chiefs of Staff, and discussions as to the most practical approach were held. Suddenly the victory at Midway in early June made an immediate attack imperative.[16] In an atmosphere of haste and despite logistical handicaps, the Joint Chiefs promulgated the directive which led to the Solomons, Papuan, New Britain, and Admiralties campaigns.

In retrospect, the directive for these campaigns stands forth as one of the outstanding decisions of the Pacific War. Within twenty months of the time that directive was issued, Rabaul had been surrounded and neutralized, the right flank to the Southwest Pacific Area had been secured, and MacArthur was thereafter able, with naval cover and support, to move along the coast of New Guinea into the Philippines. Likewise, along with earlier and unopposed occupation of the Phoenix and Ellice groups, the left flank of the Central Pacific was protected. Japanese air and surface power in the Carolines and Marshalls was drained. The eventual amphibious assaults through the Gilberts, Marshalls, and Marianas were made strategically more feasible. Finally, all of the armed services of the United States were given practical experience in the conduct of amphibious operations against relatively large land masses. Amphibious doctrine was polished, techniques tested and improved, and time was provided during which new weapons and landing craft were placed in mass production. The navy, even while carrying on a war of attrition with the Japanese in the Solomons waters, was able through repairs and new construction to accumulate that margin of fleet superiority needed to launch the offensive across the Central Pacific.

The armed services of the United States were given this valuable time interval and experience partly as a result of the stubborn facts of geography but certainly also because of audacious leadership at the highest echelon of command. In fact, King and Marshall were more audacious than single-minded in issuing the directive on July 2, 1942, for the Solomons, Papuan, New Britain, and Admiralties campaigns. Each service recognized that the employment of troops trained in and equipped for amphibious warfare and the effective application of air power were essential to success, but beyond this the difference was wide. The Joint Chiefs were unable fully to concur in specifying the initial geographical target, and to Admiral King goes much of the credit for the directive that largely shaped the future course of the Pacific War. Although all of the objectives (except for one island ultimately designated in the initial offensive) were in the Southwest Pacific Area, the stronger element of tactical air strength and all the troops amphibiously trained and equipped in the Pacific during the summer of 1942 were under the navy's control. These consisted primarily of carriers and squadrons of navy and marine planes and of the First Marine Division. Thus King's bargaining position relative to that of General Marshall was good. At one point in the dispute, King suggested that the navy would begin operations whether or not United States Army forces from the Southwest Pacific Area cooperated.[17] Under the circumstances, it is hardly surprising that the naval contention was, though somewhat altered, in the main adopted.

The Joint Chiefs of Staff always made strategical decisions for the Pacific on the basis of studies drawn up by their subcommittees in Washington, and on the basis of recommendations submitted to them by their two principal theater commanders in that ocean. All involved were agreed on an offensive in the general area of the Solomons-New Britain-New Guinea; but the region is vast, and logistical shortages would prevent a rapid follow through, much less simultaneous attacks against two or more widely separated points. The precise location of the first offensive was important because it involved the choice of command over a joint task force. King wanted a navy officer, rather than MacArthur, in strategic control of the operation and the aircraft carriers involved.

The problem of who would command the first offensive in the Pacific had given the Joint Chiefs of Staff earlier trouble. The directives establishing theater commanders had postponed the decision by stating that both the Southwest and the South Pacific Areas would prepare for offensives, and a period of from eight to ten months was allowed for a build up of forces. No one had known early in 1942 that the Coral Sea and Midway battles would occur, and that they would radically change the whole strategic outlook. Now that an offensive was to be launched earlier, neither the South nor the Southwest Pacific Area had sufficient strength. Under the circumstances, both Nimitz and MacArthur in May 1942 submitted proposals which would draw men and materiel from the adjacent theater.

The manner in which aircraft carriers were to be employed was the pivotal consideration in the dispute. Marshall and MacArthur recognized the value of these ships, and the fact that their use would speed the advance of troops out of Australia and Port Moresby by beating down enemy air strength and by lengthening the stride taken at any one time. Without carrier air, each advance along the relatively large land masses in MacArthur's theater would be restricted to the operating radius of land-based fighters, and further delays would ensue while the logistical and engineering problems of rolling air fields forward were solved. MacArthur was sending tentative plans to Washington which, in the eyes of navy officers, would expose carriers to almost certain loss. The navy did not consider its carriers so highly expendable.

MacArthur was recommending a series of rapid thrusts from the

Papuan Peninsula against Rabaul. Ships covering and supporting such movements, including carriers, would be compelled to enter the Solomon Sea. This body of water was surrounded on three sides by Japanese land bases, all a part of the Rabaul network. On many of these bases were navy planes and navy pilots well trained in the low-altitude attack tactics then essential to sea warfare. Furthermore, the Solomon Sea was so full of foul ground as to be most dangerous to navigation. Charts of the sea were a century old. Maneuvering would be exceedingly difficult and at times impossible, and of course room to maneuver was essential to any ship squirming under an air attack. The Solomon Sea was far worse than its companion waters to the south, the Coral Sea, of which a competent mariner has said: "The place is reef-littered, treacherous, ill charted, and unlit . . . . a nightmare, a reef-filled backwash of the misnamed Pacific Sea." [18]

A premature incursion into the Solomon Sea might have given the Japanese an easy revenge for Midway. They already had navy planes and navy pilots land-based in the target area, and these could be reinforced by other carrier-type planes and navy pilots winging southward from a web of internal bases, as well as by craft flown from Japan's remaining carriers, which in turn could be deployed with complete immunity from counterattack. Later in the war, after the United States had better types of carrier aircraft and a greatly increased number of floating antiaircraft batteries of a vastly improved quality, American carriers did operate adjacent to large land masses and hundreds of Japanese navy and army planes, and did, with the help of Army Air Forces, isolate such targets as Rabaul—but never for extended periods in waters comparable to the Solomon Sea.

Another aspect of MacArthur's theater planning incensed ranking naval officers as much as his desire to send carriers into the dangerous waters of the Solomon Sea. MacArthur had one United States Army and two Australian divisions in combat readiness, but none was either amphibiously trained or equipped. He was therefore requesting that the First Marine Division, early elements of which were already en route to New Zealand, be placed at his disposal. He continued to request these marines even after they had been committed to Guadalcanal, in August 1942. Since they would be the only amphibiously competent troops at his command for a speedy sweep into Rabaul, his headquarters contemplated using them with a rapidity which even on paper was breathtaking.[19] Navy and marine officers were aghast at this strategic plan and tactical schedule. The Commandant of the Marine Corps, Lieutenant General Thomas Holcomb, urged that MacArthur never be permitted to command either the fleet or ship-to-shore aspects of an amphibious operation. King's war plans officer bluntly asserted, "MacArthur . . . has no conception of the factors that enter

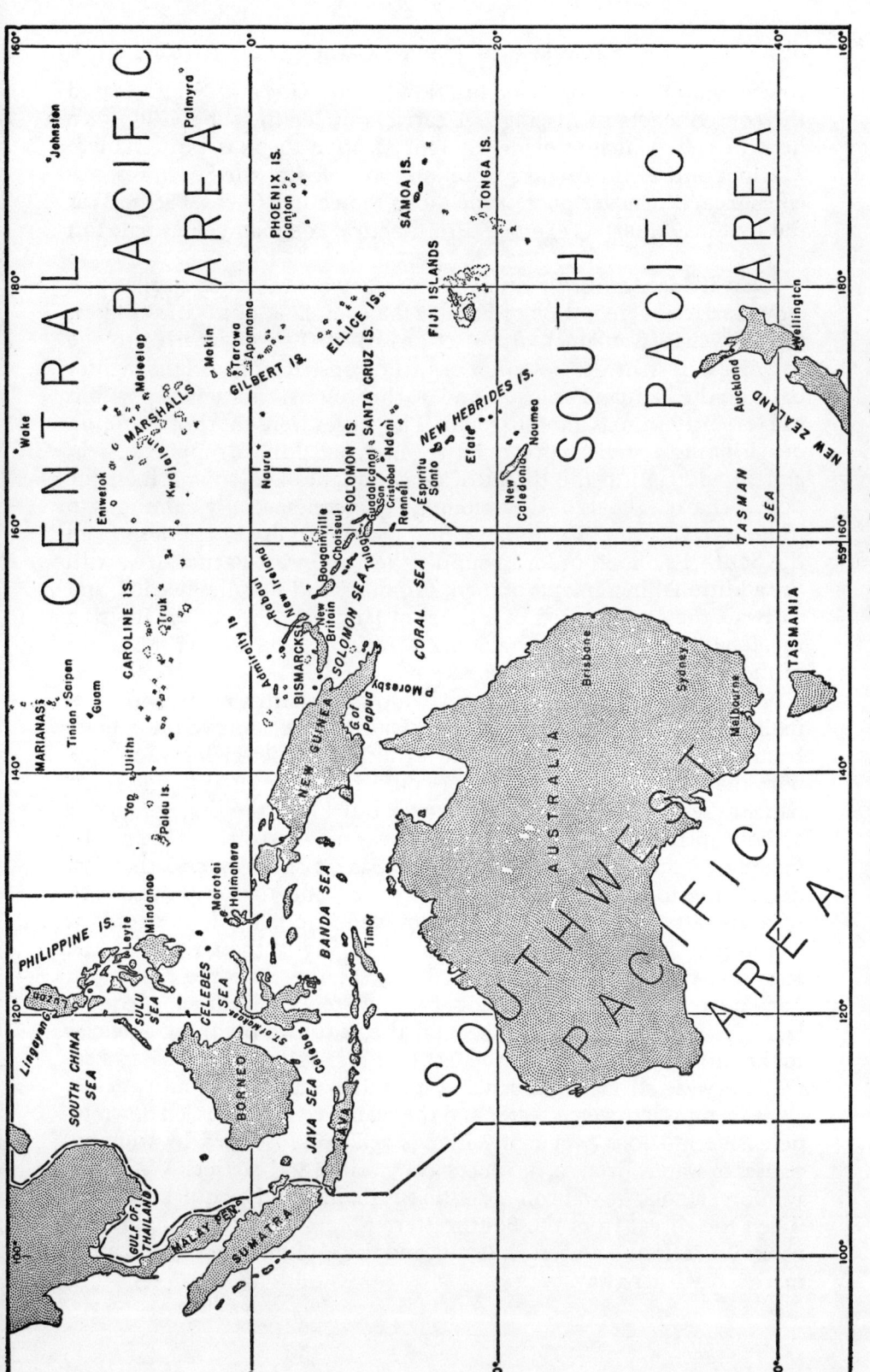

MAP 2. Theater boundaries, showing change made by the July 1942 directive.

into an amphibious force organization." Both King and Nimitz feared the consequences of placing fast carriers under the supervision of a headquarters which so evidently looked upon them as expendable.[20] Marines and escort carriers were later assigned to the Southwest Pacific Area, but never once throughout the course of the Pacific War did that headquarters exercise direct tactical command of a single fast carrier.

Even if MacArthur's plan of May 1942 were modified so that precious carriers were not placed under the command of an army officer, the navy had fundamental objections to it. The alternative to the use of carriers in the Solomon Sea, the construction of land fighter bases on the Papuan Peninsula and on the western and central portions of New Britain, was almost as bad. The Allies were short of amphibious shipping as well as covering, screening, and gunfire support vessels, and in addition to the threat of enemy planes and submarines, the poorly charted shoals of the Solomon Sea were especially hazardous to inshore navigation. Time was a vital factor. To divert strength from the South Pacific in order to supply the Southwest Pacific Area with the additional increments of men, shipping, and supplies needed, and to await the construction of a series of land bases, would be inviting the Japanese to outflank the entire venture by continuing south out of the Solomons into New Caledonia.

MacArthur's plan had some merit, although hardly enough to offset its inherent disadvantages. An offensive in his theater would operate from more secure land bases, and would enjoy better logistical support than the South Pacific Area could for some time provide. On paper at least, MacArthur's plan struck quickly at the heart of enemy activity in the Southern Pacific. He reasoned correctly that only by moving directly into Rabaul could Japanese shipments to that fast developing fortress be immediately cut off, and that otherwise each separate attack in the New Britain-New Guinea-Solomons sector would meet violent enemy reaction, especially in the air and on the sea. MacArthur rightly contended that at the time the Southwest Pacific Area alone had the necessary intelligence personnel, adequate facilities for air reconnaissance, and the requisite planning agencies for an offensive. He stressed the fact that his available land-based strategic air was a stronger offensive weapon than that of the South Pacific, since its numbers were greater and the planes were not so tied down by defensive missions over many islands relatively isolated by wide expanses of water. Even so, he must have marines and carriers. With such reinforcements, he was confident that Rabaul could be quickly seized. Then the threat from the Southeastern Solomons against the line of communications between Australia and the United States would automatically wither away.

Thus the basic question was whether MacArthur with carrier and marine components should mount the first offensive up the Papuan Peninsula toward Rabaul, or whether a navy officer, who might be expected to be more considerate of carrier vulnerability, should move from the South Pacific Area into the Southeastern Solomons. More than a limited offensive was beyond the capacity of the navy. Not even a limited undertaking could be inaugurated unless carriers could cover and support the attack with relative safety, or at least with an even chance of survival. For this reason, among others, American navy planners looked for a means of striking the enemy under auspices more favorable than those offered by the New Guinea-New Britain project. The principal objective of the navy's counterproposal was to remove quickly the threat against the Allied line of communications. Its immediate effect, in terms of planning and the availability of means, was to slow down the movement of MacArthur across New Guinea and into New Britain until enemy air strength in the region of Rabaul had been in large part depleted by an advance from a different direction; but one may maintain that the end result was to speed up MacArthur's advance toward the Philippines by diverting Japanese strength from New Guinea into the Solomons and by helping to secure his right flank, thus facilitating his sea-borne leaps.

The geographical target selected by the navy was Ndeni of the Santa Cruz group and the island of Tulagi, located in the Solomons less than 600 miles southeast of Rabaul. (See map 2.) The enemy had occupied Tulagi early in May; but contrary to his usual procedure, apparently because of naval reverses, he failed even to begin an airfield until July, when he started work on a site along the lower reaches of the Lunga River on Guadalcanal, some twenty miles south of Tulagi. Nor had the Japanese by that date completed any strong bases in the Central Solomons. Knowledge of this procrastination made a landing in the Southeastern Solomons attractive in the eyes of the United States Navy.[21]

Still other features fastened naval attention to the lower tip of the Solomons. About 800 miles south of Tulagi lay New Caledonia, on which island, at Nouméa, American installations were being erected. Southeast of Tulagi, and roughly 250 miles closer to that objective than Nouméa, was situated another scarcely begun Allied establishment on Espiritu Santo, in the New Hebrides. Carriers supporting and covering an attack against Tulagi would be removed from enemy land-based air, and could rely on antisubmarine and reconnaissance patrols from Espiritu Santo.

Also attractive was the wide expanse of water suitable for carrier maneuverings southeast and south of Tulagi. The enemy had not yet overrun the islands in this region, notably the Santa Cruz group and Rennell and San Cristobal of the Solomons chain. East and slightly south of Tulagi by little more than 325 miles was Ndeni of the Santa Cruz cluster. If this promising airsite could be developed, carriers sending planes over the Southeastern Solomons, in addition to more efficient performance in every other respect, could enjoy the security of land-based fighter combat air patrols.

MacArthur's plan and that of the navy were premised on two diverse strategic concepts, one calling for a direct stab at the principal target, the other requiring the gradual reduction of the outer positions as essential preliminaries to an onslaught against the main objective. These differences were harmonized in Washington, for in spite of them Marshall was informed by his War Department planners that they could reconcile all disagreement with their counterparts from the Navy Department except the question of command.

When MacArthur was informed by Marshall of the navy's opposition to his plan, he insisted that it had been misunderstood. He did not intend to strike directly at Rabaul because he lacked the land-based airpower to support such an operation. Rather, he wished to make a progressive advance against the Solomons and the north coast of New Guinea to secure the airfields necessary to launch an attack against Rabaul and to cover the naval forces. To carry out this modified offensive he still wished to employ the naval forces requested for the original plan. MacArthur's modification of his earlier plan removed one of the major differences between the army and navy proposals but left the question of command still unresolved. MacArthur again insisted that he should be in charge of the first operation because his theater possessed the better planning and implementing agencies. He felt that only confusion would result if ground forces from the Pacific Ocean Areas, responsible to a distant navy officer, were employed in the Southwest Pacific Area.

While negotiations between the War and Navy Departments were still going on, King despatched on June 25 a warning order to Nimitz for the Tulagi-Ndeni undertaking. During the week following this order, King and Marshall met personally to reconcile their final difference. Command of the initial attack went to the navy, but Marshall was so convinced of the importance of the Southwest Pacific Theater that, although he was willing to direct MacArthur to lend air and Australian naval support to the first attack, he refused to deplete MacArthur of trained troops and insisted that the occupation forces for Tulagi-Ndeni be drawn from the South Pacific rather than from the Southwest Pacific Area. Moreover, the directive to which Marshall agreed provided that, after the completion of the Tulagi phase of the New Guinea-New Britain-Solomons campaigns, MacArthur would take over.[22]

This compromise was embodied in the formal directive of the Joint

Chiefs of Staff issued on July 2, 1942. Singling out Rabaul as the final objective of a series of forthcoming offensives, the directive named Tulagi and adjacent positions, plus the Santa Cruz group, as targets for the first offensive, and set August 1, 1942, as the planning date for this attack. To give the navy officer in command of this operation full freedom of action from MacArthur, the directive moved the Southwest Pacific Area boundary westward to 159° east longitude, thus shifting the entire Southeastern Solomons to the control of Nimitz. (See map 2.) Later offensives at times unspecified were called for, all to be under the strategic direction of MacArthur. These were the occupation of the remaining Solomons; the seizure of Lae, Salamaua, and the northeast coast of New Guinea, and then the conquest of Rabaul and adjacent positions.[23]

3. Significance of the July 2, 1942, Directive

Historically, the campaign for the Southeastern Solomons went far in determining the future role of the army and naval forces in the Pacific War. This, in the final analysis, rather than the command of carriers and marines, was the fundamental problem. MacArthur acknowledged it in one of his despatches to Marshall. To quote an official Air Force historian: "MacArthur expressed a fear that the Navy's proposals would reduce the Army's functions to subsidiary ones and implied that army forces would be used largely for garrisoning the islands." [24] This fear, while exaggerated, was based on a brilliant insight into the real significance of the pending directive of July 2, 1942, and it is likely that the fear increased rather than diminished once the naval drive across the Central Pacific began, late in 1943. The question was which service, army or navy, would play the major part in defeating Japan. The directive favored the navy, and having gained the upper hand in this instance, neither King nor Nimitz relented.

Before and during the course of the Pacific War, two broad concepts for the defeat of Japan developed. One of these was MacArthur's, and the other that of King and Nimitz. The navy's concept called for the constant employment of fast carrier forces over waters most suitable to their maneuverability in order to gain and retain control of the sea and air. The most favorable waters were to be found east and south of the Solomons and in the Central Pacific. A progressive advance through the Central Pacific depended, of course, on amphibious operations against land masses so small that the amphibious assault was inevitable. This was the type of warfare which later dominated the march across the Central Pacific. The July 2, 1942, directive helped to make it possible by protecting the left flank of the Central Pacific, by draining Japanese strength from those waters, by affording the United

States Navy time to build up its fleet and amphibious strength, and by giving the amphibious forces experience adjacent to the large land masses in the Solomons. It should be further noted that in so far as MacArthur's concept was that of the United States Army, the nearly independent status obtained by the Army Air Forces during the war gave added weight to the navy's concept, for in Nimitz's theater were the best bases and the most readily available logistical services for the very long-range bombing of Japan by B-29's. Otherwise, although admittedly important, land-based aircraft in the naval drive across the mid-Pacific served as an auxiliary to carrier air.

MacArthur sought to reverse this concept, making carriers the auxiliary weapon. This is a crucial consideration in any treatment of the development of amphibious techniques. Had his concept been adopted, an effort would have been made to employ naval air-sea power only for offensive amphibious thrusts from bases situated around the southwestern and eventually the western rim of the Pacific basin. These operations would always have been conducted adjacent to relatively large masses of land. The mission of the navy would have been to secure and hold the line of communications into the Southwest Pacific Area, and to neutralize rather than bowl over Japanese strength in the mid-Pacific. The naval role would have been to provide carrier air as a supplement to land-based planes, the fields for which would have been rolled forward by transporting troops and supplies in regions where a relative abundance of suitable beaches and airfield sites would lessen the danger of opposition to a ship-to-shore movement.

Whereas the navy, in the best tradition of Alfred T. Mahan, wished to employ carriers as continuously as was possible in order to gain and hold command of the sea and air, it seems clear that MacArthur wanted to use carriers in deliberate thrusts and to rely on land-based planes to retain his advances. It is not known, of course, how far MacArthur's views were shared by the army, but certainly he was not alone.

In the final analysis, even had MacArthur's unmodified plan for the first offensive in the Pacific been accepted in Washington, it is hard to see how his strategy could have prevailed throughout the Pacific War. The navy's job was so important that its concept would have emerged as decisive. It could not long function in unfavorable waters. The only way the navy could clear MacArthur's right flank was by driving up the Solomons and then through the Central Pacific—in other words, by becoming the predominant service in the Pacific War. Time after time, MacArthur was unable to move until the Navy, assisted by Army Air and Ground Forces and committed principally from Nimitz's theater, had reduced such obstacles as Rabaul to MacArthur's advance. Two similar reductions later in the war further illustrate this point. MacArthur entered Dutch New Guinea only after the navy, working in the Central Pacific, had neutralized the Japanese base at Truk in the Caroline Islands; and he returned to the Philippines only after Palau had been invaded by forces under the command of Nimitz.

This is not to say that since the navy's concept was supported, MacArthur's theater was unimportant. The compromise which Marshall effected was backed by sound political and logistical as well as sound strategical considerations. By directing the initial Pacific offensive into the Southeastern Solomons, the Joint Chiefs of Staff assured continued communications with Australia, and a build up for MacArthur. In fact the thinking among Washington planners in the summer of 1942 was predominantly defensive in nature. King, in his published report, refers to the Southeastern Solomons campaign as "the offensive-defensive," in other words as an offensive effort to improve a defensive position.[25] Moreover, MacArthur's theater was important not only in guarding the Anzac countries but also in retaking the Philippines and, along with American submarines and carrier aircraft, in thus severing Japan's vital line of communications. During 1943 and 1944, cutting this line and reaching the beleaguered Chinese became the principal objectives of the coordinated drives which the Joint Chiefs of Staff directed Nimitz and MacArthur to undertake. Also, the Southwest Pacific offered suitable land masses for the deployment of large bodies of men and for mounting an invasion of Japan. But, as operations in the Central Pacific picked up momentum, and as B-29's began rolling in numbers off the assembly lines, Nimitz and the Army Air Forces were able to strangle and pound Japan into submission. For this reason, historically, MacArthur's theater occupied a secondary role during the Pacific War. He held the navy's flank while fast carrier task forces seized command of the sea and air and made possible the launching of amphibious assaults in the mid-Pacific.

Subsequent events proved that the Joint Chiefs of Staff in the summer of 1942 made the best possible decision under the circumstances. Even if the men, supplies, and amphibious shipping for the rapid execution of MacArthur's original plan had been available, it is highly doubtful that such an undertaking would have been successful at this stage of the war. The reason was a shortage of fast carriers. Assuming that an overall army command would have been as considerate as the navy of these vessels, it would have been suicidal, at this time, to send them into the Solomon Sea, or into any of the waters within striking radius of the Japanese navy pilots who were flying from the Rabaul network of land bases. As it was, American carrier strength was barely sufficient for the limited Southeastern Solomons undertaking. On two critical and separate occasions during this offensive the Pacific Fleet was reduced to a single fast carrier at sea, and at one of these junctures that carrier was damaged and unable to work at full efficiency.[26]

Despite all the favorable circumstances that surrounded the attack against Tulagi and Guadalcanal, the navy was unable to hold continuous command of the sea in the target area. This subjected the marines to logistical hardships and inadequate reinforcements. For good reason the campaign in the Southeastern Solomons earned the sobriquet, "Operation Shoestring."

CHAPTER V

INITIAL OFFENSIVES,
SOLOMONS–NEW BRITAIN–NEW GUINEA

RAINFALL in some places in the Solomons–New Britain–New Guinea area exceeds two hundred inches annually. Under such a deluge it might be considered more appropriate had the area been shaped like a fish, but on the map the islands sprawl like a torpid winged monster between northeastern Australia and the equator. "Bird's Head" (Vogelkop) was the name the Dutch long since thought appropriate for the northwestern end of New Guinea, and from there the island bellies abruptly southeastward, whereupon it again narrows at the Gulf of Papua and the Vitiaz Strait. Dangling on to the southeastward, legs poised as if in awkward flight, is the Papuan Peninsula, which gives way soon to clawed feet—reef fringed spots of land and coral abutments still carrying the labels of the adventurous French, D'Entrecasteaux Islands and the Louisiade Archipelago. The ruffled tail of this giant bird stretches eastward from the Vitiaz Strait to include the Bismarck Archipelago and the Solomon Islands. The largest land masses in the Bismarcks are unimaginatively named New Britain, New Ireland, New Hanover, and Manus. Southeastward from New Ireland trails the Solomons group, beginning with the islands of Buka and Bougainville, and then dividing for a time into two parallel chains, between which is a body of water nicknamed by Americans "the Slot."

The strategic purpose of the July 2, 1942, directive of the Joint Chiefs of Staff was to envelop the Solomon Sea which lies southeast of New Britain between the Papuan Peninsula and the North Solomon Islands, and to breach the barrier of the Bismarck Archipelago at two points. (See map 3.) The first was, by climbing up the double-chained Solomons and by seizing Rabaul, to gain control of the St. George Channel at the eastern tip of New Britain; while the second was to mount the Papuan Peninsula in order to force the Vitiaz and Dampier Straits, situated at the other extremity of New Britain. Marines played an important role in both prongs of this coordinated endeavor.

The first target was the Southeastern Solomons. Preliminary plans for this offensive got underway when King's warning order for Tulagi-Ndeni reached Pearl Harbor on June 25, and Ghormley's headquarters at Auckland, New Zealand, on the same day (June 26 east longitude

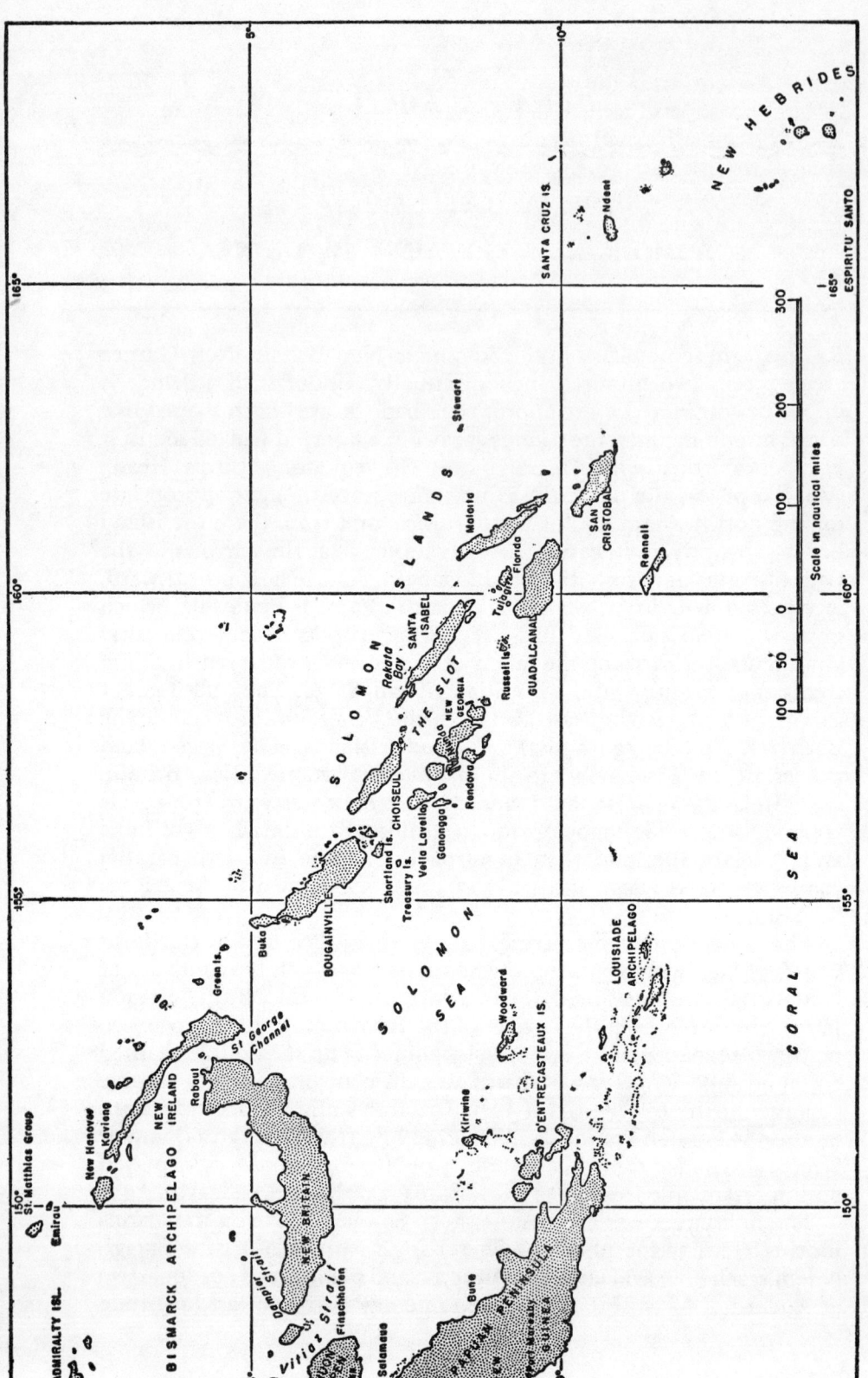

MAP 3. The Solomons-New Britain-New Guinea region.

date). A week later the warning order was confirmed by the Joint Chiefs of Staff, and four days after their directive was issued, ranking naval planners learned that the Japanese had begun an airfield on Guadalcanal, an island just south of the previously designated principal objective of Tulagi. This knowledge put a premium on early launching of the initial offensive, already set by the Joint Chiefs as August 1, 1942, for it must precede completion of the Guadalcanal airstrip lest it encounter land-based aerial resistance. In addition, a landing on Guadalcanal became necessary in order to take over the enemy's runway, and this led to the subsequent grueling struggle for that island.

Guadalcanal and Tulagi face one another across a body of water later christened "Iron Bottom Sound" in homage to the many ships sunk beneath its surface. (See map 4.) It is formed by Guadalcanal to the south, circular Savo Island to the west, Sealark Channel to the east, and Florida Island to the north. Both Guadalcanal and Florida are large and oblong in shape, with the long axis of each running west-northwest to east-southeast. Nestling south of Florida is the smaller island of Tulagi, which shelters water for the best harbor in the region; and for this reason Tulagi had been built up, at least in a fashion bearing some resemblance to the semi-modern, by the British as the seat of their Solomons Government.

South of Tulagi by some twenty miles was the portion of Guadalcanal picked for occupation. This was a small section of the north central coast of the island, an alluvial plain chiefly formed by the delta of the Lunga River. A few other such plains were nearby, but these constituted the exceptions on an island otherwise a maze of mountains with a rugged coastline.

The beauty of Guadalcanal and the Lunga Plain is striking as one looks from shipboard, enjoying a freshening sea breeze several miles from the coast. Mountains cutting the island lengthwise resemble an uneven wall of blue and green, with peaks tapering into the cloud masses of a brilliant tropical sky. From these high ranges, fingers of coral ridges, sometimes covered with kunae grass, reach down toward the beach. Roughly paralleling and bisecting the ridges are many streams swiftly carrying the heavy rainfall north out of the jagged interior, and bringing with them along their precipitous banks the lush verdure of the jungle.

Ashore, as many thousands of Allied and Japanese troops learned of all islands in the Solomons–New Britain–New Guinea area, the place lost its beauty. A long struggle for possession of an air base on Guadalcanal was waged against a foe noted for such deceptive tactics as sniping, outflanking, and night infiltrations, all of which were facilitated by the terrain—rivers with many tributaries and each bordered

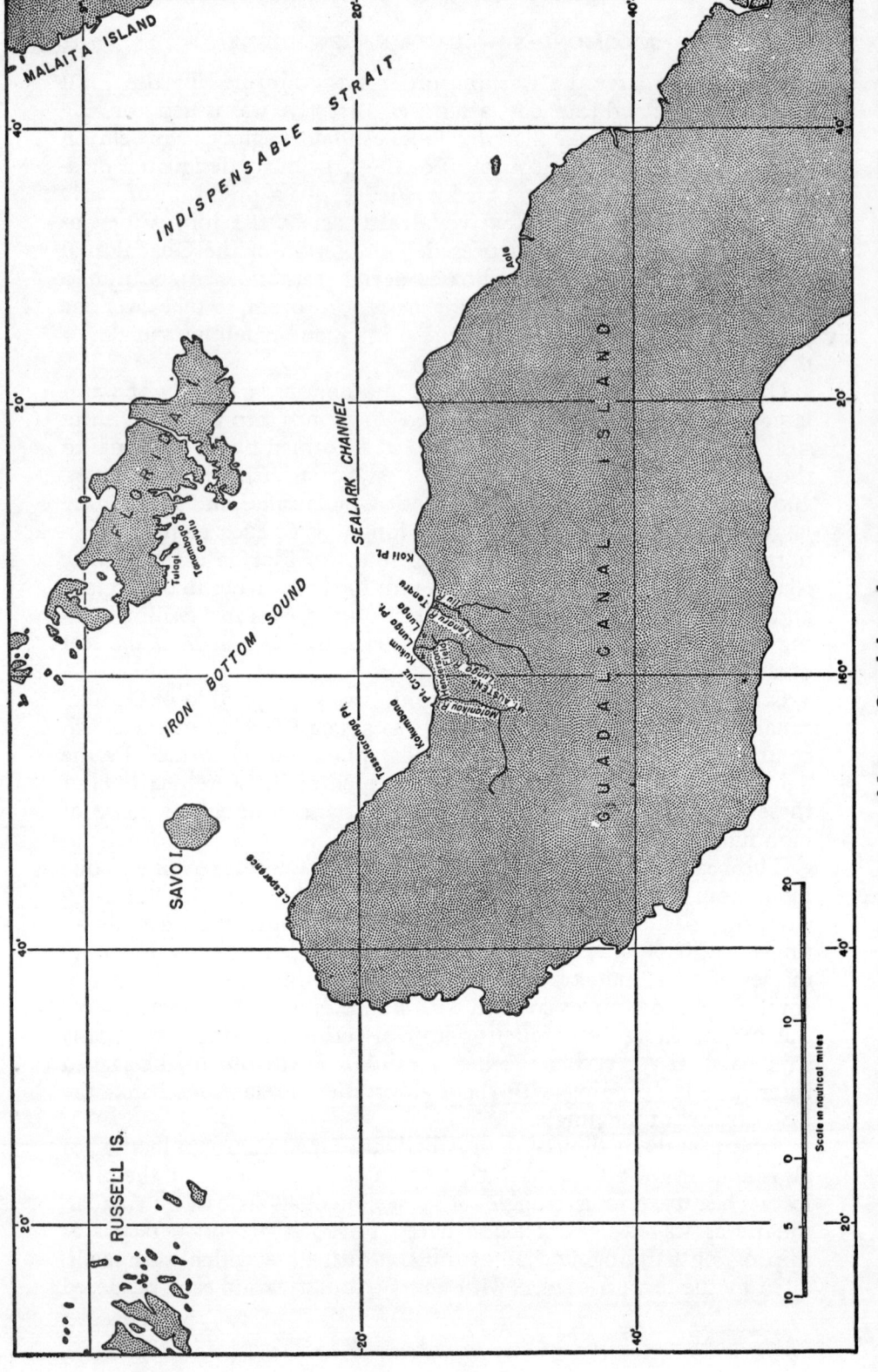

Map. Guadalcanal

by jungle growth so entwined as to black out the sun and to slow down the progress of a man with machete in hand to a very slow pace; bladed kunae grass high enough to saw at the throat; coral ridges covered with stones sufficiently sharp-edged to cut the sole of a shoe. To complete the picture, wash this land with a rainfall scarcely equaled in density elsewhere on the globe; throw in stinging ants and black flies, plus other numerous insects, including malaria-bearing mosquitoes; and add heat to create a humidity that debilitates the body and infects its skin with running sores.[1]

1. Theater and Subtheater Plans

In this festering Guadalcanal jungle United States Marine units fought from four to six months without respite. This was an uneconomical use of amphibiously trained troops, who, as MacArthur realized, should be employed in this type of warfare to seize and secure a beachhead and then be pulled out for the next advance, but there was no alternative at Guadalcanal. Vice Admiral Robert L. Ghormley had barely broken out his flag as Commander South Pacific Area and South Pacific Force when the warning order for the Tulagi attack reached him. His subtheater was in no condition to launch a proper offensive, nor was he cognizant of the fact that the Japanese were even less prepared to counter such a blow. Shortly after Ghormley was relieved of his command in mid-October 1942, but before he could accurately evaluate the great strategic success of the Southeastern Solomons campaign, he complained that planners in Washington had no adequate conception of the vast geographic distances and the lack of bases and equipment which he faced. To illustrate his predicament, he recalled a pertinent remark made by the Undersecretary of the Navy, who in August 1942 inspected his command. "Mr. Forrestal said to me that if the people of the United States knew on what a shoestring we were operating, lack of supplies, facilities, air service and ground forces, there would be a revolution at home." [2]

Since Marshall and MacArthur were eager to build up Australia and refused to allow Ghormley to tap Allied ground strength from the Southwest Pacific Area, there was no relief for the marines on Guadalcanal. It is true that in mid-1942 the ground forces in the South Pacific were almost as numerous as those under MacArthur. Over and beyond elements of the First Marine Division, Ghormley controlled two United States Army divisions, a marine and an army regiment, and other assorted units; but, aside from the First Marine Division, these men were immobilized by having been committed to island bases. Since success in the first stage of the Southeastern Solomons campaign was uncertain, Ghormley was reluctant to move these units forward.

If Guadalcanal fell, they would be critically needed in rear bases. Ghormley's chief army subordinate concurred in this decision. He was Major General Millard F. Harmon USA, an airman and an excellent soldier who became commanding general of the United States Army Forces in the South Pacific Area late in July. After looking over the situation, he joined with his navy superior in opposing the forward displacement of troops guarding South Pacific bases. As Harmon noted, Ghormley had been ordered to give first priority to defending the line of communications to Australia.[3] The navy searched everywhere, but in the planning phase and during the early weeks of fighting on Guadalcanal could find no army units, except for a lone fighter squadron, to send into the combat zone. Surely it was an act of desperation when King again suggested to Marshall that MacArthur be directed to garrison the Southeastern Solomons with United States Army or Australian troops.[4]

Because of the few ground forces available to the Western powers during 1942, the decision of the United States Navy to expend trained amphibious troops in defensive land warfare can be, in the case of the Southeastern Solomons, both explained and excused. Sufficient shipping and materiel, as well as army personnel, for simultaneously building up English bases, attacking North Africa, defending Australia, and furnishing full relief in the Solomons were lacking. The strategical gain was ample excuse; frequently in war the end has justified the means. An important function of the Corps is to seize bases needed for projecting the fleet into those waters which the enemy must continue to control in order to fight effectively. In the first Pacific offensive, the marines exhibited readiness and tactical flexibility. Although essentially an offensive arm, highly specialized in amphibious warfare, they showed that they could wage a sustained defensive land action, which under ordinary circumstances would have been an army job. Hardly ordinary were the circumstances during the planning and early phases of the struggle for the Southeastern Solomons. The adjacent sea was in dispute; gaining its command was a naval task; the contribution of the marines, a part of the navy, was to hold an airfield.

The insufficiency of ground troops in the South Pacific was bad enough, but Ghormley had other equally serious deficiencies to worry him as plans for the Guadalcanal-Tulagi operation took shape. He visited MacArthur in Australia principally to coordinate air reconnaissance and support from the Southwest Pacific Area. The two officers, however, concurred that the main need was additional landbased air, and found themselves in agreement as to the doubtful feasibility of the first offensive. Together they radioed Washington requesting an extensive delay in its inauguration. The Joint Chiefs refused. King was irritated by this suggestion, but hesitated in replacing Ghormley with a more audacious commander. Also, King was not completely fair to MacArthur. He knew MacArthur had modified his earlier plans for an offensive, but he failed to acknowledge the concern of the Southwest Pacific commander over recently reported Japanese reinforcements into the Rabaul area and an increased fear of violent enemy reactions to a limited attack. "I take note," King wrote to Marshall, "that about three weeks ago MacArthur stated that, if he could be furnished amphibious forces and two carriers, he could push right through to Rabaul. Confronted with the concrete aspects of the task, he now feels that he not only cannot undertake this extended operation but not even the Tulagi operation." *⁵

Ghormley left Australia with the promise of full Southwest Pacific support in so far as that was possible, which was not very far. Southwest Pacific planes were, throughout the planning, approach, and fighting phases of the operation, to reconnoiter the western and northern approaches to the Solomons, and to handicap the enemy around Rabaul by aerial bombing. Southwest Pacific submarines were to picket the southern exit of the St. George Channel. Three Australian cruisers were to join the attack force, and one of these, rather than returning to MacArthur, helped to form the first ferrous layer of Iron Bottom Sound.

Nimitz and the Joint Chiefs of Staff had to augment Ghormley's slender resources. In late June, Nimitz gave airfield construction in the South Pacific a high priority and allotted five marine air squadrons to Ghormley; but the pilots of these short-range aircraft needed further training in carrier operations before they could be ferried in. Meanwhile, following Nimitz's request for more land-based army planes, Marshall created two mobile air forces for the Pacific, one for MacArthur's theater and the second for Nimitz. The 11th Heavy Bombardment Group, then in Hawaii, was selected as the Pacific Ocean Areas Mobile Air Force in mid-July, and within a few days its four squadrons of Flying Fortresses were winging their way toward New Caledonia.

By the end of July, Ghormley's land-based air commander, Rear Admiral John S. McCain USN, had 291 assorted planes at his disposal, based on New Caledonia, the Fijis, Tongatabu, Samoa, and Efate, and assigned to the defense of those islands. Seventy-seven of these were United States Army heavy and medium bombers, suitable for both reconnaissance and aerial attack, and thirty-one were navy patrol bombers (PBYs) which when based on tenders at Ndeni and off the coast of Malaita in the Southeastern Solomons would supplement land-based air reconnaissance over the Solomon Slot. The remainder of the

* Code names are transposed, abbreviations expanded, and capitalization made uniform in all quotations from official documents.

planes was mostly short-range navy fighters and bombers, plus thirty British craft stamped with the emblem of the Royal New Zealand Air Force and flying from New Caledonia and the Fijis.[6]

Thus to carrier-based planes was assigned the brunt of the mission of helping the navy surface forces to localize Guadalcanal-Tulagi for attack by marines. Instead of two, as originally planned, Nimitz sent three fleet carriers with a combined capacity of about 250 planes into the South Pacific. These vessels, *Saratoga, Enterprise,* and *Wasp,* were supported and screened by the new battleship *North Carolina,* five heavy and one light antiaircraft cruisers, and sixteen destroyers. All sailed under the three starred flag of Vice Admiral Frank Jack Fletcher USN, assigned by Nimitz to Ghormley as commander of the force in strategic cover.[7] Command relations between Nimitz and Fletcher on the one hand and Ghormley and Fletcher on the other were poorly established. The agreement reached as Ghormley passed through Pearl Harbor in May 1942 was that Nimitz would from time to time send task forces such as Fletcher's into the South Pacific, but Ghormley's authority over such forces was limited. He could direct Fletcher to carry out the mission already designated by Nimitz, but could interfere in the execution of that mission only if unfolding circumstances, presumably unknown to Nimitz, indicated that specific additional instructions were immediately required.[8] Ghormley was in some ways a brilliant, if methodical, planner, but he was lacking in that quality of daring needed successfully to carry out a campaign when the margin of superiority over the enemy was small. Certainly the July 2, 1942, Joint Chiefs of Staff directive superseded the earlier arrangement between Ghormley and Nimitz, for in accordance with that directive, Ghormley was expected personally in the zone of operations to supervise the Southeastern Solomons offensive. He was within his rights when he interpreted these instructions to include New Caledonia, where he set up advanced headquarters by sailing his flagship from Auckland, New Zealand, into the harbor at Nouméa; but the real point of the directive was to secure unity of command at the implementing level, and this he did not do. Having absented himself from the actual scene of hostilities, he failed to insist in the planning phase and subsequently that the commander to whom he had delegated his authority, Fletcher, be responsible for all aspects of the offensive.

Doctrine demands that the officer implementing an amphibious operation secure lines of communication into the zone of conflict and isolate the target in preparation for the attack and for the unloading of necessary cargo and equipment. Fletcher fulfilled little of this mission, and his conduct on this occasion stands in glaring contrast to the later work of Admiral Raymond A. Spruance USN, who was the top-ranking implementing commander throughout the drive across the

Central Pacific. Unlike Spruance, Fletcher hardly concerned himself with either the problems or the vulnerability of the attack force destined for Guadalcanal-Tulagi under the command of Rear Admiral Richmond Kelly Turner USN, who as Commander of the Amphibious Force, South Pacific Area, was directly responsible to Ghormley. Since Ghormley refrained from ordering Fletcher fully to shoulder his mission as unifying commander on the spot, Turner's attack force was to be exposed to the enemy, and this brought the entire operation to the brink of disaster. Here was the greatest flaw in high-level planning.

Other errors in planning were made on all echelons of command. In large measure, these were caused by inexperience, haste, and logistical handicaps; and in retrospect, they were more than offset by the ultimate victory. Ghormley, for example, never had an opportunity personally to consult with Fletcher before the attack was launched. There was no time. Likewise orderly planning of the component parts of the attack force was impossible since Turner did not arrive at the base of embarkation in New Zealand to take over his post until mid-July. By that date, despite what doctrine says to the contrary, elements of his command had already for some three weeks been making irrevocable tactical and logistical decisions.

Since McCain lacked the facilities and the land-based air needed to localize the target and to secure the lines of communications into the forward area, and since Fletcher would not squarely face these responsibilities, Turner's attack force assumed pivotal importance. The marines were embarked in three transport groups, destined respectively for Tulagi, for Guadalcanal, and for Ndeni. Tulagi and Guadalcanal were to be hit first, and the Ndeni group was to be on hand in reserve if needed in the Southeastern Solomons. If not required, these men would be disembarked at Ndeni as the attack force retired to rear bases. The men-of-war to guard these transport groups, to provide closer cover, to screen, and to furnish naval gunfire support, came from Nimitz and from the Royal Australian Navy. They totaled six heavy, one light, and one light antiaircraft cruisers, fifteen destroyers, and five minesweepers. Opposing the venture in the target area were an unknown number of Japanese ground troops. Ghormley estimated the total at about 3,100 men; while Turner set the figure at 7,125. In the Bismarck-New Guinea area, the Japanese were thought to have at least 150 planes, eleven cruisers, thirteen destroyers, fifteen submarines, twelve patrol bombers, fifteen to seventeen transports, and a number of motor torpedo boats. Back of the Rabaul network, the enemy could, through his base at Truk, stage in as much of his military and naval strength as he cared to commit; but such movements were to be, in so far as possible, observed and interdicted by Pacific Fleet submarines operating in the Carolines.

It was a large undertaking. Turner's attack force, covered and supported by Southwest Pacific planes, by McCain, and by Fletcher, was to capture the Guadalcanal-Tulagi area and to occupy Ndeni, to maintain on hand in the forward area, a sixty-day level of supplies and ammunition and a ninety-day level of building materials, to construct facilities for both land-based craft and seaplanes, and to establish radio stations, harbors, inshore patrols, hospitals, and underwater defenses.[9]

The South Pacific Area was unprepared for this campaign. Ghormley's staff was inordinately small, and was notably deficient in communications personnel; yet it was thrown into the midst of an important operation before it could coordinate its activities and solve the tremendous problems of supply, defense, and distances involved in Ghormley's huge subtheater. Logistical obstacles were the greatest. The immediate base of supply for the Southeastern Solomons at Espiritu Santo typifies Ghormley's chief worry. It was operative as an advanced air base only a week before the offensive began. In all other respects, it was little more than a beachhead on an unoccupied island.[10]

Despite the problem of logistics, General Harmon was critical of the Ghormley-Turner plans. In essence, this criticism goes again to the heart of the command dispute culminating in the July 2, 1942, directive. Whether or not army officers could properly employ carrier-based air, naval officers were slow in comprehending the importance of land-based air and the desperate need for speed in constructing facilities for aircraft operations. The campaign in the Southeastern Solomons, said Harmon, was "viewed by its planners as [an] amphibious operation supported by air, not as a means of establishing strong land-based air action." In mid-September when visiting Guadalcanal, he noted the paucity in supply and the complete absence of such essentials as adequate construction and service personnel, gasoline, steel matting, bulldozers, dirt carts, trucks for handling fuel and bombs, pumping equipment, and bomb hoists. He concluded that airdrome construction was going to be "disappointingly slow." Harmon tended to overlook three important considerations, the haste with which the operation was planned, subtheater shortages in materiel and shipping space, and the fact that the waters of the Southeastern Solomons were in dispute; but there is still merit in his claim that "the plan did not have as its first and immediate objective the seizure and development of Guadalcanal *as an air* base." [11]

This flaw in theater and subtheater planning ranks second to the lack of a clear command relationship between Ghormley and Fletcher, and there were other threadbare seams in the fabric so hurriedly patched together by Nimitz at Pearl Harbor and by Ghormley and Turner in Auckland, New Zealand. The schedule for the initial landings was comprehensive, yet the navy was lacking in more than ground troops, it was unprepared to follow up with any type of reinforcements. The example of motor torpedo boats reemphasizes the uncertainty early in the operation as to the ability of the Allies to hold Guadalcanal-Tulagi. The waters around Guadalcanal were in dispute for fourteen weeks. The Japanese were compelled during this period, principally because of the presence on Guadalcanal of a few marine and navy dive bombers, to send in their own reinforcements under cover of darkness. A motor torpedo boat squadron would have been of great value in harassing such inshore shipping, yet a squadron was towed into Tulagi sixty-five days after the base had been won. Ghormley's staff assigned earlier deliveries of these craft, while the intense period of fighting on Guadalcanal was in progress, to rear bases.[12]

Nor did the Ghormley-Turner plans for Guadalcanal-Tulagi so much as refer to a systematic resupply.[13] Since the target area was not fully localized, this aggravated the situation for the marines. They fought for over six weeks on half rations, and that much was available only because the enemy failed to destroy his own Guadalcanal-Tulagi stockpiles. The shortage developed, however, largely because Fletcher ran off with his carriers, which along with poorly coordinated beach logistics during the landing on Guadalcanal meant that the attack force was unable to unload all of its amphibious shipping.

2. Marine Planning, Embarkation, and Rehearsal

The First Marine Division was ordered to load and prepare for an amphibious operation with sustained air and sea support, but the navy, according to Fletcher, was incapable of carrying out anything other than a hit-and-run raid. Marines were dumped on isolated beaches. They faced a long and arduous defensive campaign, fought with inadequate supplies and equipment over unknown and disease-infested terrain. They too made mistakes, but tenacity and hard fighting were keys to victory. Despite adverse circumstances, they secured and held a critically situated land-based airdrome for a navy woefully short of carriers; and marine, army, and navy pilots continuously used this base regardless of its primitive nature. Partly for this reason, the Japanese fleet was worsted in the war of naval attrition that characterized the fighting up the Solomons chain.

Pending Turner's arrival at South Pacific headquarters in Auckland, Ghormley dealt directly with the marines who were to comprise the landing force. Major General Alexander A. Vandegrift, commanding general of the First Marine Division, attended a conference at Ghormley's headquarters on June 26. It was called originally to discuss training plans for the First Marine Division, but on that day the

Tulagi-Ndeni warning order arrived from Pearl Harbor, and the gathering became far more serious than had been expected.

Vandegrift, whose outstanding qualities of command were patience, optimism, and persistence, was in this instance perturbed. King had told others of his anxiety for an offensive in the South Pacific during the fall of 1942, but for some reason had not taken into his confidence the man who would surely command the landing force. Vandegrift had reached New Zealand less than a fortnight before the warning order was received and, in accordance with his instructions, was anticipating at least six months of continuous and rigorous training for his men before they would be thrown into an offensive mission. Later, recalling this conference, he admitted his shock and concluded that the undertaking had been ordered for "reasons of the most compelling nature . . . seldom had an operation been begun under more disadvantageous circumstances." Only one third of his division, the Fifth Regiment reinforced, was in New Zealand, setting up camp outside of Wellington. The First Regiment reinforced had just embarked from home ports to join the division. As for the Seventh Regiment, it had been detached in March and sent to garrison Samoa, and would not reach the target area until mid-September. Other units of the division had been drained of precious equipment to supply the Seventh Marines for this defensive mission, and now the men going into an offensive were at a disadvantage. Vandegrift quickly voiced his anger to Washington: "It is considered highly dangerous to strip one organization to equip another and should only be resorted to when every other source of supply has been exhausted." [14]

No one yet knew exactly what units would constitute the First Marine Division reinforced as it went ashore, nor were the precise objectives fully set, but it was clear that little time had been allowed for the assimilation of information, tactical planning, combat-loading, and rehearsal. The target date, August 1, was a bare six weeks from the day Vandegrift learned of the offensive. Turner, who would have tactical command of the naval attack force as well as overall administrative control of the marines, was not at hand. Normally his operation plan would have been used by the marines as a basis for their own, but in this case, the procedure must be reversed. Nor was it the last time normal procedure was of necessity disregarded in the Southeastern Solomons campaign.

Little was known either of the target area or of the Japanese order of battle there. Difficulty was experienced even in finding Tulagi on immediately available maps and charts. Throughout the planning period and the first weeks of combat, division intelligence was the weakest component in Vandegrift's staff. The importance of personnel for the intelligence section of the newly created division staff was not immediately realized. Nor were the regimental and battalion intelligence teams well integrated with one another and with their division counterpart.[15] The price of these oversights would have to be met.

Handicapped by a weak intelligence section, the staff set about planning the Southeastern Solomons landings. The division intelligence officer was sent forthwith to Australia to collect all obtainable information. This officer was a lieutenant colonel, but under him were no officers above the rank of lieutenant. The operations section of the staff had to take over many of the functions of intelligence, and operations officers were immediately dispatched to Port Moresby. From there the cruising radius of a Flying Fort barely gave them an aerial view of Guadalcanal-Tulagi. Other operations officers, as was their duty, flew to the Fijis to locate a rehearsal area.[16]

Plans could be drawn only after information had been collected and evaluated. Meanwhile there was no time to waste; plans or no plans, combat-loading had to get underway. Here the decade of Corps experience in tailoring its tactical organization to ships paid dividends. Regardless of the scheme of maneuver later adopted for the beaches selected, the battalions and their supporting units could be loaded neatly as combat landing teams aboard transports and cargo ships. This would permit them to fit into the order of landing ultimately devised. Although the terms "battalion landing team" and "regimental combat team" were yet to be introduced, the basic organization of such units was already established.

Steaming from Wellington to the rehearsal area in the Fijis required six days; and from the Fijis to Guadalcanal-Tulagi, a full week. That left only four weeks for combat-loading, and the second echelon of the First Marine Division, comprising the First Regiment reinforced, was still en route from the United States to Wellington. Perhaps it was just as well, although there would be little opportunity to let the First Marines unlimber after their long voyage in confined quarters. Only Aotea Quay in Wellington was available, and it could berth but five ships at a time. Twenty transports and cargo vessels carrying the First and Fifth Regiments into Wellington must be stripped down from their organizational stowage and twelve of them must be combat-loaded. The job had to be done in relays. The Fifth Regiment received orders to begin work immediately, in the hope that the dock could be cleared in time for the second echelon.

In New Zealand, it was winter. Rain was frequent and cold. The quay soon became a quagmire. Paper containers split apart; dry cereals, cigarettes, and packages of rations were squashed under foot. There was shortage of shipping space in any event, and no effort was made to lift more than two-thirds of the normally allotted rations, one-half of ammunition, and one-quarter of heavy motor vehicles. All of the 155-

millimeter howitzers were left behind. As matters turned out, these items if carried could hardly have been unloaded, but their absence was to be acutely felt.

Combat marines did most of the job. Pioneers (the newly formed shore party battalion) could not handle the task alone, and New Zealand dock labor, since security prevented an explanation of the gravity of the task at hand, refused to give up any of its hard won gains, war or no war. Civilian hands were used only for such skills as crane operators. Three shifts of marines worked around the clock. The division supply officer did a remarkable job of directing the whole arduous task. It was difficult in a few instances to keep the marines on the job. They sought shelter from the rain. They were, after all, fighters, not longshoremen. Nor was there any incentive. For reasons of security, the word had been passed that a normal training cruise was afoot. Then why all the haste? [17] The reaction of one marine was inscribed on the latrine wall in the Hotel Cecil, "All wharfees is bastards." [18]

Concurrently with the work at the dock, plans were being drawn up. Two factors hampered the division staff as it did this job. First was the necessity of making decisions which would effect the organization and performance of the naval attack force. These decisions must be and were made on a unilateral basis, in the hope that Turner would later approve.

More important was the dearth of reliable information on which to base plans. The British, who until recently had controlled the target area from a residency at Tulagi, could furnish little aside from charts a generation out-of-date and maps which inaccurately displayed coastal tracks, principal buildings and pier facilities. Contact was made with refugees from Guadalcanal-Tulagi who were at the time either in New Zealand or Australia. These consisted of former superintendents of copra plantations, mariners, government officials, and one blackbirder. Eight were taken along with the troops; they cooperated enthusiastically, but the total information from all left much to be desired. Emphasis was correctly placed on the hope for strategic surprise, which prevented sending in reconnaissance parties. There was no similar necessity for such caution in later advances up the Solomons, and only later in the war did patrols pass beyond the experimental stage of their development.[19]

Much the same can be said for aerial reconnaissance and photography. This technique of gaining information is less suited to a jungle terrain than actual patrols, but it is essential to the drawing of operational maps. Although several aerial photographs were obtained from the Southwest Pacific Area, none was satisfactory. An army officer on MacArthur's staff later remembered having compiled a full set of maps from photographs of Guadalcanal and having flown them to New Zealand; but if this was done the precious shipment sank into the morass that was Ghormley's overburdened staff, and was never seen. The meager resources of Ghormley's land-based air commander, McCain, permitted only three flights over the target area. The first of these took pictures, but was made before the warning order had arrived from Pearl Harbor; no photographs were shot during the second; and the third was made too late to permit a wide distribution of its mosaic until after the landings had been made. Throughout the first months of fighting, because of the lack of bases and of aerial photographic equipment and experience, as well as trained personnel for photogrammetry, the provision of operational maps remained an insoluble problem.[20] Planning and execution were adversely affected, but only after the Southeastern Solomons campaign was over did the situation materially improve.

From unreliable cartographic data, maps for the use of the troops and their air and naval support arms were traced. The results, especially on Guadalcanal, were anything but satisfactory. Rivers on that island, believed to be fordable, turned out to rise and fall with the tide, and in the most shallow zone to reach a depth of fifteen feet. (See map 4.) Streams were misnamed, but this confuses the historian today more than it upset the marines at the time. Mount Austen, the most important terrain feature in the zone of combat on Guadalcanal, was truthfully described as commanding the entire delta of the Lunga River, on the plain of which the Japanese were busily constructing an airstrip. This elevation, it was said, could easily be occupied after one day's hike. So it had seemed, perhaps, to an unmilitary-minded plantation superintendent drinking gin and tonic in the shade of his coconut grove, but the jungle made it a tactical march of several days. As the situation ashore on Guadalcanal developed, a division had to defend the airfield; and although in the hands of the enemy Mount Austen constituted a splendid observation post and potentially an even more serious threat if artillery were emplaced on its slopes, yet more than a division, an entire corps was required before the perimeter could be enlarged to include this elevation. Relying on faulty intelligence, Mount Austen was listed as an objective for the day of the initial landings—it was finally seized by army troops after the First Marine Division had been evacuated in December.[21]

Kelly Turner arrived to take up his duties as Commander, South Pacific Amphibious Force, while the division staff was drawing up plans. He came a few days after the First Marine Regiment reinforced had pulled into Wellington on July 11 and had in turn begun its combat-loading. He accepted the scheme of maneuver for the landings almost intact, but much planning remained to be done. Hydrographic considerations and anxiety to get his amphibious shipping out of the danger zone as quickly as possible compelled him, as was his prerogative, to veto night and delayed landings. This was lucky for the marines, whose peacetime exercises had failed to drive home the inherent disadvantages of making night landings in force. Turner's insistence on flying his flag and that of the division commander on the transport *McCawley*, however, was troublesome. *Hunter Liggett* had been chosen because it offered better communication facilities, and *McCawley* had already been loaded to full complement. The shift was made, and during the approach this increased the difficulties in maintaining contact with the coastwatchers, who had been left behind in hiding by the British when they evacuated the Solomons. These valuable espionage agents were keeping South Pacific Area headquarters abreast of enemy activities among those islands.[22]

It was estimated that the field the enemy was building on Guadalcanal would be functional around August 15, and delays in loading caused Ghormley to postpone the scheduled date for the landings from August 1 to August 7.[23] Getting onto the island would be a close race with the availability to the Japanese of land-based planes with which to strike the Allied expedition, but that was part of the plan. Shortage of amphibious shipping prevented lifting more than a small portion of the heavy equipment engineers would need to build an air base. As the chief of the supply section of the division staff noted laconically: "It was hoped that most all of the construction of the airfield on our island objective would have been completed for us by the enemy prior to our arrival. . . ."[24]

By mid-July the composition of the First Marine Division reinforced for the Guadalcanal-Tulagi-Ndeni operation had been formally decided by King, Nimitz, and Ghormley.[25] Embarking from Wellington were the First and Fifth Regiments, supported by most of the First Division's artillery arm, three battalions of the Eleventh Marines, two employing 75-millimeter and one firing 105-millimeter howitzers.[26] Various other divisional components such as the amphibian tractor, engineer, pioneer, boat, medical, and special weapons units, as well as the highly trained First Marine Parachute Battalion, also left from Wellington.

Other units needed to bring the division to full triangular infantry strength, reinforced, were met for the first time in the rehearsal area, Koro Island in the Fijis; and there for the first time Vandegrift was able to brief the commanding officers on the pending operation. A third reinforced infantry regiment, the Second Marines, was attached temporarily from the Second Marine Division and embarked directly from San Diego under escort of the fast carrier *Wasp*. The hand-picked and well-trained men of the First Marine Raider Battalion reached Koro from New Caledonia aboard four destroyer transports. Finally, the Third Marine Defense Battalion from Pearl Harbor, once ashore and fully equipped, supplied antiaircraft and coastal protection.[27]

The Wellington detachment sortied with naval escort on July 22. Except for the vessels carrying the Third Defense Battalion, which hove in sight five days late, it met the other groups at Koro on July 28, an excellent feat of navigational planning by Ghormley's staff. A three-day rehearsal was scheduled at Koro.

Vandegrift termed the rehearsal "a complete bust." [28] The location had been hastily and poorly chosen, and possible damage from reefs to the boats precluded most of the landings, which in turn impaired the usefulness of the air-support trial runs and naval gunfire practice. It was seen that the ships' gunners lacked experience against shore targets, and for the safety of the boat waves, it was decided to use percussion rather than time fuses in the target area. "Peacetime training," admitted King's headquarters, "has not prepared the navy for efficient bombardment procedure." [29] Thus, even had reconnaissance uncovered suitable naval gunfire targets, there is reasonable doubt that these could have been destroyed. The navy had a long way to go before it could differentiate sharply between area neutralization fire and the pinpointed destructive aim essential to assaulting a very heavily defended beach with acceptable losses. Beyond a partial realization of that fact, all that was accomplished in the rehearsal was a debarkation drill, which could have been held in any waters sheltered from the open sea. This drill did lead to the formation of boat pools, which at the scene of the landings smoothed out movements to the beaches.[30]

Koro was of value principally because of the conference held there between implementing commanders. Vandegrift had been working with Turner for almost two weeks, and McCain had begun to lay plans for the employment of his slender land- and tender-based air strength on the day the warning order arrived from Pearl Harbor; but Vandegrift had yet to consult with Fletcher, who by seniority as well as operational order was the top-ranking implementing commander and who had come down to Koro directly from Pearl Harbor with two of the three heavy carriers to be employed, *Saratoga* and *Enterprise*. Also at Koro for the first time both Vandegrift and Turner met Rear-Admiral Victor A. C. Crutchley RN, who sailed into the rehearsal area from the Southwest Pacific and who under Turner had tactical supervision of the larger unit of close supporting and naval gunfire vessels.

At Koro, Fletcher simply refused to assume the full responsibilities which were his. He, like Spruance later in the mid-Pacific, had a tactical commander of the covering and supporting carriers, their escorts, and oilers. This was Rear Admiral Leigh Noyes USN, yet Fletcher in effect personally filled the spot rightfully belonging to Noyes. Ghormley had delegated to Fletcher the mission of integrating the operations of the carrier force with the work of the amphibious expedition, but in practice Fletcher cast Turner and Vandegrift loose to solve their own problems unassisted.[31] That an amphibious operation must have unity of command was clearly emphasized in the Southeastern Solomons undertaking, and later reemphasized by the misunderstandings surrounding the Battle for Leyte Gulf in October 1944.

As Samuel Eliot Morison has concluded, Fletcher was a timid commander, and at Koro he was tired as well.[32] For eight strenuous months previously, he and his carriers, the tangible remnants from December 7, 1941, had ranged far and wide over the Pacific, from Coral Sea to Midway. These were the only ships capable of stopping Japanese naval advances. Nor could Fletcher shift his thinking from defensive to offensive strategy. He declined to endanger the carriers more than was absolutely essential, and since Ghormley clung to his May 1942 arrangement with Nimitz and trusted Fletcher as the man in the know at the scene of battle, the decision as to what might be essential in terms of cover and support was Fletcher's alone. He flatly refused to allow carrier planes to cover the amphibious shipping or to support the troops ashore beyond the fourth day of the operation, August 10; and, soon after leaving Koro, without advance warning to either Turner or Vandegrift, he began considering an even earlier withdrawal from the zone of conflict.[33] Fletcher, in other words, translated his mission into a raid rather than a localization of the target, and this caused logistical hardships ashore and a critical loss of warships without commensurate damage to the enemy.

Both Turner and Vandegrift were disturbed by Fletcher's decision, and they would have been shocked had they learned at Koro that Fletcher would begin withdrawal on the 8th rather than the 10th of August. Turner, after all, had been King's principal war plans assistant in Washington at the time the high-level decision for an offensive in the Southeastern Solomons was being made, and he had participated in conferences with Nimitz in Pearl Harbor en route to his South Pacific assignment. It is evident that neither King nor Nimitz had contemplated the course of action Fletcher would pursue, for Turner had planned the operation and loaded his shipping for a normal amphibious operation. Only at Koro could Turner have learned how limited the initial Solomons offensive was to be, and therefore he could hardly have been expected to give Vandegrift an early warning. The truth was now apparent—the Japanese with a division of fast battleships and at least five carriers at Truk and Rabaul, plus the potential of deploying planes from those bases and from carriers into the Northern Solomons, had command of the sea and air in the area of the objective, if they chose to exercise it.[34]

Fletcher's delay in briefing Turner and Vandegrift in his estimate of the probable naval situation around Guadalcanal at the time of the attack was unforgivable. Vandegrift was sent with almost 19,000 men some 550 miles beyond the most advanced friendly base. For six weeks he had planned and organized a full-scale amphibious landing which depended upon complete naval support, with accompanying mastery of the sea and air. Only after his transport and cargo vessels had been loaded and were at a steaming distance of six days from their base of embarkation did he learn that the navy would have to dart in and out of the target zone, that only through luck would there be time to unload the amphibian shipping which his men, with sacrifice of energy and morale, had stowed.

The pillars of Vandegrift's planning collapsed at Koro, nor was there anyone to whom he could appeal. Ghormley was represented by a naval officer who had just made two stars, Rear Admiral Daniel J. Callaghan USN; radio silence was mandatory lest the play of the hand be tipped, and Callaghan obviously could not overrule Fletcher. Full command of the amphibious expedition, by Fletcher's default, devolved upon Turner, who like Vandegrift was certainly not one to retreat. A compromise was reached wherein Turner and Crutchley would stay in the target area as long as possible, and Vandegrift received a promise that land-based air would be ferried into Guadalcanal on the morning after the carriers presumably would depart, that is on August 11. As an eyewitness has testified, this conference at Koro took place in an atmosphere of "let's get on with the war." [35] Never except in the most optimistic frame of mind would Turner have pledged aircraft deliveries at Guadalcanal by August 11. He and his superiors had been making strenuous efforts to expedite plane allocations, but problems were manifold. With the exception of one fighter squadron, army deliveries were weeks distant. No belly tanks for light naval planes were then to be found in the subtheater, and flights would have to be made from the deck of an escort carrier. Ghormley was having trouble finding available fighter and light bomber pilots with requisite experience. Only in July, and then in haste, did the marine airmen at Pearl Harbor scheduled for the Southeastern Solomons begin intensive training in carrier operations.[36] Execution of planned deliveries was underway, but had been inaugurated too late to meet the deadline, even if the shipping were not already otherwise committed. The amphibious expedition was carrying few aviation supplies, and those few could scarcely be unloaded. Even if this miracle were to occur, aviation maintenance personnel would not be available, and a serious shortage of aviation gasoline, lubricating oil, spare parts, bombs, and ammunition would quickly develop. Nor could any of the vessels carrying the First Marine Division be turned around and reloaded. Combat-stowage prevents such flexibility; each vessel carries tactical units essential to integrated combat. More than anything else, Vandegrift regretted the faulty information which had, as circumstances unrolled toward a horizon of hardship, caused him to misload. He would have preferred to cross the beaches with but few supplies and few units of fire (the quantity of ammunition per weapon within the division normally expended in one day of fighting). Had he been able thus to plan his logistics, the remaining ships could have been moved forward in echelon with cargo and personnel for later and relatively safer delivery.[37]

The best Vandegrift could do was to assume that the Japanese would have their field on Guadalcanal nearly finished, and to hope that planes would be sent to this field on the critical planning date of August 11. As his men steamed west from Koro toward the target, he recast his plans in a fashion which was to shape their long ordeal on Guadalcanal. Clearly only the first few hours of his undertaking were offensive in character. He suddenly began thinking in defensive terms. "Even in the original order for the defense of the islands, prepared during the approach to the Solomons," reads his action report, "it was stated that the primary means of defense would be [land-based] aircraft and this concept was never departed from throughout the period of our occupation. The defense was to be reciprocal. The mission of the air force was to be that of disrupting attempts at a major landing. The mission of the ground forces was to protect the airfield by destroying hostile forces ashore and, by unceasing vigilance, to prevent a surprise attack from the sea by night." [38]

3. *Approach, Landings, and the Battle of Savo Island*

Eighty-two transport, cargo, and warships approached Guadalcanal-Tulagi without incident. Efforts had been made to get either MacArthur or the British to feint toward the Netherlands East Indies, but to no avail. A group of marine raiders did strike in the Gilberts, but belatedly, and this seems to have had no appreciable effect on the operation in the Southeastern Solomons.

Of greater pertinence to the job at hand, Flying Forts of the 11th Army Bombardment Group based on the recently completed strip at Espiritu Santo struck the Guadalcanal airsite and suspected supply dumps and antiaircraft positions in the target area for seven days previous to the landings. (See map 3.) Also, McCain had moved tender-based seaplanes up to Ndeni, and was preparing to shift others to the east coast of Malaita. These and other aircraft were reconnoitering the quadrants over and to the eastward of the Solomons and south to the Fijis. MacArthur was sending planes to investigate the north and west approaches to the Solomons, and to bomb enemy bases in the northern part of that group and in New Britain. Submarines from this area and from the Pacific Fleet were concentrated around Rabaul and Truk.[39]

While the Japanese were being thus observed and harassed, overcast skies curtained the amphibious expedition. Then the weather cleared during the early hours of August 7, and this good omen opened the stage to the attackers. Landfalls were easily made, and the ships separated as scheduled. A northern group headed directly for Tulagi, while a southern group turned for the transport area off the coast of Guadalcanal. (See map 4.) That island and Tulagi were to be taken first. Turner retained two battalions of the Second Marines under his control. These troops were alerted as division reserve, but he expected them to perform during the second act on Ndeni, after the Southeastern Solomons had been won.[40]

Along the southern coast of Florida, itself undeveloped, were seven islets marked for seizure. The largest was Tulagi, where fierce inland fighting developed. Close by were Makambo, Mbangai, Kokomtambu, and Songonangona, and each was taken with little or no resistance from the enemy. The other two islets, Gavutu-Tananbogo, towered precipitously out of the water a mile and a half east of the southeastern tip of Tulagi. They were connected with one another by a causeway, and were surrounded by reefs. On them alone, as it turned out, Japanese opposition at the beach compelled the marines to deliver an amphibious assault.

Landings on Guadalcanal and Tulagi were made almost simultaneously, about three hours before noon. Then at midday came Gavutu-Tanambogo. The carriers, steaming about 100 miles south of the objectives, sent in two squadrons of fighters at first light on August 7, with the duty of destroying any aircraft found on Guadalcanal as well as the seaplanes known to be at Gavutu-Tanambogo. These sweeps were followed by two squadrons of dive bombers, striking antiaircraft and coastal defense positions on Guadalcanal and Tulagi, and then covering the landing as boat waves were formed. Over and beyond these scheduled missions against ground targets, fighters and bombers remained continuously on call during daylight hours for the purpose of rendering close air support to the troops, and, beginning at one hour after sunrise on August 7, flew combat air patrols over the transport areas.

A majority of the troops, the bulk of the artillery, and a greater portion of naval gunfire were committed to the more important seizure of Guadalcanal where, although it was rightly anticipated that surprise and a carefully selected beach would preclude initial opposition, intense fighting was expected before the airfield could be taken. Vandegrift personally supervised the Guadalcanal landing, turning tactical control in the Tulagi area over to the assistant division commander, Brigadier General William H. Rupertus USMC. Three heavy cruisers and four destroyers were assigned gunfire missions on and adjacent to the Guadalcanal beach. Destroyers also served as control vessels for sending the boat waves toward the shore. This arrangement was awkward, for a warship can hardly be expected to maneuver to deliver accurate naval gunfire bombardment, and at the same time to hold position and control boat waves. Both the destroyers and the cruisers, having sent naval gunfire liaison parties ashore with the first waves, delivered call fire in close support of the troops as requested. Scout planes from the cruisers spotted this fire, and reported enemy movements to the commanders afloat and ashore. Fortunately for the pilots of these planes, there was no opposition at the beach on Guadalcanal. Underwater demolition teams were as yet unformed, and one of their principal missions, that of marking the extremities of the selected beach, fell to the province of the scout planes. This required six passes at low altitudes, and if the enemy had been present with antiaircraft guns, the slow cruiser float planes would have been splashed immediately.

Two additional scout planes as well as other naval gunfire liaison parties operated across the channel. Landings on the islets adjacent to Florida were staggered in order to gain the maximum effect with available naval gunfire and air support. Boat wave control at Tulagi was delegated to the four destroyer transports carrying the raider battalion, and five minesweepers were to clear Tulagi Harbor; while a light antiaircraft cruiser and two destroyers furnished gun support. Even Tulagi was too small to permit the effective employment of artillery, and only one battery of 75-millimeter howitzers was sent ashore. Almost full reliance was placed on the naval and air arms. In addition to neutralizing fires and strikes on the beach, ships furnished call fires, and a pyrotechnic signal was arranged whereby the tactical commander ashore summoned down a barrage of shells and bombs on the expected center of enemy resistance. When this mission was completed, the ships and planes were free to devote their attention to Gavutu-Tanambogo.

As for the troops, the least-trained got the tasks promising to be the less difficult. That battalion of the Second Marines already released to division control was broken up and committed by units to those terrain features of Florida which were believed to be unoccupied but which overlooked the boat approaches and beach areas on the nearby islets. The highly trained First Marine Parachute Battalion, minus its parachutes and led by Major Robert H. Williams, received a blood bath on Gavutu-Tanambogo. Under the aggressive Lieutenant Colonel Merritt A. Edson USMC, the First Raider Battalion made the initial landing on Tulagi, followed in close support by one battalion landing team of the experienced Fifth Marines.

The remaining two battalion landing teams of the Fifth Marine Regiment, whose commanding officer was Colonel Leroy P. Hunt, were first ashore on Guadalcanal, and secured flanks of the beachhead while the less thoroughly trained First Marines, organized as a regimental combat team comprising three battalion landing teams under the overall command of Colonel Clifton B. Cates USMC, landed in rapid succession. Cates was concerned about his men. As they crossed the Pacific he had prayed they would have time to receive full equipment and to train intensively before being thrown into combat. This was not to be. They "have had less than three months of battalion training," he noted regretfully. "Not once have we had a regimental problem, much less training with planes, tanks, and other units"; but the regiment was filled with youths, the average age being under twenty years. Here was a comforting thought. "Maybe we can make up in guts what we lack in training." [41]

The bulk of the artillery units was attached to the combat waves of the First and Fifth Marines, but the 105-millimeter howitzer battalion and headquarters of the Eleventh Marines, Colonel Pedro A. del Valle commanding, plus the engineers, pioneers, and special weapons battalion, comprised the support group for Guadalcanal. The final tactical entity ashore was the Third Defense Battalion, the larger portion of which was slated for Guadalcanal, with the remainder scheduled for Tulagi.[42]

Until the afternoon of August 7, almost everything clicked as though it were being coordinated by a beautifully timed machine. The initial phase of the debarkation, said Vandegrift, "proceeded with the smoothness and precision of a well-rehearsed peacetime drill. All boat formations crossed lines of departure promptly and moved inshore toward assigned beaches with all boat groups in good order and under excellent control." [43]

The beach on Guadalcanal lay about four miles southeast of Lunga Point, and was thus removed from the defenses surrounding the airfield, which turned out to be weak. (See map 5.) Division intelligence had estimated slightly more than 5,000 Japanese to be on the island. Of this number roughly 2,000 were thought to be laborers, while the remainder were labeled first-class troops. The only part of this estimate which proved correct was the total for laborers. Troops certainly numbered less than 600, which was the figure reached by a subsequent estimate compiled by the intelligence section of the division, and these few men seem to have been overage. In any event they, like the laborers, either fled to the westward of Lunga Point or took to the interior as the marines approached. Stores and equipment were left behind unmolested. The only record of attempted sabotage pictures one lone Nipponese hacking with a heavy instrument at the sparkplugs, distributor, and carburetor of a truck.[44]

Lunga airfield was occupied a day behind schedule, not because of enemy resistance, but because of the lack of reliable maps, the necessity of bridging a deep stream, cutting trails, and carrying equipment through the undergrowth or kunae grass. It was soon evident that heavy machine guns and 81-millimeter mortars were too burdensome for jungle operations, and that each man needed two canteens rather than one. Also, the marines were overcautious. The battalion leader on the right flank of the advance, though his coconut grove terrain presented fewer obstacles than that encountered by other units, was inordinately slow until his regimental commander personally pushed him along. He was later relieved of his command, and Vandegrift strongly recommended that inept officers in charge of tactical units be weeded out before going into action. Otherwise, the overcaution exhibited by the marines during their first hours on Guadalcanal resulted from insufficient training, and from the facts that most of the men and many of the officers were new to jungle terrain, that all anticipated the predicted opposition, and that their patrols were functioning poorly.[45]

Unlike intelligence estimates for Guadalcanal, the estimate made for the Tulagi area was, when compared with the later claim of enemy dead, amazingly accurate.[46] It is probable, however, that, after the attack was over, the intelligence section of Rupertus' staff exaggerated the number of Japanese sealed up in caves. Granting that for this one time in the planning phase of the Southeastern Solomons campaign some American made a good guess, the intelligence section was unable to break down the total for the Tulagi area and to predict what opposition would be met where. The consequences of this were serious for the marines. Tulagi was believed to be more strongly defended than it actually was. In fact, Gavutu-Tanambogo, which the British had developed as a seaplane base and which the Japanese were known to be using for the same purpose, had a greater strength in terms of effective manpower and advantageous terrain than Tulagi; yet, over 2,000 marines were thrown into Tulagi, while the capture of the smaller islets was at first assigned to about 400.

Not that less were needed on Tulagi. Stiff resistance was met before the islet was secured, and it was surprising and fortunate that only a few snipers interdicted the beach. The section of the shore picked for the landing was removed from the more inhabited southeastern end of the islet, but the coastal perimeter was small, and a tight beach defense had been expected. It was later surmised that the enemy, taken unawares, believed a mere surface raid was impending, and had dived for his underground shelters rather than jumping to his beach defenses; but in contrast to his brothers on Guadalcanal, the enemy in the Tulagi area, trooper and laborer alike, fought virtually to the last man.[47] This introduced an important tactical characteristic of the enemy. Normally, he always fought to the end when cornered, but wisely retreated (if possible) when he knew he was outflanked.

Once ashore on Tulagi, the raiders took quick advantage of the favorable situation, whipsawed the narrow portion of the elongated objective, and pivoted southeast to clear out the Japanese from the more developed end. Then, at about noon, the going got tough. Planned naval bombardment and air strikes failed to soften the way. Reinforcements from the supporting battalion of the Fifth Marines were placed in the line, but the enemy took advantage of rough terrain and had to be dug out of caves and intricately constructed underground defenses. This type of inshore fighting, far more than that experienced during the long struggle for Guadalcanal, was to characterize the march across the mid-Pacific. The night of August 7/8 fell on Tulagi with little additional ground gained. During darkness the Japanese weakened their defensive strength by unleashing the first in a long series of World War II night infiltrations and banzai attacks against the marines, and failed to break contact seriously between units. On the next day marines pocketed the enemy in a zone which was taken under fire from three sides. By nightfall on August 8 the objective was secured. Although a few annoying snipers were still at large, around 200 Japanese special naval landing troops, about one-half the division estimate, were dead.[48]

Almost as many first-line enemy were even better holed up on Gavutu-Tanambogo, plus about the same number of laborers who showed every inclination to fight until killed. In the attack there were, at first, only 395 paratroopers.[49]

Gavutu and Tanambogo are little more than steep hills rising sharply from shallow reef-bound beaches. The scheme was to capture Gavutu first, and then to overrun its brother. Here the Japanese had no choice but to begin their defense at the beach. This they were able to do despite preparatory naval gunfire and air strikes. Supporting arms did little more than daze an enemy well-protected by caves and prepared installations. Even the neutralizing effect was dissipated by poor coordination, which seems to have been caused by the unusual length of the boat approach, 14,000 yards. Premature lifting of the support fire gave the harassed enemy time to recover his defensive equilibrium, when to his pleasure, he found that the naval guns had been in an important way beneficial to his cause. The shells had turned the concrete ramp which was to be used in the beach assault into a heap of rubble, and it was necessary for some of the men to angle off to the right and to cross a pier standing some six feet out of the water. The Japanese were ably led. They held their fire until the first wave had landed; then with the offshore support of the attackers masked by friendly troops on the beach, the defenders opened up. Those on Tanambogo joined, taking the marines under a raking enfilade fire. The pier was swept by a stream of lead. This was an amphibious assault under singularly adverse circumstances. Several hours passed before the paratroopers could emplace their mortars and, assisted by a flight of planes strafing Tanambogo, relieve the pressure on their right flank. Ten per cent of those set ashore by the first boats were casualties. The commanding officer was seriously wounded, communications broke down, and the marines, functioning as individuals or as small independent groups, slowly shouldered their way to the top of Gavutu, sealing caves and dynamiting installations. Only a highly trained and aggressive outfit could have moved forward under such handicaps. The executive officer later admitted that command communications had been severed from the beginning, but added that the "battalion had a plan of attack which under the circumstances was carried out to a large degree. Each man . . . knew what the plan was and exerted every effort to carry out his part. . . ."[50]

Stiff resistance on Tulagi and Gavutu had the fortunate consequence of causing Turner to release the last two rifle battalions of the Second Marines to division control. Exaggerated casualty reports from the First Raider and the First Parachute Battalions reached Vandegrift at about midnight, August 7. He immediately requested that the division reserve be turned over to Rupertus, and Turner complied. Ndeni would have to be delayed. That was just as well; the Second Marines would be desperately needed at Guadalcanal-Tulagi.[51]

They were, in fact, used the next day. An abortive and ill-advised attempt late in the evening of August 7 to take Tanambogo with less than 100 men by assault under cover of darkness was followed by a stronger and better organized effort on August 8. With a company of the Second Marines in assault, two tanks in the van, a destroyer firing at point blank range, and an additional platoon of the Second Marines assisted by a few paratroopers moving across the causeway to flank the defenders, Tanambogo was secured by nightfall. Except for patrolling Florida, to which a few Japanese had escaped by swimming, this finished the mission entrusted to Rupertus. It is impossible to say exactly how many Japanese lost their lives in the Tulagi area, but the probable number is in the vicinity of 600. This is roughly one-third the total estimated by Rupertus' staff. American casualties, heaviest in the parachute battalion, were slightly under 250, with a few more than 100 killed.* [52]

American casualties in the Tulagi area would have been fewer if naval guns and close air support had functioned efficiently. Naval headquarters in Washington damned the fire on targets in the Tulagi area as "very poor." [53] Here again the fault lay with the lack of time for the assimilation of intelligence, for planning, and for coordinated training. Nothing occurred during the landing on Tulagi or the assaults on Gavutu-Tanambogo to alter the established doctrine for either of these two arms. The big deficiency was the absence of proper reconnaissance. Aerial photography is essential, preferably supplemented by amphibious patrols or by obliques taken from submarines, depending upon hydrographic conditions and whether or not the land mass is extensive. Otherwise defensive installations and centers of resistance can at best be approximated, rather than accurately plotted. Experienced naval gunnery personnel can make certain hits on pinpointed targets not in defilade, and those so blocked can usually be struck by dive bombers; but only if the target is described can there be allocated the type and quantity of shells and bombs needed to produce the desired effect.

Such intelligence was lacking for the harbor islets. The three naval gunfire ships repeatedly used high-capacity ammunition where armor-piercing alone would have done the job. It was like blasting hard rock with dynamite placed on the surface, where a drill hole packed with TNT was required. Area coverage with high-capacity ammunition was, however, excellent. Most notable was the obliteration of the enemy on Palm Islet, a tiny grove of coconut trees crawling with snipers which barely rises from the water close to Tanambogo; but area coverage with high-capacity ammunition over terrain where the enemy was well dug in, aside from cutting his communications, was without great or lasting effect. These Japanese had either to be flushed or sealed up by foot troops, who as yet were unequipped with flame-throwers.[54]

Naval gunfire liaison parties did not perform as efficiently as they would in later and better-planned operations, because they lacked well-trained personnel as well as lighter and more dependable radio sets. There were more fundamental difficulties in the execution of close air support. Since time was short and opportunities to train the navy carrier pilots in ground operations were limited, the air support plan emphasized simplicity at the expense of exactitude. Scheduled strikes were delivered on time, but like the naval gunfire, and for much the same reasons, failed to knock out well-constructed targets.

* All casualty figures in this volume have been, in so far as possible, checked for accuracy by the Personnel Accounting System, Headquarters, USMC.

As for call strikes, the communications system was so complex as to preclude flexibility. The naval attack force commander retained complete control over supporting aircraft, and the air-ship network with Turner's flagship *McCawley*, which was anchored in the Guadalcanal transport area, was too involved to permit the immediate delivery of all attacks needed. Sometimes it was impossible to obtain call strikes, which meant that air strength was wasted. Frequently pilots hovering on station in wait for specific orders were forced to jettison their bombs when returning to the carriers to refuel. When delays were involved, the advancing marines were sometimes endangered. Several navy flyers recognized a fundamental weakness, one which had been foreseen and which Vandegrift again brought to the attention of the Navy Department in Washington, namely the need for direct communications between the planes and the tactical commanders ashore. One pilot believed it "essential that ground forces in an operation of this type have radio communication directly with the liaison planes or Air Group Commander in order that maximum support may be afforded ground personnel." [55]

Marine airmen would have better understood the reconnaissance needs and tactical problems of the troop commanders. This fact is well illustrated and probably exaggerated by an exchange of messages between a navy pilot on reconnaissance and division headquarters on Guadalcanal. The pilot reported 200 men in column, adding, "seems to be a continuous stream of men to that area." Back to his plane were shot pertinent queries. Whose men? What area? The troops, it appears later to have developed, were cattle.[56]

Such misinformation only aggravated an already serious situation on Guadalcanal. It fed the fear that an estimated 3,000 Japanese first-line troops were deploying to attack the beachhead. Although aware of a growing congestion of supplies on the beach, Vandegrift felt it unwise, in the initial phase of the landing, to divert combat troops from their normal duties and thus solve a dire shortage of shore party hands. He believed himself, to use his words, "in close proximity to a large enemy force which possessed complete knowledge of his dispositions and movements, while he . . . was unable to make contact with the enemy or to gain information as to the direction from which he might appear." Under the circumstances it is difficult to criticize Vandegrift, for as he insisted he was "constrained of necessity to dispose all his forces tactically." That battalion holding the eastern flank of the beach must remain alerted, and the artillerymen and other personnel except the pioneers attached to Colonel del Valle, who commanded the artillery and the support force, must continue to guard the rear of the beach, while the First Marines and the remaining battalion of the Fifth swung in a quarter-wheeling motion west and southwest toward Lunga Point and the airstrip.

Vandegrift correctly added that shortages of shore party hands "had so often been pointed out in peacetime maneuvers," but there was little that could be done about it under existing circumstances. The chief of the division's logistics section, for whose actions Vandegrift was responsible, had conferred with Turner's commander of transports, and had agreed to the use of combat troops in shore party work. This understanding had been formally incorporated in the division's operation order. Later landings would see the employment of replacement battalions for this job; but the First Division had no such battalions. An element of discord was thus introduced. Since the Japanese did not contest the Guadalcanal beachhead, the combat troops seemed to be wasting their time, and some at least exhibited poor discipline and did not act as if they were ready to fight. Close by, pioneers and sailors sent in to assist sweated until they vomited from the strain.[57] A coast guard officer commanding a transport was disgusted with the marines. He claims his men spent too much time unloading "cases of pickles, butter, and fine cheeses which melted away in the hot sun"; while "hundreds of marines, many of them truck drivers, tank crews, special weapons and support groups whose equipment had not been landed, lounged about the beach in undisciplined idleness, shooting down cocoanuts or going swimming." [58]

Relatively fewer supplies were discharged on Tulagi. The plan was to move the shipping into the harbor and to utilize available wharf facilities, and delay in overrunning the islet upset this scheme;[59] but the situation on Guadalcanal was far more serious since the cargo vessels were concentrated there. The Guadalcanal beach had neither depth nor width. No disposal dumps were nearby. Amphibian tractors totaled less than 100. These valuable landing craft were yet to be employed tactically, but they early proved their worth logistically. In the words of Vandegrift's operations officer, "they saved our life, there is no doubt about that." [60] Ramp boats were few, and most of the load had to be manhandled item by item over the gunwhales of obsolete landing craft. The beach congestion grew on Guadalcanal until by midafternoon on August 7 it was necessary to recognize an already hopeless situation and temporarily to stop the ship-to-shore movement altogether. Not until the morning of the second day did Vandegrift feel tactically secure enough to extend the beach lengthwise, to the westward toward Lunga Point; but it was too late. For all practical purposes, unloading ceased after the first day of the landings. That meant that the amphibious shipping would depart for the south with but a fraction of its cargo disembarked, and for this the marines because of their inadequate shore party were partly responsible. The nature of the records prevents an exact estimate, but it is clear that because of enemy air attacks and a congested beach, a total of only twenty-four hours was spent in actual unloading. Making a liberal allowance for the wastage and pilfering in which, until the seriousness of the situation was clearly evident, some of the marines and bluejackets indulged in to a disgraceful degree, it is believed that the transports were cleared of about ninety per cent of the few supplies aboard, while the cargo vessels, in this connection the important consideration, were able at most to disembark twenty-five per cent of their rations and other war materiel. The marines could eat and shoot for at most thirty days, but in almost every other regard, there were either grave shortages, or complete absences of supplies and equipment from the start.[61]

A more serious hindrance to unloading was the Japanese air reaction to the landings. Three raids, one of them heavy, were staged out of Rabaul and the Northern Solomons during the first forty-eight hours of the operation. Coastwatchers up the Slot gave ample warning of these approaching planes, and when these messages arrived, transport and cargo vessels knocked off unloading and stood out for maneuverable waters. The ensuing delays were, in consideration of the condition on the beach, of little import; but the fact that the enemy could launch such raids formed the basis for a decision to retire the transports and cargo ships two days ahead of the schedule arranged at Koro Island, that is on August 9 rather than August 11.

Total injury from the raids was small. Turner was himself a flyer and was a brilliant tactician under air attack. A transport already void of marine personnel was gutted by fire and two destroyers were damaged, one subsequently sinking. The first raid, however, had apparently continued south in a vain search for the American carriers. Such a threat, plus a claimed shortage of fuel and the loss of twenty-one fighters in combat and to operational hazards, combined to cause Fletcher to seek safer waters to the south. He began retreating and then radioed headquarters South Pacific Area during the evening of August 8 for permission to retire. Ghormley had ordered the carriers fueled to capacity during the rehearsal at Koro, and a study of ships' logs indicates no pending fuel crisis; nor could plane losses be considered acute or even heavy. Ghormley had strongly protested previous suggestions that the carriers withdraw at such an early date, but now he gave in.[62] Nimitz later assumed that Fletcher was right and oil was low, but wondered why the carriers were not refueled one at a time, thus leaving air cover over the transports, and providing aircraft critically needed at first light on August 9 to strike a group of Japanese cruisers. Admittedly these carriers were precious—but, as Nimitz pointed out, only because they could be used. Thinking of the marines in short supply on Guadalcanal, and of serious losses in Allied warships while the enemy was virtually untouched, Nimitz termed Fletcher's decision "most unfortunate." [63]

Perhaps even more unfortunately for the marines, notification of Fletcher's departure came to Turner almost simultaneously with the receipt of bad news from Australia. A Southwest Pacific Area reconnaissance plane, on the morning of August 8, had spotted a Japanese task force headed down the Slot. Transmission of this vital information had been delayed almost seven hours. The pilot was an inexperienced and not very intelligent Australian. He winged blithely on to complete his reconnaissance leg without breaking radio silence and sending this crucial information from his plane. He then landed at his base and nonchalantly drank his tea before reporting. This prevented tracking the Japanese force, and the Australian was none too clear as to what he had seen. His message indicated at least one seaplane tender accompanied by cruisers and destroyers. On learning of the approach of this enemy force, Turner, like Fletcher, also began to feel the burden imposed by an accumulation of adverse developments. He was responsible for the safety of a group of transports and cargo vessels which at the time was irreplaceable. Air raids, followed by the withdrawal of his air cover and the threat of a Japanese naval force, threw him into a pessimistic frame of mind. He could think only of dangers from the sky. He did not seriously consider other capabilities of the enemy force, and acted on the assumption that it was headed for some such roadstead as Rekata Bay, on the northwestern tip of Santa Isabel Island. (See map 3.) He felt sure that the Japanese would, the next morning, launch float planes armed with torpedoes for a strike against his amphibious shipping. He decided, with Ghormley's permission, to clear out shortly after dawn on August 9, before these deadly aircraft could arrive. The enemy's clear capability of delivering a night cruiser attack was discounted almost completely.

Four United States and two Australian heavy cruisers were guarding against such a threat in dispositions adjacent to Savo Island. Turner called the commander of this Allied screen, Admiral Crutchley, to a midnight conference aboard *McCawley*. Crutchley, although aware of the approaching Japanese force, left his ships without an officer in overall tactical command, and cruised in his flagship, *H.M.A.S. Australia*, to attend the conference. Vandegrift was also summoned from his command post on Guadalcanal.

The enemy struck while Vandegrift and Crutchley were aboard *McCawley*, being given reasons for a decision already made. This was the Battle of Savo Island. Destroyer pickets, in the days before radar was highly developed, failed to warn the Allied vessels. The five Allied cruisers close to Savo Island were taken unawares by five heavy and two light Japanese cruisers and one destroyer. The action lasted only a few minutes, and when it was over, *Australia* was the only undamaged Allied heavy cruiser in the vicinity. *Chicago* and a destroyer were badly injured, and *Quincy, Astoria, Vincennes,* and *H.M.A.S. Canberra* were sunk. Most of America's battleships had been put out of action at Pearl Harbor, and the Battle of Savo Island reduced Allied strength in heavy cruisers in the Pacific by more than thirty-three per cent.[64]

Then the tide turned. Bad judgment on the part of the Japanese admiral aided the marines. He knew nothing of Fletcher's withdrawal, and was uncertain because of low visibility as to the extent of damage inflicted on Crutchley's leaderless ships. He retired quickly in an effort to get beyond range of an early dawn strike from the carrier planes. He failed to carry out his orders to penetrate the transport areas and demolish the amphibious shipping. This would have been almost as simple as shooting sitting rabbits with charges of canister. He must not be given another chance. Turner had no choice but to leave with everything of importance left afloat.[65]

Even near disaster had its compensations. This naval defeat made the task of the marines ashore far more difficult than had been expected, but at the moment there was a psychological advantage. Had Turner departed for any reason less tangible than the Savo battle, the marines ashore would have rightly felt abandoned. Troop morale would have declined abruptly. Now, news of the naval reverse quickly spread ashore, stimulated by a rumor that the Japanese were landing reinforcements on Guadalcanal. Companionship eased adversity. The marines steeled themselves for the worst, which the navy had already suffered.[66]

Also, the battle postponed withdrawal of the amphibious shipping for some ten hours. Obviously after the night of August 8/9, there was little reason to expect a torpedo attack launched from a seaplane tender; and the battle was followed by confusion and rescue missions which held up departure. Two or three hours of such unloading as was possible onto the still congested Guadalcanal beach were squeezed into August 9. The transports, cargo vessels, and remaining warships left before dusk.

If not supplies and equipment, almost all the marines had been disembarked. The notable exception was slightly less than 1,400 men of the Second Marines. The infantry battalions of this regiment, originally scheduled for Ndeni, had been committed on August 7–8 as demanded by the exigencies of the tactical situation. The rifle units only, rather than full battalion landing teams, had been set ashore, leaving the commanding officer, headquarters, and reinforcing elements still ship borne, and they were taken back to Espiritu Santo. It was early October before these men rejoined their parent organization.

A combination of factors worried Vandegrift after the naval withdrawal on August 9, but chief among them was the need for a defensive employment of his five infantry battalions on Guadalcanal. The airfield above all else must be protected, but the enemy for the moment fully commanded the sea and air. The terrain adjacent to the airstrip was such as to require for its defense the services of several times the number of troops Vandegrift had at hand. It is true that five additional infantry battalions, less some of the reinforcing elements but plus the paratroopers, had been drawn into the more intensive fighting on the harbor islets, but none of them could be transferred by boat across to Guadalcanal until air cover for such a movement was available, which meant finishing the airfield, flying in planes, and from somewhere by some means obtaining the ground crews and most of the supplies needed to service aircraft.

The Japanese high command failed to take full advantage of the American predicament at Guadalcanal. The Battle of Savo Island gave the enemy the upper hand over the waters of the Southeastern Solomons, but the attack of August 7 had pinned him on the sharp horns of a dilemma, and he was unable to extricate himself. He was on that date planning a vigorous drive against MacArthur in New Guinea, and was regarding his Guadalcanal-Tulagi holdings as cover for the more ambitious undertaking across the Solomon Sea. The Allied offensive disrupted these plans, but the single-minded Japanese hesitated until too late to throw overwhelming strength into the Southeastern Solomons. Rather they clung tenaciously to their New Guinea offensive, all the while weakening it to throw more and more units, piecemeal, onto Guadalcanal. It might be said that, with the full cooperation of a few marines, the Japanese defeated themselves in detail.

Hanson Baldwin, military editor of the New York *Times*, aptly phrased the situation on Guadalcanal after the Battle of Savo Island: "It is as if the marines held Jones Beach, and the rest of Long Island were loosely dominated by the enemy." [67] Wartime security doubtless prevented his completing the figure by adding that Long Island Sound (that is Iron Bottom Sound) was strongly dominated by the Japanese. The Battle of Savo Island, in other words, might well have been a decisive engagement had the enemy followed it up with energy instead of slowly committing forces piecemeal. Not only that, but the Japanese made poor use of the arms at their instant disposal. Most of the First Division's available supplies were piled high on the Guadalcanal beachhead, constituting a heaven sent target for the Japanese planes.

submarines, and destroyers which for two solid weeks roamed freely night and day above, below, and on the surface of the waters between Guadalcanal and Tulagi. Never once were these supplies molested. Instead the enemy tried to hit bivouac areas and bombed and shelled the airfield. Such tactics were of nuisance value only, causing a few marine casualties and plastering the airfield with holes that could be repaired in a few hours' time. Had the Japanese set fire to the supplies towering high on the Guadalcanal beachhead, to quote Vandegrift, "the consequences might well have been incalculable and ruinous." [68]

Disposing of these supplies was one of the three arduous tasks Vandegrift immediately set for his men isolated on Guadalcanal. If combat marines had avoided labor details during the ship-to-shore movement, they made up for it in the desperate weeks ahead. Not only were pioneers few in number, but the engineering regiment was unequal to its many duties. Frequently riflemen would fill in as pioneers or engineers all day and stand guard all night.[69] That was the program marines faced while their navy drew another breath before seeking command of the Southeastern Solomons.

Available trucks and boats were used to haul the supplies to the Lunga River. A peculiar thing had been observed about Japanese bomb bursts. The shrapnel showered the air two feet above the ground, but not below that height. So, along the east bank of the Lunga River, the supplies were cached when possible in low lying dumps.

Simultaneously steps were taken to protect the airfield from the counterlanding expected in the vicinity of Lunga Point. Such a step was the most dangerous capability the enemy had while he dominated the waters of Iron Bottom Sound. Vandegrift expected the Japanese immediately to counterattack Guadalcanal in overwhelming force, and the marines simply had to dig in and try to hold. Defensive equipment was in short supply. The need most acutely felt from the start was barbed wire, all but a few spools of which remained aboard the departed cargo ships. A little was salvaged from coconut plantations nearby, fields of fire were cut, machine guns set, and the five infantry battalions on Guadalcanal established in positions for beach defense. The critical limitation was men, nor could any of the marines landed in the Tulagi area be transferred to Guadalcanal until friendly planes arrived to cover such a movement. The defensive line faced the sea to the north. (See map 5.) Its right flank was refused (that is, bent out of regular alignment along the beach and anchored with strong points on favorable defensive terrain) slightly to the interior, along a short sluggish stream which was being called (incorrectly) the Tenaru. (Since the Navy Department has officially named a battle for this river and has called it the Tenaru, this designation is retained in the text and on the maps.) From the mouth of this river, the beach front stretched westward slightly less than five miles, crossing the Lunga to a junction just beyond the village of Kukum. There the left flank was refused, so far as was possible, along a hill overlooking the beach. It was recognized that a much better anchor for the left flank lay about three miles further west, along a swift flowing river named the Matanikau, whose easily defended precipitous banks followed its course almost to the sea, but it was early October before reinforcements made this extension practicable.

The beach line was backed by prepared emplacements for antiboat guns and available artillery weapons, which were actually set up in locations near the airfield, from where they could support any point of the defense line, front or flanks. The Third Defense Battalion mounted its antiaircraft guns, but would have to wait a full month before its 5-inch coastal batteries could be returned, unloaded, and emplaced. Engineers, pioneers, and artillerymen, in addition to their normal duties, were given the responsibility of defending the airfield installations against night infiltrations from the south. The artillery report termed this employment of cannoneers "an expedient of questionable virtue"; [70] but in view of the grave shortage of men, the alternative left the rear dangling and unprotected. In this operation, as in the earlier defense of Wake, the Marine Corps policy of giving all men basic infantry training paid dividends.[71]

A hasty inventory of supplies on hand revealed other serious shortages. One of these was food. Troops were cut to two meals a day, and these were less than normal rations. During the early phases of the operation, to quote the verdict of the chief medical officer of the division, "captured enemy supplies were the difference between a starvation diet and one well above that point in caloric value. . . ." [72]

Vandegrift was less emphatic, but noted that captured materiel "represented an important if unforeseen factor in the development of the airfield and beach defenses and the subsistence of the garrison." [73] In addition to rations, the Japanese left behind undamaged such items as timber, steel girders, tools, hospital supplies and equipment, dirt carts, road rollers, petroleum products, power plants, rails and moving stock including motor transport, switchboards, telephones, and cable systems, radio units, and rice sacks convertible to sandbags. Since no American radar had been landed, an effort was made to finish the installation of a Japanese radar warning set, but was later abandoned. These things were of value because not even fast destroyer transports could be run into Guadalcanal until mid-August. Thanks to the Japanese and the stores unloaded principally on the first day of the landings, the marines would survive until something approaching a regular system of resupply could be established in November.

Critical shortages, over and beyond food and barbed wire, turned out to be artillery and aviation ammunition, high octane gasoline, antiboat, antitank, and antipersonnel mines, and 155-millimeter guns along with the sound and flash equipment needed for effective counterbattery fire. Long in coming was a well-organized naval base force, equipped not only with an adequate number of landing craft and other small boats, but also with spare parts and repair facilities, as well as stevedores and construction personnel. Finally, the division staff lacked control over its base depots, and, along with other items of less importance, was never able to convince the rear echelons or the navy that heavy motor transport was needed and could be used on Guadalcanal.[74]

Before aviation supplies could be employed, the field must be leveled and planes flown in. The Japanese fled from a strip almost finished. They had been working in an awkward fashion, from both ends toward the middle. Using their equipment, marine engineers plugged the gap and had surface adequate for light planes ready on August 11. Work continued, but it required weeks, more supplies, and a naval construction battalion before proper drainage and steel matting could convert this to an all-weather strip, and months elapsed before facilities permitted the mounting of long-range bomber raids.

Aircraft had been promised for August 11. They were desperately required for combat air patrols, reconnaissance, shipping strikes, and close air support. But it was the 15th before destroyer transports loaded with aviation supplies and ground crews braved a night trip to Guadalcanal. On the 20th the first components of Marine Air Group 23 (Colonel William J. Wallace) of Brigadier General Roy S. Geiger's First Marine Air Wing set down on Henderson Field, so named in honor of a marine hero lost in the Battle of Midway. These first planes totaled nineteen Grumman fighters and twelve Douglas dive bombers, ferried within range by the escort carrier *Long Island*. Two days later an advanced echelon of the 67th Army Fighter Squadron followed, flying with belly tanks from Espiritu Santo in obsolete fighters, intended for the British in Burma but luckily discharged in the South Pacific.[75]

4. The Critical Phase of Fighting Ashore, August through October

Planes on Guadalcanal altered substantially the situation in the waters of the Southeastern Solomons. After the shock of the Battle of Savo Island had diminished, after new allocations of American warships had been completed, and after marine dive bombers were flying from Henderson Field, control of these waters was under bitter dispute. Beginning in late August, for seven weeks, the Japanese prevailed by night; the Americans, thanks mainly to the aircraft on Henderson Field, by day. The enemy tried during this period to land by daylight, which was the only way he could get heavy equipment and artillery ashore, but he was never wholly successful.

All of the naval action around Guadalcanal, which before the campaign was over totaled six major and several minor battles, resulted from efforts by both sides to pour men, equipment, and supplies onto that island. For this reason, a listing of the Japanese and Americans ashore at critical junctures of the land fighting becomes the important box score of the Campaign for the Southeastern Solomons. Troops in the Tulagi area may be disregarded here, since the fighting there ended on August 8, and since Vandegrift, as soon as he had friendly aircraft in the sky, brought most of those marines over to Guadalcanal. The following table gives an estimate in round numbers on important dates, of the contestants on Guadalcanal alone: [76]

JAPANESE AND AMERICAN TROOP STRENGTH ON GUADALCANAL

	JAPANESE	AMERICAN
August 7	2,200	10,000
August 20	3,700	10,000
September 11	9,000	11,100
October 12–20	22,000	23,000
November 12	30,000	29,000
December 1	25,000	40,000

During the time when adjacent waters were in dispute (which was also the critical period of the fighting ashore), it was marine airmen, assisted by navy and army pilots, who were instrumental in saving Guadalcanal by making it difficult for the Japanese to land reinforcements. American planes were drawn from every imaginable source. For understandable reasons, none of those aboard fleet carriers could be spared; but Henderson Field itself was a most strategically located "flattop." One by one the fast carriers available to the Pacific Fleet were either sunk or were knocked out of action and compelled to limp away for repairs. As this happened the fighters, dive bombers, and torpedo craft remaining flew to Guadalcanal. One pundit, an army officer who may or may not have been trying to make the best of an otherwise desperate situation, cynically observed: "What saved Guadalcanal was the loss of so many carriers." [77]

After August 20 there were always some planes on Guadalcanal, but at times the serviceable total ran dangerously low. They were used for reconnaissance and shipping strikes, and to cover the disembarkation of friendly troops and supplies by day. Pilots of these machines, although by no means completely able to keep the Japanese from getting men and supplies onto Guadalcanal, made the work costly for the enemy, and forced him to rely chiefly on the famed "Tokyo Express," that is, fast warship runs at night when darkness kept the Guadalcanal aircraft immobile. The Tokyo Express rang up full steam at dusk when barely within the cruising radius of the light aircraft on Henderson Field, disembarked troops and cargoes at around midnight, and then made a rapid exit before dawn.

Since the sortie from rehearsal at Koro, Vandegrift had been relying on planes as his principal weapon of defense. They were to serve simultaneously as a means of stopping the enemy from getting ashore whenever possible, as protection for American shipping, as an instrument to disrupt Japanese bombing raids, and as a reconnaissance and supporting arm for the ground defenders. The arrival of the long-delayed first installment of American planes boosted the morale of the marines, who were beginning to compose ditties about the navy and broken promises. Friendly aircraft in the sky on August 20, Vandegrift declared, marked a "major turning point" in the operation. One of his regimental commanders was more vivid: "We had reports that our planes were coming in for the last week, and it was an inspiration for all to see them arrive. As they circled the field over the cocoanut trees, the men cheered and threw their helmets into the air and there was much rejoicing. I actually saw tears of joy running down the cheeks of some of my youngsters and, I must admit, my eyes blurred and I had to shake myself to keep from doing the same." [78]

Day in and day out, Grummans in dogfights with Zeros and Japanese bombers were watched with awe by marines on the ground. The American fighter pilots soon learned to wipe the oil from their guns to prevent freezing when, warned by coastwatchers and later by their own radar of an approaching raid, they rose to 25,000 feet altitude or above and waited. The Japanese usually came in twenty-six bombers at a time, wedged in a V-of-V's formation, and protected by Zeros. Their fighters could barely range from Buka to Guadalcanal and back, and so could not stay around very long. (See map 3.) They built an airfield at Buin, on the southern tip of Bougainville and about 150 miles closer than Buka to Henderson Field; but this was not completed until mid-October, and even then was not much of an improvement. As in the matter of committing ground forces to the Southeastern Solomons, the Japanese were inordinately slow in airstrip construction. The field they really needed for fighters, at Munda on New Georgia Island and only 200 miles from Guadalcanal, was built with great speed but was not begun until late November.[79]

Hirohito's bombers were the target of American fighters in each raid staged by the enemy against Guadalcanal. Usually the Grummans were able to pounce on the bombers at least once and to shoot down a few before being jumped by Zeros. American tactics were to come in from directly overhead or to make an above-side pass on a bomber to avoid its tail guns, and then to fire a quick burst at a Zero before scooting for home. Sometimes, however, it was necessary to dogfight with the faster, more maneuverable Zero. In this case, the American prayed a friend would shoot the Zero off his tail, since there the enemy generally clung like a leech. For this reason, the Americans quickly evolved the two-plane mutual supporting and flight section. As one fighter pilot put it, "the Zero could outmaneuver, outclimb, outspeed us. One Zero against one Grumman is not an even fight, but with mutual support two Grummans are worth between four and five Zeros." [80]

Despite the disadvantages of the American fighter, it was a sturdy craft with great firepower. Add the mutual supporting tactics evolved and the fact that fighters whenever possible avoided Zeros and took on Japanese bombers, and the result was the maintenance of a most creditable ratio of more than five kills by Americans to one for the Japanese.

The dive bombers, later reinforced by torpedo craft, were also naval-type planes, and on Guadalcanal as at Midway and in the Coral Sea, proved they could come in low and sink ships. The marine pilots, however, were at the outset inexperienced, and September was a poor month for them and their navy colleagues. Thereafter their skill began to show, and the Japanese so respected these aircraft that from September on they centered their plans for retaking Guadalcanal about the pivotal consideration of pounding Henderson Field and everything connected with it into a pulp. No higher compliment could be paid these American flyers.[81]

As for the army pilots of the 67th Fighter Squadron, their obsolete planes were entirely too slow for combat, and were unequipped for high-altitude performance; but their armament was heavy, they could carry small bomb loads, and Vandegrift pressed them into service in a capacity presumably the marines' speciality, close air support. These airmen learned quickly, and in this work they soon won unstinted praise from all sides. They tried early in the game to take on Japanese Zeros, but as their squadron historian testified, they felt "like a herd of cows being attacked on every flank by agile wolves." Soon they confined themselves to air support of ground troops, and jokingly renamed their outfit "the 67th Bombardment Squadron (Very Light)." [82]

Even before Vandegrift had friendly planes in the sky, he was determined never, if it could possibly be avoided, to let the Japanese get poised ashore for an all-out assault against the airfield. Knowledge of what the enemy intended to do was necessary to this type of fighting, and the jungle terrain plus the absence of a photographic reconnaissance squadron as well as planes of low operating speeds were handicaps; but dive bombers could investigate the sea approaches and coastwatcher reports from the Central and Northern Solomons were of great value. This intelligence made for the most effective employment of available naval strength, and assisted the ground forces as well.

Nowhere, however, was there a substitute for foot patrolling, and this got off to a bad start immediately after the landing. Within a week there occurred a patrol which was exceptionally poor both in concept and execution. A captured Japanese testified that so far as he knew many of his countrymen to the west of the Matanikau River were willing to surrender. The division intelligence officer formed a weak patrol with intelligence and medical personnel included, and set forth in the darkness on a mission more humanitarian than military. The patrol was wiped out,[83] and the repercussions of this incident reverberated throughout the Pacific War. The intelligence section of the First Marine Division lost key personnel; and, more serious, hatred for the Japanese seared the heart of the Marine Corps. This episode, preceded by the treachery of Pearl Harbor and followed by devious trickery, such as playing dead before tossing a grenade, made it difficult to indoctrinate marines on Guadalcanal and later with the necessity of taking prisoners of war for the purpose of gaining information. Such an attitude, combined with the adamant refusal of most Japanese to surrender under any circumstances, hobbled intelligence work in the field.

Early in the operation Vandegrift was highly critical of the ability of his men to patrol, but in this instance he seems to have expected entirely too much from troops who by his own estimate were not thoroughly trained.[84] From the first, despite inexperience, it was infantry patrols which, in conjunction with sea reconnaissance by air, allowed him to employ his consistently inadequate tactical reserve to best advantage. The terrain to the west and especially to the south of the airfield was a maze of ridges, jungles, and ravines which beggared description. This fact, plus the aptitude of the enemy for concealment, accounted for the two occasions upon which the defenders were somewhat surprised by the direction from which the attack came. Well before the end of the Guadalcanal fighting for the First Marine Division, patrols were functioning at near peak efficiency, thanks in great part to training in the field, supervised by a master at the art of jungle warfare, Colonel William J. Whaling USMC.[85]

With information about the enemy at hand, Vandegrift whenever possible struck first. This active defense was made difficult by shortages of boats, of transport destroyers, and of naval gunfire support, which frequently forced exhausting overland marches in place of simple shore-to-shore movements, and sometimes compelled the marines to attack with inadequate gunfire preparation and support. Despite such drawbacks, the tactics were highly successful, and in only two instances was failure in part the fault of the marines or their leaders. In the first, a battalion commander was unable because of terrain obstacles and enemy opposition to protect his right flank, and was pinned down by machine gun and mortar fire. He requested permission to withdraw, which was received amid some confusion, and he was unjustly relieved of command. Since the Japanese withdrew from their strong positions that night, the attack was pushed home the next day. Over-aggressiveness caused the second failure. What was intended as a limited movement in force happened to meet determined and well-led Japanese resistance. The marine commanders of the attacking battalions were determined never to quit. The division staff lost sight of the original plan, and threw in reserve after reserve, until finally the danger was seen, and a withdrawal effected.[86] Otherwise, Vandegrift's active defense was effective and would probably have been uniformly successful, but for the large number of Japanese who could threaten the airfield from all directions. Repeatedly attacks to the west of the airfield were called off, and the troops moved back to defensive positions because the enemy was or was thought to be landing to the east.

The first Japanese effort to retake Henderson Field did come from the east. The enemy high command on August 7 began to recognize the threat posed by the Guadalcanal landings, and ordered the Seventeenth Army to recapture the Southeastern Solomons. This benefited MacArthur's command enormously, for that army had been previously assigned the mission of spearheading an overland attack across the Papuan Peninsula and the Owen Stanley Mountains against Port Moresby.

Lieutenant General Harukichi Hyakutake IJA commanded the Seventeenth Army. Allocations of tactical units to his command were made a few at a time; but in addition to reinforcing elements of all types, Hyakutake eventually expended four principal infantry components in attempting to retake Guadalcanal. These were the Ichiki Detachment, the equivalent of a reinforced battalion built around amphibiously trained shock troops; the experienced Kawaguchi Brigade; the 2nd or Sendai Division, renowned throughout Japan and named for the city of its birth, a place of a quarter of a million population not far from Tokyo; and the 38th Division, which had seen battle against the Chinese, had overrun the British at Hong Kong, and was reassembled in late September 1942 from easy conquests in Java, Amboina, Timor, and Sumatra in the Dutch East Indies.

Hyakutake's troops on August 7 were spread all over the so-called coprosperity sphere. This fact plus a grave shortage of shipping got him off on the wrong track. He began committing his outfits bit by bit, and never stopped. Even when his men were fresh and almost equal in numbers to the battle-weary Americans on Guadalcanal, he divided his forces and attacked in such a fashion as to preclude coordination. The individual Japanese soldier was brave and tenacious, if unimaginative in battle, but his command was abominable. Hyakutake, his staff, and his chief subordinates possessed good information. Their nationals had, after all, built the airfield, and they should have known something of the terrain being defended. Early in the operation their troops occupied Mount Austen, giving them a clear view of the entire delta of the Lunga River. The Americans were wide open to simple observation. A Marine Corps lieutenant on a patrol of Mount Austen early in November looked back into his own lines and was amazed: "Sniping could be done at range of 150–1,000 yards with an abundance of lucrative targets always in sight . . . our camouflage and camouflage discipline is almost nonexistent. Enough activity and noise could be observed of our lines and of the ridges behind to keep a dozen enemy observation posts snowed under sending dope in. If bush hides our bivouac areas, enough yelling and shouting is furnished to give away the position. Sandbag emplacements were very easy to spot and a continual flow of foot traffic over the ridges was always in evidence. Jeep drivers racing motors accurately designated the course of our roads." [87]

The inability of the Japanese leaders to evaluate the data at their disposal is almost incredible. They continuously underestimated the numbers opposing them. This fact, plus their failure to comprehend the nature and force of the fire power fundamental in modern warfare, meant defeat.[88]

The Japanese objective was always the same—Henderson Field. Assaults against it began on the day after marine aircraft landed. The Ichiki Detachment, having landed under cover of darkness to the eastward of Lunga Point, struck early on August 21. (See map 5.) Presumably heavy air raids and intermittent naval bombardment had cleared the way. The Japanese commanding officer, Colonel Kiyono Ichiki, did not even await the arrival of the bulk of his artillery support. Instead, he tried to force the sandbar at the mouth of the river bordering the eastern marine flank, which was being called the Tenaru. Apparently he believed that darkness and Japanese valor and flamethrowers were all he needed; but some such move from that quarter was expected, for a marine patrol had ambushed a group of well-fed, well-clothed army troops the day before.

The Ichiki Detachment was stopped in its tracks by machine guns, canister, and artillery. At first light on August 21, the marine battalion in reserve crossed the upper Tenaru and enveloped the Japanese; fortunately Ichiki had held back no reserve, and the weakly covered right flank of the enveloping marines was not attacked. Meanwhile, American light tanks roared out across the sandbar. By nightfall, the enemy dead ran upwards of 900, almost nine times more than the total American casualties.[89] This, the Battle of the Tenaru, was the first in a long procession of Japanese attacks. Later they improved somewhat in ingenuity, and mounted in ferocity and in numbers of men committed against the tired defenders so that the airfield, at least twice, was placed in jeopardy.

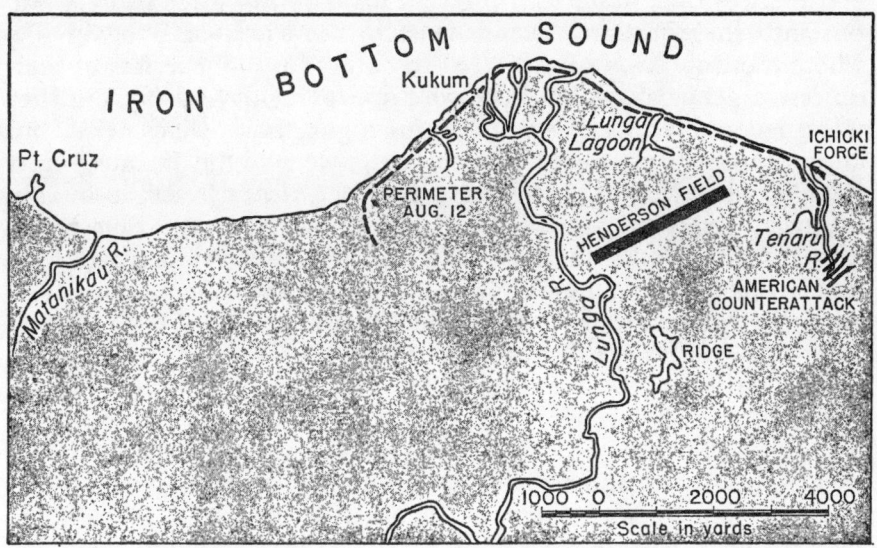

MAP 5. The Ichicki attack on Henderson Field, August 1942.

Arrival of friendly aircraft allowed Vandegrift to begin moving men from the now quiet harbor islets to Guadalcanal. The remaining battalion of the Fifth Marines was first on this schedule, supplying reinforcements for the weaker of the two flanks, to the west.[90]

Patrols made it obvious after Ichiki's fiasco that the Japanese were still strengthening their forces, both to the west and to the east of the airfield. These were advanced elements of the brigade totaling some 6,000 men and named after its commanding officer, Major General Kiyotake Kawaguchi. The first effort of the Japanese to land troops by day was made with the main body of the Kawaguchi Brigade. The plan was to bring the bulk of Kawaguchi's men and equipment in on transports, covered and supported by sea-air forces, but the naval Battle of the Eastern Solomons intervened on August 24. Fletcher sped north from the vicinity of Santa Cruz, and a carrier task force engagement ensued. The American fleet carrier *Enterprise* was badly damaged, but eleven of her homeless dive bombers thereupon reinforced the marine and army flyers on Guadalcanal. Six days later, after an enemy submarine had thrown a torpedo into the heavy carrier *Saratoga*, twenty-four additional fighters landed on Henderson Field.[91] The Japanese at the Battle of the Eastern Solomons won a tactical victory in losing only the light carrier *Ryujo*, which was deployed away from the main covering force as bait; but their covering force turned back.

The Japanese attack force commander of the Kawaguchi transports and their escorts, upon learning that his covering force had retired, put into the Shortland Islands, just to the south of Bougainville, where the troops were transferred to barges for night ferries to their objectives. Guadalcanal's pilots were improving day by day, but they were never able to make a successful night attack. They tried, but always missed. First blood in such tactics went to the Japanese early in 1943, when they sank the heavy cruiser *Chicago* (repaired in vain from her heavy beating in the Battle of Savo Island). This attack caused fear that the Japanese possessed highly developed radar for such air tactics, something it would take the United States more than an additional year to perfect; but the fear was groundless. The enemy was relying on his eyes, and the best defense was simply not to fire the antiaircraft weapons aboard ship.[92]

The Battle of the Eastern Solomons on August 24, 1942, was the first of the efforts by the American navy to recoup from the Savo sinkings. At the time, and for weeks to follow, it seemed as though the Japanese were keeping the upper hand; but this was an illusion, fed by full knowledge of American losses, while the reverses inflicted upon the enemy were not accurately known and were underestimated. The Imperial Naval Staff had agreed to make every effort to get Japanese army units ashore on Guadalcanal. This led to a steady attrition of the enemy's naval power, and the ships lost were irreplaceable. Equally important, the planes on Guadalcanal, assisted by those from United States fleet carriers, drained Japanese naval air strength, both the carrier squadrons and the naval land-based units at Rabaul and in the Northern Solomons. This proved to be a continuation of the process begun at Midway. The Japanese were slowly losing their experienced naval pilots. The process of feeding in airmen less well-trained was becoming cumulative.

Also, the Battle of the Eastern Solomons gave Guadalcanal dive bomber pilots their first major opportunity to deliver a shipping strike. Concurrently with the movement of the Kawaguchi Brigade, the remaining elements of Ichiki Detachment, principally artillery, headed toward Guadalcanal. This group was under a separate naval commander who, although he must have learned of the withdrawal of his naval cover, was not ordered into the Shortlands. He kept coming.

American land-based planes from Guadalcanal and Espiritu Santo hit him, sinking a transport and a destroyer, and damaging a cruiser. Then he put into the Shortlands with all he had left.[93]

Both tactical commanders, however, got most of their troops to Guadalcanal under cover of darkness. Most of the Kawaguchi Brigade landed to the east of the beach defense. Vandegrift struck quickly. Having just brought Edson and his raiders with the paratroopers attached across from Tulagi, he sent these men on a shore-to-shore expedition, and they burned out a principal Kawaguchi base. The undertaking involved grave risks, but was highly successful. Most of the Japanese escaped, but the loss of a part of their supplies and equipment weakened their ability to attack. Also, valuable documents were captured, but no thanks were due to division intelligence. The new chief of this staff section was working hard and learning fast, but his subordinates were still amateurs and as he admitted during this particular raid "it did not occur to any of the intelligence personnel present to collect any of the large amount of documentary material that was lying among the rest of the supplies . . . a newspaper correspondent on his own initiative, collected a poncho full of maps, diaries, and orders and brought them to me personally." [94]

The raid against the Kawaguchi base soon proved its worth. Patrols to the east, southeast, and south indicated strong enemy forces in that direction, and Vandegrift took steps to extend his flanks and to strengthen his rear. The raiders and paratroopers were placed in hastily constructed defensive positions astride a ridge which rose just south of the airfield and stretched on southward into the jungle. (See map 6.) Engineers, pioneers, and amphibian tractor personnel covered the flanks of this newly and as yet only partially established series of small defensive points, tying up in so far as possible with the beach flanks to the east and west. Thus in effect the marines had developed something which Vandegrift would later formalize in an operation order—a perimeter or cordon defense, roughly rectangular in shape, entirely surrounding the airfield.

Not a day too soon. On September 12–14 followed an engagement sometimes called Edson's Ridge, but more accurately described as the Battle of Bloody Ridge. A large portion of the Kawaguchi Brigade crossed the head waters of the relatively short Tenaru, and fell at night without warning on the positions held by Edson's men. The marines on the ridge were outnumbered two to one. Nor could reinforcements be sent in until the second day. Enemy air raids and night naval bombardments had increased in tempo, slowing down the movement of reserves; and the division staff was unable at first to determine from what direction the main Japanese effort would come. Although poorly coordinated, the Kawaguchi attack was accompanied by feints in force against both the west and east flanks. Edson was, however, reinforced by the Second Battalion, Fifth Marines, in the midst of Kawaguchi's strongest effort.

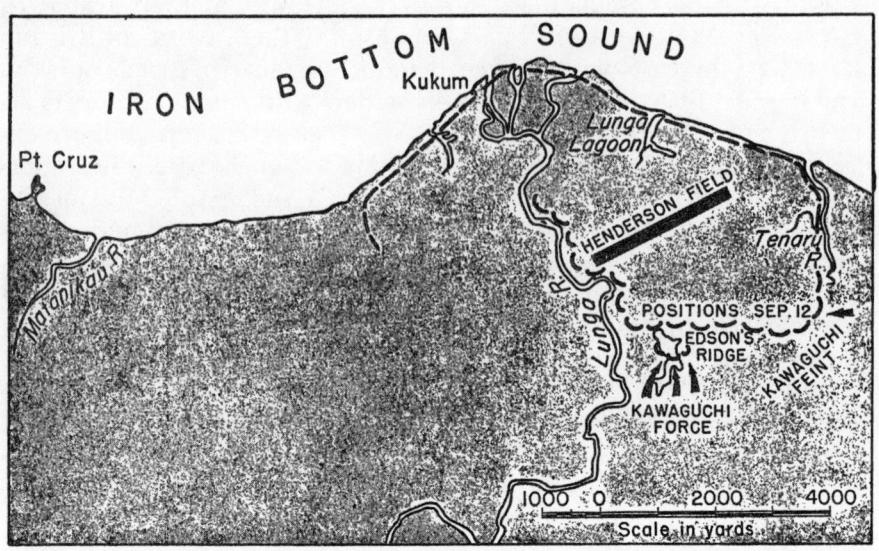

MAP 6. The Kawaguchi attack, September 1942.

Sheer weight of the Kawaguchi assault drove the marines back to the northern end of Edson's Ridge. Just below them lay the airfield; but the Kawaguchi assembly areas were raked with artillery fire, which despite poor cartographic data and the necessity of firing 105-millimeter howitzers at under the minimum range, performed superbly. Those Japanese who escaped the artillery were stopped by mortars, machine guns, rifles, and grenades, but three screaming battalions of Japanese surged forward in wave after wave. They revealed their intentions not only by jabbering and shouting among themselves to arouse their emotions to the frenzy of each rush, but also by the use of flares to signal another effort; and these foolish actions brought down on their heads additional barrages of 105's which at times of poor observation were fired by ear. Otherwise the enemy fought well. He lacked heavy artillery; but, as in the entire Pacific War, he used his mortars expertly, took advantage of each terrain feature, and resorted to every deceptive device known to generations of warriors. He shouted insults to get marines to expose themselves, and attempted to disorganize his opponents by yelling "Gas!——Gas!" But only isolated patrols filtered through the marines. Four Japanese reached Vandegrift's command tent and killed a marine sergeant with a sword before they were shot down.

Soon after this battle Edson, whose quiet manner of speaking belied his determination in action, gave his verdict as to the meaning of the struggle for Guadalcanal. "I hope the Japs will have some respect for American fighting men after this campaign," he softly declared. "I certainly have learned respect for the Japs. What they have done is to take Indian warfare and apply it to the twentieth century. They use all the Indian tricks to demoralize their enemy. They're good, all right, but I think we're better." [95]

By morning of September 15, twenty per cent of the men under Edson were casualties; but only a remnant of the Kawaguchi Brigade was left, a broken group of men who, harassed by aircraft, tramped through the jungle to the west of the Matanikau and joined other starving and malaria-infested Japanese in that area.[96]

Meanwhile, the naval war continued. The Japanese varied their tactics, and while building up a fresh attack, relied temporarily upon a concentration of submarines in the operating area of the American carriers. The objective was to prevent reinforcements and supplies from reaching the marines.

Enemy underseas craft met with success. The United States Navy became more discouraged than ever, but the Japanese had grasped the shadow and missed the substance. Fleet carriers *Hornet* and *Wasp*, the only two remaining in the Pacific while *Saratoga* and *Enterprise* were in for repairs, were covering a convoy of American troops and supplies headed for Guadalcanal. Vandegrift's insistent demands for reinforcements were being met. In the process, enemy submarines sank *Wasp* and the destroyer *O'Brien*, and damaged the new battleship *North Carolina;* but Turner, commanding a group of transports and cargo vessels, was untouched en route by Japanese torpedoes and reached Guadalcanal on September 18. This was another major turning point in the Guadalcanal campaign. Into the perimeter for the defense of Henderson Field stepped the Seventh Marine Regiment reinforced, joining its parent division from Samoa. This command numbered more than 4,000 men, and with them came almost 150 vehicles, three additional batteries of 75-millimeter pack howitzers, ammunition, and miscellaneous supplies including badly needed fuel and foodstuffs. Combat troops were restored to full rations. The paratroopers, badly battered by the actions at Gavutu and along Edson's Ridge, were evacuated from the island.[97]

Thus was Henderson Field reinforced, and it was certainly worth as much as a heavy carrier, a destroyer, and a damaged battleship. Also, because of this destruction at sea, more navy planes and pilots, along with marine and army aircraft replacements, descended on Guadalcanal. From late September on, except for a few dark days in October Vandegrift could always count fifty to seventy operational planes on

Henderson Field. Flyers endured the same hardships as the ground troops, but General Geiger was molding them into a cohesive striking team. Units dissolved in combat and under operational hazards aggravated by soft spots in the strip caused by rain, by lack of elementary services, and by enemy bombardment; but units were of no great importance. New faces were always in evidence, and heroes one by one were lost. Some pilots proved to be psychologically unsuited to this barbarian type of warfare, but the majority flew not knowing whether their wingman to port or starboard was marine, navy, or army, and in full confidence not caring.[98]

Leaving only one rifle battalion on Tulagi, Vandegrift now had forces adequate to man his perimeter defense. These totaled eleven infantry battalions, including the raiders, supported by four battalions of artillery, a nearly complete defense battalion, a small provisional battalion of light tanks, and a growing air force. The work of preparing additional installations and cutting wider fields of fire, however, carried over into October, even with the assistance of the Sixth Naval Construction Battalion, the majority of the personnel of which had been run in by destroyer transports. Nor was Vandegrift any too satisfied with the defensive arrangements. Since the early part of World War I, the cordon or perimeter defense had been dropped from the text books. It was too vulnerable to artillery fire, and when broken at any one point, the previous commitment of men to the line lessened the number in ready reserve and prevented the rapid deployment of troops to plug the gap. Defense in depth, the experts had agreed, was the most feasible means of withholding an attack in an era of intensive fire power; yet Vandegrift's perimeter technique had grown up almost imperceptibly. It met the needs of his peculiar situation. His motor transport remained small. Only with difficulty could enough trucks be pooled to lift a single battalion; and his lines, although interior, ran across difficult terrain, depending upon bridges which easily washed out. Finally, the Japanese had proved themselves notoriously poor artillerymen. They apparently had no fire director center, failed to use forward observers, and were untrained in massing fires. Nor had they shown any indication of consolidating all available power into a single pointed attack. On the contrary, there was every reason to expect the enemy to continue to divide his forces and to attempt night assaults and infiltrations. Against such tactics, in a jungle terrain, a perimeter defense was the best solution.

With aircraft arriving on Guadalcanal in a steady stream, and a new fighter strip within the perimeter almost completed, Vandegrift's fear of a direct assault on Lunga beach lessened. He shifted his infantry battalions to his flanks and rear, and moved his engineers and pioneers into the already prepared beach positions. (See map 7.) This exchange proved to have administrative as well as tactical advantages.[99]

Having failed with the Ichiki Detachment and the Kawaguchi Brigade, the Japanese next moved a division into Guadalcanal. Utilizing darkness and men-of-war as well as barges, and bringing in transport and cargo vessels at night and in broad daylight, the enemy got almost the entire Sendai Division ashore, reinforced with miscellaneous infantry units, engineers, tanks, and some large 150-millimeter guns with which to bombard the airfield.

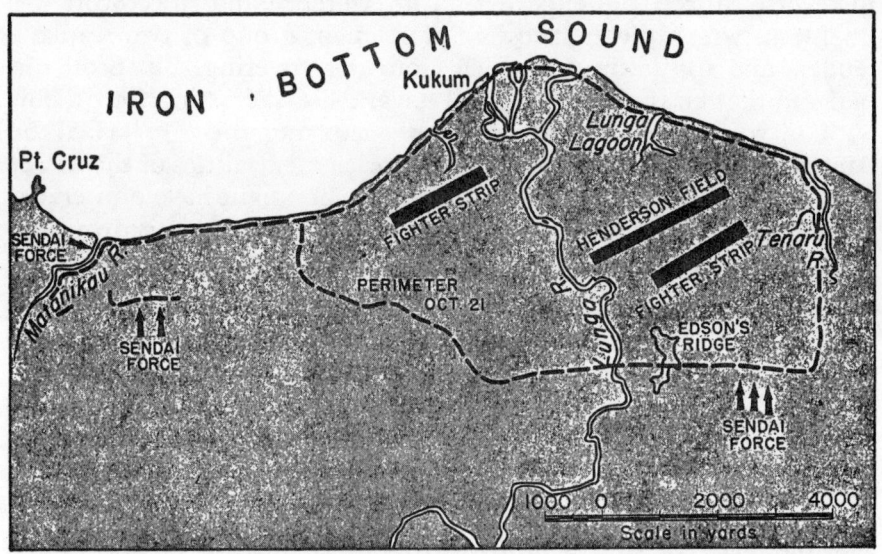

MAP 7. The attack of the Sendai, October 1942. The westernmost fighter strip was not completed until early November.

In fact, Henderson Field became the target for all Japanese arms. A conference of the Japanese high command at Truk had set October 21 as the target date for retaking Guadalcanal. Battleships and a host of smaller fry were to bombard the air installations of the Americans and thus ease the landing of Japanese troops, equipment, and supplies. The show began on October 11 with a thirty-five-plane bomber raid, protected by thirty Zeros, but clouds covered Henderson Field, and all bombs missed. That night ensued the naval Battle of Cape Esperance, the first important tactical surface victory for the American navy in Guadalcanal waters, but in spite of this the Japanese got through a night shipment of men, artillery, and tanks to Guadalcanal.

Rear Admiral Norman Scott USN with two heavy and two light cruisers and five destroyers received orders from Ghormley on October 7 to derail the Tokyo Express. Henderson Field reconnaissance planes informed Scott during the evening of October 11 that a Japanese cruiser force was headed down the Slot, and the American admiral deployed his warships in the waters between Guadalcanal and the Russell Islands which lie just to the northwest of Cape Esperance, the northernmost tip of Guadalcanal.

Rear Admiral Aritomo Goto IJN blithely sailed toward Guadalcanal and his mission of bombarding Henderson Field with three heavy cruisers and two destroyers. This was the Battle of Savo Island in reverse, since Goto expected no interference and since Scott was unable to wreck the Japanese reinforcement group of two seaplane tenders and six destroyers which Goto was covering. But Scott did perform that classical dream of all naval officers, crossing Goto's bow with his own guns laid at broadside—crossing the "T." Had the American admiral been aware of the great potentialities of the newer type of radar aboard some of his warships, he might have obliterated the Japanese covering force without serious damage to his own command; but few men in the United States Navy in 1942 knew exactly how to use radar. A Japanese heavy cruiser and destroyer were sunk, and another heavy cruiser badly damaged. Goto was killed, and his battered survivors turned north. Scott, however, lost a destroyer, and two of his cruisers and another destroyer were damaged. He also was forced to retire from the environs of Iron Bottom Sound.

Since Goto was unable to reach his position for bombarding Henderson Field, naval pilots were free on the morning of October 12 to take up where Scott left off. Sixteen dive bombers escorted by twenty-four fighters rose at first light to strike the remnants of Goto's force and to interdict the enemy's reinforcement group, which had already unloaded men, artillery, and tanks to the westward of the Matanikau River. Two additional strikes followed the first, and the Japanese lost two more destroyers before they got their ships out of range.

Despite the tactical defeat of the Japanese at the Battle of Cape Esperance, their effort mounted in fury. On October 13 neither coastwatchers nor American radar gave warning in time, and Japanese planes bombed Henderson Field, tearing holes in both runways, damaging planes, and sending 5,000 precious gallons of aviation fuel up in smoke. This was the beginning of a series of attacks which nearly meant the end of American aircraft installations on Guadalcanal. That night, October 13/14, began ominously when some of the enemy's newly arrived 150-millimeter shells began falling on the western end of Henderson Field. Since Vandegrift had no counterbattery weapons or equipment, there was nothing to do but sit and take it. Then, shortly after midnight, the heavens breathed fire. A Japanese battleship force stood off of Guadalcanal and for ninety-seven minutes accurately chewed up the field. Along with smaller caliber shells, an estimated 918 rounds of 14-inch projectiles were expended. Only four American motor torpedo boats, which had arrived that morning, were on hand to stop this bombardment, nor was this night one in which the mouse bested the elephant. The enemy fired for area neutralization, and probably for this reason only forty-one Americans were killed; but burning gasoline turned Henderson Field into a river of flames, and the strips, revetments, and taxiways were gouged with holes. The next morning only four of the thirty-nine dive bombers present could fly. Even so, by dodging pits, reconnaissance planes took off at first light, and located two Japanese surface forces bound for Iron Bottom Sound. Enemy aerial bombardment of Henderson Field continued, but construction personnel worked on the strips, and ground crews repaired planes. By late afternoon thirteen dive bombers and seven fighters were air borne and scored several hits, probably sinking a transport.

October 14/15 was another night of miseries for the marines on what they now called "Sleepless Lagoon." A Japanese surface force again bombarded the field. Dawn rose on October 15 to exhibit Japanese transports lying-to only ten miles away, off Tassafaronga Point, west of the Matanikau, unloading men and supplies. Only three dive bombers could fly, and two of these crashed trying to get off the damaged strip. The elements then began to conspire with the Japanese. Rain fell in torrents, and for several hours at a time turned the recently built and as yet unmatted fighter strip into a rectangle of oozing paste. Aviation fuel was at a premium. The division supply officer on a personal tour managed to round up only 400 drums of high octane gasoline, enough for roughly two days of operation; but Marine Air Group 25 flying in transport planes out of Espiritu Santo brought in more, and the men on Guadalcanal were never for long without at least a reassuring sight of friendly planes in the air.

More than a reassuring sight was required. A few American fighter planes annoyed the Japanese as they unloaded, but all the torpedo craft had been destroyed, and it was mid-morning on October 15 before Geiger's First Marine Air Wing could patch up twelve dive bombers. Flying Forts from Espiritu Santo assisted while the Henderson Field planes struck, reloaded, and, despite the presence of Zeros over Tassafaronga Point, struck again and again until nightfall. Three Japanese transports together with most of their supplies, including a considerable amount of artillery ammunition, were sunk or burned out; but most of General Hyakutake's troops and the major portion of their supplies and equipment got ashore.[100]

On the other side of the picture Kelly Turner was likewise busy getting everything he could to Vandegrift. During the day, the United

States Navy continued by a narrow margin to operate in Iron Bottom Sound. Protected by Henderson Field fighters, Turner landed the 164th Infantry Regiment of the United States Army's Americal Division on Guadalcanal. This was the only unnumbered division in the army, and had been pieced together at Nouméa under Major General Alexander M. Patch. Also *Hornet* planes swept in on the 16th and raided Rekata Bay on Santa Isabel, and then struck the Japanese transports remaining at Tassafaronga Point. On the following day two United States destroyers threw 2,000 rounds from their 5-inch guns into enemy positions west of the Matinakau, effectively doing what the Japanese had failed to try immediately after the Battle of Savo Island. The Japanese admitted the loss of "large quantities of ammunition and rations," and according to one of their ranking planners, this "was the most fatal reason for further failures." [101]

Concern for Guadalcanal at this critical juncture permeated the American high command. President Roosevelt, worried about the Russian front and deep in the planning for landings in North Africa, penned a note to the Joint Chiefs of Staff ordering them "to make sure that every possible weapon gets into . . . Guadalcanal, and that having held it in this crisis that munitions and planes and crews are on the way to take advantage of our success." [102] Nimitz was doing all he could. "It now appears that we are unable to control the sea in the Guadalcanal area," he said. "Thus our supply of the positions will only be done at great expense to us. The situation is not hopeless, but it is certainly critical." [103] But getting more guns, men, and planes to Vandegrift was a thing of the future. He was compelled to face the assault of the Sendai (some 22,000 strong, most of the men recently landed) with roughly 23,000 Americans, predominantly tired marines whose malaria rate was beginning to rise alarmingly.

It was Vandegrift's active ground defense, plus mid-October reinforcements, which turned the tide. Assured before the Sendai landed that he would receive a full army regiment, Vandegrift pushed his western flank over to better defensive terrain along the Matanikau River. (See map 7.) This was done early in October. Simultaneously the Japanese tried to occupy the same key ground, but as usual the marines were beforehand. The sand bar at the mouth of the Matanikau was the one feasible route across which the enemy could haul artillery and really pulverize the airstrips. Vandegrift had only enough men to form forward positions shaped like a horseshoe along the eastern bank of the lower Matanikau, refused to the right by newly constructed beach defenses, and partially refused to the interior, the left, along a grassy ridge that overlooked the first crossing up the river.

This flank extension marred the plan of the Sendai. They were never able to reach one of their pivotal jump off positions, and their assault from the first was thrown out of phase. Another factor which caused it to misfire was the extremely difficult march of eight or nine infantry battalions with supporting artillery arms across the upper reaches of the Matanikau, from where another effort to take the airfield was prepared. The journey was so arduous that, although again the marines were somewhat surprised by the direction, the enemy's timing was further upset.

Preliminary maneuvers of the Sendai were well underway by midOctober. The Battle for Henderson Field began on October 21. Renewed efforts to take the Matanikau sand bar came first, and resulted in a slaughter of the enemy, despite his employment of light tanks and artillery, similar to that of August along the Tenaru. Then, uncoordinated with the fighting at the mouth of the Matanikau because of faulty communications and jungle terrain, the Japanese released their major assault on the night of October 24/25. This fell into the same pattern as the Kawaguchi attack, a drive northward from the interior toward the airstrips. The enemy's ability to deploy a body of troops for such an attack was a feat of great endurance and considerable ingenuity, but heavy weapons were necessarily abandoned along the exhausting march over steep ridges and down through jungle mud, and the jump off positions were situated in such jumbled terrain that the Japanese generals in command of the two flank components were unable to coordinate their own endeavors. More important, Vandegrift had his freshest troops deployed to his rear. These were the Seventh Marines and the newly arrived United States Army troops. These men of the 164th Infantry Regiment, a National Guard outfit from the Dakotas, were on an average ten years older than the marines; but they were excellent fighters, and fully measured up to the need for more troops—a need further aggravated by the evacuation of the badly depleted First Marine Raider Battalion, which had left as the soldiers came ashore. The Americans held firm, and the major assault of the Sendai spent itself during the second night. Again the 105-millimeter howitzers emplaced around the airfield were of invaluable assistance to the men defending the perimeter. Colonel Masajiro Furumiya, the Japanese commander of the 29th Regiment, known throughout the homeland as a unit that had never been defeated, burned his colors and killed himself. "I am ashamed of my lack of training," he wrote as the death entry to his diary. "I am sorry that I lost my troops uselessly." Then he added a lesson for his countrymen: "We must not overlook fire power." [104]

The final effort of the Sendai was hopelessly out of phase. It should have come first, and had been so intended, but it was led by that rare exception in the Japanese army, a braggart and a coward, Colonel Akinosuka Oka. For no excusable reason, his attack against the left flank of the Matanikau horseshoe was late by two days or more. Even so, the marine line was thin, and the Japanese met with some success until a marine officer rounded up a nondescript group of cooks, messmen, communications personnel, company runners, and regular riflemen, and drove the enemy from the commanding terrain. That was the end of uncoordinated efforts by the Sendai and their reinforcing elements in the Battle for Henderson Field to recapture Guadalcanal from United States Marine and Army troops.[105]

Just as the last shots were echoing from the broken ranks of the Sendai, the United States Pacific Fleet carriers were engaged in their second major duel with their Nipponese counterpart in the Solomon waters. This was the Battle of the Santa Cruz Islands, October 26–27, 1942. The Japanese were ready, to quote Admiral Isoroku Yamamoto's orders to his subordinates, "to apprehend and annihilate any powerful forces in the Solomons area, as well as any reinforcement." For this task they had a superiority of forces, five carriers, fourteen cruisers, and forty-four destroyers, backed by about 220 naval type planes in the vicinity of Rabaul. Against these ships and planes, the new American carrier commander, Rear Admiral Thomas C. Kinkaid, mustered the *Hornet* and some sixty aircraft on Guadalcanal, reinforced by the repaired *Enterprise* and the fast battleship *South Dakota* on October 24, plus six cruisers and fourteen destroyers. Operating separately from Kinkaid was Rear Admiral Willis A. Lee USN, with a battleship, one heavy and two light cruisers, and six destroyers.

The Japanese plan, despite the plastering they had given Henderson Field in mid-October, was cautious. It was to cover another reinforcing group destined for Guadalcanal, but the run in was to be delayed until the Sendai had captured the airfield. This was not to be, but before the Japanese could retire, a carrier air engagement took place. The box score indicates an American defeat. *Hornet* and two destroyers were sunk, and *Enterprise, South Dakota*, and the cruiser *San Juan* were damaged. The Japanese lost no ships, but a heavy and a light carrier were damaged, and about 100 pilots were shot down. This last was a bitter blow. Their experienced flyers were so few that their admirals were unable to furnish any carrier cover for the next attempt to take Guadalcanal. Indeed, not until June of 1944 did the Japanese carriers again venture forth for battle.[106]

Thus ended the final massive effort of the Japanese to take Henderson Field. Before they could collect another division and the required shipping at Rabaul and stage fresh troops down the Solomons Slot, the United States Pacific Fleet won mastery of the waters in the Southeastern Solomons.

5. Command Relations and Control of the Sea

From August 9 through the hectic days of October, Vandegrift had barely managed to stave off the attacks of the Japanese and to keep planes flying from Henderson Field. As early as the rehearsal at Koro Island, when learning of Fletcher's contemplated early retirement, Vandegrift had realistically reappraised his situation and had decided that his mission was predominantly defensive, which in turn required as high a degree of concentration of his land strength as could be obtained. Turner thought otherwise. Irrespective of the naval situation, he continued to regard the mission of the marines as offensive in nature. On three separate and distinct occasions it required a crisis at Guadalcanal-Tulagi, rather than a correct appraisal of the situation by the attack force commander, to prevent Turner from landing reinforcements outside the perimeter.[107] Turner said he wanted the Japanese in the Guadalcanal-Tulagi area mopped up, when it was all Vandegrift and the marines could do to prevent being mopped up themselves. This was, of course, an unwarranted effort to interfere with tactics ashore; but the picture was not clarified until after Ghormley was relieved in mid-October.

Several factors can be marshalled in support of Turner and Ghormley. Both wanted to divert forces to occupy Ndeni, and in this desire they were supported by King and Nimitz. From a purely navy point of view, the Ndeni operation made sense. These four officers were keenly aware of the fact that if the troops and construction personnel and supplies could be located and run into Ndeni, then an airfield could be built which would help guard the line of communications into Guadalcanal and would greatly ease the problem of operating carriers in the waters east and south of the Solomons. All such forces, however, were critically needed on Guadalcanal. There simply was not at this time in the South Pacific Area sufficient strength to occupy Ndeni and still to hold Guadalcanal.

Turner was as hard-fighting a ranking commander as emerged from the Pacific War, but he was slow to understand the tactical situation ashore. His performance adjacent to large land masses, when the warfare resembled that associated with the army, is open to criticism. His well-deserved reputation was made later in the war, in the Central Pacific, where his immediate superior, Admiral Spruance, was an outstanding leader, where a marine officer as obstinate and outspoken as himself, Major General Holland M. Smith, occupied a parallel position on the echelon of command, where the land areas, except for Okinawa, were relatively minute in size, and where therefore the navy-marine policy of giving the naval attack force commander extensive powers in influencing the tactics of the fighting ashore worked satisfactorily. During the critical fighting on Okinawa, as in the last stage of the campaign for the Southeastern Solomons, the ranking commander ashore was an army officer, and once on land he was not subject to interference in tactical matters from admirals afloat.

Also it must be emphasized that, after the Battle for Savo Island, Turner recognized that the waters around Guadalcanal were clearly in dispute, and, given his limited means, he did a superb tactical job of bringing in supplies and reinforcements. But he did not fully realize that the marines, like the navy, were having a tough time remaining on their feet during the critical days from August 9 through October.

He lost no time in attempting to carry out his tactical ideas ashore. The rifle battalions of the Second Marines, which he wished to set ashore on Ndeni, were committed to the fighting in the Tulagi area on August 7–8, but Turner carried the reinforcing elements of this regiment, totaling almost 1,400 men, back to Espiritu Santo. Despite the fact that Lieutenant Colonel Evans F. Carlson USMC already commanded the Second Marine Raider Battalion, Turner formed the core of these reinforcing units of the Second Marines into another Second Marine Raider Battalion. This action, which was later rescinded by higher authority, he took without consulting Vandegrift, who, as the Commandant of the Marine Corps, Lieutenant General Thomas Holcomb, "noted with regret," was "particularly qualified and concerned" to pass judgment on such matters.[108]

Turner was apparently continuing to think of marines as small components aboard a warship, rather than as divisions and corps, in which capacity they were then and would continue to fight the Pacific War. He announced shortly after the landings in the Southeastern Solomons that the employment of a full division for any task in the South Pacific appeared "less likely" than the use of one or at most two marine regiments. He no longer agreed with "the previous concept that Raider and Parachute Battalions are always division or corps troops. . . ." He intended to weaken the rifle components of the marine regiments then in the South Pacific by forming raider battalions from their organic strengths, and he recommended that, without increasing the size of the regiments, each such outfit sent to the subtheater in the future have, "as an integral part of its organization, either a Raider or a Parachute Battalion." This change was needed, he said, to solve the problem of "mopping up outlying detachments" of the enemy.[109]

Other ranking navy officers agreed with Turner. Thus it was that during the most bitter period of the struggle on Guadalcanal, when the enemy had ashore the most powerful composite group of the substantially more than 40,000 men he expended throughout the contest for that island, the Navy Department in Washington, as recommended by Ghormley and Turner, continued to force Marine Corps Headquarters to form additional raider battalions.[110] On Guadalcanal at the time, one such unit was being intensively employed as a normal infantry battalion. It is true that raider and parachute battalions in the contest for the Solomons proved their worth in slashing behind Japanese lines, and in diverting the enemy's attention from principal offensives; but these were the exceptions, and Holcomb had pleaded in vain that such tasks could just as well be performed by any marine rifle battalion. Throughout the war in the Pacific, amphibious divisions and even larger tactical units, rather than independent battalions, did the bulk of the fighting. This flurry of interest by navy officers in raider battalions sprang in part at least from admiration for British commando tactics; [111] but raids do not hold terrain. Training and equipping raiders slowed down the organization of additional marine divisions, and for a time lessened the attention given to the coordination of tactical units on the regimental and higher levels.

Something might be said for Turner's recommendations had the United States Pacific Fleet been able to control the seas of the New Guinea-New Britain-Solomons area. The contrary was not only true, but was made readily apparent by the Battle of Savo Island. Even if control of the seas had been easily obtained, the size of the marine units needed for "mopping up" would have depended upon the opposition encountered at any given target. As long as the enemy retained the capability of reinforcing his bases, even the best of intelligence was of no help in making estimates of the landing force needed to seize any given objective in the future.

When Vandegrift persuaded Turner in early August that the Second Marine Regiment of the Second Marine Division should remain in the Guadalcanal-Tulagi area, he had simultaneously asked that the Seventh Marines of the First Division be displaced forward from their defensive position on Samoa. When the Seventh Marines became available for offensive employment in early September, for a time it looked as if they might be sent to General MacArthur, who was still demanding amphibiously trained troops; but Turner scotched this idea. "Adequate air and naval strength," he protested, "have not been made available to insure Guadalcanal and Tulagi's security, and in the absence of these forces much greater dependence must be placed on troop defense." [112] He won his point, but he wanted to land these reinforcements in men and supplies, first at Ndeni and then outside the defensive establishment on Guadalcanal. He was convinced that the only way to prevent the enemy from consolidating to assault the Lunga position was by occupying strong points along a stretch of Guadalcanal coast forty-five miles long. Splendid tactics, if the men and shipping had been available, and the sea under his command, in which case such outposts would have been unnecessary. A personal visit to Vandegrift's headquarters just as the Kawaguchi attack began mounting in fury along Edson's Ridge was enough to impress upon Turner's mind, temporarily, that concentration, particularly when on the defensive, is sometimes mandatory. The Seventh Marines were landed inside the perimeter.

The third crisis on Guadalcanal which gained Vandegrift more reinforcements came with increasing evidence of the October assault by the Sendai Division. At this juncture it was Ghormley's army commander, General Harmon, rather than anyone connected with the navy, who correctly analyzed the situation in the Southeastern Solomons. Although headquarters South Pacific was aware of the pending effort by the Sendai, both King and Nimitz were still eager to occupy Ndeni, and in late September Turner went so far as to suggest withdrawing a rifle battalion of the Second Marines from Guadalcanal for the execution of this task. Ghormley rejected this possibly fatal course of action, but tentatively agreed to such an allocation of the first army regiment available for forward displacement. Only because of Harmon's vigorous objection did Ghormley overrule Turner. Ndeni, Harmon emphasized in a memorandum for his superior, would be valueless without Guadalcanal, which unless reinforced immediately, could be retaken by the Japanese. The loss of Guadalcanal, he spoke with simple logic, "would be a four-way victory for the Jap—provide a vanguard for his strong Bismarck position, deny us a jumping off place against that position, give him a jumping off place against the New Hebrides, effectively cover his operations against New Guinea." [113] Thus was the 164th Army Infantry Regiment of the Americal Division landed inside the perimeter in time to help stop the Sendai.

The constant danger facing Vandegrift of having men and supplies diverted into Ndeni or scattered around on Guadalcanal rather than concentrated about Henderson Field where they were required is illustrative of Ghormley's greatest weakness as a commander. He was unable to appraise the situation and firmly to reach a decision. He was relieved on October 18, 1942, by Vice Admiral William F. Halsey, Jr. USN, who immediately began a study of the still pending Ndeni operation and within forty-eight hours summarily canceled it. All that King and Nimitz needed was to be told by the subtheater commander that the proposal was infeasible. After October 20, 1942, nothing more was heard of Ndeni.

Ghormley deserves recognition for his meticulous planning and early logistical implementation of a critical operation when shackled by few bases, little shipping, and a paucity of resources. Halsey's greater success, when contrasted with Ghormley's seemingly insurmountable difficulties, is attributable in large measure to the fact that by mid-October the South Pacific Area was far stronger in terms of military and naval power than it had previously been. But also, Halsey's aggressive personality within itself injected new vigor into the South Pacific Area, and at the same time resulted in better collaboration between all services.[114] Vandegrift in December said of Guadalcanal that "if the surface navy continues to perform as they have since Admiral Halsey took over, then this place is safe for democracy." [115]

Ghormley was deficient in that attribute of command which, regardless of adverse circumstances, instills confidence and a fighting spirit in his men. One explanation for this was that from the outset he joined with MacArthur in doubting the feasibility of the undertaking,[116] and an officer who fears defeat almost invariably infects the ranks with a similar attitude. Nor did Ghormley give his small staff a chance to unify itself and counteract this growing sentiment, but rather kept it divided between Nouméa and Auckland. Such a split was doubtless caused in part by the intransigeance of the so-called "Free French" officials who ruled New Caledonia and who refused to furnish adequate quarters ashore at Nouméa; [117] but it burdened farther a staff already sorely beset, and gave added credence to the gnawing belief that American forces would be driven from New Caledonia as well as from the Southeastern Solomons. Halsey, on the other hand, by canceling the Ndeni operation told all and sundry who came in contact with him that the major battle was 330 miles west-northwest of the Santa Cruz Islands, on Guadalcanal, and that the major battle would be won. Also, he immediately consolidated the headquarters of the South Pacific Area at Nouméa, and brought into that city most of the staff personnel he had employed in his earlier fast carrier task force operations in the Central Pacific. While this may have been detrimental to planning and executing Pacific Fleet carrier operations in the immediate future,[118] only a larger staff could keep pace with events in the South Pacific. Better coordination resulted. One example will suffice. Until mid-October the First Marine Division was not on the distribution list of the routine day-by-day intelligence data being disseminated by South Pacific headquarters. Of course, Vandegrift's intelligence officer, who by this date was exhibiting considerable ingenuity in assimilating and evaluating information, was equally culpable in not requesting this service, but he knew nothing of its existence until after army officers of the 164th Regiment had landed on Guadalcanal.[119] Under Halsey, such major gaps in staff performance did not recur.

Halsey was unable, however, quickly to veto all of Turner's plans as to how the marines should hold Guadalcanal. Even after the Ndeni operation had been sacked, Turner continued to try and was finally successful in dispersing the forces he put ashore. This was done despite a command conference held at Nouméa on October 20. Halsey then asked Vandegrift: "Are we going to evacuate or hold." To this the marine replied, "I can hold, but I've got to have more active support than I've been getting."

"All right." Halsey responded. "Go on back. I'll promise you everything I've got." Yet early in the next month Turner landed men and supplies some twenty-five miles east of the Lunga Point perimeter, at a place called Aola, where a new airstrip was begun. (See map 4.) Of course all the airstrips possible were advantageous to the American cause, but aside from the pressing requirement of tactical concentration ashore, this construction at Aola was undertaken against the advice of men who knew the terrain was unsuited for an airfield. Both General Geiger and Rear Admiral Aubrey W. Fitch USN (who on September 20 had relieved McCain as Commander Air, South Pacific Area) argued strenuously that Aola was nothing but a swamp. Turner, however, carried the day. Halsey later abandoned the Aola project,[120] and since American naval and air arms proved sufficiently powerful to seize command of the sea and to cut off the flow of Japanese troops attacking Henderson Field to a trickle, the momentary dispersal of troops and supplies had no serious repercussions.

Six major naval battles and the resolute flying of marine, army, and navy pilots from Henderson Field, supported by the dash and courage of American torpedo boat crews operating on the surface of Iron Bottom Sound by night, wrested command of the waters of the Southeastern Solomons from the Japanese. From the Sabbath which dawned after the Battle of Savo Island through the hard fought but inconclusive Battle of the Eastern Solomons in September and the Battles of Cape Esperance and Santa Cruz during the following month, domination of these vital waters seesawed back and forth uncertainly. Finally in mid-November came a series of night sea and land-based air engagements collectively known as the Battle of Guadalcanal. This brought victory to the American navy. Japanese forces in the Southeastern Solomons were mortally wounded, but their surface forces recovered once more and during the Battle of Tassafarongo in late November came near duplicating the earlier performance at Savo Island. This, however, was the enemy's final grasp for the Southeastern Solomons. He then withdrew beyond the horizon through the Slot.

The naval Battle of Guadalcanal determined which side, Japanese or American, would pour reinforcements onto Guadalcanal. The Nipponese at Rabaul had additional miscellaneous group support units and the 38th Division (less two battalions already committed with the Sendai, but plus 3,500 special naval landing troops) ready for action; while the Americans at Nouméa and at Aola had the remainder of the Americal Division, and were moving another regiment of the Second Marine Division, the Eighth Marines, into the zone of conflict. The enemy's carrier squadrons were too depleted after the Battle of the Santa Cruz Islands to permit the active employment of carriers in strategic cover, but the Japanese navy had about 215 operational aircraft in the Rabaul network, plus 85 that could be staged from carriers. The fighter strip at Munda was not yet begun, however, and the Japanese still depended on land-based air spotted through the Northern Solomons. On the sea their superiority was great—five battleships, twelve cruisers, and around forty-eight destroyers, plus eleven transports for the troops. Opposing this array, Halsey had four transports and three cargo vessels embarked with reinforcing units and the 182nd Infantry Regiment (less one battalion) of the Americal Division, two new battleships, eight cruisers, and twenty destroyers. Rightly, however, the Japanese planners at Rabaul and Truk surmised that American carrier strength was also at a low ebb. Actually, the only fleet carrier available was the damaged *Enterprise;* but another fighter strip was being completed within the perimeter at Lunga Point, and marine artilleryman Pedro del Valle (promoted to Brigadier General) received 155-millimeter guns on October 30, plus the sound and flash ranging equipment needed to knock out the enemy artillery across the Matanikau River. Henderson Field was currently playing host to seventy-four naval-type planes plus twenty army craft, including eighteen improved army fighters (P-38s). Crippled *Enterprise* could ferry seventy-eight additional craft onto Guadalcanal, and a total of 111 American planes were based on Espiritu Santo.[121]

Henderson Field was the thorn in the flesh of the Japanese. As during the October approach of the Sendai Division toward Guadalcanal, the enemy again decided to send in warships by night to pound the airstrips and ground the planes so that transports could once more land troops, supplies, and equipment by daylight. Earlier, in the Sendai attack, he had been in great part successful, but to no avail thanks to American marines and soldiers at the Battle for Henderson Field. A month later disaster overtook the bulk of the 38th Division before it could set foot on dry land.

November opened with Vandegrift making his largest offensive outside the perimeter to date, but he had to call it off to concentrate for the expected attack of the 38th Division. A few destroyer borne enemy troops were run in at night, but sometimes motor torpedo boats turned back the Tokyo Express and on other occasions dusk and dawn flights from Henderson Field harassed the enemy warships. Intensive efforts began on November 11 with the first Japanese air strike against Guadalcanal in over a week. This performance was repeated the next day, but Kelly Turner managed on November 12 to unload both battalions of the 182nd Infantry Regiment and about ninety per cent of his supplies and equipment. That night the Battle of Guadalcanal got under way in earnest. The Japanese bombardment force composed of two battleships, a light cruiser, and fifteen destroyers, entered Iron Bottom Sound. Awaiting Vice Admiral Hiroaki Abe IJN was Rear Admiral Daniel J. Callahan USN and an outnumbered and greatly outgunned force of two heavy and three light cruisers and eight destroyers. Again, poor use was made of the superior American radar, but Callahan was a man of courage. He closed to 3,000 yards before opening fire. In the ensuing mêlée, Callahan and his immediate subordinate Rear Admiral Norman Scott were killed, two light cruisers and four destroyers were sunk, and most of the other ships damaged; but Callahan was the victor. The Japanese had been unable to get through to bombard Henderson Field. They had lost only two destroyers during the surface action, but the battleship *Hiei* had been hit with several score 8-inch armor-piercing shells and had lost control of her steering gear. At first light, planes from Henderson Field assisted by army flyers from Espiritu Santo pounced on the wounded Japanese giant. That finished off *Hiei*.

The enemy was more successful the next night, November 13/14. A Japanese bombardment force built around two heavy cruisers met no opposition except from motor torpedo boats in the Sound, and for forty-seven minutes pumped around 1,000 high-capacity 8-inch projectiles into Henderson Field. Two torpedo boats, like gnats attacking giants, launched six torpedoes, but scored no hits. It is possible, however, that these boats caused the enemy to depart earlier than he had planned. Nor was the damage to Henderson Field as great as it would have been had the battleships been allowed to run free on the previous night. The strips were quickly repaired; two fighters were destroyed and sixteen other planes were hit by shrapnel, but most of these were back in operation by the end of the day. At dawn of November 14 the regular searches from Henderson Field were investigating the Slot. They found three cruisers and four destroyers, and assisted by *Enterprise* planes sank one cruiser and damaged another. On the day before, since *Enterprise* was incapable of her usual fast flight operations, Admiral Kinkaid had flown fifteen of his planes off with orders to report to Vandegrift for land-based duty. Now on November 14, convinced that the Japanese had no carriers in the area, he emptied the flight deck and retired. Henderson Field became the only functional "carrier" in the Pacific.

There was work aplenty for American pilots on this fateful day, and they later referred to their flight formations as "buzzard patrols." The carcass was the amphibious shipping of the 38th Japanese Division. A Japanese naval officer aboard a destroyer screening these lumbering transports later recalled: "We were very happy because we thought the bombardment groups had succeeded in destroying your planes the night before." But at shortly after noon and for the remainder of the day, this shipping was slaughtered from the sky. Seven out of eleven vessels were sunk, but the Japanese still came on. They managed to beach four damaged transports on Guadalcanal that evening, but the next day American flyers again swarmed down on the foe, and helped by the accurate 5-inch fire of the destroyer *Meade,* gutted the remnants of the Japanese reinforcing group. About one-third of the roughly 15,000 troops got ashore, but almost all of their equipment and supplies were lost.[122]

Another night surface engagement occurred on November 14/15. The Japanese belatedly sent in another bombardment force, formed around the battleship *Kirishima,* which was destined to join her sister ship *Hiei* beneath the waters of Iron Bottom Sound. Rear Admiral Willis Lee rushed in the battleships *Washington* and *South Dakota* to turn the trick. Among Lee's ships, *South Dakota* and a destroyer were damaged. Despite these wounds, it was a notable victory for the United States Navy. President Roosevelt stopped worrying about the possibility that Guadalcanal might have to be evacuated. James Forrestal said "the tension that I felt at that time was matched only by the tension that pervaded Washington the night before the landing in Normandy." As Halsey later testified of the four-day air-sea struggle for Guadalcanal: "If our ships and planes had been routed in this battle, if we had lost it, our troops on Guadalcanal would have been trapped as were our troops on Bataan. . . . Unobstructed, the enemy would have driven south, cut our supply lines to Australia and New Zealand and enveloped them." [123]

The contrary was the outcome, and between November and the following January, American naval strength in the South Pacific increased by leaps and bounds. *Enterprise* and *Saratoga* were both back in full operation. The battleship *South Dakota* was away for repairs, but *Washington* and *North Carolina* were on hand, backed by four old battleships, now far stronger especially in antiaircraft armament than at the time of Pearl Harbor. Several new cruisers and submarines were present, plus new transports and cargo vessels, and a host of destroyers and torpedo boats. On November 20, the planes on Henderson Field jumped beyond the 100-mark. From that time on, America commanded the seas adjacent to Guadalcanal. This is more apparent to the historian today than it was to the participants at the time, but as early as November 22 Nimitz adjudged the situation "past the most critical period." Not even the clumsiness of an American cruiser force which on November 30 in the Battle of Tassafaronga lost one cruiser sunk and three damaged to a skillfully executed night destroyer torpedo attack changed the picture. Concern continued that the Japanese might attempt another big push, but after toying with the idea they abandoned the Southeastern Solomons as a bad investment.[124]

6. Final Fighting on Guadalcanal

While the surface navy and Henderson Field pilots were breaking the backbone of the 38th Japanese Division, Vandegrift and his foot troops were engaged in an active defense preparatory for the worst should the enemy get ashore intact. As grim October passed and November began, the marines and soldiers were operating in force across the Matanikau in an effort to eliminate all traces of the Japanese artillery in that area. News of the impending effort of the 38th Division, however, caused Vandegrift to bring all forces into the perimeter and wait. Soon advanced elements of the 38th Division landed at night to the eastward of Lunga Point, and Vandegrift struck with speed. The Japanese were surrounded, and the majority of them killed. Those who escaped into the jungle to the south were followed and many exterminated by Lieutenant Colonel Evans F. Carlson's Second Marine Raider Battalion, a well-trained body of fighters. Carlson, for this job, was detached from the Aola perimeter, where he and his men had been helping to guard construction details. While this effort was being abandoned, the Second Raiders came in handy. They scouted around the Lunga Point perimeter, destroyed isolated groups of the enemy, and brought Vandegrift the reassuring information that the enemy remaining on Guadalcanal, except west of the Matanikau, was disorganized.[125]

For a short time in early November the Americans ashore were outnumbered by the Japanese, but most of these were shattered remnants of the Ichiki Detachment, the Kawaguchi Brigade, and the Sendai Division, infested with malaria, starving, and underequipped. Soon American reinforcements and supplies began arriving in abundance, barbed wire, ammunition, and facilities for mounting long-range bomber raids. Even war dogs entered the scene. "Two were sent to my Regiment," wrote a marine colonel, "and the first night we had them, they barked all night at the animals in the jungle. The next day, I sent them to the battalions and one was taken on a patrol towards Mount Austen. The dog passed out after going about a mile and a sergeant had to carry him back. Upon reaching our lines, the sergeant also passed out. The next night, the sergeant took him out beyond our barbed wire to a listening post and the dog immediately went to sleep.

Evidently, the sergeant went to sleep also, as the dog was urinating on him when he woke up. Some trained dogs!" [126]

Such incidents relieved the tension of the battle-weary First Marine Division troops until dawn of the day for beginning their departure, December 9, 1942. Sea control in friendly hands had virtually ended the fighting on Guadalcanal for these men. Three weeks transpired after the naval Battle for Guadalcanal before sufficient reinforcements, marine and army, arrived to permit Vandegrift to withdraw his men; but so far as was possible in the interim, he refused to employ them for difficult tasks. These were assigned to more recently arrived troops.

Battle casualties in the First Marine Division were light because of excellent leadership. Dead for all units attached to the division totaled 1,057 (the navy had lost 1,270 dead and 709 wounded in the Battle of Savo Island alone), and those wounded by gunshot were just under 2,170, but exhaustion and sickness were widespread, malaria cases within the division proper mounting to almost 6,000, and others by the score would develop this fever in their rehabilitation area.[127] The First Marine Division was spent, but it managed to get relieved only through a complicated exchange of forces which reached more than halfway around the globe. A fresh United States Army division headed for MacArthur was diverted to the Southeastern Solomons, and in exchange the First Marine Division was shipped into the Southwest Pacific Area. This simultaneously satisfied two demands. MacArthur received troops trained and experienced in amphibious warfare; and the Australians, who had been crying that one of their crack divisions then participating in the hard Libyan campaign should come home to help guard them against the menace of Japan, felt safe when protected by the heroes of Guadalcanal.[128]

Vandegrift was understandably in a jocular mood as he turned his command responsibilities over to Major General Alexander Patch USA and departed with his marines. "So now," he wrote shortly after the mid-November air-sea battle, "it is a mopping up job and the Army can do that." [129] He was surely joking, probably for the benefit of such officers as Kelly Turner. In the first place some of the artillery of the First Marine Division and all of the Second Marine Division remained behind to help complete the campaign, and a part of one unit of the Second Division, the Second Marine Regiment, had landed before any other American touched foot ashore in the Southeastern Solomons, on Florida Island early on the morning of August 7. The Second Marines continued to fight for more than a month after the First Division had evacuated, and the men of the other two regiments of the Second Marine Division, the Sixth and Eighth Marines, were in to the finish. In the second place, Vandegrift's own First Division had faced the 20,000 or so Japanese in the rugged terrain west of the Matanikau too often for him to fail to realize that large scale fighting was ahead before the island could be cleared of the enemy. One of his regimental commanders underscored the difficulties in store for Patch's XIVth United States Army Corps, comprised of the Americal Division, the 25th Infantry Division, and the Second Marine Division: "The terrain has a series of ridges, some unscalable, which is ideal for a defense. In some places the Japs have emplaced their machine guns on the reverse slopes, so it is almost impossible to reach them with artillery or mortars." [130]

In the drive from the Henderson Field perimeter westward across the Matanikau and on to Cape Esperance, naval gunfire support performed with effectiveness for the first time in the fighting on Guadalcanal. (See map 4.) Units of the Second Marine Division reinforced by army battalions handled the right flank of this drive, bordering on Iron Bottom Sound, and thus were the chief beneficiaries of support from naval guns. These could be maneuvered at sea and in many cases reach targets hidden from the impact of artillery or mortar explosions.[131] Even so, the marines of the Second Division, two regiments of which were experiencing their initial combat, found progress slow. More difficult terrain faced army troops in the interior, and it was unsuited to naval gunfire. This zone was assigned to the 25th Infantry Division, reinforced in some instances by units of the Americal Division. It included such formidable ground obstacles as Mount Austen. Early February was at hand before the westward drive was finished and the island cleared of all organized resistance.

More time would have been required had not unaggressive fighting ashore and faulty naval leadership permitted the Japanese high command to evacuate around one-half of their troops on Guadalcanal. The enemy excelled at deceptive tactics covering a withdrawal. Halsey, not for the last time, jumped for the decoy and missed the real target. Neither he nor his staff could believe the Japanese contemplated evacuation. While a small rear guard ashore on Guadalcanal held the army and marines at bay, the Nipponese navy feinted in a manner which led the Americans to expect another major effort at reinforcing Guadalcanal. With the opposition off balance, the enemy in early February 1943 evacuated upwards of 13,000 men.[132] Among those who escaped was Lieutenant General Harukichi Hyakutake, commander of Japan's Seventeenth Army.

That ended the ground fighting on Guadalcanal, six months of bitter struggle in a steaming jungle terrain. American casualties, army and marine, totaled 6,111, including 1,752 killed or missing in action; but it was a major turning point in the Pacific War. Captain Toshikazu Ohmae IJN, one of the foremost of his nation's naval planners, said: "After Guadalcanal, in the latter part of 1942, I felt we could not win." This statement was echoed by a former deputy chief of the Japanese Army's General Staff, who declared: "As for the turning point (of the war), when the positive action ceased or even became negative, it was, I feel, at Guadalcanal." How was this American victory achieved? Fleet Admiral Osami Negano IJN summarized with these words, "The cause of our setback was our inability to increase our forces at the same speed as you did." [133] Add to this explanation the vigorous active defense of Vandegrift, utilizing whenever possible amphibian techniques in rapid shore-to-shore strikes, and the poor tactical leadership of the Japanese, and the story is complete. When reminded of the Battle of the Tenaru River fought on August 21, a Japanese naval officer observed that "it was the first time the Japanese Army had been defeated. The Army had been used to fighting the Chinese Army." [134]

The United States Navy won Guadalcanal in a costly struggle of naval attrition, but America could afford the losses better than Japan. No small part of the credit for this victory must go to the men who seized, and throughout the desperate days of August, September, October, and November, held a critically situated airfield. In the final analysis it was Henderson Field, serving as an aircraft carrier for a long procession of marine, navy, and army flyers, which made it possible to hold Guadalcanal. As Vandegrift had planned while steaming into the Southeastern Solomons, the defense by foot troops and airmen was "reciprocal." Teamwork took and kept Guadalcanal.

7. *Climbing the Solomons and Neutralizing Rabaul*

Rabaul, the principal objective of the July 2, 1942, directive of the Joint Chiefs of Staff, still loomed as a powerful bastion 550 miles northwest of Guadalcanal. The American decision to by-pass the enemy's key base in the New Guinea-New Britain-Solomons area was not reached until late in 1943, and meanwhile plans for the intermediary and final pincers on Rabaul were made under MacArthur's strategical direction. Halsey could take only one further step toward Rabaul before he crossed the boundary between his subtheater under Nimitz, and spilled over into the Southwest Pacific. That step was the occupation of a nest of islands 100 miles northwest of Henderson Field, the Russells, which lie just to the eastward of 159° east longitude. (See map 3.) Seizure of this group was first planned in part as a means of blocking supposed Japanese reinforcements onto Guadalcanal by barge; but even after the elimination of the enemy from Cape Esperance, the Russells were needed for fighter strips and for the installation of radar warning facilities in order to furnish better protection for Henderson Field's bombers. Amphibious reconnaissance patrols first investigated the group, and it was occupied by army troops on February 21, 1943. Resistance at the beach was neither expected nor met, but the army landing force commander was prepared for such an emergency by having a small number of marines at his disposal.[135]

Some new command relationship, at least in the eyes of the navy, was now imperative. King was perplexed. He freely admitted to Marshall that he had miscalculated. When beginning the Southeastern Solomons campaign, he had failed to realize that further advances up that chain of islands would require the continued employment of large units of the Pacific Fleet. Now that the contrary was evident, he was reluctant either to suggest another shift in the South Pacific line, or to allow sizeable components of first-class warships to operate under MacArthur.[136]

The arrangement reached was unusual, and the fact that it worked so well reflects great credit on Halsey and MacArthur. Halsey's strength remained attached, strategically, to Nimitz; but overall planning for the employment of that strength became MacArthur's responsibility. Some such superior direction as that afforded by MacArthur was essential. Both commanders had a common goal, Rabaul; and MacArthur was careful to integrate the operations of both in such a manner as to approach the principal geographic objective expeditiously and with a minimum cost of lives. Some would say that Halsey served two masters, and that this was a violation of the basic principle of command; but it worked well in practice, mainly because Halsey was given great freedom of action by both MacArthur and Nimitz.

MacArthur must have felt, as Nimitz later complained, that Halsey wanted to fight the entire nation of Japan nowhere but in the Solomons. Six weeks after Halsey had assumed his post, he sent MacArthur a bluntly worded despatch. Halsey believed that the capture of Rabaul could best be accomplished via the Solomons climb. He pointed out that land communications in New Guinea were non-existent, and that until American forces controlled the Solomon Sea (that is Rabaul) the seizure and supply of bases along the northeast coast of New Guinea by the Allies was not feasible. He explained that this was true because, until the Solomons and Rabaul were swept by his broom, movements by naval forces in MacArthur's theater would remain flanked by enemy bases. He asked MacArthur to rely on South Pacific naval strength to prevent an amphibious attack on Port Moresby, and while maintaining a ground defense, to strike at as much enemy shipping as the various arms of the Southwest Pacific could reach. Halsey concluded that the sound procedure was for MacArthur to play a secondary role.[137]

How far this despatch influenced MacArthur is not known. It was little more than a repetition of the naval argument in the weeks preceding the July 2, 1942, directive; and from all indications the degree to which MacArthur followed the course outlined by Halsey came more from necessity than from choice. Already in the closing weeks of 1942, Australian and United States Army forces in the Southwest Pacific, having halted the Japanese overland drive across the Owen Stanley Mountains against Port Moresby, were putting the finishing touches on an attack against Buna-Gona, villages on the eastern coast of the Papuan Peninsula. (See maps 2 and 3.) The fighting was at times desperate, and MacArthur, unable to get all the amphibious shipping he desired, made great progress in improvising logistical support by air. Of course, the diversion onto Guadalcanal of Japanese troops previously earmarked for the effort against Port Moresby was of great benefit to the Allies in completing the Campaign for Papua, which was done early in 1943.

Thereupon, MacArthur began rapidly rolling land-based planes forward until by the end of September 1943 he held the Huon Peninsula, adjacent to the Vitiaz Strait. For each of these steps, he utilized little in the way of naval support other than a bare minimum of covering and escorting vessels and of amphibious shipping, which was organized as the Seventh Amphibious Force under Rear Admiral Daniel E. Barbey USN. Also, it is notable that MacArthur's air arm, commanded by Major General George C. Kenney USA, was becoming proficient not only in logistical support, in strategical bombing, and in reconnaissance, but also in tactical support for ground troops and in antishipping strikes. Kenney's Fifth Air Force was apparently alone among the United States air commands in the Pacific in perfecting the low-level tactics needed to demolish shipping. The Battle of the Bismarck Sea early in 1944 bears testimony to the degree of skill achieved. Southwest Pacific airmen battered an enemy convoy of sixteen vessels, sinking a total of twelve, and four of these were fast maneuverable destroyers. Such proficiency went far in covering MacArthur's sea borne movements, and of course Halsey's activities in the Slot gave added protection. Finally, MacArthur brilliantly planned all his New Guinea landings to make the most of his air support, logistically and tactically, and to avoid serious opposition at the beach.[138]

The Vitiaz Strait is one-half of that body of water separating the western tip of New Britain from the northeastern coast of New Guinea. The other portion, to the eastward of Umboi Island, is called Dampier Strait. In other words, while Allied operations in the Solomons drained Japanese strength and covered the movements of the Southwest Pacific Area, MacArthur worked himself into a position from which, once Rabaul was sufficiently weakened and Dampier Strait controlled, he could break the Bismarck Barrier at its western extremity and continue forward along the New Guinea coast. Once at the Vitiaz Strait, however, unable alone to crack the obstacle of the Bismarcks, MacArthur turned eastward and ordered Halsey onto Bougainville, which lay within fighter and light bomber range of Rabaul.

Halsey had been busy getting into position to advance to Bougainville by occupying or reducing enemy holdings in the Central Solomons. This required four months of planning and roughly sixty days of fighting. It fell into two phases, the New Georgia and the Vella Lavella operations. (See map 8.)

The first of these had as its objective the seizure of the Japanese airfield at Munda, about 100 miles northwest of the Russells. This enemy base was so well camouflaged that it was not discovered until early in December, at which time it was nearly operational. It was steadily pounded by warships and by bombers out of Guadalcanal, but they were unable to render it totally ineffective for more than a few hours at a time.

Although air support to a degree hitherto unexperienced was available from four fields on Guadalcanal and two on the Russells, planning the New Georgia operation was difficult for a number of reasons.[139] The lack of amphibiously trained troops was acutely felt. Both the First and Second Marine Divisions had been exhausted on Guadalcanal, and were now undergoing rehabilitation, the First at Melbourne and the Second at Wellington. The Third Marine Division arrived in the subtheater in April 1943, but was not ready for combat until it had gone through an intensive six-month training period. That left, besides army troops, only marine raider battalions, which throughout the fighting in the Central and most of the Northern Solomons, were employed as normal infantry landing teams on beaches where opposition might conceivably be met.

Even if troops trained in the technique of the amphibian assault had been available, and a frontal attack across a defended beach had been justifiable on other grounds, hydrographic conditions around Munda would have prevented such a course of action. Nor was the navy yet confident of its ability to render adequate gunfire assistance.[140] This was admitted by a ranking naval officer in the South Pacific, Rear Admiral Theodore S. Wilkinson USN, who became Commander of the Amphibious Force, South Pacific Area in July 1943, thus allowing Kelly Turner to take up the more important role of commanding the amphibious aspects of the coming drive across the Central Pacific.

Also, it was just as well that at this juncture army troops predominated in the South Pacific. The area headquarters was handicapped by an inefficient top marine command. The First Marine Amphibious Corps had been created on paper in October 1942, and had been acti-

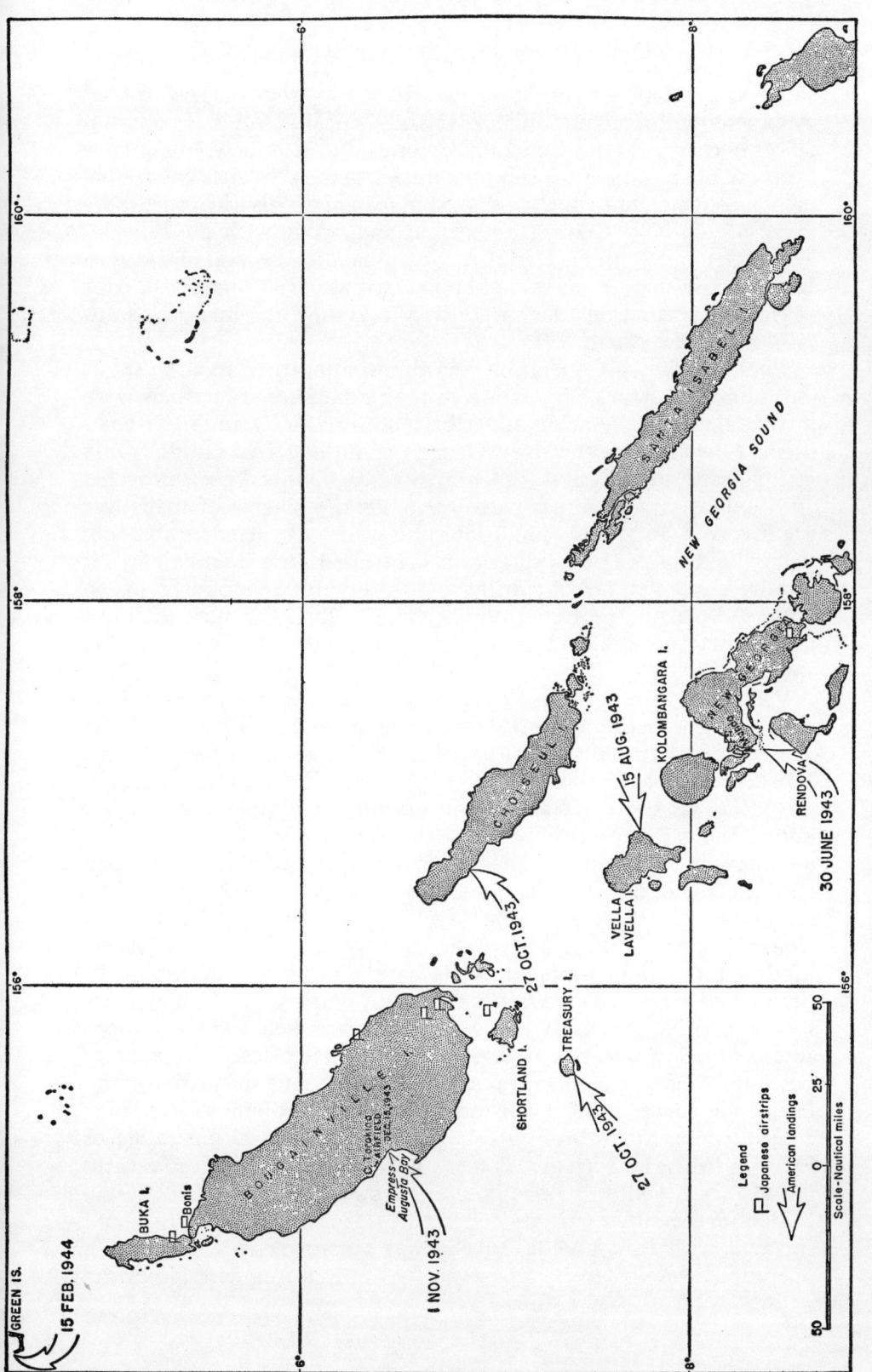

Map 8. Landings, Central and Northern Solomons, June 1943 to February 1944.

vated in the field the following month. It was from the start a dual command, with both administrative and tactical duties.[141] The initial officer in charge, Major General Clayton B. Vogel USMC, seems to have been unable to master his complex duties, and weeks after the recommendation had gone in, was relieved of his post. This was done in the midst of the New Georgia operation; and, along with the relief of Major General John H. Hester USA, commanding general of the 43rd Infantry Division, it was brought about with such an unpleasant odor of charred reputations that, according to Halsey, the lingering scent "still makes me cough." [142]

The New Georgia operation was almost altogether an army show. (See map 8.) It was complex. More than a half-dozen landings were involved, with two marine raider battalions participating in three of them. The hope was that New Georgia could be seized rapidly. Only insignificant opposition was met on any beach, as had been expected after extensive amphibian patrolling; but the scheme of maneuver was involved, and jungle conditions plus well-constructed military obstacles held up progress. Americans controlled the sea and air, yet it required over a month of fighting and the employment of over 30,000 army and marine troops, outnumbering the Japanese more than five to one, before the Munda airfield was finally seized in early August 1943.

Vella Lavella was taken in mid-August. It was an easy operation, thanks to the first opportunity that arose in the South Pacific for the application of an old strategical principle. This was by-passing. The Japanese command at Rabaul was determined to make every island in the Solomons another Guadalcanal or another Munda, costly if not impregnable. For this reason, before the New Georgia fighting reached a climax, they busied themselves fortifying and reinforcing Kolombangara Island, a circular land mass just north of Munda and less than fifty miles southeast of Vella Lavella. Halsey simply leapfrogged Kolombangara, bottling up the enemy thereon and leaving them behind to starve. In planning the Vella Lavella undertaking, amphibian patrols and aerial reconnaissance were fully employed. Through these mediums, suitable naval base and airsites were chosen, and army troops accompanied by a marine defense battalion were placed ashore unopposed on August 15. New Zealand soldiers were used in driving the last of the enemy from the island. The Central Solomons were now controlled by the Allies, but Rabaul was not yet within range of Halsey's fighters, which at this stage of the war was a condition essential to effective and sustained bombing from shore bases.[143]

Despite the rather curious story of the seizure of New Georgia, and the ease with which Vella Lavella was taken, these two mid-1943 operations were of great importance not only to the winning of the

Pacific War but also to the development of amphibian techniques. The Japanese in evacuating Guadalcanal, did not simultaneously give up the rest of the Solomons. Rather, they retreated step by step and took blow after blow. Thus the attrition begun in the Southeastern Solomons continued up the Slot, with the outcome of each separate encounter progressively more and more favorable to the American cause. The United States Navy substantially improved its night destroyer torpedo tactics, and this along with the professional use of improved radar on all warships in night gunnery actions spelled the end of more and more Japanese shipping: warships, transports, and cargo vessels. Coordinated night tactics between destroyers and motor torpedo boats, and cooperative daylight attacks by these tiny surface craft and planes, began tearing apart the enemy's barge and small boat traffic.

Naval air losses in the Solomons were even more serious to the Japanese than their surface reversals. Early in 1943 the Imperial Navy had called upon the Imperial Army for a few aircraft and airmen to toss into the Solomons fighting; but throughout the struggle for those islands the antagonist facing Americans in the sky remained, chiefly, naval planes flown by navy pilots. Not only did the Japanese navy sacrifice the cream of its land-based air squadrons in a vain effort to hold the Solomons, but also threw carrier components onto land bases and then into the slaughter. Plane losses were not critical, since home production was mounting; but experienced navy pilots were lost, and this was a stunning blow from which the enemy's navy never fully recovered.

With increasing frequency, United States Marine, Navy and Army pilots encountered poorly-trained Japanese in the air. Not only that, but the Americans now manned superior aircraft. The marines, for example, began flying the Corsair fighter before the New Georgia operation began. The performance of this craft was in every department better than the Zero. Not even the Japanese night bombers were safe, as the Americans, assisted greatly by the English who had turned the trick in the Battle for Britain, perfected their radar and began shooting hostile raiders out of the starlit skies of the South Pacific. Another outstanding British assist was the introduction of magnetic mines in Japanese-held waters. These were sown from surface craft or from the air, and were satanic in construction. Five enemy ships might pass over them in safety, but a sixth would trip the explosive mechanism and be blown skyward. Also they were set to demolish themselves before advancing American shipping entered the mined waters.[144]

Better planes in the hands of marine pilots, and more of them, permitted improved all-round performance. Although assisted by army and navy planes and pilots, the air aspect of the advance up the Solomons was predominantly a Marine Corps job. A notable record was turned in as regards combat air patrols over amphibious shipping, as well as in sinking enemy vessels and in bombing Japanese ground targets. Equally important, marine airmen began improving their techniques of close air support.

On New Georgia, close air support was a mixture of success and failure. Strikes by marine and navy pilots against enemy installations along the various beaches were usually effective, but efforts to knock out emplacements hidden in the jungle and holding up the advance of American foot troops were disappointing. A recommendation of Vandegrift's from Guadalcanal was being met. This called for the attachment of air liaison parties to the staffs of tactical commanders ashore, with direct communications to airmen in the sky. Marine air liaison parties were being formed in the United States, and were being given rudimentary training; but since none had arrived in the South Pacific by mid-June 1943, such parties were improvised. Their radio equipment, however, was poor, and their efforts to designate inland targets by smoke were unsatisfactory, especially since the Japanese quickly caught on and confused the pilots by throwing a few smoke shells themselves.

One example will show not only the failure of the air liaison party at this early stage of the game, but also the inherent fallacy underlying the concept of the marine raider battalion—being designed to raid rather than to take and hold terrain, it lacked combined arms such as artillery. The First Marine Raider Battalion, now commanded by Lieutenant Colonel Harry B. Liversedge and rested in New Caledonia, was brought back for the New Georgia operation. To it was attached a battalion of the 148th Infantry Regiment, and with these two battalions Liversedge was assigned the mission of making a separate landing and cutting the enemy's land communications between Munda and Rice Anchorage, some fifteen miles due north of the Munda airstrip. It was an important mission, for otherwise the enemy might reinforce the primary objective, Munda, from his base at Rice Anchorage; but Liversedge was given a man-size job without the necessary artillery. He ran into a well-entrenched enemy and bogged down. Another marine raider battalion and a second United States Army infantry battalion were sent in, but still the Americans could not advance. Air strike after air strike was brought down on the enemy hidden in the jungle, but to no effect. Liversedge was a competent officer leading aggressive men, but he had to call off his attack because he lacked artillery.[145]

Other than the prospect of much better close air support, additional improvements in amphibious techniques and tactics ashore were introduced in the conquest of the Central Solomons. On New Georgia a set of ground tactics was outlined which later would be polished and become routine in the Central Pacific. This was the integration of artillery, tanks, and infantry equipped with flamethrowers to overcome strong enemy positions; but such work on New Georgia was handicapped by the lack of medium tanks with which to crush well-constructed installations. Also on New Georgia, Americans for the first time in the Pacific War set up shore-based artillery on an unoccupied beach in order to neutralize or destroy possible enemy opposition on an adjacent island. Great as is the value of naval gunfire, shore-based artillery should be used whenever possible, particularly if an amphibian assault is expected to develop.[146]

Improvements in amphibious techniques were notable. Newly devised ships and craft, mass produced, and recently delivered to the combat areas were responsible for these advancements. It was now possible to embark supplies and men on landing vessels capable (with favorable hydrographic conditions) of being beached, and these were then disembarked directly onto the target without the necessity of being transferred from a transport into small boats or landing craft. These new logistical and in some cases, tactical weapons, along with the prewar design and mass production of amphibian tractors, led to unprecedented economies in the use of transport and cargo vessels, lessened the tremendous labors facing shore parties, and greatly speeded all aspects of beach logistics, thus facilitating what had probably been the most vulnerable part of an amphibious operation.

Heading the list of the new craft was the diesel-powered seagoing infantry landing craft (LCI), with space for almost 200 men and more than thirty tons of cargo, and with twin ladders on either side of the bow, which lowered to discharge its complement directly onto the beach. Ultimately the dual-purpose antiaircraft guns of this craft would, in some cases, be supplemented by 4.5-inch rockets, providing an auxiliary beach fire which, although of limited destructive potential, had a devastating psychological impact on the defenders.

More useful was the seaworthy tank landing ship (LST), followed early in 1944 by two similar vessels, the larger dock landing ship (LSD) and the smaller medium landing ship (LSM). The tank landing ship (LST) cruised at roughly ten knots, had a shallow forward draft, was ramp-equipped, and was capable of beaching to disgorge its vehicles and personnel directly ashore. It was also commodious enough to transport, by one means or another, not only amphibian tractors but also any one or all of the following newly devised craft.

None of the others was fully seaworthy. Next in size and brought across the Pacific lashed to the tank landing ships, were the tank landing craft (LCT) capable of lifting four tanks or 150 tons of cargo. Next in descending order of size were the medium landing craft (LCM), followed by the vehicle and personnel landing craft (LCVP).

As early as 1936 the marines had initiated the experiments leading to these new developments, and after 1939 an added impetus was given to the program by British ingenuity and interest; but delays were inevitable. Aircraft production and warship construction had higher priorities, nor was it possible to standardize the types until combat experience had dictated the needs and the army had decided on the size and characteristics of tanks and vehicles to be used in landing operations. In terms of procurement, the marines had no choice but to use the weapons that the army accepted. Thus eighteen months elapsed between Pearl Harbor and the time the new amphibious craft and ships were rolling off production lines in a quantity sufficient for use in combat.[147]

These new landing ships and craft made it easier to by-pass, a strategy that lends itself readily to amphibious warfare. At little risk and with great economy of means, sea-air power is then able to harass the isolated enemy, shatter his morale, and leave him to die, unsupplied and ineffectual, far behind the zone of combat. Unlike warfare on continental land masses, enemy groups isolated on islands by amphibious warfare have no opportunity to engage in partisan or guerrilla tactics. And, where for the purpose of obtaining land-based air installations it was necessary to land on a relatively large island occupied by the enemy, the Vella Lavella operation saw the Americans in the South Pacific introduce yet another refinement. Experience had shown that captured Japanese fields were not nearly up to American requirements. With sufficient naval construction personnel on hand, trained in infantry tactics by marines and assigned as either corps or division units, the question arose: Why land and immediately overrun an enemy defense of one of his airfields, when better air installations will result at less cost by going ashore on a large island at a suitable point distant from the enemy and constructing an altogether new field? At Vella Lavella, New Zealand troops were given the distasteful job of mopping up the island; but at Bougainville this strategy was perfected still further. There a strong perimeter was established around a recently built airfield, and the Americans sat down and waited. It was the Japanese who were forced to march over mountains and through jungle mud, hauling heavy equipment. Then, tired and diseased, they dashed out their brains against the American perimeter.

Launching the Bougainville operation was complicated by limited means. The Third Marine Division, reinforced, was ready for amphibious employment and land-based air power was great, but operations in the Central Pacific were pending, and especially in amphibious shipping and surface supporting and covering men-of-war, other strength was small.

The enemy in the Northern Solomons was powerful, but relatively immobile. He had been successful in withdrawing some troops from both the Southeast and Central Solomons, and these had brought his total up the chain to something in the vicinity of 50,000 men. (See map 8.) On Bougainville and its neighboring islands south and north, six airdromes were operational, and several others were under construction. Further, the enemy would be able to deploy fighters directly from Rabaul over most of the Northern Solomons. The Allies were confident that the Japanese could be outfought in the air and on the sea, but his ground superiority seemed to necessitate a series of limited offensives. In all probability, without MacArthur's intervention, the first step out of the Central Solomons would have committed scarce men and supplies to a target of secondary strategical value.

MacArthur was anxious to get through the obstacle posed by the Vitiaz-Dampier Straits. He insisted that Halsey place himself during the closing months of 1943 in a position to send land-based fighters over Rabaul. For this reason he excused Halsey from any assistance to unfolding Southwest Pacific operations, and in effect ordered him directly onto the island of Bougainville.[148]

The exact location of the landings was yet to be determined. In the absence of continuous carrier cover it was essential that the beaches be within fighter radius of Munda and Vella Lavella bases. That restricted the region to south central or to southern Bougainville.

Southern Bougainville and its off-lying islands were too heavily defended to be struck with the means at hand, even if common sense had not dictated avoiding an amphibious assault if it were humanly possible. North of this zone, however, South Pacific headquarters was unable to decide between the lower east central and the lower west central coast. (See map 8.) In the long run, this indecision was beneficial to the Americans. Two plans were drawn. The west coast, with a landing in the northern portion of Empress Augusta Bay, was selected; but the plan for an eastern landing sufficient to divert the enemy from the principal movement was retained.[149]

The scheme of maneuver selected by the attack force and landing force commanders was involved but brilliant. Cooperation between these two officers, navy and marine, left nothing to be desired. Wilkinson, who had taken over Turner's job in mid-1943, showed a far better grasp of conditions surrounding amphibious operations adjacent to large land masses than his predecessor had ever exhibited. The man who relieved Vogel, Major General Charles D. Barrett, Commanding General, First Marine Amphibious Corps, South Pacific, initiated the planning for the Bougainville operation, but suffered an accidental fall which led to death from cerebral hemorrhage on October 8. He was followed by Vandegrift, now a lieutenant general, to whose experience and keen sense of tactical judgment most of the credit for the success of the Bougainville undertaking, which began on November 1, 1943, should be attributed.

With Vandegrift in charge, and working on a parallel echelon with a cooperative naval attack force commander, it is hardly accidental that the Bougainville operation resembled that of Guadalcanal—minus most of the errors.

Aside from similarity of terrain, the strongest resemblance to Guadalcanal is that from the outset the plan, by design rather than by reaction of the enemy, called for a perimeter around an airfield. This time the marines were evacuated once the perimeter had been expanded to its strongest terrain features. The major landings were removed from the known center of enemy strength, and land communications on Bougainville were such that an estimated three months would elapse before the Japanese could move the bulk of their strength into positions needed before attacking the perimeter.

Also, the plans made provision for moving in an army division on the eighth day of the operation. Thus the Third Marine Division seized and held the beachhead against attacks from the air and against counterlandings by sea, both of which were anticipated and both developed. Then, as the marines fanned out to secure the perimeter, their units were displaced laterally, turning over to the army the relatively quiet sectors. The marines devoted their full attention to occupying the difficult but commanding terrain and to enlarging the perimeter so as to prevent the enemy from eventually registering artillery on the airstrips. The problems on Guadalcanal would have been fewer if Mount Austen and the lower reaches of the Matanikau could have been thus secured early in that operation.

Further army assistance in the Bougainville operation was fundamental to the plan. Once the airstrips were operational and marine fighters were ready to clear the enemy's combat air patrol from Rabaul, marine ground troops, save for the highly trained antiaircraft and coast defense battalion, were evacuated altogether. This was economical employment of well-trained amphibious personnel. A corps of army troops, backed by artillery, moved into a prepared perimeter and waited for the Japanese to attack. Since the seas remained under American control, the heavy fighting came just as had been anticipated. It took the enemy three months to deploy two divisions from southern Bougainville and adjacent positions for an all-out assault on the perimeter. Once the Japanese had spent themselves struggling with heavy equipment over mountains and jungle trails and ramming into the stone wall of a prepared defense, the army troops in turn were moved out to fight in the Philippines, and the perimeter was turned over to raw Australian militia. The Bougainville perimeter stands as an example of the manner in which the entire Solomons fighting should have been waged, if the means and the time had been available.

Nor does the story end there. The shortage in amphibious shipping was greater for this operation than at Guadalcanal, but Vandegrift and Wilkinson were as good in logistical as in tactical planning. Only eight transports and four cargo vessels were available to lift an entire division, reinforced, plus the necessary antiaircraft defensive units, engineers, and air service personnel and equipment for construction of the airfield. To solve the logistical problem thus created, a branch unit of a marine base depot was rolled forward to Vella Lavella; and, after amphibian patrols had investigated the terrain, a brigade of New Zealand troops was sent into the Treasury Islands five days before the major landing was made, for the purpose of carving out an advanced naval base. (See map 8.) These islands are situated some seventy-five miles southwest of the selected Bougainville beaches. They were well located to allow motor torpedo boats to harass the enemy in the region of southern Bougainville, to prevent Japanese barge traffic into the main zone of conflict, and to protect the right flank of the sea approach from the mounting bases in the rear, via Vella Lavella to Empress Augusta Bay. Thus the occupation of the Treasuries helped to immobilize the enemy and assisted in shuttling the transport and cargo vessels rapidly back and forth a second and a third time between Vella Lavella and Bougainville. These vessels and tank landing ships ferried the troops, supplies, and equipment needed to hold the perimeter and to build the airstrips.[150]

The Treasury Islands fulfilled another important function. On one of them, before the main operation began, long-range radar was installed. This warned the commanders in Empress Augusta Bay of enemy planes approaching from Rabaul and improved the performance of combat air patrols over the beaches and the amphibious shipping.[151]

One final item was of importance in the period preceding the major landing. Unless a diversion were made, the seizure of the Treasury Islands, southwestward of Bougainville, would alert the enemy and help him to analyze the situation, perhaps causing him to move all available forces into Empress Augusta Bay. To prevent such an outcome, two days after the Treasuries were occupied, the Second Marine Parachute Battalion boarded destroyer transports and made a raid on the northwest coast of Choiseul. This carrot-shaped island stretches for some eighty miles south and slightly east of Bougainville. These paratroopers like all their colleagues in the Marine Corps were never chuted into action, principally because there was never an inland communications center in the South or Central Pacific suitable for such an attack. It was far safer to land them on Choiseul by boat, and once ashore they created sound and fury enough to convince the Japanese that a landing in force was under way, preparatory to a main effort on the east, rather than on the west coast of Bougainville.[152]

The Bougainville landing was made on and to the north of Cape Torokina, Empress Augusta Bay, at slightly more than an hour after sunrise, during the morning of November 1, 1943. (See map 8.) For weeks previously, marine, army, and navy land-based pilots under Major General Ralph J. Mitchell USMC, Commander Aircraft, Solomons Area, had been neutralizing enemy air bases in southern Bougainville and on islands close by. A cruiser and destroyer task force assisted this process by bombarding both the southern Bougainville area and the Buka-Bonis region to the north of Bougainville just before the landings began; and planes from fleet carriers, which approached from the eastward, worked over the Buka-Bonis base shortly thereafter.[153]

Little was known of the beaches and terrain selected, not because of the lack of amphibious and aerial reconnaissance, but because the decision as to the exact location of the landings had been so long delayed. An amphibious patrol had been sent in during late September, in common with two others, one to the east central coast of Bougainville and another to the northwest coast of Choiseul; but the Cape Torokina patrol had been overloaded with missions and was unaggressively led. The beaches at the time were undefended, the interior was suitable for airstrips, and little else was learned. Fortunately, the submarine *Guardfish* which took this patrol to Empress Augusta Bay was commanded by an alert officer, who took low-level photographs of the beaches. These revealed reef conditions unsuspected from aerial photographs, and this information was of great value in marking out the transport and naval gunfire areas, and in planning the ship-to-shore movement. Also, the submarine captain was a good navigator. He noticed that the Army Air Force chart then in use was seven miles off as to the location of Cape Torokina, an error which, undetected, might well have upset the entire landing.

Aerial reconnaissance subsequent to this amphibious patrol showed unmistakable enemy activity in the vicinity of Cape Torokina, but it later developed that the enemy was preparing in a limited way for a landing to the south of that cape, rather than to the north. Unaware of this fact, Vandegrift was worried. The navy had been able to furnish him with only four destroyers for naval gunfire support, although one heavy and two light cruisers and six destroyers had been requested. Nor had any of the assigned destroyers participated in a shore bombardment before the rehearsal in Efate, New Hebrides, October 17-19.

Belatedly, Vandegrift sent in a second amphibious patrol. Its members subsequently came into the perimeter, but it never forwarded any information. Radio communications failed. Under such circumstances, the instructions were to signal the incoming attack force by smoke if the beaches were defended by less than 300 men. From the transport area early on the morning of November 1, Vandegrift looked in vain for smoke. None was visible. The patrol was either captured, or the beach more heavily defended than expected.[154]

Vandegrift had reason for concern. He was relying heavily on intelligence that indicated little or no resistance at the beach, and had so arranged his landing waves as to expedite the handling of beach logistics. His chief fear in planning had been Japanese air reaction from the vicinity of Rabaul. In addition, he was going into an operation with a recently formed outfit, inexperienced as yet in combat. Most noticeable was the fact that the Third Division lacked a competent shore party. Neither Marine Corps Headquarters in Washington nor the staff of the top marine command in the South Pacific had taken cognizance of one of the principal lessons of the landing on Guadalcanal. Since Vandegrift took over command of the First Marine Amphibious Corps only a few weeks before the landing was scheduled for Bougainville, he is not open to criticism in this regard; rather, given his intelligence, he is to be commended for that fact that he refused to see the confusion of Guadalcanal beach repeated. There is no evidence that he allocated to the division commander, Major General Allen H. Turnage USMC, more than a modicum of control over beachhead logistics.

This time Vandegrift from the outset called upon combat marines to engage in the mundane labor of logistics, but in doing so he had necessarily lowered the striking impact of his ship-to-shore movement. So the lack of word from his amphibian patrol ashore worried him. He had already assigned forty per cent of the men comprising the first echelon to work the holds of the ships, to accompany the cargo to the beach, and to sweat with the shore party. These were mostly non-riflemen, everything from replacement companies to personnel more important to actual fighting, such as artillerymen and stretcher bearers. Amphibian tractors were to come in later, with the tank landing ship echelons; but even so, some of the tractor crews would be kept busy for the first eleven days of the operation, carting supplies from the beach to inland dumps.

Vandegrift would have had no cause for alarm had his patrol, which was intact, been able to carry out instructions. He had made the correct decision in stressing efficiency in beach logistics, even at a sacrifice of tactical momentum at the water's edge. At most there were not many more than 300 Japanese (if that) in the vicinity of the beaches.

Not only was there plenty of labor for handling supplies and equipment, the total materiel carried in the first echelon was reduced to a bare minimum. The few amphibious ships available were filled to full complement with personnel, and at that they could lift only two-thirds of the division, roughly 14,000 men; but their cargo space was left largely empty. The idea was to carry no more than could be unloaded in a single span of twenty-four hours, interrupted as it would surely be by air attacks. The total tonnage was 6,200, an average of under 525 tons for each of the twelve transports and cargo vessels involved. This consisted of the supplies and organic equipment necessary to live and fight for ten days, plus enough ammunition to last, normally, for only three days (that is, three units of fire).

Rubber boats, medium landing craft, and vehicle and personnel landing craft were accumulated in sufficient number to set one-half the first echelon ashore in the initial wave. Nor did Vandegrift this time wait a full day before extending the length of the beach. Eight battalion landing teams reached the shore simultaneously, using a total of twelve beaches, one for each transport and cargo vessel available, although several of them later proved impracticable for the purpose selected.[155]

The logistic planning was excellent. Had the naval gunfire from the supporting destroyers preliminary to the landing been even passably accurate, little trouble would have developed. The naval attack force commander, in a masterpiece of understatement, observed that the "gunnery performance of our destroyers left much to be desired." Then he expressed himself more adequately: "Some ships fired short for almost five minutes with all salvos landing in the water. . . . Although a short bombardment practice had been fired at Efate it was not sufficient."[156]

Clearly, the naval gunfire overlay for Torokina Point noted "Gun Positions under Construction."[157] This turned out to be a single 75-millimeter weapon, but even after it had opened up, it went unscathed. At least one commander aboard ship was relieved when the marine pilots brought their planes in on schedule, and began bombing and strafing the beach; but as the aircraft departed and the first wave was about 500 yards offshore, the Japanese again fired their rifles, machine guns, mortars, and the lone 75-millimeter gun. Four planes each armed with a 2,000-pound bomb had also missed this target. Even so, close air support by marine pilots was better in the landing phase than was its naval gunfire counterpart. From the beginning, air liaison parties who had trained with the division served ashore with combat troops, and, having direct contact with the planes on station, arranged for the immediate delivery of call strikes.[158]

The Japanese 75-millimeter gun, assisted by small arms and mortar fire, created confusion on the morning of November 1. Boats were disabled, command of the assault wave broke down, several dozen casualties were suffered, and the men went ashore in a mixture of units. Tactical control by higher echelons was impossible, but the marines knew what to do. Rifle groups were quickly formed and the Japanese were dug from their crude pillboxes. A marine crept up to the 75-millimeter gun and killed or dispersed its crew before he died of his wounds.[159]

Thereafter the operation went as planned, although some heavy fighting was ahead before the marines cleared the perimeter. An enemy effort at a counterlanding was weak. The roughly 500 Japanese hastily set ashore at night to the west of the beaches were cut apart and wiped out. But the enemy moved all personnel immediately available into the surrounding terrain, and these had to be blasted by artillery or dug out by flamethrowers, tanks, or charges of explosives.[160] On one occasion, close air support by marine pilots directed onto an enemy strong point by air liaison parties (now well-equipped with communication facilities) was so perfect that it eliminated a group of Japanese which even artillery and mortars had failed to reach. The pity was that these expert marine bombers could not be transferred to escort carriers to support their marine comrades across the beaches of the Central Pacific; but the tactical situation early in the mid-Pacific drive demanded that all carriers be manned by pilots whose principal skill was in sinking ships (in which activity, it must be added, these Solomons airmen excelled, although the naval high command believed navy pilots were better). Later, a few marine pilots were carrier borne, at the time of Iwo Jima and Okinawa; but the experienced marine airmen of the Solomons never had an opportunity to show what they could do in supporting men engaged in the amphibious assault. From the Solomons they were shifted to the Philippines, where their performance in close air support amazed and delighted United States Army troops.[161]

Another event occurred at Bougainville to remind Vandegrift of Guadalcanal. The Japanese sent a cruiser task force toward Empress Augusta Bay; but this time the Americans were alert, although the crews had participated in two shore bombardments over the course of as many days. Commanded by Rear Admiral Aaron S. Merrill USN, the force of cruisers and destroyers which had been assigned to cover the amphibious expedition met the Japanese during the early morning darkness of November 2 and turned them back with severe losses.

The most damaging enemy reaction was, as expected, from the air. The marines had attacked the threshold of Rabaul, where the Japanese possessed five principal airdromes as yet scarcely harmed from the sky. Air reaction to the landing, and confusion caused by enemy fire from the shore, prevented the few supplies aboard the transports and cargo ships from being unloaded on the first day. Some of these vessels returned the second day, but the Japanese continued to harass the beach and to keep the ships maneuvering rather than at anchor and unloading. The plan was for MacArthur's land-based planes, which had been attacking Rabaul for over a year, to begin pounding that harbor heavily on October 15, and to continue to neutralize it for a month. MacArthur's air commander, General George C. Kenney, set up a detailed timetable to fulfill this mission, but bad weather between his bases and the target interfered frequently, and Halsey was bitterly disappointed with the support he was getting.

Immediate and drastic counteraction against the Japanese at Rabaul was necessary. Combat air over the beaches at Bougainville and emplaced antiaircraft guns could not handle the problem alone. To beat down enemy air strength in Rabaul and to disrupt a second cruiser surface raid which the Japanese were obviously preparing in that harbor, Halsey, with some trepidation, sent carriers northward into the waters of the Solomon Sea for an early dawn raid on the New Britain fortress. The peril of dispatching carriers into the Solomon Sea in November 1943 was small compared to that in August 1942. Japanese bases, except those on the Bismarck Archipelago, were either overrun or neutralized. The eastern portion of the Solomon Sea, in contrast to the western, had few shoals and little foul ground. Finally, the operation involved was a quick strike rather than a sustained endeavor, and the old heavy carrier *Saratoga* plus the new light carrier *Princeton* were furnished a strong combat air patrol by navy pilots based on Munda and Vella Levella. Rear Admiral Frederick C. Sherman USN was able to put ninety-seven planes over Rabaul on November 5. Despite bad weather, these carrier pilots drilled in and damaged four heavy and two light cruisers, and two destroyers. Admiral Merrill's exhausted covering force need fear no further enemy surface effort against Empress Augusta Bay.

But enemy planes flying from the airfields around Rabaul were still a menace to the amphibious shipping off Bougainville. Combat air patrols could not stop them all. Nimitz hastened reinforcements to Halsey. Three fleet carriers, *Essex*, *Bunker Hill*, and *Independence*, under Rear Admiral Alfred E. Montgomery USN, were scheduled to help with the invasion of the Gilbert Islands in the Central Pacific on November 20, but they were loaned to the South Pacific for a few days in the interim. On November 11, Sherman and Montgomery made a coordinated approach against Rabaul from the east and from the south. Foul weather and a scarcity of shipping made pickings meager, but airfields were bombed and strafed, and more than fifty Japanese planes were shot out of the sky. Japanese air reaction against the Bougainville beachhead then subsided.[162]

On November 10, Vandegrift relinquished his command and returned to Washington to take up new duties as Commandant of the Marine Corps. His successor in the South Pacific was Roy S. Geiger, the marine airman whose improvisation on Henderson Field had earned him promotion to major general. Early in December, Geiger turned a completed Bougainville perimeter over to the XIV United States Army Corps. Along with these prepared positions, the marines and their naval construction comrades left extensive beach facilities, road nets, and one finished and two partially completed airstrips. The marines had counted approximately 2,500 Japanese dead, and had suffered losses amounting to 118 killed or missing and 907 wounded in action.[163]

United States Army Air Force bombers (assigned to the Fifth Air Force in the Southwest Pacific and the Thirteenth Air Force in the South Pacific) had been attacking Rabaul for months before the landing on Bougainville was made. Airsites on that island enabled the fighters and light bombers of the South Pacific to take up where the carrier pilots left off. At the beginning of November the Japanese had some 373 naval type planes at Rabaul. By the end of that month the Rabaul air garrison had ceased to be a strong offensive weapon, though still strong enough to be a threat of considerable proportions. This was caused principally by the forays of the carrier forces and the losses to marine aircraft covering the Bougainville beachhead. The first American airstrip at Torokina was completed on December 10, and from that time on marine and army fighters and light bombers laced Rabaul without mercy. Japanese air strength declined so rapidly that MacArthur could safely start his operations against Dampier Strait on December 15. Raids from the South Pacific, aided by Sherman's carriers, continued throughout December. New Year's eve was no time for joy at Rabaul. January saw its air strength dwindle to insignificance, and its shipping destroyed or chased away. The only mobility left the Japanese in Rabaul was by submarine and barge. Photographs taken at the end of February revealed 427 barges, but even this traffic was slowly strangled and three months later no more than eighty-six barges could be located. No mail from Japan got through to Rabaul after February 1944.

Thus marine airmen climaxed their work in the Solomons. They were responsible for a large slice of all the Japanese amphibious shipping lost to air strikes in that area from late August 1942 through the early months of 1944. To a far greater degree, they deserve credit for having knocked the enemy out of the sky in the Solomons and over

Rabaul. Claims and counterclaims of losses inflicted on the enemy vary. The Navy and the United States Marine Corps figures do not agree, and Japanese admissions of losses are so contradictory as to defy interpretation. Careful research into this problem by Robert Sherrod in his study of Marine Corps Aviation in the Second World War has resulted in no firm conclusion. It is well, under the circumstances, merely to list Marine Corps claims, and to comment that the evidence indicates these are not very far out of line with what actually happened. Japan in the Solomons and over Rabaul lost something in the neighborhood of 2,500 planes, of which marine aviators claimed 1,520⅓ in aerial combat alone. Total marine aviation figure for enemy planes shot down in the Pacific War is 2,382⅓ planes, so that it is apparent that over sixty-four per cent of the results by the Marine Corps throughout the war were gained in the Solomons.

Figures, even if true, can be deceptive. The contribution of Marine Corps aviation in the Solomons should not rest on so obviously a weak foundation as unreliable statistics. Two more significant considerations are at hand. To Americans, Japanese plane and pilot losses during the dark days at Guadalcanal were many times more important than later enemy losses; and it was in the early weeks of the critical Guadalcanal struggle that marine fighters virtually alone began shooting down Japanese bombers and Zeros. Secondly, the enemy's aircraft losses in the Solomons were predominantly naval, and more significantly, navy pilots. In other words it was the destruction of planes in flight, not on the ground, that bore fruit. This immobilized the Japanese carriers. In accomplishing this, marine fighters played an important role. In terms of numbers they were the majority throughout the ascent of the Solomons, and man for man and plane for plane they were certainly the equal of any American in aerial combat. Thus they were, after all, of great benefit to their comrades who stormed beaches in the Central Pacific, even though absent when that drive transpired. They had already drained land-based Japanese air into the Solomons from the mid-Pacific, had killed off trained navy pilots, and had thus made more feasible the operations of navy fast carrier forces in isolating amphibious targets in the Central Pacific.

Attrition of Japan's naval pilots in the Solomons was so great that when the Japanese navy again sortied carriers for action, at the Battle of the Philippine Sea in June 1944, the resulting slaughter of some 400 inexperienced Japanese pilots was dubbed by United States Navy airmen as the "Marianas Turkey Shoot." Not until the Japanese took recourse during the final months of the war to kamikaze tactics did they manage, after the ordeal of the Solomons, again to come up with an effective naval air arm.[164]

8. Opening the Bismarck Barrier, Slamming the Door on Rabaul

With Rabaul under ceaseless attack from Bougainville, the time had come for the forces of the Southwest Pacific to break free from the restricting waters of the Solomon Sea. In December 1943 but one obstacle remained, clearing the Dampier Strait, which could be done only by controlling Cape Gloucester, the western tip of New Britain. (See maps 3 and 9.) For this task MacArthur, despite vigorous protests from the navy in Washington,[165] had retained the First Marine Division under his command. From the east and from the west, marines were used in principal operations which sealed Rabaul.

A year had elapsed since the First Marine Division was evacuated from Guadalcanal. After a few hectic weeks in the hot malaria-infested environs of Brisbane, Southwest Pacific headquarters had moved the rehabilitation camp to the cooler and more salubrious region of Melbourne.[166] There, under a new leader, the former assistant division commander, William H. Rupertus, now promoted to major general, replacements were received, rotation of personnel completed, and a period of intensive training conducted. Also, full advantage was taken of the recreation facilities offered by a metropolitan community. The marines were liked by the Australians. When their next operation was announced, a Melbourne newspaper carried the headline, "OUR Marines Invade New Britain." [167]

The First Division repeated few of the errors it had committed on Guadalcanal. The intelligence section functioned smoothly, assimilating the extensive data brought into headquarters by amphibious patrols and aerial reconnaissance; and in combat, intelligence personnel showed tremendous improvement. As their chief remarked, "the importance of enemy order of battle is comparatively recent doctrine with the First Marine Division." The logistics section likewise was a more smoothly functioning outfit, the shore party was well trained and integrated its work neatly with its navy counterpart, and every advantage was taken of new developments in landing craft.

Such improvements were everywhere apparent in the division. Individual marines amazed army observers with their discipline and cool determination under fire. There was a tendency to kill every Japanese who came into view, regardless of circumstances. This refusal to trust a surrendering enemy could be easily explained by a Guadalcanal background of devious tricks; but prisoners of war frequently contributed valuable tactical information. The intelligence section had attempted to indoctrinate the men with this fact, and was making progress in that direction.[168]

Planning and execution of the Cape Gloucester operation was conducted under the supervision of Lieutenant General Walter Kreuger

USA, who was MacArthur's chief subordinate in the field and who commanded the Sixth United States Army. Excellent air support was furnished by Kenney. The purpose of the undertaking was to seize the principal Japanese airfield on the western end of New Britain, in order to deny its use to the enemy, and in order to establish Allied naval and air bases to control the Dampier Strait. (See map 9.) The landing was scheduled for the day after Christmas, 1943. A preliminary operation two weeks earlier was originally designed to capture a secondary Japanese airfield at Gasmata, on the southwestern coast of New Britain, but because of a lack of shipping and amphibiously trained troops, was executed with the more limited purpose of seizing an advanced naval operating base at Arawe. The Arawe landing would serve two important ends. Motor torpedo boats would deny barge movements along the southwest coast of New Britain to the enemy, and would divert Japanese attention from the principal effort on the northwest coast.

The Arawe operation contained a flaw which is startling when contrasted with the seizure of Cape Gloucester. Army troops were employed, the 112th Cavalry Regiment, a part of the 1st Cavalry Division. The landing on the chief beaches was made after daylight and with the assistance of fire from naval guns and from infantry landing craft converted to gunboats; it was virtually unopposed, but an auxiliary landing by a group of 150 soldiers to the westward of the principal beaches suffered fifty per cent casualties.

The approach to Arawe had to be made during a period of a three-quarters moon, for the timing was dependent upon the schedule of the more important undertaking at Cape Gloucester. Seizure of the terrain to the westward of Arawe Peninsula was also mandatory, since it controlled a native trail and was the only way to immobilize the defenders. Otherwise, they could have joined their comrades in the vicinity of Gloucester, or could have been reinforced from that region. In spite of the facts that the auxiliary beach selected was the only suitable one in the vicinity and was certainly defended, and that in all probability the moon would silhouette boat targets for the Japanese, the army officer in charge of the landing force, against the advice of the naval attack force commander, insisted upon attempting to gain tactical surprise. He requested and was granted a predawn landing by rubber boats for his auxiliary beach, without naval gunfire preparation.

The expected happened. The first wave was taken under small arms fire from the beach, and casualties mounted. The warships on call for naval gunfire were unable to locate targets ashore, because in the words of the naval attack force commander, "the darkness and the merging of the landing boats with the jungle background made it im-

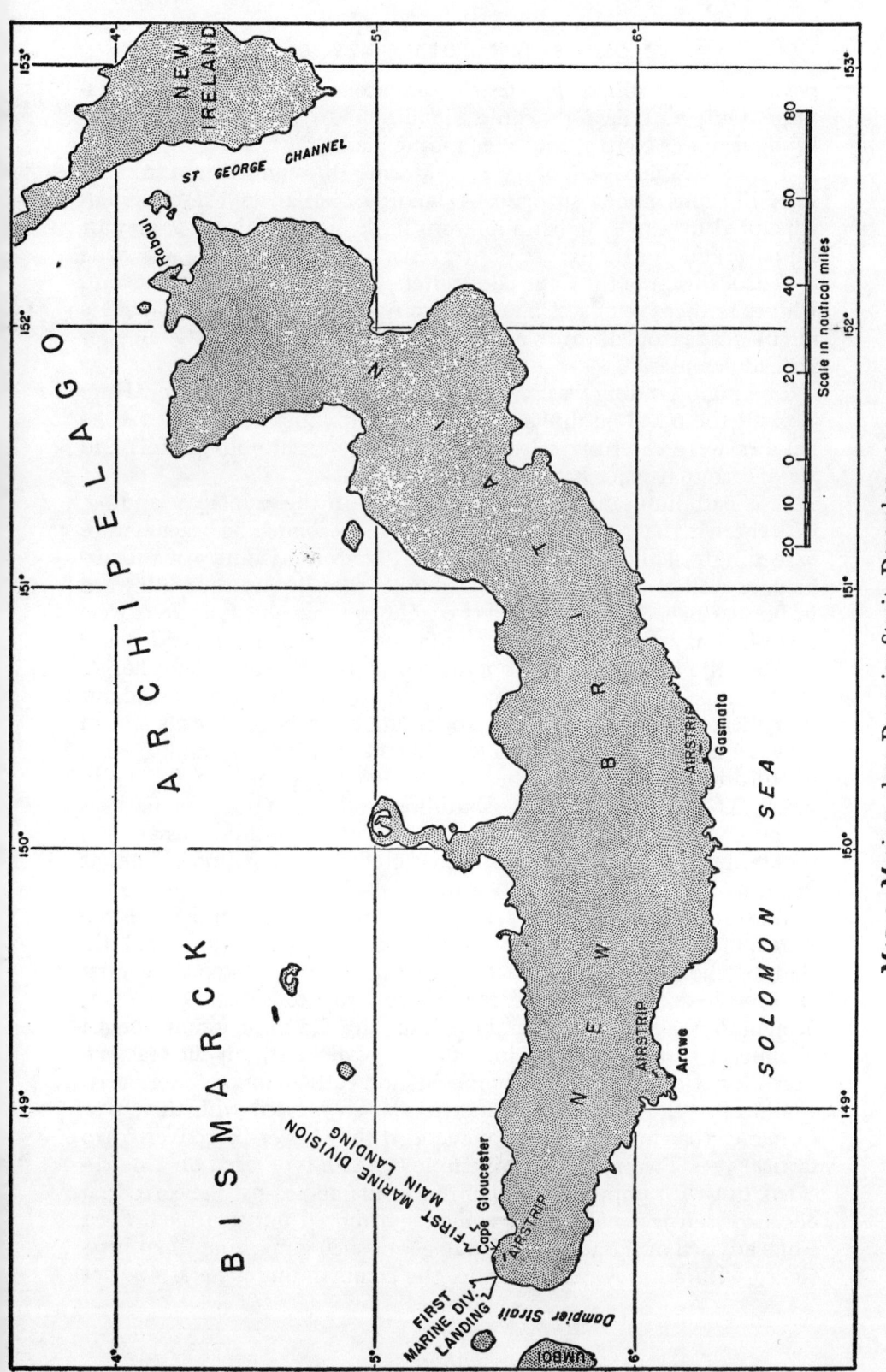

MAP 9. Marines clear Dampier Strait, December 1944.

possible for the supporting destroyer to accurately appraise the situation." Only with daylight could the mistake be remedied, the troops brought under control, and the landing made.[169]

The experienced staff of the First Marine Division suffered from no such illusions about surprise. A landing similar in principle was scheduled by a marine battalion, but in daylight, with naval and air support; and this time there was no resistance. This landing was made to the southwest of the Cape Gloucester airfield, along Dampier Strait, with the objective of sealing off the only trail by which the Japanese might escape from or throw additional men into their Cape Gloucester airfield defenses.

The main landing was on the east coast of Cape Gloucester. Here also, all the naval gunfire and air support obtainable was used. The beaches were carefully selected after both amphibious patrols and aerial reconnaissance had scoured the terrain.

Five battalion landing teams were used in the principal landing, with three in the initial waves and two in the second. The beaches were exceedingly shallow but were removed from the vicinity of the airfield, as well as from the better-defended coastline to the southward in Borgen Bay. Two heavy and two light cruisers plus four destroyers furnished naval gunfire; and medium and heavy bombers strafed and bombed the beaches, also dropping white phosphorus smoke charges on the suspected enemy observation post atop a hill which looked out over the coast. Just before the troops landed in rubber boats and in infantry landing craft, rockets were discharged from a gun-boat. No opposition was met at the beach; the defenders had fled their pillboxes. The First Division was building up a reputation for itself as an outfit which was lucky enough to avoid amphibious assaults, a reputation that would be rudely shattered in its third operation, at Peleliu.

With the beachhead seized, a perimeter defense was quickly established, tank landing ships came ashore, lowered their ramps, and discharged their amphibian tractors. Again these craft stood the First Division in good stead. It seemed almost always to rain at Gloucester, deep mud was everywhere; and when the sun did shine for any length of time, it turned the mud into a thick paste. Without the tractors, beach logistics, even with a competent and fully manned shore party, would have broken down. Rupertus was so pleased with their performance that he strongly recommended they never be converted to tactical use. Two models were employed: the type used on Guadalcanal, but with improved mechanism insulated against the corroding effects of salt water; and a new model, armored but unarmed. Even when advised of the tactical advantages of such a machine when jury-rigged with a heavy machine gun, the commanding general was not impressed. To make tactical weapons of the Alligators would greatly lower their cargo carrying capacity; [170] but in the Central Pacific, Rupertus' recommendation went unheeded.

Leaving three battalions to guard and enlarge the beachhead, two were deployed directly toward the airfield objective. Taking every advantage of artillery support, this was seized as expeditiously as the mud, and light enemy opposition, would allow. Three days after the landings one of the regiments, which had been retained by Kreuger in reserve, was placed ashore, and Rupertus began intensive patrolling of the western tip of New Britain. Principal components of the enemy were discovered marching overland towards Rabaul, and in a series of sweeping shore-to-shore movements, the fleeing Japanese were carved apart. Something less than MacArthur's generous communique estimate of 10,000 Japanese were killed or left to die of malnutrition, at the cost of slightly more than one-tenth that number of marine casualties.* [171]

Kreuger's liaison officers with Rupertus' command were uniformly impressed with the ability of these American troops. "The Marines are careful, brave fighters," declared one. He believed that "with combat experience army personnel will be just as good." Marines in the front lines, he continued, were superb. "These men were in splendid physical condition and were spoiling for a fight. They were like hunters, boring in relentlessly and apparently without fear. I never heard a wounded marine moan. The aid men, unarmed, were right up in the front lines getting the wounded. Fire discipline was excellent."

Another admired the manner in which the crews handled their medium tanks in jungle terrain; but reserved his wholehearted praise for the integration of the artillery regiment (the Eleventh Marines) with the division as a whole. "The 1st Marine Division," he observed, "is very artillery conscious. They claim to have the best artillery in existence and use it effectively at every turn." [172]

Three unopposed landings after the Gloucester operation closed the door on Rabaul. The first was the employment of New Zealand troops on February 15, 1944, to seize and occupy the Green Islands, lying between Buka and the southern tip of New Ireland, closer to Rabaul than Empress Augusta Bay, and hence of value as a fighter and light naval base. (See map 8.) No opposition was expected, and naval gunfire preparation was to be used only in an emergency, lest the natives be harmed.[173] Next was a Southwest Pacific undertaking, the occupation of the Admiralties, which were reconnoitered in force in late February 1944, and the situation appeared so favorable that rein-

---

* The First Marine Division on Cape Gloucester lost 311 killed and 924 wounded in action.

forcements were hastened in, the small Japanese garrison destroyed, and construction of a major naval base begun.[174] (See map 3.)

MacArthur thereupon instructed Halsey to go through with the planned seizure of Kavieng, situated on the northwestern tip of New Ireland, the principal remaining outlying base protecting Rabaul. Halsey demurred and made the counterproposal that the island of Emirau, one of the Saint Matthias group, be occupied and developed, thus simultaneously slamming Japan's front gate to both Rabaul and Kavieng. Since MacArthur was already through the Bismarck barrier, it is hard to see what could have been gained by attacking Kavieng. Both Rabaul and Kavieng were already subject to persistent bombing and although strong defensively (Rabaul, the better defended of the two, had 90,000 men, 350 antiaircraft guns, and more than 6,500 field pieces), were of no further offensive use to the enemy. Capturing Kavieng would have been a major undertaking, possibly as bloody for Americans as Palau. The decision to by-pass Rabaul had been made as early as August 1943, and Kavieng certainly fell in the same category. Fortunately, the Joint Chiefs agreed with Halsey. Emirau was seized in March 1944, the last offensive landing launched in the South Pacific subtheater.[175]

So weak were Rabaul and Kavieng in offensive potential that, in the words of the transport commander of the Emirau expedition, "the unique feature of this operation was the fact that insofar as known, not a single enemy contact, air, surface, underwater or ground, was made during the entire period from departure to return of the Task Group to Guadalcanal. . . ." [176]

Fittingly enough, the last South Pacific landing was made by marines, the Fourth Regiment. This outfit was given the same designation as the marines who surrendered on Corregidor and was composed of the raider battalions which had seen extensive duty throughout the march up the Solomons, almost invariably employed as normal infantry battalions. At last they were combined as a regiment and subjected to training as such, of which the Emirau landing was a part. The Fourth Marine Regiment later landed on Guam, and then became a part of the Sixth Marine Division, which participated in the Okinawa operation.

Much had been learned in the Solomons. Some of it, such as the tactics of jungle fighting and malaria control, would benefit Mac-Arthur's command more than it would the marines in future operations, for the type of terrain of interest to the marines changed radically with the mounting of the Central Pacific drive.

Other lessons were of equal value to both the marines and the army. These had to do with the use of the most advanced models of amphibious landing ships and craft, and the proper employment of personnel and logistical support in order more rapidly to utilize the ground seized. It was evidently foolish ever to cross a beach without full naval gunfire and air preparations; and likewise, with proper use of reconnaissance, it was inexcusable ever to select a beach known to be defended, unless circumstances were of the most compelling nature. This principle the marines had learned well. The army could continue to abide by the principle, but circumstances compelled the launching of amphibious assaults in the Central Pacific.

For this reason, landing operations in the Solomons-New Britain-New Guinea area were of importance over and beyond the direct strategical gains. Almost two years elapsed between the attack on Pearl Harbor and the assault against Tarawa by the Second Marine Division. This time was needed to get ready for the amphibious assault.

During these twenty-three months, the fleet was repaired and new units added. By employing fast, recently built carriers, battleships, cruisers, and destroyers in the covering force, the navy was able to assign its pre-Pearl Harbor warships, supplemented by escort carriers, to the attack force commander. These arms, integrated with a landing force sent ashore in the most recently perfected ships and craft, were the weapons employed in the Central Pacific. Officers and men, army, navy, and marine, had gained experience in coordinating these weapons while they conducted amphibious landings in the South and Southwest Pacific. Now, at Tarawa, came the first real amphibious test.

CHAPTER VI

THE FIRST MAJOR ASSAULT, TARAWA

THE lessons derived from landings in the Solomons-New Britain-New Guinea area were valuable, but much remained to be learned. This became evident when the drive across the Central Pacific began. Here for the first time a major amphibious assault was delivered, and the Second Marine Division sustained some 3,300 casualties in taking Tarawa, the only strongly defended atoll in the Gilbert Islands.

Tarawa was a notable victory and would have been worth the cost even if the casualties had been double those incurred. Strategically it opened the road to Kwajalein Atoll in the Marshall Islands and inaugurated the march across the Central Pacific with a tempo that mounted rapidly in momentum to stop only with the advent of peace, at the threshold of the home islands of Japan. Tactically it established the pattern of warfare which above all others would defeat the enemy; it gave valuable experience in the amphibious assault.

Knowledge gained at Tarawa led to improvements in every field of amphibious warfare. Many of these were directly related to a more effective delivery of air and naval gunfire support. The experience pointed out the necessity for new types of amphibious craft, for improvement in the technique of shore party control and in the tactics of offshore, beach, and inshore fighting best suited to storming small objectives surrounded by coral and to overrunning strong enemy emplacements. Tarawa, in short, was the testing ground for the amphibious assault. Therein lies its true significance.

1. Geography and High-level Planning

Seizure of the Gilberts was a necessary preliminary to entering the Marshalls. This was true because the problem of localizing a target for an amphibious operation was complex, and especially so since the Japanese navy was still believed to be a most formidable adversary, and because land-based planes were desired to help neutralize the Japanese in the Marshalls. Most important, however, was the fact that carrier-based aircraft were incapable of integrated photographic reconnaissance and only land-based photographic planes could furnish the information absolutely essential to storming the Marshalls. This lesson was clearly indicated by America's early amphibious experiences both in the Pacific and in the Mediterranean. Land-based photographic planes have long legs, but in 1943 the United States had none that could reach enemy bases in the Marshalls from fields already established. After the war Holland M. Smith concluded that taking the Gilberts was an error, that the first Central Pacific offensive should have struck directly into the Central Marshalls. To this Admiral Raymond A. Spruance replied: ". . . I do not agree with General Holland Smith's thesis that Tarawa was a mistake and that we should have gone directly to Kwajalein. I feel sure that he would have been most unwilling to attempt the capture of any defended island without adequate aerial photographs, and . . . those of Kwajalein became available only after we had taken the Gilberts and built airfields on them." [1]

The Gilbert and Marshall Islands, separated from one another by three degrees of latitude, lie in the west central portion of the Pacific basin. (See maps 1 and 10.) The Gilberts, sixteen atolls, straddle the equator north-northwest of the Ellice group by 700 miles and west-northwest of the Phoenix Islands by 900 miles. American land-based bombers and reconnaissance craft were operating within range of the Gilberts from both the Phoenix and Ellice Islands, and from Baker Island, 660 miles east of Tarawa.

To the northwest of the Gilberts are the Marshalls, totaling thirty-six atolls. Kwajalein is the core of this group, and lies 700 miles northwest of Tarawa, heart of the Gilberts. The principal atolls in the Eastern Marshalls, Majuro, Maloelap, and Wotje, are between 150 and 270 miles from Kwajalein; while the westernmost of the Marshalls, Eniwetok, is 350 miles northwest of Kwajalein. Important atolls in the Southern Marshalls, Jaluit and Mili, are between 200 and 340 miles southeast of Kwajalein. Truk, key enemy base in the Central Carolines, sprawls 700 miles southwest of Kwajalein.

The idea of driving through the Marshalls toward Truk had been the most favored naval plan of operating against Japan since the early 1920's; but circumstances, largely brought about by earlier Japanese successes, delayed formal approval of this scheme until mid-1943.

Late in 1942, however, Admiral King began reopening the question of Pacific strategy within the Joint Chiefs of Staff, and he continued the discussion until the Casablanca Conference with the British early the next year. The British were worried lest Pacific commitments involve the United States so deeply as to jeopardize success in Europe, but King countered with an accurate surmise. His overall objective was to place and keep unremitting pressure on the Japanese. He insisted that the longer the Pacific foe was given to strengthen his holdings and recent conquests, then the stronger he would become. King wanted more power injected into the war with Japan. He suggested thirty per cent of the Anglo-American total war output; and he wanted this additional strength used to open up the Central Pacific front and ultimately to recapture bases in the Philippines. These he considered essential to keeping China in the struggle and to defeating Japan. The result at Casablanca was the drawing up of a new statement of intentions for Pacific operations in 1943, in which the British made important concessions to King's point of view. Operations to reopen the Burma Road, to recapture the Aleutians, and to seize Rabaul were agreed upon, and in addition an offensive in the Central Pacific was included. The general consensus was that the Central Pacific front would be opened up only after Rabaul had fallen, but the final draft of the conference report said that this would be done "as practicable."

King thus concurred with General Douglas MacArthur on a basic point, the desirability of returning to the Philippines. But King intended to use the Central Pacific route for the principal drive, while MacArthur was proceeding on the assumption that the main effort would be made from the Southwest Pacific Area. While the Casablanca Conference was in full swing, MacArthur's headquarters were well along with plans for reconquering the Philippines. His staff believed that the capture of Rabaul and islands in the Bismarcks would provide adequate bases to support entry into Mindanao in the Philippines, if the United States Navy could be prevailed upon to protect the right flank of this offensive.

Soon after the Casablanca Conference, the Joint Chiefs directed their planners to study long range Pacific strategy in the light of recent decisions made by the Combined Chiefs of Staff. By late April 1943, after a series of Washington conferences in which both Nimitz and MacArthur were represented, future strategy in the Pacific began to take shape. MacArthur's concept that the main offensive against Japan should originate in the Southwest Pacific was not accepted. Two of the most important agencies working under the Joint Chiefs of Staff seem to have been instrumental in shaping the ultimate decision. These were the Joint Strategical Survey Committee, composed of experienced and highly independent senior officers of all services, and the Joint Staff Planners, which labored over the details of strategical problems and the allocations of men and materiel and was thus also influential in shaping military policy.

The Joint Staff Planners reasoned that before the war could be brought home to the Japanese people, large air bases and their supporting arms and services would have to be built up in China, and this would require the possession of a port somewhere along the China coast. Hong Kong looked good, and the best route to it lay through the Celebes Sea. The most feasible approach to the Celebes Sea ran through the Marshalls and the Carolines. This was true not only because it was shorter than the route through MacArthur's area,

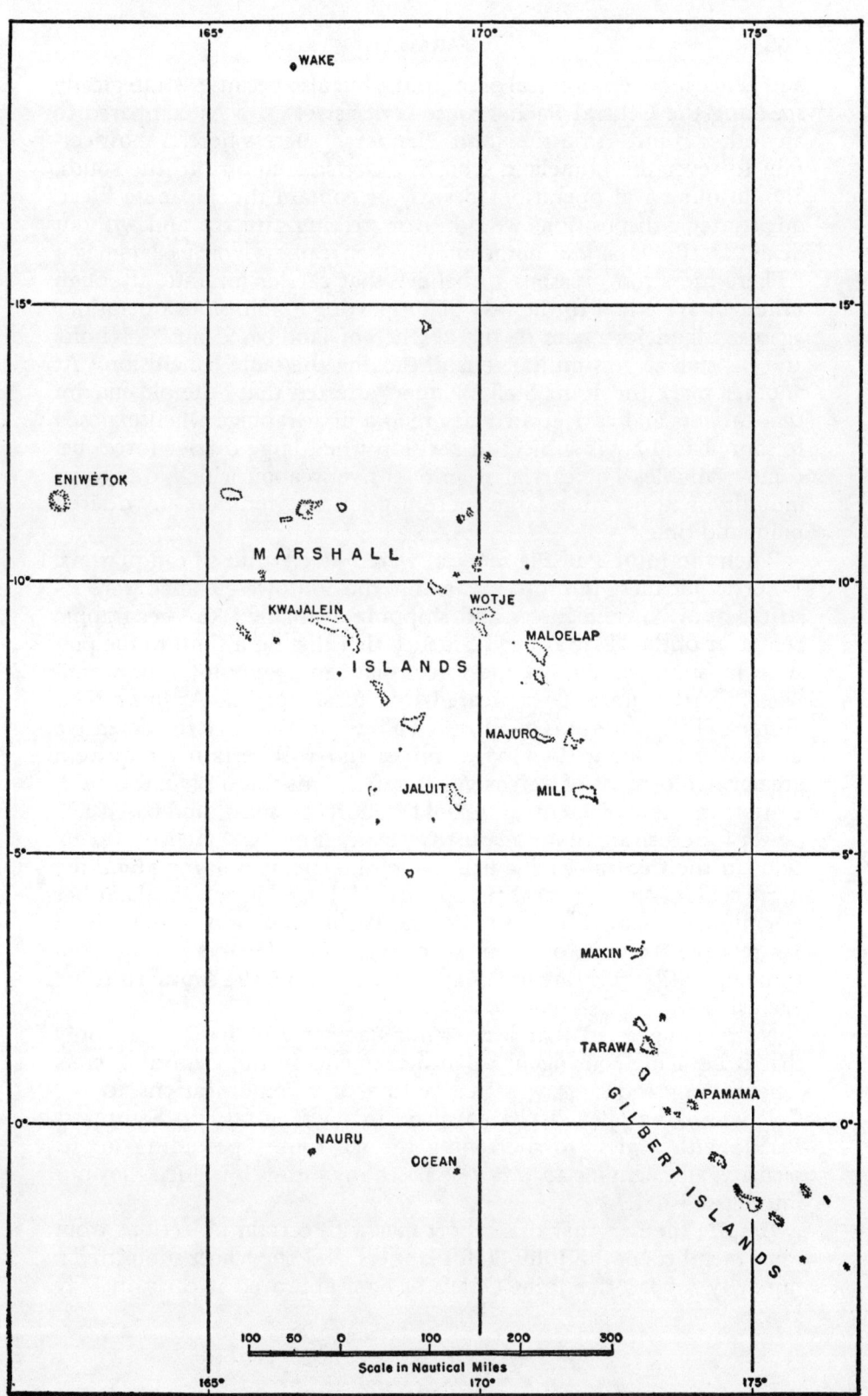

MAP 10. The Gilberts and Marshalls.

and hence more economical of shipping, but also because "strategically speaking the Central Pacific route is decisive. . . . As compared to any other route," said the Joint Planners, "success here is most certain to sever the homeland from the overseas empire to the south. Should our naval operations destroy or contain the Japanese Fleet, our strategic dispositions would favor striking directly, and without delay, at the Japanese homeland." Then came vigorous language: "There are strong reasons to believe that carrier aircraft, although untested, are equal to the task of supporting amphibious operations against island fortresses in the absence of land-based air." [2] Nimitz and his staff were simultaneously reaching the same conclusion.[3] At another place the Joint Staff Planners asserted that "the old maxim that carriers and carrier aircraft are at a disadvantage when exposed to shore-based air is subject to revision when large carrier forces become available. The carrier is an offensive weapon which, due to its mobility, will permit a large concentration of aircraft at any desired point and time." [4]

Then the Joint Staff Planners answered MacArthur's headquarters. Whereas Japanese reinforcements into the Southwest Pacific were restricted only by the forces and shipping available, "the geographic character of the Central Pacific is such that there is a limit to the possible Japanese air and ground forces that can be employed to advantage." Furthermore it was feared that to accept MacArthur's New Guinea-Philippines axis of approach alone "might force the defensive dispersion of our greater naval forces and will certainly require a greater deployment of defensive aircraft." This was a pivotal consideration in view of General Arnold's efforts to mass land-based airpower for crushing blows against Germany. Finally, "offensive operations in the Central Pacific flanks [sic] the enemy holding along the north coast of New Guinea, but operations along that coast will neither eject him, nor flank him in the Central Pacific bases and he could hold his relative freedom of naval maneuver. The Japanese could continue operations on our flanks and rear if we use the southern route exclusively."

No one suggested that MacArthur's advance be halted, but only that it be made contingent upon movements in the Central Pacific. The recommendation was that a line of communications to the Celebes Sea be opened "by advances in the Central and Southwest Pacific with a view to shortening the sea routes, providing for its security, and denying to Japanese bases any means by which they can interfere with it." [5]

Despite the fact that this report met with certain objections from some members of the Joint Staff Planners, and one officer submitted a minority report, the Joint Chiefs of Staff approved it early in May

1943, and later that month the allocation of the necessary men and materiel was agreed to by the Combined Chiefs of Staff meeting in Washington. The aim of the Joint Chiefs was "to maintain and extend unremitting pressure on Japan," and in the most expeditious manner possible to gain positions from which the unconditional surrender of the Japanese could be forced. Such surrender would probably come by invasion of the home islands after repeated air strikes on her industrial cities, but prophetically these words were used: "It may even be that the scale of such an air offensive can be great enough to ensure unconditional surrender without invasion." [6]

MacArthur's reaction was immediate. He was ignorant of the inner workings leading to this high-level decision, and repeated his belief that "the best course of offensive action is a movement from Australia, through New Guinea, to Mindanao." As for the decision made: "A move through the mandated islands will be a series of amphibious attacks with the support of carrier-based aircraft against objectives defended by naval units and ground troops supported by land-based aviation." He apparently believed that the American victory at the Battle of Midway had been one of land-based versus carrier-based air, and warned that "Midway stands as an example of the hazards of such operations." He disliked this revival of the navy's prewar plans, since to his mind the circumstances had been "greatly altered by the conquest of Malaya and the Netherlands Indies, and by the availability of Australia as a base." [7]

A group of War Department planners came to MacArthur's support, and it was Nimitz who pushed through an acceptable compromise. The original plan was to withdraw two divisions from MacArthur's command into the Central Pacific. Nimitz, however, did not wish to go directly into the Central Marshalls, as proposed, since it would result in by-passing the Japanese-held Gilberts, Wake, and the Eastern Marshalls. He lacked the necessary sea-air strength for such a move, as well as the troops. The Joint Staff Planners replied that, since MacArthur objected so strenuously to giving up any of his forces, the date for knifing into the Central Marshalls could be set back to permit additional troops to be trained and made available from the United States; but King rejoined that this defeated one of the primary purposes of the plan, which was to prevent the Japanese from strengthening their positions further.

With all proposals and counterproposals in, the Joint Chiefs again instructed their planners to review the problem. The directive issued to Nimitz on July 30, 1943, was to invade the Gilberts and Nauru (an island 360 miles due west of the Gilberts) as preliminaries to the Marshalls. This would permit land-based bombers and reconnaissance planes to support first the Gilberts and then the Marshalls campaign, and would allow carriers to concentrate in two separate attacks, thus avoiding the spread of their strength too thinly over a wide area. By supervising the timing of the Central Pacific operations and those already approved in the South and Southwest Pacific, especially the landing on Bougainville, the Joint Chiefs gained strategical coordination. The target date for the first Central Pacific campaign was set for November 15, 1943; with the second to follow six weeks later, on January 1, 1944. No forces for the Marshalls were designated at the time, but for the Gilberts and Nauru, Nimitz was instructed to use the Second Marine Division, then resting and training in New Zealand, and one United States Army division from the Hawaiian Islands. Also, Nimitz got three marine defense battalions, and three army engineer and construction battalions. In terms of naval strength, he was told to expect five new battleships, seven old battleships, six heavy and four light carriers, seven escort carriers, eight heavy and four light cruisers, sixty-six destroyers, twenty-seven attack transport and cargo vessels, and nine merchant ships for additional transport and cargo duties, provided antisubmarine warfare in the Atlantic continued to go well and nothing unforeseen happened.[8]

Thus the Gilberts campaign was largely instigated by Nimitz as an essential means of obtaining a jump off position for entering the Marshalls. Two objective areas were suitable for this purpose, Wake and the Gilberts. The first lay 600 miles north of Kwajalein, and the second 700 miles south and slightly east of that important atoll in the Marshalls. The Gilberts were selected because they lay nearer friendly bases in the Southern Pacific, because once seized they offered several dispersed land-based airsites, and because once overrun, without awaiting further fighting, the supply route to the South and Southwest Pacific Areas would be shortened and bases throughout the Southern Pacific would be made more secure.[9]

Aside from the coordinated Central Pacific-Southwest Pacific movement toward the Philippines and the China coast, only one other means of bringing the war to the enemy's homeland existed. This was the Aleutian-Kurile route through the North Pacific. It was undesirable because weather conditions would prevent maximum employment of sea-air and land-based plane strength, and because, unless the United States wished to jeopardize Russia's neutrality with Japan, the next land operation after the Aleutians had been recaptured must of necessity strike the Kuriles, which were thought to be strongly defended. Nor was American sea-air power deemed sufficient to prevent the Japanese from reinforcing the Kuriles at will from their home islands. The threat of an American move westward from the Aleutians was therefore of limited but important usefulness. It caused Japan to be cautious in her dealings with Russia, which in turn helped the

Allies to win the war in Europe. At the same time, however, Russia's military deployment in Siberia and the Maritime Provinces remained of some benefit to the United States throughout the Pacific War. It, and the presence of America forces in Alaska and the Aleutians, kept Japanese land and naval strength dispersed in Manchuria and the Kuriles, and hence distant from the actual zone of conflict. As long as the enemy responded thus to the retaking of Attu and Kiska, these amphibious operations had achieved their purpose. They had cost little, having been conducted in May and August of 1943 with no resistance at the beach in the first instance and no opposition whatsoever in the second. Air raids out of the Aleutian fields and a small naval force in the North Pacific were enough to retain the strategic gains of the Aleutian campaign; and almost to the end of the war, Nimitz stood prepared for a major redeployment of forces in the event that Russia entered the conflict against Japan.[10]

The Central Pacific drive was needed to bring increased pressure on the Japanese and to facilitate MacArthur's reentry into the Philippines. Even with the neutralization of Rabaul, he could not obtain the full fleet support essential to an amphibious advance along the northeast coast of New Guinea into the Philippines until Truk, the pivotal Japanese base in the Carolines, had been seized or contained. Otherwise, MacArthur's water communications in both the Bismarck and Philippine Seas would be outflanked and vulnerable. As in the case of the first Joint Chief directive in July 1942, MacArthur was again compelled to permit the United States Navy, operating as it saw fit, to move toward Truk and the Celebes Sea.

King and Nimitz together deserve the bulk of the credit for pushing through the strategical concept of using fast carriers to isolate targets in the mid-Pacific for amphibious operations. They were responsible for coordinating America's growing carrier strength with her constantly improving amphibious techniques. It was this strategy that gave the Central Pacific drive its great momentum. While operations in the Solomons-New Britain-New Guinea area were, after the landing on Guadalcanal, restricted for a long period to the range of land-based fighters, in the Central Pacific, with aircraft carriers supplying the agility and marines the muscle, leaps from the outset covered record distances.[11]

As Nimitz and MacArthur moved Pacific bases closer to Japan, logistical support of America's increasing fleet of submarines was improved, as was their performance in hacking at the Japanese coprosperity life line which dangled from the homeland down through the South China Sea into the Netherlands East Indies.

In addition, the basic intent of the July 1943 directive was to reach China quickly and to mount bombers against Japan, as well as to strew

Japanese home waters with magnetic mines. However, by the time the very long-range bombers were being mass produced, it was seen that the Mariana Islands were, logistically and tactically, better bases for the B-29's; and the Marianas became, to use Admiral King's figure, the "key" to Pacific victory.[12] Anxious to begin bombing Japan as soon as possible, the Army Air Force joined with the Navy in pushing operations along the axis of the Central Pacific.[13] And now it was realized more clearly than ever that a body of troops expertly trained in amphibious fighting was an essential ingredient of a well-balanced fighting force. The navy had long since recognized this prerequisite to obtaining bases required for its air, surface, and subsurface strength. Now, and for a similar reason, the Army Air Force needed troops who could implement the amphibious assault. The two new techniques of warfare to emerge from the Pacific, very long-range strategic bombing and the amphibious assault, complemented each other as effectively as the navy and the marines had always done in the past.

The curtain on the Central Pacific drive went up with the Gilberts campaign, which, principally because of hydrographic considerations, began on November 20, 1943, five days later than scheduled by the Joint Chiefs of Staff.[14] Nimitz created a new command in order to achieve unity of control at the implementing level. This was the Central Pacific Force, headed by Vice Admiral Raymond A. Spruance. The quality of Spruance's strategical and tactical planning had already gained him an enviable reputation, and in the early months of the war he had exhibited firm abilities as a commander afloat. He became the officer responsible for all phases of the Gilberts offensive, and to him were assigned the forces earmarked for that campaign.

From the outset, Spruance's decisions were governed by a paramount consideration—namely, the pressing necessity of completing the attack with the utmost speed, once it was launched. In the Gilberts campaign, fear of enemy counterattack placed a premium upon speed. Violent Japanese subsurface and air reaction from land bases in the Marshalls was anticipated. It was rightly felt that the Bougainville operation would tend to immobilize the Japanese fleet, but the threat of a major naval engagement in the vicinity of the Gilberts remained a distinct possibility.[15]

As it happened, no such threat materialized, and the enemy was able to offer only token counterstrokes in the air and under the sea. The reason for this weakness—unexpected and unknown to American intelligence at the time—is now apparent. Operations in the Solomons, in addition to speeding up MacArthur's advance along the New Guinea coast and through the Bismarck barrier, had also drained enemy naval and air strength from the Central Pacific. Beginning in September 1943, the Japanese suspected an American advance into the Central Pacific, and sent reinforcements to the Marshalls; but when this attack failed to develop, fleet units returned to Truk. On the 30th of that month, Imperial Headquarters in Tokyo designated Rabaul as "the ultimate point of resistance," and this was followed by throwing more naval pilots into the Solomons slaughterhouse. During the next month, the Japanese again thought action in the Central Pacific imminent and once more sent the bulk of their fleet into the Marshalls; but nothing happened, and on October 24 the naval units retired to Truk. Then the Bougainville landing got under way, and the Japanese fed still more naval pilots into Rabaul, expended precious cruisers and screening destroyers at the Battle of Empress Augusta Bay, and in early November lost temporarily other cruisers and destroyers in Rabaul Harbor to the carrier planes of Rear Admirals Frederick C. Sherman and Alfred E. Montgomery. By the time the Gilberts offensive was launched, few reinforcements were available to the Japanese for the Central Pacific. Their carriers lacked pilots, and their heavy surface units were inadequately screened. Finally, their submarine potential in the Central Pacific was weak. The American strategy of by-passing in the South and Southwest Pacific was having its effect. The Japanese were already using some of their underseas craft logistically rather than tactically.[16] Nothing better illustrates the value of the initiative in warfare than this period in which the Japanese shuttled strength back and forth between the Marshalls and Rabaul. As Robert Sherrod comments, by the time of the Gilberts attack, the ranking Japanese naval officer at Truk "was turning his head faster than a man watching a tennis match." [17]

American commanders, however, could not gamble in planning for the Gilberts. An amphibious expedition is a vulnerable target and one difficult to protect. A torpedo into a loaded transport might easily result in more deaths than an amphibious assault. It was agreed that the Gilberts had to be taken in a hurry. Strategic surprise was mandatory, and this ruled out any concentration of preliminary aerial bombing and naval bombardment (that is gunfire and air preparation against a target previous to the arrival of the troops in the transport area and the beginning of disembarkation). In order to keep the enemy guessing, the preliminary air and naval gunfire preparation must be spread over several possible geographical areas. Once the Japanese learned the Americans were headed for the Gilberts, the land objectives had to be taken at once, and the carriers and amphibious shipping withdrawn before the full fury of the anticipated Japanese air and subsurface counteraction could be mounted. At most, a few days could be allowed. No one wanted tactical surprise ashore, since efforts to obtain it would sacrifice the far more valuable air and naval gunfire preparation that could be squeezed into the early morning hours before the landings. For this reason it was necessary to concentrate the greatest possible volume of bombing and naval gunfire in a brief period of time. In the end, however, this decision—determined by naval considerations of the most compelling nature—forced marines to go ashore in a withering crossfire from the beaches.

2. Plans and Preparations by Implementing Commanders

The demand for speed permeated the commands that implemented the Gilberts campaign. Spruance as the top-ranking officer was also named Commander of the Fifth Fleet. This was his important command since it was operational, and in this capacity he retained under his supervision the covering naval force of new fast battleships, heavy and light aircraft carriers, and a quota of cruisers and destroyers. These ships had the dual mission of protecting the amphibious expedition from hostile surface intent, and of neutralizing or standing guard against enemy bases to the west and to the north of the target area. Subordinate to Spruance and assisting in this work, as well as administering preliminary bombing and carrying out the necessary reconnaissance missions over the Gilberts, was the land- and tender-based air command of Rear Admiral John H. Hoover USN.[18]

Spruance's amphibious commanders, navy and marine, occupied a peculiar but successful mutual relationship. Rear Admiral Richmond Kelly Turner had been recalled from the South Pacific in July 1943 and made Commander Amphibious Force, Pacific Fleet, and thereupon he began planning the amphibious aspects of the first Central Pacific campaign. Turner was brought under Spruance's supervision a month later when he was made Commander Fifth Amphibious Force. At the same time, in August 1943, Major General Holland M. Smith USMC was given tactical duties. As Commanding General Amphibious Corps, Pacific Fleet, he had been in charge of the amphibious training of all troops under Nimitz. Now Holland Smith was named Commanding General Fifth Amphibious Corps.

Initially Holland Smith was subordinate to Turner in every respect, a condition distasteful to the hot-tempered marine general and contrary to the better interests of his men. He was soon able to obtain a far-reaching modification of this status. There could be only one top amphibious commander at times of actual training maneuvers and fighting, and Turner continued to occupy this position; but during the highly important planning period of this and all subsequent Central Pacific campaigns in which Holland Smith participated, he ranked equal with Turner on Spruance's echelon of command.

Duties in the Aleutians delayed Holland Smith's arrival in Pearl Harbor until September 5, 1943, whereupon he was instructed, with two reinforced divisions plus garrison troops, to plan the seizure and occupation of the Tarawa and Apamama Atolls in the Gilberts, and of Nauru Island. The Second Marine Division reinforced, to be embarked from Wellington, was scheduled for Tarawa and Apamama, while the 27th Infantry Division, embarked at Pearl Harbor, was assigned to Nauru. Evaluation of information, however, soon made it apparent that Nauru, because of defenses and hydrographic and terrain features, could hardly be taken with the forces available. There was insufficient amphibious shipping to lift two reinforced divisions plus the necessary garrison and construction echelons. Holland Smith recommended that a much weaker target, Makin Atoll, northernmost of the Gilberts and only 100 miles distant from Tarawa, be substituted for Nauru. This was done, but there were annoying delays in allocating to Turner and Holland Smith the ships and troops to be employed, which in turn complicated lower echelon planning, training, and rehearsals. "For future operations," complained the marine general, "it must be remembered that an early assignment of forces is absolutely imperative." [19]

The operation plan issued by Nimitz in early October directed Spruance to prepare the way for entering the Marshalls by taking Makin, Tarawa, and Apamama; to cover the amphibious expeditions involved; and with carrier planes vigorously to deny the enemy use of land bases adjacent to the Gilberts, in the Marshalls and on Nauru.[20]

Preliminary planning on a divisional level had begun in August. The army's 27th Infantry Division was led by Major General Ralph C. Smith. With both the division and its commander, Holland Smith would have trouble throughout the Central Pacific. He relates in his memoirs that at Pearl Harbor before the Gilberts campaign he had doubts about the capabilities of the 27th Division, but it was destined for Makin which was known to be weakly defended. There were only about 250 first-line Japanese troops plus a few prepared installations (some of the gun emplacements later turned out to contain dummy weapons). Since Holland Smith could lift only a part of the 27th Division, he assigned the most thoroughly trained army regimental combat team, the 165th, to Makin. Then he picked a regiment from the Second Marine Division, the Sixth Marines, for his corps reserve.

This choice was momentous. It meant that the Second Marine Division would have only two reinforced rifle regiments, the Second and the Eighth, with which to plan the seizure of Tarawa. Conservatively Tarawa was, and was known to be, at least ten times more heavily held than Makin; [21] yet the Sixth Marine Regiment reinforced was committed to corps reserve. It was to accompany its parent division to Tarawa, but was to be released only with the permission of Turner, as well as that of Holland Smith. It was to be employed at

Makin, Tarawa, or Apamama, as might be necessitated by tactical situations ashore. Of course it was used at Tarawa, but the commanding general of the Second Marine Division was unable to plan on such a development. Holland Smith was belatedly criticized for such an allocation of forces. "Under present conditions," said Nimitz, "it is necessary to plan for the employment of not less than one division for the capture of an enemy position comparable in strength to Tarawa." [22]

A third Smith, Major General Julian C. Smith USMC, quiet and unassuming, commanded the Second Marine Division. His navy counterpart at Tarawa was Rear Admiral Harry W. Hill USN, and the command relationship between these two officers was identical with that between Kelly Turner and Holland Smith on the next higher echelon. Hill and Julian Smith were also given the task of taking Apamama. This atoll, some eighty miles south and slightly east of Tarawa, was very lightly held, and for the purpose of reconnoitering it in force, Julian Smith was allotted three platoons of the Fifth Amphibious Corps Reconnaissance Company. The fourth platoon of this company would help army troops at Makin.[23]

Although Julian Smith had been advised in August of his part in the Gilberts offensive, it was mid-September before his division was transferred from the First to the Fifth Amphibious Corps. Not until early October did he and members of his staff have an opportunity to confer with Holland Smith in Pearl Harbor, and to establish liaison between the two headquarters.

Weakened by one-third, the Second Marine Division was ordered directly into the heart of Japanese strength in the Gilberts. No other course was open. To occupy lightly defended atolls and neutralize Tarawa by air would turn the conflict into a struggle of attrition. The navy had had enough of this type of warfare in the Solomons. It would jeopardize warships, transports, and cargo vessels, and unduly delay the pending advance into the Marshalls. Similarly, the requirement of speed deprived Julian Smith of the possibility of fully utilizing his artillery on Tarawa Atoll. Less than three hours of naval gunfire and air support were being scheduled during the morning before the landing. Julian Smith would have felt more confident if given an opportunity to emplace his artillery at first light on a strip of land within Tarawa Atoll adjacent to the islet of Betio, which was the principal target since it contained the enemy's airfield and the bulk of his defenses. (See map 11.) Such use of artillery, however, would require too much time. It would divert naval gunfire and escorting men-of-war from the main objective. Assaulting Betio without artillery assistance was a necessary concession to haste and a shortage of naval support. Julian Smith was himself devising a thoroughgoing replacement plan, should any of his battalion landing teams be sent to the bottom of the sea.[24] Even though Japanese air and subsurface reaction was far weaker than expected, a single event during the Gilberts campaign proved that the navy's caution and insistence on speed were justifiable. An enemy submarine off Makin Atoll sent a torpedo into the escort carrier *Liscome Bay*. The loss of life in this single sinking ran almost as high as the total marine dead on Tarawa.

Even if the navy had been willing to grant the time necessary for the establishment of artillery adjacent to Betio, it could not have been done. Holland Smith had so depleted the Second Marine Division that his subordinate no longer had the forces for an auxiliary landing. It had long been recognized that in assaulting a defended shore, the attacker should have at least a three to one superiority over the defender. By concentrating all men and firepower left under his control, Julian Smith could expect to land only twice the strength the Japanese were known to have on Betio Islet. Automatically this ruled out either a diversion or a preliminary landing on an adjacent islet. Julian Smith's chief of staff, Merritt A. Edson of Guadalcanal fame, now a full colonel, brilliantly summarized the problem: ". . . the relative superiority of strength with the troops now available to us as opposed to the hostile strength on Betio alone, which is our primary objective, does not permit the detachment of any part of the Second Marine Division for secondary landings. Reliance must be placed on supporting air and naval forces to neutralize or destroy hostile weapons which may successfully interfere with our landing on Betio." [25] Julian Smith, in other words, had no freedom of action. He asked his superior to make this clear in his operation order, and Holland Smith minced no words. He directed the Second Marine Division reinforced (less the Sixth Regimental Combat Team) to "land on Betio Island, seize and occupy that island; then conduct further operations to reduce the remainder of Tarawa Atoll." [26]

The Second Marine Division had been evacuated to Wellington early in 1943 for rehabilitation and further training following extensive ground operations on Guadalcanal. It was a seasoned outfit, but with the exception of one regiment had as yet to participate in an amphibious landing, much less an amphibious assault. The Second Marines had served in the Guadalcanal area from August 7, 1942, until mid-January 1943. To this experienced regiment and a battalion of the Eighth Marines went the difficult job of being first to cross the beaches at Betio.

The commanding officer of the Second Marines was ill and unequal to the task ahead, and was replaced by a young aggressive lieutenant colonel, spot-promoted a grade. This officer was David M. Shoup. A battalion of the Eighth Marines was attached to Shoup's regiment, thus giving him four full reinforced rifle battalions. The plan was to land three battalions abreast, and to hold one battalion from the Second Marines in regimental reserve. Shoup's reinforcing elements were strong. He had a company of medium tanks, the special weapons group of the Second Marine Defense Battalion, combat and shore party engineers, eight shore fire control and air liaison parties, medical and service units, and a battalion of 75-millimeter pack howitzers.[27] The artillery and support groups were placed under Lieutenant Colonel Presley M. Rixey of the First Battalion, Tenth Marine Regiment. Beachhead logistics were to be supervised by Lieutenant Colonel Chester J. Salazar of the Second Battalion, Eighteenth Marines, the Second Division's regiment of engineers.

Strengthening Shoup weakened Julian Smith's division reserve. It consisted principally of Colonel Elmer E. Hall's Eighth Marine Regiment reinforced, less one battalion and its attached components. The support group for the division, headed by Colonel Cyril W. Martyr of the Eighteenth Marines, contained one battalion of artillery and miscellaneous personnel.

Not under Julian Smith's control, but ordered to the transport area off Tarawa along with its parent division, was the Sixth Marine Regimental Combat Team. The three reinforced infantry battalions comprising this command were under Colonel Maurice G. Holmes.

Tarawa is situated in the north center of the Gilberts group. It is shaped like a right triangle. (See maps 10 and 11.) The hypotenuse forms the northeast side, and consists of elongated islets; the southern leg is similarly formed; while to the west the islets disappear, and on that side only a reef shelters the lagoon. There is but one navigable entrance to the lagoon, a break in the western reef just north of the northwest end of the islet of Betio. Betio is at the southwestern corner of the atoll, forming, along with the western reef, the right angle of the geometric figure. Betio, like the other islets of the atoll, is entirely surrounded by a fringing coral reef. Before the war it had served as the center for British economic and governmental activities in the Gilberts, and for this reason, on the lagoon side, was equipped with a stubby wharf which could take small boats at high tide, and a more serviceable pier which ran into the lagoon to the edge of the reef.

Taking advantage of these facilities, the Japanese had converted Betio into their principal base in the Gilberts. They reconnoitered Tarawa in December 1941, and came back in September 1942 to construct an airfield suitable for medium bombers. As the marines planned to capture the objective, the enemy was busy completing formidable ground defenses on Betio.

Submarines and aerial photographic reconnaissance was the chief Allied means for obtaining information on Tarawa in general and

Betio in particular. A periscope showed Betio as a flat lying cluster of palm trees and undergrowth, with the terrain height everywhere less than ten feet. The place was without natural defilade positions. The attacker would have to come in from the water organized and fighting. There was only one possibility of taking cover from the enemy's fire, and that was to seek the protection of man-made defenses.

From the air, Betio appeared thin. There would be very little maneuver room ashore. The long axis ran east-west for a distance of two and one-half statute miles. The small body of land was shaped like a crescent, with the southern shore gently concave toward the open sea. The western end was relatively wide, some 800 yards; but as the islet ran eastward a sharp cove or reentrant cut for a short distance into the lagoon side, and then even more suddenly turned northward toward the lagoon, restoring the width to its 800 yards. There, in the east center portion of the islet, the Japanese had built an airstrip, which with its two adjacent taxiways looked from the air as if a triangular branding iron had seared the belly of the islet. From the eastern end of the airstrip, the convexing lagoon coast tapered slowly on southeastward to form a long narrow tail, dipping into the shallow reef about 4,000 yards short of neighboring Bairiki Islet—on which Julian Smith would have liked to land artillery before the assault on Betio was made.

Photographic reconnaissance of Betio was so good that an estimated ninety per cent of the enemy's defensive installations were pinpointed before the target date. The bulk of this work was done by Nimitz's highly efficient Joint Intelligence Center, Pacific Ocean Areas. The services of this organization were of great benefit to the marines throughout the Central Pacific drive.

From an analysis of enemy construction, as well as other data, it was possible to determine with fair accuracy the number of enemy personnel on the islet. After the battle the total was set at slightly less than 5,000, of whom more than one-half were first-line special landing force troops. "Naval units of this type," noted Julian Smith's intelligence officer in late October, "are usually more highly trained and have a greater tenacity and fighting spirit than the average Japanese Army unit." [28]

Large-scale maps of Betio were drawn. On them were blocked out enemy defenses and other constructions, and this intelligence was of utmost value to the marines and their supporting arms. Not yet, however, had the beach underwater demolition party been organized, nor had the kodachrome technique of determining hydrographic conditions within the vicinity of geographic objectives been perfected. Apparently Holland Smith's intelligence officer was unaware of the possibility of such a development. *"It should be emphasized,"* he said after the operation was over, *"that accurate depths of water cannot be determined from photographs."* Rear Admiral Harry Hill showed more foresight. He believed that black and white photography would turn the trick, and advised that in future operations photographic missions prior to the target date be flown at widely varying times in an effort to determine the periods of tides and to reveal beach obstructions and mines with an accuracy sufficient to permit their being plotted on a chart.[29]

Absence of accurate hydrographic data complicated the planning of the Second Marine Division. Tide tables and reef soundings for Tarawa were unreliable and incomplete. The British in 1941 had been using charts made by an American exactly a century earlier. As in the planning phase of Guadalcanal, British shippers and pilots were called in for consultation. Again they cooperated enthusiastically, and again their memory left much to be desired.[30]

The fringing reef around Betio was a natural obstacle which would block most landing craft. The Second Division staff did everything in its power to solve this problem. The decision was to employ amphibian tractors tactically. This was an innovation. Previously they had been used only logistically, and marines fighting in the jungles argued that to load them with weapons and protective plate for tactical use would curtail their cargo-carrying capacity. The men planning the Betio assault had no choice but to disregard such advice. The Second Division's amphibian tractor battalion managed to collect seventy-five serviceable craft of the vintage used at Guadalcanal. With the cooperation of the navy,[31] extensive tests were held to prove the feasibility of crossing reefs with these vehicles; machine guns were mounted forward; and efforts were made to armor the craft by riveting on boiler plates.

Seventy-five amphibian tractors were not enough. Finally the staff was able to procure fifty additional new models, armed with machine guns and partially armored. These were in San Diego. There was not time enough to get them to the division for tests and rehearsals. They were dispatched in tank landing ships via Samoa, where they were met by a special amphibian tractor company formed by the division. On the morning of the target date, November 20, 1943, they met the division at Tarawa.

Nor were 125 amphibian tractors sufficient. Julian Smith's preferred plan, which was used, called for the employment of 100 in the first three assault waves. Twenty-five of the older models were held in division reserve,[32] which showed excellent judgment for otherwise few would have remained for necessary logistical services. Since, however, only the amphibian tractor could cross the reef off Betio, it meant that after the first three waves were ashore, the assault bogged

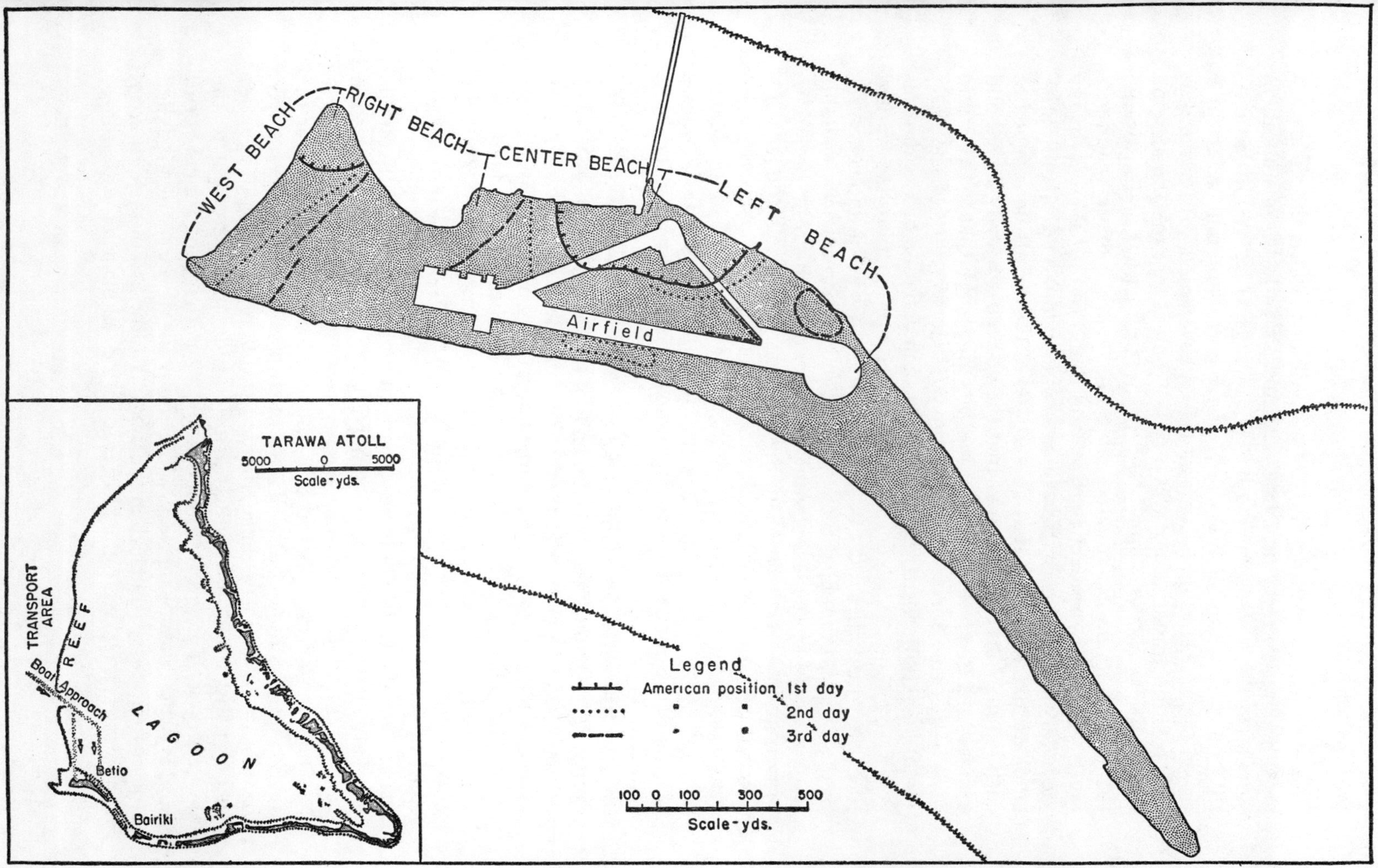

MAP 11. Betio Islet with insert of Tarawa Atoll.

down. Above everything else the amphibious assault should pack a sustained wallop. That at Tarawa did not. The number of amphibian vehicles at Betio was sufficient barely to win the islet, and little more. "Without the amphibian tractor," asserted Holland Smith, "it is believed that the landing at Tarawa would have failed." After the war, Julian Smith was asked for the precise moment that the Japanese on Betio were licked, and he replied (perhaps somewhat optimistically) that their morale suffered irreparable damage when they saw amphibian tractors belly up over the reef and then head for the beach. Immediately after the operation he recommended (and Holland Smith emphatically approved) that at least 300 of these craft be assigned to each amphibious division, and that they be more heavily armed and armored, be given more speed, and be equipped either with a ramp or a light crane for unloading cargo.[33] Undersecretary of the Navy James Forrestal concurred with this recommendation and with characteristic energy translated it into increased production. He warned that heavy casualties must be expected in future amphibious assaults in the Pacific, but added that the more amphibian tractors available the less would be the loss of American blood "in this most hazardous of military operations, the landing on a hostile shore in the face of a determined, experienced, well-equipped enemy. . . . Success of invasions to come will depend upon the sweat that we put in these landing craft today. The sooner they are built, the sooner will the war be over and the lower the cost in human lives. They must be built quickly." [34]

More and better amphibian tractors, however, were a thing of the future. They would not help the men of the Second Marine Division at Betio, whose planners knew that the number available was insufficient to get more than the first three waves of Shoup's three assault battalions onto their beaches. Thereafter, unless the tide were favorable, the assault would lose its punch. The remaining two waves (principally reinforcing elements) of the first three battalion landing teams must be boated in landing craft. These required at least four feet of water over the reef. There were only enough tractors to lift roughly one-half of the personnel in Shoup's three beach assault battalion landing teams.

The question of tides and the absence of sufficient water over the reef to float landing craft at Tarawa will probably never be resolved satisfactorily. The tide range, that is the difference in depth of water between high and low tides, varies considerably according to the moon's cycle. The greatest range occurs when the moon is new or full and is called the spring tide; while the point of least range is called the neap tide and occurs when the moon is in the first or third quarter. Tarawa was attacked in the neap tide period, and (since the assault for logistical reasons and because of tactical commitments in the South and Southwest Pacific could not be delivered earlier than it was) the question arises: why not wait seven days and land with a spring tide? The answer is that the times for peak water points of neap and high spring tides progressively change to complete a full cycle of twenty-four hours. During late November 1943 the spring tide was coming in either during darkness or relatively late in the day. Tactically a landing at either of these times was unacceptable. The first would preclude air and naval gunfire support; and the second would allow insufficient daylight to secure a beachhead. Only by delaying the operation from November 20 to December 27, or thereabouts, would the spring tide occur at the time of day that the assault, for sound tactical reasons, must be launched.

Of course, these general considerations of tides were well known by all concerned in planning Tarawa. Beyond such general knowledge, however, there was an area of ignorance because, while the tidal and reef data for Tarawa was the best that could be compiled, it was full of inaccuracies. Thus the absence of sufficient amphibious tractors posed the basic problem of whether to delay a month and go in with the spring tide, or to try and determine on the basis of data at hand whether or not it was feasible to get landing craft over the reef on the day that the neap tide coincided most nearly with the hour the assault should be made. If it were feasible to land in late November, then to postpone the operation another month was out of the question, since this would in turn set back the entire Central Pacific offensive and give the Japanese just that much longer to fortify the Marshalls and all other future targets. The planners decided that a landing in late November was feasible. The decision was correct, but the calculation of water over the reef turned out to be faulty, and according to the estimate of an eyewitness, low water increased casualties fifty per cent. Assuming that this estimate is correct, one may conclude that American lives would have been saved by awaiting a properly timed spring tide. Another possible conclusion, however, is that the delay, while saving marines at Tarawa, would have probably cost a far greater number of marines and soldiers at Kwajalein, Eniwetok, the Marianas, Palau, Iwo Jima, and Okinawa. The second conclusion seems the more valid. Strategical momentum, in short, is apt to be more economical of means than tactical momentum. Admiral King realized this in July 1943 when, having taken cognizance of the heavy pressure being brought on the Japanese in the Solomons-New Guinea area, he concluded: "It appears to me urgent that we take the maximum advantage of this situation by mounting the operations in the Gilberts-Marshalls at the earliest convenient date practicable, even at the expense of not being completely ready." Admiral Spruance, who at the time of the planning for Tarawa was personally concerned with both the performance of the amphibian tractors over coral reefs and with the number available, emphasized the same point after the surrender of Japan. "War is a tough business," he said, "and often we gain more than we lose by pressing forward against the enemy before we are entirely ready. This was certainly true against the Japanese in the Central Pacific." [35]

On the basis of the best calculation possible, the most favorably timed neap tide for late November would begin to flood rapidly at roughly half-past eight o'clock on the morning of November 20. The entire operation was planned around that moment. Most of the British acquainted with the Gilberts promised five feet of water over the reef by the time the non-amphibian craft were wanted on the beach. Since four feet would be adequate to float the landing craft, then there would be (if the data and the overwhelming majority of the people experienced in navigating the waters of the Gilberts were right) twelve extra inches of depth over the reef, and the assault would carry through with sustained momentum.

One British officer who stood out against his compatriots, however, happened to be right. He was Major F. L. G. Holland of the New Zealand Army who had lived on Tarawa for fifteen years. He predicted something he called a "dodging tide" for around November 20. The United States Coast and Geodetic Survey, however, is unfamiliar with the term "dodging tide." Holland had been around Tarawa long enough to have sensed, at least, that the tidal and reef data being used was unreliable; but he had at his disposal none that was better. His ominous prediction for November 20 created grave doubts in the minds of Julian Smith and others, and caused them to drill the marines in what to do in case of low water. As far as men can ever be mentally prepared, they were prepared for the contingency that the boats would ground at the edge of the reef and some of them would have to wade in. But there was no other choice than to plan the time of the landing on the most highly scientific basis possible, and to hope that it was correct. Had the accurate hydrographic data compiled after the capture of Tarawa been available, it would have been obvious that there would not be enough water over the reef at high neap tide to allow non-amphibian landing craft to reach the beach.[36]

Deciding which beaches to use in assaulting Betio was painful, but hardly difficult. Hydrographic consideration and the Japanese defenses, combined with the requirement of speed and the withdrawal of one of the regimental combat teams from the Second Division, dictated that Julian Smith select the northwestern lagoon beaches.

The Japanese had approximately 200 coastal defense, antiaircraft, antiboat, and beach defense guns on Betio. These ranged in size from

8-inch naval cannon to mortars and light automatic weapons. A slightly greater number of emplacements, most of them well-constructed with coconut logs or reinforced concrete and mounded up with coral and sand, seems to have existed. Except for the 8- and 5-inch coastal batteries, everything on the island could be used against landing craft. All antiaircraft weapons, for example, were dual purpose, and were emplaced for beach defense.

Nor was this all. In addition to the natural obstacle that was the fringing reef, the Japanese had planted in the water immediately surrounding the islet a large variety of man-made barriers. These included concrete tetrehedrons, piles of coral rock, fences of heavy coconut log, antiboat mines, and aprons of defensive wire. Along almost the entire length of the coast, with only a few gaps and interspersed breaks permitting inshore guns to fire, a beach barricade had been constructed from coral stone and from coconut logs. This was designed to house light and medium antiboat weapons, and was integrated with the more solidly built emplacements just inshore which contained larger caliber guns. Fields of fire were superbly laid. Full enfilade was the purpose. Attackers would be channeled by the reef, the man-made obstacles, and the beach barricade into a crossfire of all types of weapons. "The Japanese at Tarawa Atoll," reads the post-operational verdict of the Joint Intelligence Center, "organized Betio Island for an all-around, decisive defense at the beach." [37]

Study of the preoperational aerial photographs and low-level submarine camera shots showed that the Japanese expected a landing on the south or west coast of Betio. (See map 11.) Defenses in those sectors were heavier and more nearly complete. Of the two, the west coast offered the better possibility of effecting a landing. Here the coast line was short, only 800 yards, but once occupied, there would be no land to the right or left of the attackers and hence no enemy flanking fire. However, the high surf which characterized the seaward beaches was feared, and immediately inshore from the west beach the cove along the northwest lagoon coast would sharply curtail maneuver room. In addition, just south of the reentrant, which cut the width of the island to a mere 450 yards, was the western end of the enemy airfield, roughly 150 yards wide, and this could be swept by Japanese machine gun fire. An assault on the west coast, in other words, looked like plunging into a hangman's noose.

If the southwest coast were struck, maneuver space as ample as was possible on tiny Betio would open to the assaulting units, but here in addition to the surf and the heavy defenses, the concaving coast line would facilitate flanking fire. Similar reasoning, plus a lack of maneuver room, ruled out the southeast coast.

The lagoon coast was convex. This would tend to mask at least some enemy fire. The northeastern beaches were, however, unsuitable. They offered no maneuver room once ashore and reaching them would require a long run into the lagoon while flanked by defenders' guns. The lagoon itself was poorly charted and was known to be treacherous with coral heads; and it might be mined.

Only the northwestern lagoon beaches remained. They had to be used. Enemy weapons on the eastern lagoon coast would be partially masked, but unless friendly naval gunfire and air supporting arms did their jobs well, the reentrant itself would form a small and deadly pocket. These arms, especially the naval guns, should be able to take out the defenses along these beaches. Heavy warships could lie to off the west end of Betio, outside the lagoon, and enfilade the northwestern beaches.

Other considerations pointed to these beaches. Here the Japanese installations were, relatively at least, weak. By first seizing the long pier and then straddling its base with two beaches to the right and one to the left, the attackers could utilize this crib-like obstacle, rising eight to ten feet out of the water, to reduce enemy crossfire in the immediate vicinity of the coast. Once in friendly hands, the pier would greatly facilitate the problem of beachhead logistics.[38]

The scheme of maneuver adopted was to send in a scout-sniper platoon to clear the long pier, and then to land three reinforced battalions abreast on as many northwestern lagoon beaches. Each of the beaches was about 600 yards in length. As the marines raced southward in 100 amphibian tractors over lagoon waters onto the northwest coast of Betio, their right flank beach stretched from the northwestern tip of the islet eastward to include the entire reentrant; the center beach ran from that point in the same direction to the eastern base of the long pier; and the left flank beach continued eastward beyond the wharf to the eastern extremity of the airstrip.

While the staff of the Second Marine Division was evaluating the information available on Tarawa, selecting its beaches, and planning the training, rehearsal, and operational features of its mission, higher echelons were working on the overall strategical and logistical aspects of the Gilberts offensive.

In addition to the land- and tender-based planes under Hoover, Spruance had a mighty array of naval power. His covering force consisted of six new fast battleships, six heavy and five light carriers, two heavy and two light cruisers, and twenty-one destroyers. Operating as four fast carrier task groups, these warships entered the area of combat early, delivered air strikes and naval bombardment against the geographical objectives, and then proceeded to the north and west of the Gilberts and continued the neutralization of certain enemy bases while guarding against Japanese air attacks from others. It was the successful strikes of this covering force which localized the target area and kept the Japanese air reaction down to minor night harassments; but in another important respect, the work of Spruance's covering force was a failure. It was scheduled, on the two days immediately previous to the target date, to take over from Hoover's land-based planes the chief responsibility of hitting the atolls marked for seizure. A variety of islands were taken under attack, to keep the enemy confused as to the ultimate goals, but major attention was devoted to Tarawa. The principal targets were the coastal defense guns on Betio, which must be taken out before the transports and cargo vessels could operate adjacent to the atoll. These enemy weapons were concentrated on the three tips of Betio. They were pinpointed on aircraft and gunnery charts. Spruance's presumably accurate carrier-based bombers dropped almost 200 tons of explosives at these targets, and then a cruiser division tried to work the installations over with naval bombardment. The enemy weapons remained intact. Fortunately, the American gunners accompanying the attack forces would be more competent because they were better trained in shore bombardment, but this was a good indication of the lack of efficiency, when striking ground objectives, of all carrier pilots then in the Pacific. Failure of the preliminary air and surface strikes caused no forebodings because the results were not accurately known; pilots reported exceedingly weak antiaircraft fire, and concluded that all worthwhile targets on Betio had been demolished before dawn of November 20.[39]

Spruance allocated other men-of-war, as well as the transports and cargo shipping, to Turner. These constituted the two naval attack forces, one to Makin and the other to Tarawa. The three platoons of the amphibious reconnaissance company destined for Apamama were carried in a submarine.

Turner decided to accompany the expedition to Makin. That atoll was closer to the Marshalls than Tarawa, and was therefore in the danger zone of probable Japanese air and subsurface reaction. It was the critical naval target, and Turner's choice was sound. Holland Smith accompanied his naval counterpart on the echelon of command, and was absent from the bitter Tarawa fighting.

Since Makin was the more dangerous target from a naval point of view, it meant that the army troops taking that atoll had a greater potential volume of naval gunfire support than the marines at Tarawa. Fewer escort carriers were assigned to Makin, but three of the four fast carrier groups were operating in that vicinity. Allotting preponderate naval support to the weaker of the ground targets was necessary for a number of reasons. The transport area at Makin required the stronger antiaircraft guns, as well as the more powerful combat air and antisubmarine patrols. Finally, there was always the possibility that the enemy fleet would sortie, and the fear of such a development would mount if an equatorial weather front closed in over the Marshall Islands and hampered American reconnaissance. The warships accompanying both amphibious expeditions might have to drop other duties and deploy for a naval engagement.[40]

Accompanying Turner and under his immediate control at Makin were four old battleships, four heavy cruisers, and six destroyers. Turner's flag was in the old battleship *Pennsylvania*. Three escort carriers furnished direct air support, assisted by planes from one fast heavy and two fast light carriers during the early phase of the operation. Combat and garrison troops for Makin were lifted in nine assorted transport and cargo vessels, plus three tank landing ships, and a dock landing ship, accompanied by a minesweeper and screened by six destroyers.

Turner and Holland Smith delegated full tactical control of operations at Tarawa to Rear Admiral Harry Hill and Major General Julian Smith. Hill picked the old battleship *Maryland* for his flag. The choice was poor, but the best available since Turner had *Pennsylvania*. *Maryland* was overcrowded, and her communication facilities were antiquated. She was necessarily a part of the naval gunfire support group, and every time she fired a salvo, her communications were apt to go dead.[41] The naval attack force commander was not well situated to fulfill his duties, and Julian Smith was even worse located to keep abreast of progress ashore; but the problem of accommodating the attack and landing force commanders remained unsolved until the construction of amphibious force flagships equipped with special communication facilities (AGCs).[42] Two vessels of this type were first used in the Marshalls.

Including *Maryland*, naval gunfire at Tarawa was furnished by three old battleships, two heavy and three light cruisers, and nine destroyers. Five escort carriers were on hand for close air support, supplemented on the first day of the assault by aircraft from two heavy and one light fleet carrier. Thirteen transports, three cargo vessels, three tank landing ships, and a dock landing ship lifted the marines and their equipment to Tarawa, accompanied by two minesweepers and screened by seven destroyers. The Tarawa and Apamama garrison troops, principally composed of the Second and Eighth Marine Defense battalions respectively, were echeloned forward in tank landing ships with additional destroyer escort.[43]

Logistical planning on the higher echelons was, with one exception, good. The supply section of Nimitz's staff was a highly efficient well-integrated body of men, and by late 1943 was functioning smoothly. This section handled the logistical details for most of the Gilbert attack forces, and followed through with complete resupply plans. The high caliber of this work was indicative of the future excellence of Nimitz's supply section. Not only did it, in cooperation with the Navy Department in Washington, perform near miracles in base developments, but also it devised a floating train capable of keeping the Pacific Fleet at sea for weeks on end. This in turn reduced the number of advanced bases required, and eased the burden on assaulting marines.[44]

Shipping shortages plagued the supply section of Nimitz's staff and delayed the assignment of transports and cargo vessels to the attack forces. The logistics section of the Second Marine Division staff was unable at a convenient date to obtain reliable data on the characteristics of the vessels involved. Under the circumstances, combat-loading was well done. Only in one instance was there an annoying passage of several hours before meeting a demand for light tanks which had been bottom loaded, and this was not the fault of combat-loading since it was caused by a transfer of cargo in the transport area while lying to off Tarawa.[45] Few pallets (bulk packaging of supplies in an effort to facilitate beach logistics) were used because the necessary equipment arrived late at Wellington.

Julian Smith's supply section did an excellent job. It made no effort to lift more than five units of fire and thirty days of supplies. Motor transport was cut to what seemed to be a bare minimum, and that was more than was needed.[46]

Some marines complained that they carried more on their backs than could possibly be used in an operation like Betio. Evidence indicates, however, that at least a few carried more than their administrative order specified, and thus they had only themselves to blame. After the battle, some argued that the combat pack was cumbersome and should be discarded, that it cut down efficiency and lessened mobility. While men storming a coral atoll neither ate, slept, nor moved their bowels during the period of intense fighting, a pack of some description was necessary. Arms, ammunition, water, salt tablets, the intrenching tool, the gas mask, and dextrose and a bar of hard chocolate were essential—and as early as Guadalcanal it should have been learned that water supplementary to the canteens should be brought ashore in porcelain containers, otherwise it tastes of rust.[47]

The Second Marine Division finished its loading in time to sortie from Wellington on November 1 and to arrive for simulated combat landings at Efate in the New Hebrides Islands from the 7th through the 12th of November. This set of rehearsals, said Julian Smith, "was satisfactory but not complete." This was, to quote Holland Smith, "because the forces had such a short time to prepare and coordinate the rehearsal plans." The corps commander could have been more specific if he had singled out the absence of carrier pilots. This does not include those on the fleet carriers assigned to Tarawa, who, while the rehearsals were going on, were busy striking Rabaul; but it does include those on the escort carriers. These airmen needed to practice their mission; yet, up to the time of the actual assault, the squadrons of three of the five escort carriers which furnished the bulk of the air support at Tarawa, had not operated together as a group.[48]

Two separate rehearsal landings were made. They were principally of value in continuing to acquaint the men with the novel employment of amphibian tractors tactically. The verdict of the marines as regards their training for the Tarawa assault was generally favorable, but not universally so. There was a tendency to get ready for another jungle operation, for another Guadalcanal rather than for an assault against heavy fortifications on a coral atoll. Holland Smith, perhaps unwittingly, reaffirmed this misconception after Betio had been taken. The members of the Second Marine Division, he stated, "were veterans of a campaign and needed little training other than amphibious training." [49]

More than amphibious training was required. Some riflemen complained that in large part they were readied for jungle fighting, rather than for the type of warfare in which they had to coordinate their work with tanks and engineers. Julian Smith counters that of the 14,500 men evacuated from Guadalcanal in the spring of 1943, a total of around 12,000 had malaria. Rehabilitation was essential before training could begin, and rotation plus a large number of replacements further complicated the problem. The principal concern of the staff was, correctly under the circumstances, amphibious training, and with the assistance of the navy this was carried out. But coordinated tactics to take out heavy installations were not sufficiently stressed, a fact admitted by Julian Smith. He and his staff were somewhat surprised by the type of obstacles encountered on Betio. While the Japanese perfected a static defense tied down to heavy construction along the beaches and solid block-houses just inshore, the Americans planned their offensive with minds steeped in occidental warfare, with its sector defensive zones, defensive mobility, and greater reliance on artillery. The skill of the Japanese in erecting low-lying massive strong points as nearly as possible impervious to the flat trajectory of naval gunfire was enough to startle anyone; and their tactics of standing pat in individual groups well-protected by defensive installations until the last man was killed, rather than obtaining the sector coordination conventional in defensive fighting, surprised western minds. Under the circumstances, it is notable that after the battle both Julian Smith's engineers and his tankmen praised the practice they had received in coordinating their demolitions, flamethrowers, and firepower to the end of knocking out well-constructed emplacements. The missing link, in so far as there was any, was the absence of polished teamwork between riflemen on the one hand and demolition engineers and tankmen on the other. Had the training been more complete, one of the more serious flaws to appear in the struggle on the beach and inshore would have been corrected in time. This was the lack of communications between the tactical infantry commanders and their supporting tanks. In this connection it is evident that coordination between the riflemen and the light tanks was better than that between the men worming forward on their stomachs and the medium tanks. The reason was simply that the light tanks were with the division throughout the training period, whereas the medium tanks were lifted in a dock landing ship directly from New Caledonia and, like the new amphibian tractors from San Diego, were never fully integrated into the battalion landing teams. Thus a combination of circumstances is responsible for faulty riflemen-tank communications. "We did not lose a man inside the tanks," recalled the commanding officer of the Second Marine Tank Battalion, "but most of them were lost getting out and trying to communicate with the infantry." [50]

Rehearsals were of value in further acquainting the naval gunfire and air liaison parties with their duties. Personnel for these billets were scarce, and it was necessary to draw upon men in the artillery regiment of the Second Marine Division; but the plans for the use of these groups were more advanced than in any previous operation. Each battalion landing team was to have its own air and naval gunfire liaison groups, which, once communications were established ashore, were to help supervise close air support and call fires.[51] Such a decentralized system was essential. Integration was gained through the use of regimental, landing force, and naval attack force air and gunfire control officers, who monitored requests from the lower echelons and supervised the planes and gunfire ships held in reserve. Despite the use of pilots poorly trained in ground support duties and despite grave difficulties in establishing and maintaining communications ashore, the system proved its worth. Emphatically, the most effective periods of both air and naval gunfire support came after the troops were ashore.

Great strides in the direction of better naval gunfire support had been taken in September 1943, when headquarters of the Fifth Amphibious Corps and the administrative command for the cruisers and destroyers of the Pacific Fleet had established training facilities for naval gunfire ships and their shore fire-control parties in the Hawaiian area. Arrangements were made to evaluate scientifically the ability of naval gunners against shore targets, and the training improved marksmanship and shore control greatly as the Central Pacific drive gained momentum. Unfortunately, this gunfire course was set up too late fully to benefit the Tarawa assault. Only a few of the ships involved ran through the course.[52]

Although flaws later appeared in naval gunfire support, Tarawa stands as the dividing point between the discrediting of naval gunfire at Gallipoli and its vigorous and successful employment in the amphibious assault. Both marines and navy officers collaborated in drawing up the naval gunfire plans for Tarawa, and alike must share the praise for its merits and the criticism for its shortcomings. Praise, however, should far outweigh criticism when one considers that a lack of appropriations had hamstrung experimentation in the years between the wars, that a critical shortage of warships and fighting amid the jungles and large land masses of the Solomons-New Britain-New Guinea area had afforded no clear-cut opportunity to polish naval gunfire support, and that moving both heavy and light men-of-war into point blank range of a shore line in the face of coastal batteries was a revolutionary procedure.

Nerves were taut and tempers ragged as the rehearsal ended at Efate. A press conference was held, and the implementing commanders hid their concern, fears, and doubts behind a cloud of confidence. This was as it should have been. The navy officers were particularly proud of the fact that they were going to bore through with their ships until gun muzzles almost touched the coast. Reporters were told in detail how this concept was new, untried, dangerous. But it was necessary to get the marines ashore. One of the ranking navy commanders rose to heights of eloquence (and exaggeration) as he said of his chief gunnery target, Betio Islet: "We do not intend to neutralize it, we do not intend to destroy it. Gentlemen, we will obliterate it."

The Marine Corps has never been deficient in the art of public relations. Julian Smith listened to such talk as long as he was able, and then rose to say: "Even though you navy officers do come in to about 1,000 yards, I remind you that you have a little armor. I want you to know that marines are crossing the beach with bayonets, and that the only armor they'll have is a khaki shirt." [53]

3. *Approach and the Seizure of Makin and Apamama*

The Tarawa attack force departed its rehearsal area on November 13, and rendezvoused at sea with the army troops headed for Makin five days later. The approach of both attack forces was without serious incident. As Spruance had expected, the Bougainville operation and carrier strikes against Rabaul were timed perfectly to assist the Gilberts offensive.

Army troops destined for Makin had been trained amphibiously under the supervision of Holland Smith's staff, and were rehearsed in the Hawaiian area. They were attacking a target with overwhelming strength, since they had something in the vicinity of a six or seven to one superiority in numbers and firepower. Defenses on Makin were light, concrete and heavy coconut log emplacements being the exception rather than the rule, and for this reason the air and naval gunfire supporting arms were much more effective than at Tarawa. Over 1,700 tons of naval shells alone were poured into the principal geographical objective, Butaritari Islet of the Makin Atoll, before the landing began. Failure of the army troops once ashore to use naval gunfire on call indicates the lack of heavy opposition, as well as the fear of men inexperienced in the value of this excellent support that it might rain down on their own heads. Shore fire-control parties, however, had been trained, army personnel had been incorporated, and these were landed. Naval ships stood by to deliver fire, but, said Holland Smith's naval gunfire officer, "there was no fire called for by battalion or regimental shore fire-control parties." [54]

This was the first time the 165th Infantry Regiment had met the enemy, and under the circumstances it carried itself well. Forty-eight amphibian tractors lifted the initial waves to the beaches. There, fortunately for the soldiers, no resistance, or very little, was met. "The major difficulties encountered," reads one official army version, "came from the terrain. . . . The ineffective Japanese opposition to the landings . . . ceased in less than ten minutes." Another official account quotes the commander of the leading battalion landing team: "I jumped down from my boat and stood straight up for two or three minutes, waiting for somebody to shoot me. Nobody shot! I saw many other soldiers do the same thing."

There was trouble in getting tanks and artillery ashore, and the troops were hesitant to move without them; yet even inland, opposition was desultory. As the troops moved out to secure their beachhead, again quoting an army historian, "only insignificant rifle fire was met, the main obstacles being the debris and the water-filled craters resulting from the air and naval bombardment." At noon of the first day, "the American troops were opposed only by snipers." [55] Four nights passed, and the soldiers showed their lack of basic training by indiscriminate firing, revealing their positions and causing their casualties to mount. The regimental commander was killed trying to spur his men forward against sniper fire. He seems to have been a competent and energetic officer, but on the whole Holland Smith had reason to be annoyed with the performance of the army leaders of all ranks. It was not the fault of the men. They simply had not been well indoctrinated and were not being well commanded. The operations officer of the Fifth Amphibious Corps noted this emphatically: "On the land the heavy growth was such that visibility was limited so that even a squad leader could not observe his entire squad, if deployed, from a single location. The necessary control required a great deal of personal supervision by commanders of all grades. There was an evident lack of such supervision and fire discipline, which may account for entire units being held up for rather long periods by sniper fire. One such instance was observed when a battalion was held up by sniper fire for approximately four hours." [56]

This was certainly a poor showing when contrasted with what the marines did on Tarawa. Despite the weakness of the Japanese on the islet of Butaritari, it took the army longer to seize it than the marines needed to overrun Betio. Such a contrast, however, is grossly unfair. Since this was the first action for men of the 165th Infantry Regiment, a more valid basis of comparison exists with Guadalcanal. There the marines on Tulagi and Gavutu-Tanambogo showed up well in their first contact with the enemy, but those on Guadalcanal, and especially the battalion on the right flank of the movement toward the airfield, had been slow. The men of the Second Marine Division who landed on Tarawa were experienced in combat. It would be foolish to contend that there was any inherent difference between the men of the 165th Infantry Regiment and those of the Second Marine Division. Both came from similar families and had enjoyed similar backgrounds. Both had been given basic training in ground tactics from the same field manuals. It is true that marines are imbued with the compelling naval requirement of speed in such operations as that at Makin; while the army is accustomed to fighting on a larger land mass, and for this reason is anxious to employ advantageous terrain with artillery rather than naval gunfire support; but this consideration alone fails to account for the slowness with which Makin was seized.

As well as inexperience, inadequate basic training and poor leadership unquestionably delayed the capture of Butaritari, and increased the number of army casualties. The best way to prevent the enemy from reorganizing and stiffening his resistance again and again on a small objective such as an islet on a Central Pacific atoll was to drive relentlessly forward. Relative to opposition encountered, army losses were higher than those of the marines, who endured a beach assault at Tarawa. American casualties ashore on Makin were 216 dead, wounded, and injured; and at that, it was the supporting naval arms that really suffered at this northernmost objective. Including the men on the ill-fated *Liscome Bay*, the navy's losses were more than 1,000. Over 750 of these officers and bluejackets were dead.[57]

Apamama turned out to be a simple job, but one filled with excitement. The amphibious reconnaissance personnel aboard the submarine *Nautilus* came near being lost because of gunfire from an American destroyer. On the night before the morning of the Tarawa assault, she upped periscope off Betio to observe the enemy on that objective, but when she headed eastward toward Apamama, of necessity submerged, she encountered an unfavorable current. Having lost precious time, she surfaced to regain position as the Tarawa attack force approached, and an escorting United States destroyer suspecting hostile intent sent a 5-inch shell through her conning tower. *Nautilus* dived to 300 feet before control was regained, and after this additional delay went on to fulfill her mission.

Another countercurrent at Apamama during the night of November 20/21 carried the rubber boats of the three marine reconnaissance platoons out of position, but the men got ashore without additional mishap and proceeded to investigate the atoll. Resistance was encountered early the next morning. *Nautilus,* assisted later by a destroyer, provided naval gunfire, and most of the twenty-four Japanese on Apamama, conveniently for the Americans, committed suicide. The marines lost one man dead, one wounded, and a third suffered a hernia in unloading supplies.[58]

4. *Tarawa: Gunfire and Air Preparation and Disembarkation*

Tarawa was the difficult target in the Gilberts, and this assault would have been easier if the supporting arms had been better coordinated and more accurate. Almost from the moment the transports arrived in the vicinity of Tarawa, things began going contrary to schedule. Once introduced, the confusion of shifting times became cumulative, and the ill-effects lasted until the principal objective had been seized.

The major fault of both naval gunfire and air support was the lack of flexibility in delivering preparation once the planned schedule had broken down. The touchdown of troops on the shore is the important moment in planning an amphibious assault. All calculations must be premised on the precise minute when the first wave of troops is expected to hit the beach, and about this moment in turn revolves a long and complicated timetable for the supporting arms before, during, and after the run in from the line-of-departure to the shore. Doctrine recognizes, however, that should the time of the first landing be altered by the circumstances of execution, then all other scheduled activities must be shifted forward or backward as the case may be. In naval parlance, the time of the touchdown is normally called "H-hour," and all other activities move around H-hour, whatever that may turn out to be. This introduces such terminology as "H-hour minus 27 minutes" or "H-hour plus 48 minutes."

During the planning phase, however, it is necessary to equate H-hour to the precise moment that the landing is expected to begin, and this pegs all other undertakings on the dial of a clock. Thus regardless of doctrine a certain amount of rigidity is seemingly introduced into the schedule; and actual experience was needed to drive home to both naval gunners and carrier pilots the point that all aspects of amphibious warfare pivot around, not an arbitrarily selected moment, but the actual time, planned or not, that the first troops touch foot ashore. There are extenuating circumstances which go far in excusing the naval gunners, but no one has yet been able to explain fully what the airmen were doing. They were overconfident and inexperienced.

Pilots were late when their strike could have been and should have been delivered on schedule. They were right on the spot when the exigencies of the situation below compelled delay. They not only failed to hit the target with their quota of bombs and machine-gun fire, but interfered with the naval gunfire and helped to dissipate its effect. Nimitz noted the performance of these airmen with concern. Some came over Betio with little semblance of order, bombing and strafing at will and apparently to the individual tastes of their flight leaders. "It was evident," concluded Nimitz, "that the carrier squadrons were not fully trained to provide efficient air support of amphibious operations." [59]

The set schedule began going awry during the early morning darkness of November 20. The amphibious shipping, following a radar beacon pulsating from a destroyer, entered the transport area in good order; but while the marines were being served a big breakfast of steak and eggs, these vessels were caught in a surprisingly strong current to the southwest and began drifting out of position. They had to get under way again, and this led to some confusion as the amphibian tractors and landing craft plowed through the darkness in search of their assigned ships.[60]

Then a more serious event occurred. Twilight had scarcely begun when the enemy's coastal batteries on Betio fired. Near misses splashed the water in the transport area. Fortunately for the marines, no vessel was hit. Either the Japanese gunners needed practice, or, more probably, their fire-control instruments had been damaged by the preliminary bombing and bombardment delivered by Spruance's Fifth Fleet.

The possibility that the Japanese coastal guns would fire on the morning of the target date had been covered in the plans. From the outset, heavy warships took counterbattery positions, and Harry Hill lost no time in ordering them to reply to the Japanese. Temporarily, the large enemy weapons were silenced. Those on the western end of Betio were not entirely destroyed until after some of the marines were ashore, and those on the eastern end were still firing on the second day of the assault. But silencing enemy guns during the early twilight of November 20 was costly to the American cause. Communication difficulties on the flagship were expected, and *Maryland* had been assigned only two types of naval gunfire support in an effort to keep her radios in trim. It was hoped that she could hold off with her main batteries until just before the marines were to land; but she had to be used if counterbattery became mandatory. *Maryland* fired 16-inch projectiles at the Japanese coastal batteries, and her transmitting facilities temporarily went dead at a most inopportune moment, when they were needed to contact carrier planes scheduled for a twilight strike. In another respect, early morning counterbattery caused the prelanding gunfire and air support to lose some of its effectiveness. It had been hoped that the first heavy strike from the carriers could be brought in at twilight to precision bomb the enemy's coastal guns; but no one expected a bomber to hit a small ground target unless he could see it. Projectiles from warships burst first on Betio, raising clouds of dust and debris that would not completely settle until the islet was in American hands. There was yet another reason for concern. At this stage of the war, it was considered unsafe for bombers to operate over a target being pounded by naval projectiles, since no scheme had yet been devised to keep airmen out of the line of fire.

But the bombers failed to arrive on schedule. No one has yet explained exactly why. Nimitz's staff was unable to ascertain the cause. "For reasons as yet unknown," he reported to King, "this air strike was late in developing. . . ." Samuel Morison, in the first draft of his volume on the Gilberts and Marshalls (written while the war was still in progress), says that the confusion arose because the fast carriers assigned to Tarawa were plastering Rabaul at the time of the rehearsals, and that their commander could not be briefed on the plans. Rather than a dawn strike at 0545, this officer, Rear Admiral Alfred E. Montgomery, planned a sunrise attack at 0615.[61]

Hill stopped counterbattery a few minutes before the planes were due. When they failed to arrive, since the coastal weapons were still firing, counterbattery was resumed. *Maryland's* radio voice was finally restored, and the planes brought in some twenty-five minutes late. The strike had neither volume nor accuracy. Dust and confusion were partly to blame. The bombers were supposed to work over Betio for a half-hour, but they were withdrawn after ten minutes. It was necessary to get the first phase of the naval gunfire support under way.

Marines and naval gunners, prior to Tarawa, generally felt it impossible to do more than to neutralize shore targets. Planning for Betio modified this concept, the intent being to neutralize the entire islet and at least to destroy the enemy on and in the vicinity of the landing beaches. Executing the Betio assault revolutionized the concept of naval gunfire. It proved that destruction was not only feasible, but essential. As Admiral Hill observed, "the assault waves were opposed by only a few automatic weapons, the total on two of the three beaches being only about five. That was five too many, and regardless of whether future landing plans provide for taking care of them by tanks or other weapons, it is considered necessary that future naval gunfire plans provide for the destruction of these strong points before the assault." [62]

Firing previous to the assault was divided into two phases. The first was to begin immediately after the early plane strike, just as the sun rose, and was to last for seventy-five minutes. At the end of this period, it was anticipated that the exact time when the marines would hit the beaches could be accurately foretold. There followed an interval of adjustment to allow all remaining preassault gunfire and plane strikes to be correctly calibrated. Naval gunners were to lessen the volume rather than cease fire altogether at the end of the first phase. They were to maintain neutralization on the tail of the islet until the marines were ashore and had turned left to clear out that sector. Elsewhere they were to continue to interdict (interdiction is slow, well-aimed fire intended to harass the enemy and to curtail his mobility) favorable targets of opportunity as their navigators checked data and most of the warships shifted position to the best fire support sectors from which to pound the landing beaches. Then the second period, one of intensive point blank firing, was to begin forty-five minutes before the moment the first wave was expected to touch the coast.

Five minutes before the time the marines reached the beaches, naval gunners were instructed to lift their fire inland. At that moment, fighters were to begin strafing the beaches, continuing up to the time of the actual landings, when naval gunfire would be lifted altogether and bombers would for fifteen minutes strike inland targets. After the first troops were ashore, the supporting arms would enter the third and final phase of their duties. This was the period of call strikes and of naval gunfire controlled by the naval attack force commander on the basis of requests by the division, the assaulting regiment, and, later, the air liaison and naval gunfire parties assigned to the battalion landing teams.

Because of the delayed arrival of the planes for the first strike, the initial phase of naval gunfire was seven minutes late in beginning, but most of this lost time was made up at the other end of the period. Firing in the first phase was done principally by capital vessels. Battleships opened up from ranges varying from five to seven and one-half miles, paying particular attention to the three strongly fortified ends of the islet. Cruisers joined as the range was closed, and in some instances came with the battleships to within one mile or less of the beach. Destroyers fired little during the first phase, but screened the heavier warships.

The first phase provided for complete coverage of the islet, with pinpointed accuracy on important targets and heavy concentrations on the areas containing strong installations. Slow, deliberate fire was called for, but the tempo of actual delivery was too great to permit full spotting and hence accuracy. Some targets were designated as requiring a high-angle plunging trajectory with armor-piercing shells. A few antiaircraft shrapnel projectiles were used, but most were of the high-capacity explosive variety. Some of the latter were armed with steel nose plugs and equipped with base fuses to give them delayed detonations.[63]

Meanwhile, disembarkation was continuing. A few minutes after sunrise, at about 0615, the two minesweepers began clearing the lagoon channel. (See map 11.) They continued eastward into the lagoon, preparing the way for the boat waves. The minesweepers were followed in close support by two destroyers. These four vessels were fired on from the lagoon beach, but smoke was effectively employed and the destroyers, although one was hit by a couple of duds, delivered splendid counterbattery fire.[64]

A combination of circumstances delayed the arrival of the first and subsequent waves at the line-of-departure. Two of the explanations seem to be based on rumor. These were the discovery that high water over the reef was going to be later than anticipated, and that what has been termed a "strong unseasonable" wind was blowing from the southeast across the port bow of the tractors and boats.[65] It is impossible to see how anyone could, on the morning of November 20, have determined just when the depth over the lagoon reef would be at its maximum, and, while the direction of the wind was from the southeast, tending to blow the water off the reef and to establish a surface current counter to the approaching amphibious craft, it was normal for the season, and it was not of undue or unexpected intensity. All told, this wind was favorable to the operation. Smoke used to hide the minesweepers and to obscure the formation of the waves at the line-of-departure was carried northwestward from the point laid. This added nothing to the dust and confusion on the islet, and thus did not further black out those targets being sought by the naval gunners and pilots.

There are plenty of acceptable reasons why the tractors and boats were late in arriving at the line-of-departure. The confusion began right in the middle of the disembarkation, when the transports had to get under way. Tractor drivers of the fifty newer models had missed the rehearsals, and their inexperience added to the time-consuming task of transloading the first three waves, at sea, from boats into the amphibian tractors. Inside the lagoon, the minesweeper *Pursuit* was so busy sweeping and then firing counterbattery that she moved to the north. She was to mark the line-of-departure, and when the amphibian tractors reached her, they still had some distance to go before getting into position. Finally, some of the older models were developing mechanical failures; and although Julian Smith does not see why this should have held up entire waves, some tractor drivers thought that it did.[66]

No one could nor did anyone desire to interfere with the movement of the first wave. It was on its way to the shore, and could travel only so fast. The point was that every other aspect of the undertaking must be timed around the estimated moment when the first wave would reach the beaches. Harry Hill, in consultation with Julian Smith, was responsible for determining when this pivotal minute would fall. He miscalculated. Circumstances were against him.

The naval gunfire ships completed seventy-three minutes of phase one fire at 0735. They readjusted positions, continuing to interdict targets of opportunity, and were ready to begin the next phase exactly on time, that is, at 0745.

Almost simultaneously, Hill received news of the first tractor wave. A liaison plane informed him that the tractors were late and at the time were still short of the line-of-departure. Immediately, the naval attack force commander radioed new instructions to the supporting arms. The predicted time of landing was set back fifteen minutes, to 0845. Again, communications broke down between *Maryland* and the aircraft. The naval gunfire ships, as ordered to do in the plans, checked fire. Phase two, scheduled for forty-five minutes, was delayed but would be delivered in full.

Most of the firing in phase two was also to be done by heavy ships. These were to enfilade the landing beaches by lying to off the western end of Betio, a dangerous practice for men-of-war, but the risk was accepted in the hope of obtaining the desired result. Throughout most of this final phase of preparatory bombardment, the plan was for the firing to remain deliberate. This would improve vision and permit accurate destruction; but just before the marines reached the beach, the tempo was to be increased fifty per cent in an effort to obtain the maximum neutralization at this critical moment.[67]

The amphibian tractors were slower than expected. Tests had been held, but it had been impossible, given available data, to duplicate accurately conditions of wind, current, and reef. Everyone during the planning and rehearsals had concurred that these tractors would cruise at four and one-half knots. At Betio on the morning of November 20, they averaged slightly less than four knots.[68]

Hill was informed at 0823 that the first wave had just crossed the line-of-departure. Here was the difficult and vital decision. He was not in a good position to control naval gunfire, since he was outside the lagoon. Betio was obscured by smoke and dust, which was being carried by the wind into the lagoon. Repeated tests had set the figure of forty minutes (the time needed to cover 6,000 yards at four and one-half knots) for the run in from the line-of-departure to the beaches. This was the calculation on which Hill must rely. He did not know exactly why the tractors were late in reaching the line-of-departure, and he had no grounds for premising his decision upon a run to the beach of more than forty minutes. He wanted to lift the gunfire before it endangered the advancing marines. At this stage of the war, few suspected that maintaining naval gunfire up to the last possible moment, even at the risk of hitting friendly troops, would in fact save American lives. Hill added forty minutes to 0820 and reset the target hour a second time, at 0900. This meant that the final phase of preparatory naval gunfire was spread over an hour rather than forty-five minutes.[69]

Precisely at 0855 Hill ordered naval gunfire lifted inland for the final five minutes of the second phase. This, as it happened, was exactly fifteen minutes before the first troops landed. The tractors came in at staggered intervals. Officers tried to keep the drivers of the newer models from forging ahead. Apparently, some were more successful than others. From right to left, the beaches were reached at 0910, 0922, and 0917.[70] Lifting the gunfire inland at 0855 was as planned (coming as it did at what was thought to be "H-hour minus five minutes"), but as Hill later confessed, he thereupon placed his faith in a very weak arm. Fighters were supposed to strafe the beaches as the tractors cut through the last few hundred yards of water. Even if the pilots had performed as well as expected, machine-gun fire against the defenses of Betio was about as effective as dropping marbles on the sidewalk.

Unlike Hill, the carrier pilots were in a position to observe what was going on in the lagoon. They failed to get word of either change in the target hour. No matter, Turner had underscored the instructions handed to these airmen. The original plans were for strafing to begin at 0825, but that was only tentative, and, Turner had specified, *"the distance of the boats from the beach is the governing factor."* [71]

Naval guns were still firing at 0825. Betio and the lagoon were as usual obscured by smoke and dust; but men in the control vessels could see that at 0825 the first wave had just crossed the line-of-departure. The ranking officer in the lagoon had made artificial smoke during the period of minesweeping, but he then stopped for fear of obscuring the progress of the boats from such friendly eyes as those of the pilots—a wise decision. Officers in Hill's liaison plane could see the delayed tractors. Apparently not so the carrier pilots. They started strafing the beach at 0825.

Finally they were reached by *Maryland's* croaking radio. The strafing was called off, and naval guns resumed their thunderous fire. The beaches were pounded steadily until 0855, and then at 0900 with two exceptions naval gunfire was lifted from the entire islet. One of these exceptions was two destroyers which continued interdiction of the southern coast until 0915. The other exception was the two destroyers in the lagoon, which were able to keep close tabs on the first wave and therefore were instructed by Hill to shoot until they were stopped by tractors loaded with marines at the water's edge.[72]

The fighters and the bombers, in a disorganized fashion, resumed the fulfillment of their mission at sometime around 0855 and 0900. The fighters had been told to make their last strafing pass when the first wave was 100 yards from the shore, but they all cleared out when the tractors were several times that distance away.[73] As they left they informed Hill that they were out of ammunition, which was the result of their premature strafing earlier in the morning. Those airmen returning to the fleet carrier *Essex* were confident. They reported that they had done their work well. The bombing, strafing, and bombardment, they said, had been almost completely destructive. Landings could be made without much opposition.[74]

This was a complete distortion of reality. Without the preassault bombing and bombardment, any type of a landing would have been impossible; but the naval gunfire and air support arms had failed to function as expected. About 3,000 tons of naval projectiles were hurled at Betio, the great bulk of it just before the landing on the morning of November 20—all this on an islet less than a half mile square. The allotted quota of bombs was not dropped, but the volume delivered was impressive. "Heavier support of this kind is not to be expected in the Central Pacific Campaign," judged Nimitz, "but increased efficiency in that support is to be expected." [75]

All hands turned to after Tarawa to improve the quality of naval gunfire and air support. One of Julian Smith's first messages from Betio went to his command counterpart, Harry Hill: "Strongly recommend that you and your chief of staff come ashore . . . to get information about the type of hostile resistance which will be encountered in future operations." [76]

The most obvious need was for pilots better trained in close air support. Holland Smith, however, was never successful in getting the type of pilots he wanted. "It is recommended," he urged after Tarawa, "that consideration be given to the assignment of at least one Marine Aircraft Wing specifically for direct air support in landing operations. This wing would make direct air support a specialty and would train specifically for this purpose. They should be given a complete background of amphibious operations and a thorough and considerable period of training."

The navy refused. Accepting such a recommendation would withdraw pilots from the decks of carriers who, in addition to air support, were needed for strictly navy functions, and possibly for use in a fleet engagement. As long as the navy judged its own flight personnel superior to marine airmen in strictly navy duties, and as long as both fast and escort aircraft carriers were scarce and the enemy retained a strong fleet, the navy's position in this regard was understandable. The decision, however, prevented marine pilots from supporting their comrades and army troops ashore in the Marshalls and the Marianas. Marine pilots in the Central Pacific before Tarawa served important defensive missions, but after that battle, since their craft were of short range, they watched the war leave them far behind. Their principal function in that section of the globe was bombing by-passed atolls.

Holland Smith doubtless anticipated a refusal of his request for a Marine Air Wing aboard escort carriers. He ended his recommendation by asking for the best possible alternative. Before the next operation he wanted an opportunity to train navy escort carrier pilots in the tactical details of fighting on the beaches and inshore. "If it is impractical to assign a Marine Aircraft Wing for this purpose," he concluded, "a suitable assignment should be made with the same objective in mind." [77]

Marine casualties at Tarawa shocked navy airmen into a better understanding of their air support mission. Aside from practice in point bombing targets smaller than any ship, studies were inaugurated to determine the size and characteristics of bombs best suited to penetrate and demolish ground installations. Never again, as at Tarawa, did the pilots fail even to try to drop those heavy demolition charges designed to destroy buildings and rip aside camouflage and undergrowth. The napalm bomb (tanked gasoline mixed with a jelly substance that would stick to any surface) later produced was of further assistance in this work. Finally, in no future operation were any half-submerged hulks off the coast or buildings along the shore in the vicinity of the beaches left purposely intact. These, notably Japanese privies built over the sea water, were allowed to stand as aids to navigation and hence gunfire accuracy. The enemy from the first employed them to conceal his sniper and other small arms fire. The error was obvious as soon as friendly troops were ashore, but then too frequently these havens for the enemy were bombed and shelled only at jeopardy of American lives.[78]

Likewise, naval gunfire, which was by far the more effective of the two supporting arms, improved because of Tarawa. Recommendations poured into Nimitz's headquarters from every echelon of command. Together, these constituted one of the more important lessons to be derived from the assault. On the basis of these recommendations, Betio's installations were duplicated on the gunnery range of the Fifth Amphibious Corps in the Hawaiian area. Data accumulated in demolishing these targets were set beside interpretations of future photographed objectives, and the needed ammunition was allotted to the fire support schedule on a really scientific basis.[79]

Up to the time of the actual landings on Betio, almost all navy and marine officers believed that their bombardment was of decisive effect. Those, however, who went in with the support waves were shocked to discover how little this belief was justified. Members of the shore fire-control parties were "quite unnerved upon closer approach to the beach to see many batteries of all calibers still firing at the waves engaged in landing." [80] One of them was more emphatic. "We did not neutralize pillbox installations," he said, "nor did we even neutralize the beaches." In amazement he added: "Six layers of coconut logs reinforced with sand, concrete, and steel formed a chain of pillboxes, gun positions, and a net of passageways along the shore. Intense prearranged direct fire from close inshore for a considerable period would have been necessary to neutralize that beach." [81]

The last quotation is an exaggeration since a small part of the selected beaches was not barricaded and since the barricade elsewhere along the western lagoon coast was usually not as strong as described. But that is not the important part of the quotation. This particular member of a shore fire-control party was, like many of his colleagues at the time, confused in his terminology. He used the word neutralization when he meant destruction.

Destructive fire requires deliberate, pinpointed accuracy. Neutralization, on the other hand, is obtained through a huge volume of explosives, and can best be gained by quickly saturating larger areas. After Tarawa, these two types of fire were specifically called for in the plans, and received rigid adherence. The naval gunfire annex to Admiral Hill's Tarawa report admitted that the plans for Betio asked for the impossible: simultaneous neutralization and destruction in the same target areas. The old precept of keeping the enemy "guessing where to jump next," was carefully arranged. This required placing sequences of fire into areas unpredicted by the previous fall of shot. To achieve such an end, gunners shifted targets repeatedly and rapidly, with a resultant loss of control, a lowering of the effectiveness of fire, and a waste of some ammunition. The precept, in short, was of value for neutralization, but unacceptable where destruction was the objective.[82]

Nor was the fire at Betio deliberate enough. Slow deliberate fire had been stressed in the plans, but here again the navy and marine officers who drew up the naval gunfire schedule stumbled over themselves by confusing the terms neutralization and destruction. The gunners threw shells too rapidly into Betio. This stirred up dust and smoke and tended to convert what should have been direct pinpointed fire into radar-controlled indirect area coverage.[83] After Tarawa this error was avoided by extending the time for delivering the fire scheduled in the prelanding phases.

Efforts at destruction were not as successful as those designed to obtain neutralization at Tarawa. One reason, in addition to the lack of deliberate firing, was found by the naval gunfire support commander, Rear Admiral Howard F. Kingman USN. The number of armor-piercing and base-fused shells was not sufficient. "Our high-capacity projectiles, with superquick fuses," he said, "made a grand display, but accomplished little if any real destruction of installations or personnel." [84] Examination of Japanese defenses after the battle revealed that, while formidable, each could have been penetrated if hit by the proper trajectory and type of shell. An armor-piercing shell with a plunging trajectory would have knocked out the strongest installation on Betio, a small command post built almost flush to the ground with a roof of reinforced concrete $6\frac{1}{2}$-feet in thickness.[85]

Likewise neutralization would have been greater if frequent shifting of target areas had been avoided in the first phase of naval gunfire support, and if while enfilading the beaches in the second phase a coverage of the water immediately offshore had been obtained. The mean center of impact during the second period was inshore, rather than along the beaches.[86] This occurred despite clear orders to the contrary, which called for enfilade fire on the beaches and in the water adjacent to detonate possible mines.[87] Such a failure was not repeated after Betio. "We must," commented one observer, "plaster the beach with prearranged fire, even at the cost of slighting inland strongpoints." [88] Fall of shot at the water's edge would have helped rather than hindered the assault. Officers were impressed by the offshore defenses at Betio, particularly those more nearly completed, along the south and west coasts. Some method must be devised to detonate mines and demolish man-made obstacles, but this task was probably beyond the capabilities of naval gunfire. This fact stimulated further thinking in the direction of the underwater demolition team,[89] first conceived by Major Earl H. Ellis USMC in the early 1920's.

Thus Tarawa showed that it was possible to destroy, as well as merely to neutralize, beach defenses, and also that it was possible to furnish a rolling barrage with naval guns. In the future this barrage moved just ahead of the troops as they landed, inshore and outward along both flanks. Landing craft mounting rockets assisted in this work. There was no time to get rockets and the necessary equipment to the Second Marine Division in New Zealand. Rockets were used at Makin, but at Betio nothing more than a token display was employed; at least so the reports indicate, although Julian Smith cannot recall the firing of a single rocket.[90] Especially, however, were destroyers needed to provide both barrage and close in gunfire support. Harry Hill was justified in making two complaints. The destroyers he had at Tarawa were armed to fight enemy planes, rather than to fire at targets ashore. They were supplied with antiaircraft 5-inch projectiles, rather than high-capacity common. The latter type of explosive possessed a smaller bursting radius, and was therefore safer for friendly troops when being laid down in a rolling barrage adjacent to their expected advance. Nor did the naval attack force commander have enough destroyers, although this of course was a continuing complaint throughout the Central Pacific drive. The lagoon at Tarawa on November 20 lacked maneuver room to accommodate more than two destroyers, but Hill pointed out that in the future, at more commodious targets, destroyers should be used in relays to furnish a rolling barrage as well as call fire after the troops were ashore. Destroyers were always running out of ammunition, so it was necessary to use them in relays; but often the sound heads with which they ferreted out enemy submarines were damaged by inshore work. It was therefore desirable to have a sufficient number of these valuable vessels in order to leave some constantly screening the transport area and the heavier warships, while others were used for naval gunfire. Hill wanted destroyers brought so close inshore that they would be able to use not only their 5-inch batteries, but also their 40-millimeter antiaircraft guns.[91]

One of the more notable features about all of the action reports on Tarawa, marine and navy, is the zeal with which the officers concerned picked out the flaws of their performance and sought far-reaching remedies. No higher commendation than this can be offered to these men; but, unless the historian is careful, their reports distort the picture, throw the operation out of its true perspective, and obscure the brilliance of the success actually gained. Another quotation from the naval gunfire support commander, Admiral Kingman, illustrates this danger. "From an observer's viewpoint," he said as he recalled the morning of November 20, "it seemed almost impossible for any human being to be alive on Betio Island. Ton after ton of explosives was rained upon an island less than 0.4 miles square, and yet, when the bombardment was stopped, Japanese manned machine guns and literally annihilated the . . . waves." [92]

That statement is a gross exaggeration, made by the man who above all others would have been responsible had it been true. If not destruction, naval gunfire did achieve a period of neutralization. The first three waves of marines got ashore almost intact. This transpired despite the interval of from fifteen to twenty-seven minutes which elapsed between the lifting of naval gunfire and the time the first tractors touched the beaches. The Japanese began showing signs of life after the first three waves were in. This fact casts an entirely new light on the operation. The critical failure at Tarawa was the lack of momentum in the assault, rather than somewhat faulty naval gunfire and haphazard air support. Blame, if there be any, should rest on the lack of amphibian tractors; or, if the reader prefers, on the absence of sufficient water over the reef to float landing craft.

The marines in the first three waves received some hostile fire while in their tractors, but their casualties began to mount after they were ashore, when they tried to scale the barricade. It was the members of the subsequent waves who were shot in the water off Betio. Since the landing craft of the later waves tied up on the reef, the assault lost its impact. Almost as important was that unfortunate set of circumstances which caused the naval guns to be lifted too soon from the beaches. Just as the marines of the first three waves needed help in crossing the barricade and overrunning the beach defenses, the Japanese, battered in their dugouts by avalanche after avalanche of neutralizing fire, shook their dazed minds free from shock, left their underground shelters, and manned their beach defenses.

The left flank of the easternmost beach provides a further case in point. In that area the two lagoon destroyers continued to fire for twenty-one minutes after the other warships to the west of Betio had ceased. These destroyers, in other words, plastered the left flank beach until the first tractors headed into that zone were only sixty seconds from the shore. The Japanese on the left flank of the assault waves were the last to rally themselves and to open fire.[93]

5. *Tarawa: The First Thirty-six Hours of the Assault*

The temporary neutralization of the northwestern lagoon coast of Betio permitted the first three waves of marines to get ashore and to gain two isolated toeholds, rather than a beachhead. Thereafter the obstacle of the reef and enemy opposition robbed the assault of its momentum. Neither the three battalions in the van nor any subsequent unit during the first thirty-six hours of the battle reached the beaches intact. Unless infantry components can cross the coast with some semblance of organization, they cannot advance against determined resistance. For a day and a half there was no fully organized American unit on Betio. Marines were shot in the water, on congested beaches seeking desperately some defilade from enemy fire, and as individuals or small groups as they tried to penetrate inland. Men with rifles, demolition engineers, artillerymen, and tanks had to make up for all the previous errors and miscalculations. As Vandegrift later said, "On Betio, our operation was assault from beginning to end." [94] And, until a unit was landed with organization intact on the evening of the second day of the contest, the battle hung in the balance.

Or, so it seemed at the time to Julian Smith and his staff. Little can be said of the Japanese side of this story. The island commander, Rear Admiral Meichi Shibasaki IJN, is dead, and few of his records were recovered from the holocaust that began sweeping Betio on November 20. One of the tiny group of prisoners of war testified that Shibasaki was a man of great drive and confidence, who had claimed that not even 1,000,000 Americans could seize Tarawa in 100 years.[95] He did his best to make good that boast. His defenses, although not quite complete, were superbly planned; and in October he had instructed his special naval landing force personnel to "wait until the enemy is within effective range (when assembling for landing) and direct your fire on the enemy transport group and destroy it. If the enemy starts a landing, knock out the landing boats with mountain gunfire, tank guns and infantry guns, then concentrate all fires on the enemy's landing point and destroy him at the water's edge." [96] It seems likely that Shibasaki intended to counterattack on the night of November 20/21, when the Americans were very much "at the water's edge." It is impossible to say whether or not such an effort would have been successful. The marines expected it and had trained for it, but it did not come.

The probable explanation is that Shibasaki's communications were destroyed by the prelanding naval gunfire and bombing. He had only begun to bury his telephone wires, and these were knocked out from the start.[97] Thereafter he had to rely on runners, who could not get through because of the constant pounding of naval shells and bombs, which were later joined by shore-based American artillery and continued to batter the Japanese on Betio after the first waves of marines were ashore. Thus Shibasaki lost control of his troops. His October orders prove that he wanted to achieve at least some mobility and to concentrate at the beaches. It is also possible that, at least in part, he desired his men to remain in their dugouts and pillboxes and to fight to the last, individually and in groups; at any rate, whether from choice or necessity, that is in the main what happened. No counterattack developed on either the first or the second nights; it finally came on the third night, after the enemy had been squeezed into the tail of the islet and there was no chance of success.

The first three waves on the morning of November 20 met no flanking fire from the long pier. The regimental scout and sniper platoon, led by Lieutenant William D. Hawkins USMC, had removed the enemy from this structure. Hawkins, like most of the aggressive junior officers and noncommissioned ratings, was later a casualty. He died of his wounds. Of him Shoup, the regimental commander, asserted: "It's not often that you can credit a first lieutenant with winning a battle, but Hawkins came as near to it as any man could. He was truly an inspiration." [98]

Inspiration was essential. The tractors met relatively little enemy fire in the water, and much of this was ineffectual. Air bursts from artillery pieces began when the tractors were about 3,000 yards out, but the cases were overcharged with explosive and the shrapnel was almost as small as sand. It was after the first three waves of tractors had hit the beaches that enemy fire rose in quantity and improved in quality. The plan was to push the tractors inland before the marines disembarked, but the beach barricade halted all vehicles but two. These two, crossing the left flank beach, found a convenient opening at the base of the long pier and took their human cargo inshore to the south side of the northwestern taxiway. All others discharged their loads at the water's edge.[99]

Even well-trained men with battle experience on Guadalcanal lost their equanimity when face to face with the coast defenses of Betio. They threw themselves at the base of the beach barricade. They sought some defilade. To one observer in the first waves, "it looked as if it was going to be impossible to get them to advance forward beyond the protection of the revetment along the beach. Had not several junior officers and noncommissioned officers actually jumped over this revetment and led their troops, the results would have been disastrous." [100]

Most of the marines who provided such inspiration and leadership were, like Hawkins, early casualties. From the outset, the high percentage of dead and wounded among officers and noncommissioned officers was a handicap. Their absence ashore was further aggravated by other circumstances. Almost all the men in the final waves of the three assault battalions, as well as those later committed to the lagoon beaches from regimental and division reserve, had to wade in from the edge of the fringing reef. Again, many of the aggressive leaders were shot, this time in the water. Or, if they got ashore, the leaders were apt to be separated from their men. The three battalion commanders of the men landing in beach assault were in the fourth wave, lifted in landing craft. In no place was there more than three feet of water over the reef, and in spots the depth was a matter of inches.[101] So, these battalion commanders were among the first to jump in and start wading. What became of them typifies the confusion along the lagoon beaches during the morning of November 20. Only one of them got ashore alive and in a position to control his men. Thus it happened that the marines, once on the beach, frequently found that the officers and noncommissioned personnel in the vicinity were strangers. Control under these conditions was exceedingly difficult. The first battalion committed to the center beach was led by an absolute stranger. The regular commander was shot in the water, and the executive officer landed out of position. An observer from the Fifth

Amphibious Corps voluntarily took over command. After trying to move a reluctant group of marines forward, he said to the correspondent Robert Sherrod: "They don't know me, you see. They haven't got the confidence men should have in their officers." [102]

It was almost a miracle that, under the circumstances existing offshore and on the northwestern lagoon beaches, any control whatsoever was obtained and retained. Certainly it is a tribute to Marine Corps indoctrination that an amount of control was maintained sufficient to clear the beach at the western end of Betio, to cross from the lagoon to the south coast and split the islet in two, and ultimately to secure a full lagoon beachhead.

Good planning committed medium tanks in the fifth wave to the lagoon beaches, and most of these got ashore at around noon on November 20. These tanks were able to lumber through water that after the reef was crossed might suddenly drop to a depth over a man's head. Wading marines were not so lucky. Some were killed outright by enemy fire; others, heavily laden, were wounded and a few stepped into water pits and drowned.

The one battalion commander who got ashore in position was Major Henry P. Crowe, whose Second Battalion Eighth Marines was attached to Shoup's Second Regiment. Crowe's men landed on the easternmost beach, to the left of the base of the long pier. (See map 11.) Assisted by the destroyers firing from the lagoon, Crowe lost very few men in the first three waves, but in the fourth and fifth waves (the fifth containing tanks), casualties jumped to eight or ten per cent. Both of his half track 75-millimeter guns broke down early, and he set up his two 37-millimeter weapons defensively. By noon he was fortunate enough to get his full platoon of medium tanks ashore, and he ordered them to attack directly to the south and knock out all enemy positions encountered. By sunset only one of his four tanks remained in action. One was destroyed by friendly dive bombers; a second by enemy fire; and the planes and the enemy cooperated on the third.

Crowe employed his tank, demolition, and infantry teams well. He early gained some depth on his right, and was able to establish lateral contact with friendly troops in that area. The difficult thing about his situation was that the Japanese were intrenched on the entire left half of his beach. At about noon, Shoup tried to send Crowe organized reinforcements. Shoup had already committed his battalion in regimental reserve to another beach, but Julian Smith released one of the two battalion landing teams in division reserve, the Third Battalion Eighth Marines, Major Robert H. Ruud, to his assaulting regimental commander; and Shoup ordered this unit to land on the easternmost beach and to move into position on Crowe's critical left flank. By this time Japanese fire across the water to the east of the long pier was intense. Ruud's first wave, dismounting from boats at the edge of the reef, was greeted by a hail of fire and all semblance of formation was lost. Subsequent waves angled to the right, over to the long pier, and followed it in along both sides to its base. Getting ashore was a time-consuming and costly process. Ruud reached the coast in the late afternoon. He found many of his officers and noncommissioned officers missing. The men remaining to him were disorganized and badly shaken. They were incapable, even if daylight had remained, of gaining ground the first day. Ruud's outfit was weaker than Crowe's, which had been fighting ashore for nine hours. Rather than on Crowe's left flank, the Third Battalion Eighth Marines was placed on the easier right flank of Crowe's position.

Crowe and Ruud, at nightfall of November 20, held not a continuous line but a series of foxhole positions running from a point just short of the base of the wharf, about 300 yards east of the long pier, for an inland depth of some 100–250 yards. The men were strung out almost due south from the coast, across the northeastern taxiway, and then westward parallel and about 200 yards distant from the main airstrip. There, at a point due south of the long pier, Ruud tied in for the night with the marines who had crossed the center beach. Both battalions of the Eighth Marines had sustained heavy casualties. They would be unable to clear out the left flank of their beach until the end of the third day of fighting, and then only with the help of very close naval gunfire support from the lagoon.[103]

The situation on the center beach at sunset on November 20 was worse than Crowe's. The unit sent in assault onto the center beach was the Second Battalion Second Marines. The executive officer of this unit was lost in the confusion. Intense enemy fire drove his party far to the right, about a half mile off his designated point of landing. He got ashore on the right flank of the westernmost beach. The commanding officer of the Second Battalion Second Regiment, Lieutenant Colonel Herbert R. Amey, was an early casualty. In the absence of the executive officer, a corps observer with Amey's command group, Lieutenant Colonel Walter I. Jordan USMC, took over the battalion.

Ashore, Jordan found the situation precarious. He set up his command post in a shell crater on the beach at about 1000. He was from the outset short of officers and noncommissioned ratings. At first he had no communications. Runners advised him that marines from his first three waves were about seventy-five yards in from the water's edge, "but could not advance due to machine gun positions to their front and flanks, and sniper fire from trees in their immediate vicinity. All information received was very, very brief and vague, so we continued to hold where we were. At this time there was no contact between elements on my right or left and I could not find out how many men of each company had landed." [104]

Jordan soon got reinforcements, although the original intent was not to assist him. Shoup, boated at the line-of-departure in a landing craft, was in communication with all of his assault battalion commanders until they reached the coast. The regimental commander was most concerned with his right flank beach. By 1000 he knew that Crowe had landed, and he had watched men cross the center beach. Everything he heard from the assault unit on his right flank, the Third Battalion Second Marines, was discouraging. Neither the executive officer nor the commander of this battalion got ashore on the proper beach. The commanding officer of this unit, Major John F. Schoettel, later reported he had withdrawn from the vicinity of his beach because of heavy fire and because he believed his first three waves "all wiped out." The regimental commander, having been advised of the mishap to the first waves, ordered the subsequent ones onto the center beach. The last Shoup heard from Schoettel was this reply:

"We have nothing left to land." [105]

Shoup had to remedy that situation at once. He felt it foolish to try again the direct approach to the westernmost beach. Even before he was ashore, he committed his regimental reserve. He ordered Major Wood B. Kyle to land the First Battalion Second Marines on the center beach, to turn right, and to work his way west to the relief of whatever marines might be on the right flank beach.

Since Kyle's men started in before those under Ruud, it was possible to try to set Kyle and the First Battalion Second Marines ashore in amphibian tractors. This was the last time an effort was made to use these vehicles tactically. Few had been lost in running the first three waves to the beaches, but on retracting and heading for the line-of-departure, a great number were struck in the stern and began succumbing to enemy fire, as well as to mechanical breakdowns. Only a small group sufficient to lift two-thirds of Kyle's battalion could be assembled, and one of his companies was forced to wait till noon for transportation. The other two companies crossed the reef and approached the center beach at about 1130. The reentrant, as had been feared, contained a threatening pocket of Japanese. Fire from this area, which extended from the right half of the center beach across most of the right flank beach, was deadly. Even the tractors, at this late hour, could not safely make the coast. The battalion sustained around 200 casualties on the beach or just offshore. One officer and slightly more than 100 men were driven far to the right by enemy fire. They landed out of position, on the western edge of the right flank beach. The others came ashore onto the left half of the center beach. They were disorganized, shaken, and without their heavy equipment.[106]

By noon of November 20, Shoup had committed the four battalion landing teams under his direct control and one of the two in division reserve. He and his party reached the beach after considerable difficulty at around 1200. Along with Shoup, among others, were Lieutenant Colonel Evans Carlson who had led a raider battalion on Guadalcanal and was now a corps observer, and Lieutenant Colonel Presley Rixey, Shoup's artillery commander. In getting ashore these officers had discovered an important fact, but it was too late fully to benefit from it. There was a way into the northwestern lagoon coast less dangerous than any other. As Carlson described it, "the only approach to the beach that was relatively secure was a corridor about 100 yards wide which extended west from the pier."

Rixey used this corridor that afternoon and evening in following Shoup's first order once ashore, and bringing in 75-millimeter pack howitzers for general support. Since Shoup as yet had no reliable communication with the division staff on *Maryland,* he next ordered Carlson back along the pier and out of the lagoon to give Julian Smith a personal account of conditions on the coast. "He asked me to say to General Smith," Carlson later recalled, "that he proposed to stick and fight it out regardless of how tough the situation became, and requested that further reserves be sent in through the center beach. His plan was to expand the beachhead at this point to the south, and to link up all landing teams on all beaches." [107]

Shoup set up his command post beside a well-built Japanese installation just inshore on the center beach. The walls of this structure gave him some protection from enemy fire, but sentries were placed to guard the entrances and vents, for it still contained more than a score of live Japanese.

At an early hour Shoup gained lateral contact with Crowe, and, being on the scene, the regimental commander was acquainted with the situation on the center beach. Three medium tanks arrived on the center beach at about noon, and aided the advance across the northwestern taxiway. By nightfall the First and Second Battalions of the Second Marines held a beach of some 250–300 yards depth, and it was also constricted laterally. To the west these marines faced strong enemy positions occupying the entire right flank of the center beach. These Japanese prevented Shoup from learning what was happening on the right flank beach, much less gaining lateral contact with the marines in that area.

Communication difficulties plagued the Americans as well as the Japanese at Tarawa from beginning to end. *Maryland's* faltering voice was more than duplicated by failures in ship-to-shore and beach-to-beach radio networks. Basically the fault lay with the sets, which were bulky and hard to handle, and which were not adequately waterproofed. Once wet, which happened to all in getting them ashore, they refused to function before drying out. This not only complicated close air and naval gunfire support once the marines were on the beaches, but more seriously it kept Shoup and Julian Smith in the dark tactically speaking, and caused them to fumble through and to make decisions on the basis of inadequate knowledge.

Although it was about sunset before the men on the right flank beach found a radio and got it functioning, they were far better off than anyone suspected. The Japanese pocket in the cove of the lagoon beaches began on the right portion of the center beach and ran continuously westward along almost the full length of the reentrant, covering, as well as one-half of the center beach, more than four-fifths of the right flank beach. It was only on the extreme northwestern end of Betio that any marines capable of fighting got ashore. It was a mixed group. One of the company commanders, Major Michael P. Ryan, took charge. Most of his men were from his own battalion, that is the Third Battalion of the Second Marines, but there were present as well marines from both battalions committed to the center beach, who had been driven off course by heavy enemy fire and had landed far to the right.[108]

These men managed to clear out the extreme northwestern tip of the islet, and about noon what was left of a platoon of tanks arrived. When Ryan wrote his report, he was not in a talkative mood. "Two medium tanks got in over the reef," he said, "and the engineers blasted a hole in the sea wall for them to come through. We put three companies abreast, took two medium tanks, but the two tanks were knocked out. It was then about 1630. We could not find a radio in communication with Division and later found the Second Battalion's." [109]

Those few words include a lot of fighting. The two tanks were early put out of action by enemy fire, but Ryan managed to push his men southward along the west coast to a depth of some 500 yards. That position could not be held for the night, however. Enemy installations had been by-passed, and Ryan lacked the heavy equipment to crush them and needed flamethrowers to kill the Japanese inside. There was nothing left to do at nightfall but to retire to the northwestern tip of the islet and dig in. At about the same time, Ryan managed to inform Shoup and Julian Smith of his night position. Hardships of communication, however, prevented a clear understanding of the course of events on the western end of Betio. Nor could Ryan predict the enemy's next move in that zone. Thus he was unable to promise that his weak force could, the next day, clear the western beach entirely. Shoup and Julian Smith believed Ryan hard-pressed in a tiny pocket on the northwestern tip of Betio. There was no reason for them to believe anything else. The golden opportunity of getting a battalion landing team ashore, intact and fully organized, across the western beach of Betio went unnoticed for more than twelve hours.

Aboard *Maryland* Julian Smith was in a tight spot. Aside from infrequent radio messages from the shore, all of them pessimistic, he was kept informed of the tactical situation by observers aloft in scout planes. He knew it was difficult to get men ashore, but he was also convinced that only utmost pressure applied as rapidly as was possible against the Japanese on Betio would bring victory. An assault fails unless the attacker brings overwhelming firepower against the defender. Julian Smith had to commit his men and commit them fast. This necessity brought the division commander face to face with two problems—where to get the men and at what point to land them.

By noon of November 20, Julian Smith had but one battalion landing team in division reserve. Before he could safely commit this unit, he needed more reserves. At 1331, having previously advised Holland Smith of the seriousness of the situation at Betio, he requested the release of the corps reserve. Less than fifty minutes later this request was approved.[110] Julian Smith now had four battalion landing teams in division reserve. For the first time he could start thinking in terms of a three to one superiority over the defenders.

The second problem was by far the more difficult to solve. It was obvious by mid-afternoon that units could not be sent intact across either the flank or center beaches. The situation on the westernmost beach was obscure and so far as was known most unfavorable. Carlson had not yet arrived aboard *Maryland* with Shoup's request that reserves be sent in to the center beach.

Julian Smith had to make his decision on the basis of information available. Elmer Hall and his headquarters group of the Eighth Marines were already boated and standing by at the line-of-departure with the First Battalion of the Eighth Marines available for commitment. After the battle was over, Julian Smith was confident that an enemy counterattack could have been successfully repulsed on the first night; but he lacked sufficient knowledge to have even a shred of confidence on the afternoon of November 20. He was still thinking that the Japanese would use zone defenses and mobility (as indeed they might have, in part, had Shibasaki been able to control his men). Julian Smith feared most of all what might be developing on the southeastern tail of Betio. As yet the Japanese in that zone were relatively untouched by either naval gunfire or bombing. They might fall on Crowe's left flank and roll the marines off the lagoon beaches. Julian Smith was desperate, and to disrupt such a move made a desperate decision. He was willing to sacrifice the First Battalion Eighth Marines. He ordered Elmer Hall to land on Betio to the eastward of

Crowe's beach. Hall would go ashore, or try to, in the late afternoon, with little remaining daylight to secure even so much as a toehold. The price was high but in Julian Smith's mind the threat from the eastern end of the island warranted the expenditure. Hall would at least divert some of the Japanese expected to strike at Crowe's left flank. The next day, if the northwestern lagoon beaches still had Americans on them, Julian Smith could send the Sixth Marines across, and then he planned to muster every marine who could walk and to follow himself with his division support group.[111]

Retrospect shows this decision to have been an error, and for once a communications failure benefited the marines at Tarawa. Hall never received these orders. Just after they were issued, one of Julian Smith's liaison pilots saw a battery of Rixey's artillery leave the line-of-departure and head for the center beach. How a single battery of 75-millimeter pack howitzers could have resembled a boated battalion is a mystery, but in defense of the pilot it must be added that by this time the lagoon was littered with boats going in all directions in confusion. He mistakenly assumed that the First Battalion Eighth Marines was entering the center beach. He so advised *Maryland*. No one knew how the mixup had occurred, but on the division's situation map, the First Battalion Eighth Marines was plotted on the center beach. Actually, Hall and his outfit spent the night at the line-of-departure, awaiting orders.

Since Julian Smith now thought he had two full regiments ashore, he was anxious to get a general officer onto the beaches to integrate the tactics of Shoup and Hall. Julian Smith ordered his assistant division commander, Brigadier General Leo D. Hermle USMC, to land on the center beach and take over tactical command ashore. Again communications failed. Hermle remained in the lagoon awaiting instructions.

During the night, while the marines on Betio were nervously awaiting a counterattack that failed to materialize, the situation as regards the First Battalion Eighth Marines was clarified. Hermle, while standing by for instructions, worked his way to the end of the long pier as he tried to get some dry communications equipment in to Shoup. There Hermle met two runners sent out to the pier by Shoup in an effort to contact division headquarters. Hermle learned what Carlson had just told Julian Smith, that Shoup wanted reinforcements over the center beach. However, Hermle knew something of which Julian Smith was unaware, namely that the First Battalion Eighth Marines was at the line-of-departure. Hermle boarded a destroyer in the lagoon and radioed *Maryland*. Hall's orders were changed; he was to try to make the center beach at sunrise on November 21.[112]

At dawn, Hall and his remaining battalion landing team, commanded by Major Lawrence C. Hays, Jr., dismounted at the edge of the reef and began wading ashore. Shoup's messengers had failed to inform Hermle of the least dangerous route. Carlson was returning from *Maryland* as this unit approached the coast. "It sustained heavy casualties on the way in," he reported. "The hulk northwest of the pier again contained snipers and machine gunners. As I waited off the pier for an amphibian tractor, planes came over and got four direct hits on the hulk, and in so doing strafed the wounded of the First Battalion Eighth who dotted the water nearby." Then he added two sentences that underline the gravity with which the Americans in the lagoon then regarded the whole undertaking. "Apparently the commander of the First Battalion Eighth Marines was not aware of the 100 yard corridor west of the pier. In fact, those on the water off the beaches at this time were uncertain of the situation ashore and were even under the impression that the enemy had reoccupied the pier." [113]

In getting ashore, the organization of Hays' battalion was shattered. He lost many of his leaders and much of his heavy equipment. Shoup fed these marines into positions facing the Japanese core to his right. By now Rixey's pack howitzers were firing at point blank range against enemy installations, but Shoup still lacked the strength to erase this enemy pocket.[114]

Likewise Crowe and Ruud, despite heavy fighting by their men during the second day, were unable to budge the enemy on their left flank. Success in terms of ground gained, in the vicinity of the long pier, went to elements under the command of Kyle and Jordan. By noon these center beach marines had reached the southern coast. The Japanese on Betio were finally cut in two.

Over on the northwestern tip of Betio, Ryan prepared during the night of November 20/21 to retrace his steps south. By the morning of November 21, he had flamethrowers and two additional medium tanks. Two separate plane strikes managed to take out as many enemy artillery weapons. Supported by close naval gunfire from two destroyers, the marines attacked at 1100. "There was," said Ryan, "little opposition." [115]

When news of Ryan's almost phenomenal success reached *Maryland*, there was cause to rejoice. This was what everyone had been praying for, a chance to get a fully organized battalion across a beach. Carlson had reported in to Shoup during the morning of November 21, and immediately was sent back with another message to *Maryland*. He was in low spirits. Shoup had "reiterated his determination to stick and fight it out," but more than stubbornness was needed and the situation was, if anything, worse than that on the 20th. But Carlson climbed aboard *Maryland* on the afternoon of November 21 to find his bad tidings out of date. Julian Smith and his staff had just learned that the western beach was clear, and that the coast south of the long pier had been reached. "I was frankly skeptical," Carlson admitted "that so radical a change had taken place in so short a time after my departure from the beach." [116]

6. *Tarawa: Securing Betio and the Remainder of the Atoll*

Carlson's skepticism was ill-founded. Colonel Maurice Holmes' Sixth Regimental Combat Team was already being boated. The plan was to land two battalions in echelon on the western beach, and to have them attack directly east, overrunning the south coast of the islet lengthwise. The first of these was scheduled to go ashore on the evening of November 21, and to pass initially to Shoup's control; but as soon as possible Julian Smith was to land, and meanwhile his chief of staff, Edson, was going onto the center lagoon beach. Edson would relieve Shoup of overall tactical command ashore. The all-out attack was to begin on the morning of November 22. Shoup was to devote his full attention to clearing out the Japanese pocket between the center and westernmost lagoon beaches. (See map 11.) For this task, he would have what was left of four battalions, all three of the units in his own Second Regiment, plus the First Battalion Eighth Marines attached. The other two battalions of the Eighth Regiment, led by Crowe and Ruud, were to revert to Hall's control, allowing him to integrate a drive to oust the enemy from the left flank of the easternmost lagoon beach.

Plans were also made for committing the final battalion landing team, a unit of the Sixth Regiment. Reports had reached Julian Smith that Japanese were crossing from the southeast tip of Betio over to Bairiki. Naval gunfire alone could not be expected to interdict this movement. It posed a threat which could not go unattended. After Betio, Julian Smith's orders were to overrun the entire atoll, and no marine wanted to let the Japanese get set on Bairiki to make another determined stand at the beach. A battalion of the Sixth Marines was sent to Bairiki, to be followed ashore by a battalion of 75-millimeter pack howitzers from the Tenth Regiment. Once the artillery was emplaced and registered, it was hoped that the unit of the Sixth Marines on Bairiki could be withdrawn to relieve Hall's depleted units on Betio. Then for the final drive down the tail of that islet, Maurice Holmes would have all three of the battalions of the fresh Sixth Regiment at his disposal.

With few unimportant exceptions, these plans were carried out. Lieutenant Colonel Raymond L. Murray landed the Second Battalion Sixth Marines on Bairiki during the late afternoon of November 21. There was no resistance. Here close air support really came into its own. About fifteen Japanese were on Bairiki, manning two machine guns. The Nipponese, for some strange reason, had a can of gasoline in their vicinity. A strafing plane hit the can with a .50-caliber bullet, and burned out the enemy. At last the way was cleared for Julian Smith to set up his artillery on Bairiki. It registered late, but was of value in helping marines to bowl over the southeastern end of Betio.[117]

Shortly after Bairiki was seized, the First Battalion Sixth Marines landed with few casualties on the western beach of Betio. The commanding officer, Major William K. Jones, was guided ashore by Ryan, who managed to warn the incoming waves that the southern portion of the western beach was heavily mined. Jones' men were loaded in rubber boats, towed by landing craft. One of the latter struck a mine and was blown apart, but otherwise no mishap occurred in landing.

Jones commanded the first fully organized unit to reach the coast of Betio. On the morning of November 22 he began a drive which within twenty-eight hours completed the assault. Two factors were of assistance in speeding up this final attack. During the night of November 22/23, after the enemy had been crowded into the tail of the islet, he depleted his strength in a series of futile countercharges. Even more important, as a post-operational study of Betio's defenses revealed, the enemy's "organization for defense inshore was haphazard. While it does not appear that they were intended for that use, the bombproof ammunition and personnel shelters inshore from the beach defenses were used in the later stages as defensive positions in depth. The fires from the doorways of these were, in some cases, mutually supporting, but by accident; for the most part, they were blind to attack from several directions in that they were not designed as blockhouses, and had but few firing ports." [118]

At 0805 on the morning of the third day of the assault, November 22, Jones began his attack. He was ordered to fight his way along the south coast between the beach and the airstrip eastward until he reached the pocket of marines already situated on that coast, due south of the long pier. Assisted by naval gunfire and effectively employing teams of tanks, flamethrowers, and riflemen, the First Battalion Sixth Marines "had little or no trouble going along the coast," and reached its initial objective, a distance of about 2,500 yards, at slightly before noon. Jones was then ordered to continue fighting his way along the south coast, and at nightfall to tie in with the Eighth Marines to his left. Finally the men under Crowe and Ruud, with excellent artillery and destroyer gunfire support, were making progress eastward along the lagoon beach.

The going became more difficult for Jones' First Battalion Sixth Marines that afternoon. Resistance stiffened, and more than ever Jones felt the need of medium tanks. He had only one of these machines, plus seven light tanks. The light tanks were, however, of little value other than psychological. Their 37-millimeter guns, even at point blank range, failed to penetrate enemy installations, and they lacked the weight needed for a crushing effect.[119] The fact that the light tanks were of little assistance in working over Japanese defenses had first become apparent on New Georgia, but this lesson came only a few months before the attack on Betio. A company of medium tanks was all the Second Marine Division could obtain for the Tarawa operation, and by the third day of the assault most of the medium tanks were lost.

At nightfall of November 22, Jones reached the eastern end of the airstrip and sent one of his companies across to the lagoon beach to assist the exhausted Eighth Marines in holding their gains of the day. Julian Smith, who had landed during that afternoon, was encouraged by the progress of the day, but expected hard fighting ahead. He did not know that the Japanese were ill prepared to fight inshore, nor did he expect them to dissipate their remaining strength in banzai charges. And, after Betio was secured, he had the rest of the islets of the atoll, except Bairiki, to capture. "Complete occupation," he advised Hermle who was then on *Maryland*, "will take at least 5 days more." [120]

Betio was seized by the afternoon of the next day, November 23. The Japanese began their counterattack during the late evening of the day before. Jones' men were in line across the width of the islet at the eastern end of the airstrip. Naval gunfire was called down in the areas where the enemy was assembling for his attack, and Rixey's artillery pieces as well as those on Bairiki joined in the massacre. The riflemen exercised splendid fire discipline, refusing to disclose their positions. When the sun rose on the morning of November 23, more than 300 Japanese were dead. Jones' casualties were light.

The next morning the Third Battalion Sixth Marines, Lieutenant Colonel Kenneth F. McLeod, passed through Jones' lines and resumed the attack to the east. Meanwhile, Shoup was continuing the arduous task of clearing out the Japanese pocket along the reentrant of the northwestern lagoon beaches. Using the remnants of the Second Marines and of the First Battalion Eighth Marines, this job was completed at about the same time McLeod reached the southeastern tip of the islet, at shortly after 1300 on November 23. Taking the rest of the islets of the atoll was relatively easy, and was done, as Julian Smith had predicted, by November 28.[121]

7. *Tarawa: Naval Gunfire and Air Support Ashore. Beach Logistics*

One reason that the fighting on Betio was finished so quickly was that both air and naval gunfire support improved during the struggle ashore. It was found that naval guns and bombers could safely work together on the same target. After a period of hesitancy and uncertainty, naval gunfire was of necessity called down less than fifty yards in front of friendly troops. Destroyers were used for these missions, and their 5-inch projectiles tore gaps in the enemy's line. Thereupon, in the opinion of Holland Smith's naval gunfire officer, "the troops gained a large amount of confidence in naval gunfire." [122] Carrier pilots also showed up better after the first landings were made, and these men and their machines exerted a psychological influence all out of proportion to their performance. Marines rejoiced as the planes struck, and the enemy was terrified; but communications difficulties prevented the airmen from being well controlled by the air liaison parties, and the flyers either could not see or failed to heed the panel and pyrotechnical devices which marked the advance of friendly troops.[123] They showed up best when striking ahead of marines who were advancing rapidly, when helping Ryan on the west coast and Jones along the south coast of Betio, and in the seizure of Bairiki. Crowe with his left flank wrinkled up by enemy pressure was not pleased by the pilots. He somewhat unjustly summarized their activities with these words: "Don't know how much good they do, but we know their bullets will kill men if they hit anything. One fifty-caliber slug hit one of my men—went through his shoulder, on down through his lung and liver. He lived about four minutes. Well, anyway, if a Jap ever sticks his head out of his pillbox the planes may kill him." [124]

Beach logistics were also essential to the marines once they were ashore on Betio. Plans for beach logistics were faulty, and by the afternoon of November 21 the supply situation ashore was becoming critical. The marines had landed with only one unit of fire, and this was being rapidly expended. As early as noon of the first day the division staff was receiving urgent requests for water and blood plasma, as well as for ammunition. On the second day some of the battalion commanders began improvising. Small parties of men were formed and given the sole duty of retrieving and repairing rifles, and salvaging ammunition from the friendly dead. This, however, was but a temporary solution to a pressing problem.[125]

Plans for beach logistics were premised upon the assumption that a beachhead would be secured at an early hour. When this failed to materialize, there was no alternate organized means of sending supplies to the coast.[126] Navy officers, understandably anxious to unload their vessels and retire, kept dumping cargo into available boats. These in turn milled around the lagoon with no place to go. Boat control was lost, since there were not sufficient control vessels and those on hand were not properly equipped with communications. Fortunately the situation in the lagoon looked worse than it actually was. In only one instance, and this too late in the period of the assault to matter much, was it impossible to round up a sufficient number of boats for a tactical movement of troops.

Some of the boats off loaded at the end of the long pier, but there was no means of screening their cargoes and, in order not to overcrowd the pier, of taking off only the items really needed ashore. From the first, amphibian tractors were of great assistance in relaying supplies from the end of the pier onto the beaches. What was needed was a means of integration and control.

This became apparent to Carlson as he worked his way back from *Maryland* on the morning of November 21. After he had reported to Shoup, he was requested to return with a second personal account of the situation ashore to Julian Smith. Shoup's lack of supplies, particularly ammunition, water, and medicines, was evident. Carlson asked for and was given permission to help organize the logistical endeavor as he went back toward *Maryland* a second time.

When Carlson reached the end of the long pier on his second outward journey he found the regimental shore party officer, Lieutenant Colonel Chester Salazar. Together Carlson and Salazar improvised a brilliant scheme in which the navy officers in the lagoon cooperated enthusiastically. Salazar established a control and transfer point for supplies at the end of the pier, and sent in nothing but selected and greatly needed items to the center beach. Carlson then proceeded to the control ship in the lagoon, the minesweeper *Pursuit*, contacted the ranking navy officer, Captain John B. McGovern USN, and sought his cooperation. McGovern was asked to dispatch to the end of the pier only those items needed ashore, and to organize all amphibian tractors available, placing them under Salazar's supervision. The tractors were to be used only in ferrying the supplies from the end of the pier, along the west wall, to the center beach, evacuating wounded on return trips. McGovern, said Carlson, "grasped the picture immediately, and promised full cooperation. While I was there he gave orders which resulted in rounding up 18 amphibian tractors and in sending boats to the pier." [127]

In view of the dire shortage of amphibian tractors at Tarawa, it was essential that such a logistical arrangement be made. Of the 125 tractors taken to Tarawa, only thirty-five were operational when the assault was over.[128]

Thus in another notable respect, beachhead logistics, the assault on Betio improved the quality of planning and of execution for future operations. This went beyond the obvious need for a greater number of better tractors. It improved the concept of ship-to-shore movement by giving the tactical troop commander, through his shore party officer, control over the priority in unloading from ship to boat. Further, it showed the need for control and transfer points offshore. Since the presence and feasibility of using a pier could not be relied upon in the future, the idea of floating stockpiles of critical supplies, loaded in boats and idling at the line-of-departure, was born.[129]

8. Tarawa and the Amphibious Assault

Marine casualties at Tarawa shocked the American people. Despite the fact that navy dead off Makin totalled almost as many as the number of marines killed at Betio, this information, even had it been made public at the time, would probably have gone unnoticed beside the glaring headlines of marine losses. When a man-of-war goes down, one expects men to die. The public did not understand the fundamental point that only after rapid seizing of targets such as Makin or Tarawa can ships and the men in them be withdrawn to safety. The point, perhaps, would have been generally accepted by the American people only if the Japanese fleet had been able, in the Gilberts or later, to move through and demolish transports loaded with marines and army troops. That would have been too high a price to pay for general understanding of a basic lesson in naval strategy.

Nimitz, his staff, and the implementing officers in the Pacific, of course, thoroughly understood this point. The Gilberts campaign showed them that fast carrier forces could localize a target for amphibious assault, and they gained so much confidence in their covering force that speed in subsequent operations was made secondary to obtaining the maximum naval gunfire bombardment and air bombing in the preliminary phase.

Tactically, Betio became the textbook for future amphibious landings and assaults. Lessons learned were widely disseminated. The necessity of coordinating the supporting arms and of timing everything around the moment the first troops actually touched the beach was recognized by all. Air and naval gunfire support observed their errors and emerged the stronger.

The experience gained at Tarawa was useful. Thirty-three hundred casualties are low when compared with the total for any other Central Pacific offensive, with the exception of the seizure of Kwajalein and Eniwetok in the Marshall Islands. Assaults against the Marianas, the Palaus, and Iwo Jima were not only more expensive in terms of lives lost—it may confidently be said that these later victories were possible at all only because of the lessons learned at Tarawa.

These lessons included, in addition to a more effective application of naval gunfire and air support, means for obtaining a smoother flow of supplies from ship-to-shore. More control boats with better communications were to become the nerve center of both the logistical and tactical aspects of future operations. Also, facts of tremendous value in the tactics of actually storming a beach were learned. The principal need was for more thorough training in teamwork among tanks, artillery, flamethrowers, demolition experts, and riflemen in isolating and overrunning strong defensive installations. Regardless of their specialties, all marines must know something of the use of demolitions, heretofore left to the combat engineers. Also, more and better weapons were required. Additional flamethrowers were essential, and since the light tank was of value for little else, the idea of converting it into a flamethrowing tank arose. Likewise, work was pushed on the development of an armored amphibian tractor which could accompany the first waves ashore and protect their flanks as they worked their way inland.[130]

Faulty communications stood out like a beacon light. The special command ship for the attack and landing force commander would not alone solve the problem. Improved portable equipment was required, lighter and more mobile, and waterproofed so that once ashore hours of precious time would not be spent in drying out instruments and batteries. Well-trained communications personnel were another necessity, especially for assignment to the fire-control parties, the air liaison groups, and the beachhead logistical parties. After Tarawa, the Joint Chiefs of Staff became interested in this problem. Following in essence the recommendations made by Vandegrift from Guadalcanal, they directed that naval gunfire, air liaison, and shore party communications personnel be pooled into joint assault signal companies, that these be trained under supervision of the Fifth Amphibious Corps, and that one such company be temporarily allocated to each division assigned to an amphibious landing.[131]

These, along with the stepped up production of vehicles capable of crossing reefs, were the chief results of Tarawa. Nor were these lessons gained in an operation of no strategical importance. On the contrary, the line of communications to the South and Southwest Pacific was shortened, and new bases were seized from which to bomb the enemy in the Marshalls and to photograph his installations. This intelligence of the enemy, plus the Tarawa experience, permitted the compilation of such superior plans for invading the Marshalls that the losses in the Gilberts were more than compensated for in the next campaign. Penetrating into and controlling the Marshalls turned out to be such an easy task that it gave the Central Pacific drive a momentum which was breath taking for the American commanders as well as for the Japanese. The enemy fleet fled from Truk without offering battle. Nimitz scrapped his earlier intentions, and advanced the target date for entering the Marianas by months.

CHAPTER VII

THE MARSHALLS, GAINING MOMENTUM

"This time we've got what it takes. This time we've got everything," said a marine happily as he watched the preparatory fires on Kwajalein Atoll in the heart of the Marshall Islands.[1]

He was right. In the Marshalls, American forces won an outstanding series of rapid victories. But the significance of this campaign rests neither in the tactical speed achieved, nor in the successful application of lessons learned at Tarawa, nor in the contributions made to the further development of amphibious techniques during the fighting in the Marshalls. The real importance of the campaign lies in its strategical consequences. It added impetus to operations in both the Pacific Ocean and the Southwest Pacific Areas.

1. Theater Planning

With an insight rare among military columnists, Hanson Baldwin analyzed the brilliance of the Marshall victories. "The amazing success, at relatively small cost, of our Marshall Island operations has been due to thorough logistical planning, the concentration of overwhelming force against the enemy and a combination of strategical boldness and carefully prepared and coordinated tactics."[2]

Credit for this "strategical boldness" is principally due to Admirals King and Nimitz. These were the men who insisted that America's mobility of carrier aircraft be used to the utmost in localizing targets for amphibious operations, and this was the strategy which crashed through the Marshalls with record speed.

Nimitz, using language similar to that earlier employed by the Joint Chiefs of Staff, stated the purpose of the Central Pacific drive in mid-January 1944. "The immediate strategic objective of the forces of the Pacific Ocean Areas," he said, "is to obtain positions from which the ultimate surrender of Japan can be forced by intensive air bombardment, by sea and air blockade, and by invasion if necessary." Obviously, he reasoned, Truk must at least be covered before either his forces or those of MacArthur could advance toward the Celebes Sea. (See map 2.) Insufficient resources continued to prevent the simultaneous mounting of major offensives in both theaters. Nimitz was willing to order the Pacific Fleet to protect Southwest Pacific movements into central and northwestern New Guinea, the Halmaheras, and the Philippines, and to transfer temporarily from his command the reinforcements in men and amphibious shipping needed, but he intended to supervise the coordination. He considered his command more important than any other in the Pacific. "When conflicts in timing and allocation of means exist," he emphasized, "due weight should be accorded to the fact that operations in the Central Pacific promise at this time a more rapid advance toward Japan and her vital lines of communication; the earlier acquisition of strategic air bases closer to the Japanese homeland; and, of greatest importance, are more likely to precipitate a decisive engagement with the Japanese Fleet." [3]

The directive from the Joint Chiefs of Staff to take and control the Marshalls was received in July 1943, along with that for the Gilberts. Thus, while plans for Tarawa and Makin were being drawn and executed, planning for the Marshalls was also taking shape. Nimitz's staff issued the first blueprint for the Marshalls in October 1943. At this time the commanding officers of the principal troop components to be used in the second Central Pacific offensive, the Fourth Marine Division, the 7th Infantry Division, and the Twenty-second Marine Regiment, knew that their task was atoll warfare in the Marshalls. It was a long time, however, before they learned their precise objectives, for the overall plans were first modified and then radically revised.

The original scheme was to take three well-defended atolls in two phases of fighting. The 7th Infantry Division, with the marines in reserve, was to seize Wotje and Maloelap in the eastern edge of the group; and then, if not earlier committed, the marines were to overrun Kwajalein Atoll in the Central Marshalls. (See map 10.) Difficulties at Betio, however, and preliminary intelligence of enemy strength in the Marshalls proved this concept overambitious. In mid-December 1943, Nimitz directed his subordinates to continue the planning for Wotje and Maloelap, but only as an alternate to a new, preferred scheme of maneuver. The new plan was to assault Kwajalein alone, and to occupy a lightly held atoll (as yet unspecified) in the eastern edge of the group. If and when intelligence discovered a suitable and lightly held atoll in the Eastern Marshalls, it could be conveniently employed to help secure the line of communications back to Pearl Harbor, to provide a staging point for tactical deployments into the Central and Western Marshalls, and to ease the problem of fleet logistics by furnishing a lagoon anchorage safe from enemy submarines.

In late December the alternate plan was dropped, and the Marshalls campaign took final shape. Majuro, a large atoll in the Eastern Marshalls ninety miles south of Maloelap, was named as the lightly held objective and Kwajalein stood alone as the difficult target. Nimitz also allocated additional troops to Holland Smith, the 106th Infantry

Regiment reinforced, a part of the 27th Infantry Division. Meanwhile, for logistical and tactical reasons, the original target date set by the Joint Chiefs of Staff became impossible, and Nimitz set the day for the principal landings as February 1, 1944.[4]

All of Nimitz's implementing commanders were opposed to taking the risks involved in by-passing strong enemy bases in the Eastern Marshalls. Holland Smith shared this feeling, despite the thesis advanced in his memoirs that Tarawa was a mistake and that the first Central Pacific assault should have knifed directly into Kwajalein. With Spruance and Kelly Turner, Smith recommended that the eastern fringe of the Marshalls group be controlled by amphibious operations as well as by air and surface strikes before landings were attempted on Kwajalein. The cogent reasoning put forward by Spruance must certainly have concerned Nimitz as he pondered the difficult decision that he had to make. The commander of the Central Pacific Force pointed out to his superior that the Pacific Fleet was scheduled, shortly after the Marshalls campaign, to be turned over to Halsey for the proposed seizure of Kavieng on New Ireland. "Under these conditions," Spruance recollects, "I argued as strongly as I could with Admiral Nimitz against Kwajalein," proposing instead that the Eastern Marshalls be taken. "My argument was based, not on any difficulty in taking Kwajalein . . . but on the insecurity of our line of communications in to Kwajalein after the withdrawal of the Pacific Fleet. Kwajalein would have stood encircled by Japanese airfields. . . . With the air pipe line through Eniwetok open back to Japan and with the activity which had been shown by Japanese air in the Marshalls in their attacks on our fleet forces during the Gilberts operation, I felt that our support shipping moving into Kwajalein would have a tough time of it. In my arguments I was supported by Admiral Turner and General Holland Smith, but I was overruled by Admiral Nimitz." [5]

Nimitz avoided a hasty decision; and he reached it finally on the basis of the correct belief that in Majuro he had found a target which, when captured, would meet the objections raised to his plan by his chief implementing commanders. The delay in finally reaching this decision was necessary, since good judgment depended upon photographic interpretation, intelligence analyses, and a correct estimate of unfolding developments. This, however, set back planning and cut down the opportunities for training, rehearsals, and critiques. In short, it helped to account for most of the few errors made during the execution phases.

Such tactical shortcomings were more than offset by the strategical suitability of the plan. The scheme selected economized America's amphibious strength. The enemy expected the Marshalls to be attacked, but he was hit at places where he was not well prepared. Contrary to American fears, the enemy had not, before the outbreak of World War II, been building up his Pacific military bases as mighty fortresses. The Japanese showed keen discernment in refusing to do so. Their resources were limited, and before the encounter they had spent the great bulk of the funds available for the navy in constructing a mobile fleet. Until there was no other recourse, the Japanese high command remained remarkably free from the Maginot-line complex of static defense. Before the campaign in the Gilberts began, the Japanese were hastily building up Wotje and Maloelap to guard the Marshalls from a thrust delivered directly from Pearl Harbor. After November 1943, they shifted their attention to Mili and Jaluit, the atolls closest to the Gilberts. United States aerial reconnaissance revealed these efforts, and this was one reason that Kwajalein, although it was known to be occupied by a larger number of defenders than any other atoll in the Marshalls, was chosen as the principal target. The capture of Kwajalein was considered to be the best means of striking at the root of Japanese power in the Marshalls and rendering useless the frantic Japanese activities on the periphery. The suitability of Kwajalein and the quality of its defensive installations, rather than the number of defenders, were the determining factors in the choice of the chief target.[6]

In one sense, the second Central Pacific offensive resembled an amphibious expedition against a large land mass. Since the Marshalls consisted of thirty-six true atolls spread over a sizeable body of water, there was ample maneuver room, and this was utilized. The island group contained many widely separated landing beaches, each feasible for the American purpose, namely to secure fleet and air bases; and thus it was possible to catch the enemy off balance. He did not know precisely where the landings were to be made until, to quote Holland Smith's intelligence officer, "our transports and landing craft were visible to him offshore." [7]

The art of devising strategical protection for amphibious expeditions in the Central Pacific had benefited immeasurably from three important lessons learned in the Gilberts. These were, first, that Japanese air and submarine potential in the mid-Pacific was weaker than earlier estimates had indicated; second, that combined strikes by American land and carrier planes were capable of neutralizing enemy bases over a wide expanse of water; and third, that maintenance of this neutralization could be extended, with a minimum of continued effort by carriers, surface strikes, and land-based bombers, until such time as the newly acquired bases themselves mounted planes and took up the mission of constantly pounding the targets so recently by-passed.

Nimitz premised his decision on these lessons, took the strategical initiative, and instructed his subordinates to maneuver and attack.

The dividends from this course of action surpassed expectations. Landings in the Marshalls were finished ahead of schedule, and forthcoming operations throughout the Pacific were made easier. "Gaining momentum" is the phrase that best characterizes all aspects of the Marshalls undertaking.[8]

2. *Implementing Plans, Embarkation and Rehearsals*

Forces stronger than those present in the Gilberts were available for the next offensive in the Central Pacific, and they were better employed. Again Spruance provided unity of command, and sailed personally with the covering force, which was built around twelve fast carriers. Land-based army and naval planes under Rear Admiral John H. Hoover USN were by mid-December operating from four newly won fields in the Gilberts. Aircraft under Spruance and Hoover undertook the task of demolishing enemy air facilities in the Marshalls and the Eastern Carolines. The plan was to attack and destroy all Japanese aircraft and to neutralize their bases throughout the Marshalls-Eastern Carolines area as nearly simultaneously as was possible, rather than, as was done in the Gilberts, to strike some bases and assume a defensive role toward the others.[9]

Turner received an armada of almost 300 vessels for the expeditionary force. One heavy, two light and eight escort carriers, seven old battleships, eight heavy and four light cruisers, sixty-three destroyers, twelve infantry landing craft converted to gunboats, and twelve destroyer escorts were on hand for direct air support, close cover, and naval gunfire and screening duties. Auxiliaries totaled fifty-five. In addition, forty-six assorted transports, twenty-seven cargo vessels, five dock landing ships, and forty-five tank landing ships lifted almost 85,000 combat, garrison, and construction personnel, with their supplies and equipment. Turner also got two additional vessels. These were newly built and equipped with special communications facilities for use as amphibious attack and landing force flagships, named *Rocky Mount* and *Appalachian*. The Marshalls campaign introduced these headquarters ships to the war in the Pacific, and they, along with improved radio equipment ashore and the concept of the joint assault signal company, eliminated many of the communications failures which had marred the assault on Betio.[10]

When Nimitz assigned the troops for the Marshalls, he advised Holland Smith to employ two full reinforced divisions in taking the principal target of Kwajalein. (See map 12.) That atoll is the largest in the Marshalls group. The reef-islet fringed lagoon is irregularly shaped, but comes to three points as if it were a triangle. It stretches slightly more than forty miles in a north-south direction, and some sixty-five miles northwest by southeast. The islets are low lying, never rising to more than fifteen feet elevation. Of the three points of the atoll, only two were of great military importance, the northern and southern extremities where the land is extensive enough for airfields. The atoll itself is named for the southernmost and largest islet, Kwajalein. North and slightly west of Kwajalein Islet lie Roi and Namur, very close together and connected by a land spit and a concrete causeway. The enemy was concentrated on and in the vicinity of both Kwajalein Islet and Roi-Namur, and the only way to get the atoll and to use its airsites was to eradicate these Japanese forces.

Holland Smith gave the job of capturing Kwajalein Islet and adjacent strips of land to the 7th Infantry Division. This was a veteran body of army fighters, experienced in amphibious warfare across the roughest waters in the world, in the Aleutians. The task of seizing Roi-Namur and their neighboring islets fell to the Fourth Marine Division, which was being embarked from San Diego for its first combat duty. In addition, five reinforced battalions steamed up to Kwajalein Atoll in reserve for employment if and when the tactical situation dictated. These were the three battalions of the Twenty-second Marine Regiment, and two of the three battalions of the 106th Infantry Regiment. For Majuro, the Fifth Amphibious Corps Reconnaissance Company was selected, and was ordered to scout that atoll. If serious enemy resistance developed, the remaining battalion of the 106th Infantry Regiment was to be on hand for employment ashore.[11]

Turner subdivided his shipping into three amphibious groups for the jobs ahead. He hoisted his flag on *Rocky Mount* and retained general supervision over the entire expedition, but kept direct tactical control only over the forces destined for the southern end of Kwajalein Atoll. Rear Admiral Harry Hill, refreshed from Tarawa by a leave in the United States, was put in charge of getting ashore on Majuro, and other shipping in his command was temporarily detached to take the troops in reserve to Kwajalein. Both Turner's group and that of Hill were made up of experienced amphibious sailors. The third group, however, was largely composed of new shipping and green crews. It was hastily assembled on the West Coast and was ordered to lift the Fourth Marine Division and to set it ashore on Roi-Namur. It is evident from the record that tactically Roi-Namur was judged the more difficult of the two targets in the Kwajalein Atoll, and that the planners wanted to use marines rather than army troops at the northernmost islets. Whether or not this reasoning was sound will be discussed after the narrative of the landings has been completed; the point here is that an inexperienced amphibious group was assigned to transport and put ashore an inexperienced division. This was the most serious flaw in the allocation of means.

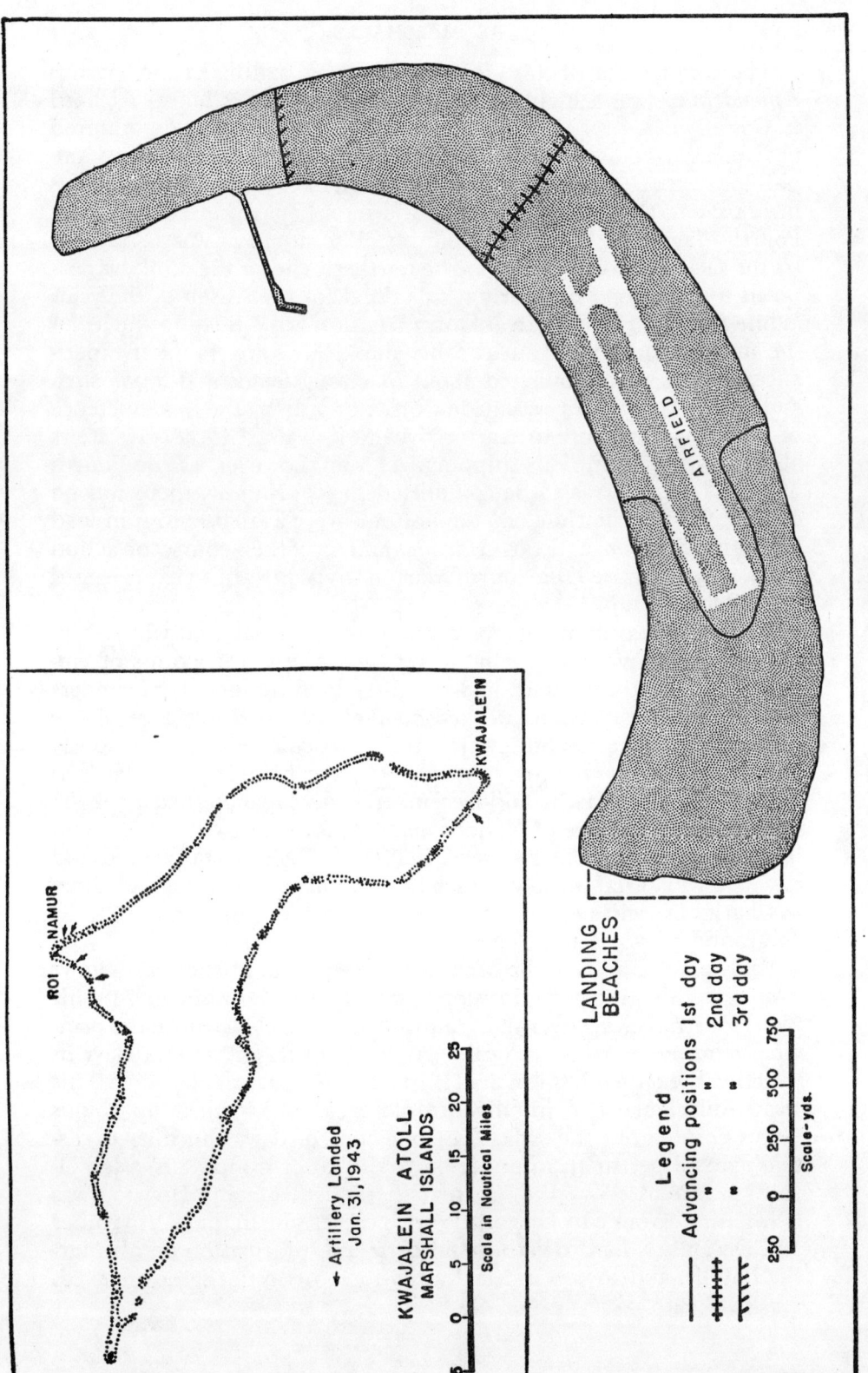

MAP 12. Kwajalein Islet with insert of Kwajalein Atoll.

The commander of this amphibious group, sailing in the flagship *Appalachian*, was a highly competent officer, Rear Admiral Richard L. Conolly USN, probably in the eyes of the marines the most admired navy officer to emerge from the Pacific War. Conolly had gained amphibious experience in the Mediterranean, but he was given precious little time to pound his new command into shape and to exercise the Fourth Marine Division amphibiously. The situation was aggravated by the fact that Roi-Namur, at the northern end of the atoll, was exposed to the strong northerly winds usual for the season of the year. While the experienced 7th Infantry Division was landed in the lee of the atoll by Turner's highly capable amphibious group, the inexperienced marines were buffeted about by strong winds and heavy surf, and their predicament was made worse not only by the incompetence of their own amphibian tractor drivers but also by the raw crews aboard their amphibious shipping. As long, however, as the Fourth Marine Division was to be committed to Roi-Namur, there was no choice. Neither the time nor the bottoms were available to transload an entire division at Pearl Harbor, and no other course of action could have furnished the Fourth Marine Division with an experienced amphibious group.[12]

While these assignments were being made official, and while shipping scurried over the Pacific to its widely scattered points of embarkation, the three attack and the three landing force commanders and their lower echelons worked on their plans. Knowledge of the Marshalls in general and Kwajalein in particular was conspicuously absent before army photographic planes began bringing their cameras back to the Gilberts in mid-December. The Japanese had held the Marshalls as a League of Nations mandate for over twenty years, and had closely guarded their secrecy. Before intelligence staffs could find any better material through which to pick, they perused such volumes as Charles Darwin's century old journal of explorations in the Pacific and found a little data on reefs.[13]

Early photographs of the Marshalls were of more benefit to Nimitz in making his strategical decision and to Spruance in drawing up his plans for strategical cover than to the tactical echelons. Since the principal landings were on the calendar for February 1, 1944, delays in selecting the targets left less than thirty days for tactical planning. This was insufficient. The intelligence officer of the Fifth Amphibious Corps pointed out the difficulties engendered. It was his duty to disseminate all pertinent information to the lower troop staffs, a job already complicated by the fact that the Fourth Marine Division was being lifted from San Diego. Also this officer, during late November and December, had to gather and correlate information on all Marshall atolls, and to pay especial attention to two not later attacked.

Photographic reconnaissance could be concentrated only after the targets had been conclusively designated. With pardonable pride the corps intelligence officer observed that despite the short time allowed, his office distributed more than 190,000 sheets of maps for the Marshalls campaign; yet he confessed the quality was sometimes poor. Not until January 29 did he receive large-scale vertical photographs of Kwajalein Atoll, and it was only on the last day of that month that he was able to issue a situation map with all defensive installations pinpointed. The commanding general of the Fourth Marine Division complained he never knew what specific areas nor what scale maps to expect from corps headquarters. As a result, in order to prepare for his own reduplications, he was forced to combat-load a considerable quantity of paper and lithographing equipment when embarking his division. The corps operations officer also criticized the map makers. In several instances the sheets furnished his section "were extremely difficult for anyone without considerable experience in map reading to read correctly." [14]

Holland Smith seconded the request for more planning time. He asked, on the basis of the Marshalls experience, that the final theater operational plan be delivered to corps headquarters at least 100 days before the execution date, that photographic coverage begin ten days later, and that the attack units be assigned to corps seventy-five days before the time of the landings for the purposes of training, rehearsals, and lower echelon planning. This arrangement he felt would allow him to issue his corps plan a month and a half before the assault began. It would ease the problems of logistics as well as training. It would improve coordination at the implementing level.[15]

Even though telescoped, the tactical planning for Kwajalein was well done. Principal credit for this should go to Spruance and to the navy, marine, and army officers who drew up the schedule for supporting fires preliminary to the principal landings. Spruance with his force in strategic cover promised to localize the target for a time sufficient for deliberate and destructive naval gunfire and carrier strikes, and to allow the troops to emplace artillery adjacent to their principal objectives. This permitted high-trajectory shore-based artillery fire to assist in preparing the main targets for landings. In addition to the localization by Spruance, the geographical configuration of Kwajalein Atoll was favorable for the scheme devised. Unlike Tarawa, the lagoon at Kwajalein is deep as well as large and is relatively free from coral heads. In seizing islets required for preliminary artillery support, it happened that the Japanese close ashore to the two main channels into the lagoon were eliminated. Thus amphibious shipping could seek the lagoon as a haven from enemy submarines.

Need for both deliberate destructive naval gunfire and air strikes and for the emplacement of artillery had of course been made evident at Tarawa. In fact, the experience at Tarawa shaped the plans for preliminary fires at Kwajalein. This is best illustrated by two of the more important studies issued by Turner and Harry Hill immediately after the assault on Betio. These were entitled "Extracts from Observers' Comments" and "Lessons Learned at Tarawa." They recommended the expenditure of at least three times the ammunition used at Betio. Otherwise it was feared that the troops in getting ashore would suffer losses greater than "we can sustain." To curtail casualties in crossing the beaches, continuous and heavy shore-based bombing attacks were called for, followed by several days of carrier strikes. Likewise heavy warships and destroyers should deliver slow destructive fire for several days before landings were attempted. Finally, both Tarawa and Makin proved that the accuracy of naval gunfire and especially air bombing could be improved.[16]

All this was done at Kwajalein.[17] Spruance, Turner, and Holland Smith prepared to carry out Nimitz's decision with daring and with painstaking attention to detail. These three men were in large part responsible for the effective application of Tarawa's lessons to the seizure of the next objective, and they were fittingly promoted during and shortly after the fall of the Marshalls. Turner spoke for the trio and their staffs when he declared: "The fellow we are working for is the fellow that walks the beach." [18]

With plans laid for thorough preparatory fires, a combination of factors determined the tactical scheme of maneuver for each of the attacking divisions at Kwajalein. These were hydrographic and geographic considerations, and the calculated capabilities of both the assaulting and defending forces.

At neither of the principal objectives did aerial and submarine photography provide all the information desired with respect to the nature of the reefs and their conditions at various stages of the tide. Fear of a repetition of the trouble at Betio caused Julian Smith's recommendation for 300 amphibian tractors per division to be more than fulfilled. The Fourth Marine Division in the northern section of the atoll had almost 350 such vehicles at its disposal. The army troops at the southern end had less than one-half this number, but the deficiency was made up by the introduction of an amphibian new to Central Pacific fighting. This was the army-developed 2½-ton amphibian truck, commonly called the Dukw. It proved its worth both tactically and logistically, and is one of the most notable contributions made by the army to amphibian techniques during the course of the Pacific War.[19]

The presence of a large number of amphibian trucks and tractors should have solved the tactical and logistical problem of the reef, but

PLATE 1. A tank landing ship manned by the Coast Guard discharging an amphibian tractor loaded with marines off Iwo Jima, February 19, 1945. To the right background, a second tank landing ship similarly engaged. (USN PHOTO)

PLATE 2. Assault marines of the Fourth Division churn from the line-of-departure toward Iwo in amphibian tractors, February 19, 1945. Control craft are in center background, a man-of-war and amphibious shipping on horizon. (USMC PHOTO)

PLATE 3. Gavutu-Tanambogo with a part of Palm Islet in the left foreground, just before the assault on August 7, 1942. The wharf on Gavutu is aflame and smoke partially obscures the difficult hill objective. (USN PHOTO)

PLATE 4. A portion of Guadalcanal. Edson's Ridge is in the center, flanked by jungle growth and the Lunga River. Beyond Henderson Field stretches Iron Bottom Sound, with Florida Island twenty miles beyond on the horizon. (USMC PHOTO)

PLATE 5. Marines covered by the sea wall, left flank beach of Betio, Tarawa Atoll, November 20, 1943. To the left background, the wharf, strands of barbed wire, and concrete tetrahedrons. The long pier is off the picture to the left. (USMC PHOTO)

PLATE 6. Betio, Tarawa Atoll, with the tide out, showing the pattern of barbed wire and concrete tetrahedrons off the south coast. Amphibious shipping and men-of-war in the background. (USMC PHOTO)

PLATE 7. Looking northwest at Roi-Namur, Kwajalein Atoll, while under preparatory bombardment. A beach defense has been hit on Roi. Two supply dumps smoulder on Namur, and its more difficult terrain is evident. (USN PHOTO)

PLATE 8. Engebi Islet, Eniwetok Atoll, under intense preassault neutralizing fire as waves of amphibious tractors approach lagoon beaches from the background, February 18, 1944. Note effects of earlier preparatory bombardment. (USN PHOTO)

PLATE 9. Portion of the narrow beaches, Tinian. Shore-beach party personnel roll oil drums from tank lighters. Amphibian tractors to the right, and a variety of large and small shipping and craft reach to the horizon. (USCG PHOTO)

PLATE 10. Vehicular and personnel landing craft circle in their rendezvous area off Guam, July 21, 1944, before running in from the line-of-departure for transfer at the reef to amphibian tractors. (USMC PHOTO)

PLATE 11. Marines hit the beach at Guam, July 21, 1944, jumping from an amphibian tractor and scrambling forward. As the beachhead expands, the tractors carry the men farther inshore. (USMC PHOTO)

PLATE 12. Tanks and troops assault a portion of the rugged Umurbrogol pocket, Peleliu, Palau Islands, October 7, 1944. Long weeks of fighting were required to clear this and similar terrain. (USMC PHOTO)

PLATE 13. Looking northwest at Iwo under preparatory bombardment, February 17, 1945, just after underwater demolition gunboats had been taken under enemy fire. Targets are on preferred beaches and along escarpments to the right. (USN PHOTO)

PLATE 14. Waves of amphibian tractors reach Iwo as the neutralizing barrage moves inshore and to the flanks of the beaches, February 19, 1945. A warship is in the foreground, and gunboats and control craft are amid the tractors. (USN PHOTO)

PLATE 15. A portion of Iwo's first terrace of volcanic gravel dominated by Suribachi, just after the initial landings while the enemy remains partially neutralized, permitting marines to dash forward standing up. A marine to the far right has reached the second terrace. (USMC PHOTO)

PLATE 16. One reason for speed in amphibious operations. A kamikaze plane attacking a light cruiser, *U.S.S. Vincennes*, off Okinawa, April 6, 1945. (USN PHOTO)

another consideration loomed large during the planning period. Fear of reefs and man-made beach and offshore obstacles caused considerable misgivings. In this connection, Kelly Turner followed through with a scheme he had been working on since the New Georgia operation in mid-1943, and formed underwater demolition teams. Beach obstructions and beach and reef mines such as those used at Tarawa were, he said, a matter of "very serious concern" during the planning period of the Kwajalein operation. For this reason he called together army, navy, and marine personnel familiar with demolition work, and instituted a training program for the job involved. He also set up a board for research into the problem; but he had no way of knowing how polished underwater demolition teams would become by the end of the war; and as for Kwajalein Atoll, he felt "little confidence" that they would be of "any great assistance." [20]

With the target date set to take full advantage of the tide, and with every possible precaution made to assure the troops of impact when hitting the beaches, other factors shaped the schemes of maneuver adopted by the division commanders and approved by their naval attack force counterparts.

The marines planned their operations in the northern end of Kwajalein Atoll carefully. (See map 12.) The wind at the time of the attack was normally from the northeast, at an average velocity of fifteen knots. The waves produced were some five feet in height, and the surf on the seaward beaches of Roi-Namur and other islets in the vicinity was treacherous. Yet, in order to get into the lagoon and to start emplacing artillery it was necessary to draw up a complex plan and to start the preliminary landings on seaward beaches. The plan was to begin landings on exposed coasts and to take the three islets just southwest of Roi-Namur during the morning of January 31. Since these islets also bordered the northern lagoon channel, their capture would permit entrance into the lagoon where much quieter waters were expected for subsequent landings, both on the islet needed for artillery support to the southeast of Roi-Namur, and on the main objectives themselves. (See map 13.)

The enemy garrison on Roi-Namur was estimated to total around 3,000 men, including laborers. Roi contained the most important Japanese airfield in the Marshalls, and was considered more strongly defended than Namur, despite the fact that Namur was uncleared for airstrips and was dotted with barracks and supply and ammunition dumps. The two islets together fitted into a rectangle, some 900 by 2,300 yards in size, with the shorter legs forming the eastern and western ends. A seaward approach to this rectangular objective, that is from the north, was ruled out not only because of the surf but also because Japanese fortifications on those beaches were known to be stronger than the defenses anywhere else around the principal targets in the north. Two considerations over and beyond surf conditions eliminated the end beaches from the preferred scheme. The coast lines were short and would permit little maneuver room once ashore; and if either end were hit, after one or the other of the islets had been overrun, the attackers would find themselves funneled onto the land spit and the connecting causeway in charging across to the remaining islet. The lagoon beaches on Roi-Namur were thus a rather obvious choice. The plan was to bring transports, cargo vessels, landing ships, and close fire support destroyers and gunboats into the lagoon, and on February 1 to send four battalion landing teams abreast onto Roi-Namur.[21]

The army gained the same basic advantages at the southern end of the atoll, but circumstances caused a number of variations in tactical approach. (See map 12.) Kwajalein Islet possessed an emergency airfield, and its defensive installations were estimated as slightly weaker than those on Roi-Namur, but it was more strongly manned. It was correctly believed to be garrisoned by some 4,000 enemy, with about 100 more first line troops than Roi-Namur and twice as many laborers.

In order to work over waters in the lee of the atoll, and to open the southern pass into the lagoon, the land areas due north of Kwajalein Islet were left to the last phase of the attack. Those to the northwest of Kwajalein, on the other hand, were listed for the first landings, on January 31, to secure entrance into the lagoon and to obtain dry land for artillery pieces. The attack on Kwajalein Islet was to begin at the same hour as that on Roi-Namur, on February 1.

The above considerations also dictated the employment of the southwest, west, or northwestern lagoon beaches of the principal target. The southwest beaches were eliminated because they were believed to be more heavily defended than the others. The shape of Kwajalein Islet precluded landings on the lagoon beaches. It is a relatively long land mass, formed like a crescent with the concave side facing the lagoon and the northern end tapering around at a 90° turn. It was feared that landing waves approaching from within the lagoon might meet flanking fire from the strong points located at both ends of the islet. The western beach was only some 500 yards in width; and more maneuver room was desirable, since only two battalions could land abreast, but nevertheless this was the best possible landing site.[22]

The 7th Infantry Division assigned to the Kwajalein end of the atoll was built around the 17th, 32nd, and 184th Infantry Regiments. These men had early come under the amphibious tutelage of Holland Smith and his staff. Later, two of the regiments had gained amphibious and battle experience on Attu, and the third had carried out a full-dress amphibious rehearsal on Kiska. The division had then been placed under a new commander, Major General Charles H. Corlett USA, and shipped to Hawaii, where Corlett instituted intensive training for atoll warfare before and after the division passed to the operational control of the Fifth Amphibious Corps in mid-December 1943. As Corlett instantly recognized, the task facing him "appeared to be a special operation radically different from anything for which the division had previously been trained." [23] He was a superior officer, who studied the reports from the Gilberts carefully and applied the lessons learned to his well-disciplined and well-led command. The results were most notable in the coordinated use of demolition engineers and tank-infantry teams, as well as in the introduction of the men to both the logistical and tactical employment of amphibian tractors and trucks.[24] Final rehearsals, held in the Hawaii group during the first eighteen days of January, were highly satisfactory. Atoll conditions were simulated, and a number of practice landings was made, some with both naval gunfire and air support. During these trial runs, logistical methods and equipment and the tactical performance of each battalion landing team were checked; and additional practice was given to the Dukw and tractor drivers, recently converted from service personnel, as well as to the newly activated battalion assigned to the division's armored tractors.

Embarking the 7th Infantry Division, while facilitated by the experience of both the army and navy personnel involved, was complicated by the task of procurement. After the Aleutians, the division had in any event to be resupplied, and warfare against a coral atoll posed entirely new problems. Supply was the duty of the Commanding General of the United States Army Forces in the Central Pacific Area, Lieutenant General Robert C. Richardson, Jr., USA, whose post had recently been established and who was unprepared for this responsibility. The presence of the staff of the 7th Infantry Division in Hawaii made it easy to coordinate planning with higher army and naval echelons, but the necessity of forwarding materiel from the San Francisco Port of Embarkation led to a hastily improvised logistical liaison. Critical items tended to arrive in Hawaii piecemeal or were late, and the supply officers of the division often had to exert every ingenuity to obtain substitutes. Under the circumstances, the fact that so large a portion of the tonnage was palletized and expertly combat-loaded reflects high credit on the staffs of both Corlett's division and Turner's amphibious group.

There was not, however, always a meeting of the army and naval minds as to the amounts of the various classes of supplies to be transported. The logistics section of the 7th Infantry Division began making its requests while the Gilberts campaign was getting under way, at a time when the staffs of both Turner and Holland Smith were otherwise engaged. The tentative logistical plan of the Fifth Amphibious Force for the Marshalls appeared in mid-October, but Corlett's staff immediately began to take issue with some of its important features.

One of the differences pertained to the number of units of fire to be loaded. Turner and Holland Smith, presumably thinking in terms of a speedy assault essential to the rapid retirement of amphibious shipping, specified five units of fire for all categories of weapons except antiaircraft guns. The army officers however were unofficially planning on ten days to complete the attack; and army pressure was instrumental, late in the embarkation phase of the Marshalls campaign, in doubling the allowance for heavy weapons and in raising that for light arms from five to eight units. Corlett's staff had, as it developed, made an excellent estimate of its needs, not in terms of time required but in terms of the volume of ammunition to be used. Army troops on Kwajalein Islet, for example, employed eighty-eight per cent of eight units in four days. Nor was this expenditure excessive, for fire discipline was good and, in any event, the expenditure of lead is to be favored over the expenditure of flesh. But the increase was a blanket order, effecting also the Fourth Marine Division. The marines were fully aware that their tactics (combining speed and firepower) required no more than five units of fire, and they neither desired nor requested more ammunition. The army troops and the bluejackets of Turner's amphibious group were sufficiently experienced in combat-loading so that the delayed decision caused no appreciable hardship; but it was different with the marines, to whom the increase was belatedly and unwisely applied. The action reports fail to clarify this matter, but it seems to have been caused by bureaucratic routine in Holland Smith's headquarters rather than by logic. Instructions to enlarge the ammunition carried, unaccompanied by any change in the tactical plan, made no sense whatsoever to the marines in San Diego and only added to the onerous burden of combat-loading being carried out by them and by navy personnel, both of whom were new to the work. "Of utmost importance," said the San Diego marines, "is the cessation of logistical planning once the loading has begun." [25]

The Fourth Marine Division had enough troubles of its own, without having them augmented by last-minute logistical changes. It was a recently formed division without combat experience. The oldest unit was the Twenty-third Marine Regiment, a rifle component in the Third Marine Division from the time of the organization of the regiment in July 1942 till early in 1943. In February of 1943 it was withdrawn from its parent organization and became the core of the new Fourth Marine Division. The next rifle regiment for the Fourth Division, the Twenty-fourth Marines, was formed toward the end of March; and about a month later a part of the Twenty-third Marine Regiment was split off as a cadre for the final infantry component of the Fourth Division, the Twenty-fifth Marines. Also, between February and June 1943, the artillery and engineering regiments were formed, designated respectively the Fourteenth and Twentieth Marines.

As was customary, both experienced officer and noncommissioned officer personnel were ordered from other duties and injected into the new division, but its units were forced to train separately on both the east and west coasts of the United States until July 1943. During that month movement was begun to collect the division at Camp Pendleton, Oceanside, California. There, even before the concentration was completed, the Fourth Marine Division was formally activated in mid-August. Brigadier General James L. Underhill USMC was named assistant division commander, and was soon dispatched to observe the Betio assault. The top post in the division went to an officer of great experience, Major General Harry Schmidt USMC, formerly the Assistant Commandant of the Corps.

The Twenty-fifth Marines were the last to reach Pendleton, arriving in early September. While the staff was busy planning for atoll warfare in the Central Pacific, units of the division were exercising in landings, field problems, pillbox reductions, and night attacks.[26] News of Tarawa, the return of Underhill and other observers from Betio, and the preliminary and final action reports from the Gilberts, stimulated the men and gave them concrete examples of their forthcoming ordeal. As Schmidt later recalled, "every effort was made to benefit by this experience, including intensified training in the utilization of amphibian tractors as assault troop carriers, and in the type of tactics required for coping with a strongly entrenched enemy on a small atoll." One of his regimental commanders was more specific. "Great stress," he reported, "was laid on the training of assault demolition teams for use against pillboxes and other fortified positions." Two types of assault teams were organized, each totaling some twenty men. Both contained demolition, bazooka, and automatic rifle groups. The first was built around a flamethrower, and the second around a light machine gun. "Selected infantrymen in all of our assault units," he continued, "received special training in demolitions in order to take their place in the above teams, and to substitute for engineers where necessary."[27]

Schmidt was well pleased with the integration of these infantry groups and his artillery, tank, and engineering arms; but from the start he was concerned lest his division fail to function smoothly with the navy. He felt the great fault of the training period was the absence of the men-of-war and aircraft which were to furnish direct support in the actual operation. The brief presence of some of these ships and planes during the rehearsal was not sufficient to satisfy him. "Due to the fact that air and naval gunfire are the principal supporting arms during the critical ship-to-shore phase," he emphasized, "it is considered highly important that maximum training with the firing ships and air groups be conducted prior to the operation in order that the infantry-air and infantry-naval gunfire teams may be welded into smooth organizations." [28]

These words overlook the constant need for keeping warships on or close to the fighting front, and in any event, as both Schmidt and Conolly realized, their big problem lay in the inexperience of the marine tractor drivers and the crews of the amphibious lift.

Combat-loading at San Diego was complicated by the problem of higher echelon liaison in Hawaii, as well as by late changes in logistical plans; but navy-marine collaboration here, unlike other phases of the operation, was good. A large percentage of the tonnage lifted was palletized, which worked out well since beachheads were quickly won and since there were amphibious vehicles available for logistical use. The supply section of the corps staff tried to obtain uniformity between the army troops and the marines in all loading, and to cut down to a bare minimum the equipment lifted, especially motor transport.[29]

The rehearsal period gave full warning of forthcoming difficulties in the ship-to-shore movement of the Fourth Marine Division. The time allotted was short, from January 1–3 at Pendleton and on San Clemente Island off the coast of California. Only a part of the naval supporting arms was present, and as in the rehearsal for the army troops, atoll conditions were simulated. Conolly believed that the rehearsal of the Fourth Marine Division accomplished much, an opinion some responsible marine officers did not share. But Conolly seems to have been more nearly correct in this judgment than the marines. Many of the tank landing ships had just been commissioned, and a large number of the amphibian tractor crews were equally green. The decision had to be made whether to take these inexperienced men along or to do without them and their precious tractors at Roi-Namur. Betio was a vivid example of how critically such personnel and their equipment were required, and the decision to use them was certainly sound. Limited though the rehearsal necessarily was, it benefited some of the men who desperately needed it.[30]

Most of the marine rifle components, however, just went along to the rehearsal for the ride. Time was so short that few men were set ashore. The commanding officer of the Twenty-fourth Marines noted that the only personnel actually landed were the headquarters of battalions and regiments; and of the rehearsal he concluded, "this period aboard ship proved tiresome and useless for the majority of troops and it is believed the time could have been better spent ashore." [31]

The criticism of the rehearsal applies only to the Twenty-third and the Twenty-fourth Marines, who were assigned to the February 1 attack on Roi-Namur. Since Conolly and Schmidt could not fully exercise all of their command, they wisely selected the men who were to begin the landings on seaward beaches on January 31, and gave them a more thoroughgoing trial run. The units involved were the Twenty-fifth Marines, the artillery regiment (the Fourteenth Marines), and a scout company. This ship-to-shore rehearsal, however, was fouled from beginning to end. The tactical marine leader of this phase of the operation was the assistant division commander, Underhill. He observed of his rehearsal, "About everything that could go wrong went wrong." The scout company never saw its boats. Some of the tank landing ships which were carrying the amphibian tractors and a part of the artillery failed to arrive, and those that put in their appearance were out of position. Not all the troops turned up, nor was the debarkation drill complete. The rehearsal ended in confusion. It was altogether too accurate a foretaste of what would happen at Roi-Namur. Unfortunately, nothing could be done about it. The tank landing ships steamed at such slow speed that it was necessary to dispatch them at once for the staging area in Hawaii. There was only time enough for reloading, for repairs to the amphibian tractors, and for the continued installation of armor on some of the tractors. Many of the amphibian tractor units had only recently come under the control of the division, and their personnel (principally marines) were inexcusably devoid of discipline. But there was no time for a second rehearsal, much less for basic indoctrination. There was not even an opportunity to point out to the amphibian tractor and tank landing ship crews the errors they had made and to attempt to get them to iron out their mutual problems. Underhill felt with reason that had he been able to hold a critique of the rehearsal with the personnel involved, and then to conduct a second rehearsal, things would have gone much better in the actual operation.[32]

Thus in the Marshalls as earlier in the Gilberts, the United States pushed ahead before all components were ready. The approach of the amphibious expedition into the Marshalls was safely made, Spruance's covering force having swept into the area at an earlier date. Although the targets had been carefully selected and the troops were optimistic, vigorous resistance was expected. As Holland Smith's intelligence officer had noted, while Kwajalein Atoll was not thought to be the most difficult target in the group, it was the "pivotal point" of the defensive system in the Marshalls. Photographic interpretation and other data permitted him accurately to predict the number of defenders on the atoll at between 8,000 and 9,600 men, including laborers; but he feared the Japanese were throwing in additional troops and their defensive potential would increase before the day of the attack. He knew that a part of the enemy's 52nd Division was in the vicinity of the Carolines and the Marshalls. He little suspected that this command was, belatedly in January 1944, being sent to Truk. He concluded Kwajalein would be harder to take than Tarawa. "Since the Japanese," he said, "have had control of the Kwajalein Atoll for some twenty-five years and have had ample time to prepare this base against assault, installations are believed to be of a more permanent nature and consequently more formidable than those found on Tarawa. It can be expected that Kwajalein Atoll will be defended against an American attack at all costs." [33]

As the troops steamed westward, this considered opinion of heavy losses was given out to the press and promptly despatched to prepare the American people. "We are invading a part of the Japanese empire," read the newspapers. "[We] will make the most audacious attack attempted . . . in this war. . . . We expect Kwajalein to be tougher than Tarawa." [34]

3. *Preparatory Fires and Preliminary Landings*

Such pessimistic predictions evaporated in the face of brilliant plans which were on the whole skillfully executed. Since mid-December land-based bombers and intermittent carrier strikes had been hitting various atolls in the Marshalls, and in addition seaplanes from Midway were neutralizing Wake. Intensive preparations began in late January when Spruance took over from Hoover the primary responsibility for pounding most of the enemy bases in the Marshalls. Carrier task forces did the bulk of the work, but also a small group of cruisers, escort carriers, destroyers, and minelayers under Rear Admiral Ernest G. Small USN followed carrier planes into the vicinity of two of the atolls being neutralized, bombed and bombarded their installations, and interdicted the lagoon channels with explosives. The combined endeavors of these pilots and surface sailors were eminently successful. "It is significant," Nimitz asserted, "that the ultimate destruction was so complete that *not one Japanese aircraft was able to attack our surface forces* engaged in the Marshalls occupation." [35]

The explanation was that the enemy had no planes left by the time the expeditionary force arrived. Japanese efforts to halt Hoover's heavy and medium bombers over the Marshalls were both vain and costly; in December 1943, for example, the Japanese lost a complete air flotilla, approximately 100 planes. When Spruance moved in on January 29, they had only 130 aircraft with which to confront 700 American fighters, scout bombers, and torpedo planes. By nightfall there was not an operational Japanese aircraft east of Eniwetok. The next day one of Spruance's fast carrier task groups moved westward, successfully demolished the planes and airfield installations on Eniwetok, and thus knocked out the key base through which reinforcements in planes might have been staged into the remainder of the Marshalls group. The entire area was localized and wide open to amphibious attack.

The covering force also devoted considerable attention to Kwajalein. Two fast carrier groups hit that atoll on the first day, January 29. Each concentrated its power at one of the two principal objectives. Planes alone hit Kwajalein Islet, while at nightfall one fast battleship and two destroyers were detached from the Roi-Namur task group to maintain harassing fire on this northern target. Both groups continued their work on January 30. More than 200 sorties were flown over Roi-Namur, augmented by a deliberate four-hour bombardment by three fast battleships and five destroyers. No counterbattery fire materialized, and the airfield, coast defense guns, and stores were hit repeatedly with good results. Almost 250 sorties were sent against Kwajalein Islet, followed by three and one-half hours of naval bombardment, involving three fast battleships and three destroyers.

By sundown of January 30 all coast defense guns on Kwajalein Atoll had been rendered useless. Each of the principal targets had been on the receiving end of more than 1,000 projectiles from 16-inch guns, and around 8,000 from 5-inch guns. Thereafter the two fast carrier task groups stood by until February 5, furnishing some close air support during this period.[36]

The regularly assigned air support and naval gunfire vessels arrived to take up their duties at Kwajalein Atoll along with the amphibious lift, during the early morning hours of January 31. Meanwhile Majuro was being captured. Oddly enough, photographic interpretation of Majuro was too correct. Pictures of Japanese construction had led to the conclusion that it was occupied by some 300–400 Nipponese. So it had been, but they were evacuated in November 1942. Only a naval warrant officer and three civilians remained behind to guard Japanese buildings and materiel. The Fifth Amphibious Corps Reconnaissance Company landed in rubber boats a few hours before midnight, January 30/31. Its first task was to scout the small islets adjacent to the lagoon entrance. The only trouble encountered was in understanding the natives and advising the admiral, Harry Hill, that the atoll was virtually unoccupied. The reconnoitering marines could not get their radios to work, and this led to a waste of ammunition during the dawn twilight, when a short preliminary naval gunfire was delivered against one of the larger islets. Finally the commanding officer of the company got a message through. The gunfire was abruptly halted and the scheduled air strike cancelled, much to the relief of the natives. The reconnaissance company scouted the remainder of the atoll, taking the warrant officer prisoner. The lagoon was quickly swept for mines, and Majuro was prepared as an advanced anchorage for major operations on to the westward. The Second Battalion of the 106th Infantry Regiment was landed as a mobile defense force only after it was seen that this unit was not needed in reserve at Kwajalein.[37]

Following the covering force, the naval attack forces at Roi-Namur and at Kwajalein Islet started their preparatory fires against the principal targets early on January 31. A small amount of air support and naval gunfire on that day was devoted to assisting the preliminary landings, but the vast bulk was directed in a deliberate, thoroughgoing, destructive manner against the primary objectives. Old battleships, for example, were maneuvered to less than 2,000 yards from the pinpointed installations on each of the important islets. The Northern Attack Force commander, Rear Admiral Richard L. Conolly, endeared himself to the marines by insisting that these elderly giants move in until their keels were almost scraping coral, thus earning for himself the sobriquet "Close-In" Conolly.

To summarize, before the morning of the principal landings, Roi-Namur had been plastered by three successive days of accurate bombing strikes and of naval bombardment, plus night harassing fire. Kwajalein Islet received similar attention. While it is true that naval gunfire on Kwajalein Islet began several hours later than that at Roi-Namur, almost the same tonnage of projectiles was hurled at each target. Whatever preliminary naval gunfire support Kwajalein Islet lacked, relative to Roi-Namur, was more than offset by the assignment of heavier regular naval gunfire support group to the Southern Attack Force, and by a greater preponderance and earlier emplacement of the army's artillery.[38]

Preliminary landings to clear the lagoon channels and to set up artillery on Kwajalein Atoll went on concurrently with naval gunfire and air strikes on January 31. The wind that morning was stronger than normal, blowing at a force of nineteen to twenty knots rather than fifteen, and both current and surf conditions deteriorated correspondingly.[39] This increased the burden on the navy personnel and on Underhill's men. Despite handicaps, they carried out their mission, but it is important to determine wherein man-made factors contributed to the confusion that arose on that day, especially since this confusion carried over and adversely affected the principal landings on Roi-Namur on February 1.

There was a certain amount of animosity between the navy personnel and the marines, nor was it restricted to inexperienced tractor drivers and tank landing ship crews. It was present, at least in a milder form, aboard some of the larger amphibious shipping. Both the navy and the marines were to blame. At least a few of the sailors and their officers had not been indoctrinated in the basic fact that an amphibian lift has but one reason for being, namely to transport troops to the target. On the other hand, there is evidence that some of the marines were not very pleasant passengers, destroying shipboard property and failing in certain essential housekeeping duties.[40]

The serious handicap at Roi-Namur, however, was the lack of cordial relations between the marine amphibian tractor drivers and the tank landing ship crews. These men not only had little grasp of their duties, but like spoiled children could not get along with one another. Doubtless the action reports exaggerate this discord, with each trying to lay the blame on the other, for if it had been as deep-seated as described by some, it is impossible to see how any landings at all could have been made. It is, finally, difficult not only to evaluate the extent of this discord but also the degree to which it caused plans to go wrong. It certainly had some influence, even though the more important consideration, and in all probability the one leading to personal animosities, was inexperience. Nevertheless, the fact is that the tractors were forced to make long runs over choppy waters, and the problem of reservicing them was poorly met. The result was a loss of many of these valuable amphibians when they were acutely needed.

To make matters worse, the procedure for getting the marines into the tractors was complex. Landing craft ferried the men from their transports to the tank landing ships, where they were transferred to amphibian vehicles for further movement ashore. Rough seas on the morning of January 31 made it difficult for the landing craft to locate the correct tank landing ship.[41] After the assault troops were aboard the tank landing ships, there was some difficulty in debarking the tractors, especially those loaded topside. "In one case, only one man in the entire crew . . . professed any knowledge of ever having seen an amphibian tractor lowered down an elevator."[42]

Even where this problem was solved, the amphibian tractors were too frequently released when still far distant from the planned position, compelling extended trips against countercurrents to the lines-of-departure, and resulting in a battering by waters that were choppy, even within the windward end of the lagoon. Some of the vehicles ran out of gas. At the time, all pumps were mechanically operated. Lacking fuel in a rough sea meant that after a short interval, unless the tractor could be beached, it sank. In some instances, at least, crews of the tank landing ships, responsible for replenishing the vehicles, insisted that they service only those they had lifted to the area. Some tractors were unable to return to their parent ship, either because of a shortage of gas, because that vessel was out of position, or because low visibility prevented identification.[43] Sunken tractors were permanently lost. Those out of gas and beached were immobilized and of no tactical or logistical use. The Fourth Marine Division went into the Kwajalein operation with 340 amphibian vehicles, but this was not enough. And, on the morning of January 31, other factors arose further to hamper execution of an orderly ship-to-shore movement.

Radio communications with the amphibian tractors broke down. No waterproofing protected these sets, and rough seas drowned them out.[44] Under the best of circumstances, lack of primary communication facilities would have made control difficult. Since marine amphibian tractor personnel were neither well-trained nor well-disciplined, the situation was worse than it should have been. Tractor crews were attached to the division too late for proper orientation. Reports from Betio led to an increase in the number of vehicles, with a consequent dilution of the relatively experienced personnel. Some tractor groups arrived at almost the last moment before sailing. "To insure getting the utmost use of attached units," complained a regimental commander when discussing tractor performance, "it is believed that they must be attached at least three weeks before departure for an operation so that they may be indoctrinated not only with the phases of the operation but with the discipline necessary for successful completion thereof." In combat, some of the tractor drivers felt themselves to be privileged individuals, and responsibility for this attitude must rest squarely on the Marine Corps. These men, emphatically concluded this regimental commander, believed "that the nature of their work entitled them to freedom from strict discipline and that idea must be eliminated."

Under this accumulation of adverse factors, it is to the credit of the navy and the Twenty-fifth Marines that they carried out their mission on January 31. (See map 12.) Although several hours behind schedule, the channel islets to the southwest of Roi-Namur were cleared, and while artillery was being run ashore in amphibian tractors and medium landing craft, the line-of-departure was shifted into the windward end of the lagoon for the run to the islet southeast of the principal target.

Here new complications arose. On departure from the staging area in Hawaii, the intent was to take only one islet southeast of Roi-Namur; but en route to the target Conolly in consultation with Schmidt added a second. This decision was tactically sound, and had been earlier discussed; but it was belatedly reached, and at least some of the tank landing ships and hence the tractor personnel never heard of the late change in plan.[45]

This multiplicity of objectives for January 31 should be noted in defense of the tractor drivers. Only about a third of the tractors were employed on the first day, in order to assure a sufficient supply on February 1 for the pressing tactical problem that Roi was thought to be. Some of the tractor crews shuttled back and forth for long distances to and from the lines-of-departure. It was, from before dawn to after sunset, an exhausting ordeal. Further delays within the lagoon established the time for taking the fourth islet at near dusk. For the fifth objective, so few tractors were available as to require a slow and tactically unsound expedient of ferrying a few men at a time. Fortunately for the marines involved, the opposition was faint and the distance from the fourth to the fifth islet short.[46]

A near breakdown of boat control which occurred inside the lagoon held up seizure of the fourth objective. Underhill, who had tactical command of the marines in the January 31 landings, was embarked on a craft either inadequately equipped or without suitable communication facilities, and could attempt to restore order only by word of mouth.

The trouble was that the primary boat control vessel inside the lagoon was trying to serve in a dual capacity. This was the destroyer *Phelps*. Choice of a destroyer as a primary control vessel was in every respect excellent: ability to enter the lagoon at an early hour, ease of identification, and availability of communication facilities all argued in its favor; but *Phelps* was also designated command ship for a fire support unit. Since the radios of the amphibian tractors were useless, control from the start was difficult; but the point at which it virtually collapsed was the moment *Phelps* departed her control station and began carrying out her fire support mission. Even so, control would not have deteriorated so sharply had *Phelps* properly designated a substitute control craft, and had she transferred to that craft the marine landing force staff officer who was alone thoroughly versed in the landing plans and schedules.[47]

All these ship-to-shore difficulties, plus those which followed subsequently in the operation, caused Schmidt, when submitting his final report, to make two far-reaching recommendations. He asked, not for an earlier attachment of amphibian tractor units to division, but that such units be made a permanent part of his and other similar commands. Finally, he requested a fundamental change in ship-to-shore doctrine, proposing that the tactical landing force commanders have full supervision over the dispatch of boat formations from the lines-of-departure, and of the time and place of the landings involved.

Holland Smith rejected both recommendations. To the first he replied that "task organizations normal for attack on one type of terrain may not be normal for another. As a consequence, divisions can not possibly retain a permanent organization of all units necessary to meet all situations." There had been, and would continue to be, he said, a limited number of tactical components such as the amphibian tractor battalion which must remain assigned to corps, ready for attachment to divisions needing them in particular operations.

The rejoinder to the more fundamental request was equally negative. "Effective amphibious doctrine," he noted, "prescribes that the Navy is responsible for the delivery of the landing force to the beach. It is not recommended that this responsibility be changed. The preparation of the debarkation and approach schedule is a responsibility of the Battalion Landing Team Commander. Through his annex to his Operations Order the Landing Team Commander does direct the time of landing of his troops, the time those formations leave the rendezvous area, and the time they cross the line-of-departure." Current doctrine, he concluded, "recommends a staff officer of the Landing Force Commander be placed aboard the control vessel: this officer to be given authority to make tactical decisions concerning the control of dispatch of troop formations crossing the line-of-departure."

Better training and discipline, longer rehearsal periods, more efficient equipment, and combat experience, rather than changes in organization and doctrine, were needed. Deficiencies in each of these former categories, most evident on the first day, handicapped the Roi-Namur undertaking. Although three battalions of 75- and one of 105-millimeter howitzers were emplaced and sufficiently supplied with ammunition to begin support at dawn on February 1, the delays involved prevented adequate reservicing of some amphibian tractors, further aggravating the shortage of these craft for the principal landings. The Twenty-fourth Marines, going into Namur, suffered. They were minus almost forty per cent of their planned assault lift.[48]

At the other important corner of the atoll, the 7th Infantry Division met few of the troubles which plagued the marines on January 31. (See map 12.) Experienced personnel, working across waters made relatively placid by the eastern and southwestern legs of the atoll, faced no great multiplicity of landings such as those adjacent to Roi-Namur; hence there was no reason to shuttle amphibian tractors loaded with men from the line-of-departure to the shore and back a second and even a third time. Landings on the channel islets were conducted by a reinforced cavalry troop in rubber boats and at night, but there was no serious opposition. One of the objectives northwest of Kwajalein was overlooked in the darkness, and its neighbor occupied; but this error was rectified at first light, and it led to the capture of a set of secret Japanese charts which proved to be very useful in forthcoming Central Pacific operations. At about the same time, the 17th Infantry Regiment began seizure of the islet marked for five battalions of artillery and of another suitable for supply dumps and repair stations. Army troops performed these tasks without serious deviation from schedule. Thus amphibian tractors at the southern end of the atoll were used to occupy only two, rather than five, preliminary objectives. Unlike their colleagues to the north, the well-trained crews of the tank landing ships and the highly disciplined personnel of the experienced army tank and service units converted to drivers for the amphibian tractors took such splendid care of their equipment that none was permanently lost, and all were available for immediate reemployment at Eniwetok. Dukws, rigged to carry 105-millimeter howitzers, and medium landing craft loaded with 155's likewise performed their mission with commendable dispatch; and no amphibian tractors lifted artillery. Most of the army's howitzers were emplaced and registered before nightfall on January 31, roughly twelve hours before the marine cannoneers were fully ready to lend similar support.[49]

Use of artillery against Kwajalein and Roi-Namur Islets was but one of the factors which converted the principal attacks into relatively bloodless landing operations. Naval gunfire and air support at each of the main objectives met the most sanguine expectations. Both marines and army troops crossed the beaches at Roi-Namur and Kwajalein Islet standing up. No opposition worthy of the name was encountered at either objective until the Americans had penetrated some 200 yards inshore. The comment of an observer at one of the objectives was equally applicable to the other: Kwajalein Islet "looked as if it had been picked up to 20,000 feet and then dropped." [50]

The enemy defenders on Roi-Namur and Kwajalein Islet were kept groggy by means of harassing fires on the night of 31 January/1 February; and during the early morning daylight hours that followed, the supporting arms reached a crescendo when shore-based artillerymen joined the bombers and the naval gunners. The landing on Kwajalein Islet was executed on schedule. Marines at Roi-Namur were held up by additional confusions and the continuing ill-effects of the ship-to-shore movement on January 31. Unlike the situation at Betio, however, all supporting arms accurately calibrated their fires, not in conformity with an arbitrarily planned hour, but with the exact position of the amphibian tractors.

The plan for the supporting arms on the morning of February 1 was identical for each of the primary objectives. Ship- and shore-based guns opened their barrage at first light. The fire, slow and deliberate, continued to be destructive. While these weapons were checked and prepared for the next phase of their activity, planes came in over both targets, bombing, strafing, and firing rockets. Then naval guns and artillery reentered the fray, paying particular attention to the landing beaches, and increasing the fall of their shell during the period just before the troops reached the shore. This fire was sustained until after the first waves were across their lines-of-departure, whereupon it was shifted inshore. Guns, more reliable than planes, were thus depended upon to keep any remaining beach opposition neutralized until it would be overrun.

Just as the artillerymen and naval gunners directed their fire inshore, infantry landing craft converted to gunboats dashed toward the beaches firing 20- and 40-millimeter guns and releasing rockets. All troop-laden amphibian tractors had machine guns, and some had rockets. Preceding the first assault waves at each objective were armored amphibian tractors, carrying no passengers but each mounting a 37-millimeter weapon and three .30-caliber machine guns. The plan was to send these vehicles across the beach and inland several score yards, from whence, having fanned to the right and left flanks of the assaulting waves, they were to furnish covering fire for the dismounting rifle components.[51]

More than superficial devastation was obtained by preparatory fires. Generalizations by men associated with each of the three supporting arms, claiming destruction of virtually all pinpointed defenses, were obvious exaggerations; inshore fighting frequently required tank-infantry-demolition coordination against enemy strongholds, but the fact remains that each of the supporting arms exhibited a high degree of accuracy. A headquarters observer flying over Roi testified to this proficiency. While describing the situation below, he suddenly ejaculated, "the whole damn island has blown up!" Asked if he were hurt, he replied: "We're a thousand feet higher up now . . . got blown there. Must have been an ammunition dump our guns hit with us right over it." [52]

Against each of the principal targets at Kwajalein Atoll, around 6,000 tons of explosives were hurled by artillerymen, naval gunners, and pilots. This figure includes neither projectiles less than 75-millimeters in size, nor rockets. On Roi, for example, the average was some three pounds of explosives per square yard of terrain. Such volumetric calculations really become impressive when the quality of accuracy is added. Both armor-piercing and high-capacity shells were fired, sometimes by direct control at point blank range. Not only did this knock out most of the opposition at the beach, but it also facilitated the fighting inshore. Even Holland Smith, perfectionist that he was, had nothing but praise for all aspects of the preliminary fires.[53]

4. Seizure of Roi-Namur and Kwajalein Islet

Preparatory bombing and gunfire on Roi-Namur was so thorough that it threw the tactical allocations of strength to the two participating regiments out of balance. It had been anticipated, on the basis of

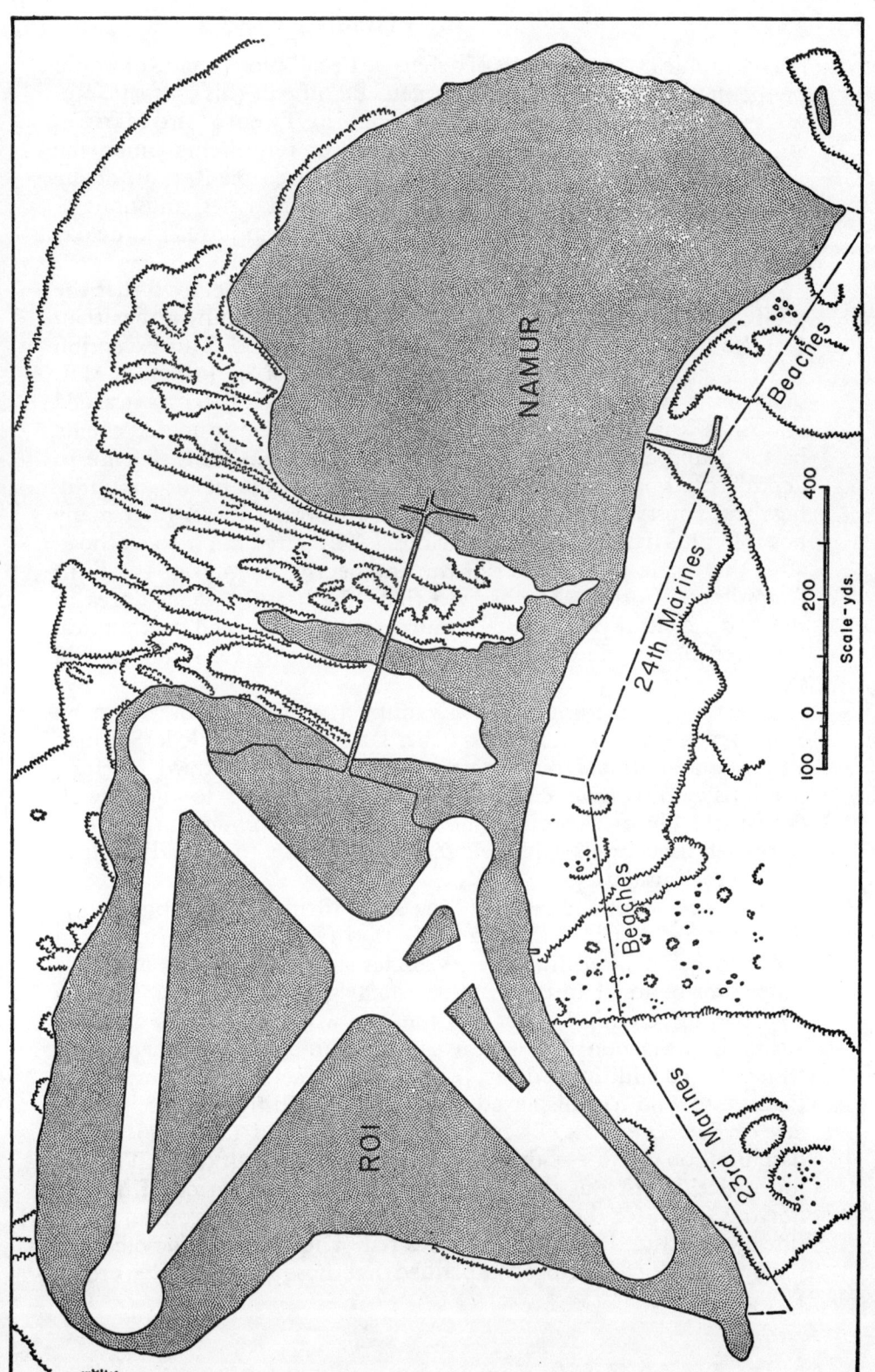

MAP 13. The islets of Roi-Namur.

photographic interpretations of defensive installations, that Roi would be the more difficult of the two targets. Because of this estimate, Roi was assigned to the oldest of the regiments, the Twenty-third Marines, and they were favored in the dispensing of reinforcing units: the single battalion of 105-millimeter howitzers fired on Roi; all of the medium tanks accompanied the Twenty-third Marines; and none of the amphibian tractors lifting this regiment was employed on the day before the principal landings.

With one exception, no navy or marine planner believed that the preliminary support would be so effective that Namur, rather than Roi, would prove to be the more difficult of seizure. This exception was Holland Smith's intelligence officer, Colonel St. Julien R. Marshall USMC, who, while most concerned over beach defenses, warned that since Roi was practically all airstrip, while Namur housed enemy barracks and ammunition dumps, a stronger "makeshift defense in depth" could be expected on Namur, "where the abundance of buildings and construction work within the island perimeter offer many possible alternate defensive positions." This prediction was echoed after the battle by the chief of the engineering section of the Fifth Amphibious Corps, who observed that "the heavily wooded area in the north central portion of Namur, a maze of fire and communication trenches, made the destruction of the enemy here difficult and slow." [54]

The time of landing on Roi-Namur, at slightly before noon on February 1, was more than two hours later than scheduled. (See map 13.) The amphibian tractors assigned to the Twenty-third Marines, previously unused in combat, had trouble getting to the line-of-departure; far more serious, however, the Twenty-fourth Marines were even longer delayed by the results of the ship-to-shore difficulties of the previous day.

Commanders of the tank landing ships lifting the tractors for the Twenty-third Marines insisted on a 0130 reveille on February 1 in order to begin launching their vehicles sufficiently early; but their intent was better than their ability to navigate. At 0700 these vessels were still fifteen miles out of position, and when they finally did drop anchor in the lagoon, they were five miles behind the line-of-departure, which caused additional delay. Nor were the tractor drivers any better than those who had displayed such lack of training and discipline a day earlier. Once the Twenty-third Marines had their two assault battalions on the line-of-departure, they had to wait until the Twenty-fourth Regiment was similarly prepared. It was a period of intense nervous strain for the men waiting to go into Roi, and control at the line-of-departure left much to be desired. The commanding officer of the Twenty-third Marines complained that those giving garbled orders to go ahead and land anyway included almost everybody: "Boat Commanders, Wave Commanders, Flotilla Commanders, Amphibian Tractor Company Commanders and platoon leaders and tractor drivers."

The situation just to the eastward, with the Twenty-fourth Marines headed for Namur, was even more confused. Only 62 of the 110 troop-carrying tractors assigned to this lift could be located, and it was necessary to boat some assault troops in landing craft, which in turn could not be assembled rapidly nor in sufficient quantity. As the minutes slowly dragged by and the Twenty-fourth Marines were still not formed for the race forward from the line-of-departure, Conolly, in consultation with Schmidt, was faced with a difficult and possibly fateful decision. Gunfire could not be continued forever, and the attack must be launched before its neutralizing effect plus that of the bombings was dissipated; equally important, the amphibians and landing craft idling at the line-of-departure were running short of fuel. Conolly had learned from the underwater demolition teams that hydrographic conditions were favorable and no man-made obstacles had been located. He had no choice but to rely on what he estimated to have been highly effective preparatory fires, for he must order the attack to begin before the Twenty-fourth Marines were fully ready, and thus rob that unit of some of its momentum across the beach. In the words of its commanding officer: "At 1112 without prior notice to the Combat Team Commander . . . the control vessel executed the signal for the first waves to leave the line-of-departure."

Conolly was aware of the possible danger of this decision. It meant a repetition of what had happened, because of adverse hydrographic conditions, at Betio. The landing on Namur lacked sustained drive. Neither of the two battalions landing in the van was organized for departure, nor had the reserve companies of these battalions so much as arrived in their designated area. And, of course, the battalion landing in regimental reserve was not prepared. This gave rise to confusion at the beach, landings which were strung out rather than compact as planned, a mixture of units, and hence a loss of the maximum effort. The landing on Namur resembled a ferrying operation more than a power-laden deployment. But neither there nor on Roi was there any effective opposition at the beach, thanks to the preparatory fires, to the weapons mounted on the landing craft and the tractors, and to the blistering mortar and 37-millimeter shells being hurled at Namur from the islet just to the southeast. Conolly, in short, as all responsible commanders are apt to be forced to do, had to make a decision on the basis of calculated risks. He could not delay the run any longer and still attack on February 1, nor because of logistical and tactical considerations could he well afford to put the landings off a day. Schmidt agreed. Conolly and Schmidt relied on their preparation as sufficient even for a somewhat disorganized landing. They were right; there was no duplication of Betio.[55]

At the same time, it must not be assumed that the faulty ship-to-shore movement had no appreciable effect on the land fighting. If anything, the Twenty-third Marines hit the Roi beach with entirely too much momentum; or perhaps it would be more accurate to say that some of the men were so anxious to kill an enemy as to exhibit a lack of fire discipline, while some of the units, especially the tank crews, were so eager to be the first to reach the seaward shore, that they side-stepped many strongpoints and swept across Roi like broken field runners. It is also possible that some of Roi's defenders managed to slip over to Namur during the preparatory period. The plan was to halt at a phase line half-way across Roi and reorganize while another barrage of artillery and naval gunfire was called down on the remaining enemy; but the phase line was overrun a bare sixty minutes after the first wave landed, and the close support had to be cancelled for fear of killing friendly troops. By mid-afternoon of February 1, no organized resistance remained on Roi; and by nightfall, despite the ability of the Japanese in snaking through the complicated web of piping that drained the airfield, shooting first from this opening and then from that, the objective was secured.

It was the Twenty-fourth Marines who needed this momentum, and yet who were denied it by confusion at the line-of-departure. Even so, they might have reformed quickly and driven forward rapidly but for two untoward events.

The first of these was opposition, not from the beach, but in the language of the regimental commander, "from the rear from our own armored tractors." The crews of these vehicles, rather than pressing forward and covering the assault waves from either flank, "halted before reaching the beach and created a menace to the succeeding waves." Even after the troop-landed tractors had managed to worm through their armored and armed brethren, the latter "continued to fire on the beach through the assault waves." This was enough to slow down any group of men.

The second untoward event was a series of heavy explosions ashore on Namur which occurred about an hour after high noon and which in the opinion of the regimental commander accounted for fifty per cent of the casualties sustained by his right flank van battalion. There were a few survivors in the immediate scene of the blasts, and their evidence indicates the explosions were touched off by marine infantry-demolition teams. But these men are open to no criticism since the enemy's pillboxes, blockhouses, and covered ammunition dumps were not only indistinguishable, but also frequently interchangeable. The first explosion was so huge that it blanketed "the entire island with a dense cloud of pungent smoke, which was first thought to be gas. Fragments of concrete, steel, wood, shrapnel and several torpedo heads rained down over the surrounding area. . . ." Within the next thirty minutes, two smaller but violent blasts originated in the same general zone.

February 1, 1944, was not a lucky day for the Twenty-fourth Marines. Two 75-millimeter half-tracks, which proved to be the most effective weapon ashore on Namur, reached the beach at around 1245, but the engine of one of them was drowned out by the surf. About fifteen minutes later, three out of five light tanks made the coast, but all three immediately bogged down in the sand. Another light tank came in at about 1400, and a second an hour later. These proceeded to extricate the earlier arrivals from the sand, and five light tanks were ready for employment, but it was already well past midafternoon.

Thus on the day of the principal landings, the Twenty-fourth Marines had to rely on half-tracks, mounting both heavy machine guns and 75-millimeter weapons, as well as flamethrowers, to carry the brunt of their attack. In neither category did the regimental commander believe the table of organization for his unit sufficient. He wanted at least seven half-tracks, and considerably more than nine flamethrowers.[56] These requests were doubtless motivated, in part, by the absence of tanks for most of the first day, and their ineffective employment on the second. Even so, the battalion on the left reached the phase line half-way across Namur at 1400, while the right flank battalion, in which area the explosions had occurred, came into line an hour later.

There then ensued a delay of from two and one-half to three and one-half hours while the light tanks and other reinforcements lumbered forward. Despite artillery, naval gunfire, and mortar support, this long interval gave the enemy time to regroup. The attack from the phase line was launched at 1730, with a company of the reserve battalion in the place of a decimated unit on the right flank; but moderately heavy resistance unexpectedly developed on the left, in the north central portion of Namur, a thickly wooded area interlocked with communicating trenches. Elements on the right reached the seaward coast, only to be forced to drop back and tie in with the left flank battalion at nightfall.

The night of February 1/2 was uneventful, except for minor Japanese infiltrations and undisciplined fire by rear area units which "seriously endangered troops at the front." The regimental commander, noticing "little effort" on the part of the officers and noncommissioned officers of this normally non-combatant personnel in curbing "unwarranted firing," ordered their weapons and ammunition taken away from them.

Namur was overrun before noon on February 2. At dawn, about 100 Japanese attacked the left flank, but were beaten back while additional ground was being gained. The marines jumped off for their final drive at 0900. Facing them was heavy debris, interspersed with several blockhouses and pillboxes, and a number of hastily constructed strong points. By this time the medium tanks had been transferred from Roi, and were employed on the more difficult left flank, but the terrain was unsuited to optimum use, and the air observer communication channel to division headquarters interfered with the frequency on which the tank radios were set, making control and coordination with the infantry difficult. On the second as on the first day, it was mainly a hand-to-hand struggle by groups of marines, who by-passed resistance points and relied principally on half tracks and flamethrower-infantry-demolition teams to keep the attack rolling. The northern shore of Namur was reached in strength at around 1100, and some three hours later all organized resistance had been overcome.[57]

At the southern end of the atoll the army troops continued to cooperate splendidly with Turner's amphibious group; and the February 1 ship-to-shore movement, despite a few trivial incidents, went off like clockwork. Again the underwater demolition teams found conditions favorable for landing. The 7th Infantry Division with two regiments abreast, each with a battalion landing team in beach assault, struck the western end of Kwajalein Islet at 0930. (See map 12.) Opposition was light, mainly consisting of scattered small arms fire. The greatest obstacle was the heap of rubble which the naval gunfire had left in demolishing a concrete barrier across the selected beaches; it was necessary to blast corridors before some of the supporting weapons, especially the medium tanks, could be brought ashore.

The ship-to-shore movement was backed with power, and the initial advance inland was rapid. Nightfall found six reinforced battalions ashore, headed lengthwise up the islet, three deep on the lagoon and seaward sides respectively. Once the airstrip was reached, however, the enemy was afforded a field of fire which permitted him to render American efforts at maintaining lateral contact difficult and time-consuming. Even so, an ineffective counterattack on the night of February 1/2 was beaten back; and taking full advantage of close artillery, naval gunfire, and air support, the 32nd and 184th Infantry Regiments with tank assistance jumped off at 0715 on the next morning. Before nightfall they had cleared the airfield and had overrun two-thirds of the islet. Still, it required two additional days to finish the seizure of this objective. Holland Smith, aboard *Rocky Mount* with Kelly Turner, was irritated by this delay, but on more mature reflection he seems to have softened his judgment. The fact is that the 7th Infantry Division in every way was a first-rate ground force. It was ably led, well-trained amphibiously, and consisted of men every inch as courageous as the marines. Yet it took six reinforced army battalions four days to advance 4,600 yards, from one tip of Kwajalein Islet to the other. The explanation lies in army indoctrination when contrasted with that of the marines. On Kwajalein there was a marked tendency to knock out most entrenched Japanese as the army troops went forward, rather than to by-pass certain strong points in order to maintain that constant pressure essential in keeping the enemy confused and disorganized.[58]

By-passing under such circumstances as those existing on Kwajalein Atoll is tactical doctrine for the army as well as for the marines. Yet in practice, in the Marshalls campaign, the marines resorted to tactical by-passing far more than did the army, and the speed of their advance was correspondingly greater. Why was this so? The question cannot be answered until certain extraneous considerations have been set aside, and the performances of the Fourth Marine Division and the 7th Infantry Division have been compared objectively.

Certainly it is not helpful to approach the problem by attempting to judge the relative "bravery" of the forces or by seeking to prove essential differences in basic training, in firepower organic to battalion landing teams, or in the efficiency of infantry-demolition-flamethrower teams. Both marines and soldiers had received their basic training from the same field manuals; both were well led ashore; both were similarly armed; and both employed team tactics. If these facts alone were considered, there would seem to be no reason why the army advance should not have been as rapid as that of the marines, the more so since the army troops had had previous combat experience and, thanks to their superior ship-to-shore movement, got a better start across the beach.

Nor does there appear to have been any essential difference between the opposition met ashore on Kwajalein and that experienced on Roi-Namur. Both were pulverized by preparatory fires, which were particularly effective against beach defenses; and both lacked prepared positions in depth. Many of the Japanese emplacements had been constructed with extremely limited fields of fire and were therefore not mutually supporting. In other words, the defenses were similar to those encountered on Betio, built with all-out opposition at the beach in mind. Again like Betio, the installations inshore on Kwajalein and Roi-Namur resembled air raid shelters more than anything else; or, to quote the corps operations officer, "many dugouts and pillboxes were obviously made to hide in, not to fight from." If the enemy had planned to alter his defensive system, or to supplement it with mutually supporting inshore blockhouses, he had not had the time to do so. As the chief of the corps intelligence section observed, "the vast quantities of cement, gravel, sand, reinforcing steel, and some lumber encountered at Kwajalein Atoll points [sic] to a contemplation of additional defenses which had not been started or completed." [59] Some army officers believed they encountered well-prepared inshore defense in depth on Kwajalein Islet, but evidence from men who examined both ends of the atoll is to the contrary.[60] The inshore obstacles faced on Kwajalein Islet, like those on Namur, were hastily improvised.

Just as there was after the preparatory fires little to choose in terms of the defenses between Roi-Namur and Kwajalein, so also were the close fires once ashore splendid at both ends of the atoll. A joint assault signal company was attached to the Fourth Marine Division, and on Namur close artillery, air, and naval gunfire support was uniformly excellent. There was no similar unit available for attachment to the 7th Infantry Division, but the substitute selected, the 75th Army Signal Company with navy officers and additional communication personnel added, was well rehearsed and smoothly functioning. There was nothing but praise for all aspects of the close support given the army troops on Kwajalein Islet, and they employed it constantly and well.[61]

Finally a comparison of the efficiency of beachhead logistics on Roi-Namur and on Kwajalein Islet throws little light on the question at issue. It is true that the Fourth Marine Division lost much of its amphibious tractor strength, but hydrographic conditions were such that a tank landing ship could beach on Namur; and Roi-Namur was so quickly taken that the problem of supply for inshore fighting never arose. This problem did exist at Kwajalein Islet, but army-navy cooperation was excellent; the innovation of tank landing ships converted to mother vessels for the proper servicing of all amphibians was so successful that it furnished a large supply of tractors and Dukws for logistical employment and became the pattern for future operations; and beachhead logistics were superbly handled.[62]

Summarizing, the following considerations seem extraneous to an examination of the problem of why the marines overran their target in less than one-half the time required by the soldiers: training, leadership, and ground equipment used; preparatory and close support fires received; resistance encountered; and the quality of beachhead logistics furnished.

Once this is admitted, however, there remains an important consideration which helps explain the discrepancy in speed between the advances on Roi-Namur and Kwajalein. The geographic configuration of the two targets and the direction of the two tactical approaches from out of the sea were not identical. To assert this would be as unfair as to compare the ship-to-shore movements to the detriment of the marines without considering the wind, surf, and countercurrents at the northern end of the atoll. Kwajalein Islet was larger than Roi-Namur. (See maps 12 and 13.) Also, the marines deployed on a two-regimental front with four battalion landing teams abreast and swept up from the lagoon broadside against an elongated objective. The marines had more lateral maneuver room than the army troops, since the soldiers were compelled to hit their narrow target at one end, with only two battalion landing teams abreast (and constricted at that), and to overrun Kwajalein Islet from tip to tip with little maneuver room.

This consideration brings the nub of the question to the fore. Holland Smith should have switched the targets. The error of lifting an inexperienced marine division in an inexperienced amphibious group has already been examined and was admittedly unavoidable. Now the question arises, why not assign the Fourth Marine Division to work at Kwajalein Islet, over the lee waters of the atoll, where the ship-to-shore movement would not have been so difficult? The answer during the planning phase was, of course, that Roi-Namur was thought to be the more difficult target. Even granting, however, that Roi-Namur had at the outset by a slight degree the more formidable installations, other factors should have outweighed this consideration. Among these were the tactical approaches to and the terrain configurations of the principal targets, as well as the fact that Kwajalein Islet was defended by roughly 100 more first-line troops and several hundred more laborers. A closer examination of the expected capabilities of the marines and the army troops would have dictated an exchange of objectives.

Army infantry divisions, no matter where they fight, cannot be expected to depart overnight from the type of tactics normal to a relatively large land mass. They are imbued with the need for maneuver to take full advantage of favorable terrain, to await tank and close mortar and artillery support, and to rely on firepower. When operating on restricted land areas against sharp resistance, by-passing becomes the exception rather than the rule. Inevitably, the advance of the 7th Infantry Division on Kwajalein Islet was deliberate, especially after the first two days when the remaining Japanese were hemmed into the tail of the objective. To state this is not to imply criticism. But the conclusion is that in terms of amphibious training, hydrographic conditions, geographical configuration of the targets, tactical approach, and availability of maneuver room, the 7th Infantry Division should have been committed to Roi-Namur. There, in striking the target broadside, seizure would have been necessarily quick.

In terms of similarity of terrain and defenses encountered, only one section of Roi-Namur was comparable to the northeastern one-third of Kwajalein Islet; this was the north central portion of Namur, overrun by the marines in slightly more than two hours, even after the Japanese had been given an opportunity to reorganize. On the other hand, it took the army as many days to clear out the pocket at the far end of Kwajalein Islet. The sector facing the army was admittedly the larger, but not enough larger to require two full days of fighting. This contention is best supported by recalling Tarawa. Betio and Kwajalein Islet were about the same length; both were bowled over from broad end to narrow tip; the enemy dissipated his strength on both in banzai charges—yet without anything approaching the quality of supporting arms later obtained, one battalion of marines seized the tail of Betio in around six hours.

The official army historian who most recently studied the Kwajalein operation grappled with the essential point but failed to carry the discussion to its logical conclusion. He emphasized that whereas the army's movement from end to end on Kwajalein Islet was thorough, cleaning out most strong points as these were encountered, the marine doctrine of rapid, selective, and frequent by-passing left a considerable amount of mopping up to be done after Roi-Namur was secured. He is correct.[63] The marines are indoctrinated with the necessity of such fighting. The target must be secured, the amphibious shipping unloaded, defensive guns (especially antiaircraft) emplaced, and base construction begun at the earliest possible moment. All of this can be and should be carried on concurrently with mopping up. Thus one of the crucial requirements in amphibious warfare is better met by the marine technique, which enables shipping to be rapidly turned around, to be removed from protracted exposure to enemy reaction, and to be made more quickly available for the next operation. The fact that the Japanese failed to counter the Marshalls landings with their fleet, and were unable to do so with land-based planes, and the fact that a lagoon haven protected the amphibious shipping from enemy submarines, diminished in no way the importance of this essential consideration.

Holland Smith accurately described the type of speedy fighting done by marines in the Marshalls. "The technique of infantry-tank teams pushing rapidly forward," he said, "closely followed by demolition and flamethrower teams is concurred in by this Headquarters as sound." He wished, however, to stress "that it must be a continuous movement in which light enemy resistance is neutralized and by-passed by the forward elements of the infantry-tank teams, then the supporting elements of the infantry equipped with demolitions and flamethrowers reduce these isolated enemy positions before they can recover and fire on the rear of our troops moving forward." Selective by-passing, combined with a quick sustained thrust to keep the enemy disorganized and tactically off balance, would in the end lower American casualties. "This technique," he continued, "is particularly effective in searching out the real strong points and thereby avoiding holding up the attack by weak and scattered resistance. When a strong point is encountered, the infantry-tank team and demolition-flamethrower team become integrated and operate together until the strong point is reduced." Such tactics permitted the maximum employment of close supporting fires. "In reducing a strong point, emphasis must be also placed upon the value of supporting fires from air, naval gunfire and artillery. Field artillery continues to be the most reliable and effective weapon for neutralization purposes in close support of infantry. Proper use of supporting fires in reducing strong points calls for the artillery-infantry-tank team to be closely coordinated. The greatest neutralization value is gained by the infantry and tanks moving quickly into the neutralized area as artillery fires lift. The closer the advance behind our own neutralization fires the more the benefit derived from the neutralization. . . . Team work, involving firing, must be practiced in training periods to develop thoroughly the use of combined arms." [64]

These quotations assist in understanding the speed with which the marines operated ashore. Once Roi-Namur and Kwajalein Islet had been seized, there remained the final phase of the undertaking, which involved occupying, or at least clearing, all the islets other than the principal targets and those taken on January 31 for the purpose of setting up artillery ashore. (See map 12.) The tasks of the army troops and of the marines were equally difficult in this final phase. The work fell to the two regiments used on January 31, and then placed in their respective division reserve for employment on Kwajalein Islet or Roi-Namur if necessary. Since neither was used on the main objectives, the 17th Infantry Regiment and the Twenty-fifth Marine Regiment were given the job of securing the remainder of the atoll. The army troops were responsible only for the islets in the southern end, while the marines had the larger number in the northern and northwestern portions; but those taken by the army had the greater total of enemy personnel. Notable in this respect was the strip of land immediately north of the northeastern tip of Kwajalein itself, which housed the important seaplane base for the atoll, and was believed to be garrisoned by something more than 700 Japanese. The final phase of the Kwajalein operation was completed on February 8.[65]

A single question of importance concerning the seizure of Kwajalein Atoll remains to be discussed. Which was the less costly in American lives, relative to opposition encountered, the extensive by-passing tactics of the marines, or the more thoroughgoing movement of the army? Since enemy air and subsurface as well as fleet reaction to the invasion of the Central Marshalls was practically non-existent, it is possible, even if inadvisable, to treat this problem in a vacuum—that is, without regard to the vulnerability of amphibious shipping.

A word of warning is in order at the outset. No brief is held for the value of statistics in such a complex consideration as this now being placed before the reader. The desire is to challenge the widely advertised idea that marine tactics and marine leadership are unduly wasteful of American lives.

Marine indoctrination shows up to advantage when utilizing the casualty report submitted on February 22, 1944, by the Assistant Surgeon of the Fifth Amphibious Corps, Lieutenant Colonel L. K. Mantell (Medical Corps) USA. Army losses were five per cent of the troops engaged; while marine losses were only three per cent of the men committed. For every casualty sustained by the 7th Infantry Division reinforced, less than 3.9 Japanese were killed or taken prisoner; but for each marine casualty at the Roi-Namur end of the atoll, more than 5.5 Japanese were dead or surrendered.[66]

These figures, as do most statistics, introduce a number of imponderables, some of which at least, in addition to the consideration of amphibious shipping, must be mentioned. Who can say conclusively that the prelanding preparation at Roi-Namur was not better than that at the opposite end of the atoll? Nor should the muzzle blasts and the premature explosions of 155-millimeter shells in the hands of army artillerists, resulting in forty-five American casualties, be overlooked. On the other hand, the marines sustained losses in the heavy surf, a condition unknown in the lee of the atoll; and the explosions on Namur were costly—but presumably to the Japanese as well as to the marines.

Contrasting army and marine casualty statistics in this manner must not be allowed to warp the overall picture, for the truth is that relative to the Japanese, American losses were exceedingly light. The joint effort of the forces of the United States, experienced and inexperienced, army, navy and marine, came through to a brilliant victory. The mobility and striking power of carrier aircraft were geared perfectly with America's constantly improving amphibian techniques. The Japanese in the Marshalls were localized, and those on Kwajalein were immobilized, were pounded by preliminary fires, and were left for ground forces to eliminate in detail. Something in the neighborhood of 8,122 Japanese died, more than twenty-seven times the number of Americans who were killed by enemy action.[67] This goes down in history as a world's record for the type of operation involved.

The success was so complete that the entire Central Pacific drive picked up speed. Nimitz, with characteristic modesty, told the press that "the capture of Kwajalein Atoll in the Marshall Islands will result in a quickening of the tempo of the Pacific War. . . ." When drawing up his plans earlier in 1944, he had feared that "with a likelihood of some delay," the Marshalls campaign could not be completed with the seizure of the westernmost atoll, Eniwetok, until sometime in the early spring of that year, and he had set May 10, 1944 as the target date.[68] But the Kwajalein victory was so overwhelming that the five battalion landing teams taken in reserve to that atoll had not yet been employed. These men were available for instant commitment. On February 17, 1944, they began the occupation of Eniwetok.

5. Plans for and Seizure of Eniwetok

The loss of Eniwetok, lying 375 miles to the northwest of Kwajalein, thwarted Japan's hope of ever again ferrying planes into either Wake or the by-passed atolls in the Marshalls; its capture moved America's reconnaissance planes forward, and brought land-based air within striking range of enemy positions in the Central Carolines. (See map 2.) Also, the final operation in the Marshalls campaign provided the Central Pacific drive with perhaps its best anchorage for servicing submarines and for supplying the fleet, as well as a staging base for amphibious expeditions to the westward. "The capture of Eniwetok," summarized Spruance, "gave us complete control of the Marshalls. It gave us a base for the next operation, whether it was to be against Truk or the Marianas." [69]

This fitting climax to the Marshalls campaign was concluded at minimum cost to American strength because Nimitz took full advantage of the momentum already acquired and because the enemy had failed to fortify his atoll positions in depth. Only in January, after an attack somewhere in the Marshalls became evident to the Japanese, did they hastily throw a sizeable garrison into Eniwetok; but this action increased rather than diminished the magnitude of their defeat. Time to consolidate the position was unavailable. Knowledge of these circumstances spurred the Americans to greater speed.

Nimitz and his principal subordinates gave thought to a rapid occupation of Eniwetok while planning for the Kwajalein operation, but the hope of obtaining it was too small to elicit formal plans. Holland Smith, however, had a tentative plan for Eniwetok tucked in his baggage, and Spruance confirms that a desire for haste was in the air. "We received our first aerial photographs of Eniwetok at Pearl Harbor shortly before I was due to sail for the Marshalls operation," he writes. "A study of them failed to show any defenses at all comparable to Tarawa or to the other Marshalls bases. Our intelligence indicated the reenforcement of the Eniwetok garrison by several thousand troops." Spruance then describes a conversation with Nimitz: "I said that I wished we could proceed with the capture of Eniwetok after Kwajalein, instead of having to send the Fleet to the South Pacific for the operation there [Kavieng] and to wait until it returned, thus permitting the additional troops at Eniwetok to strengthen greatly its defenses; but that I presumed the schedule set up by the Joint Chiefs of Staff would have to be adhered to."

It was the dispatch with which the Central Marshalls were taken and controlled that gave time for another attack. "The Kwajalein operation," Spruance continues, "went through so quickly and with such small losses that Admiral Nimitz sent me a radio asking my recommendation on going ahead as soon as possible with the capture of Eniwetok and on covering it with a carrier strike on Truk. The latter, it was hoped, might enable us to bring on an engagement with the Japanese fleet. After consultation with Admiral Turner and General Holland Smith as to ways and means for taking Eniwetok, I was glad to be able to recommend approval." [70]

Planning for Eniwetok was complete although hastily done. The Fifth Fleet was again relied upon, this time to widen further its scope of localization and to neutralize enemy air bases in the Carolines and the Marianas. The mission was performed with excellent results. Harry Hill's amphibious attack group, lifting the troops originally sent to Kwajalein in reserve and commanded by Brigadier General Thomas J. Watson USMC, was unmolested by enemy surface, subsurface, or air reaction. Thus it was able to blast Eniwetok Atoll with all types of supporting arms, again immobilizing the defenders and leaving them for the ground forces to liquidate in detail.

Although smaller than Kwajalein, the lagoon at Eniwetok was relatively free from coral heads and was large enough for the entire Pacific Fleet. (See map 14.) The atoll, fringed with sharp coral especially on the seaward side, is slightly oval in shape, some fifteen by twenty miles in diameter, with the long axis running northwest by southeast. Most of the islets, and all of those of any military importance, are along the eastern semicircle. There are two principal channels into the lagoon, Deep Entrance to the southeast, and Wide Passage at the south.

From the first, Harry Hill planned a bold stroke. He was determined to take his attack group directly into the lagoon, thus avoiding any landings on seaward beaches. This was possible at Eniwetok since no coast defense guns bristled alongside the lagoon entrances. Hill's navigational estimates were excellent; but, he wrote, the capture at Kwajalein of complete sets of Japanese secret hydrographic charts for enemy possessions and occupied territories in the Pacific "probably saved a few gray hairs from my head." [71] In order quickly to seize Eniwetok and to begin base developments, it was necessary to strike first at the most heavily defended islet, Engebi by name. This was at the northern end of the atoll, and on it the Japanese had built an airfield. The scheme of maneuver was to send minesweepers through both of the main channels into the lagoon, followed by most of the attack group, battleships included, and to proceed directly to the designated transport and naval gunfire areas off the lagoon beaches of Engebi. Capture of the important channel islets and of the remainder of the atoll would come later.

Working within the lagoon from the outset facilitated every aspect of the Eniwetok operation. Even a seaplane base was established, easing the problem of servicing the battleship and cruiser scout planes, and allowing the immediate delivery of air borne supplies.

Nothing captured on Kwajalein, however, permitted an up-to-date estimate of enemy defenses and personnel on Eniwetok. Evaluation of aerial photographs throughout January and early February showed that reinforcements were being thrown in, but unlike any previous Central Pacific objective, there were few above-ground structures on the atoll except for Engebi, and the more formidable ones there were lightly constructed with unreinforced concrete. Most of the defenses throughout the atoll were underground entrenchments, covered with green coconut logs, skillfully camouflaged, hence difficult to evaluate from photographs alone. At first it was believed that only Engebi held a garrison of any strength, but a despatch from Nimitz's intelligence section just as Hill's task group departed Kwajalein on February 15 confirmed suspicions that additional Japanese had landed on the atoll. These were Japanese army troops, most of the First Sea Borne Mobile Brigade. Subsequent photographs showed hasty activity on both Parry Islet, just south of Deep Entrance, and Eniwetok Islet, directly east of Wide Passage. Beginning at 700 men, the estimate of the atoll's defenders shot upward to something between 2,400 and 4,000.

Actually the number of Japanese later buried was approximately 3,400. Engebi was the most heavily defended, followed by Parry and then by Eniwetok Islet. Last-minute changes in the estimate of the Japanese situation necessitated quick alterations in General Watson's landing plans. American troops, army and marine, outnumbered the enemy only slightly more than two to one; but the Japanese were isolated on three objectives, and these were to be taken one at a time. Beginning with the islets adjacent to Engebi on February 17, the final target, Parry, was mopped up six days later.[72]

Like Kwajalein, Eniwetok was also softened by carrier strikes and prepared for assault by a combination of air, naval gunfire, and artillery support. A fast task group built around one heavy and two light carriers, having neutralized Engebi on January 30, returned during February 10–12 to continue its foray against aircraft and air installations, to knock out Engebi's coastal guns, and to attack the radio direction finder thought to be on Parry. Passing to the operational control of Harry Hill on the following day, this carrier group covered the approach of the assault shipping, and struck Eniwetok Atoll a third time on February 16.

The three remaining task groups of Spruance's covering force hit Truk on February 16–17, and long-range bombers continued the neutralization of Ponape, Kusaie, and Wake. While the fast carrier group under Hill's control was providing closer cover for the amphibious shipping, and searching a radius of 250 miles on a wide arc north, west, and south of Eniwetok, the rest of Spruance's fleet attacked the Marianas on February 22.[73]

The naval attack group arrived at Eniwetok early on February 17. Present in the gunfire support sections were three old battleships, three heavy cruisers, and seven destroyers; three escort carriers were on hand to lend tactical air support. A marine battalion of 75-millimeter pack howitzers and an army battalion of 105-millimeter howitzers were lifted in two tank landing ships to furnish artillery support. After a slight confusion occasioned by the sweeping of an enemy deep water mine within the lagoon, and a mix-up as to which tractors would carry ashore the Reconnaissance Company of the Fifth Amphibious Corps, two strips of land southeast of Engebi were found to be devoid of enemy; artillery was taken inland by Dukws, emplaced, and before sundown registered on Engebi.

Meanwhile planes and naval guns, the latter firing from both within and without the lagoon, were working over Engebi. This islet is triangular, about a mile on each side; and the airstrip ran east and west along the northern seaward coast. (See map 14.) Toward dusk on the first day, an underwater demolition team, assisted by fire from men-of-war and from infantry landing craft converted to gunboats, found the beaches picked for assault neither mined nor in any other way artificially obstructed, and marked the boat approaches and coral heads with buoys. After nightfall, while harassing fire was maintained on Engebi, a second marine scout company attempted to land from rubber boats on the islet due west of Engebi. Darkness and countercurrents confused the party and upset plans; only one-half the company got ashore, and these men were out of position. By maneuvering eastward along the reef from one land strip to the next, the selected islet was reached at 0230 on February 18. The Japanese had evacuated all these positions; and the mission assigned the scout company, however inefficient the execution, was accomplished. Engebi was bottled up. Meanwhile, gunfire support vessels stood guard day and night off Parry and Eniwetok Islets to harass the enemy and prevent a concentration at the southern end of the atoll.[74]

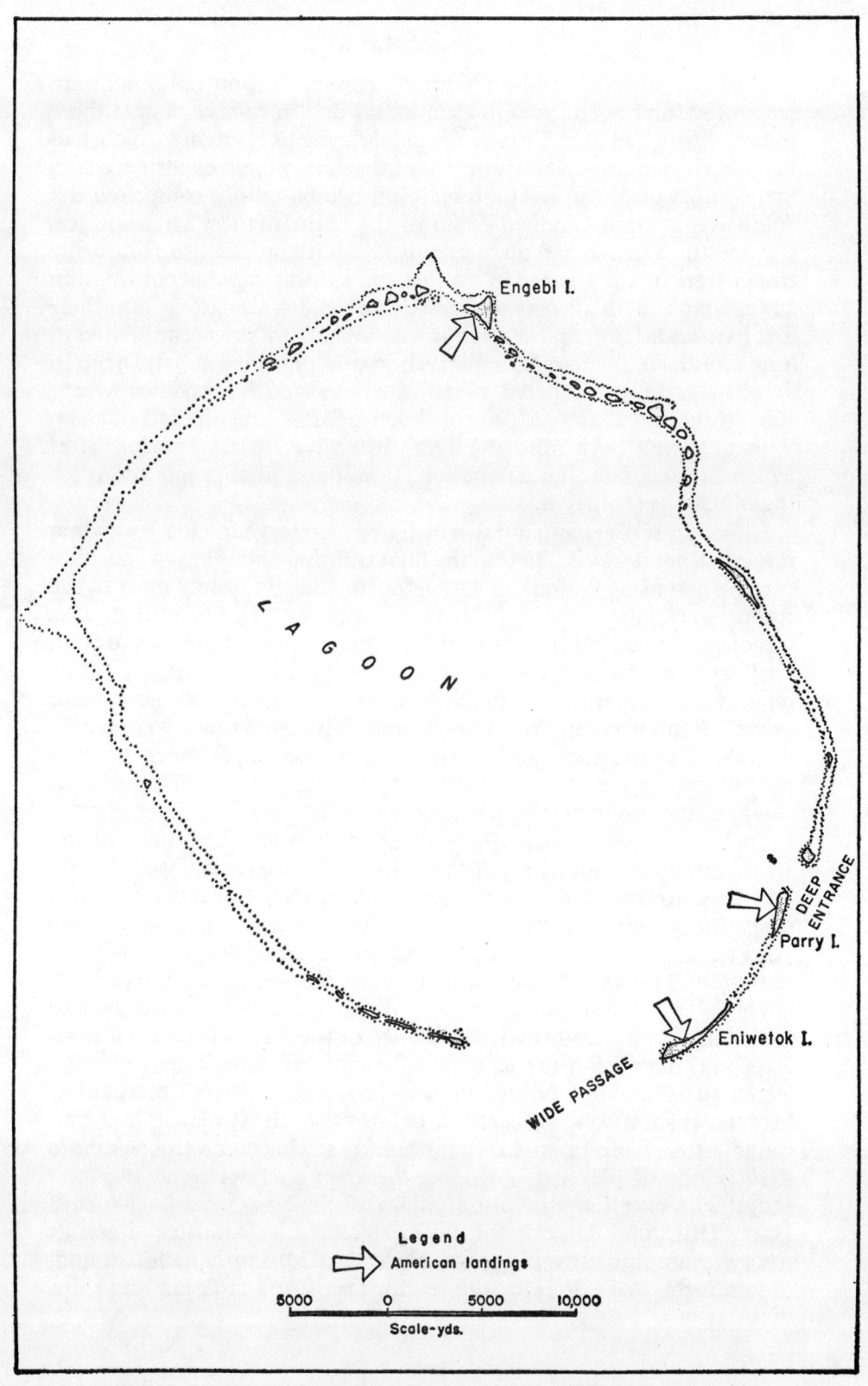

MAP 14. Principal landings on Eniwetok Atoll, February 1944.

Three of the five battalion landing teams at Watson's disposal were scheduled for Engebi, two in assault and one in reserve. These three units constituted the Twenty-second Marine Regiment, which had been activated for over twenty months but which experienced its first combat on Engebi. The remaining two battalions comprised the 106th Regimental Combat Team of the 27th Infantry Division, less the battalion which had already moved ashore on Majuro. The army troops were inexperienced in combat and exhibited poor coordination at Eniwetok. The Twenty-second Marines were also going into their first battle, and they approached it with an enthusiasm accumulated in long months of maneuvers and garrison duty. Formed at San Diego in June 1942, their unit had departed the next month for Samoa, where it had functioned as a part of the defense force until the fall of 1943. This duty had been followed by an intensive training period, after which the regiment left Samoa for Hawaii and final preparations for the Marshalls campaign.[75]

Since Watson's command was assigned as reserve for the Kwajalein undertaking, it was slighted in the final training and rehearsal periods. "In the actual operation" at Eniwetok, testifies Watson, "most of the troops were landed in amphibian tractors for their first time. . . . Troops did not land in rehearsal supported by naval gunfire, air and artillery fires to accustom them to actual attack conditions. . . . The rehearsal . . . permitted no appreciable advance inland, no combat firing, no infantry-tank team movement. The troops had no opportunity to rehearse attacks against typical Japanese emplacements and to practice in the use of demolition and flamethrowers against such targets and in mopping-up such areas." [76]

Lack of a better rehearsal handicapped the two battalions of the 106th Infantry Regiment, but the marines did extremely well despite Watson's protest. This was due not only to long training and heavy preparatory fires, but also to the fact that the marines, as well as the army troops, were carried ashore by the 708th Army Amphibian Tank Battalion. This was the unit which had done such a good job at Kwajalein Islet. Almost 120 of its amphibian tractors were attached to Hill's task group, and the performance of their crews, admittedly always working within the lagoon, was again first-rate. The drivers effected three major landings in five days, and although mechanical breakdowns resulting from continual use at both Kwajalein and Eniwetok Atolls were in part responsible for setting some troops ashore slightly out of planned positions, the tractor crews stood the long ordeal with excellent discipline and fortitude. Navy personnel aboard Harry Hill's tank landing ships cooperated fully. Transfer of assault troops to amphibian vehicles was always expeditiously handled; and, to lessen the work done by the tractor crews, the tank landing ships were sometimes anchored less than 1,000 yards from the lines-of-departure. The result was an efficient ship-to-shore team.[77]

Preparatory fire against Engebi was similar to that delivered at Kwajalein Atoll, but of shorter duration and lighter in quantity. Nevertheless, the almost 1,200 tons of naval shells, as well as additional bombs and artillery projectiles, hurled against the first objective at Eniwetok were said by a prisoner of war to have killed about one-half the defenders prior to the landing, and an eyewitness of both operations testified that Engebi was more devastated than Kwajalein Islet had been.

The First and Second Battalions of the Twenty-second Marines, each with two companies abreast, hit the lagoon beaches of Engebi three minutes ahead of schedule at 0842 on February 18. (See map 14.) Subsequent waves followed with the cadence of a pile driver, and the assault from the first had impact. The only flaw occurred on the right-flank beach, when some of the tractors, because of mechanical failures and because their crews were partially blinded by the smoke and dust kicked up by the preparatory fires, guided on the right flank gunboats as these swerved to the starboard after firing their rockets. As a result, the right flank was overextended, and the situation was further complicated by the failure of a platoon to turn up on time.

Movement inshore on the right flank was delayed until the medium tanks assigned to that sector arrived, while elsewhere penetration up to 100 yards was made with little opposition. Resistance then stiffened, but the medium tanks of the Second Separate Marine Tank Company were landed fifteen minutes after the first wave, and these renewed the forward thrust all along the line virtually before it had halted. No other unit in the Eniwetok operation performed as efficiently for as long a period as did this tank company. Its personnel took part in three landings; they were either in battle or repairing and reservicing their weapons and machinery for five full days and nights.

Within an hour after landing, some of the medium tanks turned up at the far northeastern tip of Engebi. Coordination between the tank crews and the infantry was almost perfect. Preliminary fires had obliterated almost everything above ground, and tank-infantry teams, followed by flamethrowing-demolition-infantry groups, raced across Engebi and tore apart organized resistance within slightly more than six hours after the initial landing.

A full discussion of the type of enemy resistance encountered on Engebi will assist in understanding the remaining fighting on the atoll, for elsewhere the Japanese defenses, while not as elaborate, were equally ingenious. There was no system of blockhouses and pillboxes, but the defenses were difficult to destroy by preliminary fires, and once overrun a considerable number of enemy were left still to be mopped up. Back of the beach entrenchments, the defenses consisted of a series of strong points, each with exits toward every corner of the compass. Underground communications were so numerous that the marines aptly termed the defense as one of "spider webs." Construction of these hideouts was simple and crude, frequently affording the enemy extremely limited fields of fire, but they were expertly camouflaged. The walls of the center compartment were generally fashioned from light wood to prevent a cave in of the sandy soil; and the flat top, flush with the ground level, was composed of corrugated iron sheets held in place by light-weight angle iron. A relatively small charge of high explosive was all that was needed to destroy the hub once it was found; but its occupants frequently scurried to temporary safety through radiating tunnels composed of oil drums laid end to end under the ground, and then popped up from all directions to snipe at the back of advancing marines.[78] The process of flushing these Japanese reminded one marine of "a prairie-dog town in Texas, where they burrow and burrow under the ground and then come up in little holes at the end." [79] Regardless of the difficulty in mopping up Engebi, the islet was secured so rapidly that the marine battalion in regimental reserve was barely used, and the by-passing tactics extensively employed were so inexpensive of American lives as to permit the two forward battalions to be withdrawn virtually intact for the invasion of Parry Islet.

Engebi was secured on February 18, although it was yet to be completely mopped up. The next target was Eniwetok Islet, assigned to the army's 106th Regimental Combat Team, less one battalion. Originally, this strip of land was thought to have been only lightly defended, but intelligence from Nimitz's headquarters and an evaluation of information captured on Engebi pointed to a garrison of several hundred men. For this reason Hill and Watson immediately began revising their plans for operations on February 19. Naval gunfire support and air strikes for Eniwetok Islet were increased, but no preliminary artillery preparation could be offered. The two marine scout companies, threading their way southward along both sides of the atoll, were yet to reach either Wide Passage or Deep Entrance; and Parry, some 5,000 yards northeast of Eniwetok Islet, was also known to be more heavily defended than expected, and could not be taken until the two battalions of the Twenty-second Marines which had rushed across Engebi were disengaged and given some rest.

The Third Battalion of the Twenty-second Marines, however, was on hand to provide a floating reserve for the army troops at Eniwetok Islet. This marine unit had landed in reserve on Engebi about two hours after the first wave on February 18, but had not been committed to heavy fighting at the northern end of the atoll. It had done a little mopping up on that day, and had then been evacuated, along with the medium tanks, for use on the 19th at Eniwetok Islet. Simultaneously, the army battalion of 105-millimeter howitzers had been relifted to be landed across the beaches on Eniwetok Islet in support of the attack against that objective. Meanwhile the First and Second Battalions of the Twenty-second Marines on Engebi dug in preparatory to a hazardous night of Japanese infiltrations, February 18/19. It was here for the first time in the Pacific that Harry Hill began using star shells from naval guns. These were far superior to those fired by artillery pieces, and assisted the marines in their all-night vigil. The results were excellent, and the technique was continued throughout the war. The marines mopped up the enemy that remained on Engebi the next day, while a landing was being effected on Eniwetok Islet.[80]

With arrangements made to strengthen the army troops in every way possible, the landings on Eniwetok Islet got under way on the morning of February 19. The men of the 106th Infantry Regiment, however, were slow. It required the two battalions of this regiment, assisted by the same medium tanks which had served on Engebi and for a time by the fresh battalion of the Twenty-second Marines, four days to secure Eniwetok Islet.

It was unfortunate for the speedy success of the Eniwetok operation that the army regiment was not given more preliminary support. The best estimate of enemy buried seems to be 1,300 on Parry; 1,200 on Engebi; and 900 on Eniwetok.[81] Engebi alone contained any sizeable number of above-ground defenses, and since it was the first taken, an examination of its "spider webs" allowed the navy gunners to alter their technique for both Eniwetok Islet and Parry. Close in fire with a very flat trajectory was not suited. A deeper, plunging fire was required; and a direct hit with a smaller caliber shell or bomb was more advantageous than the blast effect from a projectile fired by the main battery of an old battleship or from a heavy bomb.

Yet the great deficiency at Eniwetok Islet was, oddly enough, the failure to employ a large number of the heavier bombs and projectiles. This strip of land is the highest in the atoll, something in the neighborhood of 20 feet, giving the defenders greater depth for their complicated entrenchments. Finally, the islet, shaped like a blackjack with the handle tapering to the northeast, was covered with a thick foliage, with a heavy undergrowth in some places. (See map 14.) Since this improved the enemy's camouflage and made it more difficult to locate his strong points, it should have been stripped by the blast effect of the larger projectiles or burned by incendiary bombs. But, Hill's force did not have the ammunition required; and the napalm bomb, which would have been admirably suited to the terrain, was still a thing of the future.

The task of ferrying the medium tanks from Engebi delayed the attack on Eniwetok Islet. The beaches selected were on the lagoon side, about half-way between the middle of the islet and the southwestern broad extremity. The plan was to split the objective in two by driving to the seaward coast. One battalion was then to pivot northward in a holding line, while the other battalion drove southward to clear out the southern end of the islet for the emplacement of artillery to support the later attack to the north.

The two army battalions landed on adjacent beaches, each with two companies abreast, at about two minutes after the time finally designated, 0915. On the whole, the troops were set ashore in planned position, but the attack never gained any appreciable momentum across the beach. This should not have been the case; for, although the tonnage of naval gunfire expended against Eniwetok Islet was less than that for Engebi, the beaches had been well covered with 5- and 8-inch projectiles almost up to the time of the landing. A sudden rise of ground just inshore from the shallow beach, however, prevented the tractors from effecting the initial penetration, and the troops hesitated after dismounting. This lead to a serious congestion as the subsequent waves came in.

The beach congestion was somewhat cleared, and the short distance to the seaward coast covered by slightly before noon, but then the attack completely bogged down. It developed that the Japanese had made their best preparations for beach defense along the southern coast of the islet, and the American scheme of maneuver was threatening these positions from the rear. For this reason, the southern end of the islet had the preponderate number of the enemy, who counterattacked the army battalion and halted its southern advance.

Shortly after noon, the reserve marine battalion was thrown into the fighting. It crossed the beaches and took over the left flank of the attack to the south. This unit, supported by medium tanks, infused for the first time some momentum into the attack. The terrain covered was the most difficult on the islet, and the positions overrun were the best prepared. As an official army historian has noted, "at about 1830, the swift movement of the marines on the left of the line had reached the principal Japanese defensive position in the southwest corner of the island." The attack was continued after dark, but the marines advanced so rapidly that they lost contact with the army unit to their right; the Japanese seized their opportunity to strike at this gap, drove to the marine battalion command post, and inflicted serious casualties. But the penetration was quickly wiped out, and lateral contact between the Americans regained. Early on February 20 the marines continued to break down opposition on the southern end of the islet, but were soon withdrawn for rest before their scheduled commitment on Parry.

The Third Battalion of the Twenty-second Marines, although in the line for less than twenty-four hours, carried the brunt of the attack on Eniwetok Islet. They were principally responsible for clearing the enemy from the more heavily defended and larger end of the islet, yet the 106th Infantry Regiment required two more full days, through February 22, despite the availability of close air, naval gunfire, and artillery support, to overrun the northeastern end of the objective.[82] Once again a unit of the 27th Infantry Division performed poorly. The men of the 106th Infantry, like those of the 165th Infantry on Makin Atoll in the Gilberts, were neither well-led nor well-trained. As Watson summarized: ". . . the 106th Infantry . . . did not move forward rapidly from the beaches . . . did not operate in close cooperation with tanks and failed to realize the capabilities of and to use to the fullest extent naval gunfire and close support aviation." [83]

The final landings were made on Parry Islet. Its shape is similar to that of Eniwetok, except that its width is more uniform throughout, and the tail points southwestward. (See map 14.) It was prepared for the attack of the Twenty-second Marines, with the two marine scout companies attached, by a volume of fires slightly larger than that for Eniwetok Islet, including air strikes, naval gunfire, and artillery emplaced on an islet just across Deep Entrance to the northeast and on Eniwetok Islet to the southwest.

With the 106th Infantry still committed on Eniwetok Islet, no floating reserve was available for Parry. This deficiency was met, in so far as was possible, by alerting 500 marines who were present in a defense battalion for garrison duty; but it was not necessary to employ them.

The attack against Parry was a duplication of that against Engebi, except that naval gunfire hit two of the gunboats as they ran close ashore to release their rockets, and that it required some four additional hours to smash organized resistance ashore. Landings were made across the northwestern lagoon beaches on February 22, seventy-two hours after the army had hit Eniwetok Islet; but final resistance on both of these objectives was mopped up on the same day, February 23.[84]

6. Amphibious Lessons and Strategical Significance

The Marshall Islands were thus occupied or controlled at a loss of less than 3,000 marine and army casualties. The low figure illustrates vividly the lessons learned at Betio, and for the same reason little new in amphibious warfare not already conceived and under development was added in the Marshalls. Nevertheless, five novel techniques are notable; and two were supplied entirely by the 7th Infantry Division working in conjunction with Turner's group at Kwajalein Islet. These were the use of the Dukw, which earned for itself a permanent place in both tactical and logistical employment, especially in the ship-to-shore movement of artillery and ammunition; and the concept of establishing repair stations on unoccupied islets or of converting tank landing ships to mother vessels for servicing both amphibian tractors and Dukws and their crews, which had worked out so successfully that it had been in part responsible for supplying Harry Hill with a large proportion of his assault lift at Eniwetok. More important, at least psychologically, was the use of tank landing ships as temporary hospital wards. This was convenient since the amphibians evacuated wounded from the shore, and it expedited medical attention to the seriously injured before transfer to regular hospital ships. The fourth contribution of consequence resulted from the faulty ship-to-shore movements at the Roi-Namur end of the atoll. Holland Smith was determined to remove at least one cause of the confusion, and he set his staff to work on a standard operating procedure for lifting the assault elements to the target area. The central problem was to simplify the process of getting the assault troops into their amphibian tractors. At Kwajalein the procedure had been this: on arrival in the transport area, the assault troops were loaded from their transports into landing craft, and were then run to the tank landing ships for further transfer to the tractors. The solution was, thanks to an increase in the number of tank landing ships available, to make the exchange from the transports to the tank landing ships at the staging base immediately before beginning the last lap of the approach to the target. This meant that for the final miles of the journey to the objective the beach assault troops were, along with their amphibians, passengers aboard tank landing ships. The fifth innovation of value in the Marshalls was the successful employment of naval star shells at Eniwetok.

On the whole it may be said that in terms of both amphibian techniques and tactics ashore, the Marshalls campaign merely drove home the value of Tarawa to the development of amphibious warfare. As Holland Smith reported after the fall of the Marshalls: "Recommendations made and acted upon by this Corps as a result of the Gilberts offensive proved sound." The technique of capturing targets like Tarawa, Kwajalein, and Eniwetok had been mastered. "In the attack of coral atolls," he continued, "very few recommendations can be made to improve upon the basic techniques previously recommended and utilized in the Marshalls campaign." Not again during World War II, however, did an amphibious assault develop in the occupation of a coral atoll. Holland Smith probably foresaw such a possibility, and concluded his Marshalls report with a warning: ". . . there is still much to be desired to improve planning, improve the coordination of efforts and prepare for the attack of more difficult objectives." [85]

The significance of the Marshalls campaign lay in the realm of strategy rather than that of tactics and techniques. The degree to which this rapid and inexpensive success quickened the tempo of the Pacific War may best be seen by examining the change in overall planning it was instrumental in causing. Not only were all of the Marshalls occupied and controlled in February 1944 rather than during the following May; but as a result the Japanese fleet hastily evacuated the Carolines and retreated behind the Philippines-Netherlands East Indies-New Guinea barrier. Nimitz would have preferred a major naval engagement, but it pleased him to be able to order the supposed fortress of Truk by-passed, and to set the target date for the Marianas forward almost twenty weeks.[86] The fact that the Marshalls campaign was sufficient to deny Truk to the Japanese fleet became apparent to Nimitz and his planners in mid-February 1944.

American naval officers had overestimated the strength of Truk because they believed the enemy had been building up that base ever since acquiring it during World War I. At the outbreak of the Pacific War, however, Truk was nothing more than a fleet anchorage. Once the Japanese offensive of 1941–1942 jolted to a halt, the enemy concerned himself with fortifying the outer rim of his newly acquired territories. Little, however, was added to the defensive potential of Truk over and beyond what nature had provided. This by itself gave pause to the attacker. The lagoon was large enough to accommodate an entire fleet plus its train. Truk was a group of islands which aggregated, for an atoll, a sizeable land mass. Islands bordered by rugged cliffs interlocked with caves, surrounded and towered from the lagoon, which in turn was fringed with a knife-sharp reef.

Even so, Truk was a sham. Early in 1944, Japanese army troops constituted the principal defensive components, and their numbers totaled less than 8,000 men. Their emplacements, equipment, and supplies were meager because American submarines had curtailed the ability of the Japanese to reinforce. The job of disgorging them would have been costly to the Americans, but not nearly as arduous a task as it was at the time supposed. The ranking Japanese admiral stationed at Truk during the middle period of the war testified that he would listen to the American radio proclaim Truk "the impregnable bastion of the Pacific" and then he would become apprehensive that the United States might learn the real truth. Nonetheless, the enemy decision to pull back his fleet lowered the number of marine and army casualties in the Central Pacific. The atoll was kept neutralized by carrier aircraft, by planes mounted from surrounding bases in the Marshalls and the South and Southwest Pacific, and, toward the close of the war, by training flights of very long-range bombers out of the Marianas.[87]

In short, operations into the Marshalls destroyed the myth of Truk. The Japanese had failed to establish logistical facilities or to fortify that atoll strongly. Fuel was scarce, and drydock repair for anything larger than destroyers was nonexistent. The commander of the Combined Fleet of the Imperial Japanese Navy began making arrangements to retreat as soon as the first United States reconnaissance plane, piloted by marines from the Solomons, flew over the atoll early in February, while the fighting in the Marshalls was under way. Within a week he had sortied his principal components, temporarily for Palau, ultimately for Singapore and Tawi-Tawi in the southwestern Philippines. A few days later, on February 16–17, American carrier aircraft arrived over Truk. Their pilots found fewer targets than expected. More than two-thirds of the enemy's 365 land-based planes were demolished. Approximately 140,000 tons of shipping were sunk, but war vessels were hard to locate. Carrier pilots of the Pacific Fleet for the first time in the war staged a successful night bombing attack, and this along with daylight strikes sent an aircraft ferry, two converted submarine tenders, and three converted light cruisers to the bottom. Five days later, on February 22, the same American pilots swept through the Marianas. Again shipping was scarce, but the entire strength of the Japanese First Air Fleet then in the Marianas, 120 planes, was destroyed. This was an inopportune time for the enemy. The center of his new defense line in the Central Pacific was assailed at the very time he needed desperately to strengthen it.[88]

By mid-February 1944 United States naval forces commanded the waters east of the Nanpo Shoto-Marianas-Palau line. Marines at Betio pierced the skin of Japan's defenses. Action in the Marshalls proved that the outer portion of the coprosperity fruit was soft. "The incredible seemed to be true," commented a serious American periodical. "Japan's . . . defences were vulnerable." [89]

The rapidity of the Marshalls campaign and its strategical results were of course reflected in the directives handed down by the Joint Chiefs of Staff. At the Cairo Conference in November and December 1943, the decisions taken earlier were reaffirmed: that is, the coordinated advances of Nimitz and MacArthur toward the China coast were recognized by the Anglo-American Chiefs of Staff as the principal offensive effort of the Pacific War. The Cairo proposal called for an intensification of operations in the China-Burma-India theater, and General Arnold planned to bomb the Japanese home islands with B-29's from Chinese bases beginning May 1, 1944, and from the Marianas by the close of that year. In line with Arnold's principal interest in the Pacific, the decision reached at Cairo moved the pivotal strategical area in the Pacific north from the Celebes Sea to the Formosa-China Coast-Luzon triangle, and asked for a major assault into that triangle before the typhoon season in the spring of 1945. Also, it was again stated "that operations in the Central Pacific promise at this time a more rapid advance toward Japan and her vital lines of communications. . . ."

The Cairo Conference was followed by a meeting at Pearl Harbor during the early weeks of 1944, attended by Nimitz and his chief staff advisers, and by a group from the Southwest Pacific headquarters led by Major General Richard K. Sutherland USA, MacArthur's chief of staff. Two major points were at issue: first, the continuing question as to which command, that of Nimitz or that of MacArthur, would mount the principal drive against Japan; and second, which theater would absorb the bulk of the strength from the South Pacific Area, since Halsey was rapidly reaching the point of having no more Japanese to fight. MacArthur wanted, in effect, to close off the Central Pacific drive, to absorb all possible military and naval strength (naming Halsey as his ranking naval commander), to by-pass the Marianas as well as the Carolines, and to move via the New Guinea axis and the Palaus into the Philippines. Little was accomplished at Pearl Harbor, although the discussions were enlightening to all concerned. King took note of these developments, and observed to Marshall that MacArthur should busy himself with Southwest Pacific theater plans and not question overall strategy; but after Sutherland left Pearl Harbor for Washington he was followed in a few weeks by Nimitz.

Meanwhile the Joint Strategical Survey Committee had been instructed to review the conflicting opinions, and it reported to the Joint Chiefs of Staff on February 16. The committee recommended that the Joint Chiefs of Staff clarify the decision taken at Cairo by assigning first priority to attacks made in the Pacific Ocean Areas. MacArthur's advance should continue, but should be relegated to a position of secondary importance. This recommendation was written for the most part by Vice Admiral Russell Willson USN, and on learning of it Sutherland expressed strong opposition. The army's counterpart on the Joint Strategical Survey Committee, however, Lieutenant General Stanley D. Embick USA, vigorously upheld Willson's position. Regardless, the Joint Chiefs deferred decision until the fighting in the Marshalls had been finished and the entire problem had been canvassed by the Joint Staff Planners.

Sutherland's bargaining position in Washington was weak because of the brilliant success being registered in the Marshalls. At this juncture, acting on the recommendation of General Kenney, who commanded the air arm of the Southwest Pacific Area, MacArthur decided to move immediately into the Admiralty Islands, almost six weeks ahead of schedule. The operation began in late February as a reconnaissance in force, and by March 4, 1944, an American victory was assured. Although the basic strategies varied, competition between MacArthur and Nimitz was altogether healthy for the American people. With the picture in both Pacific command areas clarified, and with Sutherland and Nimitz in Washington, the Joint Chiefs of Staff quickly reached a decision. Sutherland found his chief remaining trouble coming from non-naval quarters. He had tried in vain to interest Arnold in basing B-29's in the Southwest Pacific Area for the purpose of bombing Japanese oil installations in the Netherlands East Indies. But, in the words of the official Air Force historian: "Since the early fall of 1943 the AAF had shown an active interest in the possible use of Marianas bases for B-29 operations against the Japanese homeland, and Sutherland reported to MacArthur on 9 March that Brig. Gen. Haywood S. Hansell, Jr., representing the AAF on the Joint Staff Planners, was supporting an early occupation of the Marianas."

Having received the report of the Joint Staff Planners and having listened to both Sutherland and Nimitz, the Joint Chiefs of Staff issued the first of two March 1944 directives on the 12th day of that month. MacArthur was told to complete the isolation of both Rabaul and Kavieng (which was not to be occupied) with a minimum of forces, to attack Hollandia in Dutch New Guinea on April 15, to work his way to the Halmaheras and to be prepared to invade Mindanao in the southern Philippines on November 15, 1944. Nimitz was instructed to neutralize and by-pass Truk, and to cover that base from the north by invading the Southern Marianas on June 15. He was then to take the Palaus (an operation favored by both Nimitz and MacArthur) on September 15, 1944, which would cover Truk from the west and secure MacArthur's right flank into the Philippines. Both Nimitz and MacArthur were directed to coordinate their planning, including the details for a Central Pacific operation against Formosa on February 15, 1945, to be accompanied on the same day by a Southwest Pacific offensive into Luzon.

In other words, the Joint Chiefs again refrained from designating which of the two coordinated drives was to have first priority, and in effect the Joint Chiefs continued to keep the top Pacific command in their own hands. Their second directive, handed down on March 25, provides a clue to their reasoning. This involved the apportionment of the South Pacific forces to MacArthur and Nimitz. The Thirteenth Air Force went to MacArthur, but was to be employed as requested by Nimitz, to help neutralize the Carolines. MacArthur also received the XIV United States Army Corps Headquarters and corps troops, plus six army divisions, as well as miscellaneous navy and marine air units, and a substantial increase in his amphibious lift. Nimitz, however, got most of the naval components, including the First Marine Amphibious Corps (soon to be redesignated the Third Marine Amphibious Corps) and corps troops, plus the First and Third Marine Divisions. Thus MacArthur's ground strength was increased from six to twelve United States Army divisions, while Nimitz controlled four marine and six army divisions. The balance in overall strength, when one considers the mobility of the Pacific Fleet and the designated use of B-29's, favored the Pacific Ocean Areas.[90]

The merit of MacArthur's overall strategy will long be a subject of dispute. Exactly how he contemplated using the Pacific Fleet is not known, but there are indications. Already in Seeadler Harbor, Admiralty Islands, he had an excellent base for embarking an amphibious force, but he apparently continued (until directed otherwise) to desire another naval base in the same general region, at Kavieng. The intent must have been to deplete the Central Pacific of the bulk of its naval power, and to attempt to unhinge the remaining Japanese in that theater by operations around the western rim of the Pacific basin. He favored taking Kavieng, but opposed capturing the Marianas. Aside from the effort to divert B-29's to a role that appears in retrospect to have been of secondary importance, it seems clear that naval power could best cover MacArthur's theater by operating from Central Pacific bases. In fact, the Marshalls campaign, by taking out Truk, gave him all the strategical naval cover he needed up to the threshold of the Philippines (that is, up to the point that the Palaus must be neutralized or seized). To have called off the Marianas campaign and to have based the Pacific Fleet in MacArthur's area would have been to waste its power for more than six months. Nor was any such arrangement necessary. Nimitz capitalized on carrier mobility and, in between Central Pacific operations, sent MacArthur the Pacific Fleet for tactical air support in the Hollandia attack. This enabled the Southwest Pacific commander to range beyond his land-based fighters, to vault across Wewak, and to begin the establishment of another embarkation base in the west central portion of New Guinea in April 1944. Thereafter, and without a sizeable fleet, his advance continued to be rapid. Wakde-Sarmi was taken in May; and during the early summer, in coordination with Central Pacific operations in the Marianas, Southwest Pacific troops after considerable inshore lighting seized Biak Island in Geelvink Bay. This added another air base to those already sending planes over Truk, and brought Palau within bomber range. Noemfoor Island was next, and on July 31 Southwest Pacific soldiers in a shore-to-shore movement took Sansapor, on the northwestern tip of New Guinea. This poised MacArthur on the crown of the "Bird's Head," Vogelkop Peninsula. If and when Central Pacific forces removed the menace of Palau, the final thorn in his right flank would be extracted, and his return to the Philippines facilitated.[91]

More important for the marines, the sudden discovery that Japanese defensive strength in the Marshalls was weak and that Truk was untenable speeded the assault across the Central Pacific. Nimitz wasted none of his amphibious power. After the Marshalls, he set as his next objective the Marianas. Among those islands, in the summer of 1944, bases were won for the intensive bombing of the Japanese home islands by B-29's. Off the Marianas, for the first time since Bougainville, the Japanese offered naval battle.

Marine and army personnel trained in amphibious warfare were on hand for a rapid deployment into the Marianas because of several significant developments. Overrunning the Eastern and Central Marshalls had not only proved easier than anticipated, but also the advanced bases won at Majuro and Kwajalein had allowed a rapid displacement westward of Nimitz's well-organized logistical arm, thus permitting an almost instantaneous staging of the unused Kwajalein reserve against Eniwetok. Tentatively, Nimitz in January 1944 had allocated the task of seizing Eniwetok to the Second Marine Division and two regimental combat teams of the 27th Infantry Division. As it turned out, these men were not needed in the Marshalls, and were rested for the advance into the Marianas. The decision to by-pass Truk was even more important in this connection. In January 1944, Nimitz had earmarked five divisions plus a regiment for the work of taking Truk and adjacent atolls. Three marine divisions, the First, Third, and Fourth, and the Fourth Marine Regiment, were to lead the assault, backed by two army divisions in the next echelon, the 7th and 77th.[92]

Success in the Marshalls and the decision to by-pass Truk made it possible to furnish the Second, Third, and Fourth Marine, and the 27th and 77th Infantry Divisions, plus a marine regiment, for quick dispatch into the Marianas. Likewise, there was available for the Palaus a thoroughly rested First Marine Division (in so far as any rest could be found in its camp on rain-soaked Pavuvu Island in the Russells, where it had gone after taking Cape Gloucester).[93] Indirectly the Marshalls campaign, along with a later decision not to assault Yap in the Western Carolines, allowed Nimitz to transfer the 7th and 77th Infantry Divisions to MacArthur for use in the Philippines.

The Battle of Midway ended the Japanese offensive in the Central Pacific, and fighting in the Solomons-New Britain-New Guinea area drained the enemy of shipping and experienced pilots. Early 1944, however, marks the point at which American forces broke almost completely loose from the restraining leash of short-range land-based fighters, and relying on carrier mobility began advancing rapidly toward the coprosperity life line extending from Japan southward into the Netherlands East Indies. The decision to by-pass Truk along with Rabaul and Kavieng released most of the men required to seize the Marianas and the Palaus, and some of those used in the Philippines. It was principally the Marshalls campaign, plus simultaneous operations in the South and Southwest Pacific, which closed the enemy's front door on Rabaul and Kavieng, and imparted a momentum to America's offensive in the Pacific War which the Japanese were never able to halt.

Walter Lippmann found more than military victories in the Marshalls campaign and in the strikes against Truk. He discovered a spiritual rejuvenation of the American people. Noting that the Americans were confused and worried by successive failures in diplomacy and war, he observed that "Kwajalein and Truk are memorable not for the quality of power which has been assembled in the Pacific. . . . They are memorable for the quality of the planning and command that has been demonstrated; of this we had become dreadfully uncertain in the cynical, sentimental, materialistic days between the two wars." He judged the navy to be the nation's chief means of defense. "This is why we must put such great store upon the proof which has been given in the Marshalls and at Truk that the Navy has mastered the art of combining all arms in order to strike successfully across the seas. We shall learn from it, as the proof sinks into our minds, that we need doubt no longer the capacity of the nation to meet its tests and to fulfill its destiny." [94]

CHAPTER VIII

THE MARIANAS, BASES FOR THE A.A.F.

IN NOVEMBER 1945, Marquis Koichi Kido, Lord Keeper of the Privy Seal of the Imperial Japanese government, was asked by American interrogators at what date had he first given up hope that Japan could win the war in the Pacific. He answered, "rather early—after the fall of Saipan. It was my opinion at that time that it was advisable to give consideration to discontinuing the war." When further asked what were the particularly significant results stemming from the fall of Saipan, he listed two: "First, the fall of Saipan meant the intensification of American air attacks upon the Japanese home islands. Second, the failure of the navy, upon which our Japanese people in general had placed a great deal of reliance. . . ."[1]

Other high ranking Japanese civilian and military personnel agreed. Tojo's cabinet resigned immediately upon the American capture of Saipan, and intelligent Japanese in all walks of life could foresee only disaster.[2]

They were justly apprehensive. The invasion of Saipan, followed by the capture of Tinian and Guam, gave to American forces in the summer of 1944 complete control of the Marianas Islands and adjacent waters. This represented the furthermost thrust of American power toward Japan and her strategic line of communications into the Netherlands East Indies. The Marianas are over 3,200 miles from Pearl Harbor and over 1,300 miles from Kwajalein. The operation resulted in considerable, though not decisive damage to the Japanese fleet and in the destruction of large numbers of Japanese carrier and land-based aircraft. Casualties to enemy ground forces numbered more than 43,000 men.[3] Staging and submarine bases were moved up much closer to Japan with a great increase in the effectiveness of America's undersea warfare. Finally, and most important, the United States obtained excellent air bases from which the very long-range bombers (B-29s) could strike industrial and military targets in the heart of Japan.

1. Geography of the Southern Marianas and Theater Planning

The Marianas chain stretches in a curved line for almost 500 miles from Farallon de Pajaros on the north to Guam at the southern tip. (See map 15.) Only the southern islands were large enough to use as naval and aerial bases in the war against Japan. Of these the largest are Saipan, Tinian, and Guam.

Saipan, the northernmost of the three, is approximately fourteen statute miles long and five miles wide. (See map 16.) It is irregularly shaped and contains two harbors, Tanapag on the northwest and Magicienne Bay on the southeast coast. The southern portion of the island is a flat plateau bordered by hills and ridges. It was here that the Japanese had built Aslito Airfield, which was to become the first important objective of the American troops. The middle section of the island is mountainous, dominated by Mount Tapotchau, an extinct volcano rising above 1,500 feet. North of this mountain, the land is hilly but levels off gradually to a coastal plain some 700 yards in width. The high terrain, especially in the central region around Mount Tapotchau, is very rugged with steep cliffs and deep ravines abounding. Only a small portion of the island was under cultivation when the marines landed. A large and almost impenetrable swamp surrounds Lake Susupe on the west coast in the area of the assault beaches. The rest of the island is covered with pines, willows, sword grass, and tangled ground vines.[4]

In short, Saipan was to present a combination of problems entirely new in the Central Pacific theater. For the first time in this area the invading troops were called on to conduct large-scale operations on a comparatively large land mass characterized by semi-jungle vegetation and volcanic mountains and cliffs.

The island of Tinian, to the southwest of Saipan across a channel only three miles wide, was far less formidable. (See map 17.) It is only about twelve statute miles long and six miles across at its widest. Along the northern coast runs a moderately high plateau culminating in Mount Lasso, which rises to a little over 500 feet. South of that point, most of the ground is flat or rolling until the very southern tip. Then a high plateau, surrounded by cliffs and escarpments, makes attack from either land or sea dangerous. Much of the terrain in the southern part of the island was under cultivation when the marines attacked, and consequently was far easier to penetrate than the semi-jungle areas of Saipan. Also a good road system made the transportation problem fairly easy. Although the Japanese had an airfield near Ushi Point at the northern end, Tinian contained no harbors large enough to berth any sizeable number of ships.[5] Indeed, its military value would have been negligible had it not been for its proximity to its northern neighbor and its adaptability for an air base. For these reasons it was essential for the invading forces to capture the island; otherwise it would have been the source of constant harassment against the ships, planes, and personnel of the occupying forces on Saipan.

Guam is the largest island of the Marianas group. (See map 18.) About 100 miles south of Saipan, Guam is shaped somewhat like a peanut. About thirty-four statute miles long, it averages seven miles in width and contains some of the most difficult terrain in the Pacific. The southern part of the island is dominated by volcanic hills, the highest of which is Mount Tenjo, about 1,000 feet in elevation. These hills level off just north of the east-west axis into a fairly flat plain which terminates on the north coast in another range of volcanic hills, the highest being Mount Santa Rosa on the northeast. The whole island is covered with thick tropical growth except for small patches of cultivated land, and the hills themselves are covered with thick cane grass instead of trees. The lowlands consist mostly of swamps, rice paddies, and dense sword grass. Among the worst features from the point of view of amphibious assault troops are the high bony cliffs that jut out to the sea on many parts of the western coast. Since this coast offered the only practical beachheads, the landing force would inevitably have to scale these cliffs at the very outset in order to secure these beaches. This unenviable job was to fall to the lot of the Third Marine Division.

Yet, in spite of these difficulties, the value of Guam as an advance naval base in the war against Japan was greater than that of any of the other Marianas. It had the only nearly adequate water supply in the entire group, and in Apra Harbor on the west coast it offered easily the best anchorage in the entire area.[6] Furthermore, the very fact that it had formerly been United States territory made its recapture all the more desirable, for reasons of morale.

Two factors, however, led to the decision to initiate the Marianas campaign against Saipan rather than Guam. First, the former was some 100 miles closer to Japan and therefore more practicable as a base for very long-range bombing raids. Second, the prompt capture of Saipan by United States forces would deny to the enemy the use of its landing fields for air raids against shipping in the remainder of the Southern Marianas. Japanese planes staging out of the Nanpo Shoto or the homeland would have to fight at the end of their run, but if the capture of Saipan were delayed until Guam had been secured, they could use the former as a base for aerial attack on American forces to the south.[7]

Terrain was not the only hazard facing the American forces in their attack against the Marianas. Distance was another. These islands were a part of the enemy's inner defensive line and far from the nearest friendly base. Saipan lies some 1,200 miles from Tokyo and a mere 625 miles from Iwo Jima in the Nanpo Shoto. Eniwetok, recently taken by the United States Pacific Fleet, is 1,050 miles from Saipan. But none of these considerations was weighty enough to eliminate the Marianas as a priority target in the sweep across the Central Pacific. As Admiral Nimitz had made clear when outlining his ambitious plan for 1944, he was anxious to place Japan proper under intensive air

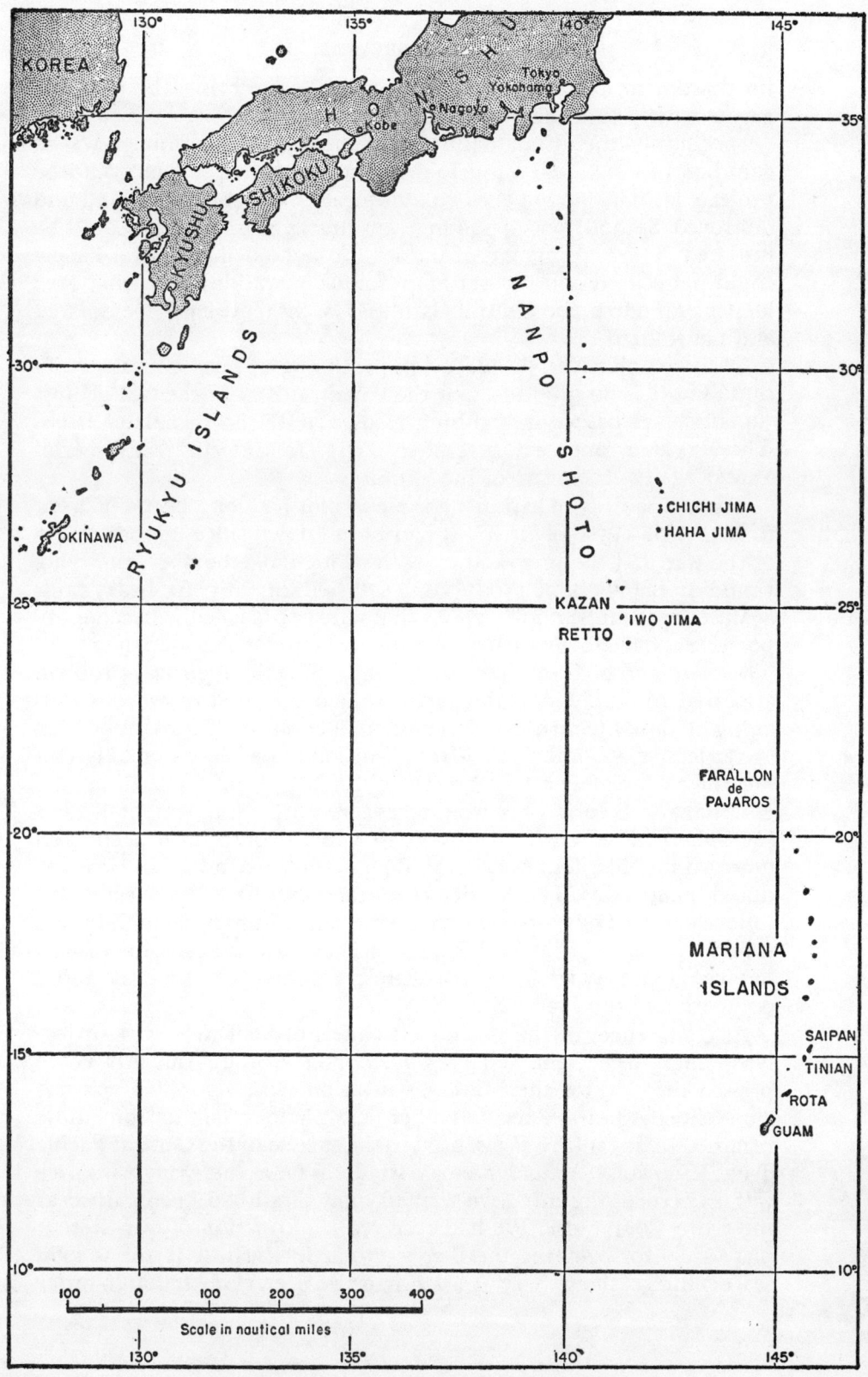

MAP 15. Japan and islands to the south.

bombardment and naval blockade, as well as to bring about an engagement with the enemy's fleet.[8]

Specifically, the ultimate purpose of the Marianas campaign was to gain bases from which a fourfold thrust against the enemy could be projected. First, Japanese sea communications might be attacked and destroyed. Second, very long-range air attacks against Japan could be initiated. Third, command of the sea throughout the Central Pacific could be secured and further amphibious operations from that area launched. Fourth, the Central Carolines might more easily be isolated and neutralized.[9]

Of these objectives, the second proved to be by far the most significant. There is no question that their main utility in the war against Japan was as bases for bombing raids against the homeland itself. They became "anchored aircraft carriers" for pressing heavy aerial attacks against the heart of the empire.

The desirability of capturing these islands had long been apparent to Army Air Force planners. It had been known since the beginning of the war that the proposed new very long-range bomber, the B-29, would probably not be produced in sufficient quantity for heavy raids against Japan until mid-1944. As that date approached it became imperative to have adequate bases for them close enough to Japan proper. The mainland of China was a possibility, but the logistical problem appeared insoluble, and the Japanese had captured or were threatening all suitable airports closer than Chengtu or Chunking, which are at least 2,000 miles away from Tokyo. These were not only vulnerable to Japanese attack but their distance made a refueling stop essential for B-29's. This would have required supplemental bases somewhere closer to the China coast which would have been even more vulnerable. Otherwise, the B-29's would have had to carry reduced bomb loads. The Marianas, on the other hand, were some 800 miles closer to Tokyo than either Chengtu or Chunking; and Nimitz's superior logistical arm in the Central Pacific stood ready for instant service. Hence Army Air Force planners were anxious for the rapid occupation of the Marianas.

At conferences of the Combined Chiefs of Staff held in Cairo in November 1943, General Henry H. Arnold of the Army Air Force pressed the case for the Marianas invasion with vigor. He was not alone, since Admiral King and other navy planners had for some time regarded their capture as essential to the success of the Central Pacific drive. In any case, Arnold later reported, "as far as the Army Air Force was concerned, the thing we wanted most of all had been gained at the Cairo Conference. We had received confirmation of our present plans . . . for bringing the B-29's into action against Japan as soon as we could get them there. . . . It had also been evident that in order to use them we must at first operate from bases either in the Marianas or in China. . . . The Marianas, specifically Guam, Saipan, and Tinian came closer to filling the bill than any others."[10]

Theater planning for the Marianas was already under way early in 1944, when Nimitz on January 13, as directed by the Joint Chiefs of Staff, outlined the successive steps by which United States forces would drive across the Central Pacific almost to the very door of Japan. Nimitz stood ready to coordinate his schedule with MacArthur's concurrent advance along the New Guinea-Halmahera-Philippine axis, but as earlier noted, he insisted that priority in the allocation of forces go to the Central Pacific. This drive picked up such momentum in the Marshalls campaign that Nimitz was able to scrap his earlier timetable. Success in the Marshalls, plus decisions to by-pass Kavieng and Rabaul as well as Truk, supplied both the opportunity and the means for rapid movement into the Marianas.

Under Nimitz's plan of January 13, 1944, the Marianas campaign was to be divided into three phases: first, the seizure of Tinian and Saipan to commence about November 1, 1944; second, the attack on Guam, to be launched by December 15; and, third, the extension of United States control over the whole Marianas area by whatever means necessary.[11] As events proved, Nimitz's timetable was conservative. The rapidity and comparative ease of the Marshalls campaign allowed him to advance the target date in the Marianas by four and a half months. In early April it was decided to by-pass Truk in favor of an immediate execution of the Marianas plan.[12] Landings on Saipan were set for June 15, and for Guam they were to be on June 18.

To accomplish this ambitious plan it was soon recognized that a much larger force than hitherto employed in the Central Pacific would be necessary. Consequently, responsibility for the land phase of the operation was allotted to two distinct corps. The Fifth Amphibious Corps, located in the Hawaiian Islands under the command of Lieutenant General Holland Smith, was assigned the task of seizing Saipan and Tinian. For purposes of this operation, the corps was designated Northern Troops and Landing Force and consisted chiefly of the Second and Fourth Marine Divisions reinforced with the 27th Infantry Division of the United States Army in reserve. Holland Smith had a dual responsibility, first as Commander Northern Troops and Landing Force for the Saipan-Tinian phase, and second as Commanding General of all Expeditionary Troops including those assigned to Guam. The job of seizing the latter went to Major General Roy S. Geiger USMC, whose Third Amphibious Corps was designated Southern Troops and Landing Force. This corps was stationed on Guadalcanal and consisted of the Third Marine Division reinforced plus the First Provisional Marine Brigade, that is the Fourth and the

Twenty-second Marine Regimental Combat Teams. The 77th Infantry Division at Pearl Harbor was, at the same time, alerted for employment in Expeditionary Troop reserve, and was subsequently assigned to the Third Amphibious Corps for the attack on Guam.[13]

Since all Central Pacific operations were under navy jurisdiction, overall command was assigned to Admiral Spruance. Command of the Joint Expeditionary Force attacking the Marianas went to Vice Admiral Kelly Turner. His force was divided into a Northern Attack Force for Saipan and Tinian, direct command of which he retained himself, and a Southern Attack Force for Guam headed by Rear Admiral Richard L. Conolly.

Thus, by early April, the main objectives of the forthcoming campaign had been defined, the assault dates established, and the troops assigned for the job. This same month was spent in outlining the minute details of the operations, acquiring new intelligence where possible, providing against every foreseeable contingency and rehearsing the troops. Holland Smith issued his preferred operations plan on May 1. Each division and regiment followed suit. Slight modifications in the original plan followed, and alternate plans were devised to be put into execution in the event intelligence of the strength and disposition of Japanese forces should prove grossly in error, or other unexpected difficulties should arise.

Smith's estimate of the enemy situation on Saipan was based largely on information captured in the Marshalls and on aerial photographic missions flown from late February through mid-April. These showed that, as of May 1, there were probably from 11,400 to 12,000 enemy troops on the island, including both army and navy units. Three airfields had been sighted. (See map 16.) The largest of these was Aslito Field, located in the far southern section of the island; another at Marpi Point on the far northern tip and one at Charan Kanoa near the southwest coast were thought to be only partially completed. These fields contained an estimated eighty-two planes. By the end of May, however, it was evident that troop strength had greatly increased. These later estimates placed the total Japanese defensive forces at a possible 18,900 army and navy personnel, plus 3,000 home guards. Rapid improvements of defenses throughout the island were also indicated, and it was recognized that troops would probably keep pouring into the island until intercepted by American forces.[14]

Holland Smith's original plan for the capture of Saipan called for an initial assault landing of two divisions abreast on an 8,000 yard front. The beaches designated lay along the west coast to the north and south of Afetna Point. These were chosen in part on the assumption that the enemy expected landings at Magicienne Bay on the east coast and would concentrate his defenses there. Furthermore, the site straddling Afetna Point was wide enough to permit the landing of eight battalion landing teams abreast. It also offered the shortest practicable route to Aslito Field and would give the attacking troops their best chance to split the enemy forces by driving quickly across the island to Magicienne Bay.[15]

The specific assignment of beaches was as follows: The four located to the south of the town of Charan Kanoa were allotted to the four battalions of the Fourth Marine Division designated for beach assault. After landing they were to proceed inland as rapidly as resistance allowed and capture Aslito Field, then await further orders. Two battalion landing teams of the Twenty-third Regimental Combat Team would be on the left flank, while two battalion landing teams of the Twenty-fifth Regimental Combat Team would cross on the right. The third regimental combat team of the division, the Twenty-fourth, was assigned to division reserve with the duty of landing and supporting the attack whenever so ordered.[16] To the north of Charan Kanoa, the men of the Second Marine Division would also land on four beaches. On completing their seizure of the beachhead line, they were to drive further inland to Mount Tipo Pale and Mount Tapotchau, seize those strongpoints and protect the left flank of the attack. The Eighth Regimental Combat Team was assigned to the right flank, the Sixth to the left, and the Second was to be in division reserve and land when directed.[17] The two reserve regiments, the Second and Twenty-fourth Marines, were to make a diversionary landing movement toward Garapan. The 27th Infantry Division was designated as floating reserve to land only if enemy opposition proved too stiff for the operation to be completed in the scheduled time. Originally, it was also planned to embark the First Battalion, Second Marines, aboard destroyer transports and land them at selected beaches on Magicienne Bay sometime before the major assault, but this scheme eventually had to be abandoned in view of the subsequent discovery that Japanese defenses were heaviest at this point.[18] Otherwise, no substantial changes were made in the final execution of the main landing plan.

The underlying principle behind the plan was this. Assault troops would be landed in such a fashion as to permit the seizure of a beachhead both broad and deep enough to allow ease of deployment on the ground. Breadth would be assured by putting ashore eight battalions of infantry in line abreast in the first few waves. Depth, it was hoped, would be gained by landing these troops in amphibian tractors, the first two waves of which would proceed inland to a distance of about 1,500 yards before debarking their troops. They would then establish a perimeter defense along favorable terrain in order to protect the beachhead. In this task they were to be assisted by the 75-millimeter guns of the armored amphibians which were to precede them. Subsequent waves could be employed to mop up resistance by-passed by the first two waves. This was a new trick in amphibious tactics and its projected employment was based on the following considerations: that preliminary bombardment would effectively neutralize the defenses on the landing beach area until after naval gunfire lifted; that the shock action of the armored amphibians would temporarily prolong the stunning effect of the naval gunfire; that elements of enemy resistance by-passed by the leading assault waves could be mopped up by later waves; and that troops could debark more easily in defiladed areas to the rear of the shore line.[19] It failed to take into account the difficulties of the terrain which the tractors would have to traverse. It overestimated the capabilities of both the armored amphibian and the unarmored amphibian tractor as land-travelling vehicles. These shortcomings were recognized by the commanding general of the Second Marine Division, who protested such use of the amphibians and was given permission to alter their employment. However, in the case of the Fourth Marine Division, the error was costly, and the miscalculation accounts in part at least for the eventual collapse of plans on the first day of the operation.

For artillery support the Tenth Marines were assigned to the zone of action of the Second Marine Division, and the Fourteenth Marines were to support the Fourth Marine Division. In addition, Holland Smith had under his direct control the United States Army XXIV Corps Artillery consisting of 155-millimeter guns and howitzers. Air support was to be furnished by Vice Admiral Marc A. Mitscher's fast carriers, organized as Task Force 58 directly under Spruance, and by the escort carriers of Turner's Northern Attack Force supplemented by those of Conolly's Southern Attack Force which began their work at Saipan before moving down to Guam. Strikes against beach defenses, heavy fortifications, land planes and facilities of Aslito Field, as well as all transportation and communications facilities on both Saipan and Tinian were ordered for the two days before the target date. Then carrier planes were to step up their strikes, concentrating particularly on the landing beaches just before the first waves hit, and were to continue thereafter to knock out various enemy defenses as the troops drove inland. Naval gunfire support was to be furnished by the fast battleships and destroyers of Spruance's Fifth Fleet beginning two days before the attack, and followed the next day by the slower battleships and supporting men-of-war of Turner's attack force.[20]

By early May, basic plans for all echelons involved in the coming operation had been largely completed, and the remaining time had to be spent in rehearsing and loading. Rehearsals, as usual for troops embarking from the Hawaiian area, were conducted on the islands of Maui and Kahoolawe. Between May 15 and 19, both marine divisions practiced all phases of the ship-to-shore movement ending in a full-scale simulated landing under the protection of naval gunfire and aerial bombardment. Similar rehearsals were conducted by the 27th Division the following week.[21] Back in Pearl Harbor, last-minute loading was completed, and the greatest task force yet assembled in the Central Pacific sortied in echelon, the last tractor group carrying troops of the 27th Division leaving on June 1.[22] The ships lifting the two marine divisions staged through Eniwetok, where the units destined for beach assault were shifted from their transports to tank landing ships, which were already carrying the amphibian tractors. On June 11 the last shipload of troops departed Eniwetok for the larger but far less hospitable shores of Saipan.

2. *The Landings and Fighting Ashore on Saipan*

On the same day, Mitscher's carrier-based planes swept across Saipan, Tinian, Rota, and Guam, both localizing the selected beaches and beginning the preinvasion bombardment. This took place two days earlier than planned.[23] American aircraft gained quick control of the target area, and strikes continued the next day, June 12. Seven fast battleships began working over Saipan on June 13 while underwater demolition teams and minesweepers searched the shores and adjacent waters for mines and underwater obstacles. Next day, the old battleships of Turner's and Conolly's attack forces, joined by cruisers and destroyers, combed the two islands of Saipan and Tinian with counterbattery and harassing fire from dawn to dusk and throughout the night. In the early morning twilight of June 15, troops aboard the transports and tank landing ships got their first look at Mount Tapotchau. Before dawn their ships had come to anchor in the transport areas off the landing beaches.

The seizure and occupation of Saipan, as events worked out, divided itself roughly into three phases.[24] (See map 16.) Phase one, lasting from the 15th through the 19th of June, consisted of the assault landing, seizure of the beachhead, the capture of Aslito Field, penetration by marines and soldiers to the eastern coast, and the isolation of elements of enemy forces in the southeastern tip of the island (Nafutan Point).

Time for the initial landings was originally established at eight-thirty in the morning. Soon after daylight, the troop-laden tank landing ships began to disgorge their amphibian tractors, and the movement toward the line-of-departure began. Unavoidable delays in getting the amphibian tractors into the water necessitated postponing the landings ten minutes, but with this single exception the disembarkation of troops proceeded as planned. As the tractors crossed the line-of-departure, they were preceded by infantry landing craft converted to gunboats whose job was to give the landing beaches a last-minute shower of 40-millimeter, 20-millimeter, and 4½-inch rocket fire. From left to right (north and south) the battalion landing teams were disposed as follows: on the four beaches north of Afetna Point, the Second and Third Battalion Landing Teams of the Sixth Marines, and the Third and Second Battalion Landing Teams of the Eighth Marines, all a part of the Second Marine Division; on the four beaches to the south, the Third and Second Battalion Landing Teams of the Twenty-third Marines, and the Second and First Battalion Landing Teams of the Twenty-fifth Marines, all from the Fourth Marine Division. To the north, in the area of Tanapag Harbor, the Second Regimental Combat Team of the Second Division and the Twenty-fourth Regimental Combat Team of the Fourth Division were boated in amphibian tractors to conduct a diversionary feint off Garapan.

Artillery and mortar fire from the shore peppered the water as the troops approached the edge of the abutting reef. It was not dense enough to retard the ship-to-shore movement seriously, and the first wave hit the beaches with precision. Within twenty minutes some 8,000 men were ashore. The tactical plan, however, broke down early. In most sectors, tractor drivers would not or could not proceed to the beachhead line as ordered, but instead disembarked their troops near the water's edge causing untold confusion and congestion. The Second Marine Division was landed through unavoidable error some 900 yards north of the assigned beaches and hence had to fight in two directions, south as well as east. Contact between the two divisions was consequently lost, creating a dangerous gap which was not to be closed for four days. Resistance was fierce, and casualties were unexpectedly heavy. Yet, in spite of these obstacles, by the end of the day the marines had established a front of about five miles with an average depth of 1,500 yards. Artillery regiments of both divisions had landed a large portion of their weapons and personnel, and the most hazardous phase of the amphibious assault had been successfully executed. But the enemy still held both Agingan Point and Afetna Point, and the danger of infiltration and counterattack was great.

That danger was realized in the early morning hours of June 16 when well-organized counterthrusts were carried out at various points in the zones of both divisions. These were repulsed, but only with severe losses to the marines. Not until afternoon of the second day of the operation were the American lines well enough reorganized to allow the launching of an offensive drive toward the line selected for protecting the beachhead. The extremely heavy losses and the intensity of the enemy's resistance had induced Holland Smith to revise his initial plans. While the Second Marine Division consolidated its posi-

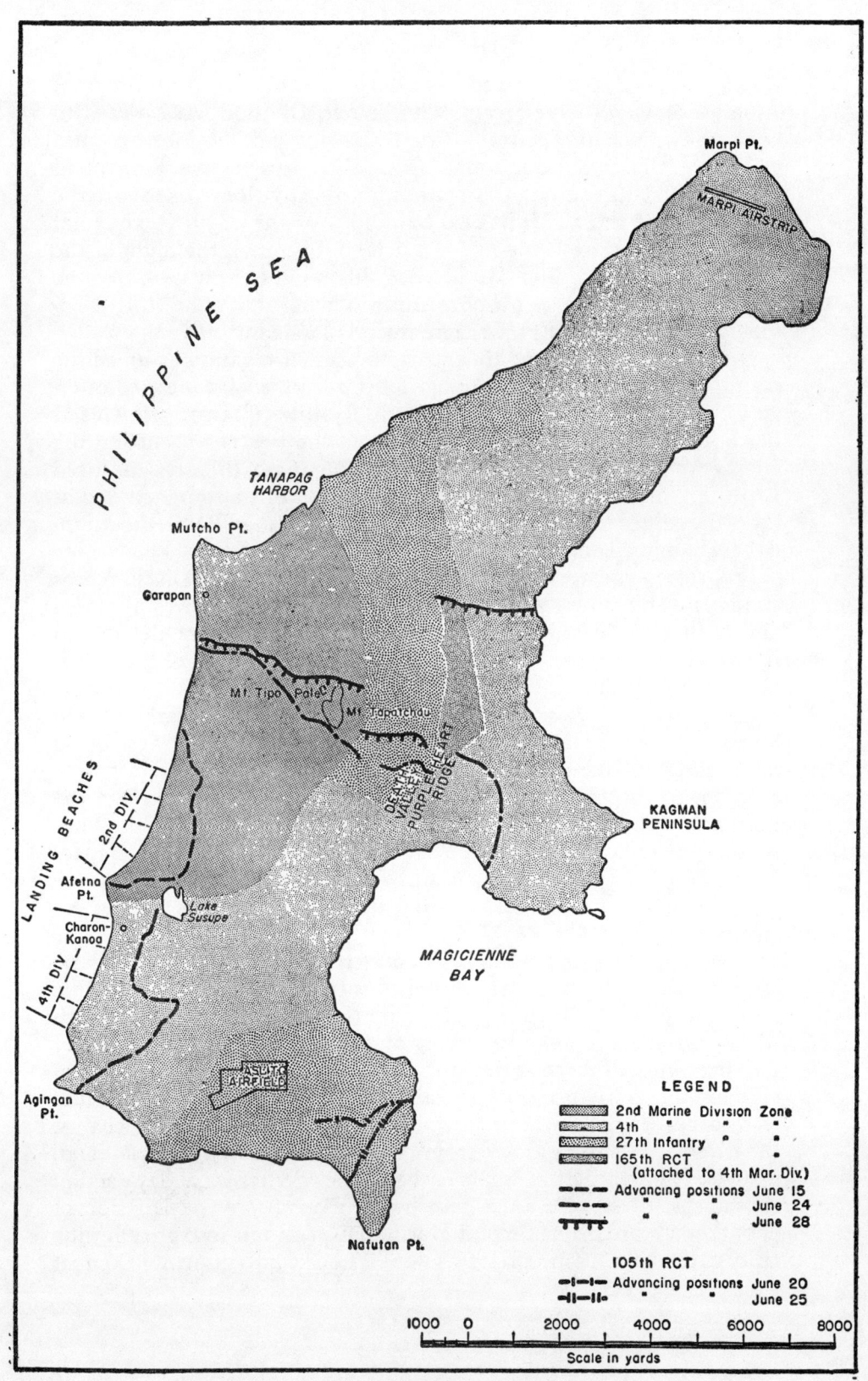

MAP 16. The struggle for Saipan, June–July 1944.

tion and moved southward to close the gaps in the line in the area of Afetna Point and Lake Susupe, the Fourth Division was ordered to press the attack on Aslito Field, by-passing pockets of resistance which were later to be mopped up by the corps reserve. Smith had thus decided to commit the 27th Infantry Division to support the attack against the airfield. Two battalions of the 165th Regimental Combat Team were landed with much confusion on the night of the 16th, and the remaining battalion of this regiment plus most of the 105th Infantry were put ashore the following day. The third regiment, the 106th Infantry, was not entirely landed until June 20.

During the period June 16–19, marines and army units assumed the offensive in spite of a fierce though uncoordinated Japanese counterattack in the early morning of the 17th. By June 18, two regiments of the Fourth Marine Division had reached the east coast, cutting the enemy forces in two. On the same day the 165th Infantry captured Aslito Field, and on the following day army units also penetrated as far as the east coast and some 1,500 yards into Nafutan Point, the southeastern peninsula of the island.

Progress in the north, the zone of the Second Marine Division, was slower, but by June 19 the gap between the two divisions was closed and both were in a position to pivot northward against the second line of enemy defense. Thus, by June 19, the first phase of the operation was completed.

On the same day, far out to sea, American ships and carrier-based aircraft routed a major Japanese naval task force set on destroying or at least paralyzing the attack force. Over 400 enemy aircraft were shot down; three aircraft carriers and two tankers were sent to the bottom by American planes and submarines. This Battle of the Philippine Sea guaranteed to the American forces uncontested control of the seas adjacent to Saipan and freed the troops ashore of any future danger of isolation or full-scale counterlandings by the enemy.[25]

Phase two of the operation began on June 20. On that date Holland Smith ordered the two marine divisions to attack northward in line abreast, the Second Marine Division on the left (west) and the Fourth Marine Division on the east coast of the island. The 27th Infantry Division with all three regiments now ashore was assigned the task of clearing out resistance on Nafutan Point. For two days the marines were occupied in a wide pivoting movement which would change the direction of their attack from east to north. Then, on the 22nd, a full-scale forward drive was launched. The results of that day's action on the east coast were a net gain by the Fourth Marine Division of about 2,500 yards. The Second Marine Division ran into greater difficulty in its zone, and progress was slow. The Sixth Regimental Combat

Team seized the crest of Mount Tipo Pale during the afternoon, but except for this important gain little advance was made.

Even before the Second Marine Division encountered such stiff resistance, Holland Smith had determined to feed large elements of the 27th Infantry Division into the front line to gain momentum in the northward drive. After consultation with Major General Ralph Smith USA, commanding general of the army division, it was decided to commit the 106th and 165th Infantry Regiments to the center of the line, thus permitting the Fourth Marine Division to fan out to the eastward in order to occupy Kagman Peninsula. Only in this manner could an unbroken front be maintained across the entire island which was wider in this area than further south. At the same time, it was decided that one battalion of the 105th Infantry would be sufficient to mop up the remaining enemy on Nafutan Point. The rest of the 105th was to go into corps reserve.

The next week saw the fiercest fighting encountered since the initial assault. On the left, the Second Marine Division had the unenviable task of scaling the well-defended cliffs and ravines of Mount Tapotchau. On the right the Fourth Marine Division was assigned the less difficult job of seizing Kagman Peninsula. In the center, Ralph Smith's two army regiments were poured into one of the best fortified pieces of land on the island. This area, known later as Death Valley, contained two parallel defensive lines of caves and strong points which in turn ran parallel to the line of advance and made swift movement virtually impossible. On the left it was flanked by the sheer cliffs of the Tapotchau Range, and on the right by a high and densely wooded ridge, soon to be known as Purple Heart Ridge. It was here that the attack to the northward by these divisions bogged down. As marines on the right and left moved forward to seize their respective objectives, army troops could make no headway against the center. Thus the flanks of the marine divisions were threatened with dangerous exposure, and they were compelled to retard their advance until the center of the line could be brought forward.

After one and one-half days of fighting by the 27th Division, during which very little penetration into Death Valley had been made, Ralph Smith was relieved of his command by his superior, Holland Smith, on June 24. He was replaced by Major General Sanderford Jarman USA, who was removed from his position as Commander, Garrison Troops, to take temporary command of the 27th Division. Four days later Jarman was relieved of his temporary command by Major General George W. Griner USA.

Meanwhile both marine divisions had been advancing as rapidly as was possible under the circumstances. On June 25 Kagman Peninsula fell to the Fourth Marine Division with comparatively little opposition, and the crest of Mount Tapotchau was taken by the Second Division after encountering severe fighting and suffering heavy casualties. By now General Jarman, following the plan devised earlier by Ralph Smith, had abandoned the attempt to carry out a frontal attack through the valley facing his troops and instead had decided to move along the crest of Purple Heart Ridge. By June 27 his division had occupied all but the northernmost of the series of hills which comprised the ridge, and the next three days were spent in mopping up the remaining enemy strongholds in the valley below. The Fourth Marine Division made no attempt to move forward during this period, since its lines were already well in advance of the army division. On the left the Second Marine Division moved down off the peak of Mount Tapotchau and was able to command the area in front of Garapan Harbor. By July 1 the lines were once again consolidated and phase two of the operation completed. Tipo Pale, Mount Tapotchau, Death Valley, Purple Heart Ridge, and Kagman Peninsula had been secured. A penetration by some 500 Japanese through the lines of the Second Battalion, 105th Infantry, on Nafutan Point in the early morning of June 26 had not seriously upset the advance even though these Nipponese succeeded in reaching Aslito Field as well as the command post of the Twenty-fifth Marines before being recognized and liquidated. Everything was in order for the third and final phase of the operation.

Holland Smith's plan for this last phase contemplated a three-divisional movement in a northwesterly direction, the first objective being the seizure of Mutcho Point and Tanapag Harbor. As these localities were reached, it was understood that the Second Marine Division coming up the west coast would be pinched out and then go into reserve. Thereafter, the 27th Infantry Division and the Fourth Marine Division would complete the occupation of the remaining northern segment of the island. In only three days, the first objectives were reached. By July 4 the town of Garapan, Mutcho Point, and Tanapag Harbor had been secured, and the attack was ordered to shift to the north. The last quarter of the island was to be captured by the army moving up the west coast and the Fourth Marine Division on the east and center. A slight modification of this plan was ordered on July 6, when Holland Smith decided to swing the left flank of the marine division to the northwest coast and thereby cut off the retreat of enemy elements in front of the army troops. To accomplish this, he attached the Second Marine Regiment to the Fourth Division, thus leaving only two regiments of the Second Marine Division in corps reserve.

Although progress of the marines was steady against relatively light resistance, the army met stiffer opposition, and little advance was made. Then, in the early morning hours of July 7, Lieutenant General

Yoshio Saito, ranking Japanese army commander, issued his orders for a last desperate banzai charge against the American lines. Probably 3,000 fanatical enemy soldiers participated in this charge, although some estimates run as high as 4,300. Pledging "seven lives to repay our country," and armed with everything from machine guns to knife-tipped bamboo poles, they fell with fury against the weary American troops. The brunt of the attack was lodged against the unlucky 105th Regimental Combat Team of the 27th Division, which was not well disposed to meet the assault. A 300 yard gap lay between the First and Third Battalion, and a breakthrough was easy. These two battalions were forced to fall back, and remnants of the regiment were eventually surrounded with their backs to the sea. Two batteries of marine artillery about a mile to the rear of the front line were overrun, although by that time, the full force of the attack was almost spent. By nightfall the 106th Infantry had recovered the artillery positions and about half of the lost ground, although the command post of the 105th Infantry was still isolated.

The next day the Second Marine Division was ordered to relieve the 27th Division which returned to corps reserve (except for the 165th Infantry which was attached to the Second Marine Division). Thereafter, the advance to the north coast was rapid. On July 9, as hundreds of Japanese soldiers and civilians leaped to their death on the rocky shoals below Marpi Point, Holland Smith declared the island secured. Although for weeks afterward mopping up caves and pillboxes continued, all organized resistance had come to an end.

3. Amphibious and Tactical Aspects at Saipan

The capture of Saipan was, as had been the case in all previous marine operations in the Central Pacific, primarily amphibious in the purest sense of that word. That is to say, it was initially a large-scale assault on a hostile shore carried out by specially trained troops who were embarked from distant overseas bases and lifted to their destination by combat-loaded ships. Nor did the amphibious aspects cease once the troops had been landed. Throughout the operation men-of-war and carrier-based aircraft continued to support the ground troops by providing gunfire and bombing where artillery could not do the job.

The essentially naval character of the entire operation was explicitly recognized from the outset when Admiral Spruance, and under him Admiral Turner, were put in overall command of the undertaking. Yet the seizure of Saipan presented problems considerably different from previous operations in the Central Pacific in which the Marine Corps had participated. It was a comparatively large land mass. This fact, plus the varied nature of the terrain, required solutions unknown to atoll warfare. Some 77,000 troops had to be maneuvered over this area, and they had to be adequately and promptly supplied over land distances greater than those ordinarily encountered in Marine Corps operations. Also, for the first time in the Central Pacific, a large body of ground forces were deployed on a single land objective. Three reinforced divisions, plus a separate artillery unit, the United States Army XXIV Corps Artillery, were used ashore, and this greatly complicated the problems of liaison and coordination. All of these inherent difficulties were rendered still more complex by the fact that one of the infantry divisions and the corps artillery were army organizations thrown in beside unfamiliar marine units and serving under a marine commanding general.

For these reasons an analysis of the successes and failures in the various phases of the Saipan operation must take into consideration many factors. The amphibious and tactical aspects can be broken down into several parts. These are combat-loading and approach to the target; beach logistics; preliminary and close support fires, which also involved, once the troops were ashore, the coordination of both air and naval gunfire support with land-based artillery; and the ship-to-shore movement. As indicated above, however, this does not cover the whole story. Consideration must also be given to the infantry tactics employed by the enemy and by both army and marine units, to command relations throughout the operation, and to liaison between different command echelons. Since this particular operation precipitated a difference of opinion between two participating services and resulted in the relief of one army general and a great deal of bitterness between the Army and Marine Corps, it will also be necessary to examine the origins of that dispute if for no other reason than to indicate the difficulties inherent in joint operations.

COMBAT-LOADING AND MOVEMENT TO THE TARGET

Launching the attack against Saipan put the heaviest load on naval shipping that had yet been known in the Pacific War. A total of 209 transports, cargo vessels, and tank and dock landing ships were required to lift the men and material of the Northern Troops and Landing Force to Saipan, exclusive of those needed for resupply. Also, as usual, there were not enough bottoms to satisfy all the needs of the expeditionary force, especially since the problem was complicated by the need for embarking the Southern Troops and Landing Force. Hence, although logistics officers, troop and transport quartermasters, and ship captains made every effort to comply with the tested doctrine for combat-loading, complete success was not always achieved.

Holland Smith's two staffs, working furiously at Pearl Harbor, screened all equipment lists from lower echelons and cut their requests down to the bare bone before submitting their shipping requirements to Turner for approval. They were handicapped constantly, not only by shipping shortages, but by constant changes in shipping assignments and loading dates, and particularly by the general absence of adequate ships' characteristics data. In the case of vessels which failed or were not ordered to submit these vital statistics in time, it was impossible to prepare loading plans until the time they put into the port of embarkation and their holds and deck space could be measured.

It is therefore no surprise that much necessary equipment for Saipan was left on the dock or misloaded. For example, the vessels assigned to transport the men and equipment of the Twenty-third Marine Regimental Combat Team did not have space to carry more than one-half of that regiment's authorized 1-ton trucks, to say nothing of vital items of engineer, medical, and ordnance equipment. Yet the same ships took on board a supply of naval shells, some of the equipment and personnel assigned to Fifth Amphibious Corps, and a part of the headquarters load of the Fourth Marine Division, plus that of two artillery battalions which were not to reinforce the regiment. The 27th Infantry Division suffered in the same way when more than fifty per cent of its motor transport, engineer, and other combat equipment had to be left behind or stowed elsewhere because the ships assigned to the division were loaded with corps troops and materiel.

But despite these shortcomings in the execution of the loading schedule, no serious consequences ensued. The test of any combat-loading plan is whether or not it permits an expeditious unloading of the ships in the target area to meet the exigencies of the tactical situation ashore. In other words, is the materiel arranged aboard ship so as to permit its being unloaded fast enough and in the proper order to meet the requirements of the troops ashore? To this question, an affirmative answer can be given for Saipan. Although the troops suffered some shortages in the earlier phases, particularly in transportation and equipment, this can be laid to the inadequate number of ships and not to the method of loading them. For the most part, transports and tank landing ships were systematically loaded according to sound doctrine, and the errors noted above, whether avoidable or not, did no vital damage to the progress of the operation.[26]

BEACH LOGISTICS

On the other end of the logistical equation, however, greater difficulties were to appear. It is axiomatic that it is harder to unload a vessel in an amphibious operation than to put the cargo aboard, even when the latter has been stowed perfectly. Saipan was no exception, and innumerable obstacles appeared, some avoidable and some not, to plague the various beach and shore parties in their effort to get the required equipment ashore in the proper place at the proper time.

Some of the delays in unloading and the movement of supplies ashore stemmed from natural or man-made obstacles over which the attacking forces had no control. Others were imposed by the navy's policies adopted as a result of real or anticipated dangers from enemy sources. Still others arose out of the failure or inability of Holland Smith's headquarters to cope with the tremendous complexities involved in supplying three divisions with the necessary equipment at the right time.

Although the Japanese had not installed artificial barriers along the western beaches, the natural reefs fringing them hampered the rapid movement of supplies ashore. At low tide only Dukws and amphibian tractors could be used, and there were never enough of these on hand to meet all the demands of the troops promptly. Also, at least until the fifth day of the operation, most of the beaches were under frequent enemy artillery and mortar fire which, of course, handicapped beach logistics.[27]

A more important reason for the tardiness of supplies was the fact that throughout the beach assault phase of the operation the navy and not the landing force commanders made the decisions as to what should be landed and when. Although in theory these decisions were to be made after consultation with the proper marine or army officers, in practice the navy commanders usually made them unilaterally.[28] This resulted, in some instances, in ships leaving the area before unloading high-priority goods, and also in dumping ashore equipment intended for troops which had not yet been landed. Another cause for delay was Turner's decision to stop all unloading during the hours of darkness. This may have been a necessary precaution under existing circumstances, although in later operations the navy was to permit night unloading. Finally, the forced withdrawal of practically all the transports during the five-day period when the Battle of the Philippine Sea was being waged, far to the west of Saipan, caused shortages ashore for many of the troops. These shortages were particularly acute in the case of the 105th and 165th Infantry Regiments, which had been put ashore with almost no transportation or supplies and had to depend upon the charity of marine divisions while their transports and supporting vessels were still at sea.[29]

Not all the logistical bottle necks were the product of naval policies or decisions. One of the worst tie ups on the beaches occurred when the 165th Infantry was landed on June 16 on the coast to the rear of the Twenty-third Marine Regimental Combat Team. All traffic bound for the marine regiment was temporarily stopped, and when the army unit eventually got ashore there was almost hopeless congestion on the beaches due to the confusion of Army and Marine Corps supplies. The Fifth Amphibious Corps had issued no directives to coordinate the shore parties of the two units and made no subsequent attempts to do so.[80] Apparently the possibility of one division's landing immediately behind another had simply not been considered when plans were being evolved.

In the lower echelons, no serious shortcomings in the operation and functioning of the shore parties themselves were observed. Under the circumstances, they performed with distinction. The occasional withdrawal of engineers from shore parties to perform such functions as road building and repair for the troops further inland was unfortunate but unavoidable. The divisions simply were undersupplied with combat engineering personnel.[81]

With all the difficulties and shortcomings listed above, and many more unmentioned, the navy was able to unload all the assault shipping, with the exception of one transport division, within the first eleven days of the operation,[82] and most of this found its way into the hands of the appropriate troop units. The only serious shortages suffered by the men ashore were in certain types of ammunition and in transportation. The first was due to the failure of the corps planners to realize the great potentialities of 60- and 81-millimeter mortar fire on islands the size of Saipan. The second, which was far more serious, was due in part to the shortage of cargo space and in part to corps' insistence that its own motorized equipment be loaded at the expense of that belonging to the divisions. To the extent that this disproportionate allocation of shipping deprived the ground troops of their essential mobility, corps headquarters was responsible. Otherwise it was unavoidable, given the amount of shipping assigned to the operation.

PRELIMINARY AND CLOSE SUPPORT FIRES

To observers watching the invasion beaches on Saipan a few minutes before the assault began the destruction wrought by the preparatory bombardment from naval ships and aircraft seemed terrific. On June 11, planes from Mitscher's task force had struck heavily at Saipan, Tinian, Rota and Guam, for the first round of preliminary bombardment. Two days later seven of Spruance's fast battleships worked over Saipan with their heavy guns, while minesweepers covered the adjacent waters, and swimmers from naval underwater demolition teams stroked their way to the shore line in futile search for underwater obstacles. On the 14th, the day before the landings, the fire support ships of Turner's task force took over and poured a still heavier concentration of fire onto the beaches and into adjacent areas. Meanwhile naval aircraft were striking inland coast defense guns as well as the beach defenses in the area between Garapan and Agingan Point. (See map 16.) Beginning at dawn on June 15, Turner's support ships moved to within 2,500 yards of the shore and stepped up their fire against the landing beaches and their flanks. At seven o'clock naval gunfire lifted momentarily to permit a heavy air strike by bombers and fighters parallel to the beaches. When this was terminated, the battleships and cruisers resumed their fire until the troops were a mere half-mile offshore. Five-inch fire from the destroyers arched over their heads and landed on the beaches until they reached the 300-yard line. Then, as the big ships' fire lifted inland, the gunboats let go with their 20- and 40-millimeters, and 4½-inch rockets in a last-minute effort to extend the neutralization of the landing areas for as long as possible.

Yet, in spite of the apparent magnitude of this intensive bombardment, Japanese artillery and mortars which many assumed would have been silenced opened up on the assault troops as they began to cross the reef. The fire grew heavier as the troops hit the beaches and continued throughout the day of the initial landings to decimate the marines and to check the anticipated rapid advance from the shore to the line marked for securing the beachhead. Casualties for the first two days reached the appalling figure of 4,000—far in excess of what had been predicted on the basis of high confidence in the effectiveness of preliminary and preassault naval and air bombardment. Preliminary or preparatory fires are those delivered before the day of the attack; and preassault fires, those on the morning immediately before the initial landings. The inadequacy of both at Saipan was one of the main reasons why Holland Smith committed all of the 27th Infantry Division. Since that left no floating reserve for Guam, Nimitz was forced to postpone that operation.

The truth is that at Saipan neither air nor naval gunfire support was adequate. A still more unfortunate truth is that these deficiencies might have been remedied in time had naval planners properly read the lessons of previous operations in the Pacific. Certainly by June of 1944 it should have been clear that heavy casualties at Tarawa were due, in considerable part at least, to faulty bombardment, while the relative ease with which the Marshalls were taken could be ascribed in no small measure to the very effective naval, aerial, and artillery preparation before the landing. A month after Saipan was taken, the quick reduction of Guam, which was defended almost as heavily as Saipan, was to be attributed by many to the fact that for thirteen days before the assault naval vessels and aircraft subjected Guam to a carefully planned, methodical, and concentrated bombardment. Only two days of such preparation were allowed for Saipan.

Not only was the preliminary naval gunfire at Saipan insufficient in amount, but in many instances it was ineffectively executed. This was especially true of the bombardment delivered by the fast battleships of Spruance's Fifth Fleet on June 13. These vessels had fallen down at Betio, but apparently had performed well at Kwajalein. Saipan, however, was a different type of a target. Firing there made it evident that the crews of these ships had been trained chiefly in the traditional techniques of naval surface warfare, and their gunnery personnel were not adequately educated to the requirements of shore bombardment. Since Spruance needed these fast battleships as floating antiaircraft batteries for his fleet carriers, he could ill afford to allow them to close within range of shore batteries. Thus these battleships, even though their gunnery crews were relatively inexperienced in the work at hand, were forced to fire from ranges of over 10,000 yards. Important targets were obscured, and the gunners tended to concentrate their fire on large buildings and other easily sighted objects of insignificant military importance. The old battleships and supporting vessels of Turner's task force did a far better job the following day. They had had more experience and practice in naval gunfire support and were allowed to move within effective range of the priority targets.[33] Even so, captured Japanese documents revealed that most artillery positions away from the water's edge escaped destruction entirely and were able to remain in operation for four days after the assault began.[34]

As soon as the initial wave landed, naval fire slacked off, and immediately the marines on the beach were subjected to a shower of enemy shells and mortars from Agingan Point, Charan Kanoa, and the low ground to the rear of the landing beaches. (See map 16.) The old battleship *Tennessee* took Agingan Point under fire but failed to silence most of the guns in that area. These were, in fact, not put completely out of action until June 17, two days later. Had more naval fire been concentrated on the flanks of the assault troops and had the ships employed a box barrage (fire blocked successively ahead and to the flanks of the beaches as the marines moved ashore and inland), much of the damage done in the early hours of the landing could have been avoided.[35]

Unfortunately, too, the shortcomings in naval gunfire were not offset by aerial bombing. Navy aircraft were assigned the duty of neutralizing all artillery positions and troop movements east of a line 1,000 yards from the beaches, which was the terminus of naval gunfire responsibility. This neutralization was not accomplished, either because an insufficient number of planes was assigned or because their pilots were inadequately trained in this type of action. Ground reconnaissance, after the beachhead line had been seized, showed several enemy field pieces, located in open terrain without any concealment from the air, that had been left intact. A Marine Corps board set up in 1945 to evaluate the effectiveness of air operations during the war, concluded that at Saipan "it was obvious that the preparatory bombardment was inadequate and did not approach the optimum neutralization desired." [36]

Subsequent failures in naval gunfire on the first day ashore were due chiefly to enemy artillery. It had been planned that naval close support of troops would be controlled by shore fire-control parties attached to each battalion, headed by a marine spotting officer and a naval gunfire liaison officer. These parties were furnished by joint assault signal companies which were landed on Saipan with the early waves. They suffered severe casualties and were consequently unable to perform their duties adequately until replacements could be obtained. Thus the deficiencies of the preliminary and preassault bombardment snowballed into near disaster in the first phase of the operation. The failure to knock out all but the shore line enemy positions meant that proper communications with ground troops could not be maintained after the landing had been effected. Hence, until artillery was landed in the afternoon of the first day, the marines were virtually powerless to do anything other than hold grimly to the beaches. Against the heavy concentration of enemy artillery, advance to the line needed to protect the beachhead was virtually impossible.[37]

Happily, the record of naval gunfire support after the first day of the operation offsets somewhat its earlier failures. In spite of its inherent limitations, naval gunfire is peculiarly adapted to the requirements of island fighting. Naval guns are generally not as accurate as land-based artillery, and the flat trajectory of their shells vitiates their effectiveness against targets located on the reverse slopes of high hills and mountains. These unavoidable defects, however, are more than offset by the high degree of maneuverability of which ships are capable. The terrain on Saipan offered ample opportunity for naval vessels to demonstrate their virtuosity as a supporting arm to the ground troops. Although the main ridge runs in a generally north-south direction through most of the length of the island, frequent outcroppings occur more or less at right angles to the mountain range and the shore line. As the troops moved northward, these lesser ridges obstructed their advance. Artillery alone was incapable of clearing out all the enemy defenses in the valleys behind these hills. But ships firing perpendicular to the line of advance could easily penetrate into these positions and destroy them. Marine and army personnel alike were unanimous in their praise of naval gunfire both close and deep, and one Japanese officer concluded that this was the greatest single factor contributing to the American victory.[38]

Four battleships, five cruisers, and thirty-nine destroyers were on call early in the operation, except for the interruption occasioned by the Battle of the Philippine Sea. Requests for close support ordinarily originated from the battalions and were monitored by naval gunfire liaison officers assigned to the regimental, division, and corps headquarters. This supervision by higher echelons permitted proper coordination of fire and, for the most part, caused no serious delay in the execution of the requests. Destroyers were usually assigned to pinpoint firing missions against known enemy gun positions, one destroyer to each battalion being the usual allotment. They were almost uniformly accurate and prompt. For heavier saturation fire, cruisers and battleships were normally used and were very effective. Thus in the zone of action of the Second Marine Division the navy laid down a three-day barrage, reducing the town of Garapan to a shambles and permitting its occupation against only nominal resistance.[39]

The innumerable caves which honeycombed the island also offered a novel opportunity for naval vessels. Many of these caves faced the sea and were therefore invulnerable to artillery fire. Infantry landing craft converted to gunboats, first used in the Marshalls, were especially adept at reducing these cave positions. These homely little craft, because of their shallow draft, could move close ashore and wipe out machine gun nests with comparative ease. For heavier anti-cave work, destroyers and occasionally even cruisers were assigned, and to good effect.[40]

Another useful service performed by the navy was night illumination, thanks to Harry Hill's innovation at Eniwetok. Star shells fired either at regular intervals or on request from the ground troops provided an effective deterrent to enemy infiltration after dark. Since the Japanese relied so heavily on this sort of tactics, their defensive power was considerably weakened. Ground troops would have preferred an even steadier rain of star shells, but within the limitation imposed by shipping space, the supply was steady and the delivery well executed.[41]

As compared with the assistance given to the fighting troops by naval ships, close air support was decidedly inferior. In the early part of the operation, close support missions were flown exclusively by navy planes, and only toward the end of the operation were army aircraft based at Aslito (renamed Isely Field after Commander Robert H. Isely USN) employed for this purpose. At no time were specially trained marine pilots available for this type of work.

The deficiencies in close air support can be attributed to a number of factors. Inadequate training of the pilots, overcrowding of radio circuits between ground troops and aircraft control agencies, an unwieldy system of liaison and control, and poor coordination between air, naval gunnery, and artillery were the chief reasons for the failures. Navy pilots had received only nominal training in support of ground troops, and army aviators almost none at all. Again, the task at Saipan was more difficult than that at Kwajalein. It was believed necessary that the army airmen identify targets by means of dummy runs before executing their missions and this, of course, necessitated frequent delays, since both infantry and artillery had to halt while these practices were being held.[42]

From the point of view of the ground troops, the chief defect in close air support was the long delay often experienced between the request for and execution of air strikes. To each battalion and regiment was assigned an air liaison party made up of one officer and five enlisted men. Requests for support missions originated with these parties and had to be approved both by division headquarters and by the Commander Support Aircraft, stationed aboard ship. After final approval had been given, the Commander Support Aircraft then designated the agency to control the strike, which would normally be either his own staff, the flight leader of the aircraft unit assigned, the air coordinator, or occasionally the Commander Aircraft for the Landing Force, who was stationed ashore. This complicated procedure inevitably slowed down the execution of desired missions as requests and orders moved with majestic pace up and down the chain of command. Only one radio circuit, the support air request net, was assigned to these communications, and it proved inadequate. It was hard enough to serve the forty-one air liaison parties and the various control agencies and aircraft on station, but even more serious was the fact that the carriers themselves had precedence over all other stations on the net, even for merely administrative communications. It is therefore not surprising that the average time lag between requests and execution was something over an hour, nor that marines and army troops were skeptical about the efficacy and flexibility of the air arm as a close supporting weapon. The experience at Saipan only reinforced the Marine Corps' long-held conviction that greater decentralization of control and better communications were needed, that its own pilots were the best indoctrinated for close support missions, and that in future amphibious operations escort carriers manned chiefly by marine aviators should be assigned exclusively to this duty.[43]

Unlike close air support, artillery on Saipan for the most part functioned efficiently and greatly aided the forward advance of the infantrymen. Deep support was normally provided by the 155-millimeter guns and howitzers of XXIV Corps Artillery. In addition, under the latest table of organization, each marine division was allowed an artillery regiment consisting of two 105-millimeter battalions (twelve howitzers each) and two 75-millimeter pack howitzer battalions (twelve pieces each). On Saipan an additional howitzer battalion was assigned from the Fifth Amphibious Corps to each division, giving them a total of five artillery battalions. Initially, divisions released their artillery to regimental control during the landing phase of the operation, although this procedure was subsequently reported to have been a failure by one division commander.[44] After the assault phase, artillery was returned to corps or division control so that as many as eighteen battalions were capable of massing fire in support of the three-divisional attack to the north. This was considerably more than the marines were accustomed to and was fully appreciated by the men.

Terrain features, to be sure, occasionally hampered the artillery. Caves which opened to the sea could not be touched by land-based guns or howitzers, and elsewhere defensive positions were sometimes so well protected that they could only be eliminated by demolitions or flamethrowers. Each infantry regiment controlled organically four 75-millimeter guns (half-tracks) which could sometimes be employed for such direct fire missions.

Artillery was also handicapped by the uneven movement of the various divisions in the northward attack commencing June 23. On frequent occasions requests for fire in the 27th Division's sector were refused on the grounds that the marines were so far ahead on either flank that their lines would be endangered. As it was, the Eighth Marines were shelled by American guns on five different occasions and the Sixth Marines once during the period of the northern sweep.[45] In spite of these difficulties artillery support was generally well handled and of great value to the infantry troops.

THE SHIP-TO-SHORE MOVEMENT

Obviously the most critical period of any amphibious operation is during the ship-to-shore movement and the first few hours of the landing, before artillery can be emplaced. At Saipan this transfer of troops from tank landing ships and transports to shore was carried out on a larger scale than at any time previously in the Pacific and was in general a marked success. Landing eight battalions abreast over a treacherous reef through which there was only one channel was a monstrous task. Small boats could not traverse the reef, so amphibian tractors had to be relied on exclusively for getting the first waves ashore. They were preceded by armored amphibians whose job was not only to lay down a last-minute preparatory fire (75- and 37-millimeter) along the beaches, but also to support the assault to the beachhead line about 1,500 yards inland.[46]

This line was reached in places, despite the unexpectedly heavy artillery fire from the beaches which began as the troops crossed the reef. But in several sectors plans miscarried. Amphibian tractors whose speed was slightly faster than that of their armored counterparts sometimes crowded the latter and in some cases, actually passed through them, thereby masking the fire of the armored amphibians. In the Second Marine Division's zone a more serious mistake was made when the troops were carried off course and landed considerably north of their scheduled beaches. (See map 16.) The Second Battalion Landing Team of the Eighth Marines, intended originally for the division's southernmost beach, was actually put ashore about 900 yards to the north of its designated spot. Since this battalion was on the right flank, it threw off the entire division's landing, and worse still, widened the gap between the Second and Fourth Divisions.[47] This error exposed the flanks of both divisions and was not rectified until the second day of the operation, and then only temporarily. The error was due in part to an unexpected northerly drift of the current and in part to heavy fire on the southern approaches which persuaded amphibian drivers to veer to the north.[48] In spite of this error and in spite of mounting opposition from the shore, the movement can generally be considered a success. Within twenty minutes after the first wave landed, over 8,000 troops were ashore—an achievement unequalled in any previous amphibious operation.

Once the shore had been reached, all did not go so well. The basic plan of operations used by the Fourth Marine Division had prescribed a blitz amphibious assault, continuous from shipboard to the first high ground about a mile inland. At that point, or near it, the tractors were to discharge their troops, who would then set up a perimeter defense supported at first by the 75- and 37-millimeter guns of the armored amphibians. This, it was anticipated, would permit the establishment of an initial beachhead of sufficient depth to permit the deployment of assault troops on the ground and to land reserves on the beach, and for mopping up the area immediately ahead of the shore line. These plans broke down almost as soon as the first tractors hit the water's edge. On the extreme right of the Twenty-fifth Regimental Combat Team's sector, on the southernmost beaches, opposition was very heavy, and with some exceptions tractors in the assault waves were unable to proceed any great distance inland. This meant that troops had to debark at or near the water's edge, causing much confusion as succeeding waves came in. For the first hour of the assault the troops extended only twelve yards inland. On the regimental left, hostile fire was not so heavy, and tractors were able to clear the beach to as far as 700 yards inland before debarking troops. But the initial plan for armored amphibians to furnish the fire support for these early waves failed entirely. Of the twenty-four armored tractors assigned to the Twenty-fifth Regiment, only seven ever got as far as the designated beachhead line, and these were all with the left battalion. Northward, the Twenty-third Regimental Combat Team was experiencing similar difficulty. As the first wave landed, some armored amphibians went as far inland as fifty or seventy yards, but others were seen wandering aimlessly up and down the beach, some drivers refusing, even under orders, to advance. As succeeding waves of tractors hit the shore, increasing numbers disembarked their troops on the beaches regardless of prior plans or orders. In both assault battalion sectors of this regiment, only eight armored and eleven troop-laden tractors reached the beachhead line.[49]

Above Charan Kanoa, the area of the Second Marine Division, similar difficulties were being encountered despite the fact that Major General Thomas E. Watson, commanding the Second Marine Division, had persuaded Holland Smith to accept a modification of the original plan in his sector. According to this change, the armored amphibians would proceed inland and clear only the immediate beach areas. The first wave of troop-laden tractors would follow them and discharge their men beyond the beach. All subsequent waves were to debark on the beaches themselves.[50] In most cases thirty yards was the extreme limit reached by these tractors before they unloaded troops. Heavy casualties were incurred by the armored amphibians, which explains in part the reluctance of their drivers to go farther. Three were knocked out in the water and another twenty-eight disabled on land.[51]

The conclusion is inescapable, then, that this part of the assault (especially in the Fourth Division sector) was a failure and that the failure rose out of an initial error in the conception of the potentialities of the armored and troop-laden tractors as land vehicles. Japanese artillery and mortar fire, of course, contributed in no small measure to the general confusion. Had the preparatory fires by ships and aircraft lived up to expectations, casualties would have been greatly reduced. Even the armored amphibians were too lightly protected to withstand anything heavier than light machine guns. Once out of the water, they were too vulnerable to warrant their use as tanks, which was essentially the function they had in this instance. But aside from the unexpectedly heavy enemy opposition, neither the armored amphibians nor the passenger-carrying tractors were capable of maneuvering over the terrain faced by the assault troops. Debris in and around Charan Kanoa, the swamp in the area of Lake Susupe, tree stumps, shell holes and ditches made movement all but impossible. Once stalled in their attempt to find passable avenues inland, they lost their momentum, and their formations broke down. This, in turn, rendered them still more vulnerable to enemy fire. Better intelligence as well as more effective preliminary and preassault bombardment might well have avoided some of the confusion that existed.[52]

JAPANESE AND AMERICAN TACTICS ASHORE

In spite of the heavy casualties on the first two days of the operation (June 15–16), the choice of the western beaches was wise. As previous intelligence had shown, heavy Japanese defenses were concentrated in the Magicienne Bay area, and even as late as June 19 General Saito continued under the illusion that a landing in that area was forthcoming. There can be no doubt that a measure of tactical surprise was achieved by the attack. The Japanese plan of defense was based on two hypotheses: first, that the American forces could be contained within the initial beachhead; and second, that the Japanese fleet could destroy them there along with the transports and their escorts that had brought them to the island. The first hope was dispelled by June 17, as the marines slowly worked their way inland. The second went down with the lost carriers in the Battle of the Philippine Sea. Thereafter, Saito was compelled to fall back on the Mount Tapotchau line and fight a delaying action as best he could.[53]

Against these tactics, the marines' doctrine of aggressive, hard-hitting warfare was to prove extremely effective, and once the initial beachhead had been secured, not as costly in lives as some critics have maintained. About one-fourth of all marine casualties occurred on the first two days of the operation. Marines had long been indoctrinated with the value of speed in the amphibious operations. As a military organization whose primary function was to seize advance bases for naval use, the Marine Corps had for years constantly stressed the necessity of a rapid seizure of the beachhead line as the controlling principle of all their tactical plans. Holland Smith, both by training and character, was singularly suited to put this doctrine into action. As he described it, his overall tactical plan, like that in the Gilberts and Marshalls, was based on the principle of maintaining constant and unremitting pressure on the enemy and "of by-passing strong points of resistance for mopping up by reserve elements, in order to press the attack to better ground, to reach and destroy the enemy, and to prevent him from utilizing the terrain to its best advantage." In order to establish security in by-passed areas, he insisted on the maintenance of vigorous antisniper patrols at all times. Where possible, advances were directed along ridge lines rather than in the undergrowth of valleys. Saipan was, as he described it, primarily "a battle of movement and perpetual patrolling."[54] In the end, after the main force of the enemy's defensive action had been spent, he had to be dug out of his caves and retired positions by demolitions, hand grenades, flamethrowers, and bomb and shell fire.

During the war and since, there has been much theorizing about the alleged differences in tactical doctrine between the Marine Corps and the Army. Saipan itself touched off a good deal of this because of the bitter controversy precipitated when Holland Smith relieved Ralph Smith, commanding general of the 27th Infantry Division. It is commonly believed among laymen and sometimes asserted within the two services themselves that the Marine Corps sacrificed lives in its insistence upon speed, while the Army was more conservative of manpower at the expense of time; that the marines relied relatively little on artillery and heavily on infantry, while the army seldom launched an infantry drive without previous heavy gunfire and aerial preparation; and that the by-passing and mopping up technique was typically a Marine Corps tactic whereas the Army believed in driving the enemy back on a solid front until his defenses crumbled.

In fact, as was observed on Kwajalein, there are few if any important theoretical differences in tactical doctrine between the two services. Marine and army officers alike are trained in the same basic field manuals. The training given by the Marine Corps Schools, in both basic and advanced infantry tactics, differs in no significant detail from that imparted to army personnel. In each case stress is put on the necessity for a balanced employment of all arms—infantry, artillery, and air support, in the proportions most suited to the occasion. It is impossible, of course, fully to prove or disprove the allegation that marine commanders are generally more prodigal of manpower than their counterparts in the army. Comparative casualty figures for different operations are almost always meaningless, since all the pertinent factors such as terrain and quantity and quality of enemy defenses are never constant. Even in battles like Saipan, where the two services fought side by side, such comparisons are of little value. In this operation, in fact, the percentage of casualties after the 27th Division began to come ashore was probably somewhat higher for the army division than for either of the two marine divisions.

This cannot be conclusively proved because of the admitted unreliability of casualty reports for the first day and because of the fact that the Fourth Marine Division submitted no casualty reports at all for June 15. But an estimate can be made. The Second Marine Division listed 1,575 casualties for June 15 alone, or more than one-fourth of its total (5,870) for the entire operation. If this figure is subtracted from the final casualty report for the capture of Saipan, the remainder is 4,295, which represents the casualties after June 15. This means that after the first day's action losses sustained by the Second Marine Division were 19.7 per cent of its total manpower. In the 27th Division, which did not begin to go ashore until after June 15, the percentage was 20.9. Since the Fourth Marine Division also suffered heavily on the first day, it can be assumed that a comparison between its casualty figures and those of the 27th Infantry Division would lead to similar results. In fact, if one considers that it was not until the sixth day of the operation, or well after the beachhead had been secured, that all units of the army division came ashore, the differential between percentage casualties in the army division and those of the two marine divisions during the post-beach assault phase is probably much greater than these figures indicate, the army's being still higher. This, though inconclusive in itself, detracts somewhat from the argument that army tactics on Saipan were particularly designed to save lives.[55]

As to the theory that the marines were more parsimonious of their artillery than was the army, there is no evidence in this operation to substantiate it. It is true that according to the tables of organization at the time, marine divisions had, in deference to their amphibious character, lighter organic artillery than did their army counterparts. Whereas the artillery regiment of each marine division was allowed two battalions of 75-millimeter pack howitzers and two of 105-millimeter howitzers, the army division had three battalions of 105-millimeter howitzers and a battalion of 155-millimeter howitzers.[56] Thus, as far as *organic* artillery was concerned the army division was, on paper at least, considerably stronger.

But the difference was more apparent than real. Actually, on Saipan during the first phase of the operation, marine divisional artillery was strengthened by the addition of one 155-millimeter howitzer battalion to the Second Marine Division and one 105-millimeter howitzer battalion to the Fourth Marine Division.[57] Once all Fifth Amphibious Corps artillery was landed, all three divisions depended on it for deep support. Also, on more than one occasion elements of the 27th Division's artillery were attached to corps for purposes of supporting marine troops. In other words, although theoretically weaker in organic artillery than the army division, in practice the two marine divisions were just as heavily supported when the occasion demanded. Holland Smith's headquarters could and did allocate artillery support in whatever quantities they thought necessary to whatever infantry units they believed needed it most, regardless of the uniform they wore. At the same time marine commanders had just as much respect for artillery as did army officers, and called for it in the quantities and at the time they felt the particular ground situation warranted. The limiting factor in marine divisional artillery was not a distrust of supporting fire or foolhardy reliance on the prowess of the individual infantryman. Rather it stemmed from the fact that lack of shipping space and the inadequacies of the earlier landing craft made it impossible to transport or to land over a beach the numbers of larger weapons assigned to army divisions.

One other distinction between Army and Marine Corps basic divisional organization deserves comment. That is in the organization of the rifle company and its component parts. In both the Army and Marine Corps each infantry regiment had three battalions, each battalion three rifle companies. The companies were in turn broken down into three platoons each consisting of three rifle squads. The rifle squad contained twelve men in the Army and thirteen in the Marine Corps. These men, carrying either Browning automatic rifles (BARs) or Garand rifles (M-1), spearheaded the infantry attack.[58]

In early 1944 a further breakdown was authorized in the Marine Corps, although the exact dates when this change was introduced varied among divisions.[59] Each squad was subdivided into three "fire teams." Each of these consisted of one BAR-man and three riflemen, the thirteenth man being the squad leader. The purpose and the result of this change was to spread the responsibility of leadership. Whereas under the old organization, the responsibility and authority of command reposed on only one man in the squad (the squad leader), now it rested on four—the squad leader and the three fire team leaders. By this devolution of authority it was believed that the principle of military leadership would be more widely disseminated and that the efficiency and aggressiveness of the rifle squad would be enhanced.

The army table of organization and equipment in 1944 allowed only one BAR per squad, and did not provide for a breakdown into fire teams. Although the army rifle company on paper at least was considerably stronger than its marine equivalent in supporting weapons such as machine guns and mortars, it was weaker in rifle power on the squad level by two BARs.[60] Thus, in theory, the marine rifle squad was more capable of independent action than was its army counterpart. On the occasions when artillery and supporting weapons could not be used to their optimum advantage, a marine squad would tend to be less tied down than an army squad, if for no other reason than because of its superiority in automatic rifles.

But here again the difference is more on paper than in fact. Regardless of the tables of organization and equipment, the 27th Infantry Division was issued many more BARs than were allowed. As far as practicable these were issued on the basis of one extra per squad and the squads were divided into two fire teams.[61] Thus the army squad on Saipan approximated if it did not quite duplicate that of the marines in fire power and organization.

One other alleged point of issue between Army and Marine Corps tactical doctrine was the question of aggressive by-passing tactics as against slow methodical destruction. To state that by-passing enemy pockets of resistance was a doctrine peculiar to the Marine Corps is pure fantasy. High ranking army officers in other operations in the Pacific used or favored the use of tactics similar to those employed by Holland Smith on Saipan. Major General Alexander M. Patch's first field order after taking over command of XIV Corps on Guadalcanal reads in part as follows: "Isolated points of enemy resistance will be contained and by-passed; they will be reduced later. . . ." [62] Major General George W. Griner USA, who eventually took over command of the 27th Division on Saipan and who was most critical of Holland Smith during that operation, was the chief advocate of precisely the same by-passing tactics on Okinawa a year later.[63]

SMITH VERSUS SMITH

All this is not to say that the interservice dispute engendered at Saipan was inconsequential. It resulted in the relief of a general officer of the United States Army, which though not unique in the history of World War II was certainly an unusual and alarming occurrence. It set off a train of charges and countercharges that were to strain Army and Marine Corps relations severely throughout the rest of the war and afterward. Hence the facts of the case deserve careful attention, not only for their own sake but also for the light they throw on the difficulties inherent in joint operations involving more than one branch of the armed services. But it must again be stressed that the real issue at stake was not a theoretical difference between Army and Marine Corps as to basic tactical doctrine. Nor was it limited to the incidents leading to the relief of Ralph Smith on June 24. Fundamentally, the issues were two: the military efficiency of the 27th Infantry Division as demonstrated throughout the entire operation (both before and after Ralph Smith's relief); and the competence of Holland Smith and his corps staff to command an operation of the size and complexity of the Battle for Saipan.

An examination of the first question will require a recapitulation of the activities of elements of the 27th Infantry Division during four separate periods of the operation: (1) the conduct of the 105th Infantry on Nafutan Point and of the 106th and 165th Infantry Regiments in Death Valley between June 22 and 25, which led to the relief of Ralph Smith (see map 16); (2) the subsequent record of the 106th Infantry in the Death Valley sector; (3) the escape of a Japanese contingent on Nafutan Point through the lines of the 2nd Battalion, 105th Infantry, during the night of June 26/27; and (4) the breakthrough of a Japanese counterattack north of Garapan in the sector of the 105th Infantry in the early morning of July 7, which led to the relief of the 27th Division (less the 165th Infantry) from further active participation during the rest of the operation.

On June 21 it was apparent that the army's four-battalion attack against Nafutan Point had succeeded in breaking the back of defenses there and that all that remained to be done was to mop up the remaining Japanese forces, which the 105th Infantry estimated to number between 300 and 500 men.[64] Meanwhile the two marine divisions to the northward were reaching a position where they would have to spread out laterally as the Fourth Marine Division approached the base of Kagman Peninsula abutting eastward.

Consequently, in the morning of June 21, Holland Smith issued his Operation Order #9-44, which stipulated that one battalion of the 27th Division plus a light tank platoon was to complete the occupation of Nafutan Point. The rest of the division was to revert to corps until ordered into marine lines on the main front. At five o'clock that afternoon Ralph Smith phoned Holland Smith, protested that one battalion would be insufficient to do the job, and recommended strongly that the entire 105th Infantry be allowed to remain on its present front lines.[65] For the rest of the day the 105th was unable to make any appreciable progress against Japanese resistance, so corps headquarters agreed to follow Ralph Smith's suggestion and keep the entire regiment, less one battalion in reserve, to clean up Nafutan Point.

This change of plans was issued by corps headquarters in a mailbrief received by Ralph Smith early in the morning of June 22; this ordered one regimental combat team of the 27th Division to "continue the mission in the Garrison Area [Nafutan Point] of cleaning up remaining resistance and of patrolling that area." Meanwhile Ralph Smith, following his telephone conversation with Holland Smith, issued his own Field Order #45-A. This directed the 105th Regimental Combat Team to "hold present front lines facing Nafutan Point with two battalions on the line and one battalion in regimental reserve . . . reorganization of the present front line to be affected not later than [11 A.M., June 22] and offensive operations against the enemy [to] continue. . . ."[66] Holland Smith, later, in requesting Ralph Smith's relief, claimed that this field order was in direct contravention of his own order #9-44, as modified by the subsequent mailbrief, which he said placed the 105th Infantry under his control with instructions to mop up the remaining resistance on the point.

This charge of direct contravention of orders was flimsy at best and was probably chosen for legalistic reasons rather than for its intrinsic merit. In neither the operation order nor the mailbrief from

Headquarters, Fifth Amphibious Corps did Holland Smith specifically designate the unit concerned. Nor did any orders issue directly from corps to the 105th Regimental Combat Team. If Holland Smith intended to remove this regiment from division control it is certainly not clearly stated either in his original order or in his mailbrief. His omission of any specific designation of the unit involved would hardly indicate any clear intention on his part to resume corps control over the 105th Infantry. Hence Ralph Smith was not deliberately, directly or indirectly, flouting his superior's orders when he issued his field order. Furthermore, Ralph Smith's instructions to "hold the line" until eleven o'clock on the morning of June 22 did not in reality contradict Holland Smith's order to "mop up resistance," since the delay was undertaken merely to permit the units of the 105th Infantry in the line to be shifted, after which offensive operations were to be continued.

By the afternoon of June 22 it became apparent that two regiments of the army division would have to be committed in the center of the main drive to the north between the Second and Fourth Marine Divisions. In order to provide a reserve for these troops Holland Smith decided to withdraw two battalions of the 105th from Nafutan Point, leaving the job of mopping up solely to the 2nd Battalion of that regiment. He communicated his intentions to Ralph Smith who at nine o'clock that night issued his Field Order #46 on the basis of these verbal instructions. About an hour later Headquarters, Fifth Amphibious Corps, released its Order #10–44, although this was not received at division headquarters until eleven-thirty that night. For this action, Ralph Smith was charged with usurping his rightful authority by issuing an order to a unit (2nd Battalion, 105th Infantry) not under his tactical control but under that of corps.

Actually, no such deliberate intention on the part of Ralph Smith is apparent. Technically speaking, no doubt, he was somewhat forehanded in issuing his Field Order #46 before actually receiving in hand the written order from corps to do so. However, there was no basic difference in the sense of the two, and in fact the phraseology is almost identical. Corps Order #10–44 stated that the 2nd Battalion, 105th Infantry was to continue operations at daylight "to mop up Nafutan Point," and "upon completion this mission revert to corps control as corps reserve." The only real difference between the corps and division orders was that the former made daylight the time of attack whereas according to the latter it was to be delayed until ten o'clock. Nevertheless this single discrepancy can be excused on the grounds that Ralph Smith's headquarters did not receive Order #10–46 until late at night and had felt compelled earlier to issue some orders to the 2nd Battalion to cover the next day's action. This single difference does not warrant the charge of contravention of orders that was subsequently brought against Ralph Smith. Nor does corps' later contention that the 27th Division's commanding general was exceeding his authority by issuing orders to a unit (2nd Battalion, 105th) not under his control seem justified. The inclusion in the corps order of the phrase "upon completion this mission revert to corps control" would seem to indicate that at that time at least the battalion was considered still to be under division control.[67]

The following day a more serious occurrence took place in the ranks of the 27th Division which was to strain "Howlin' Mad" Smith's never ample patience to the breaking point. This was the first day of the main three-divisional drive against the Mount Tapotchau line. Two battalions each of the 106th and 165th Infantry Regiments were ordered to relieve the Fourth Marine Division in the center of the line, after which the latter were to move eastward to occupy Kagman Peninsula. The line-of-departure for the 27th Division was established as the *"front lines held by the Fourth Marine Division at the designated jumping off hour,"* which was ten o'clock on the morning of June 23.[68]

At dawn the 165th Infantry moved to the line-of-departure and was prepared to launch its attack at the designated hour. However it was held up by the 106th Infantry on its left which arrived late and the attack was delayed for at least fifty-five minutes. This delay resulted in complete confusion along the entire line. The two marine divisions which had pushed forward as ordered, soon found their flanks exposed and had to retard their progress. By nightfall almost no advance had been made by the army troops. The fact that also on June 23 the 2nd Battalion, 105th Infantry, had been ordered to attack at dawn and to clean out Nafutan Point, but had failed to jump off until thirty minutes past one o'clock in the afternoon only served to strengthen the corps commander's ever growing conviction that the 27th Division was something less than an efficient and aggressive military unit.

On the following day, June 24, Holland Smith requested and received permission from Admirals Turner and Spruance to relieve Ralph Smith of his command.[69]

Certain points should be made in extenuation of the actions of the army units along the northern front on June 23. In the first place, the terrain and character of enemy defenses in the 27th Infantry Division's zone of action were unquestionably far more difficult than corps intelligence had supposed. This was the entrance to Death Valley and the location of a part of the main Japanese line of defense against expected landings in Magicienne Bay. Secondly, as one army observer concluded, "there is reasonable question as to whether or not corps allowed the division adequate time to prepare for the attack and move its troops and artillery forward to make the main effort." [70]

Although the division commander had cognizance of corps plans for the morning of June 23 by late in the preceding afternoon, the final corps order did not come through until eleven-thirty on the night of June 22. There was not enough time for the 165th Infantry to conduct proper reconnaissance of the roads and trails leading to the front line in their sector. As they moved out at daylight the 165th took a wrong road and became tangled with parts of the 106th as well as with rear elements of the Fourth Marine Division. As army units approached the marines' front line, they discovered that it did not correspond with the line-of-departure shown in the previous day's corps order, since some elements of the marines had withdrawn several hundred yards the day before under heavy enemy gunfire.[71]

None of these facts, however, fully exonerates the division's tardiness in jumping off or its failure to push forward throughout the remainder of the fighting on June 23. A night march along the road used to supply the Fourth Marine Division was feasible, if difficult. Reconnaissance parties could have been dispatched early in the morning to determine the exact location of the marines' lines and might have avoided the confusion that took place concerning the true location of the line-of-departure. The fact that the marines had withdrawn the previous afternoon, if anything, made the task of relieving them easier, since the division commander's field order designated the line-of-departure as the front actually held by the marines at the time of their relief.

Whatever the merits of the specific charges brought against Ralph Smith, the truth of the matter seems to be that the 27th Infantry Division was not performing with the degree of combat efficiency that Holland Smith expected and usually got from the marine divisions under his command. In his memoirs written after the war, he made no pretense that the specific legalistic charges brought against Ralph Smith had any significant bearing on the relief. Holland Smith's real reasons, as revealed here, were his convictions that the 27th Division had shown "all-round poor performance" and that "Ralph Smith has shown that he lacks aggressive spirit." Thus Holland Smith replaced Ralph Smith with Major General Sanderford Jarman USA, who had originally been assigned to the operation as Garrison Commander.[72]

Whether the succession of misfortunes that befell the army division were due, as alleged, to poor leadership, or to faulty training, inexperience, poor liaison with corps headquarters, or just bad luck is impossible to say and really irrelevant. The corps commander had reason to be dissatisfied, and if some of the specific grounds upon which he chose to ask for Ralph Smith's relief appear weak in retrospect, the general conduct of the division up to that point and later in the operation seems to justify the action. It was a command decision, made in the heat of combat and inevitably without benefit of a careful and prolonged sifting of all the evidence pro and con. The 27th Division had been slow to take Nafutan Point and had retarded the advance of the two marine divisions. A far more patient corps commander than Holland M. Smith might reasonably have concluded that a command shake up within the division was necessary. Holland Smith was not a patient man.

In this connection it is certainly germane to cite Ralph Smith's own testimony on the question as reported later by Jarman, who relieved him. Jarman, at Holland Smith's request, visited the division command post in the afternoon of June 23, where he relayed the corps commander's deep concern over the division's progress and added his own opinion that it was "not carrying its full share." Ralph Smith, according to this report, "immediately replied that such was true; that he was in no way satisfied with what his regimental commanders had done during the day and that he had been with them and had pointed out to them the situation. He further indicated to me that he was going to be present tomorrow, June 24, with his division when it made its jump off and he would personally see to it that the division went forward. . . . He appreciated the situation . . . and stated that if he didn't take his division forward tomorrow he should be relieved." [73] In fact, the division failed to make any significant headway the following day, and the relief was effected.

THE 27TH DIVISION AFTER RALPH SMITH'S RELIEF

The subsequent performance of the 27th Infantry Division confirmed in Holland Smith's mind his previous opinion of that command. Failure of the 105th Infantry Regiment to press the attack against Nafutan Point on June 22 was never adequately explained, and this failure had consequences dangerous to the entire operation. (See map 16.) Major General George W. Griner USA, who took over command of the 27th Division from Jarman on June 30, himself wrote: "It would appear from basic report that a faint-hearted attack was made. The means were available for complete success had a determined attack been made." [74] Then, on the night of June 26/27, about 500 Japanese escaped through the lines of the battalion without interference. Part of the force attacked Isely Field, and elements struck the 27th Division artillery installations as well as the command posts of the 2nd Battalion, 105th. The major part of the body, however, moved north and spent itself in a futile attack against the Fourteenth Marines and the Twenty-fifth Marines and was destroyed—but only after holding up a scheduled attack against Kagman Peninsula.[75]

Meanwhile, to the north in the area of Death Valley, the two marine divisions continued to be held back on either flank until June 29 when the army division finally completed its drive and the lines were straightened out. Without question, the terrain and the concentration of enemy positions in this sector made the going extremely difficult, and it is probable that neither Holland Smith nor his staff ever fully appreciated the problems involved. But there is also evidence that the quality of fighting exhibited by the 106th Regiment left much to be desired. At least, that was the opinion of Jarman who wrote on June 30: "Based on my observation of the 27th Division for a few days, I have noted certain things which give me some concern. They are . . . a lack of offensive spirit on the part of the troops. A battalion will run into a machine gun and be held up for several hours. When they get any kind of minor resistance they immediately open up with everything they have that can fire in the general direction from which they are being fired upon." He went on to say that if "a patrol comes in around their bivouac area they immediately telephone in and state they are under a counterattack and want to fall back to some other position. . . . I found that troops would work all day to capture well-earned terrain and at night would fall back a distance varying from 400 to 800 and sometimes 1,000 yards to organize a perimeter of defense." He concluded, "I had to, in the brief time I was in command of the 27th Division, issue an order that ground gained would not be given up, that the perimeter of defense was to be formed on the ground captured, and troops in the rear would be brought up."[76]

Finally, in the early morning of July 7, another and more serious breakthrough occurred in the zone of action of the 105th Infantry. Around five o'clock in the morning a banzai charge of the now desperate Japanese struck the front lines of the 105th, which was on the extreme left (west) flank of a two divisional front moving northward to complete the island's occupation. Estimates of the enemy's strength vary from 1,500 to over 4,000, but Major General Harry Schmidt USMC, who put the final figure at 2,500 to 3,000, is probably most nearly correct.[77]

Within an hour and a half the main enemy force had overrun the 1st and 2nd Battalions, 105th, had penetrated through a gap in the positions of the 1st and 3d Battalions, and reached batteries of the Third Battalion, Tenth Marines. After overrunning these, the enemy was finally stopped, at about seven-thirty in the morning. Two battalions of the 106th Infantry which were in division reserve were ordered up to retake the lost ground. By one o'clock they had recaptured the artillery positions, but they failed to pursue the counterattack further or to relieve the two westward battalions of the 105th Infantry which were now completely cut off and eventually had to be evacuated by sea after extremely heavy casualties. At this point Holland Smith ordered the Second Marine Division, then in corps reserve, to pass through the lines of the 27th Division. This was accomplished the following morning, July 8, thus removing the 105th and 106th Infantry Regiments from any further part in the operation.[78]

This incident precipitated another dispute between Army and Marine Corps commands. General Griner placed a large part of the blame for the disaster on the fact that corps had failed to honor his requests for additional tank support, "obviously because Headquarters did not accept my version of the importance of the action then in progress." He believed that the Fourth Marine Division, then facing minor opposition on the northeast, could easily have spared the tanks. Also he resented the fact that Holland Smith had seen fit to remove the bulk of his division from further combat operation even though they had succeeded by midafternoon of July 7 in reforming their lines and retaking part of the lost ground. He added later that it was his firm opinion that Holland Smith was "so thoroughly prejudiced against the Army that no Army division serving under his command alongside of Marine divisions will receive fair treatment." [79]

As in most of these disputes engendered on Saipan, where entirely different and often contradictory sets of facts and interpretations were adduced by each service, an objective conclusion is difficult to reach. As to the specific charge that Holland Smith's refusal to commit marine tanks was in any way to blame for the success of the Japanese counterattack, the records do not support it. Actually Griner's request for tanks was not made until eleven o'clock on the morning of July 7, at least six hours after the Japanese attack had commenced and well after its fury had been spent.[80] Holland Smith's refusal to send tanks at this juncture may have slowed up the recovery of lost ground but could hardly have had any influence on the main course of the Japanese attack.

It does appear clear on the other hand that Holland Smith underestimated the number of enemy involved in the counterattack. As late as July 15, he was arguing that it was probably not more than 1,500,[81] although both Spruance and General Harry Schmidt accepted the figure 2,500–3,000 as being closer to the truth.

There can be little doubt that the 300-yard gap between the lines of the 1st and 3rd Battalions of the 105th Infantry was one of the reasons for the success of the breakthrough. Spruance concluded that "the gap between the 1st and 3rd Battalions 105th Infantry could have been readily closed by swinging the left of the 3rd Battalion forward.

In any case, this gap should have been covered by local reserves and/or planned machine-gun fires." [82] Yet, while the initial responsibility for neglecting to close this critical gap lies at the door of the battalion commanders, it must be said that the constant pressure which was applied by corps headquarters on all lower echelons in the name of speed more than once discouraged them from taking precautions which common sense and standard procedure alike dictated. In this particular case, it is pertinent to note that on the night before the Japanese counterthrust two battalions of the 105th Infantry were pushing the attack until six-thirty, too late to permit them to consolidate their lines before nightfall.[83]

The army was not alone in criticizing corps' repeated failure to take into sufficient account factors of time and space when handing down orders. Marine regimental commanders made frequent complaints on this score. On one occasion, on June 22, the Twenty-third Marine Regiment was given less than three hours to move up out of reserve, cross an area of extremely rough terrain about 2,500 yards distant, and launch an attack. The regimental commander considered the time allowed entirely insufficient. On another occasion the Twenty-fifth Marines were allowed only an hour and a half to move across 10,000 yards of enemy-infested country and launch an attack. Regimental commanders also complained that corps' insistence on pushing the attack until only a half-hour before dark often left their troops on untenable ground and that the policy of jumping off right after dawn gave them too little time for reconnaissance.[84]

Undoubtedly, Holland Smith on occasion demanded the impossible. Be that as it may, there can be no doubt that in the long run the corps commander's hard-hitting tactics paid off in results. The most formidable enemy island fortress yet to be broached by American forces was taken in twenty-one days, with about 24,000 Japanese killed and almost 1,000 captured.[85] A forward naval base was firmly secured—not the best natural harbor in the Pacific but useful for providing logistical support for future operations. A key enemy airfield was captured and, more important, American fields were soon to be established as bases for intensive, very long-range bombing operations against the heart of the Japanese Empire. As an exercise in amphibious doctrine, the Saipan experience was to prove invaluable to future landings. No outstanding deficiencies in standard doctrine had been made manifest. Certain defects in execution had been revealed, notably in the delivery of air and naval support and in the employment of armored amphibians as land tanks. Some of these errors were to be remedied in subsequent island assaults. None of them proved fatal at Saipan.

With the island declared secured on July 9, troops, ships, and planes of the expeditionary force were now free to take up the offensive against the remaining two targets in the Marianas—Tinian and Guam.

4. The Conquest of Tinian

The capture of Tinian was in some ways unique in the annals of World War II amphibious warfare. True, in some respects the operation resembled other landings completed or yet to be undertaken in the Pacific. The assault troops were transported aboard tank landing ships to the island at night, arriving at the transport area approximately at dawn. They then were debarked in amphibian tractors and moved from the line-of-departure to their assigned beaches in normal wave formation. The way had been prepared by prolonged naval and aerial bombardment conducted according to standard procedure. The character of the enemy defense differed in no material respect from those already encountered in island warfare, and the tactics employed by the marines to overcome these defenses were essentially the same as on Saipan and elsewhere.

But here the similarity to other Pacific operations ceased. Tinian was different for two reasons. First, it was only three and one-half miles away from Saipan, which was already in use as an American base. Second, the most strategically located beaches, and those which were used by the landing forces, were somewhat less than 600 yards in width, and of this area less than 200 yards could be traversed by amphibian tractors or trucks. Because of the first fact, many of the difficulties that plagued the marines on Saipan were eliminated or at least reduced to manageable proportions. Naval and aerial bombardment before the assault could be more prolonged and deliberate. Artillery based on the southern tip of Saipan could easily destroy and neutralize enemy positions in the northern sector of the neighboring island. Intelligence was greatly simplified. There was virtually no limit to the number of aerial reconnaissance sorties that could be flown over the island. Beach reconnaissance and documents captured on Saipan completed the picture and gave the attacking force minute and detailed information concerning Japanese defenses and troop dispositions. Supplies could easily be transported from Saipan to Tinian in small craft on a purely shore-to-shore basis.

Yet the narrowness and contour of the beaches chosen raised difficulties not hitherto encountered in the Pacific and considerable ingenuity was required to overcome numerous complications. Under these circumstances congestion of troops, vehicles, or equipment at the water's edge might have been fatal and had to be avoided at all costs. This called for a modification of the standard ship-to-shore technique, and, more important, necessitated a radical revision of the normal shore party procedure.[86] Both of these ends were accomplished with utmost finesse, thus demonstrating the high degree of flexibility which standard amphibious doctrine had achieved by this time. In fact, as a study in pure technical skill and amphibious virtuosity, the assault on Tinian excels any other landing in the history of the war.

Planning for the operation began in late April, before the departure of the attack force from the Hawaiian area. En route to Saipan, Holland Smith's headquarters drew up a tentative draft of the operation plan which was submitted to the general when the convoy reached Eniwetok. The original concept envisaged a landing on northern Tinian by what was essentially a shore-to-shore movement. The reason for choosing this part of the island was to permit full use of shore-based artillery emplaced on southern Saipan.[87] Subsequent events were fully to justify the choice.

Early in July, as the fighting on Saipan was reaching its conclusion, Holland Smith began holding daily conferences to work out the details of the next operation. By that time frequent aerial photographic sorties had been flown over Tinian, a number of revealing Japanese documents had been captured, and considerable information had been gleaned from prisoners of war on Saipan. From these data it appeared that the original concept of the attack was basically sound. There were only three possible landing points on the island. First, excellent beaches existed in the area of Sunharon (Tinian) Bay on the southwest coast. (See map 17.) These were by far the best of the entire island, but for that very reason the enemy chose to place his major defenses in that area. A second possible landing area appeared to be in Asiga Bay on the east coast. This, too, was heavily mined and defended, and was exposed to the northeast trades. The third and remaining landing area consisted of two extremely narrow and coral-choked beaches on the northwest edge of Tinian. This was obviously the best place to land if the Saipan-based artillery was to be fully exploited. Yet it was questionable if amphibian tractors could negotiate beaches of such limited width, or if two divisions of marines could be landed and supplied across them.

To answer the first question, it was decided to dispatch the newly organized Amphibious Reconnaissance Battalion of the Fifth Amphibious Corps to reconnoiter both the northern beaches and those on Asiga Bay. On the two successive nights of July 11 and 12, detachments from this battalion, joined by naval underwater demolition personnel, successfully completed this mission. Under cover of darkness these hardy individuals were launched in rubber boats from destroyer transports and paddled to points about 500 yards offshore. The rest of the distance they swam—stealthily enough to avoid de-

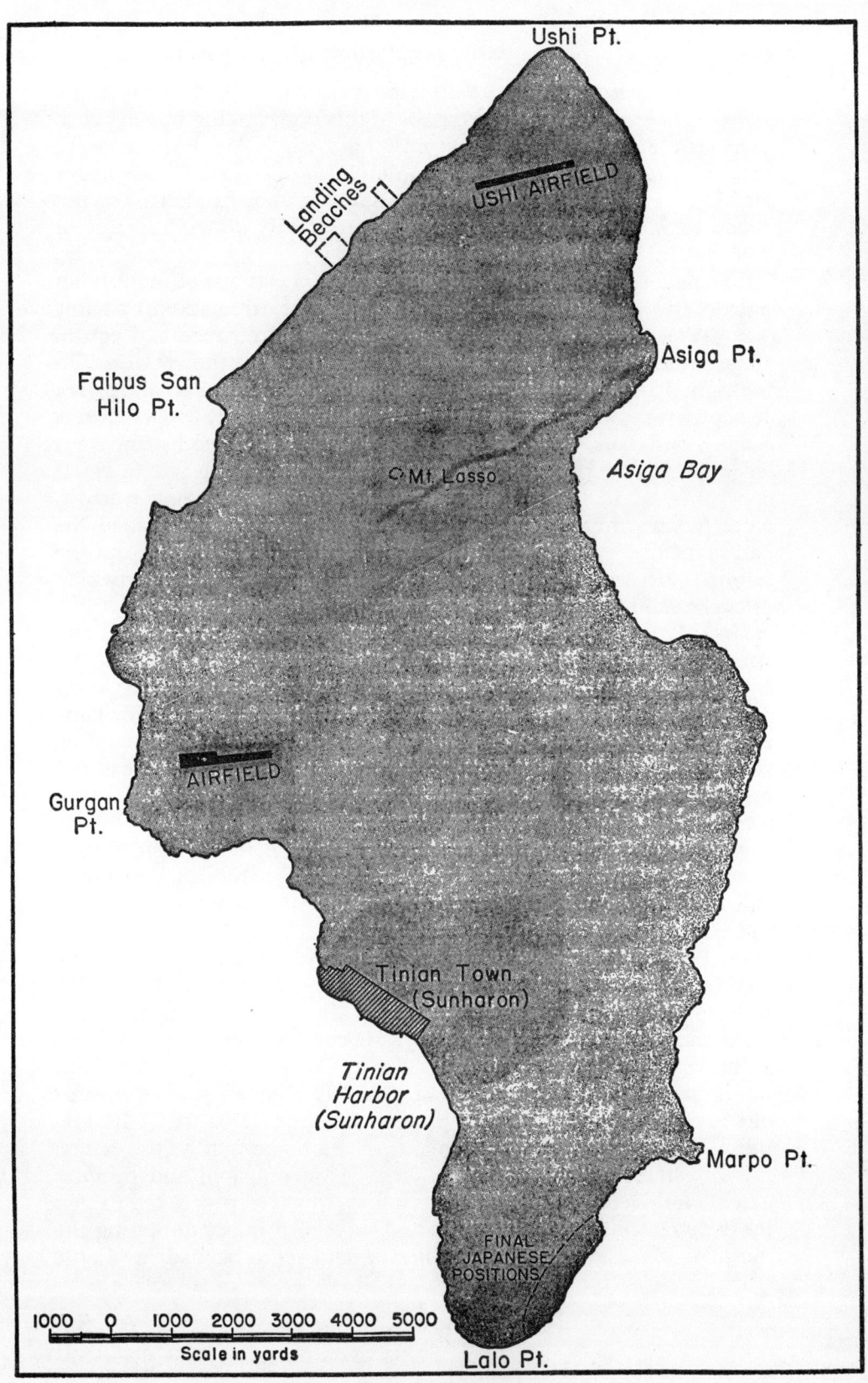

MAP 17. Tinian.

tection by enemy patrols who on some occasions walked within a few yards of their operations. The result of this undertaking was to prove what had already been suspected, that Asiga Bay beaches were heavily mined, flanked by unscalable cliffs, and beaten by a heavy surf. On the other hand, the reconnaissance of northwestern beaches closest to Saipan indicated that they were lightly mined and free of excessive surf.

On the left flank beach, the area usable for passage of amphibian tractors and vehicles was about sixty yards in width, backed by a low coral ledge which was sufficiently fissured to permit men and equipment to be debarked and to move inland through the crevices. On the right flank beach it was discovered that there was a sandy area of about 160 yards in width, but of this about ninety-five yards was covered with coral boulders, and it, too, was obstructed by low coral ledges. Altogether then, the two beaches offered landing area of about 600 yards, of which only 125 were usable by Dukws or tractors. Nevertheless the advantages of artillery protection outweighed the hazards of the forbidding beaches, and it was decided to carry out the original plan, trusting to preparatory fire and a novel shore party plan to overcome the difficulties involved.[88]

On July 12, Major General Harry Schmidt USMC relieved Holland Smith of command of the Fifth Amphibious Corps and of the Northern Troops and Landing Force, although Smith still retained overall command of Expeditionary Troops in the Marianas. Major General Clifton B. Cates USMC took over Schmidt's job as commanding general of the Fourth Marine Division.[89] Three days later Rear Admiral Harry Hill relieved Turner as commander of the naval attack force to be committed to the capture of Tinian.

None of these shifts, however, made any change in the basic plan of attack, which was finally approved by Spruance on July 18. The target date for Tinian was set as July 24. Cates' Fourth Marine Division was to bear the brunt of the beach assault. It was to land two of its regimental combat teams, the Twenty-fourth and Twenty-fifth Marines, on the left and right flank beaches respectively, to seize the line needed to secure the beachhead, and then, on division order, to make the main effort toward Mount Lasso. The Second Marine Division, after a diversionary movement against Tinian Town, was ordered to land on the same beaches to the rear of the assault force, and prepare for offensive operations on corps order. The 27th Infantry Division, minus the 105th Infantry Regiment, was to be held in corps reserve.

While these plans and orders were being prepared and promulgated, intelligence sections of all echelons involved proceeded to step up their reconnaissance missions and succeeded in accumulating the most detailed and accurate intelligence data yet to be made available to marines in the war. From July 5 to 22, seven photographic missions were flown by various squadrons attached to corps or to naval attack force headquarters. From these, excellent mosaic maps of the entire island were constructed and distributed to all echelons down to battalion commanders. Obliques of the landing beaches and of terrain inshore were equally useful. To be sure, one divisional commander (Cates) criticized the aerial photographic interpreters for tending "to call every shell hole or ground scar some form of enemy position," but he added that on the whole photographic coverage was excellent and far better than on Saipan. Schmidt was of the opinion that photographic reconnaissance for the operation "left nothing to be desired." [90]

Personal reconnaissance was also carried out to a degree never before witnessed in the Pacific. In the Fourth Division, not only the commanding general and his staff, but all regimental and battalion commanders and even some company commanders made several flights over the island in order to familiarize themselves with the terrain on which they would have to fight.[91]

Aerial photographic sorties, beach reconnaissance, interrogation of prisoners of war on Saipan, and captured enemy documents all combined to provide a far more accurate and complete picture of the enemy situation than assault troops had in the past enjoyed. They revealed that the main enemy defenses were centered around Tinian Town, that the Japanese would concentrate initially on the beaches, and if thrown back would retire to set up a direct defense of the two airfields on Ushi Point and Garguan Point, of Tinian Harbor and of gun positions in the southern area of the island. Schmidt's intelligence section estimated the total enemy strength, consisting of the 50th Infantry Regiment reinforced (commanded by Colonel Ogata IJA), plus several independent air and naval units, to amount to 8,350 troops. In addition there were 3,000 home guards of dubious military value. Data accumulated after the fight was finished showed the latter figure to be too low by about 550 men, but the error was of no great importance.[92]

On the other side of the picture, it is apparent that the Japanese on Tinian were in complete ignorance of American plans and totally miscalculated American strategy, even though the occupation of Saipan had given them conclusive warning of the inevitability of an attack on Tinian. As late as June 25, orders from the Japanese commander's post east of Mount Lasso read: "the enemy on Saipan as far as conditions can be determined can be expected to be planning an attack on Tinian. The area of that landing is estimated to be either Tinian Harbor or Asiga Harbor." Again on June 28, Ogata issued his "Battle Order" which set forth only two basic plans: (a) in the event the enemy lands at Tinian Harbor, and (b) in the event the enemy lands at Asiga Bay. No plans or dispositions of troops were made in anticipation of a landing on the northwest coast.[93] There can be no doubt that in doing so the marines achieved complete tactical surprise.

On the night of July 23, thirty-seven tank landing ships at anchor off Saipan were fully loaded with the troops, vehicles, equipment and ammunition of the Fourth Marine Division, designated for the initial assault on Tinian. Close at hand rode the ships of the two transport divisions which would carry two regiments of the Second Marine Division on a diversionary feint against Tinian Town and would later disembark them along with the third regiment across the northwestern beaches. Battleships, cruisers, destroyers, and other vessels of the fire support groups had steamed out to sea on assigned courses which would bring them back to Tinian by daybreak. Before daylight the troop-laden ships weighed anchor and proceeded toward their assigned areas. At dawn the island of Tinian, which had suffered a considerable beating since July 11 from planes, ships, and land-based guns now received the full fury of the attack. Three battleships, three heavy cruisers, three light cruisers, sixteen destroyers, and thirty gunboats saturated the beaches and adjoining areas with their fire. A total of 244 navy and army planes made repeated strafing and bombing runs. From Saipan sounded the guns and howitzers of thirteen battalions of artillery, 156 field pieces in all.[94] After a ten-minute delay, the armored amphibians and troop-carrying tractors proceeded toward their assigned beaches, astern of the rocket-firing gunboats.

On the left the Twenty-fourth Marines hit their beach at about seven forty-five on the morning of July 24. To their right the Twenty-fifth Regimental Combat team landed about ten minutes later. Some machine gun and rifle opposition met the two regiments as they approached the shore, but it was insignificant compared to what they had seen on Saipan. The four assault battalions rapidly overcame the rather feeble opposition at the beaches and advanced inland in good order. The reserve battalions were all landed by eleven o'clock. Shortly after noon, the division artillery reached land and within four hours both the Tenth and Fourteenth Regiments had two battalions each ashore and in position. By dark the reserve infantry regiment, the Twenty-third Marines, had landed and had taken over the right sector of the expanded line, and one battalion of the Second Marine Division had been landed in reserve for the Fourth Marine Division.

Meanwhile, ten miles to the south, the transports lifting the bulk of the Second Marine Division's troops carried out their feint against Tinian Town. Empty landing boats were sent in as far as the line-of-departure off the beach under cover of naval gunfire. The demonstration drew heavy fire from coastal defense guns and the main reserve of the island garrison was held ready to counterattack a landing that never materialized.[95]

By the close of the day on the northwestern beaches, the marines of the Fourth Division had occupied a beachhead approximately 4,000 yards wide and 1,500 yards in depth. The price for this day's successes was phenomenally low by usual standards—only fifteen men killed and 225 wounded in action.

Early the next morning, July 25, the enemy sallied forth as anticipated in a full-scale and well-organized counterattack. Beginning about two o'clock in the morning, Japanese infantry and tanks hit all along the line. The marines were ready for them. By seven o'clock the full weight of the attack had been spent. However, one group of Japanese soldiers managed to filter through a gap between the Twenty-fourth and Twenty-fifth Regiments and to attack battery positions of the division's artillery, but these enemy troops were obliterated in short order. By mid-morning, mopping up operations were finished and a total of 1,200 Japanese dead were counted in the area, as well as five disabled tanks. It was during these few hours of morning fighting that the Fourth Division, in the words of General Cates, "broke the Jap's back in the battle for Tinian." [96]

The remaining eight days of the operation, though not exactly uneventful, were spent in rapid pursuit and destruction of a now thoroughly disorganized enemy. Most of the Second Marine Division got ashore on July 25 and by the afternoon of the following day had penetrated to the east coast against nominal resistance. On the same day the Fourth Division occupied Mount Lasso, the highest elevation on the island. For the next three days both divisions moved rapidly down the island, meeting no resistance worthy of mention. By now it was evident that the Japanese were withdrawing to the hills and caves of the southern coast to take up their last stand. Troops and tanks made an average advance of almost 3,000 yards a day across the rolling farm country, covered with sugar cane fields and studded with small patches of woods. Morale was high—the marines were "heading for the barn."

On July 29 the Second Marine Division ran into somewhat stiffer opposition on the east side of the island, but not enough to check progress seriously. On the same day the Fourth Division was slowed up somewhat as it drove through heavy cane fields hiding small elements of the enemy. On the 30th the Second Marine Regiment of the Second Division, on the extreme left flank, met sudden and stiff resistance, but it was promptly eliminated by artillery fire. By nightfall the Second Division had reached the enemy's final defensive position in the high plateau on the southern tip of Tinian. Routes of access were few and difficult, as all the approaches were blocked by cliffs and jungle growth. Meanwhile the Fourth Division was running into heavier opposition as it approached Tinian Town. Japanese holed up in caves had to be liquidated by infantry-tank teams using demolitions and flamethrowers, but the town itself was in ruins and was easily taken. On those beaches, the advancing troops discovered heavy mine defenses, placed there in anticipation of a main assault landing in that area.[97]

The next two days saw the heaviest fighting since the initial landing. As the marines approached the southernmost ridge of the island where the Japanese had retired for their final stand, they at last came up against hazards of terrain and fierce enemy fighting more reminiscent of Saipan than anything they had hitherto encountered on Tinian. In the early morning hours of July 31 the Fourth Marine Division repulsed a counterattack on its right flank while at the same time the Second Division came under heavy mortar fire. From dawn until eight-thirty that morning the southern tip of the island was placed under an aerial, naval, and artillery preparation which was probably the most intense and the most effectively controlled of any bombardment thus far witnessed in Pacific amphibious operations. As the day progressed, the troops found the going steadily tougher. Counterattacks were repulsed in both divisions' sectors. The passages up the side of the cliffs were heavily studded with mines, and half-tracks and tanks were unable to negotiate the roads in many cases. Yet in spite of these difficulties, an average advance of about 2,000 yards was made, and both divisions had elements on top of the southern ridge by nightfall.[98]

Early in the morning of August 1 two small banzai charges were delivered against the Second Division but were beaten off. For the rest of the day the opposition was disorganized and light, although the terrain still made progress difficult. Both divisions advanced to the southern coast, and shortly before seven o'clock in the evening Schmidt declared organized resistance to have ceased. The island was considered secured except for mopping up remaining pockets of enemy soldiers.[99]

The American forces had suffered only 2,289 casualties of which 399 were deaths. On the other hand, over 5,500 Japanese soldiers were killed and some 400 captured.[100] In his final summary, Schmidt's intelligence officer attributed the rapid and relatively inexpensive capture of the island to several factors, the largest of which was the tactical surprise achieved by landing on the northwestern beaches. Other reasons were the efficiency of naval gunfire and artillery in destruction of enemy positions which had been accurately located by intelligence, and the close coordination between artillery and ground forces. Finally, not the least cause for the complete success of the operation "was the aggressive spirit of the assault troops that contributed in large measure to the surprisingly rapid conquest of the island of Tinian." [101]

5. *Amphibious and Tactical Performance at Tinian*

The preassault bombardment of Tinian was superior to that of Saipan. Targets were more easily ascertainable, the firing and bombing was more prolonged and deliberate, and both ships and aircraft benefited greatly from the experience they had received in the earlier operation. Naval bombardment of Tinian began on June 13, two days before the landing on Saipan. Initially it was designed mainly to prevent enemy interference with operations on the larger island, but as soon as ships were available a program of deliberate and methodical destruction of enemy defenses was instituted. Commencing on June 27, and continuing for a period of about a week, three light cruisers were assigned to daily destructive fire missions on pinpoint targets. After Saipan was secured this program was stepped up rapidly and successfully coordinated with artillery and aerial bombardment. On July 16, and for a week thereafter, one destroyer a day was assigned to the artillery officer of the Fifth Amphibious Corps to fire on designated targets from mid-morning until sunset. Every night destroyers harassed the beaches of Tinian Town and Asiga Bay in an effort to knock out enemy personnel working on the beach defenses and to confuse the Japanese as to the selection of assault beaches. Heavy cruisers joined on July 20 and finally, on the day before the landings, July 23, a total of three old battleships, two heavy cruisers, three light cruisers and four destroyers worked over the island. From dawn until the moment of the landing on July 24, a large assemblage of naval vessels, ranging in size from battleships to gunboats, bombarded the narrow beaches and surrounding areas with a merciless rain of shells and rockets.[102]

While naval guns were striking at all known targets they could reach from sea, aircraft were bombing, and artillery was saturating the northern part of the island with 155-millimeter shells. Artillery fire against Tinian was begun just as soon as the XXIV Corps Artillery landed on Saipan. By July 17 a total of thirteen battalions were in position to fire against targets on the northern part of the island, and by the day before the assault they were executing as many as 155 firing missions a day. Air strikes began on July 15 and were gradually stepped up until July 24, when they concentrated chiefly on the landing beaches. Fire bombs were dropped in the thick brush immediately inland to clear the area of cover in which the Nipponese might conceal themselves. Just before the landing, bombers and strafers were able to detonate several mines off one of the beaches which underwater demolition teams had been unable to reach the night before.[103]

The notable success of all this preparation by supporting arms was due in large measure to the close coordination between air, naval gunfire, and artillery. Shortly after the capture of Saipan was completed, definite sectors of responsibility for covering Tinian were assigned. Artillery was to engage targets in the northern sector; aircraft and naval vessels covered the southern two-thirds of the island. Conferences were held daily among representatives of the three at Holland Smith's headquarters and were continued when Harry Schmidt took over command of Northern Troops and Landing Force. At these meetings a careful study was made of each target, its location and terrain, before assigning it to the appropriate support weapon. Daily reports were made of results obtained during the previous day's bombardment. Fire was continued on priority targets until destruction was reasonably sure, and in some instances enemy positions were successively turned over to each of the supporting weapons to make triply certain of their obliteration.[104]

Thus the burden imposed on each arm was considerably lessened, and the net result was that enemy defenses were almost completely disorganized before the landing took place. But disorganization is not synonymous with total destruction, and in some instances reports from firing ships were overoptimistic and lulled the landing troops into a false sense of security. Thus, on the morning of the landing, 6-inch coast defense guns located south of Tinian Town caused some damage to the attacking forces, and the next day 155-millimeter guns on Fabius San Hilo Point opened up on the beaches. Yet Admiral Hill's ships had reported both of these installations to have been previously destroyed.[105] Evidently, there was still some fight left in the enemy in spite of the heavy beating he had taken before the landing began.

Close naval gunfire support on Tinian was even more efficient than on Saipan, where it had proved such a useful weapon. Preparation fire was delivered on request of division commanders prior to the morning jump off whenever it was felt that artillery could not adequately cover the area under attack. A particularly heavy and intensive bombardment coordinated with artillery and air was delivered in support of the final attack on the high ground in the southern part of the island. A total of 6,410 rounds of 14-, 8-, 6-, and 5-inch ammunition was fired on this occasion, and the barrage was delivered so close to the front line that the marines had to be ordered to dig in during the bombardment. Counterbattery, interdiction, and destructive fires were delivered daily on call. Harassing missions usually began at sunset and terminated at dawn. As the troops forged down the island, and the area occupied by the enemy was rapidly reduced, coordination between air and naval gunfire became increasingly difficult, and congestion of ships in the firing areas created a serious problem.[106]

Night illumination was used even more effectively than on Saipan, especially during the counterattack on the morning of July 25. In general, call-fire procedure was carried out more expeditiously than on Saipan, chiefly because of the experience gained on the latter and because all personnel both afloat and ashore had been carefully briefed. Shore fire-control parties functioned well. In spite of the fact that replacements were obtained for some of the casualties suffered in the earlier operation, there was still a shortage of personnel in the First Joint Assault Signal Company assigned to the Fourth Marine Division.[107] The only major deficiencies reported were in coordination of fires. According to Cates's operations officer, coordination of requests for preparatory fires within the Fourth Marine Division "still left much to be desired due to the lack of workable regimental naval gunfire nets and due to the time element after receipt of attack orders." He also noted that improvement in the coordination of air, artillery, and naval gunfire for counterbattery work was needed.[108] The worst example of this occurred on August 1 when a heavy strafing aerial attack was flown by mistake into an area on the southern part of the island already under bombardment by ships. No great damage was done, but the naval vessels had to cease fire before completing their mission.[109]

Air support for Tinian was furnished by army P-47's flown from Isely Field as well as by carrier-based aircraft. As was the case on Saipan, all requests from ground troops for air strikes had to be approved and were directed by the Commander Support Aircraft on the attack transport *Cambria*. A subordinate officer, designated Commander Support Aircraft Ashore, remained at Isely Field to direct operations there and to assist in apportioning missions between army and navy planes; another subordinate, the air borne Air Coordinator, was stationed over Tinian. Air liaison parties were organized and attached to battalions, regiments, and divisions in the same manner as on Saipan, except that the divisional parties were each alloted two extra officers. As before, it was their job to request and direct close support missions via the support air request net and to keep their unit commanders advised of all air strikes in every zone of action. In this manner it was presumed that troop commanders would be made aware of the disposition of planes over the entire area and would be in a better position to coordinate their own requests with those of other units.[110]

Soon after the troops landed, enemy artillery and mortar fire began to fall on the beach area. In a short time planes were flown in on request of the Fourth Division's Air Liaison Party, and most of the firing pieces were silenced. During the next few days, as the marines moved forward on Ushi Point plain toward the airfield and toward Mount Lasso, navy and army planes continued to knock out enemy mortar and artillery positions and, what was more important, practically isolated the battlefield by interdicting enemy troops and vehicles attempting to move northward to reinforce the defenses there. As the American front swung rapidly southward from Mount Lasso plateau, air support was used with great success in supplementing artillery preparations before the troops jumped off each day and in knocking out artillery positions in defilade. Finally, on the morning of July 31, aircraft played an important role along with naval gunfire and artillery in delivering the final blow to the remaining enemy troops who had holed up in the caves and ravines of the island's southern plateau. At shortly after seven o'clock that morning, all artillery and naval shelling ceased in order to permit a large-scale air strike. For thirty-eight minutes, 111 planes dropped sixty-nine tons of bombs. The results were more than satisfying. Prisoners of war later reported that the shock felt from the attack was almost unbearable. Great strips of land were blasted clear of underbrush, and the smoke and concussion blinded and confused the defenders. There can be no doubt that the blast and fragmentation effect of this mass bombing contributed signally to the final destruction of the Japanese defenses in their last bastion. This is in spite of the fact that in one regimental sector it was reported that approximately thirty-five per cent of the bombs landed in the valley north of the proposed target line.[111]

In general, it appears that close support aviation for Tinian was a more flexible weapon than for Saipan. All flights of support planes were arranged on a time basis, each flight being scheduled to be on station an hour and a half after the preceding flight. Carrier-based planes alternated with army P-47's so that, in theory, there should have been planes on station at all times, ready to render immediate aid to the troops on request. In practice, however, this was not always the case. On several occasions a particular flight of planes, having expended all its ammunition, flew back to its carrier or to Isely Field long before the expiration of the one and one-half hour period to which it was assigned. Thus, the troops in the area in question were left without any air protection until the next scheduled flight put in its appearance.[112]

Troop commanders felt again, as on Saipan, that there was excessive delay between requests and execution of air strikes. Even when planes were on station, it usually took them from twenty to thirty minutes to act on the requests; and if they were not on station, delays of an hour were not at all uncommon.[113]

Radio nets were not overcrowded as they had been in the Saipan operation, but, as was the case there, the support air request net was still sometimes used for communications to and from carriers about matters not connected with close support. Another difficulty arose out of technical deficiencies in the communications equipment aboard *Cambria,* which broke down on several occasions to add further complications to the already cumbersome system. Another delay was caused by the practice of closing down the support air request net while arrangements were being made for an air strike and while the strike was in progress. This sometimes resulted in a piling up of requests from air liaison parties who were unable to get access to the Commander Support Aircraft until a particular strike had been completed. In one instance it was well over an hour before one of the parties could get on the air to submit a request for a strike to take place later. Even though this particular request was ultimately denied, the unit commander involved was at a loss to know how to use his other supporting arms until he could make certain whether or not aircraft would be assigned to him. There were times also when the Commander Support Aircraft failed to pay proper attention to the order in which requests had been submitted. One air liaison party had to wait nineteen hours before securing the requested planes although fully assured that the strike would be executed much sooner. In the face of these difficulties, it is little wonder that many troop commanders remained skeptical of the efficacy of close air support, at least under the complex organization then existing. But both divisional commanding generals agreed that the air strikes, when executed, were far superior to those on Saipan. Pilots were more familiar with the terrain, had a better appreciation of close air support requirements, and were better briefed.[114]

One novel feature of the aerial bombardment of Tinian was the employment for the first time of the napalm bomb. This was a fire bomb consisting of a jettisonable tank to be carried under the belly of a fighter plane and containing a mixture of gasoline with about six per cent napalm jelly. Just before the beach assault on Tinian, a naval expert on the subject arrived aboard *Cambria* and by showing a motion picture of the bomb's effect on land targets persuaded Harry Hill to try it out on an experimental basis. Since there was very little napalm on hand, it was decided first to use a mixture of oil and gasoline as a substitute, and several tests were subsequently made against different types of terrain. The results of these tests showed that the oil-gasoline mixture was effective against cane fields and wooden buildings (when a direct hit was scored), but comparatively ineffective against stands of ironwood. On the day before the landings, about thirty fire bombs (some containing napalm) were dropped in the area of the selected beaches, and burned off a considerable amount of the surrounding brush cover, although the effects on personnel were not clearly determined. Throughout the entire operation, a total of 120 jettisonable tanks were dropped, of which twenty-five contained napalm, and the balance a mixture of oil and gasoline. Napalm bombs proved to be considerably better against cane fields, shrubs, and wooded areas than either white phosphorus or thermite, the standard incendiary agents. Against personnel in open shallow foxholes or trenches, it was extremely effective, although its lethal effect on personnel in covered dugouts or blockhouses was considered doubtful. The final conclusion reached by Hill on the basis of reports from marine and navy observers was that the bomb gave great promise of success as an amphibious weapon in future assaults against densely covered islands.[115] Forthcoming operations were to corroborate this opinion and prove the value of the Tinian experiment.

Artillery, last but not least of the three supporting arms, functioned with almost unqualified success in the operation against Tinian. The two divisions were able to call not only on their organic artillery regiments but also had at their disposal the entire XXIV Corps Artillery, reinforced by the 27th Division's artillery. Such a heavy concentration of fire in an area of only eighteen miles square was considerably more than the marines had been accustomed to in past operations.

As soon as Saipan was secured, joint plans were prepared by all three supporting groups to render maximum effective support for the projected assault on Tinian. In view of the excellent artillery set up, this group was designated coordinating head of the combined agency.[116] Certainly the central factor governing all planning for the operation was the ability of artillery emplaced on Saipan to bring the northern beaches under fire immediately before the landing. As the troops approached the shore, fires were lifted inland, and Mount Lasso was effectively covered with smoke shells, in order to conceal the beaches from the view of enemy positioned there. On July 24 alone a total of 186 firing missions were completed by Corps Artillery, firing a total of 20,100 rounds.[117]

For the initial landing the Fourth Marine Division had, in addition to the corps artillery, four battalions of 75-millimeter howitzers which were ashore and firing by four-thirty on the afternoon of the first day. Each of these battalions had been preloaded in Dukws and embarked on a tank landing ship. Since ammunition was likewise preloaded, it was possible to land sufficient personnel, equipment, and ammunition to support the attack.[118]

During the first four days after the landing, corps artillery provided preparatory fires in advance of the daily jump off of the marines; but after that date, due to a shortage of ammunition, that particular job was left to the organic artillery of the divisions and to naval gunfire.[119] Harassing and interdicting fires continued to be delivered from Saipan, but as more and more units were moved to Tinian, less reliance was placed on the pieces remaining on the larger island. Their primary responsibility had been the northern half of Tinian, and once the marines had penetrated south of Mount Lasso their deep support was no longer vital.

If land-based artillery was responsible in no small measure for the success of the initial landing, the decision to place so much reliance on it raised new problems which no amphibious planners had yet been compelled to face. Specifically, the decision to land on the northwest beaches in order to exploit to the fullest the field pieces on Saipan necessitated a radical revision of standard logistical procedures. Something less than 200 yards of these beaches were usable, which made it essential that all beach congestion be eliminated. To avoid any such breakdown, it was necessary to develop a supply plan which would provide that all supplies cross the beach on wheels and be moved directly to supply dumps inland without any rehandling on the beaches themselves.

After a careful study of the amounts of supplies necessary to support the action and of means available to land them, a plan was evolved to exploit both Saipan and the available shipping as supply bases. Loaded trucks and trailers were to be put aboard the various small amphibious craft and shuttled back and forth between base supply dumps on Saipan and division supply dumps on Tinian. For the transfer of material from ship-to-shore, amphibian trucks and tractors would move directly to inland dumps on Tinian or, if necessary, to the front line units themselves. In addition, it was decided to maintain barges loaded with fuel in drums immediately off the reef; these would be accessible to amphibious vehicles in the quantities desired. For the movement of assault troops, equipment, and supplies, a total of eight transports, two dock landing ships, twenty tank landing craft, 195 smaller amphibious craft, 657 amphibious vehicles, and nine pontoon barges were employed.[120] This was a tremendous flotilla indeed, considering the size of the operation.

Initial supplies were provided by preloading thirty tank landing ships and two dock landing ships at Saipan with top deck loads consisting of balanced amounts of water, rations, and ammunitions sufficient for the whole attack force for the first three and a half days of the operation. These same tank landing ships carried the troops and amphibian tractors of the Fourth Marine Division, and four of them transported the division's artillery. The two dock landing ships lifted in their holds eighteen medium tanks each mounted on amphibious craft. This heavy top-deck loading was made possible for three reasons: the short distance to be travelled; the elimination of fuel items by the employment of floating pontoon barges; and the emplacement of all artillery over 75-millimeter initially on Saipan.[121]

Once the assault troops were landed, unloading proceeded rapidly. On the first day the amphibian tractors and trucks carrying troops and ammunition were unloaded from the tank landing ships, and all were waterborne by nine in the morning. Two trips to the beaches were made to debark all of the Fourth Marine Division, after which about 148 short tons of ammunition, rations, and water assigned to the division were carried to the inland supply dumps from the beaches. Also on the same morning the two dock landing ships discharged their thirty-six medium tanks and were on their way back to Saipan for another load well before noon. By the close of the following day the thirty tank landing ships had unloaded all their supplies, and in addition the transports carrying the troops and equipment of the Second Marine Division were almost emptied.

In order to facilitate unloading over Tinian's rough and narrow beaches, two novel devices were employed. Ten special ramps mounted on amphibian tractors were brought over from Saipan in the second trip of the dock landing ships. At the water's edge, these ramps carried vehicles over the abutting beaches until heavier pontoon causeways could be placed in position. Two of the latter were launched in the late afternoon of the first day and sent in to the shore. One struck a coral head en route and promptly capsized, but the second reached its destination and was successfully put to use by tractors landing supplies. The next day the remaining eight pontoon causeways were launched, of which six were landed and put into operation, the other two being swamped on their way in to the shore by the wash from a couple of incautious Higgins boats.[122]

The second and on the whole more successful scheme for artificially enlarging the beach area was the employment of two causeway piers which were assembled on Saipan, using sections of a partly destroyed Japanese pier at Charan Kanoa. These were towed to Tinian the afternoon of July 24, and one of them was in operation by six o'clock the following morning, although the second could not be moored properly until the 27th because of enemy mortar fire. They were put to good use and helped considerably to expedite unloading until a heavy storm on the night of July 29 broached one and wrecked the other. Thereafter, until Tinian Town was secured and its docks put into operation, all unloading was by Dukws and tractors, whose efficient handling in spite of heavy surf was one of the highlights of the operation.[123]

Shore party functions were performed for each division by its organic pioneer battalion assisted by the 1341st Army Engineer Battalion, which had been temporarily detached from the 27th Infantry Division. For the most part, all executed their jobs with exemplary efficiency, and a minimum of confusion was evident on the beaches. But back at the supply dumps some difficulty was experienced due to the manner in which supplies were apportioned to the two divisions. In order to be certain that each division received a just share of rations and ammunition, Dukws crossing either of the two landing beaches were dispatched alternately to the Second and Fourth Division dumps. Since Second Division dumps were to the rear of the left flank beach and Fourth Division's were behind the right flank beach, this entailed a great deal of criss-crossing by the amphibian trucks and caused an unnecessary delay. Had single dumps for rations, ammunition, and other classes of supplies been established, from which both divisions could have drawn, much of the traffic congestion might have been avoided.[124]

On Saipan, moreover, the shore party command group charged with responsibility of loading resupplies bound for Tinian ran into considerable difficulty. This group consisted at first of only three officers and six enlisted men, with three officers and twenty enlisted men temporarily attached. This was far too small a number to shoulder the responsibility of executing the major part of the resupplies from Saipan to Tinian. The causeway which they had to use for loading supplies was inadequate. On July 30, heavy seas washed out most of it, leaving only one section usable for both incoming and outgoing traffic, and later the pontoon was completely destroyed, making it necessary to move all operations to Tanapag Harbor. Beginning on July 25, the rapid movement of corps artillery from Saipan to Tinian greatly complicated the resupply plan, since it took six tank landing craft out of operation for the shipment of other supplies and equipment, and seriously overcrowded the already limited dock space. At no time did the loading group have sufficient motor transportation or a motor transportation officer competent to handle the technical problems of truck control and maintenance. In fact, most of the officers were engineers with little or no training in quartermaster functions, which was what the situation required.[125]

In spite of these difficulties on the Saipan end, no serious shortages, except for fuel, developed on Tinian as the operation progressed. Two merchant ships anchored close offshore from July 27 until the island was secured, and a steady stream of Dukws to and from these vessels maintained ammunition supplies at a fairly high level. As to rations, the records indicate that a reserve supply of approximately two days was maintained throughout the operation. In addition to those transported in the usual manner, by sea, some 3,300 rations were flown to the airfield on Ushi Point.

The initial plan for resupplying fuel was to ferry 400 drums a day via amphibian trucks, but this system proved slow and the rapid advance of the troops increased the demand so much that the reserves dwindled rapidly. Commencing on July 27, a daily supply of 600 to 800 drums was provided via pontoon barges. Tractors delivered the fuel from barges to beach dumps. However, before an adequate reserve could be built up on shore, the tail end of a typhoon hit the area, and no further unloading into the tractors could be risked. Fortunately, large quantities of Japanese gasoline were captured, and this averted any serious shortage which might otherwise have been felt. In spite of the fact that heavy seas lasting from July 28 to August 1 made the causeways unusable and stopped all night unloading across beaches by amphibian vehicles, the supply situation never became acute.[126]

Indeed, the successful execution of the supply plan against great natural odds remains in the end the most remarkable feature of the Tinian operation. In the words of General Schmidt's supply officer: "This operation was in many ways a remarkable demonstration of the fact that preconceived notions and amphibious doctrine can be altered radically on the spot. In effect, a reinforced corps was landed over less than 200 yards of beach and over a difficult reef, and was supplied throughout nine days of heavy combat without handling so much as one pound of supplies in the usual shore party manner. Everything rolled in on wheels. When a violent sea made impossible the landing of trucks, the Dukws took over all supply, supplemented to a minor degree by incoming air evacuation planes bringing in rations. The troops never lacked what they required at the time it was required." [127]

There was nothing particularly remarkable about the ship-to-shore movement at Tinian except that it was carried out with relatively little opposition and with few of the hitches that usually marred this delicate and difficult operation. Partly because of the experience on Saipan and partly because the nature of the beaches would have precluded it anyway, it was early decided not to send the armored amphibians or the amphibian tractors inland with the first wave of assault troops. Otherwise the movement proceeded as usual. Gunboats moved ahead first in line abreast and were generally more effective than on Saipan because the reefs permitted them to get within better rocket range of the beaches. Then came the armored amphibians, followed by troop-carrying tractors. They met with very little gunfire as they approached. Mines remained on the left flank beach, and three tractors were lost when they nosed onto the shore. Otherwise there were no casualties. As the armored amphibians approached the beach, they retired to the flanks for supporting fire to permit the tractors behind them to unload their troops at the water's edge. Although the leading wave of troops was dispatched from the line-of-departure ten minutes later than planned, favorable conditions of wind and tide enabled it to pick up lost time so that it was landed only six minutes behind schedule. These conditions continued, and the three leading battalions landed within two minutes of the prescribed times, and all other waves came ashore within one minute of their schedule. One regimental commander reported that there were several instances where amphibian tractors landed too far to the right or left of the defined landing area and blamed it on inadequate indoctrination and training of the crews and drivers. But this was the only reported instance of any such miscarriage, and the same report admits that in the three opposed landings in which the Twenty-fourth Marine Regiment had used tractors this was the first time they were used successfully. At Namur their landing plan had not been executed on schedule because there were not enough tractors available at the proper moment, and at Saipan there had been some delay in getting ashore for the same reason. At Tinian, the report continued, "adequate tractors were originally assigned and landing was accomplished as intended." [128]

Some difficulty was later occasioned in the beaching of artillery and tanks. The headquarters and service battery of the Tenth Marines was afloat on a tank landing craft for eighteen hours, overnight, and the two 105-millimeter battalions had the same experience. This was caused primarily by the lack of proper control at the chief control vessel anchored off the beaches. Despite repeated radio messages informing that vessel that the artillery was afloat and waiting to land, no action was taken and the pieces were finally moved onto the ramp without authority. On the right flank beach, the Fourth Division had trouble getting its tanks and shore party equipment ashore. The reef edge was rough and had wide, deep fissures. On the first day, two bulldozers were taken ashore by a tank landing craft, but a third fell into a fissure and was lost. Thereafter, all bulldozers were landed on the beach to the left, which proved much easier. Tanks also had difficulty landing to the right, and although eventually an entire tank company was brought ashore there on the first day, it was a slow process. But in spite of the natural obstacles, all this heavy equipment was landed in such a manner that at no time was the beach blocked either to the continued landing of personnel or of artillery.[129]

No radical new developments in infantry tactics occurred during this operation, but certain marked improvements in standard techniques were notable. Outstanding among these was the employment of tanks and the functioning of the tank-infantry teams. This was due partly to the fact that the terrain of Tinian was more favorable for tank operations than that of Saipan and partly to the experience that had been gained in the earlier operation. Although Mount Lasso and the high ground around it, as well as the plateaus and cliffs at the extreme southern end, were hard to traverse, the gentle undulating ground on the rest of the island afforded good opportunities for well-directed and excellently coordinated tank-infantry attacks. Each regiment was assigned one reinforced medium tank company totalling eighteen tanks plus a platoon of four flamethrower tanks and two light tanks. These same companies supported the respective regiments to which they were attached throughout the operation, and thus the disadvantages experienced on Saipan of having different tank units serve the same infantry unit were overcome.[130]

Patrols also were used more frequently and effectively than on Saipan. The crushing defeat sustained by the enemy in his counterattack during the early morning of July 25 and his subsequent withdrawal to the southern end of the island, coupled with favorable terrain, permitted the employment of daily patrols from 500 to 1,000 yards ahead of the front lines. Normally when these lines were stabilized for the night, patrols would conduct reconnaissance and return before dark. The Fourth Division Reconnaissance Company twice during night reconnaissance contacted appreciable groups of enemy and made valuable observations on the withdrawal from Mount Lasso. Intelligence patrols, usually in groups of four to six, were used freely throughout the operation; and mopping up patrols were also employed frequently, especially along the southern ridge after the island had been secured.[131]

Perhaps the greatest improvement over Saipan, at least as far as lower echelons were concerned, was in the coordination and control exercised by higher authorities. Attacks were halted soon enough before darkness to permit the development of favorable ground for defense. Orders for the continuation of the attack were received soon enough to permit preliminary reconnaissance. Finally, attacks were generally better coordinated by higher echelons so as not to expose flanks unduly.

One notable feature of the Tinian operation was the high degree

THE MARIANAS 371

of cooperation between army and marine units. After the bitterness engendered on Saipan the close and efficient interservice coordination on Tinian was all the more remarkable. True, no army infantry troops fought on the island, but other army units played significant parts in the final victory. Indeed, since so much of the success of the operation depended upon artillery based on Saipan, on shore party operations, and on close air support, it can be concluded that the army's share in the reduction of Tinian was far out of proportion to the number of its personnel actually employed. In addition to artillery on Saipan, a large portion of which was army, one whole battalion of army engineers was detached from the 27th Division to perform vital shore party duties for the Fourth Marine Division, and army P-47's flew a large percentage of the close air support missions requested by marine units.

As for the Japanese, they were never able to employ any major defensive tactics except in the counterattack on the morning of July 25. The enemy's plan was to defeat the marines on the beach, to defeat them by counterattack at the beachhead if the landing succeeded, to harass them by infiltration and occasional artillery fire from concealed positions, to use artillery fire during times when the Americans were firing in the hope of creating the impression among the attacking forces that their own shots were falling short, and finally to die gloriously causing seven deaths to one in fatal banzai charges. In the end, of course, none of these measures succeeded, except perhaps that from the Japanese point of view their deaths were glorious, even though the exchange ratio was not seven to one, but for the whole Tinian operation about thirteen to one in favor of the Americans. The fact is that the weight of the combined naval gunfire, aerial bombardment, artillery, and infantry attack, and the surprise and speed with which the initial landing was effected threw the enemy for a loss from which he never even partially recovered.[132]

In nine days Tinian was secured with minimum casualties to the attackers. The campaign for the northern Marianas was completed. Meanwhile, about a hundred miles away, the Third Amphibious Corps was successfully pressing the attack against Guam.

6. *The Reoccupation of Guam*

Plans for Guam were made concurrently with the preparations for the attack on Saipan. Major General Roy S. Geiger USMC, Commanding General of the Third Amphibious Corps, flew with his staff to Pearl Harbor late in March and held daily conferences with Turner and Holland Smith, and with the naval attack force commander for Guam, Rear Admiral Richard L. Conolly USN. These conferences lasted until April 7 when the Third Corps delegation returned to its headquarters on Guadalcanal. For purposes of this operation the corps was designated Southern Troops and Landing Force. Thus Turner as Commander of the Joint Expeditionary Force and Holland Smith as Commanding General, Expeditionary Troops, under Admiral Spruance, supervised the Guam operation, but Conolly and Geiger were the principal implementing commanders.

The tentative plan for Guam devised at Pearl Harbor called for a simultaneous landing of the Third Marine Division on beaches between Adelup Point and the Tatgua River and of the First Provisional Marine Brigade on beaches to the southward between the village of Agat and Bangi Point. (See map 18.) The Brigade consisted of the Fourth and Twenty-second Marine Regiments (reinforced). This brigade was the nucleus of what later was to become the Sixth Marine Division, but it had not yet been organized to full divisional strength. For artillery support, in addition to the pieces organic to lower echelons, Geiger had attached to his corps troops a battalion of 155-millimeter howitzers and another of 155-millimeter guns, supplemented on occasion by the weapons of the Ninth and Fourteenth Marine Defense Battalions.

In order to facilitate joint planning between the naval support vessels and the corps troops, Conolly flew to Guadalcanal on April 15 and was shortly joined by his flagship, *Appalachian*. The army turned over Cape Esperance for training purposes, and for two weeks marines went through the usual dull but necessary routine of preparing themselves for the coming offensive. Late in May a full-dress rehearsal, more elaborate than usual, was held in the same area.

In spite of every effort made to simulate the attack on Guam, Guadalcanal did not offer reef, beach, and terrain features resembling those of Guam, and many artificialities had to be introduced into the rehearsals which detracted somewhat from their value. Nevertheless, these preliminaries were more than ordinarily fruitful, chiefly because of the opportunities provided for close cooperation between forces. Conolly's presence on the spot and the close liaison between his staff and those of corps and the two marine units made for a degree of coordination hitherto rare in the Pacific. Indeed, if the Guam operation is distinctive at all as an amphibious exercise, it is because marines and navy personnel fully appreciated the potentialities and limitations of each arm. The beginnings of what was to develop into an efficient fighting combination were made during the training stage on Guadalcanal, and the results were to prove more than satisfactory.[133]

The original plan had called for an invasion of Guam shortly after the initial assault on Saipan; and accordingly on June 15,

Spruance designated target date for the Southern Attack Force as June 18. Originally also the 27th Infantry Division had been designated floating reserve for any or all of the three phases of the Marianas campaign. By the end of the first day on Saipan it became apparent that these plans would have to be changed. The heavy casualties suffered by the two marine divisions on the beachhead made it mandatory to commit the 27th Infantry Division at once and thus deprive the Guam attack force of reserve troops. Also the imminence of a major naval engagement which finally materialized in the Battle of the Philippine Sea necessitated diverting part of Conolly's support ships to a stand-by status for possible fleet employment. For these two reasons, the target date for Guam was indefinitely postponed, and the impatient troops were sent back to Eniwetok to bide their time until further orders. This meant, in the end, an average of about fifty days aboard ship before these men landed. True, they were given short exercise periods ashore in the Marshalls, but the nervous and physical strain was considerable. Geiger reported later, however, that "contrary to popular opinion, the prolonged voyage had no ill effect upon the troops and they were landed . . . in excellent physical condition." [134]

On July 6, Admiral Nimitz assigned the 77th Infantry Division to act as reserve troops for the Southern Landing Force.[135] This unit was still in Pearl Harbor and had had no previous experience in amphibious operations, but it had been alerted earlier and was the only command available when the crisis at Saipan arose. July 21 was set as the day for the beach assault at Guam, and immediately wheels were set in motion for revising the original plans. Actually no significant change was made in the initial attack plan except to provide for a much more prolonged preliminary aerial and naval bombardment. The beaches allotted to the brigade and the division remained the same, and the scheme of maneuver after these beachheads were secured went unchanged.[136] As it turned out, the decision to delay the operation was a happy one, at least from the point of view of the attacking troops. No matter how much griping may have gone on as the task force shoved off for Eniwetok, the marines aboard were to have good reason to thank the fates (or the Japanese) that prolonged their temporary agonies. For while they sweltered in the stuffy holds of their transports, Conolly's support ships were subjecting Guam to the heaviest preparatory bombardment yet delivered by the navy in the Pacific. The results were altogether wonderful.

The capture of the island evolved in two stages. The first phase consisted of the landing and securing the force beachhead and lasted from July 21 until July 30 when elements of the 77th Infantry Division in the south established contact with the Third Marine Division in the north. This was the critical stage in the battle for Guam, and once it was completed the rest was comparatively easy. The second phase consisted of a coordinated attack to the north. The greater part of this task fell to the Third Marine and the 77th Infantry Divisions, although in the final wind up the brigade was thrown in as well. The attack pressed against scattered resistance as the enemy withdrew the remnants of his forces in a hopeless attempt to forestall disaster. By August 10, marines and soldiers reached the northern shore of the island, and organized resistance ended. Mopping up took longer than usual because Guam was a large island and its terrain offered excellent cover, but after August 10 there was no serious challenge to the complete occupation by American forces.[137]

The hour for landing was set at half-past eight o'clock on the morning of July 21, and no last minute revision was necessary. Troops boated in amphibian tractors reached the shore on schedule. On the northern beaches Major General Allen H. Turnage's Third Marine Division landed with three regiments abreast, the Third Marines on the left, the Twenty-first Marines in the center, and the Ninth Marines on the right. (See map 18.) Although there was some sporadic mortar fire against the troops as they approached their beaches, resistance was slight at this stage. Later in the day heavy artillery and mortar fire began pouring down from the high ground immediately inshore of the landing beaches, but it was quickly reduced by air strikes. Movement onto the beach was so rapid that the division command post was established ashore by four in the afternoon, and by nightfall most of the artillery organic to the division had been landed. Some infantry units had by then penetrated to the beachhead line, but the division's hold was nonetheless precarious. The beachhead was some 4,000 yards wide and 1,500 yards deep, but there were many gaps in the line, and the enemy was in positions along the overhanging cliffs that abutted the beaches, as well as in heavily wooded ravines just inshore. Some of these ravines ran down almost to the water's edge. The Japanese were in position to give a lot of trouble.

The situation was somewhat better along the southern beaches, assigned to Brigadier General Lemuel C. Shepherd, Jr.'s First Provisional Marine Brigade. There the Fourth Marines landed on the right and the Twenty-second Marines on the left, with the 305th Infantry of the 77th Division in reserve. Although enemy fire in this vicinity increased in intensity during the day, it did not seriously impede operations, and by nightfall the brigade beachhead was about 4,500 yards wide and 2,000 yards deep. The landing was a success, although there was still danger of violent enemy reaction.

The first night ashore saw the usual Japanese counterattack in

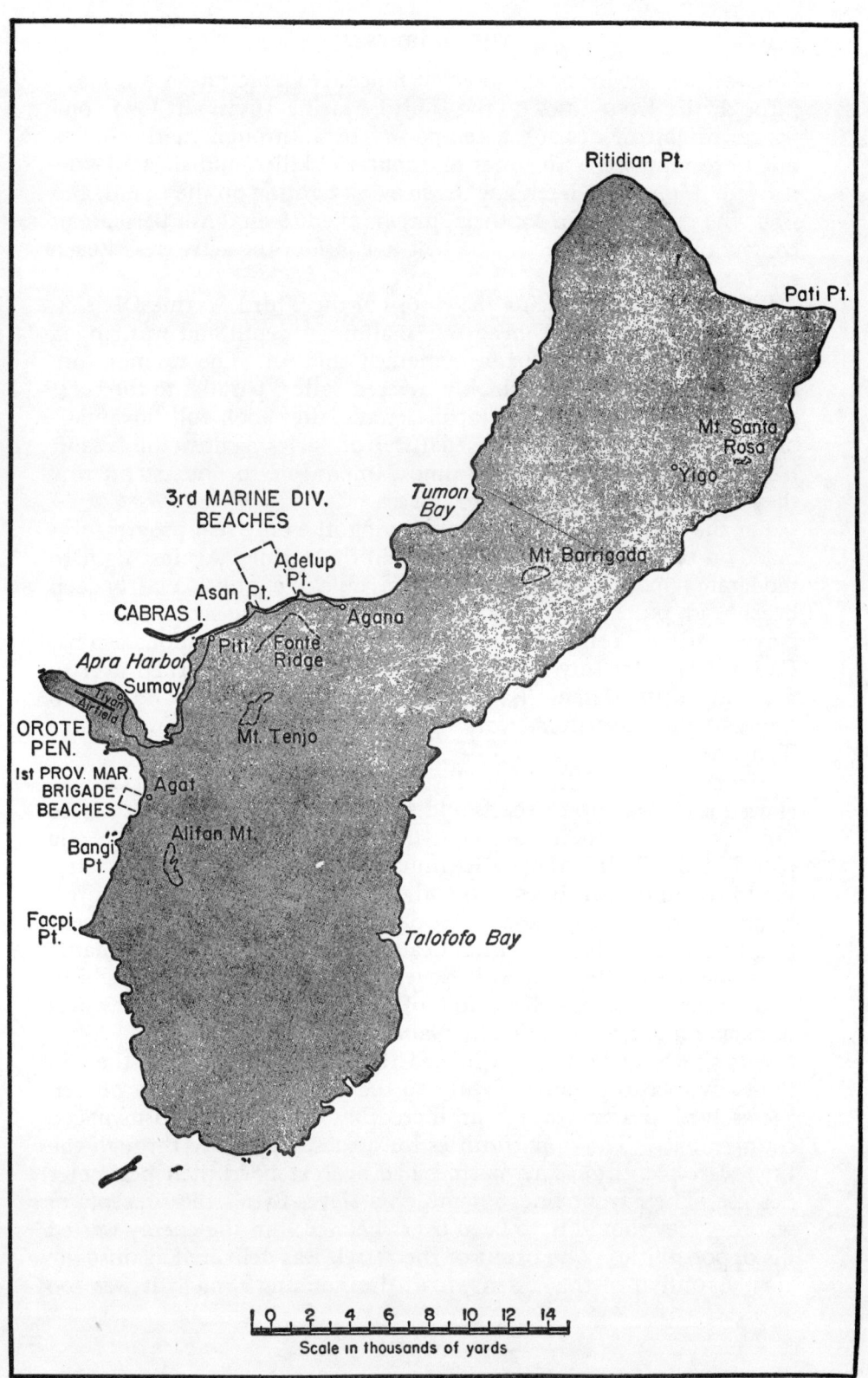

MAP 18. Guam.

both sectors, but in each instance it failed. No penetration was made through the front lines of the Third Marine Division. Two companies of Japanese made a temporary breakthrough in the south, but were repulsed with losses of about 268 killed and six tanks destroyed.[138] The next week saw the heaviest fighting on the island, and since the northern and southern forces failed to establish permanent contact until July 30, it will be best to consider the activities of each separately.

The chief obstacle facing the troops of the Third Marine Division was terrain. Their beachhead was shallow in depth and was ringed with high cliffs which made maneuver difficult. The ravines running down to sea and the thickly covered valleys parallel to the coast offered ideal cover for the Japanese, and they took full advantage of it. With these tremendous natural obstacles against the assault troops it seems, in retrospect, almost impossible to understand why they were not hurled back into the sea.

For the first two days after the landing, the only real progress was made on the division's right by the Ninth Marines. Against light to moderate opposition, this regiment was able to establish a fairly deep beachhead, push rapidly to the south parallel to the shore, seize Piti Navy Yard and conduct successful shore-to-shore operations against Cabras Island by July 23. This little island was then turned over to the Fourteenth Defense Battalion which set up its guns and searchlights for counterbattery work against Orote Peninsula and Mount Tenjo.

Meanwhile, the Third and Twenty-first Marine Regiments slowly clawed their way up the cliffs and tried, still unsuccessfully, to close the many gaps in their lines. The underbrush was so heavy that one patrol of the Third Marine Regimental Combat Team got lost trying to rejoin its own lines in broad daylight over a gap of only a few hundred yards. During these first days the most typical message sent back to regimental and division headquarters by company commanders along the whole front was "never quite gained ridge." To add to other difficulties, one battalion of the Twenty-first Marines was bombed on July 24 by friendly planes.

But slowly these marines inched their way forward, and then in the early morning hours of July 26 the Japanese obligingly offered themselves up to sacrifice in an incredibly wasteful and mismanaged counterattack. The opportunities for a successful drive through the lines were plentiful. The marines had overextended their perimeter defense. Their front lines resembled a sieve. By all the precepts of warfare, they should have been overwhelmed; but the enemy wasted his opportunities. The brunt of the attack was delivered against the First Battalion of the Twenty-first Marines, and though it was too powerful for them to stop they slowed the enemy down enough to permit the division reserves to throw up a hasty secondary defense. By daylight it was relatively easy to mop up the remaining enemy that had filtered through. On the right, through a gap between the Twenty-first and the Ninth Marine Regiments another major thrust succeeded in getting as far as the division hospital. Not until midmorning were the lines closed, and the rest of the day was spent in hunting out the snipers who had survived the previous night. Probably this weird maneuver broke the enemy's back, though not without considerable cost to the Third Division. From five to seven battalions of Japanese had participated in the thrust and a total of 3,200 enemy dead were counted in the front lines, with approximately 300 in the rear areas.[139]

Thereafter, the task of the division was considerably lightened, although by no means easy as yet. The next day the Second Battalion of the Ninth Marine Regiment, in trying desperately to make lateral contact with friendly forces to the south, staged a bloody and costly assault against Fonte Ridge and gained its nose by night. On July 28 contact was finally established with units of the 77th Infantry Division on Mount Tenjo, and for the next two days the marines in this sector spent their time consolidating their lines, mopping up small pockets of resistance, and sending out patrols which generally came back with the report that the enemy was rapidly withdrawing.

In the southern sector the First Provisional Marine Brigade, reinforced by elements of the 77th Infantry Division, was to drive inland from the beachhead, to seize the Alifan massif, then to turn northward to isolate Orote Peninsula, and finally to eliminate the remaining enemy trapped on that promontory. Taking Alifan Ridge was a comparatively easy job, but not so the movement across the base of Orote Peninsula where swamps and dense jungle growth, to say nothing of Japanese, made the going tough for the Twenty-second Marine Regiment. Not until late afternoon of July 25 did the marines reach the coast of Apra Harbor.

Meanwhile, army troops had been assigned the task of holding and extending the perimeter in order to free the Fourth Marine Regiment for action on Orote. With the Fourth Marines on the left and the Twenty-second Marines on the right, and with the help of army tanks, artillery on Cabras Island, and naval and aerial bombardment, the two combat teams slowly slugged their way out to the tip of the peninsula against desperate resistance. Not until July 29 was the area overrun. The brigade's casualties were 279 killed and about 1,500 wounded in action. In exchange, a toll of well over 3,000 enemy dead was accounted for. On the afternoon of the 29th, all hands not otherwise occupied stood by while the American flag was raised over the old Marine barracks for the first time since that dismal December day in 1941 when the Japanese had invaded in overwhelming force. The long road back was beginning to seem a great deal shorter.

Before the really heavy fighting on Guam had come to its conclusion, reconnaissance patrols and aerial intelligence had shown definitely that little further resistance was to be expected in the southern end of the island and that the Japanese were retiring hurriedly to the north, presumably to make their last ditch defense in the areas of Mount Barrigada or Mount Santa Rosa. Actually, the enemy was too disorganized to put up much resistance. With only a slight rest, the Third Marine Division and the 77th Infantry Division were committed to a line abreast drive up the northern half of Guam, commencing on July 31. The marines were on the left, the army on the right, and the brigade, which had seen bitter fighting most recently, went into corps reserve. For the first few days no real resistance was encountered. On August 2 the marines overran Tiyan Field with ease. As army troops approached the southern slopes of Mount Barrigada, they got a taste of fairly heavy delaying fire, but it was short-lived, and by August 3 Barrigada was taken against no resistance except heavy jungle growth. Meanwhile the marines were meeting little resistance with the exception of a small counterattack on the night of August 4, which was easily repulsed. Contact between marine and army units was temporarily lost when the latter was slowed down in mountainous terrain. As the island widened out to westward it was decided to commit the brigade to the left flank to avoid overextending the lines of the other two divisions, and this was accomplished on August 7. Occasional road blocks and isolated groups of enemy were encountered, but nothing serious presented itself. As army troops ran into easier terrain, they began to out-distance marine units on their left flank, which caused the latter no little chagrin and induced them to abandon their bush-whacking tactics for more rapid movement along trails and roads. Some Japanese were encountered by the army troops as they occupied the town of Yigo, but these were quickly subdued. By August 8 the 77th Division captured Mount Santa Rosa and the marines reached Ritidian Point on the northwest coast. Two days later the entire coast was occupied, and organized resistance was over. The island was secured. For the past ten days opposition had been paltry, at least by normal standards of Central Pacific warfare.[140]

By the end of the operation an estimated 10,646 Japanese had been killed against a total of about one-tenth as many American troops.[141] Fighting after the first nine days had been desultory. Yet this had never been anticipated when the operation was planned. If anything, the defenses on Guam had been expected to be superior to those on Saipan, and it was for that reason that the operation was delayed when it was discovered that the 27th Infantry Division would have to be committed to the capture of the northern island. On July 6 Nimitz estimated the number of enemy ground troops on the island to total about 20,000 with probably an additional four to five thousand navy and construction personnel attached. This proved to be an exaggeration, but the 19,000 Japanese constituting the garrison there might have been expected to put up a stiffer resistance than was encountered. Intensive fortifications had been constructed all along the most likely beach areas between Tumon Bay in the north and Facpi Point in the south, and there is no evidence that the Japanese were surprised at the choice of beachheads. The enemy put his greatest reliance on shallow beach defenses, and all along the west coast the most likely landing areas were protected by offshore obstacles and mines. The coastline was heavily guarded with trenches, machine guns, pillboxes, and heavy caliber weapons. Behind lay a network of still more machine guns and dual purpose weapons surrounding the two operational airfields. Orote Peninsula was strongly defended, and the terrain was intelligently exploited. The Japanese had built numerous trenches and foxholes in depth, supported by large numbers of pillboxes and heavy caliber weapons. The enemy had an ample number of tanks and vehicles for conducting a mobile defense once the landing was accomplished, and the road net of the island was well suited to that purpose.[142]

Yet in spite of these advantages the garrison on Guam seemed to operate in a daze. From the very beginning the Japanese appeared to be completely disorganized and incapable of anything but the most sporadic and ill-planned countermeasures. There was little or no coordination between the separate units on the island because of the almost total breakdown of their communications. On the day of the invasion, for example, the small Japanese garrison in Apra knew nothing of the landing a few miles away until four o'clock in the afternoon when a straggler from Agat finally brought the word.[143] Telephone lines had either been totally disrupted, or the people who manned the phones had deserted their stations in panic. There was good reason for panic that day. For the two weeks preceding, Guam had been subjected to the most careful and destructive bombardment that had yet pounded any island in the Pacific. For that, thanks were due chiefly to the ships of Admiral Conolly's task force.

7. *The Amphibious and Tactical Phases on Guam*

As early as June 11 the island was hit by planes from Mitscher's fast carrier task force, but not until July 5 did the preparation begin in earnest. That was the first day of a planned series of carrier-based strikes, and two days later one of Conolly's cruiser divisions appeared on the scene to initiate the surface bombardment.

Up to this time many marines had been understandably skeptical about the efficacy of naval shelling. Although impressive to watch in the hours just before the troops started for shore, it had seldom (except in the Marshalls) produced results commensurate with all the noise and smoke. Too often the bombardment was started too late or lifted too soon. Too often the ships had lain too far out to sea to permit precision firing and had been content with area bombardment which looked a lot better than it really was.

Geiger, Conolly, and their staffs determined that these defects would be remedied, and that Guam should resemble Roi-Namur more than Betio. The delay in the target date gave them an ideal opportunity, but even before that had been decided on, steps were taken to improve the accuracy and destructiveness of support fires. Immediately after Geiger returned from Pearl Harbor to Guadalcanal, his staff began a careful study of gunfire requirements necessary to get the landing force ashore. When Conolly arrived in person, these plans were rapidly matured. Joint conferences between navy and marine personnel were held regularly. Conolly's gunnery officer and Geiger's naval gunfire officer worked constantly. The importance of this preliminary cooperation between ground and naval forces cannot be overstressed. Years of indoctrination to the contrary, many officers in both the Navy and the Marine Corps were still overly suspicious of naval gunfire support. On their side, some marines failed to appreciate the navigational difficulties involved in close shore bombardment and were dubious about the accuracy of naval fire against land targets. On the other side, many navy officers clung to the old myth that "ships can't fight forts" and hesitated to risk in such foolhardy enterprises vessels which they felt should be saved for surface fleet actions of the traditional kind. This mutual distrust could only be ironed out by close cooperation and detailed planning which would permit a careful coordination of the specific requirements of the ground troops with the potentialities and limitations of the support ships. The groundwork for a truly efficient amphibious team was laid in these conferences at Guadalcanal, and they paid dividends.

On July 14, after six days of bombardment by the cruiser division and the carriers, Conolly reached Guam aboard *Appalachian* and personally took over supervision of the job. More and more support ships were added to the task force until by the day of the beach assault a total of nine cruisers and six battleships with their escorting destroyers were saturating the island with fire. Saturation is perhaps the wrong word if it implies random area bombardment. Guam was subjected to the most systematic working over of any island in the Pacific up to that time. When Conolly arrived, he brought with him an up-to-date target list giving the best information available as to the location and nature of priority targets. This was modified as new intelligence came in from air observers, captured enemy documents, prisoners of war, and other sources. A target board consisting of officers from the air, gunnery, and intelligence sections assigned all objectives for both air strikes and naval bombardment. They concentrated on coast defenses, dual purpose, and heavy antiaircraft guns. No target was checked off the list until there was good indication from aerial reconnaissance or other sources that it had been destroyed or at least silenced. After it was believed that most of the big guns had been eliminated, the board concentrated on warehouses, command posts, communication centers, dumps, and troop concentrations. For a period of thirteen days (exclusive of the target date), battleships, cruisers, and destroyers steamed close into shore and hammered away at everything that threatened the success of the assault troops. The following table of their ammunition expenditures gives an idea of the immensity of the bombardment: [144]

> 836 rounds 16-inch
> 5,422 rounds 14-inch
> 3,862 rounds 8-inch
> 2,430 rounds 6-inch
> 16,214 rounds 5-inch

In the opinion of Geiger's naval gunfire officer, Major William M. Gilliam USMC, "the extended period for bombardment plus a system for keeping target damage reports accounted for practically every known Jap gun that could seriously endanger our landings. When the morning of the landings arrived, it was known that the assault troops would meet little resistance." Conolly's staff believed "that not one fixed gun was left in commission on the west coast that was of greater size than a machine gun." [145] Although these estimates proved to be somewhat exaggerated, there can be no doubt that the effect was devastating.

On the day of the landings, July 21, the schedule of fires was stepped up as usual for neutralization, but unlike Saipan, shelling of the land behind the beaches was not stopped with the landing of the troops. Instead, naval fire was lifted inland and to the flanks in a rolling barrage and was continued for ninety minutes. To give an idea of the intensity of this post-landing barrage, the figures in the following table indicating the rounds fired on July 21 should be compared with those given above for the entire preceding thirteen day period:

      342 rounds 16-inch
  1,152 rounds 14-inch
  1,332 rounds 8-inch
  2,430 rounds 6-inch
13,130 rounds 5-inch
  9,000 rounds 4.5-inch rockets

Aside from the quantity of ammunition expended, the careful check of targets fired upon and demolished, and the use of the rolling barrage, no change in normal operating procedure for naval gunfire support was employed on Guam. The support ships were divided into two groups, a northern group under Conolly which supported the landing of the Third Marine Division and a southern attack group under Rear Admiral Lawrence F. Reifsnider USN, which performed the same function for the First Provisional Marine Brigade. Destroyers were assigned to either flank of the assault boat lanes to protect them from enemy machine guns on the way in, and nine infantry landing craft converted to gunboats preceded the first wave, laying down their barrage of rockets and gunfire.[146]

About three hours after the first landings, call fires began and continued day and night throughout the operation. During the battle for Orote Peninsula, the brigade made much use of prearranged naval gunfire preparation in conjunction with artillery and air strikes, and certainly the heavy bombardment by all three supporting arms contributed no little to the speed with which the area was captured. (See map 18.) Night programs were begun on the first day and were maintained unremittingly. Road junctions, airfields, bivouac, and supply areas were interdicted; and as usual since Eniwetok, star shells were extensively employed to discourage infiltration and night counterattacks. About 1,500 rounds of 5-inch and 300 rounds of star shells were fired nightly as well as some heavier ammunition and liberal amounts of 40- and 20-millimeter projectiles. Deep support fire from naval guns was used continuously by all elements from battalion to corps. In some units casualties which were incurred early in the operation and were attributed to naval gunfire discouraged marine officers from calling on the big ships for anything but deep support missions. However, even in the one regiment where this fear seems to have been felt most keenly, the unit commanders did make frequent use of gunboats to clear the roads along their line of advance.[147]

On the whole, the shore fire-control parties operated efficiently in spite of the fact that the Third Joint Assault Signal Company which was assigned to the Third Marine Division had not completed its training in time for the operation. To supply the deficiency, twenty-two navy officers were assigned to all battalion and regimental shore fire-control parties in the Third Division. The chief defect in the operation of these parties was the coordination of their call fire requests with requests for air strikes by air liaison officers. On several occasions, ships and planes would commence firing on the same target simultaneously, which caused considerable confusion and forced the ships concerned to check their fire in the middle of a mission.

To some degree the claims made by the proponents of naval gunfire as to the utter destruction wrought on Guam must be qualified. Both General Turnage and General Shepherd, when they got ashore, found some installations untouched. Reports from the Third Marine Division sector showed that at least two 6-inch Japanese guns were in good condition and capable of firing at the beaches when the troops were landing. But they had been deserted. In the southern area Shepherd reported that "some hits were obtained on gun positions and pillboxes with the desired destructive and neutralization effect." He added, however, that the majority of enemy installations remained intact.[148]

The point, however, is not how many enemy guns were actually disabled, but how many were silenced by naval gunfire and remained silenced during the crucial period when the marines were establishing their beachhead. In this connection, it is well to point out that on the Third Division's beaches not a single heavy gun was manned and firing when the troops landed. The real measure of the success of the preliminary and close naval gunfire support was the degree to which the enemy's general plan of defense was disrupted. As to this there can be no doubt. As an indication of the extent of the damage, the following excerpt from the medical section of the intelligence report of the Third Amphibious Corps is pertinent:

"According to the Jap plan to defend the island, defenses were to be concentrated in three areas: Agana, Orote, and Agat. Medical facilities were provided in each of these areas. . . . This plan was smashed before ever started by the preliminary air and naval bombardment inflicted on the island prior to our landing. Agana was totally unsafe for hospitals. Attempts were made to evacuate both army and navy hospitals. . . . The loss of supplies and equipment due to bombing and shelling prior to this evacuation was serious, and satisfactory care could not be given to patients up in the hills. . . . The early evacuation of the Agana hospitals by no means marked the extent of the disorganization of the enemy medical plan occasioned by our bombing and shelling. According to prisoners, the bombing of July 11, 1944, destroyed the water mains to Orote, and the ones to Agana and Agat soon followed. From June 11 until July 21, the day of our landings, the bulk of the Jap garrison was without water, except for such rain water as they could collect. This barely sufficed for drinking purposes. Many troops were forced to drink from mud puddles, and for most soldiers bathing was impossible. . . . Skin diseases flourished, and diarrhea and dysentery increased greatly. . . ." [149]

Perhaps an even more significant tribute to the efficacy of naval gunfire support came from one of the Japanese prisoners of war captured on Guam:

"We had been thinking that the Japanese might win through a night counterattack, but when the star shells came over one after another we would only use our men as human bullets and there were many useless casualties and no chance of success; also not a thing escaped the strafing of the airplanes, and regrettably it came about that we had to retreat. . . . I was horrified by the number of deaths on our side due to the naval gunfire which continued every day." [150]

Certainly not all the credit for this destruction can be given to the naval vessels of Conolly's task force. As early as June 28, carrier planes from Mitscher's task force began periodic strikes against Guam and these were increased in frequency until July 21. Then for a whole hour before the landing, three fast carrier groups sent their full deck load of planes to strike the entire west coast of the island, and a total of 124 tons of bombs was dropped on the landing and flanking beaches by 312 planes. For the rest of the operation carrier-based aircraft were under continuous call for both deep and close support missions, observation flights, and photographic reconnaissance.

But close support by carrier planes was, if anything, less satisfactory than it had been even on Saipan and Tinian. In the Third Division the lag between requests for and execution of close support missions varied from nine minutes to five and a half hours, and the average for thirty-one missions was about an hour and a half. As a result of these delays, many missions had to be cancelled. Once again troop commanders complained about the reluctance of Commander Support Aircraft to turn over control of strikes directly to the air liaison parties concerned. The support aircraft request net was still overcrowded, which accounted in no small measure for the delays.

Similar complaints came from brigade headquarters. During the first week, Commander Support Aircraft did not in many instances grant or refuse air requests within a reasonable time and thus left the ground troops in a quandary as to whether they could or could not rely on air support. Very few strikes could be directed by the air liaison parties, not only because of the highly centralized control but also because most of their vehicular radios had been damaged by salt water. Radio nets were overcrowded. Both the division and the brigade worked on the same frequency, and since the high hills lying between them prevented their hearing each other, coordination of requests was extremely difficult.[151]

Even more disturbing to the ground troops was the number of casualties incurred by planes dropping bombs within their own lines. On July 24, three bombs fell within the lines of the Second Battalion, Ninth Marines, causing a total of seventeen casualties. One strike called by the Third Marines not only came an hour late but hit the wrong target square and killed eight of their own troops. Finally, on July 28, a company of the 305th Infantry was bombed and strafed by friendly planes and only avoided casualties by the quick thinking of a private who flagged them away before they could come in for a second run. As the operations ófficer for the Third Marine Division dryly remarked, "pilot error, resulting in strafing or bombing of our own troops, did not improve the troops' confidence in close air support."[152]

Once again marines were convinced that the only way for them to get the kind of close support they wanted was to have marine pilots do the job. Geiger concluded that "the use of Marine Bombing Squadrons in preference for close (100 to 500 yards) air support of ground troops has been clearly demonstrated. . . ." He did not know whether this was due to the marine pilots' having greater familiarization with ground force problems, but was convinced that until the change was made troop commanders would remain highly suspicious of close support aviation. Holland Smith made a similar recommendation, and as he had done after Tarawa, specifically suggested that sufficient air groups be designated and trained as direct support groups and be assigned to escort carriers. This specialized duty, he continued, should be assigned to marines because "the troop experience of senior marine pilots combined with the indoctrination of new pilots in infantry tactics should insure greater cooperation and coordination between air and ground units."[153]

As for the third supporting arm, artillery, there was general agreement among ground troops that it was the most reliable of all. Shepherd expressed the opinion of most unit commanders that "artillery is the most effective weapon employed during the operation. Close support was given to the infantry in both attack and defense, and harassing fires at night were particularly effective."[154] The troops, he continued, had far greater confidence in artillery than in either naval gunfire or air strikes for close support missions.

For the Third Marine Division artillery support was provided by the Twelfth Marines, consisting of two 75-millimeter pack howitzer battalions and two 105-millimeter howitzer battalions. In the brigade, each regiment had its own pack howitzer battalion which was supplemented for the landing by one 105-millimeter army howitzer battalion and two battalions of Third Corps Artillery. In addition, two marine defense battalions were employed in this operation, the Ninth and the Fourteenth. These units consisted chiefly of antiaircraft weapons, 90-, 40-, and 20-millimeter, plus the searchlight and radar equipment necessary for antiaircraft defense. Since no Japanese aerial attacks materialized over Guam, they were put to other uses. The Ninth Battalion helped to defend the brigade's beaches once the infantry had passed beyond the beachhead line. In the north, the Fourteenth Defense Battalion was put to a more important use. By the night of July 21 the Special Weapons Battalion of the Fourteenth Marine Defense Battalion had gone into action in support of the hard-pressed Third Marines. By July 24, two batteries of 90- and 40-millimeter guns were set up on Cabras Island, where they fired at targets of opportunity on Orote Peninsula and in the caves and ravines around Mount Tenjo, and provided searchlight illumination to ward off surprise counteramphibious attacks in the area of Apra Harbor.[155]

The ship-to-shore movement on the two beaches at Guam was not especially remarkable except that it went more smoothly than usual. On the southern beaches the first wave, composed of thirty-seven armored amphibians, landed only two minutes behind schedule and was followed in regular order by successive waves of troop-laden tractors at five-minute intervals. These vehicles had been ordered to proceed inland about 1,000 yards before unloading their troops, but as at Saipan, this scheme proved unworkable. There were too many mines and obstacles inland of the shore line. But no great confusion ensued as in the earlier operation. The tractors discharged their troops in an orderly fashion and went back to the transfer line 2,000 yards off the beach to pick up supporting troops from the small boats carrying them. On the northern beaches the same procedure was carried out and with the same general success.[156]

The assault troops in both areas had to face machine gun and mortar fire as they approached the beaches in spite of the heavy previous pounding by naval vessels and aircraft. But very few mines or underwater obstacles were encountered, in spite of the fact that the Japanese had studded the shoal waters offshore with a formidable network of obstructions. Naval underwater demolition teams had done their work well. They started their reconnaissance of the beaches on July 14 and continued up to the night before the invasion. On the Agat beaches they found a series of palm log cribs filled with coral and connected with heavy wire cable, and beaches off Asan were well protected with 4-foot square wire cages filled with coral cement and located at intervals of about five feet along the entire length of the landing area. These were all blown to pieces with high explosive charges by naval swimmers who worked under the protective fire of gunboats, destroyers, and destroyer transports. The swimmers overlooked a few mines which came to light after the invasion but did no serious damage.[157]

As in other phases of the operation, unloading of supplies was conducted in general more expeditiously on Guam than on Saipan. The northern and southern beaches were similar in that each had a reef lying from 200 to 500 yards offshore. The reef off the northern beaches was dry at low water, and trucks were able to run from the shore out to the edge without much trouble. The water over the southern reef, however, was too deep even at ebb tide to permit trucks to make the trip, so tractors and Dukws had to be used as cargo carriers. Neither reef had deep enough water for landing craft to pass the edge at any time, so the main problem was to provide means for a rapid transfer of supplies from boats either to trucks or to tractors and Dukws at the reef's edge. To achieve this, shore parties had at their disposal about twenty-five small cranes on both reefs. These were either mounted on pontoon barges or set up on the reefs themselves and were largely responsible for keeping materials and ammunition running into the beach in a fairly steady stream. In the southern area, according to Shepherd's estimate, it took four men only from fifteen to twenty-five minutes to load one tractor from ship's boats at the reef's edge. In some sectors of the beach, ships' life rafts and rubber boats were employed. The rafts were coupled together and stretched out over the reef with dunnage laid on top. Landing craft could then drop their ramps on the end raft and have their cargoes manhandled into rubber boats and floated across the reef. It was largely by reliance on such improvised devices that an average of about 5,000 tons per day of vehicles, equipment, and supplies could be landed on both the northern and southern beaches. This record was subsequently speeded up so that for the first eight days of the operation an average of 6,650 tons per day was being discharged. Thereafter a period of heavy weather lasting from July 29 to August 4 slowed up the operations considerably, but by that time the basic assault unloading had been accomplished, and forty-two transports and twenty-eight tank landing ships had already sailed back to Eniwetok.[158]

Another reason for the logistical success of Guam was the fact that Conolly was willing to permit some of his ships to continue unloading throughout the critical first night of the assault instead of sending them out to sea. By midnight of July 22 enough materiel had been sent ashore to convince the navy that they need not submit to the risk of night unloading any longer, and the practice ceased. From that time, unloading was stopped between midnight and five-thirty each morning to avoid danger from hostile aircraft, since it is impossible completely to darken ships while cargoes are being shifted from holds to small boats. As it turned out no enemy planes put in their appearance, but the precaution was a sensible one. Marine and army personnel on the beaches themselves were somewhat less cautious and after the first few nights when it became evident that the enemy was unable to produce air support or to lay artillery fire on the beaches, they illuminated their beach areas without hesitation and thus made possible a more rapid transfer of supplies inland.[159]

With the seizure of Japanese port facilities by the troops ashore, the unloading problem was simplified. Shore party operations were gradually turned over to the Third Amphibious Corps Service Group, which began unloading of cargo at Dadi beach for the brigade on July 29. Northward at Piti, which was seized by the Ninth Marines, unloading operations began on July 31. Piti Navy Yard was reconnoitered and temporary piers constructed for handling cargoes from barges. After Apra Harbor was secured following the capitulation of Orote Peninsula, still more facilities were put into use.

In the early stages of the operation, shore parties found some difficulty in locating adequate areas for dumps because of the restricted beachheads and extensive rice paddies that flanked them. Also there was never sufficient motor transportation to meet the needs of the fighting troops as fast as they wanted them. There were high casualties among the amphibians, and those that did survive after the unloading of the assault echelons could not be used on existing roads in spite of their tracks. Again the Dukws did yeoman service, and about 64 of the original 100 provided to the Corps Service Group were still in operation at the completion of the assault phase. The road net, though somewhat better than on Saipan, was still a serious problem. Heavy rains and heavy traffic made the Sumay-Piti-Agana road impassable more often than not, and the roads north of Agat could be traversed only with the greatest difficulty. Probably the chief handicap to supplying troops as they moved north on the island was the inadequacy of motor transportation. Only fifty per cent of the Third Division's trucks were with the advance echelon, and this was sufficient only for the first few days of the operation. As the occupied area increased in size and as trucks began to break down, the need for additional transportation became acute, but no more was available. The remaining fifty per cent of the assigned vehicles did not show up for a full month after the landings began, and the shortage was severe.[160]

One artillery regiment (the Twelfth Marines) also complained of a critical shortage of ammunition on the morning of July 22. The reason, they felt, was that vessels insisted on lying offshore as far as seven miles even though no shore batteries of any kind had been active. This slowed up the process of delivery, and the situation was not improved by the fact that these same ammunition ships retired to sea during the first night and did not recommence unloading until nine o'clock on the following morning.[161]

But with these few exceptions, the supply system on Guam worked smoothly and efficiently. Credit can be shared by the divisional shore parties, the Third Amphibious Corps Service Group, and the navy. Their work was made easier by the fact that from the end of the first day's operations the shore dumps were practically free from enemy fire and that at no time did Japanese ships or aircraft handicap the unloading of the vessels. The greatest hindrance to a smooth solution of logistical problems on this level is always enemy opposition, and this had been reduced to a minimum on Guam.

The tactics employed by the Japanese on Guam were in general not much different from those that marines had become accustomed to in the Pacific. The most common were night infiltrations by small groups, sniping, harassment by mortars, poorly coordinated artillery fire, and the inevitable banzai charges. The only striking difference was a curious lassitude displayed by the enemy and his reluctance to take necessary defensive steps, especially during the first days of the assault. He failed to make the most effective use of his artillery, particularly in these early days. The troops on the beachhead received fire, but nothing like the concentration they had feared. The Japanese made no determined effort to prevent the removal of barriers across the landing beaches, and although the beaches were organized with extensive trench systems and many pillboxes, these were not heavily manned except in isolated positions. During the naval bombardment phase the Japanese declined to return fire in spite of the fact that many of their coast defense guns were placed at strategic points capable of hitting American vessels. One prisoner of war was a member of a 47-millimeter antitank gun crew on Asan Point and testified that his gun could easily have wiped out one of the underwater demolition teams but that he had orders not to fire until the landing attempt was under way.[162]

Apparently no thought was given to opposing the assault until the troops were actually on shore or close to it. One Chamorro woman found this out to her surprise when she berated a Japanese soldier occupying the same shelter with several natives during the preinvasion bombardment. On chiding him for hiding out with civilians when he was supposed to be fighting, she was told that the Japanese were allowing the foolish Americans to waste their ammunition, that the Americans would have to go away and get more or try to land without enough. Then, he said, "they would find the Japanese ready for them." [163]

In truth, of course, no such state of preparedness ever existed. The Japanese were not surprised by either the date or the place of the landing, so they were not thrown off balance as they had been on Tinian.[164] They were capable enough of divining the intentions of the Americans, but apparently went completely astray in anticipating their capabilities.

In the end, the fine showing made at Guam can be charged in no small measure to the degree of coordination between Army, Navy and Marine Corps units. None of the interservice bitterness that marred the Saipan operation was evidenced. The 77th Infantry Division, though entirely inexperienced in amphibious warfare, showed an aggressiveness in patrolling and later in chasing the enemy up the northern end of the island that brought them nothing but credit. From the very outset of the planning, Conolly's staff had worked in fine accord with Marine Corps officers and showed a greater appreciation of the requirements and problems of ground troops than was often found in navy circles.

Although it was always customary for commanding generals to give at least nominal credit to the other services, the enthusiasm displayed in the final sentences of Geiger's action report attests to the fact that interservice cooperation was carried out to a greater degree at Guam than in many other Pacific operations:

"This report would not be complete without inviting particular attention to the relations which existed throughout the operation between the elements of the Army, Navy and Marine Corps. . . . At no time was there a conflicting opinion that was not settled to the entire satisfaction of all concerned." [165]

8. Significance of the Marianas Campaign

Within a little more than three months after the official fall of Guam, the Marianas were being put to use as B-29 bases for the bombardment of Japan. One hundred of these bombers left Saipan on November 24, 1944, to hit Tokyo for the first time since Doolittle's raid of 1942. From that date until February 25, 1945, B-29 attacks against Japan proper were launched from the Marianas about every fifth day, flights usually remaining above 28,000 feet and targets consisting mostly of aircraft plants. On the latter date the first 200-plane attack was run—a successful high-altitude daylight incendiary raid against Tokyo. More than a square mile of the city was burned out. The capture of Iwo Jima in February and March 1945 contributed greatly to this air offensive. By March it became apparent that Japanese defenses were so insignificant as to permit low-level bombing. On March 9 the Twentieth Air Force, based in the Marianas, sent approximately 300 of their super-fortresses against Tokyo at night in a low-level incendiary raid, and these were followed by similar attacks against other urban areas. By July 1945, sorties against Japan from the Marianas rose to about 1,200 a week. And in the following August from a Twentieth Air Force base on Tinian winged the lone bomber destined for the city of Hiroshima carrying in its bay the first atomic bomb. The Marianas amply fulfilled the main purposes for which they were seized.[166]

CHAPTER IX

PALAU AND THE PHILIPPINES: MARINES IN SUPPORT OF MacARTHUR

WHILE the amphibious forces under Admiral Nimitz's command were making gigantic strides across the Central Pacific, army troops of the Southwest Pacific Area under General MacArthur were moving steadily westward up the northern coast of New Guinea. In April they had by-passed a concentration of enemy forces in Wewak and Hansa Bay and seized Japanese air and shipping bases at Hollandia and Aitape. Next month, American forces took Wakde Island and secured the entire Wakde-Sarmi area, about 125 miles west of Hollandia. Because of the need for another forward air base, Biak was invaded on May 27. On July 2 a landing was made at Noemfoor Island, southwest of Biak. At the end of the month Cape Sansapor on the Vogelkop Peninsula in western New Guinea was occupied. New Guinea was neutralized as a base for enemy operations.[1]

The time was ripe for a northward thrust, preparatory to a drive against the Philippines. The next target chosen was Morotai, and the landing date was set at September 15. A simultaneous landing was to be made on Peleliu in the Palau group.

1. Planning, Training, and Loading for the Palaus

The Palaus are an arc of islands about eighty miles long lying southwest of Guam and about 450 miles due east of Mindanao, the southernmost of the Philippines. The largest of the group is Babelthuap, and it was here that the Japanese expected an American invasion. Some thirty miles south of the main island lie Peleliu and Angaur which were finally chosen as the points of attack.

The reason for moving into the Palaus, as later stated by Nimitz, was twofold: "first, to remove from MacArthur's right flank, in his progress to the Southern Philippines, a definite threat of attack; second, to secure for our forces a base from which to support MacArthur's operations into the Southern Philippines."[2]

Planning for this operation took an involved and tortuous path. The earliest version of Nimitz's blueprint for the invasion of the Western Carolines called for the occupation of the entire Palau group starting with Babelthuap and then working south. This original concept was revised several times, and by mid-June the idea was to undertake concurrent landings on Babelthuap and the two southern islands of Peleliu and Angaur.[3]

By the first week of July, however, the situation in the Central Pacific required a radical revision of these plans. The delay in the capture of the Marianas and the consequent shortage of shipping plus the fact that the Japanese were thought to be strongly increasing their garrison in Babelthuap demanded a somewhat less ambitious project. Consequently on July 5 a new plan was issued by Nimitz's headquarters. Babelthuap was discarded entirely. The islands of Peleliu and Angaur were to be invaded on September 15 by the First Marine Division and the 81st Infantry Division respectively. On October 5, Major General John R. Hodge's XXIV United States Army Corps was to take Yap and Ulithi in the Western Carolines. Major General Roy S. Geiger's Third Amphibious Corps, which was originally to supervise the entire campaign, was now dropped from the command organization altogether. His headquarters was currently far too busy on Guam. In Geiger's place, Major General Julian C. Smith, who had led the marines on Tarawa, was named to head a new headquarters labelled X-ray Provisional Amphibious Corps.[4] Later he assumed Geiger's former designation of Commander Expeditionary Troops.

Overall naval command of the operation was to go to Admiral William F. Halsey, Jr., as Commander Third Fleet. Under him, Vice Admiral Thomas S. Wilkinson, who had succeeded Kelly Turner in the Solomons, would command the Joint Expeditionary Force for the Western Carolines campaign. Wilkinson would personally supervise the amphibious phase of the operations against Ulithi and Yap, while his subordinate in direct tactical control at Peleliu and Angaur would be Rear Admiral George H. Fort USN.

One final change in the command organization was made in mid-August after the end of organized opposition on Guam. Geiger was named corps commander of the troops destined to go ashore at Peleliu and Angaur. His new designation was commanding general of Western Landing Force and Troops, which included the First Marine Division and the 81st Infantry Division. Julian Smith, however, retained overall command of the expeditionary troops for the Third Fleet.[5] Julian Smith's command was retained because the concept at the time called for a two-corps campaign, the second phase of which would consist of landings on Yap and Ulithi to be conducted by Hodge's XXIV Corps.

Meanwhile, Halsey in far-flung fast carrier covering sweeps from the Ryukyus south through the Philippines had come to the opinion that the Central Philippines were far more vulnerable than had previously been supposed and that they could and should be attacked directly by MacArthur's forces sometime in October. He therefore recommended to Nimitz the total abandonment of the Western Carolines-Palaus campaign (except for the occupation of Ulithi Atoll, which was needed as a fleet anchorage) in favor of a prompt invasion of Leyte Island in the Central Philippines. Nimitz forwarded this recommendation to the Joint Chiefs of Staff then meeting with their British counterparts in Quebec. They received MacArthur's concurrence in the early invasion of Leyte but did not accept Halsey's recommendation that the Palau campaign be cancelled.[6]

Neither MacArthur nor Nimitz was willing to drop the Palau campaign, and it was ordered as planned. On September 15, however, the day of the landing on Peleliu, the invasion of Yap scheduled to take place on October 5 was cancelled, and Hodge's XXIV Corps was turned over to MacArthur for the forthcoming Leyte operation. This left Julian Smith in a somewhat anomalous situation. Although he still retained titular authority as Commander Expeditionary Troops, the removal of the XXIV Corps from the theater rendered his command superfluous. He was in the position of being an army commander without an army.

In spite of these various shifts in command echelons and the last-minute deletion of Yap from the plans, the First Marine Division had ample time to prepare for its particular part in the Palau campaign, which was the seizure of Peleliu. In fact, division headquarters had to assume a larger share in the responsibility for original tactical planning than was usually the case at this stage of the Pacific War. Julian Smith's X-ray Provisional Corps was stationed in Hawaii while the division was located in the Russell Islands. This wide geographical distance between the two headquarters, bridged only by personal liaison of a few staff officers and radio and mail communications, imposed a heavier than usual burden on the division staff.

It had begun its own planning for Peleliu on June 2, the date of its receipt of one of the Joint Chiefs of Staff's early studies on Palau. Although there were many changes thereafter in the chain of command and in the target date of the landing, the original concept of employing this division only on Peleliu remained constant. Hence it was able to continue its planning for the operation without making any radical revisions. By August 15, when General Geiger reappeared on the scene as corps commander, the division had a concrete plan to offer, which was taken over bodily by the Third Amphibious Corps and confirmed as a corps order.[7]

The division had had ample experience in jungle warfare, but it needed to be reoriented toward a new type of fighting which the terrain of Peleliu would demand, and much of the summer's training was directed toward that end. Also the division had had little experience in the tactical use of amphibian tractors and none in the new type of portable flamethrower (Navy, Mark 1). In July it was decided to form a new amphibian tractor battalion in addition to the one already organic to the division. This was done by splitting the old First Amphibian Tractor Battalion and then adding more vehicles and personnel as they showed up. Training was seriously impeded by the lack of amphibian tractors. These were being delivered slowly, and even up to the time of departure the division had not received all the vehicles expected.[8]

At the same time a new armored amphibian battalion was hastily thrown together. By necessity it consisted chiefly of rear echelon personnel from armored amphibian battalions, tank battalions, and the tracked vehicle school in the States. The majority had had no combat experience at all. Trained officers were lacking. The battalion commander was a motor transport officer with artillery experience, and his only knowledge of the armored amphibian was from a picture in a bulletin from the Office of Naval Intelligence. To confuse matters further, after spending the month of July training with early model armored amphibians, the battalion was surprised in August to receive fifty new models which differed somewhat in armament and equipment.[9] In view of all these harassments, the subsequent performance of both amphibian tractors and armored amphibians on Peleliu appears all the more remarkable.

Training on Pavuvu (Russell Islands) suffered from other handicaps, chiefly limitation of space, shortage of equipment of all kinds, and camp construction. There was so little room on the island that battalion problems overran camp areas, with troops maneuvering among tents and mess halls. The division had only arrived in the area in May after the termination of the Cape Gloucester operation, and there was no camp to meet them in this steamy pest-hole to which they had been retired for "rest and rehabilitation." Screened mess halls, galleys, heads, and bathing facilities had to be constructed while training for the Palaus was supposed to be going on, and the camp was not completed until July. Roads were hub-deep in mud most of the time, and there was insufficient engineering equipment to construct new ones in the allotted time. Other equipment was equally scarce. Such critical items as flamethrowers, bazookas, Browning automatic rifles, demolitions, signal and waterproofing equipment and spare parts failed to arrive until the last stages of the training schedule, and, in some instances, barely in time to be loaded.[10]

Even more serious was the inadequacy of photographic intelligence until just prior to the actual landings. Although photographs from carrier strikes and MacArthur's bombers did exist, until the end of August they were insufficient for beach defense study. The only really good photographs, taken a week before the scheduled landing date, arrived after the attack force was under way for the target area. Even these were not made available to the troop commanders, although information from them was disseminated among the various ships of the troop convoy by means of visual signal from the flagship.[11]

Because of inadequate photography, maps were also deficient. They were found to be extremely inaccurate as to the configuration of terrain, especially as far as ridge lines and other elevations were concerned.[12] However, in extenuation, it should be remarked that the main deficiencies of the available maps were attributable to the fact that the photographs on which they were based were taken before persistent naval gunfire and aerial bombardment had stripped the ridges of their jungle cover and exposed the terrain pattern underneath. In the absence of an extended period of preliminary bombardment there was no way for aerial photographers to provide an accurate picture of the hundreds of caves which were well concealed by vegetation and camouflage.[13]

In one respect the attack forces had far more precise information about the target than was customary in Pacific operations. American troops on Saipan had captured several documents which enabled Julian Smith's intelligence officers to piece together a remarkably accurate order of battle of Japanese forces on Peleliu. As a result of this information, it was estimated, as of August 28, that the total number of enemy troops located there was between 10,700 and 10,320.[14] A ration list later captured on Peleliu itself disclosed the number of troops on the island to be 10,138. Some subsequent additions were made to this number as a result of reinforcements that reached the island during the fighting; but the close similarity between the estimated figure and the actual one was remarkable, and gave cause enough for Geiger's intelligence officer to remark that the documents captured on Saipan "provided a source of information which may be unparalleled in future operations." [15]

Yet accurate knowledge of the size of the enemy forces on Peleliu did not make up for the general ignorance of the really formidable defenses which the terrain on the island would enable the enemy to construct. Ignorance lulled the attacking forces into dangerous optimism. At the critique following the last rehearsal, Major General William H. Rupertus, commander of the First Marine Division, reminded his troops of their glorious record on Guadalcanal and Cape Gloucester and stated his conviction that Peleliu could be taken in a few days.[16] As quoted by the division's official historian, he remarked: "We're going to have some casualties, but let me assure you this is going to be a short one, a quickie. Rough but fast. We'll be through in three days. It might take only two." [17]

Misfortune plagued the Palaus campaign from the very beginning. Even before rehearsals on Guadalcanal, two fire-support battleships, *California* and *Tennessee* collided when the latter's steering gear broke down. Such accidents were not unusual among the lowly gunboats and tank landing ships of the Pacific amphibious forces, but for battleships to demonstrate their fallibility in this manner was alarming. Although the damage was not serious, *California* was temporarily put out of operation and was unable to participate in the forthcoming bombardment. This decreased the already limited amount of ammunition * to be expended on the islands.[18] Moreover, while the attack force was under way toward the target two oilers ran into each other with minor injuries to both. Finally, before dawn on September 12, a destroyer transport and a destroyer collided in mid-ocean. The former vessel went to the bottom and the latter was seriously damaged.[19] Thoughtful observers might well have regarded these unhappy accidents as harbingers of calamities yet to come.

Material damage to ships was not the most serious difficulty that beset this campaign in its first stages. More fundamental were the problems which arose from loading transports and tank landing ships so as to conform to the tactical plan of the landing troops. The 81st Division was embarked in the Hawaiian area and the First Marine Division in the Solomon Islands. In both areas the material condition of many of the ships was far from satisfactory, but many of the requests from navy commanders for longer periods of repairs had to be rejected because of insufficient time. There were days when it was doubtful if all the ships of the attack force would be ready to sortie in time, and in some instances ships were drawn out of rehearsals to complete their last-minute loading. The situation in the Solomons was complicated by the fact that the First Marine Division had to be loaded at five widely separated points, namely Pavuvu, Banika (Russells), Guadalcanal, Tulagi, and Espiritu Santo. Pavuvu and Banika had neither enough docks nor beaches to provide for the assault shipping, and loading was a piecemeal process. The marine division was unable to commence its loading plans until only ten days before its ships put in their appearance and were ready to take equipment aboard. As usual, ship characteristics of the transports involved in the operation were not made available to division planners in sufficient time. Then, just before the "final" plans were completed the logistics section of the division was informed by the navy transport group commander that two of his transport divisions would

---

* According to later testimony of Rear Admiral Fort, the loss of *California* was not as serious as it sounded, since the shortage of ammunition due to the protracted length of the Guam operation was so acute as to make it impossible to fill the complete allowances of these two battleships anyway.

be in different areas than had been counted on by the division. This meant that the entire assignment of troops to particular vessels had to be revised radically so that boats and tractors of two of the three regiments in beach assault could hit their respective beaches without crossing each other en route from ship to shore. The tank landing ships presented even more serious problems. Their commander arrived in the Solomons area after loading plans and assignment of troop units had begun and immediately requested that the disposition of his ships be changed in order to conform to his desires. This was done, but only at the cost of radical revision of all previous plans. Logistics officers in the marine division complained that this flotilla commander of the tank landing ships was practically unavailable for conference regarding approval of loading plans and settlement of questions concerning stowage, since he was too busy in various areas trying to get his battered vessels ready for sea. The division requested a liaison officer from the navy with authority to make decisions in such matters, but none was ever furnished. Marine logistics officers also experienced considerable difficulty persuading the tank landing ship commander to permit "understowage," that is stowing equipment in the tank decks as against lashing it topside. This had become commonplace in Central Pacific operations, but this flotilla commander had reportedly never heard of it, and it was only with great reluctance that he finally agreed to the arrangement for such items as rations, barbed wire, pickets, and ammunition.[20]

More serious was the failure to supply adequate shipping for the First Division's organic tanks. Only two dock landing ships were provided for this purpose, and these could carry between them only thirty tanks. This necessitated leaving sixteen behind. Yet these machines were to prove of tremendous value especially in overrunning the southern section of Peleliu, and an additional number would have been more than welcome.[21]

It is little wonder that all concerned breathed deep sighs of relief when the transport groups carrying the First Marine Division finally sortied from its Solomons anchorages with all ships fully loaded and more or less according to standard combat doctrine. Even so, there were, besides tanks, other shortages. Because of the late addition of fifty amphibians to one of the division's tractor battalions, there was insufficient space for trucks and other vehicles necessary for transportation ashore. Engineers and Seabees also complained that inadequate space had been assigned for essential items of their equipment. This was true both for assault shipping and resupply. Important items for road building and airfield construction were left in the staging area. The corps engineering officer complained that combat team loading officers failed to take full cognizance of the priority assigned to engineer equipment which was supposed to rate next after ammunition and rations. This resulted, he reported, in a last-minute scramble to find space for basic items, and equipment of the various units was dispersed throughout many ships, thus adding to the confusion of unloading.[22] But despite these difficulties, the results do not indicate that shortage of equipment made it impossible for the engineers and Seabees to carry out their missions. The fighter strip, the bomber strip, and the pontoon causeway were completed on schedule; the acute water problem on Peleliu was solved; and unloading difficulties on the east coast were cleared up in good time.[23]

The plan for assaulting and capturing island bases in the Palaus was simple and differed in no important respect from previous similar campaigns in the Pacific. The island of Peleliu was the major target, and to it was assigned the First Marine Division, an organization which had demonstrated its high quality in the jungle fighting of Guadalcanal and Cape Gloucester but which as yet had had no experience in the ridge and cave warfare that would be the prevailing type of combat here. Peleliu is a small coral island, about seven square miles in area, enclosed by a coral reef which encircles the entire Palau group except the tiny island of Angaur immediately to the south. (See map 2.) Peleliu is about 450 miles north of the equator. Temperature in September, when it was invaded, sometimes runs above 100° Fahrenheit. There are no rivers, and except for a few swamps the ground drains within a few hours after a heavy rainfall. The predominant vegetation is thick scrub jungle with a mangrove-like growth in the swamps. The northern peninsula is made up of a series of jagged coral ridge lines running generally northeast to southwest. The highest point in this welter of crags, pinnacles, and coral rubble is Umurbrogol Mountain (550 feet), and from this the entire ridge system takes its name. (See map 19.) The whole area was honeycombed with natural caves which the Japanese had enlarged and lengthened so that they interconnected underground. There were no towns of any consequence on the island, but it did boast an important Japanese airfield just south of the mountainous area and close to the west coast. The whole southern section was comparatively flat, but it contained rugged coral outcroppings which lent themselves well to cave defense. It was the sharp ridges and escarpments north of the airfield, however, that proved to be the ideal positions for the defenders.[24]

According to the basic plan, the First Marine Division was ordered to land on September 15 on a 2,600 yard front on Peleliu's southwest beaches with three regiments abreast, First, Fifth, and Seventh Marines from left to right (north to south). Although some doubt has since been cast on the advisability of landing at this particular place, the consensus among planning officers both before and after the operation was that these beaches on the west coast, overlapping the airfield, were the most feasible. Although the reef in this sector was as wide as 750 yards in places, it was not unnegotiable. More important, the airfield and the comparatively level ground immediately to the south was suitable for tank operations and for the emplacement of artillery. It was believed essential to drive across the island as quickly as possible, to secure the airfield and the flat ground below it, before undertaking an assault on the high ground north of the airfield. The jumbled ridges of Umurbrogol Mountain were known to be the key terrain features of the island.[25]

The operation plan called for the First Marines on the left to land with two battalions in assault and one in reserve. In the center, the Fifth Marines were to land with two battalions in assault and one in support.* [26] On the right, the Seventh Marines would come ashore with two leading battalions in column formation. The remaining battalion of this regiment would stay in division reserve and be landed on order when the situation warranted. The scheme of maneuver called for the Fifth Marines in the center to push rapidly across the island and seize the airfield and the eastern shore as quickly as possible. On their right the two assault battalions of the Seventh would also attempt to push across to the eastern shore and then wheel right and mop up any isolated enemy units in the southern tip of the island. On the left the First Marines were to drive inland a few hundred yards then wheel left and attack the southern nose of the ridge system that extended down from the northwest peninsula.[27]

The landing was to be made in amphibian tractors preceded by a wave of armored amphibians which in turn were to be led from the line-of-departure by rocket-firing gunboats. Meanwhile, on the same day, the 81st Division, as yet inexperienced in combat, was to make a diversionary feint toward Babelthuap about thirty miles to the north. Thereafter it would be held in readiness to land in support of the marines in the event the attack on Peleliu proved more difficult than was expected. Otherwise, the army division, less one regiment (scheduled for Ulithi Atoll), was to land on Angaur, ten miles south of Peleliu, a few days after the initial landing or whenever the situation permitted.[28]

The most unusual feature of this plan was that only one battalion was kept in division reserve. With this exception, the entire combat

* The distinction drawn here between a reserve and a support battalion is a fine one. The latter has a definitely assigned mission in the landing plan, whereas the former is committed wherever and whenever the current tactical situation warrants. In this case, the Second Battalion, Fifth Marines, was a support battalion. According to prearranged plan it was to land about an hour after H-hour and take up definitely assigned positions between the two assault battalions.

strength of the First Marine Division was to be committed in the initial landings. To be sure, the corps commander had a contingent reserve in the form of two regiments of the 81st Division which were scheduled to take Angaur after it became apparent that the landing on Peleliu was successful. He also had a floating reserve consisting of the remaining regiment of the 81st Division, the 323rd Infantry Regiment, tentatively earmarked for the occupation of Ulithi. As events turned out, both of these secondary landings were ordered to be executed well before the critical stage on Peleliu had been passed. Not until September 23 were any army units made available for Peleliu. Meanwhile, the First Marine Division, with its single reserve committed in the first day's fighting, had to carry the sole responsibility for assaulting the most heavily fortified small island in the Pacific War outside of Iwo Jima. Had a more realistic view of the formidability of enemy defenses on Peleliu prevailed before the operation was launched, or even after the first day's fighting, it is doubtful that such a heavy burden would have been laid even on the strong shoulders of the First Division. But General Rupertus from the outset of the operation persistently opposed the employment of army troops on Peleliu. Even as late as September 21 when the First Marines were a badly battered outfit and obviously needed relief, he was reluctant to bring in a relatively fresh army regiment and only yielded on the point when so ordered by the corps commander.[29]

2. Preparatory Fires at Peleliu and Angaur

Before the actual landing of troops the customary preliminary aerial and naval bombardment was executed. As early as March 30, five and a half months before the invasion of Palau, pilots from Admiral Spruance's Fifth Fleet gave the Japanese defenders of the islands their first taste of American firepower in a two-day raid during which approximately 600 tons of bombs were dropped. Thereafter the Palau group was left generally unmolested until June, when bombers from MacArthur's Southwest Pacific bases flew frequent missions over the islands in support of the assault on the Marianas. During the summer months these raids were gradually stepped up, and in the last week of August and the first of September a total of more than 300 B-24's flew nine major strikes against the islands dropping over 600 tons of bombs. Thereafter the job was taken over by carrier planes. On September 6, three groups of Halsey's fast carriers (Third Fleet) stood off Palau and prepared to take the islands under aerial bombardment. After three days of moderately heavy bombing and after it had been incorrectly determined that many of the enemy installations had already been badly damaged by the B-24 attacks, these carriers withdrew in order to undertake operations in the Philippine area. While the carriers were bombing likely targets (of which not many were observed) their escorting cruisers and destroyers made several runs of their own against Peleliu and Angaur. But none moved in closer than 7,250 yards, and much fire was conducted from as far as eight miles out to sea.[30] It is doubtful if much serious damage was done from that distance beyond starting a number of fires and knocking down some buildings on the islands. The three carrier groups withdrew on September 10 to undertake operations against the Philippines, but on the same day a fourth task group of fast carriers returned from a picnic sortie against Yap and continued the aerial assault against the Palaus. It was supported by four escort carriers, which number was increased to ten by the day of the landings, September 15, when their planes performed the usual mission of last-minute bombing and troop support during the beach assault phase. All carriers left the area by September 29, by which time sufficient ground-based planes had been landed to support the operation.[31]

Meanwhile, naval support ships had arrived to add to the destruction. The original plan had called for only two days of preparatory naval bombardment. Geiger objected that this was too little and asked for four. He finally got three for Peleliu and five for Angaur which was invaded on September 17, two days after the initial landing on the larger island.[32] Five old battleships, eight cruisers, and fourteen destroyers, most of them veterans of shore bombardment and under the command of Rear Admiral Jesse B. Oldendorf USN, who was later to distinguish himself in the Battle for Leyte Gulf, arrived off Palau on September 12. Oldendorf was handicapped in the execution of his mission both in the facilities he had on hand and in the size of his staff. His flag was an old battleship, not one of the new headquarters ships whose superior communications equipment had been one of the reasons for the increased effectiveness of naval gunfire support in the Marshalls and on Guam. Also he was short on staff personnel. In spite of many previous recommendations to the Bureau of Naval Personnel in Washington he had only a cruiser division staff, consisting of four officers. To add to his difficulties all of these but one were on the sick list during the preliminary bombardment.[33]

In general the pattern of preliminary naval bombardment followed the precedents already clearly established in earlier Pacific operations. On September 15 alone, approximately 1,406 tons of ammunition were expended. Yet in spite of this weight of explosive the landing troops met with a considerable amount of small arms, mortar, and light artillery fire as they hit the beaches. The fact is that enemy casualties from the preliminary bombardment were not heavy. Prisoners of war later confirmed that most of the Japanese had remained safely in shelters until the bombardment lifted, whereupon they emerged generally unscathed and ready to fight.[34] During the bombardment prior to September 15, Oldendorf sent a despatch reporting that all known targets had been silenced and no more were available. Such a gross underestimate of the capabilities of the Japanese on Peleliu can only be explained by the sketchiness of the target maps distributed to the firing ships before the invasion. So long as the Japanese held their fire until the troops crossed the reef there were bound to be a large number of artillery and mortar positions unrevealed to ships or their aerial observers. Without accurate prior intelligence, these could only be disclosed by the attacking troops themselves.[35]

Whatever the reasons, the conclusion cannot be avoided that preliminary naval gunfire on Peleliu was inadequate, and that the lessons learned at Guam were overlooked. Guam had demonstrated without shadow of doubt that slow, prolonged, and deliberate naval bombardment could accomplish amazing results even against a strong, well-equipped, and determined enemy force. Peleliu, like Tarawa and to a lesser extent Saipan, demonstrated that the only substitute for such prolonged bombardment was costly expenditure of the lives of the assault troops.* [36]

3. Seizure of Peleliu, Angaur, and Ulithi

The plan for the actual landing of the troops on Peleliu was different in no important respect from what had become standard operating procedure in Central Pacific amphibious assaults. Early in the morning of September 15 the landing time was confirmed as 0830. By 0715 the tank landing ships had arrived at their launching area as scheduled. Weather was excellent; the sea was calm and there was almost no surf. In addition to naval gunfire the troops enjoyed the benefit of direct air strikes on the beaches immediately prior to the landing. Beginning at 0750 and until 0805 fifty carrier planes made an attack against gun positions and beach installations on and near the landing beaches. Naval gunfire was continued throughout this attack, the planes flying high enough to stay clear of naval shells.

---

* Rear Admiral George H. Fort disagrees with these conclusions. He has stated, "I cannot accept . . . [the] statement that thirteen days shore bombardment are necessarily a lot better than three. If three days are sufficient, the remaining ten days are an absolute waste of expensive and scarce ammunition." And again, "If Admiral Oldendorf broke off fire before he had used up his allowed ammunition on the grounds that there were no more targets, he was entirely correct. The idea that some people seem to have of just firing at an island is an inexcusable waste of ammunition." Even if there had been plenty of targets, Admiral Fort asserted that "some of the fire support ships reported so late that it was impossible for them to arrive at the objective until D-3. The D date was set to coordinate with MacArthur's simultaneous landing in S.W. Pacific and could not be delayed. Hence three days bombardment was all that was possible. . . ."

Troops, loaded as usual in amphibian tractors, moved in wave formations into the shore behind rocket-firing gunboats and a first wave of armored amphibians. As soon as the gunboats ceased firing, forty-eight navy fighter-bombers began strafing attacks on the landing areas, moving their point of aim inland as the tractors approached the beach.[37]

In spite of enemy fire from the moment it crossed the reef, the first wave succeeded in getting ashore within two minutes of the scheduled landing time. Successive waves landed at approximately five-minute intervals. None of the amphibian vehicles was lost outside the reef line, but as succeeding waves crossed the reef they were met with steadily increasing enemy fire. The plan called for the armored amphibians to support the infantry inshore. Once ashore, however, armored vehicles encountered unexpected difficulties. Heavy mortar and gunfire covered the beaches, especially the flanks. (See map 19.) Horned mines and buried 75-kilogram aircraft bombs were found in great quantities at the high water mark and caused quite a few casualties. An antitank ditch measuring about ten feet wide and eight feet deep extended intermittently along most of the beach front, and seriously impeded all movement inland until routes around it could be found. As late as two hours after the initial landing the situation ashore was still so confused that it was virtually impossible for the armored amphibians to contact by radio the troops they were supposed to support. Casualties among all the amphibians, including Dukws, were heavy throughout the day. The reef and beaches were quickly littered with disabled vehicles. The total amphibian tractor losses alone on September 15 amounted to twenty-six machines.[38]

Fortunately, the First Marine Division did not rely so heavily on armored amphibians to support the first waves of troops as had the Fifth Amphibious Corps on Saipan. During the latter operation, no tanks were landed for more than an hour and a half after the first troops touched shore. At Peleliu, tanks were debarked at the reef's edge only twenty minutes after the first wave had landed. Thirty medium tanks with amphibian tractors to guide them proceeded across the broad fringing reef in six parallel columns of five tanks each. Each column was guided around boulders, potholes, and bomb craters by its amphibian tractor guide. Due to the shallowness of the water inside the lagoon and the smoothness of the reef, all but three of the thirty tanks were able to get ashore within ten minutes in spite of heavy artillery and mortar fire.[39] Thus within a half hour after the initial landing the infantry had full tank support—a record unsurpassed in any previous marine landings in the Central Pacific, except the Marshalls.

Once ashore the troops encountered extremely bitter fighting all

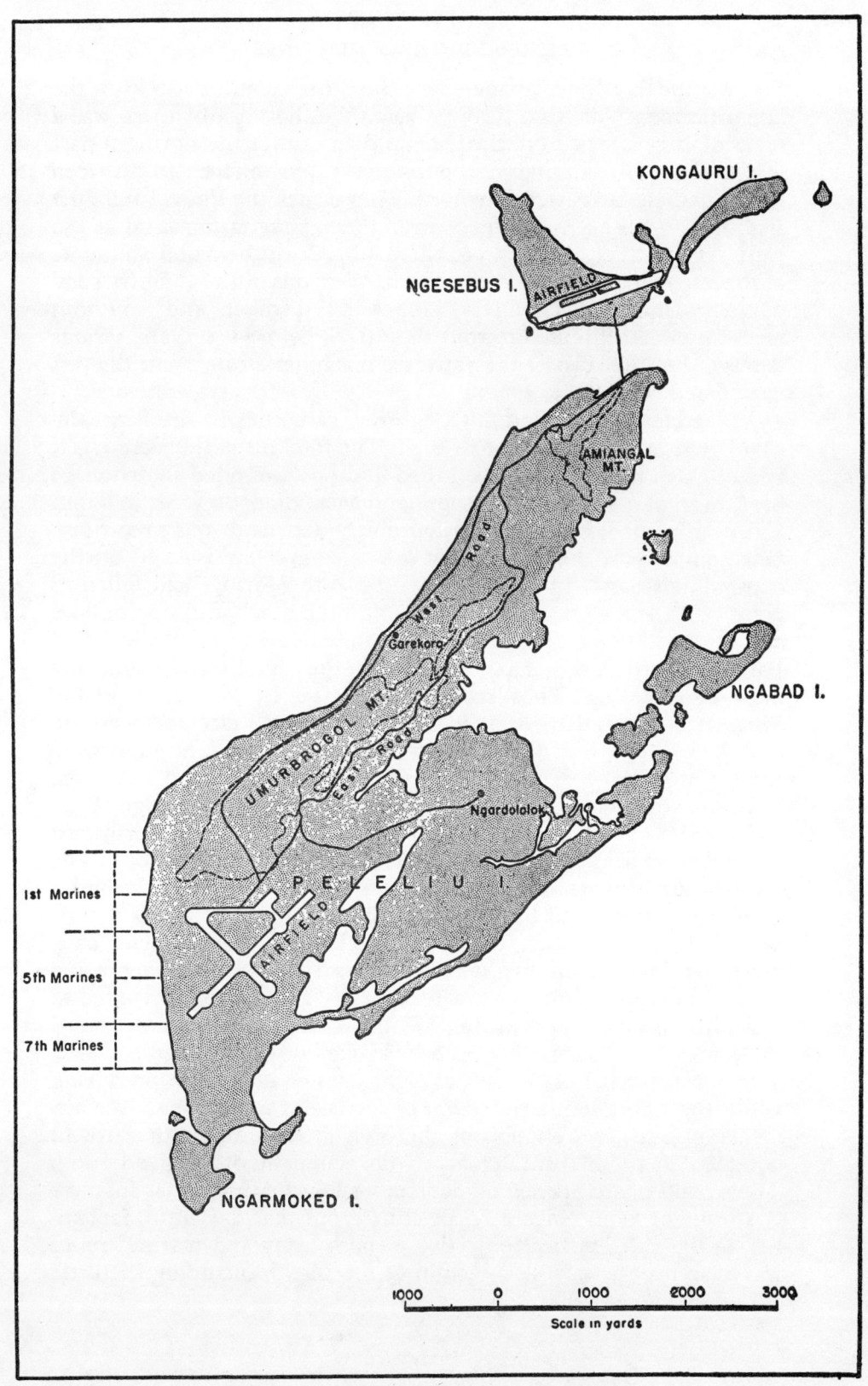

MAP 19. Peleliu and adjacent islands.

through the day. The Japanese launched three counterattacks in the late afternoon. All were thrown back. The heaviest of these was a tank-infantry attack from the general direction of the northern part of the airfield beginning at about 1700. From thirteen to nineteen light Japanese tanks were involved. They struck the lines of the First Battalion, Fifth Marines, and overran them, penetrating as far as 150 yards beyond. Yet nowhere was there a break in the front, and none of the enemy tanks reached the beach. Weapons of the infantry companies, 75-millimeter artillery, a navy dive bomber, and American medium tanks all joined to rout this attack before it did any serious damage. Possibly two of the Japanese machines escaped but the rest were demolished.[40]

At the close of the first day's fighting, casualties in the First Marine Division were exorbitantly high. The total casualties were 1,111, and of this number 210 were killed and 901 wounded in action. A beachhead of 3,000 yards in length and averaging 500 yards in depth had been gained, but the situation on the left flank was precarious. One company of the First Marines was completely isolated on the extreme left flank. In the south the Seventh Marines had failed to occupy all the area between the coast and the beachhead line inshore and were still desperately trying to tie in with elements of the Third Battalion, Fifth Marines, on their left. In the center the situation was more encouraging. The Second Battalion, First Marines, and the First Battalion, Fifth Marines, were in good contact and were established on the beachhead line facing the airfield. The most spectacular progress of the day had been made by the Second Battalion, Fifth Marines, which had penetrated across the southern edge of the airfield almost to the eastern coast and had then moved northward to the center of the airfield, an advance of about 1,500 yards.[41] The assistant division commander (Brigadier General Oliver P. Smith USMC) had established his command post ashore. The artillery regiment (Eleventh Marines) had two battalions of 75-millimeter pack howitzers in position, registered and ready to furnish supporting fires. A battalion of 105-millimeter howitzers was ashore prepared to move into position by morning.

Briefly, the fighting ashore can be broken down into three phases. The first consisted of the initial eight days of the operation during which the whole southern section of the island was overrun, the airfield captured, and enough of the high ground above the airfield occupied to permit uninterrupted development of the field itself. The second phase opened on September 23 when the 321st Infantry was brought from Angaur to Peleliu. From that day until September 29 the chief tactical objective of both army and marine troops was to secure the northern section of the island, including the little islet of Ngesebus off the northern coast, and to isolate the enemy in the Umurbrogol Mountain system. This was accomplished by September 29 when the Japanese had been largely cleared away except for those holed up in the formidable Umurbrogol pocket. From that date until long after the last marine had left Peleliu the fighting settled down into a form of siege warfare, the only possible way by which the tenacious enemy could be slowly blasted out of his mountain stronghold.[42]

The southern section of the island was assigned to the Seventh Marines. Although this area was flat by comparison to the terrain north of the airfield, it was by no means easy going. From shore to shore the region was covered with pillboxes, casemates, bunkers, rifle pits, and trenches. Once off the sand beaches there was little natural cover for the attacking forces, and the hard coral formation made digging impossible. Nevertheless the two assault battalions of the Seventh Regimental Combat Team made fairly short work of these obstacles. The Second Battalion, Seventh Marines, the division reserve, was landed on September 16 but attached to the First Marines in the north where the opposition was toughest. By mid-afternoon of September 17 the Third Battalion, Seventh Marines, one of the two battalions to the south, had overrun the whole southeast promontory and had secured the entire southeast coast. The southwestern promontory opposite it (sometimes called Ngarmoked Island) was a tougher nut, but by evening of the 18th it too had been captured by the First Battalion of the Seventh Marines. Fighting on the southern part of the island was by that date finished except for the usual mopping up. The equivalent of a Japanese reinforced infantry battalion well-entrenched in strong fortified positions had been put out of action.

The Fifth Marines also made rapid progress in the center. Their main objective was the seizure of the airfield and of the flat swampy ground on the east coast. There was little resistance on the field itself, but its location close under the towering ridges to the north made it an ideal position upon which the Japanese could register their fire. By September 16 the field itself had been to all intents and purposes captured; thereafter the line of advance of the Fifth Marines lay north and northeast across the low ground to the east of the main ridge line. On the 18th they crossed the causeway leading over into the eastern peninsula and on the 20th the whole of that area was captured. Except for seizing the few remaining islands off the northeast coast which took a few more days, the first mission of the Fifth Marines was accomplished.

It was the First Marines on the north flank that took the heaviest beating as they came up early against the cruel terrain of the

Umurbrogol Hill mass. After overrunning the building area north of the airfield the regiment on September 17 made an effort to attack northward against Umurbrogol's ridge system. By that evening a foothold had been established on the first high ground, but thereafter the fighting slowed down into a slugging match with only slight progress made, at least in terms of feet of ground gained. After six frightful days of the worst imaginable combat the regiment was definitely stopped. As of September 21, the casualties of the First Marines were reported to total 1,749. Late in the afternoon of the previous day all but one of its battalions as well as the reserve battalion attached to it were relieved by the two battalions of the Seventh Marines, which had taken the southern end of the island. To the north, a virtual stalemate had been reached.

Meanwhile on September 17, two regiments of the 81st Infantry Division (the 321st and 322nd Regimental Combat Teams) landed against nominal opposition on two separate beaches on Angaur Island. They were able to consolidate their individual beachheads on the first day, although not until the following morning could they establish contact with each other. After four days' fighting the backbone of enemy resistance was broken. One regiment was left to mop up, and the 321st Infantry was made available to be fed into Peleliu.

The second phase of the Peleliu operation consisted of a drive to seize all of the northern part of the island. (See map 19.) The tactical objectives were threefold: first, to isolate the Umurbrogol pocket of resistance and gain approaches from the north to assault it; second, to conduct a shore-to-shore movement against tiny Ngesebus which was thought to have a useful auxiliary airfield; and third, to put a stop to further enemy reinforcements being brought by boat from the islands to the north.

On September 23 the 321st Infantry landed on Peleliu and quickly moved into position to relieve the remaining battered battalion (First) of the First Marines, then on the left flank of the line stretching across the southern edge of Umurbrogol. With the Third Battalion, Seventh Marines, supporting on the right rear, the army regiment rapidly advanced up the west coast through the town of Carakero. On September 24 a strong combat patrol was sent northward about 2,000 yards and discovered only slight enemy opposition. On the same day elements of the 321st probing eastward succeeded in capturing the hill marking the northern extremity of Umurbrogol. These two events induced Rupertus to assign to the army regiment the job of sealing off Umurbrogol by driving eastward across its northern edge and at the same time to commit the Fifth Marines to the northwest tip of the island which contained a cave-ridden ridge system known as Amiangal Mountain.

Consequently in the late morning of September 25 the Fifth Marines, then stationed in scattered dispositions on the eastern peninsula and its surrounding islands, were ordered to pass through the 321st's lines north of Garekoru on the northwest coast. They assembled rapidly and within two and a half hours of the first verbal order advanced elements of the Fifth Marines were in position to launch their attack. The next day the army and marine regiments conducted a two-pronged drive eastward, both succeeding in reaching the eastern coast of the northwest peninsula. Thus both Umurbrogol and the northern tip were sealed off, and the enemy could feed no more men by barge onto Peleliu. All that remained of this phase of the action was to complete the capture of the northern tip of the island and Ngesebus and to close the gap north of the 321st and south of the Fifth Marines.

The Amiangal system of the northern tip was only slightly less well fortified and defended than the Umurbrogol pocket. It contained perhaps the largest and most elaborate cave on all Peleliu, garrisoned by more than 1,000 Japanese, and was protected not only by its own fire but also by artillery on Ngesebus. It was partially neutralized on September 27 by the combined employment of artillery and naval gunfire, by waterborne armored amphibian tractor fire into cave mouths facing the sea, by amphibian tractor flamethrowers, and, of course, by infantry. Organized resistance in the area was finished a few days later.

September 28 saw a successful shore-to-shore operation against Ngesebus. With excellent preparatory naval, aerial, and artillery bombardment the Third Battalion, Fifth Marines, landed and took the island with a minimum of casualties. The airfield proved to be too soft and sandy to be used, but at least the danger of harassing artillery was eliminated. By the 29th, marines and soldiers had cleared out remaining heavy pockets of resistance on the northwest peninsula of Peleliu, and the way was now open for the final push against Umurbrogol.

As September ended, the entire island was in American hands with the exception of the by-passed mountain stronghold which consisted of a pocket about 900 yards in length and 400 yards in width. An estimated 888 marines and soldiers had been killed and about 4,500 were reported wounded or missing in action. Of this total of 5,388 casualties, 5,044 were members of the First Marine Division. On September 30, Rear Admiral George H. Fort, in command of the Western Attack Force, declared Peleliu to be secured. This pronouncement may have seemed premature to some of the men ashore who would spend another eight weeks in reducing the single remaining pocket of enemy resistance. The cost in casualties still to come was also heavy. By November 27, in addition to those listed above, the First Marine Division lost another 281 killed and 1,170 wounded and the 321st Infantry suffered a total of more than 100 killed and 700 wounded.[43] Nevertheless, the fact that it would take another eight weeks of methodical reduction of the Umurbrogol pocket should not obscure the fact that the island *was* to all intents and purposes secured by September 30, fifteen days after the landing. By that time all of the supply beaches which were ever used were in full operation. The airfield, which was the primary target, had been captured and was in operation with only desultory interference from the Japanese. And, perhaps most important, the enemy had suffered approximately 8,800 casualties, and those remaining were compressed in a very small if still very strong area.[44]

Meanwhile, as operations were proceeding apace at Peleliu and Angaur, another American invasion (which was to have significant strategic and logistical consequences on the subsequent war in the Pacific) was being carried out at Ulithi about 260 miles to the northeast. Ulithi Atoll lies slightly south of a line between Guam and Peleliu and about equidistant from both. It consists of some thirty islets dotting a reef which surrounds a large lagoon, the northern part of which forms one of the best anchorages for large ships in the Central Pacific.

In spite of the cancellation of the Yap phase of the Western Carolines campaign, it was decided to go ahead with the original plans to capture Ulithi. The atoll was expected to be weakly defended if at all; and, since the use of its lagoon as a fleet anchorage in the operations against the Philippines and later was considered highly desirable, plans were made to send one regimental combat team from the 81st Infantry Division to take it. Accordingly on September 23, after the usual preliminary minesweeping and reconnaissance by underwater demolition teams, the 323rd Infantry Regiment landed on the most prominent islets of the atoll. No Japanese were discovered, and the natives proved friendly. Thus with a minimum of cost, the fleet gained a new harbor which was to prove of immense value in subsequent movements farther west.[45]

October brought about a change in the general complexion of fighting on Peleliu. From one of assault and aggressive forward movement the operation now settled down into a battle of attrition. In the words of Rupertus, it became "a slow, slugging, yard-by-yard struggle to blast the enemy from his last remaining stronghold in the high ground to the north of the airfield. This drive constituted within itself almost a separate operation, the rugged almost impassable terrain requiring more time to clean out than previously had been spent in clearing all the Southern Palaus." [46] Against the parallel ridges, the sharp peaks almost empty of cover, and the vertical cliffs pocked with caves and deeply gutted depressions, it proved extremely difficult to place direct fire either by artillery or naval or aerial bombardment. The only feasible tactics were flamethrowers, demolition teams, and infantry assault.

October also brought an intensification of rain squalls and wind. By the 4th of that month strong winds and high seas had reached almost typhoon proportions and the disembarkation of supplies came to a standstill. Two tank landing ships unloading at the pontoon causeway on the western shore were beached by the swells, and other craft were unable to debark. With only four days' rations on the island, troops were reduced for a while to two meals a day.

Battle casualties plus heat exhaustion were taking their toll. The First Marines who had borne the brunt of the early attack against southern Umurbrogol were so bruised and battered that it was decided to evacuate them. On October 2 they sailed for Pavuvu—not an ideal spot to lick their wounds, but at least preferable to Peleliu.

The next day two battalions of the Seventh Marines succeeded in capturing important positions on the east side of the Umurbrogol system overlooking the main road along the east coast. The 4th of October was the last day in which the Seventh operated offensively on Peleliu as a regiment. It was relieved on October 5-6 by the Fifth Marines who continued to press against the Umurbrogol pocket chiefly from the north and eventually succeeded in reducing it by about thirty per cent. Elements of the Seventh Marines were later fed back into the line at various points along the slowly shortening perimeter. On October 12, General Geiger officially declared the assault phase to be finished, and steps were commenced to replace all marine regiments with fresher troops of the 81st Infantry Division. By October 16 all marine units had been relieved of duty in the front lines, and on October 20 Major General Paul Mueller USA of the 81st Division took command of combat forces in the Southern Palaus. For all but a few marines this was the end of the show. Total casualties for the First Division as of this date numbered 1,124 killed, 5,024 wounded, and 117 missing in action. Against this figure was an estimated total of 10,695 enemy dead and 301 prisoners of war.[47] Some rugged fighting still lay ahead for the 81st Division. Not until November 27 was the last organized resistance on Peleliu declared to be over.

The Japanese had put up a stubborn and highly intelligent defense. Their application of established tactical principles differed considerably from anything previously encountered by the First Marine Division. In the first place, they did not waste their men needlessly in the hopeless banzai attacks which had typified earlier Pacific operations. Their only counterattacks occurred on the first day, and these were well organized, the troops withdrawing in an orderly fashion when repulsed. The only serious shortcomings in their tactics was the usual Japanese failure, or rather inability, to make maximum effective use of their heavier weapons. They had on hand enough artillery and heavy mortars to have made American exploitation of the landing beaches extremely difficult if not impossible—had they been able to mass their fires.

In all probability, however, the Japanese had no alternative but to pursue the course they did—that is to conceal their weapons and hold their fire until the most lucrative targets appeared. In the face of superior American naval and aerial firepower before and during the landing, and of superior American artillery after the first day's operation, this decision was forced upon them. They had to emplace most of their artillery in caves to escape the initial weight of American bombardment. The field of fire from a cave is obviously narrow and limited. Moreover, massed fires require correspondingly massive communications. And by September 1944 it had been amply demonstrated that whatever the other limitations of preparatory naval gunfire, it was uniformly successful in destroying Japanese communications unless these were well dug in.[48]

On the beaches and their approaches, the Japanese appeared to have put their heaviest reliance on mines and similar obstacles. Over 1,300 horned anti-invasion mines were later discovered to have been placed for both antiboat and antivehicle purposes on and near the edge of beaches.

But their best defense was terrain, and they made good use of it. Inland from the northern beaches they had blasted a series of interlocking caves into the almost perpendicular coral ridges. Destruction of these proved to be the most difficult feature of the operation. Their caves varied from simple holes large enough to accommodate two men to large tunnels with passageways on either side capacious enough to contain artillery or 150-millimeter mortars. Some of them were equipped with camouflaged steel doors. All of their positions were carefully chosen, well camouflaged, and presenting as good fields of fire as conditions of cave construction permitted.

Exploiting the terrain possibilities to the utmost, their plan was one of defense in depth. All pillboxes and casemates were in the best commanding positions, and all were linked in a system of mutual cover and support. When driven from coastal and immediately inland positions, the enemy was able to fall back to prepared positions on the high ground to the north and easily to cover the terrain he had just vacated with his artillery. Never before in the Pacific War had the Japanese displayed greater resourcefulness or exploited their capabilities more successfully.[49]

4. Tactical and Amphibious Aspects

For the infantryman to overcome these obstacles the best weapons proved to be the bazooka, the portable flamethrower, the flamethrower mounted on amphibian tractors, and demolitions. Artillery was employed where possible, and medium tanks proved useful especially on level ground. The bazooka was very effective against pillboxes, caves, and enemy field pieces. Marines were somewhat handicapped at first in their employment of portable flamethrowers because last-minute delivery before embarkation resulted in insufficient training. Probably the greatest deficiency demonstrated by the troops, however, was in the proper employment of demolitions. Infantrymen had not received sufficient training in the employment of explosives, and the combat engineers had too much else to do to fill the gap completely.[50] The truth is that the intricate cave system of defense on Peleliu required a much larger assignment of special demolition personnel than the First Marine Division enjoyed.

ARTILLERY AND LOGISTICS

Division artillery (Eleventh Marines) was somewhat slow in getting ashore on the day of beach assault due to heavy casualties to amphibian tractors and Dukws. The first two battalions (75-millimeter howitzers) could not get ashore and in position until half-past three in the afternoon. The third (105-millimeter howitzers) had one battery ashore before nightfall, but the remainder had to put back out to sea in their Dukws to await the next day to be brought in and emplaced. The fourth battalion (also 105-millimeter) managed to set up makeshift positions on the southern beaches and had one battery ready to fire by nightfall of the first day. In addition to its own organic artillery, the division had two battalions of Third Amphibious Corps 155-millimeter howitzers assigned to its operational control. These were fully emplaced by the second day after the landing. Observation was provided by forward and aerial observers, the latter operating initially from escort carriers until the artillery regiment's own observation planes were able to land on Peleliu airstrip on September 18.

Although throughout the operation, artillery fired many valuable missions, the size of the land and especially the rapid reduction of enemy-controlled territory limited its usefulness. The chief deficiency in Marine Corps artillery equipment was the absence of a short-range high-angle weapon as an auxiliary artillery arm. When enemy action was limited to a small pocket this lack became pronounced. The 60- and 81-millimeter infantry mortars were only partially successful, and the former were too unreliable. The army's new 4.2-inch mortars served the purpose admirably, but none had yet been issued to the First Marine Division.[51]

After the restriction of enemy resistance to the Umurbrogol pocket, artillery could seldom be used in the conventional manner. The two 75-millimeter pack howitzer battalions were among the first units to be ordered evacuated. Some of the remaining artillery pieces were used for direct fire missions at unusually short distances, and other artillerymen not thus employed were put on the line to serve as infantrymen. In the last phase of fighting by marines there were many instances of howitzers being hoisted to awkward and almost inaccessible positions to fire directly at cave mouths from ranges of only 200–300 yards.[52]

There was some difficulty in building up desirable levels of ammunition both for the artillery and the infantry regiments. This was largely due to the intense fighting and the high expenditure rate. In the early days of the battle there were shortages in 105-millimeter howitzer, 81-millimeter mortar, and 60-millimeter mortar illumination shells.[53] But there are no known instances where missions could not be fired because of acute ammunition shortages.

There were other more serious logistical difficulties. Unloading of supplies was hampered largely by the lack of any anchorage or shelter for small craft, by the long reef that surrounded the landing beaches, by mortar fire on the beach and on boats in the assembly areas, and by the necessity for clearing the beaches of the mines which the enemy had planted. In addition high winds and heavy seas virtually stopped all unloading from October 2 to 5. Not until October 12 did unloading get back to a normal rate of 1,000 tons daily. It was during this period that rations had to be flown in by planes stationed on the island. The supply situation on Peleliu was aided somewhat by the later use of Kossol Passage seventy miles to the north, off Babelthuap Island, by naval vessels. Although this was not an ideal anchorage it did provide some protection for damaged ships and those waiting unloading. By September 27 a total of sixty-six ships were anchored there.[54]

Shore party operations in the marines' zone of action were not always conducted with maximum efficiency. In the marine division each regiment was allotted a pioneer company assisted by miscellaneous personnel from various garrison units. In contrast, the 81st Infantry Division at Angaur had a shore party consisting of an engineer group headquarters and two battalions of combat engineers, thus giving each infantry regiment a full battalion for shore party duties. Geiger's engineering officer, in comparing the two, concluded that "it may be anticipated that for as long as the Marine Corps continues to throw service organizations together at the last minute from odd units and personnel the efficiency of their functioning will be decreased accordingly." [55]

It is true that the marine shore parties had to undergo far greater hazards than their army counterparts on Angaur. On the smaller island the beaches were relatively free of reefs, and there was very little enemy opposition. On Peleliu, by contrast, the beaches were surrounded by a reef, were heavily mined, and were subjected to heavy enemy fire during the most critical stage of landing operations. Moreover, essential personnel were often withdrawn from the shore parties to perform other duties. During the first days of the operation their demolition teams were frequently detached to serve with infantry units. A demolition team from Company A of the First Pioneer Battalion was assigned to Third Battalion, First Marines, with whom they worked for five days blasting caves from which the infantry unit was receiving fire. Company C was also called upon to furnish demolition personnel to the First Marines, from whose command post they labored for a period of eleven days, carrying out assault demolition missions and clearing mines and duds from the areas of advance. Also the pioneer battalion was frequently called on to send its own bulldozers to knock out enemy pillboxes in front of infantry positions, to haul supplies to front line troops directly from shore dumps, and to supply its own machine guns to fulfill infantry requests.[56] This diversion of effort prevented exploitation of the full capabilities of an organization intended for the specialized supply function.

Water supply was a problem that plagued logistics personnel from the outset of the operation. Because of the nature of the terrain on Peleliu, water drains off only a few hours after even a very heavy rainfall, and there were no natural reservoirs for its collection. Hence engineers carried with them additional distillation units. They also took the precaution to bring extra water with them from Pavuvu, but the drums and cans in which it was stored were either incompletely filled or improperly cleaned so that most of it was undrinkable. In the first days of combat with temperature rising to as high as 115° Fahrenheit the shortage was acutely felt. However, ground wells were located shortly after the landing and by September 19 a minimum of 50,000 gallons a day was available.

This comparative plenitude did not detract from the marines' appreciation of an unexpected windfall in the line of potable beverage. In a rare and wonderful gesture, Admiral Fort's flagship, *Mount McKinley*, sent her entire remaining supply of beer (500 cases) ashore just before she left the area. It was divided equally among front line troops with incalculable effects on morale.[57]

NAVAL GUNFIRE AND CLOSE AIR SUPPORT

Beer was not the navy's most important gift to the ground troops. Naval gunfire in this as in previous and subsequent operations played, within limits, a significant role in the final reduction of the enemy.

After the establishment of the beachhead, fire-support ships continued to deliver missions of all kinds in support of the troops ashore. Deep support fires by cruisers helped to reduce many positions believed to contain enemy defenses. Harassing fire was conducted nightly as requested by the First Marine Division's naval liaison officer. Since the two roads on the east and west coasts were almost the only means of moving troops or supplies, interdiction fires on these thoroughfares were maintained nightly. In the early stages of the operation, morning attacks launched by infantry were usually supported by heavy preparatory ship gunfire. Star shell illumination helped to prevent infiltrations and gave needed reassurance to ground troops at night. Ships also sailed picket patrols north of Peleliu to hamper enemy reinforcements from Babelthuap, and on the night of September 23/24 one destroyer reported the destruction of thirteen enemy barges northeast of Ngesebus.[58]

Shore fire-control parties were set up on Peleliu about two and a half hours after the first landing. The division's naval liaison officer consolidated the fire and relayed necessary information to the command ship. Naval gunnery personnel on *Mount McKinley* prepared the schedule of fires and assigned the necessary ships. When close support naval gunfire missions were no longer feasible, ships with observation planes attached were assigned missions in deep support to reduce fortifications ahead of the advance.[59]

Naval gunfire liaison officers with attached personnel were assigned to division and to each regiment and battalion. The division naval liaison officer went ashore with the advanced detachment of the division staff and operated in the vicinity of the division command post throughout the campaign. Regimental and battalion gunfire liaison officers did likewise in their respective echelons. Fire missions were ordered from all three units. Battalion requests were of course monitored by regimental and divisional naval liaison officers; regimental requests, by the division officer.

No clear directive was issued governing priorities or coordination as between air, artillery, and naval gunfire. A rather loose system of coordination was established by having all three directing elements together at the division command post. This enabled each to know what the other was doing, but no precedence was assigned to any single element of the three supporting arms. In a small operation of this sort no serious friction resulted, and the system proved fairly workable, although later in the war it was necessary to give ultimate authority for coordinating missions to artillery.

There were certain defects in the operation of shore fire-control parties, chiefly caused by lack of training. Many of the personnel attached had joined the division too late to have sufficient time to train and to become acquainted with the infantry units to which they were assigned. A more serious deviation from standard naval gunfire support doctrine was that the First Division had no marine officer serving as naval gunfire officer to work with the staff of the naval gunfire support commander. Tables of organization at the time authorized an officer of the rank of major to serve as artillery and naval gunfire coordinator, but none had been appointed within this division. During the planning phase a junior navy officer was provided by Third Amphibious Corps to assist in preparing plans for allocating naval fire to meet ground force requirements. Later, another junior navy officer was assigned to the division by Fifth Amphibious Corps for purposes of indoctrinating and instructing the marine shore fire-control parties and naval liaison officers. But nowhere in the division was to be found a marine officer fully qualified to undertake the complex duties of coordinating ships' fire with artillery and troop movements.[60]

The fact remains that even under a more efficient system of administration and control, naval gunfire would inevitably have been a weapon of limited value on Peleliu. The nature of the defenses and the configuration of terrain were certainly not ideal for the fullest exploitation of ships' fire. Lack of good points of observation made it difficult to call down fires accurately. More important, the fact that for so large a part of the operation the enemy was completely holed up underground and in heavily protected caves made it next to impossible to bring effective gunfire to bear against many positions. Even Geiger's naval gunfire officer, an enthusiast for his specialty, was forced to conclude that the "lack of good observation and the nature of the targets (i.e. caves and underground shelters) made naval gunfire support extremely difficult. The results in most cases were doubtful since it was necessary to fire on the same targets many times. . . ."[61] Geiger's operations officer was even more skeptical and warned, "it still remains a fact that naval guns cannot search defiladed areas, nor can they effectively destroy or neutralize mobile artillery or mortars. Therefore, one must guard against the overenthusiasm of naval gunfire advocates who believe that nothing can survive the heavy bombardments. It remains imperative that field artillery be landed at the earliest practicable moment and that aircraft devote their greatest attention to areas unassailable by naval gunfire."[62]

Naval gunfire experts might not subscribe to this degree of pessimism, but would be compelled to admit that at least during the latter phase of the Peleliu operation this particular weapon could be employed only with partial success.

From the point of view of amphibious development the story of close air support in the Palaus is in some ways the most significant aspect of the entire campaign. Here, for the first time on any considerable scale since the Solomons, marine pilots had the chance to demonstrate their virtuosity in the type of aerial tactics in which they claimed preeminence. They had practiced low-level bombing and strafing with marine ground forces at Culebra, San Clemente, and New River and with army forces in Louisiana and the Carolinas. In the twenties they had flown actual combat support missions in Haiti, Santo Domingo, and Nicaragua.[63] But during the war itself the bulk of marine aviation after 1943 was largely diverted from this central mission. Now on Peleliu they were awarded the opportunity to put this close support doctrine to another test. Many of the defensive installations were so constructed as to be invulnerable to anything but direct hits and not even always to those. The area occupied by the enemy was so small and so close to the front line of the attacking troops that bombing or even strafing was sometimes too dangerous to attempt. In spite of these limitations, the operation offered marine pilots an excellent opportunity to demonstrate their skill at precision bombing and accurate strafing.

During the landings on Peleliu and Angaur, direct air support was supplied by navy pilots from fast and escort carriers. From September 18, when the fast carriers left the area, to September 28, all strikes were flown exclusively from escort carriers. These included both scheduled and call missions requested by battalion, regimental, or division commanders. Within this ten-day period the escort planes flew over 300 missions and dropped a total of 620 tons of bombs.[64]

By September 16 the Fifth Marines had seized the airfield on Peleliu, and began work to make it operational. Two days later a navy torpedo bomber made a successful emergency landing, and the next day artillery spotting planes commenced regular operations from the strip.[65] On September 24 the first echelon of marine combat planes consisting of eight night fighters landed on the field. Thereafter a steady stream of marine fighters and bombers made their appearance. By the end of September a total of one squadron of fighters and half a squadron of night fighters were operating from Peleliu. By the end of October the Peleliu strip was home base for three squadrons of marine Corsairs, one squadron of night fighting Hellcats, and a squadron of navy Avenger torpedo planes for antisubmarine patrol. By that time a strip at Angaur had also been developed and was accommodating two squadrons of army Liberators and was also serving as a staging point for army transports.[66] These planes, army, navy, and marine, were all combined into a joint command designated Garrison Air Forces, Western Carolines under command of Brigadier General James T. Moore USMC.

The system set up for controlling carrier-based air strikes followed standard procedure as it had been developed in previous amphibious operations. Before the landings were made, an advance commander of support aircraft controlled and coordinated strikes with naval gunfire during the period of preliminary bombardment. The day of the assault the commander support aircraft, embarked in *Mount McKinley,* took over control, and his assistant subsequently went ashore and prepared to take over in the event the command ship was disabled. Another assistant was assigned the equivalent job for the occupation of Angaur.[67]

After the departure of the escort carriers on September 28, control passed to the Garrison Air Force commander ashore. Previously, battalions and regiments made requests for supporting air strikes directly to the commander support aircraft afloat. Upon assumption of control by division headquarters, all requests were monitored by the division air liaison officer working in conjunction with his counterparts in artillery and naval gunfire. Such requests were either granted or denied depending on whether or not the specific target could be better taken under fire by air or by one of the other two agencies.

After all the artillery was ashore by September 17, navy air was used mainly as a deep support weapon, and division headquarters instructed subordinate air liaison parties to call for close air support missions only on targets which could not be reached by artillery, that is targets in defilade or on reverse slopes. Nevertheless, there was a consistent tendency on the part of battalion and regimental commanders to use air against targets that could normally have been taken under fire by artillery or naval guns. This would seem to indicate that front line troops who were in a better position to witness the accuracy of aerial bombing were more trustful of its efficiency and safety than rear echelons. As the marines advanced northward, the opportunities for close air support decreased and by September 21 almost all air was being employed as a deep support weapon in the northern part of the island and on antibarge and strafing strikes. The exception was Marine Air Group 11, which continued to be employed in close support missions.

In general, regimental commanders were more than satisfied with air missions flown in support of their particular units. This was especially true while the fighting was going on in the level terrain in the southern half of the island, where it was relatively easy to mark and distinguish front lines and where the targets were fairly easy to pick up. After the fighting became centered in the rugged hilly area around Mount Umurbrogal, close air support was called on less frequently, although by no means discarded entirely. For one thing, it was difficult to distinguish friendly lines. For another, the maps of the hill area of Peleliu were so inaccurate that it was sometimes next to impossible to coach a pilot onto the desired target. Finally, all missions were controlled directly from the headquarters ship until the carriers left the area. In no instance until September 28 was any battalion air liaison party on the ground allowed to control missions in the sector where it had a direct and intimate knowledge.

Another defect in this first phase of naval aerial support of which ground troops complained was that the commander of support aircraft showed the usual reluctance to allow his planes to go in against a target when artillery was firing, and this slowed up the execution of missions considerably. Throughout the early part of the operation, also, ground troops complained that too often navy flight leaders failed to send word when their missions were completed. This resulted in a serious interference with artillery fires which in every case had been lifted to allow the strike to go in.

But all of these complaints made by infantry troops about the alleged deficiencies of close air support were confined to the period when it was under control afloat. After marine planes were stationed ashore, and after Marine Air Group 11 commenced operations, infantry troops were more than satisfied with the aerial support provided them. In the restrained official language of Rupertus's action report, "the missions carried out by Marine Air Group 11 were executed in a manner leaving little to be desired from a point of view of close support to ground troops." [68]

Marine Air Group 11 operated under peculiar circumstances in that its field was practically on the front line itself. As far as the ground troops were concerned this was a definite advantage since it shortened considerably the time required for air requests to be executed. It took less than fifteen seconds for Corsairs to fly from the field to positions from which they were to drop their bombs on Umurbrogol Mountain. But for air personnel the situation was not so pleasant. Heavy fighting on the ground took place within sight of their bivouac area. During their first days ashore, airmen and their ground crews found themselves being pressed into service as stretcher bearers. Some were used as riflemen and grenade throwers in support of ground troops, and several casualties were incurred in the group in their unusual capacity as infantrymen. In October, a dump of abandoned Japanese ammunition exploded near the camp area. All hands scrambled for cover and no damage was done, but the incident gave birth to a new song called "Praise the Lord, the Ammunition Passed Me." [69]

Two days after the first marine squadron (Marine Fighter Squadron 114, a part of Marine Air Group 11) came ashore, it was assigned the job of delivering preparatory bombing on the little island of Ngesebus in support of the landing by the Third Battalion, Fifth Marines. This, except for the landings on Bougainville, was the only occasion in the Pacific War when none but marine planes were employed to assist marines crossing a beach. The preparation at Ngesebus was a combination of three supporting elements. At six o'clock in the morning men-of-war began to work over the island. An hour later the chorus was taken up by land-based artillery on Peleliu. Then at eight o'clock artillery and naval gunfire ceased and the job was turned over to marine Corsairs which continued strafing and bombing for a half hour before retiring in favor of another twenty-minute preparation by artillery. The last ten minutes before the troops hit the beach was assigned again to the air squadron for a final strafing just prior to the expected landing of the amphibian tractors. The planes came in fast and not more than fifty feet above the beach. It was accurate and, according to one prisoner of war, both terrifying and effective. Unfortunately its value was somewhat vitiated by the fact that a misunderstanding had grown up between the infantry battalion and the supporting agencies as to the time when the first wave was to reach the beach. The latter were under the impression that the troops were supposed to land at nine o'clock while the former believed nine to be the time of departure from Peleliu. Consequently the precise timing of the strafing attack was thrown off. Nevertheless, landing troops experienced very little return fire and the entire program of preparatory bombardment was termed a notable success.[70]

Most of the remainder of the marine air group's activities was in delivering close support to ground troops in their protracted and bloody effort to dig the enemy out of their stronghold in the ever constricting pocket in Umurbrogol. On September 30, Marine Fighter Squadron 114 was given the job of dropping twenty 1,000 pound bombs in a target area of only about 100 yards square. Every member was briefed thoroughly as to terrain and friendly troop locations. Closest liaison was maintained with infantry troops. The infantry and squadron commanders flew over the area together in joint reconnaissance. The mission was carried out with very satisfying accuracy, especially satisfying to ground troops who were close enough to be seriously endangered if even the slightest error in bombing had occurred.

Throughout October the same sort of missions were flown frequently both in support of the marines and of army troops when the latter took over. Steep-angle glide-bombing which had been tried out in September gave way to low-level tree-top bombing using blasted tree stumps and jagged pinnacles as a means of sighting for precision drops. Tree-top drops of 1,000 pound bombs were replaced on October 12 with a trial of new napalm-filled belly tanks with instantaneous fuse mechanisms. This continued on large scale the next day when fourteen of them produced spectacular fires in the Japanese pocket. As enemy positions became more and more constricted, it became correspondingly difficult to effect precision release of belly tanks, so on October 20 a new device was tried. Fourteen tanks were dropped simultaneously in the target area without fuses and then fired by phosphorous shells from infantry weapons. This procedure became standard for the rest of the month, and ground commanders reported excellent results.[71]

5. Marine Close Air Support for MacArthur

If close air support was one of the most distinguished features of the Peleliu operation from the point of view of tactical development, it was even more spectacular several months later in the Philippines. In spite of the fact that the Marine Corps had long been theoretically committed to the doctrine of close air support, and in spite of the fact that many of their prewar pilots had had considerable training in such missions, the exigencies of war in the Pacific generally forbade concentrated and systematic indoctrination of marine flight personnel in the specialized details of maneuver, liaison, and communications required of planes acting in close coordination with ground troops. There had been instances when marine pilots had participated in such missions. But for the most part, wartime marine pilots were trained in navy flight schools and inevitably they were indoctrinated in standard navy tactics—fighter tactics to gain control of the air, dive bombing against fixed and moving targets such as shore installations or ships, torpedo attacks against shipping, and scout and search missions. At no stage in the typical early wartime naval training of a marine pilot was much serious attention devoted to closely coordinated attacks in support of ground forces.

Toward the latter part of 1944, when it began to appear that marine aviation might be more extensively employed in close support missions, some steps were taken to remedy this situation. In October, Marine Air Group 24, then stationed on Bougainville, set up intensive training courses designed to equip their pilots for this type of duty. Climax of this period was a series of practical experiments in direct communications between pilot and the ground-based air liaison party, in which the latter would actually coach the plane into the target.

By December the group had been alerted to the fact that it would be called upon to give close support to army troops in the Philippines. At various conferences before the operation it was brought out that the Fifth United States Army Air Force would furnish the support air party. This organization was comparable to the navy air support control party which, according to standard naval doctrine, controlled all strikes against given ground or sea targets. It was a higher echelon organization, not physically located on or near the front lines. Standard army doctrine, like that of the navy, did not approve of using direct communications between front line air liaison parties and support aircraft for directing strikes against ground targets. They preferred to keep control over all strikes in centralized hands so as to avoid confusion, duplication, and wastage of air power. The pilots of Marine Air Group 24 (and in other such groups) felt otherwise. They believed that accuracy, precision in timing, and general efficiency in the use of air as a weapon for close support could only be achieved by the closest coordination between air and ground. Hence they perfected a doctrine of providing their own air liaison parties which would travel close to the front lines, familiarize themselves with the terrain, and be in constant and direct communication with planes in the air for purposes of coaching them onto likely targets.[72] Although these ideas were not new in the Marine Corps, it was in the Philippines and especially on Luzon that they achieved the first wide-spread application.

MacArthur's return to the Philippines began on October 17 with landings on islands adjacent to the entrance to Leyte Gulf. The long jump past Mindanao into the Central Philippines (Visayas) was covered by Halsey's Third Fleet, which struck at Japanese bases in the Ryukyus, on Formosa, and on Luzon, and then stood guard to the northeastward of Leyte Island. The Sixth United States Army was lifted and provided with close cover and naval gunfire support by the Seventh Fleet under Vice Admiral Thomas C. Kinkaid USN. The Sixth Army began its main landings on Leyte Island against little opposition at the beaches on October 20. The naval Battle for Leyte Gulf began three days later.

The Japanese had devised a careful but highly intricate scheme for contesting either Philippine or home waters with their Combined Fleet. These were called the *Sho-Go* plans. The scheme was in fact too intricate for proper coordination and control, and this resulted not only from the enemy's penchant for deception but also from the inexorable facts of war. After the Battle of the Philippine Sea in June 1944, it was necessary for the Japanese to base their remaining fleet carriers in the Inland Sea in order to replenish their decks with hastily trained pilots. They would also have preferred to station the bulk of their surface strength to the north, but shipping losses, especially tankers, inflicted by American submarines and other arms had caused an acute shortage in oil at home ports. There was no choice but to station the Japanese battle line in the Singapore area. Thus when the Americans struck at Leyte, the Japanese Combined Fleet was divided, yet the enemy had no alternative but to offer naval battle since loss of the Central Philippines meant the complete severance of his life line with the Netherlands East Indies. (See map 20.)

American submarines opened up the Battle for Leyte Gulf by striking at enemy fleet units in the Palawan Passage on October 23. The Japanese were engaged while delivering a three-pronged naval attack, the principal objective of which was the amphibious shipping of the Seventh Fleet. A force of obsolescent warships loaded with troop reinforcements was to enter Leyte Gulf from the south via Surigao Strait. The main surface force was to exit San Bernardino Strait to the north of Leyte Island, and simultaneously to enter Leyte Gulf from the east. Meanwhile the enemy's fleet carriers were to steam south from Japan to the east of Cape Engaño (Luzon Island) and to draw Halsey's Third Fleet northward, thus permitting the Japanese San Bernardino Strait force free entry to the waters east of Leyte.

The Japanese plan worked well, but communications difficulties and American counteraction prevented coordination and resulted in a stunning reversal for the enemy. Halsey's carrier pilots pounded the advancing Japanese unmercifully on October 24, and Halsey incorrectly concluded that the San Bernardino force was out of the battle. Late that evening, on getting reports that the enemy carrier force was advancing southward, Halsey turned to meet this threat and left San Bernardino uncovered. Meanwhile warships under Kinkaid demolished the Surigao Strait force, but the stronger enemy force sortied San Bernardino early on October 25, and fell on unsuspecting American escort carriers which were furnishing close air support to the army ashore. These slow carriers were deployed to the northeast of Leyte Gulf. The Japanese commander, however, believed himself engaged with fast American fleet units. He hesitated too long, and never tried to break through the surface strength of the Seventh Fleet which was guarding the eastern entrance to Leyte Gulf; he retreated back through San Bernardino Strait before Halsey could return from the north and intercept retirement.

This battle will long remain a controversial subject. Some argue that it is another example of the folly of divided command, with the force in strategic cover under Halsey responsible to Nimitz and that in close cover under Kinkaid responsible to MacArthur. But the pivotal consideration is that Halsey and Kinkaid, although in communication with one another, failed fully to understand each other's

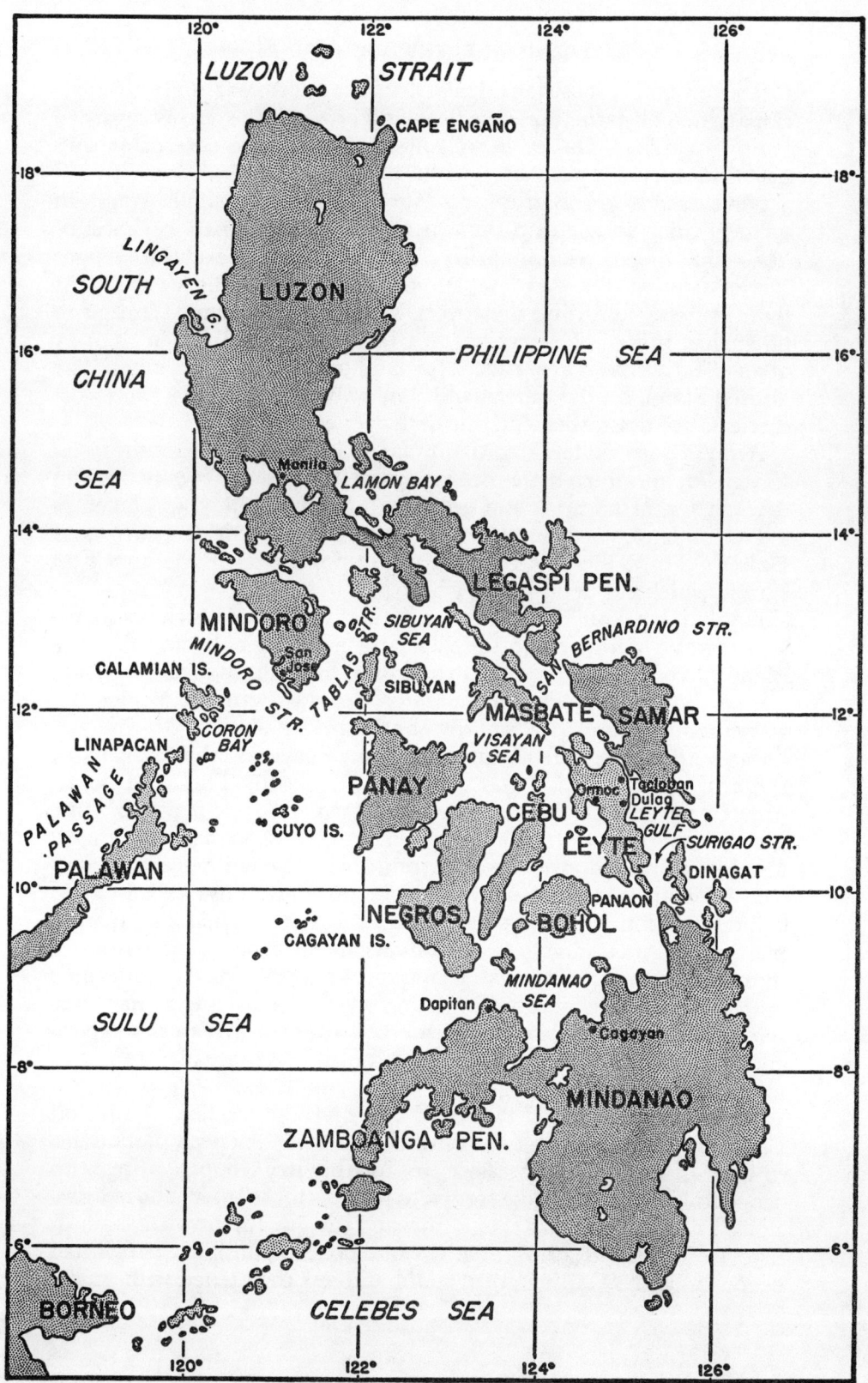

MAP 20. The Philippines.

intentions and dispositions. Halsey, furthermore, was under instructions to demolish the Japanese fleet, and however the enemy regarded his own carriers, Halsey looked upon them as the core of Japan's naval power.

Nevertheless, the Battle for Leyte Gulf was a notable American victory which speeded up the war in the Pacific. Japan lost most of her remaining carrier mobility, with one heavy and three light carriers sunk. Also, three Japanese battleships, six heavy and four light cruisers, and nine destroyers went to the bottom. Damage to other fleet units was extensive, and Japan retained little in the way of an effective naval arm except for land-based kamikaze planes. The United States, on the other hand, lost only one light and two escort carriers, two destroyers, and one destroyer escort.[73]

Army troops under MacArthur faced bitter resistance ashore on Leyte, but terminated the operation on Christmas Day, 1944. Ten days earlier, Mindoro Island, just south of Manila Bay, was taken as a site for land-based fighters, but base development was slow, and Halsey's Third Fleet was again called upon to cover the attack on Luzon, which began on January 9, 1945.

On that day, army forces landed against very weak beach resistance in Lingayen Gulf, where the Japanese had originally invaded the island three years before. After the initial breakthrough at Lingayen, the 1st Cavalry Division under Major General Verne D. Mudge USA was committed to drive rapidly southward to Manila. Marine Air Groups 24 and 32 were assigned the task of covering the left flank of the army troops which was completely exposed. The drive south jumped off on February 1, and from dawn to dusk flights of nine dive bombers patrolled the left flank and probed defenses ahead. Moreover, marine air liaison parties, manning radio jeeps, moved forward with front line army detachments and always kept in close communication with the planes overhead. For the first day, marine planes were used largely for reconnaissance purposes, but within a short time army troops began to request firing missions on unseen or inaccessible targets ahead. The accuracy of the marine airmen was remarkable. One army general remarked after the first week's experience, "I have never seen such able, close and accurate air support as the marine fliers are giving us."

For the rest of the drive, until the division reached Manila on February 3, marine pilots continued to destroy enemy installations, to level towns and afford easy entry for infantry troops, to break up concentrations of Japanese troops, and to perform other kindred missions. Later in February they supported the 6th Infantry Division in its drive to the east of Manila. On one occasion an army patrol had been stranded by falling down a cliff and was threatened with immediate extinction by a nearby enemy contingent. All efforts at relief had been foiled, and yet the colonel in command was reluctant to send in planes to attack the Japanese because of their proximity to the lost patrol. He finally consented; nine dive bombers were sent in; their loads hit within an eighty yard circle directly on the Japanese and well clear of the now exhausted American troops who were forthwith evacuated.

The efficiency of these two marine air groups in this relatively novel type of aerial warfare was attested to by General Mudge himself: "On our drive to Manila," he said, "I depended solely upon the marines to protect my left flank against possible Japanese counterattack. The job that they turned in speaks for itself. I can say without reservation that the marine dive bombers are one of the most flexible outfits that I have seen in this war." [74]

Flexibility indeed was the keynote of close air support success in this operation, and much of it can be attributed to the elimination of intermediate command channels. Most of the complaints from ground troops in other operations arose from the fact that too much time elapsed between requests for close support and execution, that strikes were controlled by higher echelons rather than front line troops, that the procedure for obtaining air support by appealing through several links in the chain of command was too rigid, and that pilots were inadequately briefed in the front line situation. Much of this was avoided not only on Luzon but in the other Philippine operations where marine air participated. The United States Sixth Army on Luzon, the X United States Army Corps on Mindanao, and the 41st Infantry Division on Zamboanga Peninsula (Mindanao) all permitted the next lower units to request support directly from the air units, although they still retained a monitor on the radio circuit and could modify or deny any requests as desired. Moreover, in the latter two cases the marine air groups involved were the highest echelon air force units present, thus eliminating at least one step in the chain of command and facilitating expeditious execution of requests from ground units.[75]

While marine dive bombers were performing excellent service in Luzon, marine fighter planes of Marine Air Groups 12 and 14 were carrying out similar duties against the Central Visayas and Mindanao from bases on Leyte and Samar. These planes did everything. They harassed the Japanese on Cebu, Negros, Panay, and northern Mindanao; they bombed and strafed enemy airstrips on these islands; they knocked out midget submarines; and they exploded trains and bridges in southeastern Luzon.

Early in March, Marine Air Group 12, operating out of Leyte, gave close support to guerrilla forces in the Visayas and Mindanao and on

March 3 took over a guerrilla-held airfield on northwest Mindanao in order to operate within range of imminent amphibious operations on the southern tip of Zamboanga. The invasion of Zamboanga Peninsula by the 41st Infantry Division began on March 10; and after the initial bombardment, Corsairs of Marine Air Group 12 flew protective cover over the landing. This group began actual support operations from Zamboanga on March 15, five days after the landing. By March 24 the dive bombers of Marine Air Group 32 arrived from Luzon, and the two groups were combined under command of Colonel Clayton C. Jerome USMC, whose leadership of close air support was spectacular.

In mid-April, Marine Air Group 24 was withdrawn from its Luzon assignment and sent to join Jerome's operation command of Marine Air Groups 12 and 32. The three groups, further augmented by one patrol bomber squadron, operated in support of the Eighth Army on Mindanao until the conclusion of this operation.

As elsewhere, they received only the highest praise from the ground troops to which they were attached. Headquarters, 41st Infantry Division stated of Jerome's flyers that "the readiness of the Marine Air Group to engage in any missions requested of them, their skill and courage as airmen and their splendid spirit of cooperation in aiding ground troops have given this Division the most effective air support yet received in any of its operations." [76] Other army general officers were equally laudatory.[77]

Although these Philippine activities of marine air groups fall somewhat outside the main story of the evolution of amphibious tactics in the Pacific, they point up one anomaly. Up to this date, marine aviation at no time had enjoyed such a full opportunity to demonstrate its adaptability to the role of close support, since marine airmen in the Solomons were principally assigned duties more closely resembling those of navy carrier-based pilots. After the Mindanao operation, at Okinawa, marine flyers would have another chance to display their skill in this type of tactics in a somewhat more systematic and orderly fashion. But not until the army called for aid did Marine Corps Aviation have a real chance to make good its ancient boast of its peculiar superiority in the field of close support of ground troops.

6. Strategic and Tactical Significance of the Palau Campaign

From 1943, until the attack on the Philippines, Peleliu was the only opportunity for marine airmen to demonstrate their versatility in close support of ground troops. In this respect the Peleliu operation was unusual, and it was this opportunity to develop techniques of close air support that was perhaps the most significant feature of the Palau campaign.

This is not to say that as a demonstration of amphibious techniques the landing on Peleliu was a failure. It was as difficult an amphibious assault as any in the Pacific War, with the possible exception of Iwo Jima. In spite of a fringing reef and heavy fire on the approach to the beaches, the assault waves came in on schedule. Tanks were landed quickly and most of the division's organic artillery was ashore by nightfall of the first day. Although logistics faltered in some respects, at no time did failures of supply seriously impede the operation of the combat units.

But in at least three respects the Peleliu operation fell short of the ideal. Previous intelligence failed in large measure to reveal the intricate nature of the enemy's defense system, and this was caused largely by terrain configuration and cover. Since the worst areas on the island were covered with dense scrub growth it is doubtful that any of the known techniques of aerial photography could have provided a much more accurate picture of Peleliu prior to extensive aerial and naval bombardment.

Naval bombardment was not up to the standard of either previous or later Central Pacific operations. The allotment of only three days for preliminary fire was insufficient. The bombardment group commander's staff was too small, and the absence of any ground force representative was both irregular and unfortunate. However, given the type of defensive system, it is questionable whether naval gunfire could have accomplished a great deal more than it did in the time allotted.

Finally, and most serious, was the failure to provide adequate reserve troops for the First Marine Division. Three regiments were committed in the beach assault with only one battalion in division reserve and one in regimental reserve. Two of the assault regiments had no reserves at all. Had the island been captured with the speed originally anticipated, this would probably have made no material difference, but when the attack bogged down in the high ground north of Umurbrogol there were no fresh troops left to feed in to the weak parts of the line.

Several alternatives might have been adopted. It might have been recognized in advance that the Peleliu phase of the campaign was a two-division job, in which case the landing on Angaur could have been deferred and the 81st Infantry Division committed on Peleliu either on the first day or shortly thereafter. Or only one army regiment might have been landed at Angaur where it was fairly certain that enemy resistance would be light, and the second army regiment used on Angaur then committed to Peleliu. Also, the capture of Ulithi might have been delayed and the third army regiment, which was in corps reserve anyway, might have been landed early on Peleliu. Almost any of these alternatives would have been preferable to the course taken.

The question remains whether the invasion of Peleliu and Angaur was strategically necessary at all, whether the gains were worth the tremendous cost in lives and materiel. In his memoirs published after the war Admiral Halsey with customary forthrightness stated that the whole campaign was a mistake. He thought so in September of 1944 and he still thought so after two years of peace. Of the Palaus he said: ". . . I felt they would have to be bought at a prohibitive price in casualties. In short, I feared another Tarawa—and I was right." [78]

Halsey's inference that the Gilberts were of little importance strategically seems unjustified, but he has a better case for the Palaus. Confirmation came from an enemy source. When naval intelligence officers interrogated Vice Admiral Shigeru Fukudome IJN, an officer of extensive staff and command experience during the war, they found him to be of the same opinion. When asked to comment as to the necessity of the Palau campaign after the Marianas had been taken, he answered: "We looked upon your operation against Palau as a step preparatory to the Philippines . . . for use as an intermediate supply base." The reasoning here is wrong, since the Southern Palaus were taken neither as supply nor as staging bases, but rather to secure MacArthur's right flank and to help cover his sea-borne movements. Thus Fukudome could rightly conclude that it was not indispensable to take Peleliu and Angaur. He observed, however, that "we had a force in Palau to be sure, but we had no intention of an all-out defense of the island, nor of increasing its air force, nor of augmenting the number of ships there. We were, then, concentrating on the Sho-Go operation which was to come next." [79]

To be sure, Halsey was the only high-ranking officer either in the Pacific or in Washington who clearly favored cancellation of the Palau campaign in September 1944. Furthermore, at that date neither Nimitz nor the Joint Chiefs of Staff could have been certain that the Japanese had written off the Palaus and had no intention of reinforcing their air strength. Had the enemy chosen to do so, it would have required some diversion of American carriers to keep the airfields on Peleliu and Angaur neutralized while American forces were moving into the Philippines. The major consideration in this connection is, of course, the effect such a diversion would have had on the Battle for Leyte Gulf, and consequently on MacArthur's return to the Philippines. The answer is not easy, for the necessity for Halsey to cover the Palaus as well as the northern approaches from the Ryukyus through Formosa and Luzon into the Central Philippines would have divided his Third Fleet; yet during the crisis of the Battle for Leyte Gulf one of his fast carrier groups was not used, since it was en route to Ulithi Atoll for resupply and replenishment.

In retrospect it appears doubtful if MacArthur's movement into Leyte was in sufficient danger of attack from the east to justify the expenditure of two months of fighting and over 8,000 casualties to the First Marine Division and the 81st Infantry Division. Had the defensive power of the Japanese on Peleliu been fully appreciated it is questionable whether the assault on that island would have or should have been undertaken. One is disposed to agree with the judgment of Admiral Jesse B. Oldendorf, that "if military leaders (including naval) were gifted with the same accuracy of foresight that they are with hindsight, undoubtedly the assault and capture of the Palaus would never have been attempted." [80]

Nevertheless certain concrete benefits did accrue to the United States forces in the Pacific as a result of the capture of Peleliu and Angaur. All possible threat of their being used as a base for enemy planes and submarines was definitely removed. American planes from the Peleliu airfield supported the later aspects of the Philippines campaigns. By mid-November two squadrons of army bombers were based on Angaur and were flying regular missions against Legaspi and other airdromes in Luzon as well as against profitable targets in the Visayas. By November 22, 1944, two more bomber squadrons were brought into Angaur for the same purpose. By the end of November, when it was determined that the heavy rains on Leyte would prevent bombers from being based there, they were permanently stationed at Angaur which was within easy range of Bicol, Visaya, and Mindanao targets. From the Southern Palaus they could also raid enemy air centers at Manila and Clark Field on Luzon Island, as soon as fighter cover from intermediate bases was provided.[81]

Moreover the entire Palau group was effectively neutralized by the capture of Peleliu and Angaur. At the war's end some 43,000 Japanese surrendered in the northern islands. These nearby Japanese garrisons were so effectively neutralized during the Palau campaign that only about 600 men succeeded in reinforcing Peleliu, and most of these arrived without weapons or equipment due to the sinking of their landing craft at the reef's edge.[82]

Finally, the occupation of Ulithi, which must be considered a part of the Palau campaign, was an asset of great value to the navy. The lagoon was some nineteen miles long and five to ten miles in breadth. Except in periods of heavy typhoon it provided an excellent fleet anchorage where ships could be fueled, provisioned, and repaired. During the months to come it proved invaluable to the Pacific Fleet.

CHAPTER X

THE SUPREME TEST, IWO JIMA

REFLECTING on the thirty-six days of unrelenting effort needed to crush the Japanese on Iwo Jima, Admiral Spruance concluded that "in view of the character of the defenses and the stubborn resistance encountered, it is fortunate that less seasoned or less resolute troops were not committed." [1]

The struggle raged on eight square miles of barren volcanic ash and soft rock newly formed from volcanic mud. Iwo Jima is less than a half century old, having only recently risen up from the sea. Its terrain features are wrinkled and jumbled, and this plus more than 20,000 Japanese troops made its seizure hell for the marines. Only in one respect, despite its semi-tropical latitude, did it fall short of ideal for the defenders. The island was still growing and fissures of steam caused by subterranean heat were evident. Surely the enemy was hot, for he was dug in.

Iwo had to be taken to permit America's B-29 attacks against the Nipponese homeland to reach the peak of their effectiveness. It stood athwart the path of the very long range bombers as they winged north from the Marianas toward Honshu and Kyushu; and seizing Iwo was, in the judgment of General George C. Marshall, "of vital importance to the air assault on Japan." [2] Thus the battle reemphasizes the conclusion that a well-trained amphibious arm was as essential to the United States Army Air Forces as to the Navy. Iwo and Tinian were the only objectives in the Central Pacific seized mainly for their air potential, but there can be little doubt that during the course of the war with Japan the Marine Corps suffered greater casualties in obtaining air bases for both the army and navy than in gaining advanced naval anchorages.

The capture of Iwo is the classical amphibious assault of recorded history. In this operation the Japanese managed to take a toll of American casualties equal to their own dead, a feat not earlier accomplished nor later repeated. Three reinforced marine divisions attached to the Fifth Amphibious Corps and led by Major General Harry Schmidt were employed, the largest body of marines ever brought under a single tactical marine command. The Fourth and Fifth Marine Divisions landed in beach assault, followed by the Third Marine Division in support; but the terrain was such that the fighting seldom varied, on the beach or inshore. There was little cover.

Iwo was, in effect, all beach. Defenses were so skillfully arranged and so expertly manned that despite the tremendous impact gained on hitting the coast, little momentum was achieved after the first two days of fighting. Iwo was taken by marines and by their demolitions and flamethrowers; the men inched forward in tanks or crawled on their stomachs, seldom seeing an enemy in the flesh and alive.

1. Strategy, Command, and Planning Preliminary Fires

A rigorous time-vise squeezed the fighting on Iwo into a narrow period, and allowed the marines on that island less than one-third the preliminary fires, including both naval gunfire and carrier-based bombing, that their tactical commander desired and requested. The beach assault against Iwo started on February 19, 1945. Barely preceding it was the landing on Luzon, and soon after came that on Okinawa. In addition to the launching of these two extensive land campaigns, the navy insisted, for good strategical reasons, on delivering carrier attacks against Honshu just before and immediately following the beach assault on Iwo Jima. Even in early 1945 the United States lacked the resources for conducting, with the desirable margin of superiority, such a rapid sequence of operations as Luzon, the first Tokyo carrier strikes, Iwo, and Okinawa; but the enemy, off balance strategically, was at a far greater disadvantage. Time was a factor more important than resources. Each day the opening of sustained preparatory fires against Iwo was postponed allowed the Japanese additional time to perfect their fortifications and to train their garrison.

First plans called for pressing forward against the enemy more rapidly than was done, but fighting in the Philippines held up all action in Nimitz's theater. The initial target date for Iwo Jima, January 20, 1945, was twice set back, and the marines destined for that island suffered all the more grievously when their recommendations for a more extended preliminary naval gunfire preparation were rejected.

The Joint Chiefs of Staff in October 1944, having agreed to put off or cancel the contemplated occupation of Formosa in favor of taking Luzon and positions in the Ryukyus, handed down the directive that shaped the Pacific offensive during the early months of 1945. In an effort to continue the momentum begun with General MacArthur's return to Leyte, precedence was given to his theater. Operations on Luzon were to start on December 20, 1944, but Japanese reinforcements on Leyte and landings on Mindoro preliminary to Luzon held up entry into Lingayen Gulf till January 9, 1945. Nor was this the only delay. An additional loss of time was caused by the attrition of naval attack vessels struck by enemy suicide planes in

Philippine waters. Adverse weather postponed air-base construction on Mindoro, and since land-based fighters were unavailable for the Lingayen landings, this tied up further the escort carriers and other support warships needed at Iwo. Also retarded was the transfer to Spruance of those fast fleet units which since August 1944, under Admiral Halsey as Commander of the Third Fleet, had been covering MacArthur's sea-borne movements.

The struggle on Iwo was likewise more extended than anticipated, but it was not allowed to cause any serious postponement in the overall schedule. The Okinawa operation was originally listed to follow the target date for Iwo by forty days; as events transpired, naval surface units were withdrawn from the vicinity of Iwo, replenished and rearmed, and sent into the Ryukyus in time to make the principal landing there forty-two days after the attack on Iwo.[3]

Before entering the Ryukyus, Nimitz was directed by the Joint Chiefs to occupy a position or positions in the Nanpo Shoto, a threadlike archipelago of small islands dangling from Tokyo Bay south and slightly east for a distance of some 700 miles. (See map 15.) Two considerations were uppermost in selecting the precise target: it must have beaches suitable for amphibious assault, and it must offer sufficient space and favorable terrain for several airfields. Among the Nanpo Shoto, only Iwo Jima fully met these requirements, and in effect Nimitz had no freedom of selection.[4] The Japanese were as aware of this fact as was Nimitz.

Iwo lies about 650 miles from Tokyo. The island is in the Kazan Retto or Volcano group of the Nanpo Shoto, that is it forms a part of the southern tip of the archipelago. It is almost equidistant from Tokyo and the Southern Marianas. On it the Japanese had built two airfields and were busy on a third. In their possession, it obstructed the employment of America's strategic bombers, and the objectives were to reverse this situation and to continue to maintain unremitting pressure on the enemy. Iwo was being used as a staging point for air raids on Saipan, Tinian, and Guam; and fighter planes were rising from Iwo to harass very long range craft en route to and returning from Japan, while a radar station on this volcanic island gave the Nipponese home defenses more than two hours' warning of an approaching ordeal from the skies. Results were attrition of the huge American bombers at their bases, circuitous flying to avoid the environs of Iwo, lack of an emergency field on which to bring down craft damaged over the target, and a declining morale among B-29 crewmen.[5]

These advantages would be lost to the enemy, and the air assault on Japan improved, once Iwo was seized. In addition, it was seen that neutralization of the Nanpo Shoto and capture of Iwo Jima would help secure the right flank of operations against Okinawa, Kyushu, and Honshu, and would provide the United States Navy with an air base from which to pound enemy shipping in home waters. Thinking of these strategical gains Lieutenant General Holland Smith, in a notable statement illustrative of the responsiveness of some of America's military officers to her political leaders, attempted to allay mounting sentiment in the United States that the taking of Iwo was ill-conceived and unduly expensive in men and materials. "Capture of Iwo Jima," he told the press late in the operation, "was considered essential by those in whose hands the destiny of our nation lies. The cost of winning this objective was no doubt weighed carefully against the importance of having this island as an operating base in speeding the ultimate defeat of Japan. When the capture of an enemy position is necessary to winning a war it is not within our province to evaluate the cost in money, time, equipment, or, most of all, in human life. We are told what our objective is to be and we prepare to do the job, knowing that all evaluations have been considered by those who give us our orders." [6]

Smith commanded the Joint Expeditionary Troops at Iwo. In the summer of 1944 he had been relieved of his tactical duties as commanding general of the Fifth Amphibious Corps, and the following fall had been made Commanding General, Fleet Marine Force, Pacific. Creation of this post was necessary on two accounts. It allowed Smith to assume both strategical and administrative supervision of the Third and Fifth Amphibious Corps when the former was added to Nimitz's direct command, and it kept Smith on a command echelon parallel to Vice Admiral Kelly Turner who had shortly before been named Commander, Amphibious Forces, Pacific Fleet.[7] But at Iwo neither Smith nor Turner exercised any immediate tactical control over the fighting forces. Both were strategical commanders, and Smith went along because the presence of his forceful personality was desired, because a marine ranking with Turner was wanted on the spot, and because a second infantry staff was an insurance against the loss of Schmidt and Headquarters, Fifth Amphibious Corps. As Smith said, "I guess they sent me along just in case something happened to Harry Schmidt." [8]

Turner at Iwo was Commander of the Joint Expeditionary Force. Both he and Smith were again subordinate to Spruance, to whom as commander of the Fifth Fleet, Nimitz delegated overall control in the target area. Turner and Smith, headed by Spruance, were responsible for the strategical aspects of the operation, and they approved or disapproved the plans coming up from lower echelons.

Intensive planning for Iwo, in other words, was done by Schmidt, the three marine division commanders, and the navy subordinates under Turner. Rear Admiral W. H. P. Blandy, heading Amphibious Group One, was given a new post in an effort to increase the effectiveness of all arms. He was made Commander, Amphibious Support Force, with the job of integrating all naval gunfire, minesweeping, underwater demolitions, and air support during the preliminary period before the day of the beach assault. On that date, which turned out to be February 19, supervision passed to Turner. The latter also delegated the remainder of his tactical duties. His second in command, Rear Admiral Harry W. Hill, Commander of Amphibious Group Two, was given the role of Commander, Attack Force. Spruance, Schmidt, Hill, and Blandy were thus the principal architects for the assault, with Turner and Smith assisting and meshing the tactical details into Spruance's overall strategical program.[9] With the single exception of the amount of preliminary naval gunfire to be delivered, there was no irreconcilable difference of opinion between the ranking navy and marine commanders during the planning phase.

Iwo's terrain and the enemy's defenses made the question of preparatory naval gunfire of paramount concern, for American intelligence forecast a difficult target. Documents captured on Saipan and Tinian outlined the essentials of the enemy's defensive plan on Iwo, and were of great aid in understanding his order of battle. After the seizure of the Marianas was begun, the Japanese hastened to complete their installations on Iwo, but photographic interpretation kept the Americans partially abreast of these developments. Final calculations of what to expect ashore were thirty per cent too low as regards the actual number of heavy and medium emplacements, and even further short of the total garrison found on Iwo.

Careful marine planners, however, added a liberal safety margin to the tallies of their intelligence sections because of several recognized facts. From the outset of the Central Pacific drive, estimates of the enemy's defensive strength had normally been low. Also, the terrain on Iwo was designed by nature to favor the defender, and especially one so facile in burrowing underground and holing up in caves; and unlike earlier defensive systems constructed of heavy materials by the Japanese, those on Iwo were known to be positioned almost altogether flush with the ground, or along ridges and escarpments and on reverse slopes, giving full play to the genius of the Nipponese for camouflage. It all added up to a most formidable target. Air photographs, the intensity of the enemy's antiaircraft fire, and the general conduct of his garrison as observed during the planning phase and later showed that the Japanese were perfecting their defenses despite the softening up by American air bombings and intermittent surface bombardments.[10]

The performance of army airmen in softening up Iwo Jima was disappointing. The Seventh Air Force based in the Marianas was assigned three missions in connection with this operation. Beginning in the early fall of 1944, these flyers were to take out enemy shipping busily engaged in building up the defenses of the Nanpo Shoto, were to neutralize airfields in that archipelago, and, immediately before the beach assault began (when there was no danger of revealing the precise target to the enemy), were to concentrate their attention on Iwo itself. The Seventh Air Force, unlike the Fifth in MacArthur's theater and the Thirteenth in the South and later the Southwest Pacific, was apparently never able to sink much shipping. Official Air Force historians seem to believe that, up through the Marianas campaign at least, this was caused by faulty command relations, and in retrospect reliance to any degree on the Seventh Air Force in taking out shipping was probably an error. In any event, these pilots were unable to come down low where they could hit shipping, and their planes were too few in number to gain success through mass drops from higher altitudes. The Joint Army-Navy Assessment Committee credits army air with sinking only one small vessel (550 tons displacement) in the area of the Nanpo Shoto during the crucial softening up period, and this ship was not struck directly from the air, but ran afoul of an army mine. That there was an abundance of shipping targets in the Nanpo Shoto is shown by other statistics. From June 15, 1944, when the Japanese intensified their Iwo build up, to February 16, 1945, when the preliminary fires began in preparation for the assault, the enemy sustained the following additional shipping losses in the Nanpo Shoto: * to unknown causes, 572 tons; to United States Navy surface men-of-war, 11,096 tons; to carrier-based air, 27,479 tons; and to submarines, 130,745 tons.[11]

Seventh Air Force pilots were probably most successful in neutralizing airfields; even so, they were none too good in hitting stationary targets. This was to be feared since each of the Nanpo Shoto was usually covered by a haze and sometimes by cloud banks, and the bombing in the softening up period was always from high or medium altitudes. Moreover, the crewmen could not be briefed in the grave importance of their work, since some might be shot down and interrogated, and for similar reason the bombing was dispersed among several islands. But whatever the damage of high and medium level bombing on the industrial heart of Japan, marines unanimously reached the conclusion that some six months of land-based strikes against the Nanpo Shoto, the last seventy-two days of which was sup-

* The area included here is 122E–145E and 22N–35N, and tonnage sunk before 1 August 1944 totaled 42,398.

posed to have been continuous against Iwo Jima with other targets thrown in, had little if any adverse effect on Iwo's defenses. There is no evidence that the Seventh Air Force either hampered the build up, stopped new construction for any extended period of time, or permanently shattered more than a very few defensive positions. On the contrary, it is believed that the effort made only increased the problem facing the marines. The judgment of Smith's intelligence officer, a man of experience in this work dating back to Guadalcanal, seems sound: "It is considered probable that the extensive air bombardments of Iwo Jima caused the underground positions to be made more elaborate than they might otherwise have been." [12]

Marine planners began discounting the effect of land-based bombing on examining photographs in the softening up period. For this reason they relied all the more heavily on the preliminary fires from naval guns and carrier-based air, especially on naval gunfire.[13] A close study of the terrain features of Iwo Jima, the landing beaches, the offensive scheme of maneuver, and the known Japanese defenses shows why.

Iwo is shaped like a pork chop. (See map 21.) From above, the island originates at its southwestern tip with an extinct volcanic cone of small diameter but rising ominously from the sea, Suribachi by name. The long axis of the island, a distance of some five statute miles, runs northeast and southwest. At the northeastern base of Suribachi is a narrow isthmus. This is the lowest point on the island, and is less than 1,000 yards across. As the isthmus moves to the northeast, it broadens gently to form two feasible landing beaches; but these drop sharply into the sea about 3,500 yards northeast of Suribachi, when the island suddenly bellies out to its greatest width, which is two and one-half miles. On the belly of the island and in the area between the two beaches were the Japanese airfields.

Profile photographs taken by submarines or low-flying airplanes from off the northwestern or southeastern coasts revealed more. The two sets of feasible landing beaches were confined to the southeast and southwest portions of the coast. Difficulties of an assault were all too apparent. Not only was the island small, but also the two prospective landing beaches were separated by so narrow an isthmus that many of the weapons guarding the one could be easily shifted to protect the other.[14] Worse, both beaches were flanked by commanding ground. Suribachi towered to 550 feet on one side, and sharp escarpments jumped to 300 feet on the other. Then as the island continued on to the northeastward, the Motoyama Plateau broadened and rose an average of some thirty feet higher, cut by gorges and ridges, some of which reached more than 380 feet above the sea. Finally, the broad northeastern end of the island terminated in a phalanx of escarpments, which dropped suddenly into the sea.

Since no reefs surrounded Iwo, strong waves had swept the volcanic ash along the isthmus into steep terraces, and the photographs showed emplaced oil drums which gave rise to the suspicion that the enemy intended to flood the beaches and offshore water with burning fuels. Marines assaulting Iwo had to fight uphill and under observation all the way—up from a possibly flaming sea onto the highest terrace, up Suribachi, up the rocky, broken, and uneven but always rising Motoyama Plateau, over its ridges and through its sulphurous pits and gorges. Only on reaching the tableland of the island would they be able to look down, occasionally, at the enemy.

Just how well the Japanese were dug into this steaming island of ashes no American knew with certainty. Of course the Nipponese were employing caves, and these were so numerous that once the battle was over, one could only speculate on the total blasted and sealed. But photographic interpretation located non-cave installations believed to house six coastal defense guns. The island was known to bristle like a porcupine with more than 240 light and heavy antiaircraft weapons, some of which were surely dual purpose; and there were at least 434 blockhouses, covered artillery guns, and pillboxes.

It was evident that these prepared defenses were carefully sited and skillfully placed.[15] Schmidt decided to use the southeastern beaches, since the prevailing winds at the planned time of assault were from northern quarters of the compass; but an alternate plan to land on the other beaches was drawn in the event the surf happened to be less on that side of the island. He wanted to employ three full divisions in the beach assault, but this plan was vetoed by Smith.[16] Regardless of which set of beaches the two divisions assigned to the initial landings used, the scheme of maneuver would remain the same: to overrun the isthmus and the airfield on the southwestern end of the island, that is Motoyama Airfield Number One; to take Suribachi and the ridges to the northeast in order to secure the beaches and to facilitate unloading; and to drive along the Motoyama Plateau and seize the remainder of the island. After the isthmus, the first airfield, and Suribachi had been captured, the troops would find themselves canalized along the plateau, and there, just northeast of Motoyama Airfield Number One, were the heaviest enemy defenses. Nowhere on the island, least of all during the attack up onto the plateau, would there be much room for maneuver.[17]

Since the island was so small, since the defenses were so many and so well constructed and camouflaged, and since the marines, once the beaches had been assaulted, would find themselves almost in the midst of these installations, there was but one period during which the large rifles of warships could be used with utmost destructive effect—that was during the time allowed for preliminary naval gunfire. No other weapon, and no other time of employment, could be fully substituted. The point under discussion here is destructive rather than neutralizing fires, but even in the latter capacity the support arms were handicapped on Iwo, and it was evident in the planning period that they might be. Once the marines were ashore, as Nimitz later said, "the proximity of our troops to enemy positions frequently denied us the benefit of adequate naval bombardment, air bombing, or shore artillery support." [18]

Both the speed with which the operation was completed and the number of casualties sustained depended on the extent of destructive preparatory fire by heavily gunned ships. By this late stage of the Pacific War, naval gunfire had reached a high state of proficiency. The question involved in the planning period was one of time, that is the number of days allotted to preparatory fires, both surface bombardment and carrier-based bombing. There can be nothing but praise for the destructive effect of the preliminary naval gunfire actually delivered at Iwo, despite restriction of visibility and weather; but on the other hand there were circumstances peculiarly favorable to accurate naval gunfire, and these were apparent to the planners. Hydrographic conditions would be good, for there were no offshore reefs and the water was too deep for much mining. As a result, deliberate, point blank fire could be used. Also, men-of-war could swing around the island for a full 360°. A target in defilade from the north, for example, could possibly be reached directly from the south. Most of all were the marines anxious to capitalize on a lesson learned in the Marianas, "that by allowing for a bombardment of considerable length prior to the day of the assault, considerable reduction can be effected in casualties among the landing troops." [19]

Marine planners first requested ten days of preliminary fires, then nine, and finally four; but the navy allowed only three days. Solving the problem of exactly why no more preparation was scheduled is complex. Available facts show that the prevailing consideration among navy officers was properly strategical in nature. There are indications, however, that Turner thought three days of preparation would be adequate, and Spruance, although ultimately authorizing his subordinate to take a fourth day if he saw fit to do so, relied on Turner's judgment.

It is wise at this point to glance ahead, and to determine if possible what were the optimum requirements in terms of preliminary naval gunfire at Iwo. No argument is made that preliminary fire should take out all defensive positions, which is manifestly impossible. Optimum preparation, however, is the destruction of most of the targets which can be reached by naval guns and low flying aircraft. An excellent post-operational study of the preliminary fires delivered during the three-day period at Iwo reveals that whereas the purely naval missions—protecting shipping from coastal defense guns, curtailing antiaircraft fire, and allowing minesweepers, underwater demolition teams, and hydrographic experts to do their work —were accomplished in the time allowed, the period required to prepare the island as thoroughly as was possible for occupation by assault troops would have been at least eight days. This study is premised upon the continuous employment of six old battleships and four heavy and one light cruisers, which, along with destroyers, were the vessels ultimately sent to fire on Iwo for three days before the assault date.[20]

Originally both navy and marine planners set up a schedule of preliminary fires which would have prepared Iwo better than was actually done; but a complicating factor entered early in the planning period. This was the feasibility of allotting the time, the warships, and the ammunition considered necessary, that is of orienting the preliminary naval bombardment of Iwo Jima into the tight time schedule set by Nimitz and the Joint Chiefs of Staff.

Planners in Nimitz's headquarters drew up the first blueprint of preliminary gunfire. It called for a cruiser division to begin bombardment eight days before the target date, and to give way five days later to seven battleships and six cruisers. In other words, two ships with large rifles would fire for five days, and thirteen for three days. Because of the small size of the objective, the need for destruction, the difficulties of spotting caused by terrain and low-lying, well-camouflaged defenses, and the limitations on communications, thirteen capital ships could hardly have conducted preparatory fire simultaneously; but the plan was to use them in rotation, thus increasing the ammunition carried and expended, and lessening the possibility of a failure of resupply at sea.

The marines wanted more preparation. Schmidt's headquarters was well qualified to face this problem, since it was headed by Colonel William W. Rogers USMC, chief of staff and a master of detail, and since the naval gunfire officer was Lieutenant Colonel Donald M. Weller USMC, a brilliant planner. Weller's conclusions were pushed vigorously by Schmidt, who in turn received the enthusiastic support of Smith. Schmidt submitted to Turner on October 24, 1944, a study of the island's defenses and a request for ten days of preliminary fire, beginning with three old battleships as well as a cruiser division. The date is important, for the document was drawn in Pearl Harbor and, taking into account the loss of a day, reached Turner's hands at the climax of the Battle for Leyte Gulf. Despite this thorough defeat of the Japanese navy, the marines at Iwo, it developed, got even less naval gunfire preparation than Nimitz's staff had first contemplated. In defense of the navy it must be remembered, however, that most of the injury done to the Combined Imperial Fleet in October 1944 was damage rather than sinkings, that the Japanese had shown a remarkable facility for both salvage and repair, and that full intelligence of the hardships imposed by American submarines and other war attrition upon the Japanese industrial system was lacking at the time. Spruance did not expect a fleet engagement during the Iwo operation, yet he had to assume during his planning that enemy surface as well as air and submarine reaction might be forthcoming.[21]

The navy rejected the request of the marines for ten days of sustained bombardment. Turner stated that limitations on the availability of ships and difficulties of ammunition replacement interposed serious obstacles to meeting the recommendation. He then proceeded to cut down the amount of fire previously planned by Nimitz's staff. The mission of the cruiser division assigned to start fire eight days before the landing was altered to retirements after short and intermittent surface bombardments, a device hardly comparable to sustained fire; and, beginning three days before the assault, thirteen capital ships were to fire. These, Turner added, would hurl more major caliber shells onto the objective than Schmidt had requested when asking for ten days. Turner was avoiding the central issue, which was the length of time allowed for deliberate, destructive fire at point blank range, rather than the tonnage of projectiles expended. Apparently he failed to notice the contradiction in his stand. Despite his concern over the problem of ammunition resupply, he promised that more projectiles would be employed than Schmidt had recommended. In any case, the problem of ammunition replacement remained, and a suggestion by the marines to spot large-caliber projectiles on Saipan and to shuttle the warships back and forth was not considered feasible by the navy.

After a further study of the target, Schmidt submitted a second recommendation for nine days, but Turner replied with a study from his own staff indicating that only slightly more than three days were needed; and Turner added that the troops would be provided with the best possible preliminary bombardment consistent with the limitations of ammunition supply, the time allowed for the operation, and the requirements of subsequent landings.[22] Schmidt was playing a losing game, despite assistance from Smith. But Schmidt refused to give up. His third request was for four days of fire.

For a while it looked as though this might be met. Turner, however, gave the recommendation a weak endorsement on forwarding it to Spruance, saying in effect that he had no objection, provided four days could be worked into the general strategical situation. With his subordinates at odds, Spruance turned down the request for four days. His principal reason was strategical in nature—the planned carrier raids on Tokyo and the industrial centers surrounding that city. As he rejected the request for four days of intensive preparation, he noted optimistically that the "shore-based air attack to be provided could be considered at least as effective as the additional day of surface ship bombardment." [23]

Schmidt now played his last card. For the fourth time, he sought a more extended preliminary naval gunfire, but seeing that three days of preparation were probably all the marines could get, he asked, as an alternative to more time, that the three days be concentrated on and adjacent to the preferred landing beaches. This would have benefited the troops in beach assault as well as the early phase of beach logistics, but here too Schmidt was unable to win his point. The navy deemed full coverage of the island mandatory for purposes of counterbattery, that is to allow warships to fire at short range, and to lower the enemy's antiaircraft fire in order to improve aerial observation and to permit low-level air support.[24]

Holland Smith in his memoirs published after the war shows little consideration of the navy's point of view, far less than Schmidt and his staff exhibited at the time. "Thus," concludes Smith, "were we defeated—a group of trained and experienced land fighters, our full realization of the necessity for naval gunfire based on many previous island operations—again overridden by the naval mind. Finding ourselves in this dilemma, we had tried our best to enlighten the high command, feeling that our judgment would be respected, but naval expediency won again." [25]

The stand taken by Spruance and Turner must be reviewed in the light of the war picture as a whole, and as it was evaluated at the time, as well as by local considerations and later knowledge.

Most damaging to the navy is the fact that Turner's response to the request for nine days of preparatory fire included a study of the island's defenses indicating the need of only slightly more than three days. This is damaging, not because the occupation of Iwo proved this total insufficient, but because it ran counter to the continued insistence of the marines and contradicted the preliminary study which caused Nimitz's staff to plan for eight days of fire.

The conclusion is unavoidable that the navy planned and delivered preliminary bombardment, not on a basis of accurately calculated requirements, but to conform with the strategical situation as the admirals estimated it at the time. The record would look better if this alone had been stressed, rather than buttressing the navy's position by a study of Iwo's defenses so obviously inadequate as that calling for only slightly more than three days of preparatory naval gunfire. Both Spruance and Turner were correctly thinking of the overall strategical picture, as well as the problems local to Iwo Jima, and Spruance's principal concern in making the carrier raids against Japan was rightly the Okinawa rather than the Iwo Jima operation. However, since the record fails to reveal a single note of dissatisfaction on Turner's part with the naval gunfire either as planned or as delivered, it must be concluded that he thought three days was enough. This was a misjudgment, even though it was probably motivated in great part by strategical considerations.

Inextricably tied with the length of fire was the problem of ammunition supply and replacement. The solution lay in increasing the number of warships and hence the amount of ammunition sent for the preparation of Iwo. Since action in MacArthur's theater postponed the release of some of the bombardment vessels assigned there, the additional rifles required at Iwo had to come from another quarter. Relying on Turner's staff study which called for only three days of fire, the navy overlooked the source of supply and the available warships and rifles needed to lift and fire this ammunition at Iwo. Turner insisted on using projectiles sparingly at Iwo in order to be ready for subsequent troop requirements, that is for Okinawa. Having only so much total ammunition to allot to the two operations, he favored Okinawa at the expense of Iwo.

While Iwo received but three days of naval gunfire preparation, Okinawa was plastered with seven days of destructive fire before the target date. Although the Japanese surprised everyone by refusing so much as a token defense of their Okinawa beaches, the disparity in preliminary fires between Iwo and Okinawa opens the navy to criticism. It is possible that even at this late date in the war the navy was failing to differentiate sharply between the amphibious assault and a sea-borne operation against a sizeable land mass. Okinawa was about seventy times the size of Iwo, and was surrounded by at least a score of beaches suitable for landing. In seizing a beachhead on that large island, it was possible to emplace artillery on adjacent strips of land to join in the preliminary fires, and then to make a diversionary feint at a landing elsewhere, thus confusing the Japanese tactically. Unlike Iwo, the most effective period of naval gunfire support at Okinawa came after the troops were ashore.[26]

Of course, firing on an undefended beach at Okinawa was a failure of American intelligence. Had the planners been aware of the withdrawal of Okinawa's defenders from the beach, they would have scheduled the landings there differently. Nor is any claim made that the Okinawa undertaking, or any amphibious operation for that matter, should have been denied naval gunfire preparation. The point is that, with the information at hand, however inaccurate, to give Okinawa over twice the length of destructive naval gunfire preparation as was furnished Iwo was a marked discrepancy. Taking into account the problem of ammunition supply, it would have been possible to augment the projectiles expended at Iwo by reducing the period of preparation at Okinawa.

The heavily gunned vessels needed to extend the period of fire at Iwo could have come only from Task Force 58, that is the fast surface units of Spruance's Fifth Fleet. Since this command was assigned the mission of raiding Honshu, an analysis of these strikes is pertinent to a discussion of the preliminary fires planned for and delivered at Iwo.

The concept of the first strikes against the Japanese homeland was excellent. The purposes were to take full advantage of the enemy's weaknesses in the air as revealed by carrier operations against the Palaus, the Ryukyus, Formosa, and the Philippines, to cover the assault at Iwo by diverting attention from that island, to blast Nipponese aircraft and air installations in the Nanpo Shoto north of the Volcano group and on the Tokyo plains, and to prepare for the Ryukyus campaign by bombing aircraft factories in the vicinity of Tokyo, Kobe, and Nagoya, thus curtailing the enemy's air potential.

Spruance's conviction that the raids on Honshu constituted a covering operation essential to the success of the Iwo assault is underscored by his insistence that the preliminary fires at Iwo be delayed so as to begin simultaneously with the first dispatch of carrier planes over Tokyo on February 16. Otherwise, since the Japanese had a great number of fields within bombing range of Iwo along a wide arc from Okinawa to Tokyo and south through the Nanpo Shoto, Spruance feared surface vessels at Iwo would be prevented by enemy aircraft from fulfilling their amphibious missions.[27]

Nor could Spruance, because operations in the Philippines delayed his taking over the fast fleet units from Halsey until January 26,[28] replenish and rearm the ships and rest the crews, and schedule the first strike against Tokyo earlier than February 16. If Spruance's decision is to be reasonably treated, he must be criticized, not for waiting until February 16 to open preparatory fires at Iwo, but for failing to extend them beyond February 18. The crux of the matter lay in the feasibility of integrating an extension of preparatory fires at Iwo with the Honshu strikes. Comprising Task Force 58 were sixteen fleet carriers, eighty-one destroyers, five heavy and eleven light cruisers, one battle cruiser, and eight fast battleships. Even with the most conservative estimates of the damage done to the Japanese during the Battle for Leyte Gulf, such a retinue of heavily gunned vessels would hardly be needed for a fleet engagement. Yet, all were taken to Tokyo. Antiaircraft gun platforms are essential ingredients of a fast carrier force.

In view of the suspected hoarding of planes on the enemy's home islands, and in recognition of the serious threat of Japan's kamikaze tactics, Spruance rightly took the most powerful possible antiaircraft force with him to Honshu. These strikes, however, along with the fighting in the Philippines, curtailed even further the preparation at Iwo. At almost the last minute before preparations were to begin at Iwo, so late that the Amphibious Support Commander, Admiral Blandy, had to make the alterations in his firing schedules by hand with pen and ink, Spruance withdrew two fast battleships mounting 16-inch guns from Blandy's force and took them with him to Tokyo. "I regret this confusion caused in your carefully laid plans," said Spruance to Smith, "but I know you and your people will get away with it." [29] The withdrawal of these two fast battleships, plus final allocations between the Southwest Pacific and the Central Pacific theaters, resulted in the inadequate preliminary naval gunfire delivered at Iwo, namely three days of fire by eleven ships with large rifles. The carriers entrusted to Spruance had to be protected, since they were essential for all forthcoming operations; but Spruance was not happy over the extent of preparation Iwo was to receive. Before leaving for Tokyo, while the softening up of Iwo was in progress, Spruance authorized Turner to take a fourth day if he saw fit to do so. In addition, Spruance assured both Turner and Blandy that the two fast battleships he had yanked from the Amphibious Support Force, which were already loaded with shore bombardment ammunition, along with two cruisers partially so loaded, would arrive off Iwo on the morning of February 19, ready to participate in a fourth day of preparatory fire if the decision should be that another day was needed. Turner, principally because of weather predictions, fear of a high surf, and anxiety for the ship-to-shore movement, refused to take the extra day. The two fast battleships and the two cruisers drawn from Task Force 58 arrived at Iwo just in time to participate in the preassault neutralizing bombardment on the morning of the landings.

In connection with the weather, short-range predictions were sometimes reliable, but long-range forecasts could be made in this quarter of the Pacific only by the Japanese and the Russians. In other words, while Turner's refusal to employ a fourth day can be defended on the basis of weather reports by those who desire to do so, forecasts played no significant role in the earlier planning, embarkation, and staging periods simply because no American could predict that a set date in the future would be favorable to the ship-to-shore movement.

No one in the navy during the planning, embarkation, and staging periods for Iwo Jima seems to have seen the course of action clearly indicated by Spruance's last-minute decision to take to Tokyo the two fast battleships already loaded with bombardment ammunition. These vessels, obviously, would be virtually useless in a surface fleet engagement; they were needed off Tokyo because they mounted powerful antiaircraft batteries. Still other fast fleet units accompanying the carriers of Task Force 58 should have been loaded with shore bombardment ammunition, and if possible given some additional briefing in the technique of firing at shore installations. The only restriction on this course of action would have been the shortage of small boats at the fleet anchorage in Ulithi Atoll, which would have made it difficult in the brief time available to off-load armor-piercing, fleet engagement projectiles and to onload bombardment ammunition; but every effort in this direction should have been made. All the fast fleet units so prepared for shore bombardment could have gone with the carriers to Tokyo, and then returned, along with the two fast battleships and two cruisers arriving off Iwo on the morning of February 19, to continue the destructive preliminary naval gunfire. If there were fear of leaving the carriers thus partially unprotected, cruisers from the bombardment force at Iwo could have replaced cruisers in the carrier task force organization. The old battleships were too slow to keep pace with fleet carriers, but the cruisers in the two forces were interchangeable. Warships with large rifles, it must be recalled, chiefly employed their primary batteries against shore targets; most of the 5-inch fire in the preliminary, preassault, and close support phases was provided by destroyers. Also, all cruisers, fleet and bombardment, were adequately loaded with 5-inch and smaller antiaircraft ammunition.

Such provision for a more extended preparatory fire at Iwo, had it been made, would have involved no great change in Spruance's Honshu plans. He contemplated hitting Tokyo on February 16–17, and if conditions warranted again on February 18. Had the third day's strike been made, the full transfer of fast fleet units to bombardment duties, after refueling, would have been delayed to February 20. After the first strikes against Tokyo, Task Force 58 was to come to the westward of Iwo and to furnish direct air support to the marines, and then another raid on Japan proper was planned for February 25. This was to be a two-day raid on the Kobe-Nagoya area, in an effort not only to hit aircraft factories but also to keep the Japanese off balance and to continue to divert their planes from the vicinity of Iwo. It could have been integrated into an extended preliminary naval gunfire period at Iwo with a few minor changes in the schedule and after an exchange of cruisers between the Amphibious Support Force and Task Force 58.

Thus it was feasible, under existing circumstances, both to raid Japan proper and to satisfy the desires of the marines for a more extended preparatory fire at Iwo. Yet the historian must not allow hindsight to obscure a risk felt at the time which did not fully materialize later. The carrier strikes were designed in part to disrupt the enemy's air reaction to the Iwo assault, and the landings had to begin before the effect of those strikes dissipated, lest the Japanese recover and hit Iwo during the critical unloading period; but this threat was reduced by the planned second raid, and in any event Spruance was willing to run the risk, as was evidenced by his authorization for a fourth day. Also, while admitting that a longer period of preparation at Iwo would probably have shortened that at Okinawa, a correct understanding of the difference between an amphibious assault and an amphibious operation against a large land mass should have dictated such a procedure.

As it happened, the raids on Tokyo were marred by several ironic twists in history. The weather was bad over Tokyo on both the 16th and the 17th of February, and the contemplated strike for the 18th was called off. Tokyo was substituted for Kobe-Nagoya on the 25th; again foul weather obscured the target, and the planned second day of this raid was also cancelled. Such ill-fortune was no reflection on Spruance's plans, since his meteorological data was necessarily inadequate. Finally, although the air facilities around Tokyo remained in workable condition, only one major strike was staged by the enemy against the shipping concentrated at Iwo. Thus, while the concept of the Tokyo raids was above criticism, in view of Japan's light air reaction over Iwo it is hard to see how Spruance's attacks on the home islands greatly benefited the assault.

Little effort was made during the three days of strikes against Japan to bomb aircraft factories, but exaggerated claims were apparently made as to the number of enemy aircraft destroyed on the ground and in the sky, 499 for February 16–17, and 158 for the 25th. A post-war interrogation of a staff officer in the Japanese army command responsible for the air defense of the Tokyo area, admittedly from memory alone, set the grand total in his outfit for February 16–17 at approximately forty planes, with but "minor damage" to the fields.[30]

A nation at the time holding back more than 5,000 aircraft was surely not stopped from contesting Iwo in the air by the Tokyo raids. Perhaps that island was too far distant from the homeland for an effective employment of suicide tactics, as long as staging points in the Nanpo Shoto were kept neutralized. At any rate, the Japanese chose to wait until the Okinawa operation before unleashing their intense kamikaze attacks.[31] Spruance, of course, could not read the Japanese mind. He was on the offensive and had to try to deal realistically with the enemy's capabilities. Schmidt agreed that, in terms of strategical planning, the Tokyo raids were necessary. Of Iwo he said, "the position was exposed and there was a constant hazard of strong enemy air attacks on shipping and shore facilities at the target." [32]

Underlying Schmidt's words is a basic problem of the amphibious operation, which Nimitz stressed after the Iwo assault. "It is a cardinal principle of amphibious operations," he said, "that shipping be localized and exposed at the objective for the minimum possible time." This principle, he continued, made "the speedy completion of the troop operations ashore of vital importance from a naval standpoint. The longer the fighting ashore keeps up, the longer will there be a large number of ships localized at the objective; and this in turn will increase the probable number of them damaged, and will curtail the time available for them to return to rear areas, reload, rehabilitate, and be ready for the next operation." [33]

Nothing would have speeded up operations ashore more than an extended period of gunfire preparation, yet this aspect was not sufficiently stressed during the planning period.

Carefully echeloned resupply lowered the number of ships localized late in the Iwo operation, but preliminary bombardment was so inadequate that the navy as well as the marines suffered. Several days passed before the enemy's artillery and mortar fire on the beaches died down sufficiently to allow the assault shipping to start full-scale unloading all along the coast. A total of thirty-six days lapsed before weary shattered marine units, largely with flamethrowers, tanks, and demolitions, overcame a resistance organized about prepared installations which were to a high degree vulnerable to preliminary destructive fire by large-caliber naval rifles. Cave positions are not included here, since they were mostly hidden from naval fire; but on the testimony of Blandy and his principal subordinates, as well as officers who later examined Iwo, there remained after three days of fire a great number of dual purpose guns, covered artillery pieces, blockhouses, and pillboxes which could have been taken out—had the planners arranged for more time.

For more than a month there were shipping targets aplenty about Iwo had the enemy seen fit to strike them. He failed to contest the island vigorously with submarines. All his air raids were trivial except for a fifty-plane suicide attack on February 21. On that day an escort carrier was sunk and two were damaged; another suicide plane hit a tank landing ship, damaging it and some tank equipment; still another injured a cargo-aircraft ferry vessel; and four kamikaze craft crashed and seriously wounded the heavy carrier *Saratoga*.

Even more directly because of the inadequacy of the preliminary naval gunfire, the navy as well as the marines sustained damage. Enemy mortars and batteries of artillery, aside from taking their toll of beach party personnel and crews of landing craft, hit over three times the number of American ships that were struck by kamikaze planes. Among those damaged by enemy fire from Iwo were a heavy cruiser and two destroyers. Potentially the most dangerous threat of all was a series of near misses from enemy artillery which, on the eleventh day of the assault, splashed a resupply ship loaded with ammunition for the troops ashore.[34]

The marines worked hard in the planning period to get more preparation. If they made any error it was in failing to stress more vigorously the close connection between an adequate naval gunfire preparation and a speedy assault. They were the experts on tactics ashore, but their tendency was to argue in terms of casualties. Of course, the navy wished to do everything possible to curtail the number of marine dead and injured, but its major concern was correctly the safety of its shipping, crews and troops, and the rapid turn around of that shipping in order to expedite the Ryukyus campaign. Smith was in a good position to put across the connection between an adequate naval gunfire preparation and a speedy assault, but did not do so. He supported each of Schmidt's recommendations to the hilt, but his approach was poor. Smith insisted on an extension of fire before the first strike against Tokyo, that is before February 16, or not at all. He believed that the sooner the assault transpired, the less time the Japanese would have to get ready for it. This was sound reasoning, but the beginning of sustained preliminary fires, rather than the day of the beach assault, was the pivotal date. Once preparations began, the enemy on Iwo must necessarily cease perfecting his defenses and hide in his positions. Nor could the preparatory fires begin at Iwo until the day of the carrier strikes on Tokyo, lest Spruance reveal his strategy and unduly jeopardize his carriers. Smith was, however, characteristically determined, and this once at least impervious to fundamental strategical considerations. He rejected the contrary advice of his own chief of staff, for he had concluded it "imperative that we should not deviate from the final target date of February 19, with or without our desired gunfire support." [35]

This determination came from overconfidence. Smith and Schmidt were fully cognizant of the necessity for a rapid assault. It is evident that they both believed, albeit with high casualties, the marines could overrun Iwo Jima, gunfire support be damned, with great speed.[86] This was asking too much, even of the United States Marines.

2. Troop Training, Embarkation, and Rehearsals

Mounting evidence of the difficulties presented by Iwo, in the face of failures to obtain more preparation of the target, made it necessary to commit more marines. Additions to the assault units and their reserve and support forces multiplied until the total exceeded 80,000 men. Also in the assault echelon were advanced parties of garrison, airfield construction and service personnel, and antiaircraft troops, bringing the number of men transported to Iwo Jima on or shortly after the target date to 84,000. Later shipments caused all troop classifications carried by Turner's command to rise above 110,000 men, most of this increase being caused by the compelling necessity of rapidly shaping airstrips for American bombers and fighters. Lifting these troops, lending strategic cover and direct support to the assault, were more than 800 naval vessels, sailed and fought by approximately 220,000 men.[37] Logistical and tactical planning for these marine, navy, and army components, as well as training, embarking, staging, and rehearsing them, was a problem of staggering proportions. With a few exceptions, it was met in a most commendable fashion.

Early plans called for four regimental combat teams, two each from the Fourth and Fifth Marine Divisions, to assault abreast. One of the two remaining regimental combat teams was to stay in Fourth Division reserve, since this command was to land in the most difficult spot, under the belly of the island, and was to pivot immediately against the bulk of the enemy in the northeastern bulge; while the other regimental combat team was assigned to corps or Landing Force reserve. The Third Marine Division was alerted at Guam in Smith's Expeditionary Troops area reserve. In other words, a division at Iwo was to have no reserve, and the entire corps was to have only a regiment in reserve. A lesson underscored at Peleliu, that a reserve is something more than the caboose on a long freight train, was being overlooked; but request was shortly made to increase the marines at the target because, to quote Schmidt, "combined with a reduction in the planned naval gunfire available . . . additional information was received during the planning period indicating a continuously higher estimate of enemy strength and a large increase in the number of defensive installations. . . ."[38]

As a result, the composition of the Landing Force was changed. First, disposition of the Third Marine Division was altered to bring it to Iwo in floating reserve on the third day after the assault began. Subsequently, the regimental combat team assigned to Landing Force reserve was released to its parent division, and one of the floating reserve regiments, the Twenty-first Marines, was ordered to arrive at Iwo in Landing Force reserve on the morning of the initial landings. Moreover, the two remaining regimental combat teams of the Third Marine Division were placed in Expeditionary Troops reserve some eighty miles from the target on the evening of the day set for beach assault.[39] Thus three marine divisions, comprising a total of nine infantry regiments with supporting arms and certain corps troops, were sent to Iwo.

In accordance with tables of organization drawn up in the spring of 1944, the engineering regimental headquarters of all marine divisions had been abolished, principally because the Naval Construction Battalion (Seabees) was no longer organic to the marine division. This change was made because Seabees were needed for continuous airfield construction, and it was unwise to keep a battalion inactive with a division between operations. Seabees went to Iwo, but as corps troops. The marine division was thus left with an engineer battalion and a pioneer battalion, each of which was broken up by companies and assigned directly by the commanding general to the infantry regiments as needed, or else concentrated if and when advisable.

The Fourth Marine Division, first employed at Roi-Namur and then engaged on both Saipan and Tinian, was led by Major General Clifton B. Cates, a veteran of Guadalcanal who had taken over the division from Schmidt when the latter moved up to command the Fifth Amphibious Corps. Regiments of the Fourth Division were the Twenty-third, Twenty-fourth, and Twenty-fifth Marines, with the cannoneers in the Fourteenth Marines. To them went the difficult task of landing under and seizing the cliffs flanking the beaches to the northeast, of taking most of Motoyama Airfield Number One, and, constituting the right flank of the corps front, of driving across the broad northeastern portion of Iwo Jima.

Still untested as a command in combat, the Fifth Marine Division was none the less highly seasoned with former raiders and paratroopers who had seen service in the Solomons. The division was activated early in 1944 and was trained at Camp Pendleton, California, and Camp Tarawa, Hawaii.[40] On Iwo, attesting to the high caliber of its leadership under Major General Keller E. Rockey, it exhibited no sign of inexperience. Its men assaulted the beaches on the corps' left, raced across the narrow portion of the isthmus to begin taking the southwestern beaches on the target date, and then pivoted southwest and northeast to overrun Suribachi and to drive the corps left flank up the Motoyama Plateau, over the escarpments dominating the southwestern beaches, and through the northern part of the island, wherein were located the final enemy pockets. Rifle regiments of the Fifth Division were also consecutively numbered, Twenty-sixth, Twenty-seventh, and Twenty-eighth, with their 75- and 105-millimeter howitzers manned by the Thirteenth Marines.

The Fourth and Fifth Divisions were, along with most of the corps and garrison troops, embarked from Hawaii; but the Third Division was lifted from Guam. The Third, Ninth, and Twenty-first Marines constituted the rifle regiments of the Third Marine Division, reinforced by the artillery of the Twelfth Marines. These men had first seen action on Bougainville, and had just completed their share of the Guam operation. Commanded by Major General Graves B. Erskine, formerly chief of staff to Holland Smith, the Third Division was an experienced well-trained body of men. Although not used in beach assault, and even though the rifle battalions of the Third Regiment failed to land at all, to this division fell the job of driving up the center of the Motoyama Plateau and splitting the enemy's organized resistance by reaching the sea along the center of the northeast coast. Comparisons as to the quality of performance of the three divisions on Iwo are impossible since the tasks assigned to each varied and since each showed up superbly. The Fourth and Fifth Divisions made the beach assault, and each occupied a wider front than the Third throughout much of the fighting. Also, the Fourth and Fifth Divisions were on the flanks of the attack up through the bulge of the island, and they crossed the more difficult terrain; but the Third Division likewise fought valiantly in the key terrain sector of the island.

Some 68,000 division troops were landed on Iwo, backed eventually by almost 14,000 corps troops ranging from two 155-millimeter howitzer battalions through engineering troops for the airstrips; for included in the orders to Schmidt was immediate airfield renovation to allow friendly planes to land at the first practicable moment.[41]

Specific training for Iwo began in the early fall of 1944. Much of the amphibious lift for the Fourth and Fifth Divisions had been recently commissioned, and every opportunity was seized to indoctrinate navy crews with their duties while continuing the amphibious exercises of these marines. Results were rewarding; but more than one-half of the amphibious tractors were in the Marianas, and despite successful efforts to get the commanders of the amphibious vehicles and their assigned tank landing ships together, incidents reminiscent of Roi-Namur occurred off Iwo Jima.[42]

Lower echelon planning proceeded smoothly, although a few of the usual delays persisted. Some of the troop transport quartermasters once again were held up in receiving details of ship characteristics, and a few regimental combat and battalion landing team commanders complained that their tactical planning was put off by the late arrival of orders from higher echelon.[43] This particularly handicapped the amphibian tractor and Dukw battalions and their corresponding inexperienced navy echelons, where according to Schmidt's operations officer "probably the weakest link in coordinated planning is still found. . . ." On the other hand, once these plans had crystallized, flexibility was hampered by the close integration of boat control to and from the line-of-departure. This made for a more compact assault, but a battalion landing team commander, for example, acting on late intelligence data, could change the composition of one of his reserve waves only after clearing his request through a maze of higher ranking navy and marine officers.[44]

Planning and training were alike improved by the excellence of intelligence, and especially by a widely circulated but closely guarded, comprehensive study of Iwo and its defenses, prepared by the Joint Intelligence Center, Pacific Ocean Areas. No other target in the Central Pacific had been photographed as thoroughly as Iwo, nor had the troops previously been furnished with photographic prints of so high a quality. One of the highlights of the planning phase was the cooperation of all navy and marine staffs of division level and above in compiling a joint enemy installation map of all known defenses. This eliminated the discrepancies that had inevitably existed when each command made its own map.

Of special value was information on the preferred and alternate beaches and the installations around Motoyama Airfield Number One. (See map 21.) Knowledge of surf and beach conditions vitally affected both logistical planning and the scheme of maneuver. Violence of the surf and the coarseness of the volcanic ash were recognized and feared, and provisions were made accordingly. Small boats proved almost useless for beach logistics, but larger craft were available; it was known that wheeled vehicles would have trouble crossing the beach until routes of egress had been bulldozed and marston matting had been laid, and every effort was made to increase the number of tracked vehicles lifted.[45]

Both marine and navy personnel were trained under the most realistic conditions possible, since indoctrination of the officers and men on the lower echelons was placed ahead of security. A training map of Iwo Jima was published, with all proper names, latitude and longitude removed, and was captioned "Island X." This map was then extensively employed in training problems and command post exercises, allowing beach and terrain characteristics to be closely simulated, and acquainting officers and men with everything from the forthcoming scheme of maneuver to the crowded conditions expected in handling supplies across the beaches, establishing command posts, dumps, and water distillation units, and emplacing artillery. "Island

X" was classified as secret, and the intent was to limit its distribution to those officers who required the map for lower echelon training, but its use in the field resulted in its being widely seen.[46]

Even so, security would probably have remained intact, since the Japanese had so zealously guarded this little-known island, but for an unfortunate incident. The Army Air Forces, presumably through Nimitz's public relations office, released to the press during the training period an oblique photograph of the Suribachi sector, identifying this as a part of Iwo Jima and describing that island as a current target of Mariana-based bombers. The picture was published in Honolulu, and as one intelligence officer remarked, "any man familiar with 'Island X' maps who saw the newspaper photos couldn't help but know our destination." There was, of course, loose talk, and in an effort to counter the damage, Schmidt's headquarters started a rumor among the habituées of the bars and hotels in Honolulu that the pending objective was Formosa.[47]

Whatever the source, the Japanese garrison on Iwo learned of the coming invasion, and also calculated the probable time of assault and earmarked the divisions to be employed. In fact, the enemy seems to have overestimated the ground forces to be hurled against Iwo. A captured Japanese diary indicated that four marine divisions and a marine brigade were to be committed, and a prisoner of war testified to a general belief among the garrison that five marine divisions were en route to the island.[48]

While releasing this photograph to the press was inexcusable, it is hard to see how harm to American troops ensued. The enemy was already building up Iwo as rapidly as he could, and a correct estimate of an obvious strategical situation, plus sightings of American shipping, the bombing efforts in the softening up period, and knowledge of available marine divisions doubtless revealed to him, at least in part, the next target, the approximate time of assault, and the probable troops to be used. In the final analysis, more was gained than possibly could have been lost by training in accord with the terrain configurations of "Island X." Such procedure along with post-embarkation briefing of all troops with plastic and rubber relief maps (an art perfected by the armed services in conjunction with the movie industries) caused one marine officer to comment that "every tank commander, cook and clerk knew what it was all about on this one." [49]

From the outset of the training period, Iwo was recognized as an objective which, even with extended naval gunfire that would furnish optimum preparation, would fall mainly because of the prowess of the assault rifle and demolition squads. This was true because of the terrain features of Iwo, and because many cave positions and some of the heavy and medium installations obviously could not be taken out before the landings began. It was the men in the front lines who would seize the island. They must utilize all possible support arms for neutralization and advance, but must rely chiefly on tank-flame-thrower-demolition-infantry coordination in destroying enemy positions. This meant that the individual marine must be proficient with his own weapon, cognizant of the value and technique of employing all other infantry weapons, and capable, if necessary, of taking over and using the weapon of a companion should he become a casualty.

Such versatility was achieved among the regular infantry troops, but the great weakness of the training period became apparent as casualties mounted. Too little attention had been paid to acquainting service and support troops and members of replacement drafts not only with elementary tactics, but also with the intricacies of the assault squad and its vital part in the forward movement. To quote the conclusions of Schmidt's operations officer, "more intensive training in weapons and basic infantry tactics is necessary in training of personnel of service troops. In many cases these troops were poorly qualified in the rudiments of infantry warfare. Additional emphasis will be placed on this training in preparations for future operations. Replacements received by divisions were in some cases inadequately trained in basic military skills and were received too late by divisions for adequate training and indoctrination by the units to which they would eventually be assigned." [50]

The triangular nature of a reinforced marine division was carried through companies and platoons to assault squads and teams, that is three teams formed a squad, three squads a platoon, three platoons a company, three companies a battalion, and three battalions a regiment. Training and coordination on all echelons was essential, but the point of interest here is the lowest echelon units, the teams and squads. A general account of their normal composition at Iwo is pertinent, since it represents the highest perfection reached in organizing the men who did the bulk of the fighting.

Each rifle platoon consisted of three assault squads, two rifle and one demolition. In each of the assault rifle squads were thirteen men, the squad leader and twelve others who were divided into three fire teams of four men each. These were a team leader, usually armed with the Garand (M-1 rifle), an automatic and an assistant automatic rifleman, and a private carrying a Garand.

The assault demolition squad also contained three teams of four men each, plus the squad leader, but each of these teams had a separate function. The "pin-up" team, with the general mission of bringing a large amount of fire to bear on a particular target such as a pillbox or a cave, was heavily armed with the bazooka, two automatic rifles, and the Garand. While the Japanese were pinned up by the bazooka team, assisted by rifle assault squads, one or both of the other demolition teams would move in for the kill. One was equipped with two sections of bangalore torpedo and at least four heavy charges of explosives, while the other carried two Ronson flamethrowers which in turn were covered by two protective riflemen.

Summarizing, each platoon consisted of nine teams of varying specialties which could be used simultaneously or in any desired combination, depending on the situation. Each of the men carried at least one weapon other than his specialty, including smoke and fragmentation grenades, Garands, carbines, and pistols. In addition machine guns and mortars, controlled by the company commander, reinforced each platoon. Finally, it was the duty of the battalion commander to supervise the employment of battalion weapons, tanks, and other supporting arms at any moment assigned to his unit. Only after the battalion commander was convinced that every ounce of his firepower was being brought to bear on the Japanese did he have any right to do any fighting himself.[51]

So great was the concentration on training the individual and small units of platoon size and lower that, according to one battalion commander, company and battalion exercises were "held to a comparative minimum." [52] Yet some officers later felt that individual and small unit training was insufficiently stressed. There is merit in these complaints, although they came after Iwo was found to be an even more difficult target than expected, and in part they arose from conditions beyond the control of corps and the divisions, such as the late arrival of personnel and tank replacements. Schmidt's operations officer summarized the training problem neatly when after the Iwo assault he observed that "in view of probable future operations against other heavily fortified positions, more intensive training of individual personnel in the use of flamethrowers, demolitions, and siege tactics is indicated, as well as continued emphasis on small unit leadership and training. . . ." [53]

Holland Smith was responsible for the state of readiness of all marines in the Pacific. He delegated much of this task as it pertained to Iwo to Schmidt, but the Commanding General of the Pacific Fleet Marine Force, along with the training section of Marine Corps Headquarters in Washington, must bear the blame for the late arrival of some of the replacements at division training bases, and for the inadequate training the replacements had received, although in this connection it should be remembered that the Marine Corps at this date in the war was no longer enlisting by volunteering, and the nation was dipping low in manpower. Yet the fact remains that these replacements were poorly trained, and Smith's operations officer willingly shouldered his part of this responsibility when after the assault he said: "A technique for the indoctrination and integration of replacements prior to and during combat operations remains one of our most urgent problems. A study is being conducted by this Headquarters, based on the recommendations of subordinate echelons towards a solution of this problem." [54]

Schmidt's supervision over training was necessarily restricted by the widely dispersed embarkation points of his corps and division troops. What control he exercised came through command conferences at his headquarters in Pearl Harbor and through frequent visits of his liaison teams with the three divisions. Except for corps troops, who were on the whole well trained considering their duties and the circumstances involved, Schmidt in turn delegated training responsibility to his division commanders, urging that it accord with the type of fighting indicated by Iwo's terrain and defenses.[55]

A discussion of training therefore revolves about the division level. These commanders were responsible for the failure properly to train division service and support units in basic infantry and assault squad tactics, but there is much to be said in extenuation. While such training is desirable, it can be effected to a high degree only under the best of circumstances, and in any case no more than a few men from such organizations can possibly be spared for the front lines. Rockey's service and support units were better prepared to enter front line fighting than were those of either of the other two divisions; and Erskine and Cates, although devoting as much attention as possible to their service and support units, were plagued with other and more grave training problems which caused them to concentrate on infantry units.

Erskine and Cates headed divisions scarred by the Marianas campaign. Rehabilitation, the meshing of prebattle or organic replacements into the infantry units, and resupply were essential, and among these first priority was given to the absorption of newly arrived men and material by the infantry components. The Fifth Division, on the other hand, had never seen combat and needed no organic replacements. Purely in terms of training, it was the best prepared of the three divisions to enter the struggle for Iwo. Not only was a portion of its personnel experienced, but it was recently equipped and up to full strength from the outset of the training phase.

One flaw in the training of the Fifth Division was occasioned by the slow receipt of its quota of flamethrowing medium tanks. These weapons, firing a long flame from the muzzles of their 75-millimeter guns, were of tremendous value on Iwo; and the troops of the Fifth Division were not fully trained in their use before the battle.

Also serious was the late arrival of the Iwo Jima battle replacement drafts assigned to Rockey's command. To each of the three divisions were allocated two such drafts, each containing seventy-five officers and 1,250 enlisted personnel. These men were distinct from organic replacements. They were to be used to bring the infantry components neither to full nor to overstrength, but were kept in pools under division control to augment the shore parties early in the assault, and were to be moved into the front lines to replace battle casualties as required. This was a new concept for the marines, to maintain the divisions at as near full strength in the field as was possible. The design was excellent but, as so frequently happens with a novel military arrangement, worked poorly in its first test. The plan was to substitute a skill for a skill, but as it turned out, and this conclusion was unanimous, most of the men in the battle replacement drafts were deficient in basic training, and altogether without proficiency as a member of an assault squad. It is believed that a better plan would have been to form the infantry replacement drafts into organized and trained assault squads or platoons, and to feed them into combat as such intact under their own leaders. As it was, individuals or groups of men were sometimes assigned to units in combat so hastily that they did not even know the name of their squad or platoon leader, nor the organization nor the armament of the other members of the fire team to which they were assigned. Even had they been well trained individually, it would have been difficult under the circumstances for them to function efficiently as members of the fighting squads. But they were not well trained individually, which was apparent when they reached the divisions. This was, however, less than six weeks prior to embarkation, and the task of acquainting them with their shore party duties prevented giving them much additional infantry instruction.

Again overconfidence in the ability of the shock troops to complete the Iwo assault with utmost speed reflected itself in the preliminary phase. Because of the extended and rigorous fighting, casualties in infantry components rose to fifty and seventy-five per cent and beyond. It thus became mandatory that members of these battle replacement drafts be put in the front lines. This was excessively dangerous for them, and at times it resulted in needlessly exposing key personnel remaining in the tanks and assault squads.[56]

Otherwise, Rockey's command entered the fray with morale at a peak, in a high state of efficiency, well-equipped, and with its personnel in excellent physical condition. There was an expected increase in colds during the first two weeks aboard ship, but these declined during the subsequent forty days en route through the staging base to the target.[57]

The Third Division had sustained some 4,390 casualties on Guam, and when training for Iwo began in October 1944 it had only recently been relieved of its duty of mopping up in the Marianas. Before rehabilitation could get under way the division faced the task of erecting its own camp, and both resupply and obtaining organic replacements were complicated by the distance to rear bases. Its artillery regiment, for example, was never altered to accord with the new table of organization which had substituted 105-millimeter howitzers in one of the two battalions previously manning 75-millimeter pack howitzers.

Worse in terms of training was the late arrival of the Third Division's quota of the recently authorized, more heavily armored medium tanks and tankdozers, and it never received any of the valuable new flamethrowing tanks (but some were borrowed on Iwo). Most serious of all was the delay in receiving both organic and battle replacements.

The first of the battle replacement drafts came in October, and the second a month later, but a combination of factors eased the problem of training these men as far as the Third Division was concerned. Its units were not to be landed in beach assault, and the training of its shore party was therefore simplified. Furthermore, it was close to the target; nor did it have to be embarked early for a rehearsal. As a result, it was able to leave Guam some six weeks after the Fourth and Fifth Divisions had departed Hawaii, and Erskine utilized this precious time in more extended training. Organic replacements were well integrated into their rifle and demolition squads, and occasion was even found to give further infantry training to the battle replacement drafts.

The Third Division also went to Iwo in a high state of efficiency. Greatest stress had been placed on a passage of lines to continue the attack, coordination of all arms, particularly infantry-artillery, and the cooperation of assault squads and tanks in knocking out pillboxes and blockhouses. In order to embark, however, the men were forced to make unusually long marches, and some blistered feet resulted. Finally, the period of transit to the objective was short, and respiratory illnesses were more common in this than in any other division. Troops of the Third Regiment suffered especially from sore feet and colds, but these men were not landed.[58]

Cates with the Fourth Division faced the most acute training problem of all. His command was likewise delayed in getting resupply, organic, and battle replacements. Most serious, it had lost over 6,400 casualties on Saipan and Tinian, and the task of handling its organic replacements was greater than that of the Third Division. In addition, the Fourth Division was not only compelled to conduct ship-to-shore training exercises of more benefit to inexperienced crews of its amphibious shipping than to its own troops, but also, since it was destined for assault and was embarked far distant from the target, was forced to board ship early and to undergo a series of rehearsals.

Earliest organic replacements reached the Fourth Division camp on September 1, but the number was sufficient for only one regiment and two additional battalions. Bringing the remaining regiment and battalion up to full authorized strength was set back to November 22, and even then it was necessary to dip into the battle replacement drafts to fill out a serious shortage in junior officers. Embarkation began thirty-six days later. There was no time to integrate properly the last organic replacements received, much less to attempt anything other than shore party indoctrination for the battle replacements. Cates alone had good reason to be thankful for the postponement of Iwo's target date because of operations in the Southwest Pacific. To him it was "obvious that had the original loading date . . . been enforced the combat efficiency of the Division would have been seriously impaired." As it was, there was time only for a minimum of reorganization and training of those units drawing last-minute organic replacements. The colonel of the regimental combat team most delayed in reaching full strength estimated that his command embarked at only ninety per cent of normal battle efficiency.[59]

Likewise Cates' command, and to a lesser degree that of Erskine, could never have properly loaded its shipping for combat without a postponement of the target date. Not only were such items as tanks received too late for full training, but other resupply equally essential to an operation barely arrived in time for the ultimate mounting out schedule. Had the originally planned embarkation timetable been confirmed, Cates' transport quartermasters would have had no choice other than to load the supplies at hand, and then haphazardly to top stow all last-minute receipts. The supply service in the new Fleet Marine Force, Pacific, while cooperating enthusiastically, was certainly not functioning smoothly.[60]

Plans on the highest command level, however, called for sufficient shipping to load out an expedition with comparative ease; but these good intentions failed to filter through the lower logistical echelons. As it turned out, a distinct improvement on earlier operations was made. While space was hardly ample, for once the shortage was not generally acute.

The transport divisions were enlarged. Each of these was designed to lift a regimental combat team, and was furnished, on paper, with an additional small attack transport and small attack cargo vessel. This made a total of four attack transports and two attack cargo vessels, but the record fails to show that by the time the ships were allotted to the regimental combat teams any one received its extra space. Properly, each of the large attack transports and attack cargo vessels was limited to slightly more than 500 and 2,000 short tons of supplies respectively, and the increase in number of ships was in the end absorbed by corps and garrison troops, with their equipment and supplies. The upshot was that for once the regimental combat team were carried to the target in what had previously constituted a transport division, namely three attack transports and one attack cargo vessel. Despite the heavier equipment assigned to the infantry components, the amount of shipping available to each of the regimental combat teams greatly reduced the need of separating men from their equipment, and permitted an unusually high degree of combat unit loading.[61]

The total number of ships in Turner's command was 495, and of these Hill, as Attack Force Commander, was assigned 172, including medium and tank landing ships, with which to lift the assault troops, their supplies and equipment.

Five units of fire for small arms, backed by ammunition resupply shipments, proved more than ample; but seven units of artillery and mortar shells, plus an emergency load in two tank landing ships, afforded no margin of safety. Enemy artillery and mortars blew up several ammunition dumps; and serious shortages, especially in 105-millimeter howitzer and 60- and 81-millimeter mortar projectiles, threatened but did not develop. Earlier operations had shown the need for more ammunition in these and other related categories, especially explosives, but Nimitz's headquarters was slow in revising the unit of fire tables, and the increases made were formalized too late to benefit the Iwo assault.

Faith in a short operation and the small size of the objective caused much heavy equipment to be left behind. Supplies which might be seriously needed, however, and which if unused could be turned over to the garrison, were loaded at from eighteen- to thirty-day levels. These included fuel, rations, and medicines. An average of fifty per cent of all supplies was palletized.[62]

Although the Third Division was given no role in the beach assault, its logistics section exhibited creditable foresight in combat-loading its units, and these were available to land individually and as required, irrespective of whether or not the beaches were secured. Most of the men and equipment of this division were carried in attack transport and cargo vessels. The plan was to set them ashore as needed in landing craft, and in Dukws and amphibian tractors borrowed from the other two divisions.

The new tanks allotted to all divisions were too heavy for medium landing craft. Those of the Fourth and Fifth Divisions were dispatched in the larger medium landing ships, while those of the Third Division were loaded in two of the altogether too scarce tank landing ships.

This left only sixty-one tank landing ships. These were apportioned between corps troops and the divisions being committed to beach assault. Here developed the only serious shortage in shipping. By the time corps artillery and other necessary corps troops were supplied with these vessels, only thirty-eight remained for both the Fourth and Fifth Divisions. Ten of these were employed by the two divisions to lift their amphibian trucks, preloaded with their artillery. Thus there were only twenty-eight of these vessels for the four beach assault regimental combat teams, and eight were of only limited logistical usefulness since they served as either radar vessels after arrival at Iwo or had to be converted to hospital receiving wards on the morning of the assault. The result was an inequitable distribution of personnel, caused by underloading the tank landing ships earmarked for radar and hospital work with the armored amphibian tractors, and overloading the remaining twenty (that is five per beach assault regimental combat team) with personnel and the cargo amphibian tractors. Conditions had been better at Saipan, where each of the assault regimental combat teams was assigned full use of at least eight tank landing ships. After Iwo, Schmidt recommended that in view of the current table of organization for division artillery, and in order to permit a uniform tactical loading of assault battalions, a minimum of twenty-three tank landing ships be assigned to help lift each division to be committed to beach assault.[63]

The Fourth and Fifth Marine Divisions, garrison troops in the assault echelon, and most of the corps troops were embarked from Hawaiian bases in late December and early January 1945. Rehearsals were held off Maui and Kahoolawe Islands, Hawaii, during the period January 13-17. These lacked realism since most of the naval gunfire vessels and direct support planes were still in Philippine waters, but particularly in the fields of communications and boat control, as well as in further indoctrination of the inexperienced navy crews, great profit was derived. Also in these rehearsals, plus the final series held in the forward area off Tinian in mid-February, elements of the joint assault signal companies of the three divisions perfected their plans and equipment, and added the finishing touches toward a first-class performance in the realms of beach logistics, shore naval gunfire control, air liaison, and artillery forward observation.

Personnel lifted from Hawaii were returned to Honolulu for a brief rehabilitation following their first rehearsals, after which the bulk of the Attack Force began moving forward in echelon via a refueling station at Eniwetok to the staging area in the Marianas. There a second set of rehearsals was held, with some of the men-of-war and escort carriers present; but rough weather interfered with plans and no troops were landed. The Third Division met the Attack Force at Tinian, but except for communications drills did not participate in the second rehearsals.

In the Marianas the Attack Force was also joined by the remaining corps troops. Three of the five battalions of amphibian tractors to be used at Iwo were taken aboard the tank landing ships, and these vessels were further loaded with the beach assault personnel from the Fourth and Fifth Divisions to be landed in the early waves by the tracked vehicles. While aircraft and submarines reconnoitered the far reaches of the Western Pacific, the Attack Force, covered by the fast carriers and screened by destroyers and destroyer escorts, began movement to the target just before and shortly after Rear Admiral Blandy's Amphibious Support Force started delivering preliminary naval gunfire and air support on the morning of February 16.[64] Joint tactical and logistical planning had been, on the whole, superior. As Holland Smith later observed: "The fact . . . that adequate troops, support, weapons, equipment and supplies were available to complete a most difficult mission without alteration of the original plans is an indication of the efficacy of that plan." [65]

3. Delivery of the Preparatory Fires

"While the enemy bombardment is going on, we must take cover in the dugouts and we must keep our casualties at a minimum."

Thus a Japanese soldier transcribed one of his "Essential Battle Instructions" some seven weeks before the advent of Blandy's warships off Iwo Jima. This order was carried out to the letter. Seldom was an enemy seen above ground; and if caught exposed, he dashed like a gopher into a tunnel, blockhouse, pillbox, or cave. For three days, the Amphibious Support Force sought to penetrate these defenses and to prepare the island for assault, but weather favored the Nipponese. Another member of Iwo's garrison, describing the morning when the bombardment began, believed that "by dispensation of heaven the characteristic mist of this Island caused the sky to be overcast. . . ." [66]

Personnel of Blandy's force performed near miracles, considering the limited time at their disposal. The Japanese refrained from opening fire, except antiaircraft, until mid-morning on the second day. This, combined with low visibility, inability to obtain good on-the-spot photographic coverage during the first two days of preparation, and the necessity of halting destructive preparation temporarily to protect the minesweepers and underwater demolition teams, handicapped the naval gunners. There were more than thirty-four hours of daylight during the period February 16–18, but the main batteries of the large warships fired an average of less than thirteen and one-half hours. Even so, roughly ninety per cent of the allotted heavy and medium caliber ammunition was hurled at Iwo. No previous target in the Central Pacific had received such a volume of preparatory shelling per square yard of terrain—nor had any other gone into the assault phase with so many of its defenses intact.

Still, the navy commanders carried out their assigned mission most creditably. Blandy's principal assistant was Rear Admiral Bertram J. Rodgers who as Commander, Gunfire and Covering Force, was in direct charge of the bombarding vessels. Both sought destruction of pinpointed installations, which, as Blandy emphasized, was a complicated task requiring "much training and experience, not only in gunnery, but also in detecting well-camouflaged targets, and in accurate observation and assessment of the results of gunfire." Otherwise, he added, "bombardments are very likely to consist only of 'area fire' which, though they may obtain neutralization for short periods, cannot be expected to achieve any appreciable destruction of enemy defensive installations."

Only on the final day of the preparatory period did these admirals reach their desired goal of effectiveness, and fortunately for the marines that day's fire was concentrated on and adjacent to the preferred beaches. This fact plus the intense preassault neutralizing bombardment and bombing on the morning of February 19 made it possible for the assault troops to secure the beaches without an unacceptable number of casualties.[67]

Blandy and his staff, lifted in a headquarters communications vessel, were well situated to supervise the preparations at Iwo. In addition to the newly formed Amphibious Support Force, two other arrangements improved the preliminary bombardment. Supplementing the catapult-launched planes of the warships were specially trained air spotters flying from some of Blandy's escort carriers. These observers, experienced in European waters, gave greater destructive value to indirect fire, and also, in view of the weather, to some fire which normally would have been directly controlled.

An agency set up to assess the effect of the preliminary fire and bombing while these were still in progress was of greater benefit. The scheme used was an improvement over that at Guam. Specific targets were kept track of individually, and when destroyed or partially damaged a notation was made of that fact. Estimates by observers were relied on as little as possible. Blandy's aerial photographic interpretation section had been expanded and these men, as often as they could get acceptable photographic coverage, did an excellent job of calculating damage and destruction concurrently with the shelling and bombing. If avoidable, nothing was left to chance. The plan was to employ both armor-piercing and variously fused high-capacity explosives, to wreck the greatest possible number of enemy defenses in the given time, and to prevent wasting projectiles on a target already obliterated. Both marine and navy air and gunfire officers had brilliantly devised this plan over a period of three months. Circumstances being what they were at Iwo, it was admirably executed.

It provided for full coverage of almost all the island. Recognizing that the Motoyama tableland afforded excellent defilade positions from which the enemy could register artillery and mortar fire on the assault craft moving ashore, these inland targets were also marked for destruction. (See map 21.) The design was to begin fire at a range of some six miles on February 16, to demolish known targets, and moving in closer, to strip camouflage. On the next two days the range was to be closed to about a mile, although provision was made to continue plunging fire into non-vertical installations. Defenses which escaped damage on February 16, and the large number of positions expected to be revealed when camouflage was blasted aside, were to be destroyed on February 17-18. Each night destroyers were to lay down harassing 5-inch barrages, to keep the garrison awake and nervous, and to prevent hasty repairs.

Highest target priority went to installations which threatened ships, aircraft, and the activities of the minesweepers and underwater demolition teams. These included coastal defense guns, antiaircraft weapons, and antitank guns near the beach. Second in order of importance were those structures of particular menace to the ship-to-shore movement, such as blockhouses, pillboxes, covered artillery emplacements, and machine guns close ashore. Third were the defenses which could oppose the troops after landing, caves, storage and bivouac areas. Not to be fired at during the preliminary period were all targets susceptible to the preassault neutralization, among others open emplacements and trenches, and hulks of grounded ships. Also, those pillboxes and blockhouses on the northeastern end of the island were to be left until after the marines were ashore.

While Blandy was staging his force through Ulithi, he realized that the delay in releasing certain ships from the Philippines had cancelled out a part of this ambitious plan. A shortage of time and ammunition compelled him, even before Spruance had withdrawn two fast battleships for the first Tokyo raid, to revise the plan for the preparatory period and to cancel the third priority targets. But all blockhouses and pillboxes, save those along the escarpments of the northeast coast, were retained on the target list, whether or not they threatened the ship-to-shore movement. This left Blandy's gunners with a staggering total of more than 700 suspected first and second priority installations. At a final conference between naval gunfire, air, and intelligence officers, the positions on the two priority lists were redivided into three groups, those most suited to high-powered naval rifles, those most vulnerable to air bombing, and those to be destroyed by both arms. This allocation was particularly useful on the first day.[68]

Things went badly for the Americans on February 16. It was eight o'clock, an hour after the appointed time, before the light mist and rain cleared sufficiently to allow fire to begin. The minesweepers functioned smoothly and range was closed, but intermittent rain squalls caused continuing poor visibility, and Blandy was forced to abandon his timetable and direct the ships to open up only when weather conditions permitted accuracy, which was generally during mid-afternoon and later. None of the known Japanese coastal defense guns was destroyed; but some progress seemed to have been made against the antiaircraft batteries which throughout the day had compelled most of the air spotters to remain above the low cloud ceiling, with a consequent deterioration of accuracy.

Visibility was excellent on February 17, and the spotter planes were able to fly at low altitudes, but firing on the previous day had been insufficient to strip the amount of camouflage needed to allow the aerial photographic interpreters to function well. The difficulty in removing camouflage was later made clear. Some of it was natural rock. More important, scheduled fires for the 17th were disrupted by operations of the underwater demolition teams.

Movement of men-of-war shooting from close range at a small island is necessarily complex, for in order to reach all targets, the full circumference of the objective must if possible be covered. This introduces the problem of protecting one's vessels from overs and ricochets. An already involved scheme of maneuver for naval vessels at Iwo was made more complicated on the second day by the necessity of shielding the underwater demolition swimmers and their craft from friendly and enemy fire.

The plan called for those warships assigned areas of responsibility on and adjacent to the southeastern beaches, to close that portion of the coast to about 3,000 yards and to deliver destructive fire from seven in the morning to ten forty-five, after which they were to retire to medium range to allow the demolition experts to work. Meanwhile, ships on the other side of the island were to bombard at medium ranges with plunging trajectories. After the underwater demolition teams had finished their task on the preferred beaches, which was estimated at shortly after noon, they were to be transferred to the alternate beaches while other heavy vessels moved in near the southwestern coast, and prepared it for the swimmers. The hour set for beginning underwater demolition team operations along the alternate beaches was half-past two in the afternoon. It was hoped that this job would be completed by four o'clock, and normal firing could be resumed for the two hours remaining before the usual nightly retirement.

That phase of fire before ten forty-five in the morning was well executed, although the ships on the eastern side were slow in closing range. Trouble really began when the underwater demolition teams, operating from destroyer transports and rubber boats and afforded close in support by infantry landing craft converted to gunboats, moved toward the preferred beaches. The commander of these swimming teams had taken every precaution possible to prevent the enemy from supposing the work of his men to be the initiation of a beach assault, but at least some of the Japanese coast defenses opened up.[69]

It is impossible to say conclusively, but evidence indicates this enemy fire was not directed by the Japanese high command on Iwo. Rather, it came simultaneously from a number of trigger-happy Nipponese gun crews.

The point is important, for if the fire was ordered from above, it is apparently the one serious error made by the ranking Japanese commander, Lieutenant General Tadamichi Kuribayashi IJA, throughout the entire operation. Otherwise his preparations and the tactical conduct of his men can only be described as outstanding. The Tokyo radio described this general as one whose "partly protruding belly is packed full of strong fighting spirit" and whose knowledge of Iwo was so thorough "that even should he be asked where a certain hole made by the rats is to be found, he would answer quickly without any hesitation." A brilliant officer, he deserved this praise. One marine, after the struggle for the island was over, said of Kuribayashi: "Let's hope the Japs don't have any more like him." [70]

Obviously the infantry landing craft converted to gunboats supporting the underwater demolition teams looked like assault craft; but they were maneuvering to fire their weapons, not to land troops, and since their total number was twelve, they surely were not lifting more than some 2,400 men. Hill's Attack Force, after all, was still several hundred miles away from Iwo. Perhaps smoke and dust obscured the visibility of the Japanese gun crews. Regardless, these twelve gunboats were taken under a blistering cross fire when some 3,000 yards from the beach, and in a matter of minutes eleven were badly damaged and one sunk.

The official Japanese news agency branded the gunboat incident of February 17 a repulsed assault;[71] but if Kuribayashi released such an interpretation, it was pure propaganda, for he quickly rectified the error that had revealed to the Americans some of his gun positions. Firm orders were issued, or more probably reissued, to hold back all weapons of possible value in repulsing the ship-to-shore movement and in the fighting to follow.

Irreparable damage had already been done to the Japanese cause. Opening up on the underwater demolition team gunboats was the one time the enemy departed from his subtle tactics of uncovering a gun or a battery, firing a few rounds, and then rehiding the weapon or weapons. This practice, in conjunction with his genius at camouflage and his smokeless powder, made the location of his light and medium artillery a hard task, and discovery of his excellent mortars even more difficult.

As it happened, the old battleship *Nevada* instantly began counter-battery against the weapons firing at the gunboats. She was assigned to the area of the preferred beaches, and rather than withdrawing to medium range had been compelled to retire toward the beach in order to stay in mineswept waters. The more powerful of these enemy pieces, which were coastal defense guns, were located at the base and along the northeastern slope of Suribachi, and amid the cliffs flanking the preferred beaches to the right. These guns were more numerous than American intelligence had suspected, and they constituted such a menace that the work begun by *Nevada* was continued throughout the remainder of that day and the next.

Thus what had been planned as a normal underwater demolition team operation had unexpectedly developed into a successful feint of great consequence. Good photographic coverage of an island partially stripped of camouflage was still more than twenty-four hours away. Without this error by the Japanese, it is probable that many threatening coast defense weapons would have remained to take a very heavy toll of men and supplies from the outset of the ship-to-shore movement. This was unquestionably the most significant role ever played by the bold underwater swimmers and their close covering gunboats in the course of the Pacific War.

Casualties aboard the gunboats were high, but the swimmers finished their work along both coasts without gunboat assistance and with remarkably light losses. No offshore man-made obstacles were located; and shoal signals were placed on Futasu Rock just east of the narrow isthmus of the island. Fear that the Japanese were preparing to flood the beach with burning oil was partially laid to rest. Optimistically, the underwater demolitions experts with a few exceptions reported the sand along the coast was coarse but suitable to landing wheeled as well as tracked vehicles.

Blasting the gunboats, however, delayed the underwater demolition teams, and this in turn interfered with planned fires for February 17. The volume expended was heavier than on the previous day, but photographic interpretation during the evening of the 17th showed little actual destruction accomplished.

The navy was shocked by the reception accorded these gunboats. Belatedly, Schmidt's final recommendation as regards the preparatory period, that if only three days were to be provided the fire be concentrated on and adjacent to the preferred beaches, was accepted. Blandy exercised good judgment, departed from his instructions, and revised plans for February 18. Fire support units responsible for the southeastern coast were reinforced, and every effort was made to increase the destructive shelling on and adjacent to the beaches destined for assault. Summarizing, the gunboat incident benefited the marines in two ways. It disclosed the positions of those guns most menacing to the ship-to-shore movement earlier than otherwise would have been possible, and it caused the navy commander on the spot to reevaluate his mission and to adopt a realistic course of action.

The excellent weather of the 17th deteriorated the next day, but was not as unfavorable as that on the first day. Visibility on the 18th was only fair, with occasional light rains. From mid-morning throughout the remainder of the day, clouds at about 1,500 feet altitude cramped the air spotters, but antiaircraft fire was weak and the pilots could fly under the ceiling. Finally, the naval gunners by this time were well oriented to their target and its terrain. In Rodgers' opinion, "this day's bombardment was worth more than all the previous softening by air bombings and gun bombardments. . . ."[72]

Two old battleships, *Tennessee* and *Idaho*, were stationed a mile offshore to blast the enemy's batteries flanking the preferred beaches; while *Nevada* and *New York*, supplemented by the heavy cruiser *Vicksburg*, destroyed other pinpointed installations in the same general area. These five capital vessels fired close ashore throughout much of the day, while the remaining six men-of-war, the old battleship *Texas*, four heavy and one light cruisers, bombarded the rest of the island. But visibility was such that most of the day passed before Blandy's assessment agency received and evaluated good photographs. As a result, some ammunition was wasted, especially by *Tennessee* and *Idaho*, who had no choice but to pound the flanking enemy weapons until these were certainly demolished.

It was three o'clock in the afternoon before these photographs, showing considerable stripped camouflage, had been studied and new firing data drawn from them. Normal night retirement was postponed thirty minutes, to half-past six. This was a calculated risk, since it ended the firing during evening twilight and increased the hazard of enemy submarines; but it was wisely and willingly taken. For three and one-half hours during the afternoon and evening of the last day, highly effective bombardment was delivered.

Concurrently with the period of preliminary bombardment, navy carrier and army land-based airmen continued attacking Iwo; but for a number of reasons this bombing was of relatively little value to the assault. Over and beyond the greater accuracy of the high-powered naval rifles, the pilots employed were inexperienced in ground tactics, their bombs were of 500 pounds weight and less and were generally too light for the defenses encountered, and the low cloud formation normal over the target detracted from the accuracy of both the carrier-based bombers and the rocketeers, to say nothing of those who released their missiles while above the ceiling.

The army pilots based in the Marianas and assigned to the Iwo operation came under the tactical supervision of Turner and his navy subordinates very late in January 1945. One of these admirals suggested after the assault that a more extended period of integrated tactical control, plus a more vigorous prosecution of supplementary bombardment from navy guns, would have considerably improved the effectiveness of the softening up period. Be that as it may, the single achievement of note made by the Mariana-based bombers was in neutralizing and keeping neutralized enemy airfields in the Bonins, on Haha Jima and Chichi Jima, just to the north of Iwo, and most of the credit for this should probably go to the navy pilots of Task Force 58 and to Blandy's escort carriers. Land-based planes were weathered out from Iwo on both the 16th and the 18th of February.[73]

Rear Admiral Calvin T. Durgin commanded the escort carrier group assigned to the Amphibious Support Force. These planes were present at Iwo from the beginning of the preparatory phase, and were invaluable in providing naval gunfire spotters and combat air and antisubmarine patrols. Also, despite camouflage, the rugged terrain, and the weather, all of which increased the difficulty of locating pin-pointed targets from fast attack aircraft, the pilots helped to ready the island for assault. Their 5-inch rockets, when fused for reinforced concrete, were particularly effective. But in most other categories their performance was mediocre. Their napalm drops were needed to help to strip camouflage and to burn away patches of undergrowth, but these were afflicted with a high percentage of duds. Nor were their bombs either heavy enough or properly fused to penetrate and destroy the installations characteristic of Iwo.[74] Blandy's supervision over the support missions of these carrier pilots was exercised through a navy officer known as the advanced commander of an aircraft control unit, who was aboard the Amphibious Support

Force flagship. After the carrier pilots had on February 18 also concentrated their attention in the vicinity of the southeastern coast, this supervising officer laconically remarked that their work "conceivably weakened the areas commanding the landing beaches." [75]

The most glaring shortcoming in terms of air support at Iwo stemmed from the small amount of influence marine officers exercised in the planning phase. The navy had been urged by marine commanders to carry heavier bombs, but did not do so. In this connection, the chief complaint of Cates regarding air support warrants examination. His Fourth Division faced the tactical problem of landing under and overrunning the terrain just northeast of the preferred beaches. (See map 21.) Photographic interpretation revealed that this ground rose abruptly in cliff formations, and then gave way into a deep pit, commonly but inappropriately called the "Quarry." On to the northeast the terrain rose and then once more fell abruptly into a area more correctly dubbed by marines the "Amphitheater." Then the ground again rose skyward just east of Motoyama Airfield Number Two, to reach a peak 382 feet above the sea.

It was evident that the Japanese had fortified this sector intensively, and that many targets were suitable to air bombing, but the terrain, save for the destruction of some of the medium weapons, was scarcely touched until the men of Fourth Division took it on foot. During the rehearsal in the forward area Cates asked the airmen to drop large "earthquake" bombs on this sector. He was seeking not direct hits but maximum concussion within ravines and all of the landslides possible which would bury the Japanese in their caves and other defenses. Such bombing would possibly have been most effective against the "Quarry." From this cavity the Japanese were extracting a fine sand clay with which to surface their roads and airstrips, and it is likely that the concussion effect would have been muffled by this soil, although not as much so as by the volcanic ash on the waist of the island. Yet the rim and sides of the "Quarry" could probably have been pushed down. The seams of rock retaining the clay around the circumference, as one observer later pointed out, were so soft that they could be "cut and shaped with a knife, axe, or pick." [76] Whether or not heavy bombs would have demolished such targets as the "Quarry," the effort surely should have been made. Although torpedo bombers could lift a large load, the navy had no heavy bombs in the forward area, but why the army supply in the Marianas could not have been tapped remains a mystery. Better still, army planes could have flown earthquake explosives from Saipan and released them over the "Quarry" at reasonable altitudes, but even after the enemy's antiaircraft fire had been reduced and the army airmen came in at around 4,000 feet, according to the testimony of marine and navy officers, they were none too accurate.[77]

So the airmen failed even to try to level one of the terrain features most suited in the eyes of the Landing Force to the air arm. The preparatory period ended at dusk, February 18.

It is impossible to estimate precisely the damage done to Iwo Jima by the preparatory fires. Admittedly no post-operational study could with complete accuracy separate the destruction wrought before the assault on February 19 from that subsequently inflicted; but joint intelligence teams from Nimitz's headquarters tried, and their conclusions are the best that can ever be obtained.

Preassault intelligence was good, but was found to be short in listing first and second priority targets by a total of more than 200 installations. Count of third priority targets was never attempted, nor was any destructive fire leveled at them during the preparatory phase. The damage done by the preassault bombardment and bombing during the morning of February 19 is necessarily included in the figures given below, but since this fire was intended chiefly for neutralization, whatever destruction was gained on that day may be reasonably lumped with the February 16–18 period.

During those three days about one-half of the sixty-five coastal defense guns actually on the island were either damaged or destroyed. Similar fate met the same percentage of the thirty-five heavy antiaircraft weapons, but only one-fifth of the 228 light antiaircraft guns were injured or put out of action. Almost all of the guns remaining intact in these categories could be and were used either against the ship-to-shore movement or during the fighting ashore, or both.

Turning to second priority weapons, there were on the island at least forty-six blockhouses, ninety-one covered artillery and antitank guns, and 450 pillboxes. Less than twenty-five per cent of these were damaged or destroyed before February 19.

Out of a grand total of 915 first and second priority installations, Blandy's force demolished or damaged only 194, or less than twenty-two per cent. Casualties inflicted on the garrison could hardly have been in a greater ratio, and were probably substantially lower since almost all bivouac areas were at least ten meters deep, and some were burrowed underground for hundreds of feet.[78]

Two conclusions are evident from these figures. First, a longer period of preparation was obviously needed. Had the Japanese not erred in opening up on the underwater demolition team gunboats, the absence of excellent on-the-spot photographic coverage would have permitted only three and one-half hours of really effective shelling. Under the circumstances, Iwo stands as a monument to the accuracy and destructive value of naval guns against shore targets; but five more days of effective preliminary bombardment were required to prepare the island adequately for assault.

Second, the enemy's tactics are revealed. As of February 19 there remained weapons capable of seriously interfering with the activities of the underwater demolition swimmers, the minesweepers, aircraft, naval gunfire vessels, and the amphibious shipping, had Kuribayashi at any given moment seen fit so to employ them. His refusal to do so was a calculated decision to prevent the destruction of his firepower and to save it for later occasions. This is not only a testimonial to his tactical astuteness, but also exhibits the awe with which he and all Japanese, by this late date in the war, contemplated naval bombardment.

In reporting by despatch to Turner during the late evening of February 18, Blandy specified that not all his allotted ammunition had been expended, and that abundant targets remained for another day of preparation; but he also correctly concluded that the preferred beaches were sufficiently cleared to make landings feasible on the morning of February 19. The decision regarding a fourth day of preparation was Turner's, and indications are that his principal concern was weather. He ordered the assault as scheduled, at nine o'clock on the morning of February 19.[79] The Attack Force started forward to Iwo Jima.

While it is true that the weather early on February 19 was favorable to the ship-to-shore movement, it deteriorated that afternoon, and the surf was so bad on February 20 that a reserve regiment could not be landed. Acknowledging that the fear Turner felt for possible Japanese air reaction and the safety of his amphibious shipping must have been acute, in retrospect it seems unfortunate that a fourth day of preparation was not taken. Given weather conditions, this would have meant delaying the landings to February 21, thus allowing a total of five days of preparation.

Such a course of action in the end would have speeded up the fighting ashore and would have localized the amphibious shipping for the briefest possible time. The beaches would have been better prepared for assault, and as a result the marines would have struck the enemy's main line of resistance along the approaches to the Motoyama Plateau with far greater impact. Finally, an opportunity for naval gunfire to work thoroughly over the installations on the Motoyama Plateau would have been gained. Spruance and Turner as well as some marines believed these defenses were in the main invulnerable to destructive fire by naval guns until ground observers could get up onto the tableland, which of course would have been too late for such fire.[80] But Blandy's Support Force was so efficient in the limited time at its disposal, and the air spotters were so well trained and so competent, that after the camouflage had been stripped and photographs had been studied, it is felt that destructive firing could have been at least partially achieved. The regret is that a serious effort in that direction was not made.

After February 18, most of the support rendered the marines was neutralizing rather than destructive in effect. It was largely up to tanks and rifle and demolition assault squads to seize the island gun by gun, pillbox by pillbox, and blockhouse by blockhouse. While concurring that the final arbiter of battle is the man with a rifle, to a far greater degree than was necessary, taking Iwo Jima was like throwing human flesh against reinforced concrete.

4. Narrative of the Fighting

Radio Tokyo announced eight days after the assault on Iwo Jima began that the American portion of the island was "not more than the size of the forehead of a cat." [81] Figuratively, this statement was too true for the comfort of the marines. By that time, upwards of 70,000 men and many thousand tons of equipment and supplies had poured ashore. These were crowded onto the waist of the island, and it was hard for Japanese rockets, artillery, and mortars to miss.

A withering neutralization of the southeastern coast during the early morning of February 19 preceded the assault, and the first waves, especially in the vicinity of Suribachi, got ashore on schedule against little opposition. (See map 21.) Well before noon, however, enemy artillery and mortars began hitting the boat lanes, the beaches, and the narrow isthmus. The task of landing men and equipment and supplies became difficult. Not until several days had passed was Suribachi captured and the northeastern flanks of both the preferred and alternate beaches completely cleared of enemy weapons. The full force of what remained of eight regimental combat teams was then thrown against the Japanese main and secondary lines of defense in a struggle which was protracted until nearly the end of March.

THE BEACH ASSAULT

On the morning of the assault, naval fire commenced at forty minutes past six, shortly before the amphibian tractors started disembarking from their tank landing ships and moving in column formations toward their rendezvous positions in the rear of the line-of-departure.

Task Force 58 had returned from Tokyo, and eleven additional cruisers, as well as the two battleships loaded with shore bombardment ammunition and the two cruisers partially so loaded, joined from time to time in the preassault bombardment. Pilots from the fast carriers augmented those from the escort carriers.

A total of twenty-six vessels with large and medium caliber guns began closing the range during the early morning twilight of February 19, firing at targets of opportunity within assigned areas of responsibility. The sun rose shortly after seven. Weather was good, and the wind was unexpectedly favorable. It was temporarily from the east-southeast, thus carrying smoke and dust away from the guns leveled at the preferred beaches, nor was it strong enough during the morning and early afternoon to cause unusually adverse surf conditions.[82]

Naval gunfire was checked but not ceased from five minutes past eight for half an hour while the heavier vessels took their final positions close ashore, and destroyers moved into the boat lanes. During these thirty minutes the major air strikes of the day lashed out against the southeastern coast. More than 200 planes were expected to participate, but roughly two-thirds of the forty-five bombers scheduled to arrive from the Marianas were weathered in at their bases, and the total on hand was 175.

After the air foray, men-of-war resumed, firing all batteries. Even a helpful breeze failed to clear away the clouds of debris kicked up by this avalanche of neutralizing fire. The sun was obscured, while Iwo trembled as if Suribachi had been awakened from its sleep. The first assault wave, sixty-eight armed and armored amphibian tractors, ran parallel to the coast along the line-of-departure. Those supporting each division were in two columns, one headed southwest and the other northeast. Then with perfect timing, just as collisions looked apparent, the vehicles turned individually right and left, and at eight-thirty started for Iwo Jima.

During the thirty-minute run in to the shore the naval vessels never stopped firing, but like the other support weapons calibrated their blasts with the position of the initial wave. A rolling or box barrage from naval guns was delivered as the marines went ashore. Fire from main and secondary batteries and from 40-millimeter antiaircraft guns was blocked step by step inland and to either flank in accordance with the expected movement of the troops, and fire-control personnel were dispatched in separate amphibian tractors to begin supervising the mean centers of impact in the event anything went wrong with communications ashore. Destroyers in the boat lanes intensified this phase of the fire. A recently perfected powder, by increasing the trajectory, made it safe to shoot over landing boats and the close in support craft.

Also a large number of gunboats, more than fifty, was employed. These were properly under the direction of the Attack Force Com-

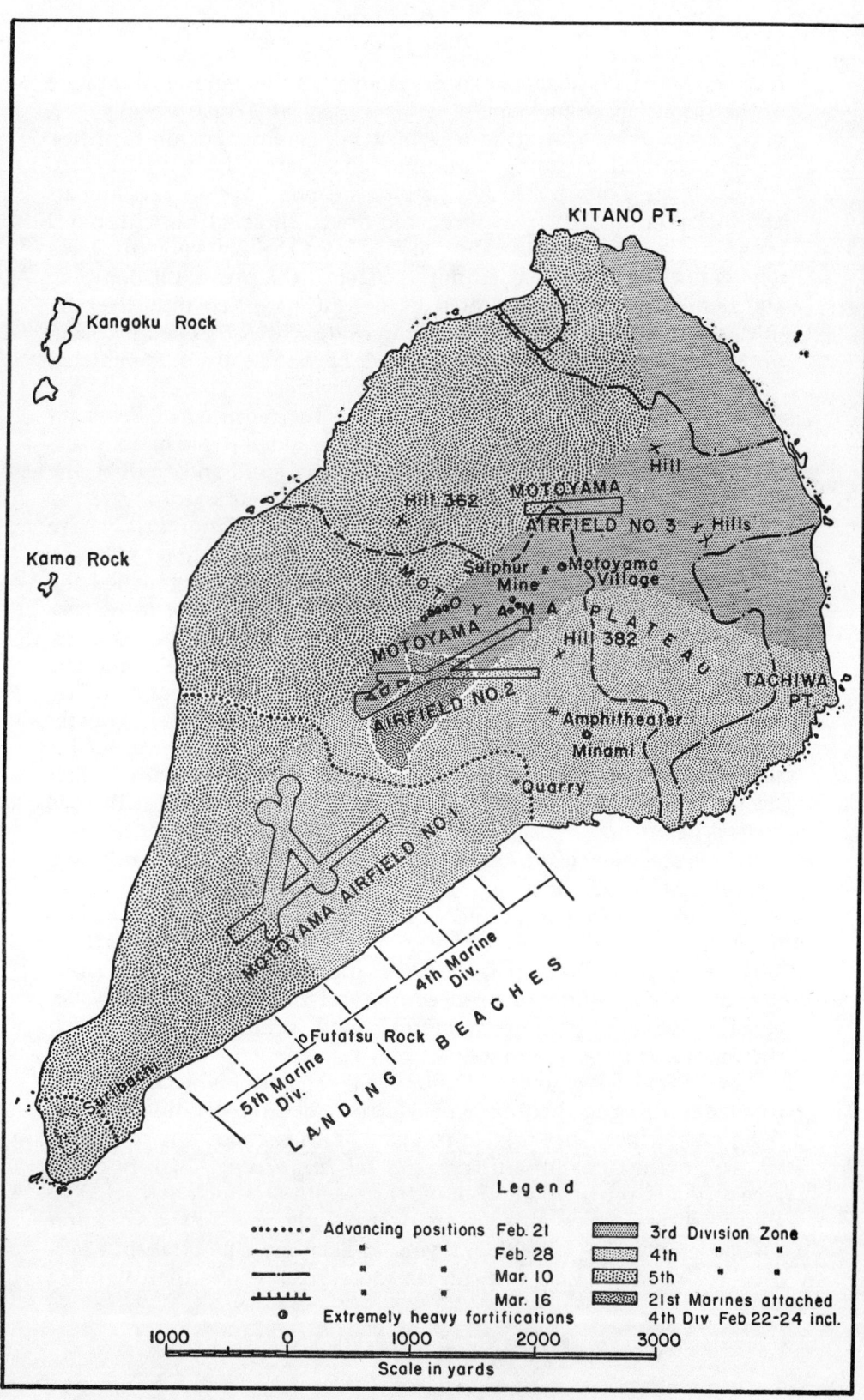

MAP 21. Capture of Iwo Jima, February–March 1945.

mander, Harry Hill, whose masterly control of the beach assault phase of the ship-to-shore movement, utilizing specially constructed supervising craft and the latest improvements in communication facilities, reflected careful planning and experience dating back to Tarawa. Mortar boats mounting heavy 4.2-inch weapons, as well as gunboats and rocket craft, ran close ashore and fired. These, along with naval shells and a last-minute strafing attack from the sky, kept the Japanese dazed and inert. The stunning effect of the preassault bombing and bombardment is illustrated by the estimate that only five amphibian tractors in the early waves were destroyed by enemy action. Finally, the plan was for the first wave ashore to be armored vehicles, firing machine guns and 75-millimeter howitzers.[83]

The ship-to-shore movement at Iwo on the morning of February 19 was no ferrying operation. It was a power-laden deployment packing the utmost momentum yet devised by the mind and engineering genius of man. This was the acme of the amphibious assault.

Any less momentum in moving up from the sea might possibly have failed to carry the advance inland. The assault was robbed of much of its thrust soon after the armored amphibian tractors touched the coast at nearly the appointed hour of nine o'clock. The word generally spread from the underwater demolition experts had been wrong. There was no hard packed sand. Rather, the beach and the entire waist of the island except for Motoyama Airfield Number One consisted of a volcanic ash, originally anchored by scrub growth. This ash was coarse, and into it a man sank to above the tops of his shoes. Only with difficulty could a marine on foot or an amphibian tractor move forward, while wheeled vehicles, unless taken in tow, bogged down.

The first terrace was too steep for the armored vehicles, and these were forced to back down and to lie offshore before obtaining a field of fire. Intelligence had predicted a sharp slope some four feet high, but it was generally double that and in places rose to fifteen feet. Lighter cargo tractors managed the incline, but it was a time-consuming and dangerous procedure, and those in the first waves generally released their men, supplies, and scaling ladders between the water and the first terrace.[84]

As well as slowing down the assault, the ash and the black dust that rose from it damaged equipment and increased the discomfort of individual marines. One private recalls that on the morning of February 19 "my mental prodding to *get off the beach* . . . refused to recognize my physical anguish and I arose to a crouch and tried to sprint up the terrace wall but my feet only bogged in the sand and instead of running I crawled, trying to keep my rifle clean but failing." [85] But in the long run the ash was a greater asset than liability to the marines. It was easily dug, bagged, and retained behind any type of bunker support; and it served as a cushion in absorbing the concussion and lessening the shrapnel burst of the enemy's mortars and artillery. Only a direct hit damaged men and equipment properly dug in. This feature of the ash, profusely cratered as it had been by naval bombardment and air bombing, was of assistance to the rifle components in the early stages of the fighting, and was later of untold benefit to service and support units.[86]

Early waves of men and equipment reached the beach with an accurate five-minute rhythm, and under cover of the rolling naval barrage the marines penetrated inland to a depth of 150 to 300 yards. There the movement slowed. Generally, only the first five waves had been boated in amphibian tractors. This constituted most of the beach assault personnel, numbering some 10,000 men, occupying almost 400 cargo vehicles. No amphibian tractors remained, however, to lift either the regimental or division reserves. These were in vehicular and personnel landing craft, and on touching the beach it was seen that these boats were generally unsuited to Iwo's surf. They began broaching, and the wheeled equipment they released, sinking to hubs in the volcanic ash, increased the clutter on the beach.[87]

Some might choose to call the landing of wheeled vehicles this early a mistake, but the advice of the underwater demolition teams had confirmed the landing waves as planned, and the boats must be brought in according to their designated order and must be unloaded. This was a power play, as in football, and some of the elements got through while others did not. Also, provision had been made to keep the assault rolling across the waist of the island. Tanks, transported in larger landing craft and in medium landing ships more suited to Iwo's coast, were called forward before ten o'clock. Among these were flail tanks for detonating land mines, and tankdozers, each carrying the commanding officer of a tank company, who sought suitable points of egress and began nosing out channels through the first terrace. Tanks followed, and although delayed by mines and the volcanic gravel, gave added impetus to the advance.[88]

The rolling barrage was timed to expand in accordance with the estimated advance of the troops, and except for the far left flank, this was slower than had been anticipated. Plans were to repeat fires in designated blocks upon request, and this was done, but the arrangement failed to function smoothly everywhere. As a result, the Japanese began little by little to recover from the daze of the neutralization period and to fire on the beaches. Those on the right flank were struck by a few mortar and artillery shells as early as two minutes after the arrival of the first wave. By noon the enemy's reaction was furious, and some sectors of the southeast coast were receiving accurate small arms fire as well as that of heavier weapons. More and more landing craft were damaged or destroyed, and abandoned in the surf—a process that was to continue until the presence of these hulks jeopardized beach logistics.[89]

Many of the enemy's installations just inland from the beaches had been demolished, but there were important exceptions. These were on Suribachi, around the first airfield, and in front of and along the right flank.[90]

The twenty-eighth Marines of the Fifth Division on the extreme left flank initially made the most rapid progress. A stubborn ex-raider from the Solomons, Colonel Harry B. Liversedge, whose giant frame had earned him the title of "Harry the Horse," was their commander. They landed in a column of battalions across a single beach 500 yards wide, with the mission of dashing across the narrow isthmus and then pivoting southwest and taking Suribachi. A highly effective naval barrage along the northeastern slope and base of Suribachi, brought and kept within 200 yards of their left flank, was of great assistance; and elsewhere in their immediate zone the majority of the enemy's pillboxes had been destroyed by naval gunfire, while but a single covered artillery emplacement remained. Elements of the Twenty-eighth Regiment reached the high ground overlooking the opposite coast within an hour and thirty-five minutes after setting foot ashore; but beach conditions and the character of the fighting led to a loss of organization, which on the first day was believed to have been caused by very high casualties. No further progress was made against Suribachi itself on the 19th.[91]

Rockey's second regiment from the Fifth Division committed to beach assault was the Twenty-seventh, led by Colonel Thomas A. Wornham, which moved ashore two battalions abreast across as many beaches just to the right of Liversedge. Enemy fire along these beaches and inland soon became intense. Also, stiff opposition was encountered off the southeastern corner of the first airfield. The Twenty-seventh was consequently slower than the Twenty-eighth in gaining the upper terrace of the alternate beaches. When the men of the Twenty-seventh turned northeast and tied in with the Fourth Division at nightfall, they were short of the Fifth Division's planned objective. Rockey's third regiment, the Twenty-sixth Marines, followed the other two ashore on February 19 in division reserve.[92]

To Rockey's right, Cates and the Fourth Division faced the tougher resistance and the more difficult mission in making the beach assault. Before the day was done, Cates had committed two of his three battalion landing teams held in division reserve. His beaches were the first to come under fire, and the reason became evident as the men moved inland. For a depth of 400 yards, thirty per cent of the pillboxes remained, and beyond that point to the airfield, the total rose to seventy per cent. Artillery, mortars, and small arms were active from the cliffs to the right. Ten reinforced concrete blockhouses, seven covered artillery positions, and eighty pillboxes were intact and directly menacing the beaches of the Fourth Division.[93] The damage inflicted by those weapons was great. Robert Sherrod, able correspondent for *Time* and *Life* who had witnessed almost every marine landing in the Central Pacific since Tarawa, said of Iwo's beaches, "nowhere . . . have I seen such badly mangled bodies." [94]

Cates held the Twenty-fourth Marines in Fourth Division reserve. Landing just to the right of Rockey's beaches were the Twenty-third Marines, led by Colonel Walter W. Wensinger. These men also went ashore two battalions abreast across as many beaches. They found themselves squarely in the center of the southeast coast, catching enemy fire from both flanks, and their losses were heavy.[95] They needed more time and more assistance from their division reserve, from the Fifth Division, and from corps reserve before they could swing their left flank across most of the field and head up the plateau against the center of the enemy's main line of resistance.

The other regiment of the Fourth Division assigned to beach assault had the most difficult job of all during the first day of fighting. This was the Twenty-fifth Marines, commanded by Colonel John R. Lanigan. Two beaches were available for their use, but the one to the far right was so close to the commanding escarpments that both Schmidt and Cates recognized the folly of attempting to employ it. As a result, the early waves of the two assault battalions were crowded onto a single beach. These were to drive inland, while simultaneously wheeling hard right to clear their second beach and to scale the cliffs onto the rim of the "Quarry." Against this obstacle they made their most important progress, seizing the top just at nightfall; but their casualties were extremely heavy. The battalion on the far right, which in scaling the "Quarry" had gone far in securing the right flank of the entire beachhead, had only 150 men left in its front line, and reserves from the Twenty-fourth Regiment were thrown in to hold the gains.[96]

All eight of Schmidt's beach assault battalions were ashore by ten-thirty in the morning, and before mid-afternoon the reserve battalions of the four regimental combat teams and both tank battalions were across the beaches. The reserve regiments for both divisions landed just before or shortly after sundown. By that time the Fifth Division had whipsawed the isthmus and had swung the Twenty-eighth Marines southwest against Suribachi. The other two regiments of the Fifth Division had turned northeast to help the Fourth Division drive over the first airfield and up to the Motoyama Plateau.

Both Rockey and Cates began expediting the landing of their

artillery during the afternoon of February 19, for a counterattack was expected that night. The weapons were preloaded along with ammunition in Dukws, but several of these had been overweighted and capsized on leaving their tank landing ships. Others were, under the circumstances existing along the beaches and just inland, sent to the line-of-departure too early. Delays ensued, worsening weather made the sea rough, and a few vehicles ran out of gas, swamped, and sank, carrying with them valuable howitzers. Yet, it was necessary to accept such risks; and considering the amount of improvisation needed to get these weapons ashore, the navy's boat control personnel, the truck drivers, and the artillery crews earned great praise. The Dukws were pulled across the first terrace by tractors or power winches; and, assisted by shore party dozers and some marston matting, most of them then proceeded under their own power to the gun positions. No attempt was made to land the corps artillery on the first day, but more than one-half of the divisional howitzers were emplaced, registered, and ready to fire during the first night ashore.[97]

Despite the obstacle of the volcanic ash, the high terrace, and enemy reaction, some 30,000 marines were landed and had seized a workable beachhead before late evening of February 19. The cost was substantial. No good estimate of the total wounded exists, but those evacuated before four o'clock in the afternoon numbered more than 1,200, and several hundred others were dead.* As usual, losses were heaviest where they hurt most, among energetic officers, key noncommissioned officers, and specialist personnel such as flamethrowers, bazooka men, and demolitions experts.[98] It was a hard beginning.

As the night settled cold and damp on marines just come from the tropics, their top commanders were concerned lest the expected counterattack strike at either one or both of the estimated weak points in the corps line. These were along the far right flank, and at the southwestern end of the first airfield, where the Fourth division joined the Fifth.[99] Even so, the beachhead could hardly have been retaken by a Japanese attack. There were too many marines with too much artillery awaiting that very development, and for three consecutive nights mortar boats tossed thousands of 4.2-inch explosives into expected centers of enemy concentration. But unfortunately for the marines, large-scale counterattacks formed no part of Japanese tactics.

* The Personnel Accounting System, Headquarters, USMC, figures the first day's casualties as follows: 377 of the Fourth Division killed and 1,058 wounded in action; and 189 of the Fifth Division dead plus 697 wounded. Total, 566 killed and 1,755 wounded in action on February 19.

KURIBAYASHI, HIS MEN AND HIS TACTICS

The enemy's commanding general was too smart to bring great numbers of his men at any time out into the open, under the muzzles of American guns, and to waste them in senseless attacks. Kuribayashi's garrison would have to be dug out or sealed up position by position, and perhaps the principal explanation for the effectiveness of such a defense was its simplicity. Rather than fanatical banzai charges, his tactics were characterized by nightly infiltrations and small well-organized counterattacks to attempt to recover key terrain features. Normally there were no withdrawals, but from time to time, especially in the early phases of the fighting, the Japanese abandoned spots hopelessly doomed, cremated or carried to the rear their dead, and retreated with their weapons. This exasperated the marines who after a bitter struggle and heavy losses overran a zone to find they had taken nothing more than a strip of ground strewn with empty shell cases.[100] Kuribayashi expected the process to wear the marines away, psychologically as well as physically, by slow attrition. That failing, he would still accomplish the utmost for his country. He would if possible make the marines pay their last penny in terms of time, lives, and equipment, before seizing Iwo Jima.

American respect for the skill of the Japanese in contesting Iwo began on February 19 and continued to rise throughout the battle. Nimitz observed that there was an undefined principle of strategy which Kuribayashi seemed to have fathomed. This was the proper ratio between the area being defended and the strength in troops and installations. Obviously too large a region cannot everywhere be fortified in depth, even by a nation with great resources. The problem on a small island like Iwo was just the reverse, that is, not to overdefend, and thus waste men and supplies by unnecessarily exposing them to extermination by the supporting arms of the attackers. "Iwo Jima," concluded Nimitz, "appears to have been close to . . . optimum in size and density of defense." [101]

As well as in the number of enemy installations, prebattle American intelligence underestimated the total garrison force, this time by around forty per cent. There were more than 20,000 Japanese on the island, plus several hundred Korean laborers who were armed and on the whole fought well. Three factors account for the faulty calculation. Whereas only several hundred naval troops were believed to be ashore, the figure was actually in excess of 7,000. Kuribayashi was thought to be on Chichi Jima, and his presence on Iwo turned that island into the focal point of Bonin-Volcano defense, lowering the number of Japanese troops elsewhere in the Nanpo Shoto while raising those on Iwo. Finally, several as yet unidentified army units were found on Iwo.[102]

The morale of the enemy troops was reasonably high, their health good, and their discipline excellent. All civilian personnel except several hundred male laborers had been evacuated months before the assault. Whether or not with a consequent improvement of morale, no evidence of "comfort" girls was found, and, indicating a long dry spell, most if not all of the few sake bottles found were empty. Empties were apparently kept for the purpose of booby-trapping. Also, these Japanese were security conscious, a condition unheard of in the Pacific War before Iwo. Orders to destroy all papers of possible benefit to the Americans were, on the whole, complied with; but true to the bushido spirit, no instructions had been given as to what to say if captured, and those few who surrendered or were taken while casualties, comprising roughly one per cent of the entire garrison, talked freely and furnished tactical information of value. Even here, however, the iron hand of Kuribayashi, a full-blooded martinet, was evident. Aware of this leakage of information in earlier operations and unable because of his code to warn against American methods of interrogation, he found another solution. Small as was the island, it was divided into smaller sections, and the personnel assigned to each were closely guarded against free movement out of their zone. The highest ranking Japanese captured, a major commanding a battalion, while volunteering information of great pertinence to his area of responsibility, was vague and indefinite about other sectors and, except in general terms, about the overall scheme of defense.[103]

Members of the garrison stayed in their set localities and worked hard. This was evidenced not only by their well-constructed defenses but also by their proficiency with all small arms and weapons up through their many antitank guns. Gone were the days of Guadalcanal when an army colonel in order to convince his tired troops that the Japanese were incapable of shooting straight at a moving target, clad himself in a fatigue cap and shorts and paraded in full view of hostile riflemen. No marine on Iwo had anything but respect for Nipponese marksmanship. "Whenever a man showed himself in the lines it was almost certain death," testified one battalion commander.[104]

Although the enemy indulged in no mass suicide, the individual Japanese exhibited no reluctance to sacrifice himself if he could exact a toll from the marines, such as blowing up his body along with a tank. Japanese antitank tactics were polished and vigorously pushed. These involved the first scientifically laid minefields encountered in the Pacific, but many of the mines were either still inactivated or improperly armed and failed to detonate, indicating a shortage of skilled personnel in the ranks. Supplementing the minefields were not only antitank ditches but also low-lying and massively constructed stone walls. Such obstacles guarded all terrain suitable for tank movement, and were covered with a multitude of well-sited antitank guns. Also, smoke shells were employed to isolate an American tank, permitting a Japanese with hand-set explosives to attack it.[105]

Probably because Iwo was so close to the homeland, the enemy was well supplied with everything from foxhole periscopes to abundant ammunition and recently devised weapons. Heading the list of more devious instruments of death were huge rockets and mortars. In the employment of mortars the Japanese had always been remarkably proficient. One new mortar was 320 millimeters in size, lobbing a shell weighing nearly 700 pounds. Shortages because of American naval action were few in number, notably tanks and barbed wire; otherwise the only deficiencies discovered were those which reflected the general hardships of the Nipponese war economy as a whole, such as a fuse fashioned from wood, and terra cotta mines planted in a soil containing iron deposits so highly magnetized that normal detectors were of no use anyhow.

Less than forty Japanese tanks were located on Iwo and, in keeping with the enemy's static defense, these were dug in to supplement his firepower from pillboxes, blockhouses, caves, and covered emplacements. Absence of unused lumber, concrete, and reinforcing steel, in view of the complete coverage of the island with defensive installations, proved conclusively that the Japanese had been provided with both the time and the supplies to ready themselves for assault. Expert military engineers had been imported from the homeland, and taking full advantage of the terrain, particularly the broken configurations of Suribachi and the northeastern bulge of the island, had fortified Iwo to near perfection. Where terrain dictated a blockhouse or a covered emplacement, there it was. Where fields of fire called for mutually supporting pillboxes to protect in turn a heavier defense, they were sure to have been built. Caves were dug to reinforce other defenses. In advancing several hundred yards through the center of the northeastern belly, for example, the men of the Third Division counted 800 pillboxes alone, obviously an exaggeration caused at least in part by confusing caves with other installations. The more intricately devised caves ran back to reverse slopes and had multi-exits, all apt to be designed with apertures in so far as possible impervious to artillery and naval gunfire. Along the broad northeastern coast, where the terrain became especially rugged, pillboxes and blockhouses tended to give way to "spider webs" far more complex and formidable than those first encountered on Eniwetok.[106]

Observers who had inspected German fortified areas in both World

Wars testified that never had they seen a position so thoroughly defended as was Iwo Jima. Comparisons are difficult, but it is probable that no other given area in the history of modern war has been so skillfully fortified by nature and by man. Certainly Kelly Turner was correct in asserting that the defenses there were "tremendously better organized and more effective" than anything previously encountered in the Pacific, and that "Iwo Jima is as well defended as any fixed position that exists in the world today." [107]

Kuribayashi lacked mobility and one might term this a weakness, but at the same time the Japanese general realistically accepted that fact and tried to turn it to his advantage. Otherwise, if the Japanese had any weakness or any serious shortage these were but two: the manner in which he employed his artillery, and a lack of drinking water.

Once again the Japanese were unable and probably also unwilling to mass their artillery fires. Marine cannoneers noticed a marked improvement over earlier performances; but on Iwo the Nipponese never fully concentrated their weapons, and after the fire on the beaches began to die down around February 25, no more than a few batteries at most massed their bursts at any given time. The full explanation of this shortcoming is not known. Probably it was a combination of faulty doctrine, poor training, and a wide diversity in types of weapons. Regardless, it along with the volcanic ash which cushioned enemy shells explains why tens of thousands of Americans could for an extended period of time crowd onto the waist of the island without unacceptable losses.[108]

There is another side to the story. Had the Japanese employed their artillery in any other fashion even with their smokeless powder, they would have found themselves in a duel not only with marine cannoneers but also with naval gunners and airmen. In other words, to have unmasked all their weapons simultaneously for concentrated fire would have invited quick destruction of those guns from the overwhelming might of America's counterbattery. Whether or not Kuribayashi realized it, his artillery tactics fitted neatly into his overall defensive pattern.

Likewise is it impossible to state conclusively that the enemy garrison suffered from a lack of potable water. Iwo had no springs suitable for human consumption, and the Nipponese were utilizing both rain catchments and sea distillation units. This water was stored in reinforced concrete wells and, more safely, in metal containers inside dugouts, caves, and other defensive structures. The sea distillation units were knocked out during the preparatory period, and the supply in the wells was probably in large part lost because of the concussion of America's bombs, naval projectiles, and artillery. Many of the prisoners of war, especially toward the middle and end of the struggle, swore that the enemy, holed up deep in the steaming terrain that was the broad northeastern portion of Iwo, was critically short of drinking water. Others, however, denied this, and it must be borne in mind that most prisoners of war were laborers, many of them Koreans, just the personnel who would be refused or at least drastically rationed on water before a serious shortage developed.[109] In view of the well-planned defense in all other respects, it seems likely that although the water situation may have caused the garrison some additional discomfort, the shortage never became acute.

On the whole, a well-equipped superbly trained and disciplined garrison awaited the marines on February 19. Kuribayashi, by the disposition of his forces about the island, called the tune for the prolonged battle. He refused to heavily man the defenses fronting the beaches. This was not only in deference to America's naval guns. Also the terraces protected the assaulting troops from fire directly inland, and flanking fire was thus mandatory as well as more deadly. On Suribachi were about 1,600 Japanese with orders to hold out till the last. Kuribayashi had pulled back into the northeastern part of the island the bulk of both his manpower and installations.

The entire island was heavily contested, but there were main and secondary lines of fortified positions. The first stretched in a broad belt from the center of the southeast coast through the "Quarry" and the "Amphitheater," across and around both ends of the second airfield, and tied in with the installations guarding the northeastern flank of the alternate beaches. (See map 21.) The secondary line was more narrow, and ran parallel to the first, about 2,500 yards on to the northeast. After both lines had been broken and marines had reached the northeastern coast, the enemy continued to hold out desperately in the northern and southeastern corners of the island.

To the individual marine, however, as a staff officer observed, "no set, definite defensive line was especially noticeable, as the defending positions were so extensive that as soon as one center of resistance was penetrated, the attackers were forced to face another." [110] In addition the fighting was monotonous, for Iwo was in effect all beachhead. It was an amphibious assault that lasted for thirty-six days. Many officers noted this fact, but a gunnery sergeant most clearly described it. Asked by a private experiencing his first combat if Iwo were worse than Saipan, the sergeant replied: "Yeah, I think it is. In this way, I mean. The shelling may have been as bad on Saipan, but there we were able to get off the beach and under cover. The beach was narrow and there were trees and jungle we could get into. But here everything is beach and you just can't get off it and there's damn little cover." [111]

The marines were headed in two opposite directions as dawn rose on their second day ashore, February 20. The men of the Twenty-eighth Regiment had turned left to tackle Suribachi, while the remainder of the Fifth Division and all the Fourth Division were wheeling right to complete the seizure of the first airfield and to take the northeastern section of the island.

THE CAPTURE OF SURIBACHI

Mottled and naked, Suribachi resembled the head of a fabulous serpent, with fangs ejecting poison in all directions from its base. Surrounding the cone of Suribachi was harder than scaling the summit. The Japanese were in several hundred emplacements, principally pillboxes, blockhouses, covered guns, and grottoes around the base of the mountain, giving way to intricately constructed tiers of caves along the slopes.

"Harry the Horse" Liversedge and the Twenty-eighth Marines of the Fifth Division began their attack against Suribachi itself early on the morning of February 20. Tanks, flamethrowers, rockets, and demolitions were used, and after more than three days of hard fighting the mountain was encircled by noon, February 23. Four hours earlier, the first American flag was raised on Suribachi. This was a small flag from a ship's boat, and raising it aloft on a short section of Japanese pipe found on the spot was the idea of some of the men who made the assault to the crest. Then at thirty-seven minutes past ten o'clock, the first flag was replaced by a larger one, erected on a more substantial staff. This was the scene of the famous photograph, taken while a fire fight in the long process of mopping up Suribachi was going on a short distance away.

Unfurling the larger and more visible flag was an event that increased the confidence of all hands and provided a picture that stirred the country. One of the greatest single factors in sustaining the morale of the marines on Iwo was the excellence of their postal service and their receipt of news and letters praising the high quality of their own fighting. The flag raising on Suribachi headed the list of stories and photographs submitted by correspondents, whose reports gained added realism because of the fact that, inadvertently it appears, some were landed on the beach receiving the heaviest enemy fire. Hoisting the stars and stripes was a momentous and inspiring occasion. Secretary of the Navy James V. Forrestal along with Smith happened to be ashore and witnessed the spectacle close at hand. Forrestal, showing great coolness under fire, also bolstered the spirits of the marines, who had just passed a cold rainy night.[112]

Ceremony aside, taking Suribachi denied the enemy positions from which to observe and fire directly onto the beaches and the waist of the island, and provided a post from which the marines could look down on the Japanese to the northeast, although visibility was such that Suribachi was of less value in this regard than expected. Conquering the broad northeastern portion of the island was far more difficult than seizing Suribachi, as the men of the Twenty-eighth Marines themselves confessed when after six additional days in mopping up the mountain they were thrown into the longer struggle.[113]

THE CONTEST IN THE NORTHEAST

The pivot to the northeast by the Fourth Division and the Fifth Division (less the Twenty-eighth Marines) had begun on February 19. In this portion of Iwo it was the character of the terrain and the nature of the enemy's defenses that caused marine officers to describe the struggle in football terms. (See map 21.) "You can't run the ends up here," one major reiterated before the landing; and a colonel added, "it has to be done right through the middle of the line." Smith later agreed that the assault was "one phase and one tactic," while Schmidt, stressing the general inability to maneuver, simply said "it was not practical to go around." [114]

A frontal assault from the first airfield up onto the Motoyama Plateau threw the marines directly into the face of the heaviest enemy defenses, but terrain precluded any other approach. The northeastern portion of the island may be divided geographically into a series of concentric circles, of which only the innermost and highest, the Motoyama Plateau, is relatively unbroken by ravines. This plateau was exceedingly difficult terrain to cross, but easier than the second and third circles, which are characterized by deep gorges leading like spokes of a wheel from the tableland outward in all directions toward the sea and the waist of the island. The outermost circles are made up of cliffs overlooking the coast line along the northeastern part of the island.

A description of the Motoyama tableland and its central approaches will give a good indication of how exceedingly difficult the fighting was throughout the northeastern portion of Iwo, for elsewhere the terrain was worse, almost beyond description. The volcanic ash characteristic of the waist of the island gave way to a solid lava as the ground rose. This lava was andesitic, soft and seemingly pliable to the hands; and even the plateau was strewn with debris and full of hidden crevices, jagged edges of stone, dangling ledges, and caves carved by nature as well as by the Japanese. Fissures of steam spewed from cracks in the ground, and evil-smelling sulphur fumes vied with the repulsive odor of decomposing bodies. Everywhere were Japanese defenses, grottoes, bunkers, blockhouses, pillboxes, deep caves, antitank ditches and walls, minefields, and a profusion of flat-trajectory antitank guns, dual purpose automatic antiaircraft weapons, and small arms, all backed by lethal mortars and rockets firing from reverse slopes. At a loss for words to describe this devil's playground, correspondents and officers writing their action reports sometimes recalled a Goya sketch or Doré's illustrations for Dante's *Inferno*.

Marines shouldering their way up the island to the northeastward from the preferred and alternate beaches, that is along both flanks of the Motoyama Plateau, confronted cliffs and ravines which within themselves and without their man-made defenses were formidable obstacles, and the thick nest of weapons on the central tableland was sited to fire down the gorges and to cover the entire coast line. Taking the Motoyama high ground was thus essential on two counts: to deny the enemy the final positions from which he could place observed fire on the beaches, and to permit marines to work from the elevated area down the ravines and over the cliffs to the sea and secure the remainder of the island. Before either the left or right flanks could advance along the northeastern front, the enemy's center had to be dented and then broken. Schmidt's highly competent operations officer, Colonel Edward A. Craig USMC, summarized the tactics which brought victory: "By a determined main effort in the center of our line just north of Airfield No. 1 the enemy forces were split. . . . This breakthrough enabled our forces to envelop enemy troops on the right and left flank and to continue the attack down the rocky corridors and ridge lines on our flanks instead of assaulting frontally these ridges and cross compartments." [115]

The marines renewed their attack on the northeastern front on the morning of February 20. The Fifth Division, less the Twenty-eighth Marines, was on the left, and the Fourth Division on the right. Important advances for the day were in the center, where the first airfield was completely seized; but then the marines found themselves flush against the main line of resistance, and gains the next day were measured in inches. By-passing single strongpoints was seldom feasible, simply because most were mutually supporting.

Effort was made to land the corps reserve, the Twenty-first Marines of the Third Division, on February 20, but the weather deteriorated sharply, and beach conditions required reembarking the regiment. It got ashore the next day, and was placed at Cates' disposal. He ordered it into line on February 22, along his left flank, in relief of Wensinger's Twenty-third Marines.

Thus was the initial regiment of the Third Division placed in the center of the northeastern front, in position to crack the main line of resistance at its only vulnerable point. Commanded by Colonel Hartnoll J. Withers, the men of the Twenty-first spent three frantic days trying to reach and cross the second airfield. The strips were heavily mined, and every inch was swept by a crossing fire from a jumble of rocks and ridge lines and from atop the plateau. Antitank projectiles were so thick that tanks were unable to lumber across— only riflemen, assisted by almost point blank support fire from the tanks' 75-millimeter guns, could turn the trick. On February 24, with the assault still bogged down, Smith released the Third Division (less the rifle battalions of the Third Marine Regiment) to corps, and the division commander, Erskine, along with the Ninth Marines and all the division artillery began coming ashore. That afternoon the central portion of Motoyama Airfield Number Two was finally crossed; and the next morning Cates was ordered to relinquish control of the Twenty-first Marines to Erskine, who sent the Ninth Marines led by Colonel Howard N. Kenyon, through the Twenty-first, and continued the assault with fresh troops. But still the line scarcely moved forward. Mainly because the men of the Third Division were denied an overwhelming concentration of supporting, neutralizing fires, two and one-half more days passed before the attack in the center began to roll. This vital center area had not been well prepared during the destructive preliminary period, and it could be captured only behind intensive and sustained neutralizing barrages.

Since Erskine had anticipated piecemeal employment of his troops, and since in any case tank landing ships were unavailable, he had necessarily decentralized his artillery when combat loading. This slowed debarkation, and adverse beach conditions delayed getting all his own artillery ashore and firing till the morning of March 1. Meanwhile, although Schmidt realized the necessity of a frontal assault up onto the center of the Motoyama Plateau and threw his freshest infantry strength and on one occasion concentrated his tanks in that sector, other considerations, in retrospect perhaps less important, caused him to push the corps front forward all along the line. The military principles of mass and economy of force seem to have been partially violated. This development, while it allowed the northeastern flanks of the preferred and alternate beaches to be cleared and thus improved logistics, in the long run probably set back the ending of the assault and made the fighting more difficult, not only for Erskine's command but also for the flanking divisions, which at times advanced beyond the center front only to be caught in flanking fires from the Motoyama Plateau and its central approaches, and to be compelled to relinquish ground gained at great cost. There were extenuating circumstances, but the error was in failing to hold back and to rest the divisions on the two flanks, and in delaying to give to the Third Division all possible neutralizing artillery, naval gunfire, and air support available to corps. This was never done to the degree demanded by the situation, and not until Erskine had most of his own divisional artillery ashore, emplaced, and registered did he make any notable progress.[116]

Before Erskine got ashore the Twenty-first Marines had been committed from the 22nd through the 24th of February with artillery support above normal to other regiments in the line, that is a battalion in direct support and another in general support, plus a battalion detached from the Fifth Division also in general support. By the time Erskine took over responsibility for the center, on February 25, all the corps artillery was ready to participate in the battle. This consisted of two battalions firing 155-millimeter howitzers with a heavy neutralizing impact; yet for seventy-two hours the men of the Third Division received no concentrated assistance from more than one-half of these weapons. The Ninth Marines tried to advance on the 25th with three batteries of their own Third Division artillery, plus two battalions attached, one from the Fourth and another from the Fifth Division. Naval gunfire including some 8-inch projectiles was used in general support throughout the day; but the corps 155's, before the attack hour that morning, massed one-half of the 1,200 rounds then expended in front of the Third Division, thereafter shifting to general support all along the active front, which was mainly the terrain facing the Third and Fourth Divisions since Rockey's right flank for a full day awaited an advance in the center. Holding Rockey back, if only for twenty-four hours, was the proper course of action, but at the same time it is important to note that Cates was also attacking and that he and Erskine together shared almost equally the benefit of the 155's.

The Third Division was not getting enough neutralization, and the Ninth Marines made no substantial progress on the 25th. A greater concentration of support the following day was in order; but on the 26th, the Third Division received less assistance from artillery than on the previous day. On the 26th, corps artillery duplicated its fires of the day before, devoting one-half of its attention to the zone of the Third Division, and the remainder to both the Fourth and Fifth Division fronts. Moreover, one of the artillery battalions attached to Erskine had reverted to its parent division on corps order, and he was unable to replace it fully with his own artillery since his three batteries ashore had by that time increased only to a full battalion. Partial compensation for this loss of artillery support on the 26th was a concentration of main battery naval gunfire before the morning attack hour; but still the assault in the center picked up no momentum.

Erskine's solution was to get the rest of his own weapons ashore. Although he was never permitted by authorities afloat to land three of his nine rifle battalions, those of the Third Marine Regiment, he was allowed to employ all of his artillery.

Four points should be reemphasized and brought into focus here. First, neutralizing rather than destructive fire is under discussion, for not even the corps 155's were big enough to destroy Iwo's heavier defenses. Second, the terrain confronting Erskine was relatively more level than that along the flanks, and the center was more susceptible to neutralization than elsewhere. Third, since the artillery regiment of the Third Division had never been brought into accord with the new tables of organization, the artillery organic to that command was less than that of the Fourth and Fifth Divisions, that is the Third Division had two battalions of 75-millimeter pack howitzers and two battalions of 105-millimeter howitzers, while the other divisions had one and three of each respectively. Fourth, Erskine's front, on the other hand, was more narrow than that of either Rockey or Cates until early in the month of March.

By the 27th, Erskine had almost two battalions of his own ashore and firing, and in addition he received continuing concentrations from one battalion of the Fifth Division, plus that from one full battalion of the 155-millimeter corps weapons, as well as heavier naval gunfire support. His direct air support seldom varied, consisting of eight fighters and eight bombers. At around noon on that day, advanced elements of Erskine's two remaining battalions of artillery were brought into line ashore, and for the first time his infantrymen really began to move. Erskine was then able to institute a rolling barrage, which with few exceptions he used to obtain a sustained neutralization for each attack. This consisted of naval gunfire and air strikes in both close and deep support, and a concentration of all possible artillery fire in close support, blocked successively forward 100 yards every seven minutes. In addition, all available automatic weapons and 60- and 81-millimeter mortars were laid down directly in front of the troops assaulting, regardless of the unit or units being pushed forward.

Erskine watched the movement on the afternoon of the 27th to detect any possible weakness along the Japanese center. None was found, and on the following morning he passed the Twenty-first Marines through the Ninth in an effort to sustain his momentum. Also on the 28th, he received additional naval gunfire support, and for the first time over fifty per cent of the fire from the corps 155's. Of some 1,700 rounds of 155-millimeter projectiles expended before the morning attack, substantially more than one-half was concentrated before the Third Division; and a similar apportionment held good for the 1,600 rounds fired while the day's attack was in progress.

Then came the break for which Erskine had waited. After the key installations of the cross-island defensive system (which lay some 750 yards due west and 200 yards north of the northernmost tip of the second airfield) had been knocked out and this terrain had been captured, a relatively soft spot developed on Erskine's right. Before nightfall a battalion had knifed rapidly ahead beyond Motoyama Village. Until the Third Division reached the northeast coast, Erskine's tactics, with one exception, were always the same. He utilized every ounce of firepower he could muster. The neutralization provided by his own guns and by corps allowed him to push forward, and he exploited each enemy weakness he discovered. Protecting his open flanks by reserves, he invariably used these reserves to widen breaches along his flanks by launching attacks through the gaps between and behind his assaulting units. That much maneuver, and no more, was possible in attacking the Motoyama Plateau.[117] Erskine's zone of action was sufficiently narrow and his reserve sufficiently deep to permit him to employ these tactics more readily than could the other division commanders who were operating on wider fronts and across more difficult terrain. Cates and Rockey were equally competent, but the Third Division was in the pivotal position.

These tactics saw Erskine's men advance across the second airfield and up onto the Motoyama Plateau, through the stench of the sulphur refinery, and beyond the shambles that was Motoyama Village. No longer could the Japanese sit atop the central ridge and place observed fire on every inch of lower Iwo. The Third Division had cut its way through the main line of resistance into the guts of Iwo Jima. The evening of the 28th found these marines looking down on the third airfield. It was believed that penetration to the coast would be easy, and the final airfield was quickly overrun, but then the secondary line of resistance was struck, and again the assault slowed and halted.

Erskine felt that his command, in splitting the enemy's principal line of resistance, had been denied proper neutralizing support. "It is believed," he wrote in his battle report, "that the zone of action assigned this division was the most suitable for making the main effort as it extended along the high ground in the center of the island. Had the bulk of all supporting weapons been allotted to this division instead of being more or less equally distributed between all three divisions, it is believed that penetration would have been effected sooner at lesser cost." [118]

While Erskine got substantially more than one-third of the fires available to the corps, he wanted more. But it must be borne in mind that the division is an important tactical organization, and that whereas Schmidt did divert organic Fourth and Fifth Division artillery to the Third Division, he had to be careful in this process not to jeopardize the two flank divisions. Schmidt properly regarded his corps command as an agency for integrating all divisional elements and welding them along with corps troops into a solid unit for the single objective of conquering Iwo, and for this reason he was compelled to provide adequate artillery to protect his flanks.

In other words, the discussion should center around corps artillery, and since this was not ashore and ready to fire until the morning of February 25, should be narrowed to the period from that time till noon on February 27, when Erskine began to move. The artillery weapons directly under corps, two battalions of 155-millimeter howitzers, were few; but it had been recognized in the planning phase that more corps weapons could hardly be emplaced on the waist of Iwo without unduly interfering with beach logistics. Nor could heavier weapons be taken, simply because Iwo was so small that the relatively flat trajectory of 155-millimeter guns rendered them unsuited to the task at hand, and 8-inch howitzers were at this date unavailable for the Pacific.

Schmidt, however, pushed his flanks along simultaneously as he tried to crack the center of the main line of resistance. For this reason, some of the neutralizing offensive strength otherwise available to corps was laid down on the flanks. Schmidt had good reason to want to advance his flanks with as much speed as possible. Weather was erratic, and this fact plus the compelling problem of supply and the cluttered southeastern coast dictated clearing both the alternate and preferred beaches of enemy weapons as rapidly as possible. To this end, the Fifth Division on Erskine's left had to clean out the cliffs commanding the northeastern flank of the alternate beaches, and the Fourth Division on his right had to move through the "Amphitheater." Finally, within the zones of the flanking divisions were terrain features which formed a part of the Motoyama Plateau, and which not only overlooked the beaches but also flanked Erskine's men as they crossed the second airfield. These were two southwesterly high points of the tableland, Hill 362 in Rockey's zone, and Hill 382 in that of Cates. The first lay 1,200 yards northwest of the far end of the second airfield, while the second was only 250 yards southeast of the same point.

As it turned out, neither of these hills was cleared until after the Third Division had swept onto the plateau. This is of course more apparent in retrospect than it was in the heat of the battle, but the record indicates that whereas Schmidt was properly willing and anxious to outflank the center approaches to the Motoyama Plateau, he and his staff correctly never considered such a development probable. Erskine's criticism is valid but should be modified. The flanks should have been held back (as the Fifth Division was held back for a single day), and every available ounce of divisional and corps neutralizing fire not required to anchor and rest the flank divisions should have been thrown into the center until momentum was gained there. Movement, in other words, should have been more carefully planned from the first. The interiors of both flank divisions, however, were pushed alongside the second airfield before the level strips were crossed by the Third Division; and yet the interior of neither flank was able to take its key hill objective. By overrunning the second airfield and climbing onto the plateau, more feasible routes of approach to both Hill 362 and Hill 382 were provided.[119]

Continuing the story of the fighting in Erskine's pivotal zone, a captured terrain sketch revealed some of the details of an important sector of the secondary line of resistance, and the marines learned the full strength of the center of this obstacle the hard way—after they had begun to assault it on March 1. Beyond the low-lying final airfield, the ground rose again sharply into a saddle, and then fell off to the sea. The high points of the saddle were two additional hill masses of almost identical height, which represented the northwestern and southeastern corners of the Motoyama tableland. These terrain features were intermingled with caves and bunkers in deep crisscrossing crevices, and were studded with huge sandstone boulders, many outcroppings, and defensive weapons of all calibers and types. Their height gave the enemy full observation of the marines to the east of the third airfield, and Erskine found it impossible to snake between them. The job was all the more difficult since there were no feasible ridge lines which could be followed onto their summits. On the contrary, just to the northwest of the right point of the saddle, commanding direct approaches to the high ground in the center, was a third heavily fortified hill, almost as high as the other two. Because of the proximity of the three hills, the two to the right were already in the zone of the Third Division, and a part of the high terrain to the left fell just outside it. Since the capture of the latter was deemed essential to the continued advance of the Third Division, it was transferred from Rockey's responsibility to Erskine's; but still, movement on Erskine's left was delayed by Japanese resistance until after the Fifth Division had pulled alongside. The center of the secondary line of resistance was broken by a frontal assault against the southeastern hill masses.

Erskine, his available infantry substantially weakened by the furious fighting of late February, moved both his regiments abreast as his front was widened and the month of March began, and prepared to crack the enemy's secondary line. Gains were negligible for the first several days. Substantial progress was made only against the northwestern high ground, but a flanking fire from the enemy in Rockey's zone prevented marines from moving down this hill over a long cliff ledge toward the sea. Erskine had no alternative but to push his right flank directly against the southeastern hills.

Efforts to advance were stopped altogether by corps order on Sunday, March 5, to allow the three divisions to regroup and reorganize, and to give the men some well-earned rest. All were tired and listless, their key personnel were largely casualties, and it was little short of miraculous that they could advance at all. Some gained comfort and a much-needed lift from a powerful drink called "Suribachi Screamer," sick-bay alcohol and fruit juice. But even where units were pulled back in corps or division reserve, there was only relative quiet and rest, because night infiltrations and minor counterattacks were constant; and day and night Japanese appeared from overrun caves and tunnels, necessitating a continuous mopping up of seized ground.

Only slight gains were registered by Erskine's men on March 6, and a bold variation of tactics proved profitable though costly the next day. This was a night attack. Earlier, units in other divisions had jumped off at first light without preparatory neutralizing fires, and had obtained an element of tactical surprise. During the late morning darkness of the 7th, illumination along the entire corps front was progressively stopped, a smoke barrage was laid down, and elements of the Third Division on the right moved forward at five o'clock against the stubborn hills in that sector. Several hundred yards were gained without a shot being fired, and dawn found a substantial advance made on the southeastern point of the saddle. The struggle was desperate and the situation highly confused, as isolated groups of marines fought hand to hand with a determined enemy, or were pinned down by intense fire from all quarters of the compass. But the Japanese had been caught off tactical balance, and many were killed while asleep in their dugouts. Even though American intelligence of the terrain was poor since orders for the attack reached the regimental commander involved after darkness and barely in time for him to work instructions forward to the men destined to jump off, the night assault was skillfully executed, and was delivered at the opportune moment. After the mêlée was over, Erskine's casualties were so high that a second night attack would probably have failed from lack of experienced personnel; but men of the Twenty-first Regiment on March 9 reached the sea along the northeastern coast and dipped up some salt water for Erskine's inspection.[120]

Not as dramatic an incident as the flag-raising on Suribachi, this was far more significant. The enemy in the bulge of the island was split, and Americans controlled the terrain approaches from the Motoyama tableland down the deep ravines to the cliffs and to the sea.

The Third Division began pacing the attack on February 27, but that only lessened the problems facing both Cates and Rockey. Men of the Fourth Division, with Colonel Walter I. Jordan's Twenty-fourth Marines at first bearing the brunt of the fighting, moved across the high ground of the "Quarry" and began dipping down into the "Amphitheater" as early as February 21. Their movements were exposed, and little progress was made toward the far side until after the center of the main line of resistance was pierced. Even so, taking Hill 382 was so gory that the men tagged it the "Meat Grinder." [121]

Cates consistently strengthened his own left in order to assist Erskine's advance and in order to move from high ground down upon the enemy. By late February, however, Cates' division was at little better than fifty per cent of normal combat strength, and continued rapidly to decline. Some units had entered the assault below full efficiency, and the fighting on the first several days ashore had caused a sharp deterioration because of casualties. The terrain had been exceedingly difficult from the outset, restricting the employment of tanks, some of which had been loaned to the Third and Fifth Divisions. While this was of great benefit to the other commands, it is indicative of the fact that the marines of the Fourth Division did the most hand to hand fighting. Finally, by-passing a large sector in the vicinity of Minami Village compelled Cates to withdraw personnel from his already depleted front lines. That the men of the Fourth Division were able in the middle and later phases of the operation to keep step behind the Third Division, and to reach the northeastern coast a day later than Erskine's command is an eloquent tribute to their fortitude and spirit. They were, however, helped somewhat by the largest enemy counterattack to occur during the struggle. On the night of March 8/9 more than 700 Japanese sortied from their holes for the ostensible purpose of reaching the first airfield, by then being used rather extensively by American pilots flying everything from very long range bombers to observation craft. Most of the Nipponese were blasted with artillery and Cates' lines held firm.[122] It is evident that this enemy sortie came after Kuribayashi had lost contact with the Japanese in Cates' zone of action.

The terrain and defenses overrun by the marines of the Fifth Division were certainly no easier than those encountered by Cates' command. To generalize, clearing the escarpments overlooking the alternate beaches and taking Suribachi and Hill 362 were difficult jobs, but hardly comparable to the "Quarry," the "Amphitheater," and the "Meat Grinder." Toward the close of the contest, however,

Rockey's men confronted the most formidable terrain obstacles found on the island, a crazy-quilt of gorges and ravines and a final pocket of prepared pillboxes, caves, and "spider webs" in which Kuribayashi was thought to have placed his command post. The Fifth Division continued the struggle, its combat efficiency below thirty per cent, for ten days after the men of the Fourth Division had begun reembarkation.

Rockey summarized the fighting his command encountered by saying it was "a battle of marine against Jap with the Jap having all advantages of cover, concealment, and fields of fire from prepared positions." Like Cates, Rockey also consistently strengthened his interior flank in order to move down on the enemy, and similarly his position was particularly exposed until the Third Division had penetrated the Motoyama Plateau.

Early advances by the Fifth Division along the northwestern coast of Iwo, with first Twenty-seventh and then the Twenty-sixth Marines commanded by Colonel Chester B. Graham, in line, were sizeable; but as soon as the front was flanked by enemy fire from across the second airfield, movement stopped. No attack was made on February 25, and seizing Hill 362 was delayed until after Motoyama Village was in American hands.

Then for several days the men of the Fifth Division kept pace with the Third Division, principally because the lay of the land along Rockey's right was highly suitable to the employment of tanks for 2,000 yards northeast of Hill 362; but then the terrain became very rugged, and the Fifth Division never touched the northeastern coast.[123]

After reaching the sea in the center of the northeastern coast, Erskine's command began following the ridge lines to the north and to the south, and eventually assisted the other two divisions in their respective zones.

Working to the southward were the Ninth Marines (Third Division). However, since the men of the Fourth Division had long since overcome the chief obstacles in their area of responsibility, they needed little help; and the Ninth Marines busied themselves with clearing out a by-passed pocket just west and southwest of the two hill masses which had anchored the right center of the enemy's secondary line of resistance. Meanwhile, the Fourth Division killed the Japanese remaining in the vicinity of Minami Village and overran the final pocket in its zone, which was in a ravine just west and slightly south of Tachiwa Point. The remnants of Cates' command started reembarkation on March 16, when organized resistance was officially declared by authorities afloat to be at an end. This announcement was not cleared through Schmidt.[124] There were still ten days of heavy fighting ahead, accompanied and followed by extensive mopping up.

Turning northward, the Twenty-first Marines (Third Division) were of great assistance to Rockey's command, since they advanced all the way up the northeastern coast and took Kitano Point. The Fifth Division was forced to halt and to surround what turned out to be the final pocket of enemy resistance. The core of this pocket was southwest of Kitano Point, and was set in a deep gorge, 200 yards wide and 700 yards long, with its long axis running almost due north and south, athwart Rockey's line of advance.

This last pocket was reminiscent of Umurbrogol on Peleliu. The neutralizing effect of artillery was largely lost because of the terrain configurations and the skillfully constructed Japanese defenses. On Iwo, Rockey secured his own artillery on March 17. The task was one for tanks, demolition teams, and riflemen, and since the advance was slow, from cave to cave and spider trap to pillbox, the front lines were hopelessly intertwined. Especially did the new flamethrowing medium tanks (unknown in the Palaus) aid the marines during these final days. Tankdozers and armored bulldozers (rigged under Harry Hill's supervision for beach logistics, but pressed into tactical use) cleared a path, and then flamethrowing tanks, followed and supported by infantry, burned out the Japanese shooting from cave entrances and spider webs. Since the men of the Fifth Division were by this time close to physical and mental exhaustion, it was March 26 before the final pocket was taken; and then some of the Japanese managed to escape and to stage their last sizeable counterattack. About 200 of the enemy slipped through into the rear areas. There they were liquidated by the Fifth Pioneer Battalion and other service troops, many of them Negroes.[125] The corps shore party commander was "highly gratified with the performance of these colored troops . . . while in direct action against the enemy for the first time. Proper security prevented their being taken unawares, and they conducted themselves with marked coolness and courage." [126]

Rockey's shattered infantry units reembarked just before and shortly after March 26, along with what was left of the Twenty-first Marines. The 147th Army Infantry Regiment had arrived seven days earlier, to comprise the mobile garrison for the island commander. Left behind to assist these army troops in mopping up were the weary Ninth Marines, the last battalion of which departed on April 13, 1945.[127]

It is believed that Kuribayashi died somewhere in the northern corner of Iwo during the final days of the battle, and although his body was never found, indications are that he committed hara-kiri. He was a man to be feared alive, but is probably even more dangerous to America dead, since he is capable of becoming a hero of a resurgent nationalism in Japan. As he prepared to die, he wrote a note to his Emperor, whose elite guard he had once commanded. Kuribayashi expressed his "most profound apologies . . . for being forced to yield this strategic point to enemy hands." Then with utmost finesse he gave vent to his dread that Japan was doomed to defeat. Asking his ruler never to lose faith in the supreme and everlasting destiny of the Nipponese, he promised after death that in order to help revive the Imperial Army, "I will turn into a spirit." [128]

America need have no recourse in the realm of such spirits as Kuribayashi's may be. Few commands in the history of warfare can equal the staying power and drive of the Fifth Amphibious Corps on Iwo Jima. Exposed to observed enemy fire across the beaches, onto Suribachi, up to and across the Motoyama Plateau, and compelled to dig out or to seal up a determined and well-trained and equipped enemy in thousands of defensive installations, grottoes, and deep caves, the men under Schmidt continued to advance, or try to advance, despite the odds against them. Many were in line day after monotonous day, their comrades casualties, themselves exhausted, and the combat efficiency of their respective units slowly ebbing into critically low percentage figures. Well might Nimitz say in admiration: "Among the Americans who served on Iwo Island uncommon valor was a common virtue." [129]

5. *Tactical and Amphibious Aspects*

Nimitz was praising not only the front line fighters but also the navy, army, and marine personnel who supported and serviced them. Without supplies and medical care the assault would have ground to a halt, and without close air, naval gunfire, and artillery support, there would have been no neutralization to permit the tank-infantry-demolition teams to advance.

ARTILLERY, NAVAL GUNFIRE, AND AIR SUPPORT ASHORE

Coordination among the three supporting arms was superb throughout the operation, a consequence not only of sound doctrine, training, and experience but also of the excellent communications supplied by the navy and marine signal units, including the component parts of the joint assault signal companies.[130] Schmidt's communications officer was concerned, however, lest the high-quality performance of these companies be dissipated. He emphasized that if they were not to be made organic to the divisions, they must at least be assigned early to those commands in order to be broken apart and acquainted thoroughly with the organizations alongside which they would work in the field. Already communications elements of the beach parties had been withdrawn and placed under exclusive navy control, and recommendations were being made to treat the air liaison and shore fire-control teams similarly.[181] The process must be halted, or there would be a retrogression to the method of Tarawa.

A Fire Support Coordination Center was established at Iwo, the theory behind it being similar to that back of Blandy's Amphibious Support Force in the preparatory period. An officer directly under Schmidt was to begin supervision of all support fires as soon as the divisional artillery was landed. For this task Schmidt selected his top corps artillery officer, Colonel John S. Letcher USMC. In practice, however, Letcher was an agent for obtaining cooperation of the three support arms, rather than in direct command of the three; and it is difficult to see how, given the location of one arm ashore, another afloat, and the third (air) both afloat and in the middle phase of the operation afloat and ashore, any other arrangement could have been made. Those who have concluded that absolute unity of command, echelon by echelon, is mandatory for military success will profit from a study of such operations as Iwo. While there was and always should be one implementing commander in control, navy or marine, afloat or ashore, the staffs of each echelon functioned at least to a degree by cooperation. The organization of the Fire Support Coordination Center best illustrates the merit of collaborative endeavor because its cohesion came altogether from the mutual interest of the three arms in advancing the American fighting front rather than from a centralization of command.

Letcher, who was always responsible to Schmidt and who was in constant consultation with Schmidt's closest staff associates, particularly his chief of staff and operations officer, was in direct command of only the two 155-millimeter howitzer battalions constituting the corps artillery. In addition, he was in continuous communication, afloat and ashore, with liaison officers assigned to each of the three divisional artillery regiments. Finally, always at his elbow was a representative of the naval gunfire officer of the Fifth Amphibious Corps, Lieutenant Colonel Donald M. Weller, and a liaison officer from the Landing Force Air Support Control Unit, headed by Letcher's senior, Colonel Vernon E. Megee USMC. Megee's presence on Iwo was the fruition of long efforts by marine commanders to control air support from Landing Force headquarters; and after marine, navy, and army squadrons began using Iwo's first airfield, Megee also functioned as Commander Air until March 7, when this post was taken over by an army officer.

Both Megee and Weller had staffs separate and distinct from Letcher's, and the Fire Support Coordination Center functioned as a clearing house of requests for close support coming in from the field. Letcher, giving orders only to corps artillery, along with the air and naval gunfire liaison officers, screened and integrated these requests, and Megee and Welter as the ranking corps air and naval gunfire officers forwarded them in the status of requests to the implementing agencies afloat. This arrangement was in effect a safeguard against unwarranted duplication of fires and against impossible demands being made on any given arm. In practice, it functioned extremely well. Modern amphibious warfare consists of highly specialized component parts. While unity of command is imperative, a great degree of flexibility is needed on the lower staff echelons. Since the single strategic objective of any given operation is simple of comprehension, and since an industrialized country like the United States produces a great amount of technological proficiency, collaboration between specialists on a basis of mutual understanding is the best procedure for obtaining integration and overall efficiency. Certainly such was the case at Iwo Jima.

Supervision was effected afloat until March 1, by which time the heavy communications equipment needed by Megee, Letcher, and Weller was set up ashore. Both afloat and ashore, however, fires were coordinated with a minimum of checking and duplication of effort. It was seldom necessary, since high-angle artillery fire was used only under compelling tactical circumstances, to halt the fire of more than a few batteries of artillery in order to bring in an air strike. All of the division, regiment, and battalion commanders, through experience as well as prebattle indoctrination, were aware of the limitations and characteristics of each arm. Various supporting agencies were summoned only when the tactical situation dictated the use of firepower beyond that at the immediate disposal of the commander involved. Finally, the commanders of divisions, regiments, and battalions in turn supervised the coordination of the air, artillery, and naval gunfire officers on their respective staff levels. The forwarding of requests for close naval gunfire was properly decentralized, since most of the destroyers and cruisers delivering this support were assigned directly to battalions in the line. But higher echelons monitored requests from below in order to integrate naval gunfire with air and artillery support.[132] The principle was simply that experts should consider their problems together and reach a solution satisfactory to all. What was said of one echelon of command was true everywhere: "The basic means of coordination between supporting arms was to achieve close and lasting personal liaison on all levels. Targets were frequently interchanged according to the method of attack best suited. . . ."[133]

The experience gained on Iwo was of value to the shore-based support coordination agency used on Okinawa. The most serious flaw to develop in the coordination of supporting arms at Iwo stemmed from the fact that both Megee and Letcher lacked the personnel needed to keep abreast of their responsibilities, and some of the men assigned to Letcher were poorly qualified for their jobs. This was especially apparent after the "Supporting Arms Tent" ashore had been set up, and may be attributed to the facts that the technique involved was new, that the assault was expected to be finished rapidly, and that the headquarters (plus some of the weapons) of the Fifth Amphibious Corps Artillery had been committed to Leyte and was thus unavailable for Iwo.

An examination of one of the consequences of undermanning the Fire Support Coordination Center will show the far-reaching effects. Blandy's assessment board which had functioned so brilliantly in evaluating the damage done to targets during the preparatory period was most inadequately duplicated after February 18. No suitable provision had been made for continuing terrain studies and pinpointing unfolding targets for deep support destruction by heavy caliber naval guns after the marines were ashore. Nor was a clearly designated bomb-line progressively drawn behind which close support planes could drop their loads when leaving station with unexpended explosives.[134] Marines watched some of these bombs disturb the fish when they might have been killing a few Japanese. Finally, the tactical maps from late February on misled the ground commanders, their troops, and their supporting arms. Unlike the waist of the island, the terrain along the Motoyama tableland and that plunging down into the sea was so jumbled that poor mosaics resulted from the high altitude photographs taken before February 16. Nor were the February 16–18 pictures much better, for by the time the troops had climbed onto the shelf, the supporting arms, admittedly without slaughtering many of the enemy, had transformed the entire landscape. Schmidt had a special company of topographical engineers at his disposal, but just at the time when they could have been most effectively employed, the navy withdrew many of its camera planes preparatory to the Okinawa landings.

In addition to the shortage of camera planes, those in use were either antiquated or poorly manned. Their shots too frequently were of terrain other than that requested, or had been improperly exposed, or the sidelaps and overlaps were so faulty as to prevent interpretation. When good photographs were obtained, both Letcher and Schmidt's intelligence officer lacked sufficient trained aerial photographic interpreters to make full use of them. Nor was the navy as cooperative in this regard as in the others. Only by accident did Schmidt's headquarters learn of one excellent photographic coverage of the entire island. This resulted in a special trip to an escort carrier to pick up the prints, but it seems that corps staff was unable to exercise any discrimination in reduplication and in forwarding aerial photographs to lower echelons.[135] At least one regimental commander requested that in the future he receive many reprints of good pictures, rather than a few of both good and bad.[136]

Schmidt was aware of some of these shortcomings, since they had occurred earlier on Saipan. "The inadequacy of aerial photography after the initiation of the attack has been previously pointed out by this headquarters," he said after Iwo. "It is understood that steps have been taken to provide the proper type planes and qualified personnel to permit the desired photographic coverage. This coverage is particularly important in uncovering targets well forward of the front lines, in order that they may be engaged before the assault troops get so close as to prevent the employment of naval gunfire, artillery, and aircraft bombing."[137] This quotation stresses but one-half of the deficiency. Only with a well-balanced Fire Support Coordination Center, working in conjunction with the corps intelligence officer, and especially with a plentiful supply of skilled photographic interpreters such as Blandy had employed, could Schmidt have reaped the full benefit of his few camera planes, his mapmakers, and his supporting arms.

To have done so on Iwo would have lessened the task facing the tank-infantrymen-demolition teams, but still it is apparent that without a longer period of preparatory bombardment, that island had to be taken on foot, the hard way. Each supporting arm alone and all together were insufficient, once the marines were ashore, to destroy the remaining Japanese defenses.

In general, the close support planes were at times too few in number, were frequently improperly armed, and some of their crews were inexperienced. As for the heavy naval rifles, since the enemy was so expert at camouflage and American aerial photographic coverage after the preparatory bombardment was so poor, they could seldom be used for destructive effect on a located target because of the proximity of friendly troops. Most of the important exceptions were in the zone of action of the Fifth Division, where destructive fires by heavy ships continued after the marines were ashore. Both the lighter naval guns and the shore-based artillery were incapable of penetrating the installations on Iwo. Support after February 18 was mostly of neutralizing value, which quickly dissipates even when furnished by heavy naval guns.

Rear Admiral Allan E. Smith, commanding one of the navy's fire support units off Iwo, summarized the disappointment of those connected with close neutralizing support. He had "the impression of a goal of effectiveness which has been far from attained." To his way of thinking, it was "best expressed by our inability to silence the mortar fire on the landing beaches and supply dumps which started shortly after the initial landings and continued for many days. None of our methods were able to prevent it." Once the troops were ashore and flush against the Japanese positions, there was too much dust and confusion for good support. "Against this well-concealed enemy fire, neither the dive bombers, napalm, marine artillery fire nor ship fire was effective; and the air spotters could not locate it. It was finally reduced by the general weight of the operation overunning the enemy positions." He was convinced the navy would find the solution exactly where responsible marines had been insisting it was for years, and especially since the establishment of the gunfire range at Kahoolawe in 1943: in fuller recognition of the grave importance of coastal bombardment, in more extensive training against shore targets for all hands, and in continuity of fire-control personnel aboard men-of-war. *"The greatest opportunity for improvement in fire support,"* he emphasized, *"lies in higher standards of gunnery."* [138]

While the student must admire the high performance of the naval gunners at Iwo, the advice of those who sought perfection demands respect. In this vein, Allan Smith's words are also applicable to the marine cannoneers; and the quality of close air support was relatively superior to that turned in during previous operations, but the airmen and their commanders still had the most room for improvement.

Close air support was most effective from the 19th through the 22nd of February, during the period when the fast fleet carriers were on hand to assist the escort carriers. In the night of February 22/23, however, the large carriers departed for their second strike on Tokyo, and after this venture were sent on a photographic sweep of the Nansei Shoto and to rearm and replenish at Ulithi.[139]

Thereafter the planes on the ten escort carriers, an eleventh having been sunk at dusk on the 21st, were inadequate for the tasks at hand. In addition to close support duties, these vessels serviced some spotting and tactical observation craft until these were all based ashore, provided combat and antisubmarine patrols, and in conjunction with army bombers from the Marianas, which also dropped explosives in deep support on Iwo throughout the month of February, continued the neutralization of enemy fields on Haha Jima and Chichi Jima. Also, weather occasionally interrupted carrier operations. The ponderous *Saratoga* furnished night combat air patrols, and dawn and dusk protection and fighter sweeps, until she was badly damaged on February 21, when *Enterprise* took her place. All carriers operated under Rear Admiral Durgin, and were withdrawn on March 11 to rearm and replenish. Thereafter, army, navy, and marine planes based on Iwo, which had begun supplementing the work of the carrier craft as early as February 26, assumed the full burden of direct cover and support until Iwo was secured.[140]

Early withdrawal of the fast carriers caused the troops to lose the support of the better pilots. As the operations officer of a regiment observed, the airmen from the fleet carriers handled their planes with greater skill and obtained higher accuracy than did those from the smaller vessels, although it should be noted that none of the latter had dive bombers. But another explanation for the superior performance of the fast carrier pilots was that ten squadrons of marine fighters were aboard Task Force 58. Thus Iwo was the one operation in the Central Pacific drive which saw marine airmen flying off carriers in close support of marines crossing a heavily defended beach. That marine pilots were on fleet rather than escort carriers as requested by Holland Smith at least as early as Tarawa was ironic, especially since it meant that their support at Iwo was of short duration.

Kamikaze tactics so disturbed ranking American navy commanders that they drastically increased the fighter complement aboard all fast carriers. Having insufficient navy fighter pilots for this sudden change, they turned to the marines until more navy fighters could be trained. Thus, indirectly, the marines landing on Iwo profited. For example, the beach strafing just before the troops landed, delivered by two navy and two marine fighter squadrons and led by Lieutenant Colonel William A. Millington USMC, was said by eye witnesses to have been one of the outstanding examples of effective precision beach strafing seen during the Pacific War.[141]

The effort to obtain a larger voice for marine commanders in planning for direct air support over amphibious assaults, and to get marine pilots aboard escort carriers for use in amphibious landings, was following a tortuous and paper-paved path between the battle front, Pearl Harbor, and Washington. Results were forthcoming, but too late for the Pacific War (marines were to be aboard escort carriers for the landings on Kyushu, which were never made).

Lieutenant General Thomas Holcomb, Commandant of the Corps through 1943, had been a vigorous proponent of marine aviation. But several considerations prevented getting marines on escort carriers. These were the shortage of manpower, the pressing necessity of feeding more and more marine air onto land bases in the Solomons, and concurrence with the navy that if and until a major fleet engagement had occurred navy pilots were required on all carriers. This situation continued during the early months of Lieutenant General Alexander A. Vandegrift's tenure as Commandant, but finally a conference with Nimitz at Pearl Harbor in the late summer of 1944 began to bear fruit. Turner, as a result of the Marianas campaign, was also asking that marines be given greater responsibility in air support. Nimitz agreed that marine aviators should take the place of navy officers in all staff posts directly involved in air support of amphibious landings, and that marine fighters and bomber squadrons should be assigned to an escort carrier division of four ships for direct support of troops going ashore. This, said Nimitz, "will more firmly integrate marine corps aviation within the Marine Corps and is therefore in the interest of naval service." Admiral King had indicated his approval, and just about the time planning for Iwo Jima began, Holland Smith hastened to polish marine pilots for carrier operations and to clear the decks for instantaneous implementation.[142]

It did him no good. Navy staff officers in Washington wrote memoranda concerning the official designations to be used for these new air components. Discussion centered about their permanence. Time passed. Fifteen marine air squadrons had been decommissioned in September 1944, and suddenly a recommendation that four additional marine bombing squadrons be abolished was originated and very nearly approved. Whatever its principal purpose, this proposal would have further disrupted plans for an escort carrier division manned by marine pilots; it was apparently rejected, among other reasons, because of fear for the continuing decline of marine aviation morale, which was badly strained throughout 1944 as marine infantrymen drove ahead but marine airmen were left far behind on land bases.[143]

Failure of the navy to acquiesce in the desires of its marine commanders in the field before the submarine menace in the Atlantic had been overcome and before Japan's mobile carrier power in the Pacific had been drastically reduced is understandable. But both these were accomplished facts by the fall of 1944, and America's total of escort carriers in the Pacific was mounting steadily. Still, the navy delayed. The decision made by Nimitz and King should have been reached earlier than October 1944, so that it could have been implemented immediately at the opportune moment.

The upshot was that the only marine airmen to support the beach phase of an assault in the Central Pacific were those from the fast carriers at Iwo. Marine aviators unquestionably made an important contribution to the tactics of close air support during and before World War II, but the regret is never once did they have a full opportunity to participate in that capacity for which above all others they were suited—namely in lending close and sustained bomber as well as fighter cover for men crossing a heavily defended beach.

Schmidt's air officer believed the quality of close air support delivered by the navy pilots from escort carriers at Iwo would have been improved not only if they had been better versed in ground tactics—a recommendation of exceedingly long standing—but also if they, the air liaison parties, and the air-support control units had been brought together before the landing for the same type of centralized and coordinated training that naval gunfire personnel had participated in. As the assault continued, however, the airmen from the escort carriers, despite terrain difficulties, showed marked improvement. Yet during the last phase of the operation it was necessary to rely on army pilots for close air support, for which they had had no training whatsoever, although they were well versed in the fundamentals of flying, were enthusiastic and anxious to learn, and under marine tutelage became fairly competent in close support missions.[144]

In the circumstances, the caliber of close air support declined once the fast carriers departed and Suribachi was seized. That obstacle was a target highly suited to the air arm, planes were plentiful, and communications were not at the time overloaded. Requests for strikes to assist the Twenty-eighth Marines surrounding and scaling that mountain were efficiently and promptly executed. Some were carried out in less than fifteen minutes, and seldom did the troops have to wait more than thirty minutes.[145] Later, however, a delay of from two to four hours was not uncommon, and the majority of the subsequent strikes were executed more than one hour after the request had been initiated. This meant that the troops were either held up, that adjacent units flanked the area and attempts to deliver the strike endangered friendly forces, or that the target was overrun before the planes arrived.[146] Erskine was worried that the faith of the marines in an important support weapon might be shattered. "Unless the time interval can be greatly reduced," he warned, "infantry units will lose confidence in support aviation and place their dependence entirely in artillery and naval gunfire." [147]

The principal reason for such delays was a shortage of planes. In addition, communications on the air support channels were overloaded, especially after the Third Marine Division came ashore. There were then twenty-four battalion, eight regimental, and three divisional headquarters on the support air request channel alone. Had the principle of supervising by monitoring not been in the main adopted for the intermediate echelons of command, the situation might easily have gotten out of hand, especially since a few operators sometimes exhibited poor communications discipline.[148]

Another cause of the long delays between requests and their fulfillment was the fact that the air liaison parties could not be fully utilized. These men showed energy and courage in keeping apace of the front lines and in advising battalion and regimental commanders of the suitability of targets for air attack; but, although equipped with very high frequency radios, the air liaison parties were not allowed to contact the pilot leader of a given strike and guide him to the objective. Rather, panels were used to mark front lines, and various pyrotechnical devices normally indicated the target. Since such techniques were susceptible to error, even if the enemy employed no ruse, a large number of dummy runs was sometimes necessary.[149] But there was no suitable alternative. Unfortunate experiences in the Marianas had caused Turner and his air advisers to doubt the feasibility of direct control of strikes by air liaison parties, and Megee, the commander of the Landing Force Air Support Control Unit, himself had little faith in the quality of most of the liaison parties, since the majority of the personnel was inexperienced. Megee and members of his staff, however, sometimes carried portable equipment forward and brought strikes in directly.[150]

Nor were the navy planes any better armed than in the preparatory period. Napalm drops continued to be characterized by a high percentage of duds. This was doubtless caused by inexperience with this type of bomb, since it had been introduced only seven months before, at Tinian. No day at Iwo was worse than February 22, when out of sixty-four napalms released, only seven were reported to have detonated.[151]

With all the deficiencies of close air support as executed, it was an important factor in the success of the assault. Perhaps the psychological impact on the Japanese was the greatest advantage gained. When planes were aloft, there was a noticeable diminution of enemy mortar and artillery fire. Observation planes were most useful in this regard. Considering the terrain obstacles involved, the pilots and crews of these craft turned in an outstanding performance. Any plane caused the Japanese to hold fire, and when they opened up, their positions were sometimes located by aerial observers, who instantly called down counterbattery.[152]

Aside from air-borne observers, the only marines used aloft after the fast carriers departed were the members of a torpedo bombing squadron. These came in along with the army fighters and were land-based. But since no provision had been made to replenish the navy planes regularly aboard the escort carriers, the marine pilots were never employed in close troop support but were pressed into service as antisubmarine patrols, for which they were also well trained. When the escort carriers shoved off on March 11, the marine flyers took over all the purely navy duties in the skies, and close support devolved on army pilots.[153]

Instruction of the army pilots in close troop support had begun shortly before this date, and they learned rapidly. Unoccupied islets adjacent to Iwo were used as practice targets, and on two separate occasions before the enemy lines were so compressed as to preclude close support the army airmen flying in P-51's with 1,000 pound bombs (twice as heavy as those used by the navy) greatly assisted the men of the Fifth Division. They were coached onto the targets by airborne coordinators, a novel technique, and obtained a number of direct hits.[154]

Close naval gunfire support was of much greater volume and of far more benefit to the marines than was the air arm. Use of the newly developed slow burning powder exceeded expectations. It not only allowed 5-inch destroyer fire to be lobbed from close in and safely over landing craft and gunboats, but also to be laid down over the front lines, sometimes within as little as seventy-five yards of friendly troops, and was effective in taking out targets on reverse slopes.[155]

Essential to well-directed close naval gunfire support were the shore fire-control parties, and, particularly since the terrain in the northeastern portion of the island was so rugged, the air-borne spotters and observers. These agencies worked in close collaboration with one another and with the firing ships. Theirs was the responsibility of supplying the data for prearranged fires before launching the daily morning attacks, and for bringing down call fires. This was dangerous work, and casualties among the shore fire-control parties were so high that more radio operators should have been assigned. Also, more compact and lighter weight radio equipment was desirable; and so successful was the practice of sending a member of a shore fire-control party aboard a man-of-war that further increase in personnel to allow such liaison to become permanent was recommended.

Destroyer fire was used chiefly for close support, interdiction, night harassment, illumination, and sometimes for counterbattery. Until the withdrawal of the heavily gunned vessels on March 7, however, the larger weapons were continuously employed. The number of major combatant ships on hand for naval gunfire support rose from eight on February 20 to thirteen the next day, and then gradually diminished to four in early March. Normally, at least one of these was assigned directly to each division, while every battalion enjoyed the services of a destroyer. The function of heavy men-of-war in divisional support was mainly to thicken deep neutralization, although they were also called upon for counterbattery, and Erskine brought some 14-inch neutralizing fire down within 400 yards of his front lines. The remaining large ships were, under the supervision of corps, assigned to deep, general support. Of course greater benefit would have been derived from these larger caliber weapons had an assessment agency existed capable of uncovering targets far back of the battle front, permitting additional heavy armor-piercing shells to destroy massive defensive installations.

Every sea-borne weapon available was pressed into service. In addition to the larger men-of-war, gunboats and armored amphibian tractors were utilized for continued close in flank support along the coast. These fired rockets, mortars, and 75-millimeter howitzers, and when so equipped added their 40-millimeter antiaircraft guns to those of the warships in covering the cliffs and in shooting at caves close ashore.[156]

The success of the rolling barrage laid down by navy guns on the first day of the assault won wide acclaim among the Americans, and caused some to wonder if the technique were not applicable for sustained neutralization throughout the assault. Despite the complicated ship maneuvers and the high degree of coordination required, Allan Smith felt such plans feasible. He would have liked to use the rolling barrage (largely conceived and planned by the corps naval gunfire officer, Weller) continuously by having a wide band of fire laid down progressively some 500 yards ahead of the advancing front, to be controlled by shore fire parties and air observers. A few of the capital ships could be assigned to destructive fire in depth, but during and after the landing the bulk of all men-of-war would be used for neutralization. To some degree, this was done at Iwo Jima, although no high amount of continuity was obtained. Allan Smith believed the technique used on February 19 could be expertly systematized and made established doctrine for close naval gunfire support, with a resulting increase in effectiveness through a decrease in ammunition wasted.[157]

Whatever the future might bring, on Iwo the bulk of the neutralization came from shore-based artillery. By dusk of February 28 there were fourteen battalions of marine artillerymen ashore with their howitzers, two battalions firing 155-millimeter weapons, eight manning the smaller 105-millimeter variety, and four shooting 75-millimeter pack howitzers.

All but the 155's were under division control, and with one temporary exception were held rigidly under the command of the three artillery regiments, according to doctrine established before Tarawa. This allowed the regimental fire direction center to function at full efficiency, gave more uniformity of performance, and permitted a rapid shift from target to target across the division front. Whereas Letcher supervised the employment of all these weapons, divisional as well as corps, neither the artillery concept nor his available personnel and equipment permitted an immediate centralization of all fires on a designated area. The small size of the island, and the nature of the terrain and of the enemy's defenses, dictated such massing of fires, and under the pressure of compelling circumstances it was achieved, but too late to please Erskine and the marines assaulting the crest of the Motoyama Plateau.

The artillery plan contemplated a loose coordination to be effected by corps. Each regiment of weapons was to be in support of its parent division. The only massing of fires expected may be seen in the provision that each of the two divisions in beach assault was to be prepared to have one of its four battalions of artillery fire in the zone of action of the adjacent division. As well as fulfilling long-range missions for corps, Letcher's 155-millimeter howitzers were to reinforce divisional artillery on request; and his staff was to effect overall coordination, but he was not authorized to exercise technical fire direction.

Without such authorization, plus the equipment and personnel to implement it, the massing of fires during the early phase of the assault would have been at best difficult. Heavy concentrations were later accomplished by mutual agreement among the commanders concerned, or by general directives issued by corps in advance every evening.

Actually, except for the delay involved, cooperation between artillery units was excellent, which under the circumstances is a tribute to the cannoneers themselves. After the first phase of the assault, high concentrations were gained and quickly shifted from one division front to another, as these commands attacked in echelon.[158]

Letcher's artillery staff received wholehearted cooperation from all quarters. The basic artillery survey, for example, was made by a skilled Coast and Geodetic Survey officer attached to one of the artillery regiments. Likewise, a full interchange of information came from all terrestrial observation posts, from the indispensable airborne artillery observers, and from flash and sound ranging stations. New ranging equipment perfected by scientists at Duke University proved compact and highly accurate.[159]

Capture of Suribachi was expected to improve terrestrial observation, but by the time it was done the northeastern front had moved up to the jumbled terrain, and this fact plus poor maps and smoke and the haze characteristic of the island hindered vision. Flash and sound ranging equipment on the mountain was of greater value, but the base line for these instruments was only 182 yards long. Nor would earlier seizure of Kama and Kanguku rocks (see map 21), small outcroppings just off the center of the broad northwestern coast taken in mid-March, have improved matters, since they were not high enough.[160]

Despite lack of good observation and ranging stations, and despite poor map coverage of the northeastern portion of the island, corps and divisional artillery performed splendidly. Their neutralizing effect was on occasion lost, however, when corps set the hour for the next morning's attack too early, allowing insufficient time for early morning reconnaissance and for resupply and tank maintenance. As a result, prearranged artillery barrages were sometimes lifted or rolled forward before the troops were ready to jump off.[161]

To lose the neutralizing punch of the artillery weapons was to lose almost all they were capable of providing. The pack howitzers were too light for any destructive fire, unless the enemy was caught in the open, which rarely happened. Only with concrete-piercing fuses and repeated direct hits did the 105-millimeter weapons gain destruction, and even the 155-millimeter howitzers failed to penetrate average installations with less than ten to twelve similarly fused armor-piercing projectiles hurled at the same spot on the same target. Such shells and such fuses were, of course, limited.[162] As a regimental commander complained, "too many anti-personnel shells, and insufficient destructive type shells were fired." [163]

Artillerists on Iwo were aware of their deficiencies and those of their weapons. Some recommended better training in precision firing. All agreed, however, that heavier projectiles were essential. The consensus was that as well as 155-millimeter guns and howitzers, Fleet Marine Force should obtain at least four battalions of 8-inch howitzers, and these weapons were indeed under procurement at the time of Iwo. Selection of corps weapons could then depend on terrain and the hydrographic conditions prevailing off the chosen objective. Certainly for Iwo, 8-inch howitzers would have been the logical choice, had they been available.[164]

Such were the limitations of all supporting arms on, over, and adjacent to Iwo, that in the words of Smith's operations officer, "the burden of reducing many fortifications fell to infantry armed with organic weapons, flamethrowers, and demolitions." Forrestal observed this fact when he was ashore, and expressed his "tremendous admiration and reverence for the guy who walks up beaches and takes enemy positions with a rifle and grenades or his bare hands." [165]

AMERICAN TACTICS AND WEAPONS

It was not quite as bad as that, but under the circumstances Forrestal's hyperbole was proper. Basically, it was the assault squad, in coordination with tanks and assisted by the neutralization of enemy defenses by one or several of the supporting arms, which seized Iwo Jima. Tactics seldom varied. Tank-infantry-demolition coordination took out position after position.

As for weapons, the light carbine was damned as lacking the impact to knock an enemy off his feet, and men armed with this gun were seen voluntarily to "lose" it and pick up the nearest Garand.

Plastic covers should have been furnished for the working mechanisms of all small arms, since there was a large amount of malfunctioning on Iwo.[166] Both the demolition grenade and the satchel charge were effective, but an explosive of intermediate weight and size was desired. Nor was there a sufficient quantity of demolition "snakes" to clear minefields, and some heavy equipment was purposely sacrificed in opening up passageways.[167] The recently perfected Ronson portable flamethrower was termed a perfect weapon, and was present in adequate numbers, twenty-seven per battalion. The bazooka was also excellent, but the folding type was superior to the cumbersome rigid weapon.[168]

In this connection, Rockey was concerned about the weight of equipment carried by members of the assault team and by the men giving them immediate support. Analyzing the loads of nineteen different specialists, seven were found to be burdened with more than 100 pounds, while five others lifted more than seventy-five pounds, and none less than fifty. The suggested solution was to increase the number of combat vehicles, especially "Weasles," a newly developed, tracked amphibian jeep.[169]

All hands sought to augment the firepower at the disposal of the battalion, regimental, and division commanders by suggesting new weapons and offering improvements for those already in use. The net result would require not only more combat vehicles, but additional personnel.

Respect for Japanese mortars turned marine attention to their own weapons in this category. A larger mortar was needed, and one suggestion was that a 120-millimeter mortar battalion be added to division.[170]

Most of all, the regimental weapons company needed refurnishing. Its equipment more than that of any other unit had fallen behind the advanced techniques of ship-to-shore movement. The 37-millimeter guns were employed offensively when possible. Their flat trajectory and high muzzle velocity could accomplish things beyond the capabilities of the howitzers, but they were awkward to handle. One regimental commander was convinced that an improved design would allow the substitution of the heavier 57-millimeter gun without increasing the problem of movement and siting.[171] Until something was done in this connection, the Japanese would continue to enjoy a superiority with their highly accurate and mobile 47-millimeter antitank and antiboat weapons.

It was also deemed possible to lighten the component parts of the rocket barrage equipment assigned to the regimental weapons companies, to increase its accuracy and range, and to enlarge its explosive effect.[172] Likewise, the 75-millimeter gun mounted on a half-track was obsolete. Already, while the struggle for Iwo raged, steps were being taken to substitute a self-propelled 105-millimeter gun, a decision Iwo reaffirmed since its weight and point-blank fire were required to knock out heavy enemy installations.[173]

The same was true of tanks. They most frequently served as the immediate base of high-velocity fire for the front line marines. "Shermans" were used on Iwo, but tanks with heavier weapons and thicker armor were feasible, since lifting the Shermans ashore necessitated the employment of medium landing ships. The newer type, heavier army tanks, "Pershings," would have been much better, but few were available in the Pacific at the time. Pershings could have been landed with greater ease, for their broader tracks would have taken a better purchase in the volcanic ash. More important, theirs was a lower silhouette, their armor was impervious to 47-millimeter fire, and they mounted 90-millimeter guns rather than 75's.

Without the Shermans, however, the assault would have failed. A total of three battalions, slightly under 150 tanks, were committed, and were, like the artillery regiments, kept under divisional control and employed where most needed. The tanks crews and their maintenance personnel were energetic and courageous, and with the assistance of their own tankdozers and of armored dozers drawn from the engineers they went almost everywhere, except up Suribachi. The Japanese quickly realized that dozers were cancelling out their terrain advantage, and losses in this category were very high. Also marked by the enemy for immediate destruction were the tank leaders exhibiting radio equipment. Difficulty of communications was the most important single hindrance to tank-infantry coordination, and all tanks should have had radios, or at least antennas.

The latest model flamethrowing tank was especially effective. Nearly all the Shermans were equipped with small flamethrowers squirting fire through one or two of their machine gun ports, but the enemy suffered most from those shooting a flame for a distance of about 100 yards directly from the muzzle of their turreted 75-millimeter guns. A greater number of such tanks was required for future operations. The Third Division had nothing but the obsolete tank flamethrowers which were limited in range and offered very narrow fields of fire.[174] The more modern types were loaned to Erskine's men by other divisions, however, and one of his battalion commanders, unable late in the operation to get his green battle replacements to close with the enemy, commented that the new type flamethrowing tank "proved the solution to the whole problem." [175]

SUPPLY, BEACH LOGISTICS, REPLACEMENTS, AND MEDICAL ACTIVITY

Supplying the front line troops and their shore-based supporting arms was highly complex. The average expenditure of artillery ammunition alone, for example, was, up to the last phase of the struggle, over 23,000 rounds daily. Such figures mean little, and in any case fail to take into account the heavy losses caused by the fire of the enemy. Ammunition of all types sufficient to fill 480 freight cars was unloaded across the beach, plus food enough to feed Columbus, Ohio, for thirty days, and fuel to form a train of tank cars several miles in length, with 10,000 gallons per car.[176]

Nor does this complete the list. Only when one considers the adverse conditions of Iwo's beaches, the enemy's artillery, mortar, and small arms coverage of those beaches throughout the month of February, and the inexperienced personnel forming the American ship crews, beach and shore parties, can one understand why it was impossible for Harry Hill's Attack Force to continue the same high caliber performance it had turned in during the time of the initial ship-to-shore movement. Errors were subsequently made by both navy and marine components engaged in the stupendous task of beach logistics. Under the existing circumstances the fact that although critical shortages of American supplies ashore threatened, none developed, is praise indeed for the personnel responsible. Plans broke down and improvisation became the compelling order of the day. "This is the toughest beach I have ever seen," said Captain Carl E. Anderson of the navy, who was Hill's beachmaster and had held this responsible post in the Aleutians, the Gilberts, the Marshalls, and the Marianas. The employment of loud speakers ashore had earned for this officer of Swedish extraction the nickname, "Squeaky." Fourteen amplifiers lined Iwo's beaches; when asked for the secret of his success by a correspondent, Anderson replied "Success, huh. I get so much hell from the Admiral I yust pass it on. Then we get things done." [177]

The weather deteriorated toward mid-afternoon on the first day, and thereafter was most erratic.[178] It was necessary to open up the alternate beaches and to shuttle back and forth in search of a lee coast. The offshore gradient was steep, especially along the preferred beaches, and waves sometimes towering ten feet broke directly on the narrow shelf below the first terrace. The downward thrust of the breakers and the outward pull of the undertow were so great that some 200 of the smaller landing craft were lost, most along the beaches. If the ramp were down, they were apt to fill with sand and water, and if not, they were likely to be broached by the next wave. The tractor and Dukw drivers, unless they rode the crest of a wave onto the terrace and secured a good purchase, also found their vehicles at least temporarily out of commission.[179]

Surf conditions were such that among the small craft only amphibian vehicles could be fully employed. This threw the major burden of running supplies ashore on the tractors, Dukws, and the larger tank landing craft and medium and tank landing ships. Since the volcanic ash was not only coarse when dry, but refused to pack when wet, it was difficult to hold the non-amphibian lighterage onto the shore. Stern anchors were useless, for plunging those weights into the gradient off Iwo was like dropping anchor in a bowl of mush.[180]

Efforts to secure beach purchase with stern anchors only complicated an already difficult job. It was best to keep all engines running forward, and double-screw craft and ships were superior to those equipped with a single screw—provided of course that an anchor line or a square of beach matting carried off the terrace by the surf did not foul one or both of the propellers. Sometimes supplementing the forward thrust of the screws were lines passed ashore to starboard and port, and secured to a tractor or a winch. Weights or long timbers sunk in the soil with lines attached (commonly called "dead men"), were useful despite the volcanic gravel, and should have been more extensively employed by ship crews to free tractors and winches for other duties.

Should one of the non-amphibian craft or ships find an unlittered portion of beach across which to unload, and without broaching or being at least cast afoul of an obstacle alongside, get its cargo ashore, its problems were by no means ended. Receiving supplies from the transports and cargo vessels was hazardous because of a rough seaway, the absence of a sufficient number of high quality fender guards, and the marked tendency of the ship crews, in their anxiety to unload and depart, to scramble cargo by dumping it haphazardly into the shallow draft vessel bobbing at the side of the larger ship. This was exceedingly shortsighted. It thwarted early efforts to get only priority cargo ashore, delayed the turn around at the beach, and added to the number of landing craft and ships forced to visit repair vessels. It had been hoped that general unloading could begin on the second day, but conditions ashore delayed this undertaking along Rockey's beaches until February 22, and along those closer to the northeastern bulge of the island until February 26. Thus the inexperienced navy crews of the first assault echelon, in their haste to depart, only added to the confusion, and some were obliged to remain around Iwo through the first few days of March.[181]

Such conduct appears to have been inevitable with inexperienced crews, regardless of the thoroughness and quality of upper echelon plans and leadership. For other reasons, control from the line-of-departure to the beach during the critical phase of unloading from the afternoon of February 19 until late in that month left something to be desired. A wide difference of opinion prevailed as to why this condition arose. Marines ashore claimed that control procedure was too highly centralized, and that navy control personnel were unacquainted with beach conditions and were unwilling to take the advice of their tactical liaison officers regarding the logistical needs of the troops. The navy retaliated that marine requests for supplies too frequently by-passed the proper control echelons. In other words, there was confusion as to just what the control system was after the waves in beach assault had landed. Circumstances, especially overcrowded communications, rather than either faulty plans or clashing personalities, were responsible.

Hill insisted on complete centralization of control over the first waves, for otherwise he could hardly assure a uniform assault on all beaches. When the moment came for the "on call" and subsequent priority supplies to go ashore, the plan was for a temporary decentralization of control, since conditions would vary from beach to beach. Thus, both the Attack Force control vessel and the two (one for each of the beach assault divisions) transport squadron control vessels, after the early waves were ashore, were to become free agents with supervisory duties, and the burden of direct control was to pass to navy officers representing the various transport division commanders floating at the line-of-departure, who were to work through the transport division beachmasters with the regimental shore party commanders along the beach. As the situation along the coast improved and general unloading began, the plan was to recentralize control up through the transport squadron control vessels, with Hill's Attack Force representative at the line-of-departure remaining a free agent with overall supervision.

Conditions ashore, over and beyond the delay before general unloading began, caused a serious modification of this plan. Since the smaller non-amphibian craft could not be fully employed, a serious shortage of lighterage developed, and it was suddenly necessary to reinstate a central control and to allot the larger landing craft and ships to the regimental beaches. It is hard to see how the confusion which ensued was the fault of any one branch of command, navy or marine. No one ashore during the critical phase of unloading (the first six days of the assault) knew exactly where to apply for priority cargo.[182]

Such confusion was alleviated by expertly handled ship-to-shore communications and by the high degree of coordination between the navy personnel and the marine liaison officers aboard the control craft, and especially between the navy beach parties and the marine shore parties. No good evidence exists to the contrary. Particularly was the degree of collaboration between the beach and shore parties commendable, for these worked under heavy fire during the first week, and were principally composed of inexperienced personnel.

All high ranking officers at Iwo sought to rectify the inferior status in which both the beach and shore parties had languished throughout the Pacific War. The success of any sustained assault depended in great part on these men, and yet little had been done to give them proper training, experience, and continuity of function. These attributes were especially desirable in view of the great technological advancements made during the war in handling supplies across the beach; pioneers and members of beach parties were no longer merely labor troops, but a sizeable percentage of them must also be highly trained specialists.

At Iwo the pioneer battalion supplied the foundation and framework for the divisional shore parties, but the personnel were mostly new. No counterpart existed in the navy's command, and as at Guadalcanal the pioneer battalion was understaffed. Some such solution as that found in the Seabee battalions was needed. The navy had to begin from scratch to build up permanent beach parties for use in operation after operation, while the marines sought improvement by enlarging the pioneer battalion, and by assigning more military police to control traffic, to hold down the pilfering of supplies, and to protect souvenir hunters, especially navy personnel who seemed unaware of the Japanese penchant for booby-trapping everything including their own dead. Also, the marines had to impress their pioneers with the grave importance of their mission.

Even with enlarged pioneer battalions, additional human muscle would be required in the critical phase of the ship-to-shore movement during an amphibious assault. Laborers at Iwo were drawn mainly from the battle replacement drafts, the division bands, and naval construction personnel, supplemented by army port troops. The number available on the first day, but of course not all used, was more than 10,000 men.[183]

Doctrine correctly calls for holding all but advanced shore and beach party elements off the coast until it has been at least partially secured from enemy fire. At Iwo such doctrine necessarily went into discard, for otherwise the front lines could not have been supplied from about February 20 until near the end of that month. There is some merit in the criticism that shore party personnel and equipment were landed too early and too rapidly, but as circumstances unfolded at Iwo there was no alternative. Advance tactical plans called for securing the beaches more quickly than was actually possible, and logistical planning depended on tactical estimates. One illustration will suffice. An important portion of the heavy shore party equipment for the Fourth and Fifth Divisions was lifted from the staging area to the objective in medium landing ships. Surf conditions were such that it was essential to use these ships in priority unloading to keep the front lines supplied, and there was no recourse but to beach and unload them. This, added to the clutter of vehicles and equipment on the beach, caused a further congestion of supplies and personnel, and increased the number of casualties.[184]

Despite the hardships imposed by the surf and the tactical situation, the beach and shore parties, the tractor and Dukw drivers, and most of the navy crews aboard the landing craft and ships, performed splendidly under fire. After routes of egress had been dozed and matted, Dukws were instrumental in resupplying artillery ammunition and evacuating casualties. Without the cargo amphibian tractors, however, and especially the later model equipped with a ramp, it is impossible to see how any advance could have been sustained, for these almost alone supplied the fighting troops during the first several days of the assault. The tracked amphibians were assisted by Weasles. These vehicles could traverse almost any type of terrain and for this reason were useful not only in supplying the front lines but also in servicing communications and returning casualties to the beach and air evacuation centers. Without exception, all commanders asked for a greatly increased allotment. The small number of Weasles provided at Iwo was partially offset by the fact that in the early period of the assault, before the rocky terrain was struck, there were fewer mechanical failures because of the soft volcanic ash. For forthcoming operations, more solid construction was desirable.[185]

Weasles, Dukws, and cargo amphibian tractors saved the day when the situation along the beach became worse than anticipated. Provision had been made for trouble. This consisted from the outset in special treatment for "hot cargo," so called because of its immediate tactical need. It was chiefly water, rations, ammunition, signal equipment, and certain medical supplies. Cargo tractors carrying the beach assault waves ashore were loaded with approximately 700 pounds of hot cargo each, which was thrown onto the volcanic ash as the vehicle turned to put to sea again. Expectation was that from one-half to two-thirds of these supplies would be lost, but that still enough would be picked up to meet demands through the first night and into the second day. Recovery satisfied the most optimistic, since from sixty to seventy per cent was either carried inshore by the troops or stacked into improvised beach dumps by advance elements of the division shore parties, which began landing with the fifth and sixth waves. The work of the advanced shore party personnel was magnificent, considering that along some beaches, after the enemy's artillery, mortar, and rocket fire became furious, their casualties mounted to above fifty per cent.[186]

The assault waves lifted only a part of the hot cargo ashore. While the 250 Dukws, three-fifths of them manned by well-disciplined army troops, and fifty of the 400 amphibian tractors were busy with howitzers and artillery ammunition, the remaining tracked amphibians returned to twenty specially preloaded tank landing ships and began ferrying in all types of ammunition, rations, water, essential toilet articles, and petroleum supplies.

Execution of these emergency logistical plans saved the Americans on Iwo. After the amphibian tractors had completed their tasks, they were pressed into service transferring cargo from some of the floating dumps, that is small landing craft incapable of being properly beached, and from the assault shipping. Day and night, the amphibian tractors furnished supplies to the front lines. These craft, along with the Dukws and Weasles, rode directly from the sea inshore, and thus provided the enemy's gunners with more difficult moving targets during the critical phase of the ship-to-shore operations. Up through February 22 across Rockey's beaches, and a day later across those of Cates, some ninety per cent of the cargo was carried directly by amphibian tractors from the assault shipping to the front lines. Then, forty-eight to seventy-two hours behind schedule, a semblance of organization began to appear on all beaches, and division dumps, easily dug and hastily camouflaged but congested as they vied for space with friendly artillery, began to appear. The supply plan ashore called for greater centralization of control than had previously been employed. Division dumps were to forward supplies automatically to front line regimental and battalion dumps, which were to be kept at a one-day level in accordance with daily strength reports. Several additional days passed before this system was functioning smoothly, and even then the terrain and lack of suitable roads in the forward areas were such that amphibian tractors were extensively employed until the island was secured.[187]

Inexperienced personnel failed to handle pallets properly, and later complained that these began arriving before suitable equipment was on the beach to cope with them. But it was conclusively demonstrated at Iwo that it is possible to begin handling cargo by machine methods at a comparatively early stage of the game. Bulk supplies should be loaded into landing craft in pallets, and special tools were readily available to the shore party and the boat crews to break the pallet straps so that the palletized cargo could if necessary be unloaded at the beach in one-man packages. The lesson learned was to train all hands in rapid methods of handling cargo.

The extensive preloading of amphibian trailers with hot cargo was also partially bungled at Iwo. Some of these were towed ashore by empty amphibian tractors, which could have lifted just as much cargo themselves. All should have been permitted to drift ashore. While this would have added to the hazards of navigation, it would probably not have been serious. An acute situation might develop after a landing where, because of combat conditions and very rough water, the drifting ashore of water-tight containers of this nature might be the only method of supplying hot cargo to troops.[188]

So great was the requirement for the full participation of Weasles, Dukws, and amphibian tractors during the early phase of the assault that one of the principal reasons for the loss of vehicles in the latter two categories must be examined. This was a low caliber performance on the part of some of the tank landing ship crews and commanders.

Since the Marshalls campaign, continuing efforts were made to improve the coordination between the amphibian vehicles and their parent ships. Landings in the Marianas were not marred by a repetition of what had happened in late January and early February 1944; but experienced tank landing ships in the Pacific gravitated into the Philippines, and Iwo Jima was supplied with some newly commissioned vessels and green crews.

Higher echelon efforts to indoctrinate these navy personnel were not wholly successful. Coordination between flotilla commanders and their marine and army amphibian tractor and Dukw counterparts in the beach assault was uniformly excellent, and it was the later activities of certain individual group commanders and tank landing ship skippers and their crews that were at fault. Once again there was a tendency to hold back from the line-of-departure and thus to increase the run in to the beach, to avoid servicing any vehicle not lifted by that tank landing ship to the objective area, and to refuse to lower ramps and take aboard damaged craft. Particularly was the situation fraught with danger when it became imperative to operate some of the amphibious tractors, never noted for their seakeeping qualities, at night. After Iwo, Turner reemphasized that each tank landing ship commander "shall assist any amphibian tractor which is in trouble to the best of his ability." [189]

Failure of some navy personnel to carry out this simple instruction caused valuable craft to be swamped at Iwo and lost at a time when they were most needed. The situation improved only when maintenance and service components could be shore-based, late on

February 23. By that time only 267 of the original 400 cargo amphibian tractors were operational, and the ranks of serviceable Dukws had been equally depleted.[190]

Other tank landing ship captains and crews, it must be emphasized, turned in outstanding performances. Some of them beached, and despite intense enemy fire stuck to the coast till unloaded.[191] Especially did the bravery and cooperation of the navy personnel aboard the medium landing ships carrying tanks and shore party equipment win the acclaim of the marines. These men brought their vessels in during the peak of enemy reaction on the first day and landed "this vital equipment," to quote Cates, "in face of the heaviest . . . mortar and artillery fire yet seen in any operation." [192]

An explanation of the unsatisfactory conduct by the inexperienced tank landing ships probably lies in the fact that their skippers relied too much on the special provisions made to rest the drivers and to reservice Dukws and amphibian tractors. One of the innovations by the navy was highly successful. A couple of tank landing ships were equipped as "mother" vessels for the personnel of all amphibious and landing craft. In providing bunks, hot baths, and food for the crews of tractors, Dukws, and the smaller lighterage, this idea bore good fruit.

Provisions for the amphibious vehicles, on the other hand, were ill-conceived. The small vehicular and personnel landing craft converted to refueling boats were dismal failures. The seas ran too high for the medium landing craft designed to resupply the boats, not to speak of the difficulties encountered by the smaller refueling craft. The boats were few in number and hard to locate, especially at night; if one were found, it was apt to be awaiting gas itself from a medium landing craft, which too frequently had neither a pump nor a winch for the transfer of a drum over the side. When a refueling boat with a supply of gas was located, it was a major task to pass and secure the necessary lines.

Gas barges were worse. Hill, expecting a favorable turn in the weather, decided to launch all portable aids to beach logistics on February 21. As he admits, this was a mistake, but he took a calculated risk. Had the surf lessened, the situation along the shore would have been greatly improved by these unloading and reservicing devices. As it was, most of the gas barges and all the offshore unloading platforms broached and added to the clutter on the beaches. The only recourse in reservicing the amphibian tractors and Dukws until their maintenance ashore could be effected was the slow expedient of running gas drums from the attack transports and the cargo vessels to the tank landing ships.[193]

Already the beaches were so cluttered that on February 20 the underwater demolition teams were sent in to assist the beach party and the shore party engineers in the critical task of avoiding chaos. The job was hard, and all hands later requested more ample waterborne salvage and repair facilities, as well as heavier equipment for handling supplies and stalled vehicles along the beach. Iwo made such an impression on their minds that little heed was given to the fact that each operation presents individual problems. Certainly it would have been advantageous to beach logistics had there been heavier tugs and more above-water damage repair vessels at Iwo, and it turned out that three dock landing ships were insufficient to handle hull casualties;[194] but getting heavier tractors, cranes, and dozers onto the beach depends on the presence or absence of offshore obstacles, either natural or man-made, and the technological advance in the construction of lighterage. The heavier the equipment, and this includes shore-based support weapons as well as the allocations to the shore and beach parties, the better; but there is for any given operation a limit beyond which it is unwise to proceed. Only the Japanese were sure that hydrographic conditions off Iwo were suitable to the landing of very heavy equipment.

It had been hoped that the corps shore party could be committed early in the assault, in order to remove a sizeable portion of the burden from the divisional units. Requests for the corps shore party went out from the coast on February 21, but the mechanics of transmitting the orders from the beach to the various transports had been poorly worked out, and dusk of February 23 found only one-third of them on the island. Thus the division shore parties labored under heavy fire on a twenty-four hour basis for from three to four days, with an inevitable loss of efficiency. Even then conditions remained so desperate that several additional days elapsed before the corps shore party commander could take over the responsibility of beach logistics from the divisions. During this interim period, corps shore party personnel were used to supplement the divisional groups.

Commanding the corps shore party was Colonel Leland S. Swindler USMC, whose administrative post was control of the Eighth Marine Field Depot. Men of this depot constituted the backbone of the corps shore party, but their duties were primarily connected with beach logistics rather than dispensing supplies from a field depot. This was the first time in which the shore party commander, with his own organization augmented by other personnel, handled the cargo from the time it landed on the beach until it was issued to the troops, and it worked out exceedingly well. Swindler was able to bring his men and equipment ashore, and to take over the functions of beach logistics just as the battle replacements were being withdrawn from the division shore parties. Furthermore, as the corps shore party took over responsibilities along the coast, some members of the pioneer battalions of the divisions were transferred inland to complete division dumps, to assist in the disposal of the dead, to help in ordnance and motor transport maintenance, and to provide additional rear area and beachhead security.[195]

Confusion was still evident along the coast as final elements of the field depot, the Third Division, and the corps artillery moved ashore on February 24–25. A contributing factor was the compelling necessity of landing airfield construction and service personnel and their heavy equipment. Schmidt was under rigid orders to get the airfields in operation rapidly, and he had no alternative but to complicate further the problem of beach logistics. But some of the bulky equipment brought in by the garrison components should never have arrived in the assault echelon, such as ice cream machines and heavy refrigeration gear.[196]

Despite all the difficulties encountered in beach logistics, no acute shortages in supply for the fighting troops developed. Mortar shells were frequently in greater demand than supply, and it was sometimes necessary to ration the ammunition expenditure of the howitzers; but air drops and later air freight from the Marianas eased the situation until the ammunition resupply vessels were squared away and priority unloading picked up speed.[197]

Clothing was ample, but the marine shoe was seen to be inferior to the recently introduced army combat boot. There was always plenty of food, but complaints arose that some of the rations dated back to 1942, and again water turned up in rusty containers or in ones previously used for petroleum products.[198] Fruit juices were especially popular, and the marines would doubtless have lynched one of the medical officers had they known he would suggest in his action report that sick-bay alcohol be carried in undistinguishable containers in an effort to lower its loss.[199]

Working hand in hand with the beach and shore parties were marine engineers, who were pleased that for once they were able to concentrate on those tasks for which they were trained, and were not demoted to what they classified as menial labor. As well as sealing up by-passed caves and blasting pillboxes and blockhouses, they cooperated with the underwater demolition teams in clearing the coast line of wrecked hulks and debris, while others installed beach equipment, cut routes of egress through the first terrace, probed for enemy mines, unrolled marston matting, and began constructing a lateral road just inshore along the coast. This last task required a transition which was inevitable and difficult, namely taking the burden of carriage across the beach and up the first terrace from the tracked vehicles and placing it on wheeled trucks. Road matting laid for the wheeled vehicles was quickly torn and mangled by the amphibian tractors. The problem could not be solved until tractor maintenance was shore-based. Then the serviceable tractors remaining were gradually given shorter and shorter hauls as the engineers spread an ever-expanding road network over the island.

In addition, the engineers helped erect supply dumps, assisted in readying the airfields for friendly operations, and set up water distillation units. The last was an imperative job. Feed lines into the sea were hard to secure, and were constantly breaking loose, only to creep back to the water's edge where they picked up large amounts of volcanic ash from the surf. One group of engineers solved this problem by running its line into an abandoned Japanese hulk along the coast. Sea water clear of sand entered the holes of this carcass, which still had sufficient plate remaining to protect the fluid from the swirling currents caused by breakers. Another group dug a surface well just inshore of the beach, hoping for a seepage from the sea. The outcome of this effort was a pleasant surprise for the marines. Rather than cool sea water, for which the distillation equipment had been designed, the engineers tapped the water table under Iwo, and up bubbled a liquid at 160° Fahrenheit and of such a high mineral content that it rapidly encrusted the distilling coils. Ever resourceful, the engineers pumped this water into a perforated pipe erected over a hastily constructed wooden floor. Thus emerged a hot mineral shower large enough for a full platoon of men. The bath, however, proved to be uncomfortably warm, and a canvass catchment was erected to expose the water to the sea breezes before entering the shower.[200]

Such jobs were completed only after the beaches were secure, that is after marines had penetrated onto the Motoyama tableland and observed enemy fire no longer plagued the beach and shore parties. From late February the situation along the beaches showed rapid improvement. Opening up the alternate coast to the reception of supplies started as early as February 25 and provided a means for avoiding the heavier surf. Corps began turning responsibility for beach logistics over to representatives of the incoming army garrison commander during the second week in March.[201]

Some of the marine pioneers and more of the corps shore party continued to help the army units working along the coasts. Most of these marines, however, moved inshore to more dangerous pursuits. Many were thrown into front line fighting.

These personnel, and especially the battle replacements, were so inexperienced in infantry-demolition-tank coordination that the decision to employ them in this work must be scrutinized. There was at least a partial alternative to such a course of action. The Third

Marine Regiment of the Third Division was not landed. In fact, Smith never released these infantrymen from Expeditionary Troops reserve. Instead, the rifle battalions of the Third Marines were shipped back to Guam on March 5,[202] just at the moment when high casualties meant that more and more battle replacements were needed for front line action.

Several times Schmidt requested that the Third Marine Regiment be released to corps, but Smith refused. Smith, after consultation with Turner, turned down Schmidt's request because enough men to take Iwo were already ashore and because of enemy fire on the cluttered waist of the island.[203] It is true that on March 5, every American on Iwo was in range of enemy machine guns, but by this date both Suribachi and the central ridge had been cleared and the waist was free from flat-trajectory fire. Artillery, mortar, and rocket bursts were still being received, but the number was relatively low and steadily declining; and this fire on the waist of the island lacked accuracy since it was pre-registered rather than observed.

Most of the battle replacements were thrown into the fighting. It could hardly have been otherwise, since casualties in one battalion of the Fourth Division reached an estimated fifty per cent on the first day; and thereafter deterioration was rapid in all units until at the end of the struggle, from sixty to seventy per cent of the personnel in all infantry components were out of action. Had no battle replacements been committed the percentages would have been higher. Some rifle companies and platoons, not counting the replacements, set their casualty figures at almost 100 per cent.[204] One battalion commander said his companies were so depleted "that appearance of a war dog and its handlers seemed like heavy reinforcements." [205]

The consequences of using battle replacements rather than landing the infantrymen of the Third Regiment and shortening the fronts of the units in the line are, in retrospect, evident. Completing the assault was delayed. Key personnel in the front lines were unduly exposed, and casualties relative to resistance encountered began to increase both among regular infantrymen and among the battle replacements.

All casualties were superbly handled by the naval medical units assigned to the marines. No one was more dangerously exposed than the marine litter bearers who treated wounds in the front lines, and carried the injured back to aid stations. During the early phase of the fighting, both aid and evacuation stations were subjected to accurate enemy rocket, mortar, and artillery fire.

Medical plans were well drawn and executed. Divisional and corps components were integrated by the medical officers on the staffs of Smith and Schmidt, and they offered the injured specialized treatment, such as transfusions with whole blood, never before realized in the Pacific War. Evacuation by both sea and air was prompt.[206] One must agree with Schmidt's operations officer who claimed that "the medical service for the Iwo Jima operation approached nearer the ideal than during any previous operations in the Central Pacific Area, and it is firmly believed that the casualties received the maximum medical care possible commensurate with the military situation." [207]

6. The Significance of Iwo Jima

Seizing Iwo cost more than 5,500 marine, navy, and army personnel killed in action, plus over three and one-half times that number wounded or otherwise incapacitated; but it was worth the price. Within three months after being secured, its fields had served as a haven for United States airmen very nearly double in number the total dead sustained in assault. Before the end of the Pacific War, more than 20,000 crewmen in crippled planes had come down safely on Iwo Jima. Roughly one-fourth of these flyers would have been lost if the island had not been in American hands.[208]

But the value of Iwo can not be correctly measured in terms of lives lost and saved. The air assault on Japan is the important consideration. The B-29 approach to Japan became direct, assisted by navigational aids at the half-way point; and long-range fighters accompanied the large bombers and protected them over their targets, thus allowing them to bomb with more precision at lower altitudes, which in turn saved even more fuel with a corresponding increase in the weight of explosives and incendiaries dropped. Iwo as a friendly base improved the morale of air crews in the Marianas; and the two fighter and one heavy bomber airfields carved on the island, along with continuing improvements and additions to the air facilities on Saipan, Tinian, and Guam, permitted a period of intense air attacks with more planes to be ushered in. American fighters and damaged bombers began using Iwo very early in March 1945; payloads of magnetic mines, explosives, and incendiaries of the very long range craft soaring northward from the Marianas to Japan jumped elevenfold during that month. Moreover, a naval air base was secured to allow low-level strikes at Japanese shipping in home waters, and the right flank of future offensives was protected.[209]

A high ranking Japanese officer on Iwo just before his death asserted that he was "spiritually . . . burning with delight and enjoying the peace of mind," since he ascribed American success in the assault to "material superiority." [210] There is a large element of truth in the excuse offered by this Japanese, but American leadership, doctrine, training, courage, and tenacity must be added. The point is that during the Pacific War every defensive obstacle manned by the Japanese in the Central Pacific was overcome by America's offensive naval power.

Just as the amphibious assault was, after Gallipoli, classified as a victim to modern developments in gunnery and aircraft, so today is it being considered, along with all amphibious operations for that matter, as terminated by the atom bomb. Resignation to such a conclusion will stifle further technological developments and will result, should the world again erupt in war, in an interhemispheric attrition destructive of civilization. America will never knowingly follow this course.

The strategy successfully employed at Iwo was a combination of control of the sea and air, plus an overwhelming firepower from naval guns and planes against the objective, and a well-equipped assault force highly versed in amphibious tactics.

Given these advantages, it is hard to conceive of a target more difficult for the amphibious assault than was Iwo Jima. The nation that could take Iwo can, by keeping abreast of technological improvements favorable to the attacker, always seize overseas objectives held by hostile powers.

The basic records on Iwo were largely destroyed during the struggle, and Kuribayashi will never be subjected to the scrutiny which Spruance, Turner, Smith, Hill, Blandy, and Schmidt must endure in the light of history; but aside from opening up on the American underwater demolition team gunboats on the morning of February 17, it is impossible from the evidence available to find a flaw in Kuribayashi's plans and in their execution. Every adverse criticism of the conduct of the Japanese on Iwo is more than countered by other considerations. Nothing underscores this more than the enemy's employment of his artillery. He was unable to mass fires, but had he done so, America's counterbattery of naval, artillery, and air weapons would have demolished the guns of the Japanese.

The conclusion is that regardless of the size of the island, the difficulty of its terrain, and the degree of its man-made defensive perfection, it can be seized by the amphibious assault if it is isolated by surface and air superiority and prepared by naval bombardment and bombing. That is the lesson of Iwo Jima. Failure of the American commanders always to keep the full benefit of their doctrine and material superiority only reemphasizes that lesson. The Japanese in Iwo's prepared defenses, by subjecting the marines to a most arduous assault, provided at the same time the supreme test for the concept of offensive warfare involved; and once any service perfects the amphibious assault, the same techniques applied to an amphibious operation against a sizeable land mass assures the success of these larger and more important undertakings.

CHAPTER XI

OKINAWA, SPRINGBOARD TO JAPAN

"The Great Lew Chew was seen from the ships, as they approached, at the distance of more than twenty miles, and, when near enough to render objects distinguishable, presented a very inviting appearance. . . . The shores of the island were green and beautiful from the water, diversified with groves and fields of the freshest verdure. The rain had brightened the colors of the landscape, which recalled to my mind the richest English scenery. The swelling hills which rose immediately from the water's edge, increased in height towards the center of the island, and were picturesquely broken by abrupt rocks and crags, which, rising here and there, gave evidence of volcanic action. Woods, apparently of cedar or pine, ran along the crests of the hills, while their slopes were covered with gardens and fields of grain. To the northward the hills were higher, and the coast jutted out in two projecting headlands, showing that there were deep bays or indentations between." [1]

The date of these remarks was May of 1853; the occasion, Commodore Matthew C. Perry's visit to the island of Okinawa en route from Shanghai to Japan. Perry's visit was viewed by the islanders with mixed feelings of amazement and alarm. He and his party were not the first white men they had seen, since they had been preceded by a British naval expedition. However, the Commodore's studious contempt for the feelings of the native population, reinforced as it was by the firepower of his naval squadron, was ill suited to allay any doubts they may have entertained about the benefits of contact with western civilization. With the typical arrogance of mid-nineteenth century occidentals in their contact with the orient, all of Perry's moves were calculated to inspire fear, respect, and suspicion. He declined to receive the lesser dignitaries of the local government because "it was not meet that he should be made too common in the eyes of the vulgar." [2] He forced his way into the royal palace at Shuri against the obvious wishes of the regent who was attending him, and generally behaved in as high-handed a manner as possible.

1. Geography and Planning

The next American intrusion upon the privacy of the Okinawans was of a more serious nature. Ninety-two years after Perry's expedition, this island became the final target in the great amphibious sweep across the Central Pacific conducted by the United States and her allies in their war against the Japanese Empire. Meanwhile it had been annexed by Japan (in 1879) and assimilated into her economy and culture. Its seizure in 1945 was considered essential to the expected assault against the Japanese homeland.

Okinawa lies near the middle of a long chain of islands stretching almost 800 miles between Kyushu and Formosa. The old name of Lew Chew by which Perry knew them has been dropped by most cartographers in exchange for the modern appelation, the Ryukyu Archipelago or, in Japanese, the Nansei Shoto. Okinawa itself is more than sixty statute miles long with a width varying from eighteen miles to two miles in the portion known as the Ishikawa Isthmus. (See maps 15 and 22.) Like most of its Pacific counterparts it is fringed with coral reef, although on the west coast this lies close to the shore and offers no serious impediment to an invading force equipped with modern amphibious gear. Along the central spine of the island runs a mountainous ridge whose highest point is 1,500 feet above sea level. The northern portion, above the coast on which the American forces were to land, is wild country, mountainous and covered with stunted pine. South of the Ishikawa Isthmus the country levels off somewhat but is cut by several east-west ridges which provide an ideal natural defense against an enemy moving down from the north. The most formidable of these ridges, cut by sheer cliffs and deep valleys, extends west of ancient Shuri Castle and was to cause untold grief to the invading forces. East of Shuri lies the Nakagusuku Wan, or Bay, an adequate anchorage for shallow-draft vessels with good protection against anything but high winds and heavy seas from the southeast. This was later renamed Buckner Bay after Lieutenant General Simon Bolivar Buckner, Jr. USA, commanding general of the American troops who was killed in action only a few days before victory was complete.

West of Okinawa by about fifteen miles lies the Kerama Retto, another little group of islands of which none is larger than six square miles. These are situated so as to provide a natural harbor in their midst, where heavy ships could be safely anchored for resupply and repairs. To the northwest barely three miles off the tip of Motobu Peninsula lies another little island, Ie Shima whose capture would be necessary to secure American control of the area. West and north of Ie were situated Aguni Shima and the Iheya Rhetto, both practically unoccupied and of no military significance except that they could be utilized as radar bases to detect enemy aircraft flying down from the mainland of Japan.[3]

Planning for this first penetration into the inner defenses of the Japanese empire began in early October 1944, even before General

MacArthur had invaded the Philippines. The strategic objectives were simple and logical. Okinawa lies only 350 miles from Kyushu and not much further from Formosa and the coast of China. Its capture by American forces would give them numerous sites for airfields from which planes of almost any type could easily reach the industrial areas of southern Japan. Its indented coast line offered some of the best fleet anchorages in the western Pacific and its size and location would make it an excellent staging base for further operations against the Japanese homeland.[4] Moreover, even if an actual invasion of the Japanese homeland were not to be carried out, American occupation of Okinawa would be of enormous strategic value to American forces in the Pacific. Okinawa was so situated as to permit American naval and air power to control the East China Sea and its adjoining waters, which include the approaches to Korea, Manchuria, Formosa and the North China coast as well as to Japan proper.[5]

Admiral Nimitz, as Commander-in-Chief, Pacific Ocean Areas, issued his warning order on October 9, 1944, designating Admiral Spruance as officer in command of the entire Ryukyus campaign, with Vice Admiral Turner to command the Joint Expeditionary Force and Lieutenant General Simon B. Buckner as the head of the Expeditionary Troops ashore. On December 31, Nimitz issued his operation plan directing Spruance to capture, occupy, defend, and develop air and naval bases on Okinawa, to gain and maintain control of the entire Nansei Shoto area, and to protect air and sea communication along the Central Pacific axis. All forces of the Pacific Fleet and the Pacific Ocean Areas were assigned supporting tasks, and the target date was designated April 1, 1945.

As the campaign opened, American forces had established air and naval bases in New Guinea, the Marshalls, Marianas, Admiralties, Western Carolines, Palaus, Iwo Jima, Leyte, Mindoro, and Luzon. Operations were continuing in the Philippines, and Iwo Jima was being slowly mopped up. Enemy naval power was still something of a threat although the Japanese forces had been so reduced that the possibility of any large-scale sortie of surface combat ships was slight. Suicide tactics by both Japanese planes and high-powered small craft were expected.[6]

According to the original plan the entire Ryukyus campaign was to be divided into three phases. The first contemplated the seizure of the Kerama Retto and Keise Shima about a week prior to landings on the main island, which were to be employed as a fleet anchorage and heavy artillery base. Following this the southern portion of Okinawa, south of the Ishikawa Isthmus, was to be seized. Phase two was to include the capture of Ie Shima and the occupation of the remaining northern part of Okinawa. Finally during the third phase the occupation of the

Nansei Shoto was to be completed by the seizure of Miyako Shima, almost half way from Okinawa to Formosa, and Okino Daito, a little island about 180 miles to the southeast of Okinawa.[7]

As the fighting developed, however, fairly drastic changes had to be made in the original plan. The last two mentioned islands were bypassed entirely, and the retirement of the main Japanese forces to the southern end of Okinawa where they put up their strongest defenses made it necessary to reverse the order in which American troops would occupy the southern and northern parts of the island.

In general, the principal strategic features of the operation were as follows. A naval gunfire and support force, by far the largest in the history of amphibious operations, began preparing Okinawa and its satellite islands seven days before the day of the main landings to soften enemy defenses, destroy aircraft, neutralize airfields, and sweep the surrounding waters for mines. The same force provided continuous gunfire support for the expeditionary troops throughout the entire period of fighting ashore. Meanwhile, prior to the scheduled landing day, planes from Spruance's Fifth Fleet under the tactical command of Vice Admiral Marc A. Mitscher struck Japan, the Sakishima Gunto, and Okinawa and thereafter provided air cover and some direct support for ground troops. A British carrier task force operating under the Fifth Fleet assisted in the neutralization of Formosa and Bakishima Gunto and covered the western flank against hostile surface and aircraft. Navy search planes based at Kerama Retto and Okinawa supported the operations through air reconnaissance of the East China Sea and attacked hostile shipping and aircraft, while other aircraft conducted antisubmarine patrol, air-sea rescue, and photographic reconnaissance. The heavy bombers of the Army's Strategic Air Force, Pacific Ocean Areas, operating from bases in the Marianas, hit Okinawa from time to time before the troops landed in order to soften up the enemy, destroy his aircraft, neutralize his airfields, and conduct further photographic reconnaissance. Another army organization, the Twenty-first Bomber Command of the Twentieth Air Force, operating also from the Marianas, contributed by striking Japan, especially airfields and installations on Kyushu. The Pacific Fleet's submarine force carried on reconnaissance, attacked enemy surface craft, conducted photographic missions, and provided weather reports.

This far-flung activity involving so many ships, planes, and men from such a variety of units was of course all ancillary to the main strategic objective which was the seizure of Okinawa and the surrounding islands. The Landing Force was the newly activated Tenth Army under Buckner's command. The assault troops were divided into a northern and southern landing force. Responsibility for the northern portion of Okinawa was assigned to the Third Amphibious

Corps under Major General Roy S. Geiger USMC, and consisted of the First and Sixth Marine Divisions. To the south was assigned the XXIV United States Army Corps under Major General John R. Hodge USA. It included the 7th, 96th, and 77th Infantry Divisions. Also assigned to that operation was a demonstration force, the Second Marine Division, and a floating reserve, the 27th Infantry Division. An area reserve, the 81st Infantry Division, was kept under Nimitz's control to be assigned to the Tenth Army only when and if needed. The total troops committed, including the Second Marine Division, only one regiment of which actually landed on Okinawa, came to 541,866 men. The ships employed to make and support the landing, exclusive of the vessels of the fast carrier task force, numbered 1,213.[8]

Okinawa was to be invaded on April 1, 1945. By a freak of coincidence the troops were to be set ashore on a day that was jointly celebrated both as Easter and April Fool's Day, a bit of irony that escaped the notice of no newspaper reporter then nor of any commentator since. Before the main landing two regiments of the 77th Infantry Division and a reconnaissance battalion from Fleet Marine Force, Pacific, supported by an appropriate task force of naval support vessels, landed on March 26 on the five principal islands of the Kerama Retto. (See map 22.) They met with minor resistance, and by March 30 Major General Andrew D. Bruce USA declared the islands secure. The next day Keise Shima, a little group of coral islets barely visible at high tide and some five miles east of Kerama, was seized without opposition by an army artillery group. A valuable base had been secured for sea planes and for refuelling and repairing surface ships. On Keise, heavy artillery could be mounted to bombard southern Okinawa, only eight miles distant. A final windfall at Kerama came in the form of the capture of from three to four hundred Japanese suicide boats. These were little plywood craft (each carrying two depth charges) whose mission was to swarm out at night among the transport vessels of the American landing force and sink or damage as many as possible while troops were still aboard. This was a tactic that had been used before but never to any such degree as contemplated in this operation. The troops and navy personnel who were now slowly approaching Okinawa had reason to be grateful for the quick work done by the Western Island Attack Group (Navy) and the men of the 77th Infantry Division.[9]

2. *Narrative of the Fighting*

The hour for the main landing was 0830 following the usual minesweeping, underwater demolition reconnaissance, and ever-accelerating naval and aerial bombardment. All along the seven mile front the landings on Hagushi beaches on the southwest coast came off on schedule or nearly so. (See map 22.) From left to right (north to south) were embarked the Sixth Marine Division, the First Marine Division, the 7th Infantry Division, and the 96th Infantry Division, each landing two regimental combat teams abreast. There was sporadic mortar and artillery fire on the beaches but not enough to cause any serious damage, and casualties for the first day were unprecedentedly low. By evening the Tenth Army with approximately 50,000 troops ashore had secured a beachhead of 3,000 to 5,000 yards inland. Eight combat teams, three artillery battalions, and approximately 15,000 service troops had been landed. Everyone from the highest ranking admirals and generals to the lowest private was amazed—and relieved.[10]

Oddly enough, the only serious casualties occurred in the ranks of the Second Marine Division, Major General LeRoy P. Hunt commanding, which was not actually committed to the main landing but whose job was to conduct a demonstration off the southern coast of the island. Shortly after dawn and well before the scheduled feint was to take place, the transports and tank landing ships carrying marines of this division made their acquaintance with Japan's most fantastic weapon of the war, the kamikaze or "Divine Wind," suicide aircraft whose mission was to crash into American vessels. This was by no means the first time the Japanese had used suicide aerial tactics, but it was significant because the Japanese exploited this weapon in the Ryukyus far more fully than in any previous campaign. In fact, the kamikaze had been organized as early as October 19, 1944, in preparation for the impending attack against the Philippines which was launched the next day. The philosophy which lay behind it was not different from that which motivated Japanese infantry troops in their famous banzai charges. As Captain Rikibei Inoguchi IJN, Chief of Staff of their First Air Fleet, later put it: "We Japanese base our lives on obedience to Emperor and Country. On the other hand, we wish for the best place in death, according to Bushido. Kamikaze originates from these feelings. . . . By this means we can accomplish peace. In view of this—from this standpoint, the kamikaze deserved the consideration of the whole world." [11]

Certainly the Second Marine Division and the navy personnel in the ships carrying them had good reason to give "consideration" to the kamikaze. One transport and a tank landing ship were squarely hit, and both put out of action. But in spite of heavy casualties, the diversionary feint was carried off successfully, as was a similar maneuver on the following day. Small craft were launched and headed in toward the beaches in waves of from nine to twelve, turned back before landing and were recovered by their mother ships. The effectiveness of the demonstration is difficult to assess, but at least one news

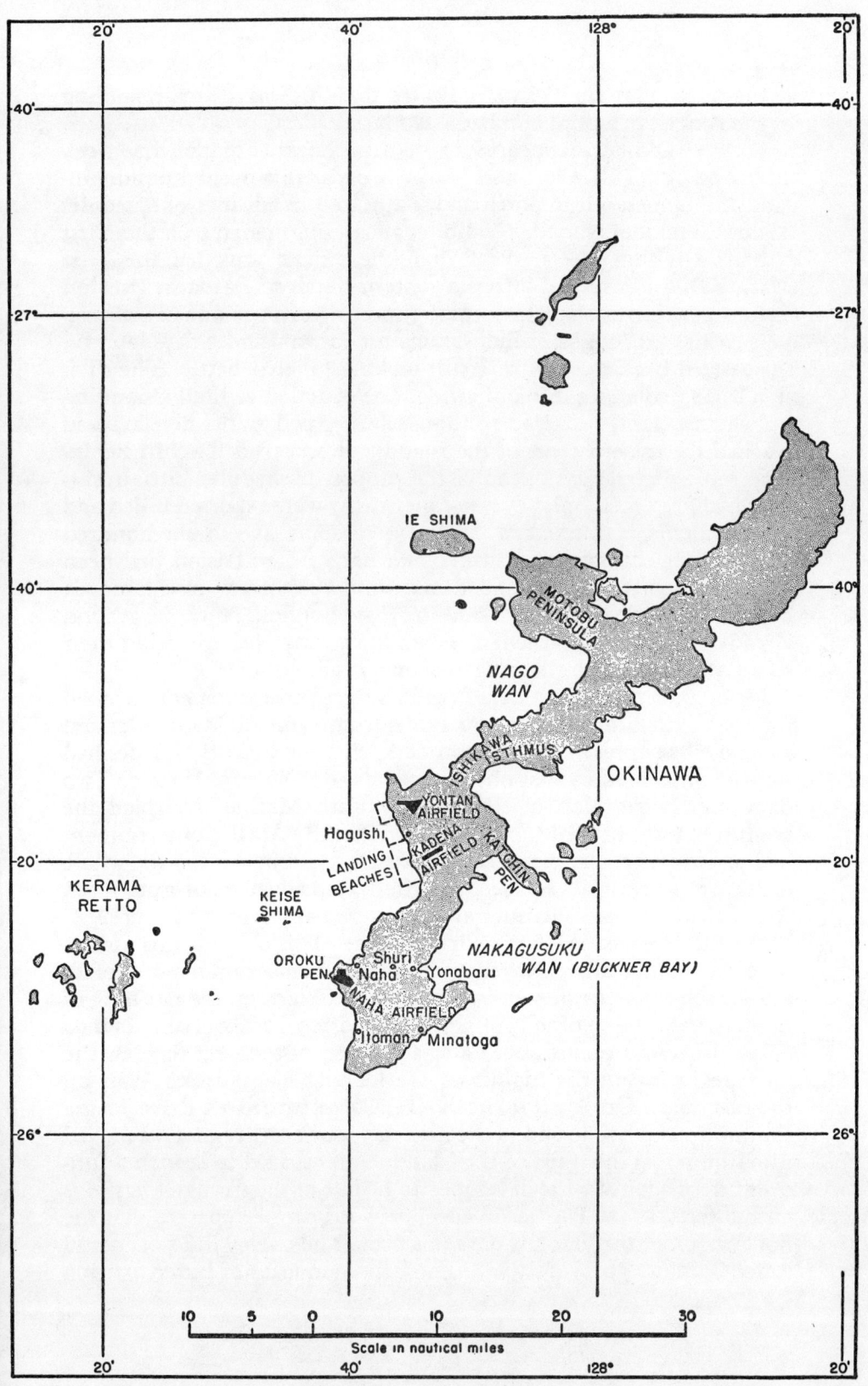

MAP 22. Okinawa and nearby islands.

broadcast from radio Tokyo, indicated that this was the main landing of the American troops and had been repulsed.[12]

Fortress Okinawa appeared to be a pushover. For the first week ashore troops of all Army and Marine Corps units pushed rapidly inland and fanned out to north and south, well in advance of schedule. Major General Pedro del Valle, commanding general of the First Marine Division, declared: "When the assault waves of the First Marine Division surged into the western slopes of Okinawa Jima on Easter morning of 1945, they came expecting to wage one of the costliest battles yet fought in the war against Japan—and 3 days later on the eastern beaches they were still looking for that battle. The division had raced across its 9-mile-wide zone of action virtually 'standing up' against light, scattered resistance." By April 4 this division had reached the eastern coast of the island and occupied Katchin Peninsula, some eleven days ahead of the proposed schedule. Little resistance had been met; only seventy-nine enemy were reported killed and two prisoners of war taken, exclusive of some five to six hundred civilians. By contrast only twelve marines in the division had been killed with thirty-four wounded in action. For the rest of the month del Valle's men had virtually nothing to do but hold on to the ground already seized, mop up the few remaining enemy pockets within their sector and keep on the alert against enemy ambushes.[13]

Meanwhile to the northward matters were proceeding equally well for the Sixth Marine Division under command of Major General Lemuel C. Shepherd, Jr. By noon of April 1 the Fourth Marines had seized and secured its first objective which was Yontan Airfield. Two days later a battalion of the Twenty-ninth Marines occupied the peninsula just north of the landing beaches. By April 4 one regiment had penetrated to the east coast of the island and by April 7 the whole of Ishikawa Peninsula was secured after rapid advances of from seven to ten thousand yards daily against scattered and light resistance.[14]

On the right flank of the First Marine Division, the two assault divisions of the army moved with almost equal rapidity although against somewhat greater resistance. By ten o'clock on the morning of the landing, one regiment of the 7th Division had overrun Kadena Airfield without opposition. Early afternoon of the next day saw the same regiment on the highlands overlooking Nagagusuku Wan on the east coast. On April 3 the XXIV Corps turned its drive to the southward and by the end of the next day four army regiments moved into line across the waist of the island and prepared to launch a full-scale attack against what developed to be one of the strongest bastions encountered in the Pacific.[15] Very shortly it became apparent that the honeymoon of the first few days was over. The enemy did not intend to let Okinawa go by default. Almost three months of bitter fighting lay ahead before the welcome news was to come to weary soldiers and marines that the island was officially "secured."

Why had the Japanese decided not to defend the beaches with anything but a nominal show of opposition? Why had they chosen instead to withdraw the major part of their forces to the southern part of the island and wage a slow war of attrition against overwhelming odds? One answer is that they were at last beginning to appreciate the lessons which had been so forcefully pounded home from Tarawa to Iwo Jima. That is they were at last beginning to appreciate the difficulty if not the impossibility of turning aside the invading forces at the beachhead. The power and accuracy of naval gunfire and aerial bombardment, the clockwork efficiency of the ship-to-shore movement, the perfected organization of the amphibious assault in all its features were convincing arguments against setting up a main defense line on the beachhead. Okinawa, although it did not develop into an amphibious assault, was in the end the highest conceivable tribute to the amphibious skills which had been slowly evolved throughout the war and for better than a decade before. American forces had apparently revolutionized one of the best established precepts of war—that an amphibious landing against a hostile shore was one of the most difficult maneuvers to execute and by the same token one of the easiest to thwart. That the reverse position was taken by Lieutenant General Mitsuru Ushijima IJA in command of the 32nd Japanese Army on Okinawa is testimony enough to the terrible potency of American amphibious warfare in the spring of 1945.

Another reason for the Japanese decision not to defend the beachhead was the development of kamikaze. Although initiated in the Central Philippine campaign and employed on a minor scale at Luzon and Iwo Jima, not until the Ryukyus invasion were these tactics used extensively by the Japanese. A definite organization was established for the employment of suicide units, and both army and navy air forces assigned to the defense of these islands were placed under a single tactical command operating from bases on Kyushu. The major attacks were carried out from April 6 to June 22 employing a total of 1,465 planes. In addition a number of sporadic small-scale attacks were launched from Formosa and elsewhere, bringing the total number of suicide sorties to about 1,900. The net result was to sink through suicide attacks twenty-six American naval vessels and to damage 164 others, causing unprecedented naval casualties during the campaign.[16]

Although this aerial frightfulness failed in the end to achieve the desired results, its employment does explain in part the withdrawal of the major Japanese forces to southern Okinawa. A decisive land battle was to be avoided at all costs until kamikaze planes, aided by the now battered surface fleet, could destroy or rout the American naval forces. Then, once deprived of naval gunfire and logistical support, the enemy could be lured into the wild mountainous country south of Machinato and bled to death in futile attack.[17]

The Japanese defense of southern Okinawa was well conceived and well executed. (See map 23.) As del Valle later remarked, "The length of the battle, eighty-two days, and the American casualties, now over 35,000 dead and wounded, bear silent witness to the effectiveness of the enemy's effort." [18] Generally speaking the defensive forces were disposed in great depth, which enabled the ranking Japanese commander, Ushijima, to stop the American advance with a minimum number of troops deployed across a comparatively narrow front. His defenses made admirable use of the terrain, which in itself constituted a strong barrier to any attack from the north. The enemy established three successive main defense lines, each of them occupying a critical terrain feature—a single ridge or series of ridges and hill masses lying generally east and west across the island perpendicular to the American line of advance. The first of these was along Kakazu Ridge, the second and strongest in the area was north of Shuri Castle, and the third ran east from the town of Itoman to Gushichan through the central terrain bulwarks of Yuza-Dake and Yaeju-Dake.

Each of these lines was held in great strength until it became untenable. Then the bulk of the enemy's forces withdrew to the next position, leaving behind small suicidal holding forces to delay the American advance through the line. Caves, which were abundant in the area, were exploited to their fullest possibility, reminiscent of Peleliu and Iwo Jima. Where there were not enough natural caves, artificial ones were dug. Each cave was made the center of an infantry strong point. Automatic weapons and sometimes light artillery pieces were placed inside well-concealed mouths, while foxholes and rifle pits guarded each against the inevitable close-quarter attack of infantry and tank-infantry teams. Since all the hills ran east and west the Japanese were ideally situated to exploit reverse slope positions to their best advantage. No hill could be secured until the rear slope was occupied and cleared of all enemy troops, a task which the Japanese opposed ferociously. Also they employed artillery more extensively and effectively than in any previous Pacific operation, although massed fire, that is fire of more than one battery on the same position, was not used here any more than it had been in earlier battles. Artillery fires were delivered primarily against front line troops and showed remarkable accuracy. In addition it became plain that the Japanese had developed an efficient defensive system against the tank-infantry team, on which American tactical plans relied more heavily for seizure of this fairly large land mass than ever before. Knowing that tanks were almost always employed in conjunction with infantry, the enemy first attempted to isolate the tank by mortar and artillery fire on it and the accompanying personnel. Once the infantry had been put out of action the isolated tank was then subjected to intense 47-millimeter fire. If none of these measures prevailed, antitank assault teams carrying satchel charges and antitank mines tried to rush the target under cover of smoke and destroy it—and presumably themselves.[19]

Such was the nature of defenses and terrain against which the two army divisions prepared to launch their drive on April 4. These were from left to right (east to west) the 7th and 96th Infantry Divisions who were ordered to drive ahead and seize as rapidly as possible the first of the more formidable natural defense barriers, Kakazu Ridge. Progress was slow and bloody. Around the Kakazu hills the Japanese had raised one of the strongest positions on Okinawa, with an ample supply of mortars dug in on the reverse slopes. An intricate system of coordinated pillboxes, tunnels, and caves enabled machine guns to be brought to bear against all avenues of approach. From the south, the area was protected by heavy and light artillery pieces emplaced around Shuri. From April 9 to 12, elements of the 96th Infantry Division drove up to the crest of the ridge, were thrown back, drove up again only to achieve a stalemate, while on their left the 7th Division was not much more successful. But the enemy was being bled. His losses on April 12 in the XXIV Corps zone of action were estimated to be about 5,750 killed against 451 for the two army divisions. A full-scale and well-coordinated counterattack delivered against the positions of the 96th Division on the 13th was stopped in its tracks and for the following week both sides stopped to rest, consolidate, and lick their wounds.[20] It became obvious that more manpower would have to be thrown into the line if the enemy was to be driven from his strongly entrenched position.

Meanwhile to the north two separate but by no means insignificant battles were being waged, one by the Sixth Marine Division for the capture of Motobu Peninsula and the northern part of the island, the other by the 77th Infantry Division for the occupation of Ie Shima, a small island lying a few miles off Motobu. (See map 22.)

Upon arrival at the base of the Motobu Peninsula, the Sixth Marine Division was confronted with the problem of reorienting for operations aimed at the reduction of the peninsula and at the same time maintaining the security of its northern flank. Consequently on April 8 the Twenty-second Marines were deployed across the island so as to cover the right and rear of the Twenty-ninth Marines, who were assigned the task of probing into the peninsula proper. The Fourth Marines were assembled in a condition of readiness in the vicinity of Ora where they might be used either to participate in the Motobu operation, support the Twenty-second Marines on the northern flank, or conduct offensive operations further north. On the morning of the 8th the Twenty-ninth Marines moved up in three columns, one along the northern and one down the southern coast of the peninsula with a third in the center, all trying to locate the enemy's main force.

There were scattered ambushes and counterattacks, but by April 12 it became clear that the main enemy force was located in the area of Mount Yaetake and that it consisted of an estimated 1,500 troops including infantry and artillery. Mount Yaetake had been intelligently selected and thoroughly organized. Its commanding elevations (as high as 1,500 feet in places) provided excellent observation of Nago Wan and of Ie Shima. The terrain was so rough that tanks and other mechanized equipment were virtually useless. Organization of the ground had obviously progressed over a long period, and all likely avenues of approach were heavily mined. Additional troops would clearly be necessary, and the Fourth Marines were thrown into the fight. A coordinated attack was planned with the Fourth Marines and the Third Battalion, Twenty-ninth Marines, driving inland in an easterly direction while the Twenty-ninth Marines drove west and southwest in an effort to reduce the enemy position by action from two flanks and isolate his forces on Mount Yaetake from those in the northern tip of the peninsula. The height of the hill mass intervening between the two assault regiments permitted the rare situation wherein two large forces could attack in opposing directions without great danger of overlapping supporting fires.

After three days of the most rugged mountain fighting, the objective was achieved. By nightfall of the 16th the Fourth Marines had seized the Yaetake hill mass while the Twenty-ninth Marines had swung their front to west and north destroying fixed emplacements and isolated enemy groups. Infantry combat was at short ranges, and the cave and pillbox positions demanded the heavy employment of demolitions. At the end of the operation, marine casualties reached 207 killed, 757 wounded, and 6 missing. The enemy loss was reported as 2,014 dead, indicating heavier resistance than had been anticipated. By April 19 the rest of the peninsula was mopped up, and two days later marines of the Twenty-second Regiment had reached the northernmost tip of the island, having completed the twenty-five mile advance in a series of tank-motorized infantry thrusts. Thereafter the Sixth Marine Division settled down to patrol the area and mop up minor pockets of resistance until May, when it was relieved by the 27th Infantry Division.[21]

With the attack on Motobu progressing so rapidly, Buckner decided that it was feasible to invade Ie Shima earlier than originally contemplated. The 77th Division, which had been resting since its capture of the Kerama Retto, was assigned the task, and the landing date was set for April 16. The usual intensive bombardment from air and sea was initiated. Underwater demolition teams reconnoitered the area, and on April 12-13 the Amphibious Reconnaissance Battalion of the Fleet Marine Force, Pacific, occupied nearby Minna Island without a contest for use as an artillery emplacement. The actual landing differed in no significant detail from what had become standard operating procedure. Battleships, cruisers, and destroyers opened fire at dawn; amphibious support ships of various types swept the landing beaches with rockets, mortars, and machine-gun fire. Planes bombed and rocketed the entire island. Tank landing ships debarked the troops loaded in amphibious tractors which were in turn escorted close to the water's edge by rocket-firing infantry landing craft. The first troops got ashore at 0758, two minutes before the scheduled landing time.

Although a fairly rapid capture of this little island only five by three miles in size had been anticipated, events proved these predictions overoptimistic. In fact, Ie Shima was much better defended than intelligence had expected, and as usual the enemy made the most of terrain features, the most distinctive being a single pinnacle-like mountain which rose to an elevation of over 1,200 feet on the island's eastern end. Not until April 21 was the summit of this pinnacle reached by elements of the 77th Division, and then only after three days of fighting which their commanding general, Major General Andrew D. Bruce USA, characterized as "the bitterest I have ever witnessed." [22] With this last threat to complete security in the northern sector of Okinawa removed, full attention could now be turned by all forces to the final job of liquidating the remainder of the enemy still entrenched on the southern slopes of the Kakazu Ridge and below it. Although less than a fifth of the total area of the Okinawa group remained to be seized, it was to take two months to do it—more than twice the time and many more times the manpower and ammunition than had so far been expended during the operation.

Initially the job of cracking the several defense rings which centered on Shuri was assigned exclusively to the army. (See map 23.) The first full-scale attack began on April 19 on a three division front. On the right (west) was the 27th Infantry Division which had been landed ten days earlier, in the center the 96th, and on the left the 7th. The first day of the attack ended in complete failure in all three sectors. Everywhere enemy artillery and mortar fire kept the attacking troops pinned down. In 27th Division's area one column of thirty tanks managed to by-pass Kakazu Ridge and penetrate into the village of Kakazu to the southward. However, since they were unsupported by infantry they were compelled to withdraw. Only eight survived the maneuver. Nowhere were any significant advances made, and the total count of casualties for this one day's action was 720. Furthermore, as a result of the 27th Division's effort to by-pass Kakazu Ridge, a mile wide gap lay between it and the 96th Division on its left. Altogether the prospects at the day's end looked dim.

For the next five days the three army divisions of the XXIV Corps attacked along the ridge line held by the enemy, and finally by April 24 the Japanese line had been so badly battered and penetrated in so many places that the enemy was forced to withdraw from this first outpost line of resistance. Kakazu Ridge and the high ground to its eastward were finally overrun. Only on the extreme west of the line in the sector of the 165th Infantry Regiment (27th Division) was progress retarded. By April 27 the regiment succeeded in clearing out the heavily defended sector which was its target area. Still ahead, however, lay Yonabaru Airfield, and two miles to the southward was the main defense line of Shuri bristling with caves, pillboxes, and with men and guns to protect them.[23]

For the next main drive against the second ring of enemy defenses a general shift of troops on the front line was ordered at the end of April. Meanwhile the original third phase of the Ryukyus campaign (the seizure of Miyako) had been cancelled, thus leaving Geiger's marines of the Third Amphibious Corps available for action on the southern front. Consequently on May 1 the First Marine Division relieved the 27th Infantry Division on the extreme right (west) of the line just north of Machinato Airfield. At about the same time, the badly battered 96th Division was taken out of the center and relieved by the relatively fresh 77th. Only the 7th Division on the left remained in position.[24]

For the next few days progress continued to be steady but slow in all zones. Then on May 4 came the first great counterattack launched by the Japanese. This was no banzai charge. It was a well-coordinated well-planned attack along the entire American line. It was preceded by heavy artillery fire, carried out by tank-infantry teams, and accompanied by a heavy kamikaze attack against American shipping and by an attempted amphibious counterlanding behind the lines of the First Marine Division on the west coast. This latter effort went awry when the enemy-laden boats put ashore to the south of their intended landing point and were intercepted by elements of the First Marine Division who easily thwarted the maneuver. To the east, however, where the main spearhead of the counterattack was thrust, one battalion of Japanese Infantry succeeded in penetrating the XXIV Corps lines between the 7th and 77th Divisions, retook Yonabaru Village and the escarpment behind it, finally reaching a point almost a mile to the rear of the American front line. There, however, the attack petered out, and finally General Ushijima realized its futility and

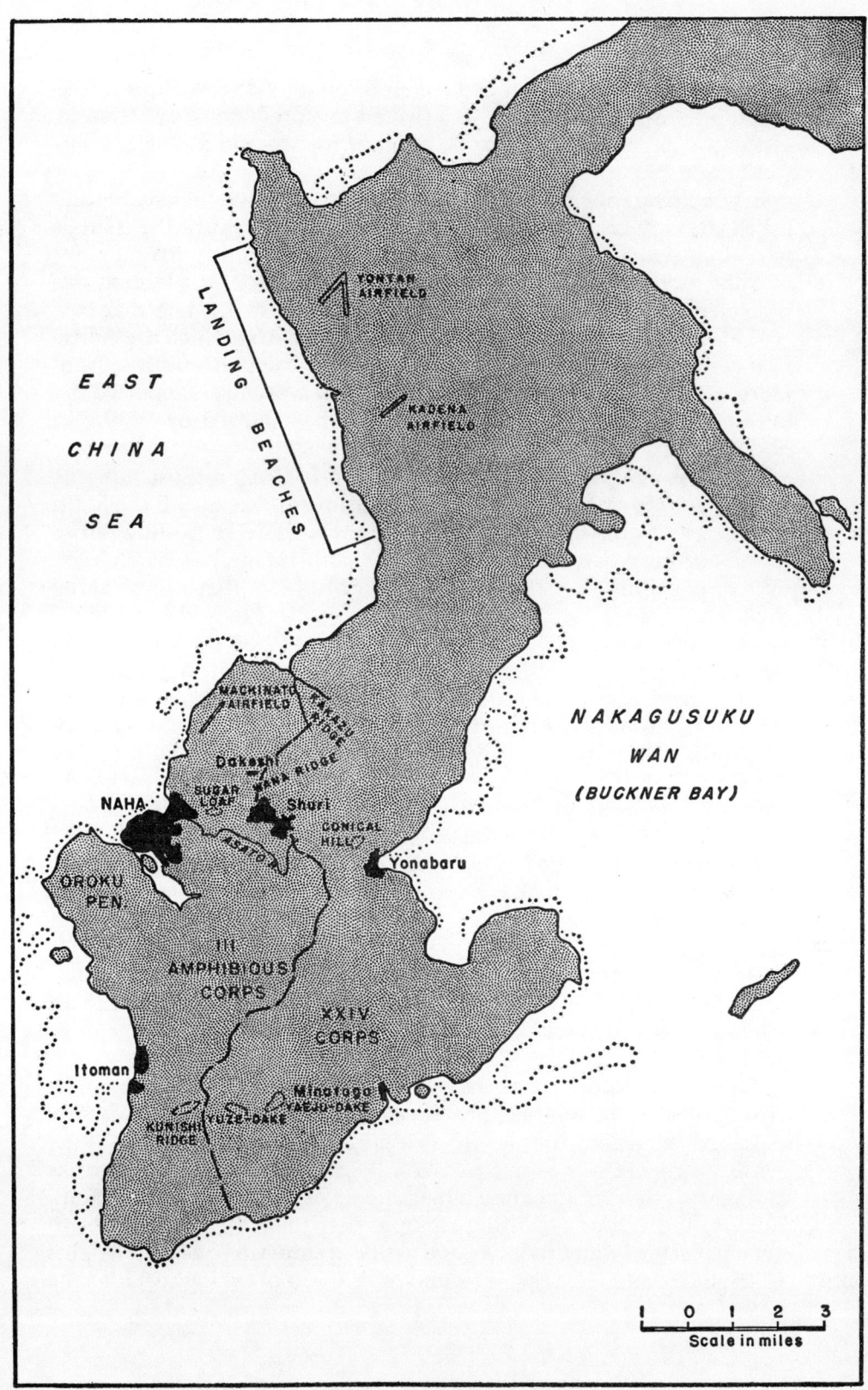

MAP 23. Southern Okinawa.

withdrew his forces, which had suffered some 5,000 casualties in the effort. Thereafter the Japanese returned to purely defensive strategy —a sound decision since it took another month and a half to overcome them.[25]

It was apparent by now that the Japanese commander had established the core of his defense at the fortress city of Shuri, the island's second largest, and had anchored it on either side at the coastal cities of Naha on the west and Yonabaru on the east. The Shuri bastion was protected on three sides by formidable cave-infested ridges that covered every approach and overlooked the ground over which the American troops would have to advance. Ushijima used his terrain advantages well. Every small emplacement was mutually supported by others, and in the end victory could only be achieved by sealing in or digging up every enemy soldier in the area.[26]

The first main attack by Buckner's Tenth Army against this line of defense was scheduled for May 11. Meanwhile on May 6 the Sixth Marine Division, which had been relieved from its patrolling duties in the northern part of the island by the 27th Infantry Division, took over responsibility for the extreme right of the southern line, taking the place of the First Marine Division which was moved to its left.[27] At the same time the 96th Infantry Division relieved the 7th Division on the extreme left. Thereafter the attack would continue on a two corps, four division front. From right to left (west to east) the Sixth Marine Division, the First Marine Division, the 77th Infantry Division and the 96th Infantry Division prepared for the big assault against the Shuri line. The plan called for an envelopment by the marine divisions on the west and the army divisions on the east, while a strong holding attack was to be maintained in the center.[28]

The principal attack was launched on May 11. As the fighting progressed it tended to break down into a series of uncoordinated battles for specific strong points all along the line. After ten days of brutal combat, the Shuri line began to crumble. The first stages of the collapse occurred on the two flanks of the defense line. With the capture of Sugar Loaf Hill on the west flank and of Conical Hill on the east an attempt at envelopment of the central fortress at Shuri could be initiated.

Sugar Loaf, just north of the Asato River and overlooking the principal city of Naha, was one member of a triangular and mutually supporting system forming the western anchor of the enemy's main defense system. It was a precipitous hill mass, well covered on flanks and rear by mortar and gun emplacements in surrounding elevations. Finally, the troops assaulting this position offered a clear target to enemy machine guns, mortars, and artillery emplaced on Shuri heights to their left and left rear. The unenviable job of taking it fell to the

Sixth Marine Division. Not yet realizing the strategic importance of the position, the Twenty-second Marines launched an infantry-tank assault on the hill in the late afternoon of May 14. After repeated unsuccessful attacks the executive officer of one battalion aptly concluded: "The only way we can take the top of this hill is to make a Jap banzai charge ourselves." Some of his troops did reach the crest of the hill, but by dawn of the 15th they were reduced to one officer and nineteen battle-weary men. For the next three days marines of the Twenty-second and Twenty-ninth Marine Regiments repeatedly slugged their way up Sugar Loaf and the surrounding hills only to be thrown back again. Finally by May 18 the position was taken; a violent counterattack that night was repulsed by artillery action and fresh troops of the Fourth Marines, which had relieved the badly shattered Twenty-ninth. The first fracture in the western anchor of the Shuri line was completed. It was the opinion of the commanding general of the division, Major General Lemuel C. Shepherd USMC, that: "Viewed in its analytical aspects, it . . . appears probable that plans for evacuation of the compromised Shuri position were initiated by the enemy upon loss of Sugar Loaf." The cost, however, was tremendous. During the ten-day period from the time of the crossing of the Asa-Kama River to the capture of this formidable hill, the division lost 2,662 marines killed and wounded.[29]

To the left of the Sixth Marine Division, the center of the Shuri line was assigned to the First Marine Division and the 77th Infantry Division. By May 15 the marines of the First Division had driven through the troublesome village of Dakeshi and the ridge that ran through it. Their next objective was Wana Ridge and the valley of the same name below it. Employing tank-infantry teams to their maximum capacity, advanced elements of the Fifth and Seventh Marines drove to the crest of Wana Ridge. By the 17th they had moved into the village for which the ridge was named, but their hold was tenuous. For four more days the outcome was in dispute, and not until the 21st was the position which lay on the outskirts of Shuri secured.[30]

Eastward in the zone of action assigned to the 77th Division progress was slow but steady. One company seized Ishimi Ridge and held on through three days of counterattacks by the Japanese with a loss of 156 out of an original number of 204 officers and men. Meanwhile on their left one battalion of the 306th Regiment succeeded in taking Chocolate Drop Hill, another important elevation commanding the approaches to Shuri. The most important action, however, took place on the extreme left in the sector of the 96th Division. With the capture of Conical Hill American troops could with relative ease pour down the corridor along Buckner Bay and attempt an envelopment of Shuri from the east.[31]

In fact, it would appear from subsequent Japanese testimony that the fall of Conical Hill was even more important than the capture of Sugar Loaf in persuading Ushijima to withdraw from Shuri. The Tenth Army's interrogation of the senior staff officer of the 32nd Japanese Army can be quoted to support that view: "On about 20 May it became apparent to the 32nd Army Staff that the line north of Shuri would be soon untenable. The pressure exerted upon the line from both Sugar Loaf and Conical Hill forced a decision as to whether or not to stage the last ditch stand at Shuri. The capture of Sugar Loaf Hill alone could have been solved by the withdrawal of the left flank to positions South of Naha and . . . would not have seriously endangered the defense of Shuri. However, the loss of remaining positions on Conical Hill in conjunction with the pressure in the west rendered the defense of Shuri extremely difficult." [32]

For the remainder of the month of May the attack slowed down almost to a standstill everywhere along the entire center of the line. Torrential rains, which began on May 22 and lasted until the 28th, rendered tanks and trucks and mounted guns immobile, and the infantry could do nothing without its armored support. In spite of the rain, the Sixth Marine Division crossed the Asato River and occupied the town of Naha, westernmost anchor of the Shuri line. These marines were now in a position to attack the center of the line from the flank and rear while those of the First Division and the soldiers of the 77th assaulted it from the front. Also on the extreme left the rested troops of the 7th Division penetrated into Yonabaru and well beyond. However, an attempt by the 32nd Infantry Regiment to envelope Shuri from the south and east bogged down in the rain. Then on May 29, ancient Shuri Castle, one time seat of Okinawa rulers and in a sense the modern symbol of the Japanese defense of the island, fell to the forces of the First Marine Division. By the last day of the month units of the First Marine Division closed their pincers on Shuri from the north and south, and, in a coordinated sweep with the 77th Infantry Division, cleared the area of its remaining enemy pockets.[33] This was the beginning of the end.

In fact, however, the decision to evacuate Shuri had been made more than a week earlier and immediately after the capture of Conical Hill on the east and Sugar Loaf Hill on the west. Ushijima decided on May 21 to move the bulk of his forces southward, and the transport of supplies and wounded began the following night. Although American pilots and observation outposts of the First Marine Division reported troop movements south of Shuri for the next few days, it was not until the 31st that the Tenth Army intelligence officers finally and fully realized that the enemy was merely holding Shuri with a thin shell of sacrificial troops and that the main part of his army had departed.[34]

In spite of the enemy's withdrawal from the Shuri line and in spite of Japanese heavy casualties, there was still considerable fight left in the enemy troops. It would take a full three weeks before the island could be declared secure. During the month of June there were two hotly contested areas which would have to be overcome by American troops. The first was the Oroku Peninsula, south and west of Naha. The second and even more inaccessible defense line was the southernmost ridge cutting east and west across the island, the Yuza-Dake and Yaeju-Dake hill barriers.

The former was assigned to the Sixth Marine Division which was ordered to conduct a two regiment shore-to-shore attack against Oroku while the First Marine Division pushed southward to seal off the peninsula at its base. Mainly because of the shortage of amphibious craft, it was determined to land the Sixth Marine Division in a column of regiments with the Fourth Marines in the van. Since continued supply by amphibious means was not feasible, General Shepherd also decided to have the little island of Ona Yama, located in the middle of Naha Harbor, seized at the same time and to install bridges from Naha to the island and from the island to Oroku so that the peninsular operation would receive adequate logistical support. The job of taking Ona Yama was assigned to the Sixth Marine Reconnaissance Company.

The two landings proceeded without a hitch. An intensive artillery and naval bombardment was laid down before the troops, embarked in amphibian tractors, made their landing. They did so shortly before 0600 on June 4, and within an hour and a half a beachhead 900 yards in depth had been secured. Later in the day the Twenty-ninth Marines were landed. Ona Yama was taken and bridge construction between Naha and the peninsula commenced. For ten days the marines gradually pushed down the peninsula, their objective being to bottle up the enemy forces there before they could escape down the southern corridor. Finally, with the Twenty-second Marines pushing from the southeast, the Fourth from the South and the Twenty-ninth from the north and northwest, the last remaining Japanese stronghold was eliminated by June 14. The fighting had been steady and bitter. Oroku was more thickly studded with mines than any other part of the island and this plus the muddy and precipitous terrain made tank employment difficult and in some places impossible. Hence the infantry were compelled to slug it out on their own. Their losses were heavy. During the ten days of fighting the Sixth Marine Division lost 1,608 men killed and wounded. It was, however, better than a fair exchange for the more than 5,000 Japanese who were killed in the action.[35]

While the Sixth Marine Division was completing its pincers movement on Oroku, army and marine divisions pushed rapidly toward the southernmost ridge barrier where the Japanese were to take their final futile stand. This was made up of the Yaeju-Dake and Yuzu-Dake hill masses, the highest on the island. By June 12 the eastern end of this line had collapsed against unremitting pressure from army troops,[36] but on the west, in the area of Kunishi Ridge and Yuza Ridge, the enemy still held against the combined assault of the 96th Division and First Marine Division. The latter had suffered severely from a breakdown in its supply system. The division was simply not equipped for a rapid advance over a large land mass, and driving rains whipped the already muddy roads into impassable mires, requiring hand carry for supplies to forward units.[37] There were only three north-south roads in this area and one of them was impassable, which meant that four divisions had to be supplied along only two roads. Not one of these was in the First Division's Zone. Furthermore, with the coming of the heavy rains, they were barely passable.[38] Not until June 8 did essential supplies begin to trickle into the front line units by way of water transportation from Naha.

The battle for Kunishi, the western end of the last ridge line, was the most costly of all those fought in the final days of the campaign. From June 12 to 17 the men of the First Marine Division (later reinforced by a regimental combat team, the Eighth Marines from the Second Marine Division) inched their way up to and finally beyond the top of the ridge. Without their tanks, which were employed extensively to carry in reinforcement troops and supplies, the job would have taken even longer.[39] Thereafter the push to the southern coast and the final elimination of organized enemy defense was rapid. Movement along all fronts was steady as all units of Army and Marine Corps pushed toward the sea. On June 22 the island was declared secured. The honor of making this announcement fell to Major General Roy Geiger of the Third Amphibious Corps, who had taken over temporary command of the Tenth Army. Buckner, who had so successfully guided the campaign through two and a half months of combat, had been killed only four days earlier while visiting a forward observation post of the Eighth Marine Regiment (Second Marine Division).

Only eight days before his death, Buckner had dispatched these words to Ushijima: "Like myself, you are an infantry general long schooled and practiced in infantry warfare. You fully know the pitiful plight of your defense forces. You know that no reinforcements can reach you. I believe therefore, that you understand as clearly as I, that the destruction of all Japanese resistance on the island is merely a matter of days, and that this will entail the necessity of my killing the vast majority of your remaining troops. . . . It is hardly necessary for me to recall to your mind the instances in the past where Japanese military commanders, in both the feudal and modern eras of Japan, have saved their forces to prevent needless bloodshed after the battle has been decided. Humanitarian considerations should impel you to make the same decision they did." [40]

The appeal to surrender was as fruitless as those made in previous operations, even though the arguments this time were more compelling. Ushijima and his chief of staff followed the customary procedure of committing suicide the night before American victory was complete. Joining them in death, more or less glorious depending on the viewpoint, went an unprecedented number of Japanese troops. As Geiger made clear in his final report of the campaign, "the Japanese Army suffered irreplaceable losses. . . . One hundred seven thousand, five hundred thirty-nine enemy soldiers were known to have been killed, and 7,401 were taken prisoner. Countless others undoubtedly lie buried in the hundreds of caves that were sealed during the battle. All of the enemy's supplies and equipment were either destroyed or captured. A large and important contribution to the destruction of the Japanese armed forces was made when this bastion in the Japanese home waters was snuffed out." [41]

3. Amphibious and Tactical Aspects

Considered purely as an amphibious operation, the Okinawa campaign was certainly far different from most of those in which marines had fought. In terms of magnitude alone it represents the culmination of amphibious development in the Pacific War. More ships were used, more troops put ashore, more supplies transported, more bombs dropped, more naval guns fired against shore targets than in any previous Pacific campaign. The mere size of the operation alone called for greater ingenuity in planning and organization, and complicated tremendously the execution of the plans once they were put into effect.

BEACHES AND PREPARATORY FIRES

Yet the most uncharacteristic feature of Okinawa, which distinguished it from almost all previous Central Pacific amphibious operations, was the lack of any but token resistance at the beaches. Kuribayashi on Iwo Jima, although he did not heavily man his beach defenses directly inshore, had concentrated deadly flanking fire on the landing areas. But Ushijima on Okinawa made the decision to withdraw from the coast altogether and to concentrate his main defenses along the Shuri line.[42] The revised concept of his basic battle plan was expressed in his "Battle Instruction Number 8" issued to the 32nd Army on March 8, 1945: "The time of opening fire will naturally vary somewhat according to the type of weapons, strength of positions, duties, etc. However, generally speaking, we must make it our basic principle to allow the enemy to land in full. Until he penetrates our positions and loses his freedom of movement inside our most effective system of firepower and until he can be lured into a position where he cannot receive cover and support from the naval gunfire and aerial bombardment, we must patiently and prudently hold our fire. Then, leaping into action, we shall open fire and wipe out the enemy, in the coastal areas and afloat." [43]

This fundamental change in plans was undetected by American intelligence and came as a total surprise to the attacking forces. Up to then it had been assumed that the photographic coverage of the island had been adequate and that the enemy would pursue his normal course of establishing heavy defenses on the beaches. Most photographic missions prior to the landing were flown by the Twenty-first Bomber Command and by planes from Marc Mitscher's fast carrier force. A definite improvement in the planning of photographic coverage was reported to have been made by obtaining adequate vertical coverage for preliminary preparation maps. Subsequently the large-scale coverage for detailed study of installations was obtained, and by that time naval interpreters thought they had a satisfactory map on which to plot their findings. These were followed by frequent small-scale coverage missions flown by B-29's which were thought to be sufficient to detect changes made in major enemy installations.[44] In all a total of five major photographic missions were flown between September 29, 1944, and March 25, 1945. Nineteen sets of photographs were prepared by the Joint Intelligence Center, Pacific Ocean Areas, and distributed by them to the Third Amphibious Corps and through them to the two attacking marine divisions.

As far as providing accurate information about the nature of the landing beaches and the approaches thereto, these sorties generally proved successful. The marine divisions prepared a detailed pictorial study of beach and reef conditions which proved to be quite correct. Water depths did not vary more than one or two feet from the estimated depths, and the character of the reef was accurately predicted.[45]

But as far as giving any reasonably valid picture of the nature and disposition of enemy defense installations or of the location of enemy troops, photographic intelligence failed miserably. The revised operation plan of the Third Amphibious Corps, which was based on studies made of photographs provided by the Joint Intelligence Center, Pacific Ocean Areas, inevitably made several false assumptions, all of which, though not fatal, were serious in nature.

Before the invasion, opinion wavered as to the strength of the enemy forces on the island. The first estimate (as of February 1, 1945) put this at between 56,000 and 58,000 troops of all varieties. Later, after further photographic reconnaissance, this figure was revised downward (as of February 12, to a total of from 37,500 to 39,500 men). Finally, the last estimate of the enemy situation made only eleven days before the landing upped the total again to 64,000 men with the possibility that subsequent troop arrivals might bring the number as high as 75,000.

All of these estimates were considerably under the mark. The final tally of Japanese military personnel on the island including army, navy, Okinawan labor troops and draftees, came to well over 100,000.[46]

This discrepancy between the predicted and actual number of enemy fighting men on the island was less serious than the miscalculation concerning the disposition of enemy forces and installations. The Third Amphibious Corps as well as the rest of the Tenth Army predicated its landing plan on the assumption that the usual type of defense at the beaches would be encountered. The corps operation plan reads in part as follows: "On the basis of the latest known information the enemy appears to have organized his ground defenses in the Corps zone of action along a general pattern which indicates a defense of selected beaches in strength corresponding with the importance of the beach. This type of defense consists of a network of mutually supporting fire trenches, machine gun pits and pillboxes, extending laterally and in some depth. . . . Although very little artillery has been located on Okinawa, there is sufficient evidence to assume that the enemy has at least two battalions of artillery in the corps zone with the possible addition of a mountain gun unit. The greater portion of this artillery will probably be so situated as to defend the beaches and approaches to the Yontan and Kadena Airfields. The high ground just north of Yontan Airfield is ideally situated for the employment of artillery and/or coastal defense guns. To date no artillery has been located in this area; the extensive cover, foliage and presence of defiladed areas could well preclude its apparent absence. . . ."[47]

As events proved, nothing could have been further from the truth. The reason may have been, as suggested here, that the foliage was too thick. Or it may have been, as intimated later by Admiral Turner, that the Japanese timely removal of guns from their installations along the coast to the easily camouflaged area around Shuri confused the photographic interpreters.[48] Whatever the reason, the attacking forces were given an entirely inaccurate idea of what to expect on landing.

To be sure none of the Americans who landed on April 1 was disappointed that these earlier predictions of heavy beach defenses proved to be so grossly in error. But in spite of the initial joy over this miscalculation, the mistake was a serious one even though at no time did it jeopardize the success of the operation. In the first place it meant that many tons of bombs and naval projectiles were dropped in areas where they were not really needed. These same bombs and projectiles could have been employed more usefully elsewhere on the island. More important however is the bearing of the whole Okinawa plan of preparatory bombardment on the earlier operation at Iwo. The force which attacked Okinawa enjoyed the benefit of seven days preliminary naval and aerial bombardment as against three for Iwo. It may be that even had intelligence of the Okinawa beaches been more accurate, the decision to bombard it for all of seven days before invasion would still have been held because of the size of the island and the necessity for neutralizing all of the alternative landing beaches. But one of Turner's reasons for limiting preassault naval bombardment on Iwo to a paltry three days was that his available ammunition supply was limited and that he had to save plenty of it for Okinawa. If the facts of the withdrawal of the Japanese from the Okinawa coastline could have been predicted and determined, a different decision might have been reached. At least one of the arguments for restricting the preparatory naval bombardment at Iwo to such a short time would have been undermined. A day or two of scheduled fires might then have been lopped off the Okinawa invasion and added to Iwo Jima, where it could have been used with great profit.

Of course the real significance of the absence of opposition on the beaches is the silent testimony it bore to the efficiency of the American amphibious machine and particularly to the deadly power of naval gunfire. No greater tribute could be made to the thousands of Navy and Marine Corps personnel who had labored so long to perfect the art of shore bombardment by seagoing vessels than this final recognition by a stubborn enemy that it was futile to contest an American amphibious assault at the shore line.

To be sure, it is impossible to assess the results of the thousands of naval projectiles thrown at the island prior to the landing. Since most of the area fired at had already been evacuated or nearly so, the most that can be said is that the damage would have been tremendous had there been many important military objectives to be damaged.

Certainly in terms of size alone, this was the most impressive display of naval preassault bombardment yet witnessed in the Pacific. The opening round in the battle for Okinawa was fired on March 24 as the advance echelon of minesweeps arrived. That day they were supported by the fast battleships and planes of Spruance's Fifth Fleet. On the following day Rear Admiral William H. P. Blandy USN arrived on the scene with his Amphibious Support Force which included, under the tactical command of Rear Admiral Morton L. Deyo USN, ten old battleships, nine heavy cruisers, four light cruisers, twenty-three destroyers, six destroyer escorts, and three seaplane tenders.* This was the day when the really heavy preparation fires commenced. Next day the small attack force assigned to the Kerama Retto made its landings and quickly completed that job, taking as additional and unexpected trophies some 300 Japanese suicide boats lying in the anchorage. The logistical value of this little group of islands was to prove tremendous. It was used throughout the operation as a seaplane base, a safe anchorage where ships of all sizes could be fueled, ammunitioned, and supplied, and last of all a forward area repair base where the victims of later kamikaze attacks could be at least in part revived. In this first phase the base's most important use was for resupply of ammunition. Because of the possibility of surface action before the landing, all of the heavier fire support ships had to carry an extra load of armor-piercing shells, which reduced their magazine space for bombardment type projectiles. A reasonably safe anchorage for resupply was hence vital, and Kerama Retto was the answer. During the six days remaining before the principal landing, each battleship was allowed one day for taking on ammunition there and each cruiser and destroyer one-half day. Eight tank landing ships had been loaded at Ulithi to provide approximately three-fourths bombardment allowance for all ships of the gunfire and covering force. From their anchorage in Kerama Retto they transferred a total of approximately 3,000 tons of ammunition, thus preventing the difficulty experienced on previous operations when support ships were practically depleted of their shells at the end of the landing day.

Only one hitch occurred in the plans for preassault bombardment. The actual presence of mines off the Hagushi beaches slowed up mine sweeping operations by twenty-four hours and meant that the firing ships could not close range until March 29, a day later than had been anticipated. But in view of the small number of targets near the shore line, the delay was of no importance. As reported by Blandy, "beach defense weapons and positions were not numerous. They were scattered and generally well camouflaged. There were a few heavy pillbox-type installations along the beaches and inland, and numerous open emplacements. Some of the emplacements contained antiaircraft weapons, but many were empty." He adds, with gracious generosity to the staff intelligence section, "preliminary intelligence studies may have overemphasized the importance of some of the suspected installations." [49]

---

* The command relationship between Blandy and Deyo was rather complex. Blandy was designated senior officer present afloat during the capture of Kerama Retto, except in the event that Deyo's gunfire and covering force was required to engage Japanese naval surface forces. Deyo also commanded this force during night retirements of his vessels. During the daytime he "loaned" them to Blandy, who was in charge of shore bombardment.

After all mine fields were cleared, the support ships moved close in to fire point-blank all along the coast line at every possible landing point. If little material military damage was done, at least tremendous havoc was created ashore. Over 13,000 large caliber shells (6- to 16-inch) and over 5,000 tons of ammunition was expended on the island and against Kerama Retto in the preparatory period.

Then, on the morning of the 29th, naval underwater demolition teams protected by destroyers, destroyer transports, and infantry landing craft converted to gunboats began to reconnoiter the Hagushi beaches, and on the following day they blasted the obstacles they had discovered. Mines and underwater obstacles were the only defenses the Japanese had set up against the invader. Approximately 2,900 obstacles made from posts and rails cemented or wedged into the coral were quickly removed by hand-placed tetryol charges. The way was now clear for the landing.

Meanwhile planes from the fast carrier force and from the escort carriers that had accompanied Blandy's support force were bombing targets inaccessible to naval gunfire. They attacked planes aground in the various airfields, bombed gun positions inshore, bridges and concentrations of enemy small craft. Finally on March 31 one army field artillery group occupied tiny Keise Shima, about eight miles west of Okinawa, and set up twenty-four 155-millimeter guns which were ready to deliver deep support fires by the day of the main landing.[50]

THE PRINCIPAL LANDINGS

Finally as dawn broke on the morning of April 1 the gigantic convoy carrying the marines and soldiers of the Tenth Army got its first glimpse of Okinawa. The day was clear but slightly hazy; visibility was about six miles. As they approached the target visibility decreased, not for natural reasons but because the supporting ships stepped up their fire to frightful proportions. Heavy ships commenced firing at 0600 on targets behind and on the flanks of the Hagushi beaches. Gradually they closed the shore well in advance of troop-carrying tank landing ships which were now disgorging their amphibian tractors. At 0755, five destroyers, two light cruisers, and one battleship moved into position only 2,500 yards from the beach, while other combat ships continued to fire from further seaward. Then the various smaller support craft moved in column formation to their positions just seaward of the line-of-departure. Four divisions of infantry landing craft, one division converted to gunboats, the others mounting mortars, and two divisions of recently perfected and specially constructed amphibious gunboats then slowly moved forward in line abreast 100 yards ahead of the first wave of armored amphibians. At a mile's distance from the shore the 4.2-inch mortar shells began to scream through the air; at a half mile the chorus was taken up by rocket salvos from the gunboats. They laid an uninterrupted blanket of destruction on the beaches. In position only 125 yards apart, each vessel's pattern of fire overlapped that of its two neighbors. Then at about a quarter of mile from the beaches gunboats lay to and let the first wave of armored amphibians, followed by troop-carrying amphibian tractors, pass through and head for the shore.[51]

The ship-to-shore movement was uneventful. None of the amphibian tractors was hit, and the troops met almost no resistance at the beaches. There was some delay because of difficulties in negotiating the offshore reef, and the first waves of both the First and Sixth Marine Divisions were from five to ten minutes late in disembarking their troops,[52] but this was of no consequence. The once most critical and dangerous stage of getting the troops from ships to land was at Okinawa little more than a ferrying operation.

NAVAL GUNFIRE, ARTILLERY, AND AIR SUPPORT ASHORE

As the nature of the Japanese defensive strategy revealed itself, it became apparent that at Okinawa as on Saipan and Peleliu the primary role of naval gunfire would follow rather than precede the initial landing. To accomplish this the navy had prepared a careful plan of allocating its firepower which proved to be the most feasible of any yet adopted, with the possible exception of Conolly's scheme for the bombardment of Guam. Responsibility for all fires delivered after the invasion fell chiefly on Rear Admiral Deyo's gunfire and covering force of battleships, cruisers, and destroyers. A similar organization had been used first at Iwo Jima, but at Okinawa a different procedure was employed. The ships assigned to Deyo's task force constituted a permanent organization whose functions were two-fold: to compose the covering force for any enemy surface action that might develop, and to supply fire support ships as required. Ships assigned to this task force remained available and were not rotated with the screen or given other duties. This was possible largely because of the ample supply and facilities for transfer of ammunition of the type needed for shore bombardment. After the main troop movement toward the Shuri defenses began, the task force was divided into four main groups, with a particular area of responsibility assigned to each. One of these undertook all fires from the western coast of the island, another from the eastern, a third anchored at Kerama Retto, while a fourth acted as a general pool. Once a ship was assigned to fire support duty in a particular area, it continued in the same sector except for periods of replenishment or repairs. This meant that ships' personnel could familiarize themselves with the terrain and with the ground force liaison people with whom they were operating. Target destruction became a continuing program. Too frequently in past operations a particular target might be fired on by one ship one day and another ship the next. Under this new system a single ship was made responsible for a single target until destroyed or at least neutralized.[53] The only interruption in this continuous program occurred on April 6–7 when a small Japanese task force was sighted about 360 miles north and 60 miles east of Okinawa. The fire support ships were immediately assembled and prepared for battle to intercept the enemy before he could damage transport shipping in the area. The precaution proved unnecessary. While the Nipponese task force, consisting of the battleship *Yamato*, light cruiser *Yahagi*, and eight destroyers was still well out to sea, it was intercepted by planes from Mitscher's fast carriers. The results were gratifying for the Americans. Both the enemy battleship and cruiser as well as four of the destroyers were sunk and another destroyer severely damaged.

This was the last effort on the part of the Japanese navy to penetrate into Okinawan waters by means of surface vessels. Thereafter, circumstances compelled the Empire's military leaders to rely almost exclusively on their last desperate weapon, the kamikaze corps. In spite of the inadequate training which many of these pilots had, they met with remarkable success. Neither radar detection, nor seaplane search, nor American fighter interception, nor the picket line of destroyers and other vessels posted between Okinawa and the homeland were sufficient to keep all these planes away from Okinawa. Their primary target was shipping, and it was the American navy that suffered the greatest loss. Apparently poorly trained in ship recognition, these pilots struck at everything from tiny gunboats to aircraft carriers. The results were appalling. Twenty-six ships were sunk and another 164 damaged. The repair base at Kerama Retto took on the appearance at times of a naval graveyard, with so many battered vessels tied up there. The chief victims were destroyers assigned to the picket screen north of the main island. In all the Navy lost 9,731 officers and men during the Okinawa operation, and by far the greater portion was due to suicide attacks.[54] Still naval support of troop movements continued unimpeded. The truth was that the American fleet at Okinawa was so large and powerful that it could and did absorb this terrific pounding, suffer the greatest material and personnel damage in the history of the United States Navy, all without any serious interruption in its main job of supporting the troops ashore.

During the first phase of the fighting ashore, with troop movements far more rapid than had been expected, there was comparatively little call for naval gunfire in close support of ground forces. But as the Sixth Marine Division moved into Motobu Peninsula it called for close fire support against the enemy holed up on Mt. Yaetake. However, the most effective phase of naval support occurred in the southern section of the island after the front lines had been consolidated before the Shuri defense line. At first, direct support ships were generally assigned on the basis of two ships per regiment. Later, reduction in the number of ships available due to casualties and departures necessitated a reduction of the normal ratio, except in case of special attacks.[55] In the First Marine Division, three ships were usually assigned, with each regiment in the line getting a minimum of one ship per day while the third was controlled by division headquarters for deep support fires.[56] In the battle for Motobu the Sixth Marine Division fared even better. Each of the four attacking battalions was assigned a destroyer or a larger man-of-war. In addition one old battleship was provided to the Second Battalion, Twenty-second Regiment, as a division general support ship for ready protection of the left flank.[57] Gunboats were put to particularly efficient use in support of this division as it drove to Naha and down the Oroku Peninsula. Starting on May 14 two divisions of infantry landing craft gunboats fired on Naha and Oroku daily with excellent results,[58] and in the latter part of the same month the 7th Infantry Division began using these vessels daily for support in their drive down the east side of the island.

In the area of the First Marine Division alone, during the entire eighty-two day period of the operation, a total of 1,063 call fire missions were handled by naval vessels, and 567 harassing or interdicting night missions were also fired. Including everything from 16-inch shells to 4.2-inch mortars a total of 7,832,338 pounds (about 3,263 tons) of naval ammunition was expended for this one division alone. General del Valle reported that the most accurate main battery fire ever delivered for his division in any action during the war was provided by the old battleship *Colorado* against Shuri Castle just before its capture. No correction greater than 150 yards was necessary, and frequently the initial salvo was a direct hit. Later when the report reached the division that the enemy was evacuating Shuri under cover of rain and low ceiling, the old battleship *New York* was requested to send up a plane to investigate. Thirteen minutes later, she opened fire. Other fire support ships, as well as artillery and air, were quickly brought to bear on the target. The results were devastating, and the roads, when the marines moved down them, were littered with enemy dead and wounded.[59]

The army was equally laudatory of the efficacy of naval gunfire. The XXIV Army Corps reported that on two successive days prisoners of war stated that naval gunfire was the most feared weapon. Of course, as Buckner said, it was not possible to judge accurately the total effect of naval gunfire since artillery and air bombing had covered the same area in many cases. However, he concluded, "there exists no question . . . that great destruction and casualties were inflicted by naval gunfire, particularly in the heavy caliber firing."

Naval fire was carried out on a twenty-four hour basis so that enemy movements at night and enemy rest would be interrupted. Star shells were fired every night and were very effective in discovering and repulsing enemy counterattacks. The use of counterbattery fire and harassing fires at night, especially after support ships were able to enter Nakagusuku Wan (Buckner Bay) were of particular benefit to the troops, permitting them to get some rest by severely restricting the enemy's artillery.[60]

Nevertheless, in spite of its general effectiveness, there were limits of destructiveness beyond which naval gunfire could not go. These limitations were imposed in part by the nature of the terrain and the size of the island, but chiefly by the particular defensive measures adopted by the Japanese. From interrogations of prisoners of war and from other sources it is clear that after the beatings suffered in the Marshalls and Marianas, especially from ships' guns, the enemy decided to abandon the log and pillbox scheme of defense. As on Peleliu they organized each hill and hill system into a sort of large-scale pillbox by constructing extensive tunnels and caves within the hill itself. These were far more impervious to American supporting arms than any pillbox would be, and naval gunners were frustrated on more than one occasion by their inability to blast this type of defensive system.[61]

When it came to neutralizing an area naval gunfire was entirely adequate to any occasion that arose. But when calls were made upon ships' guns to seal the mouths of caves not visible from sea, the results were doubtful. The commanding officer of the light cruiser *Birmingham* reported that it took about forty rounds of 5- or 6-inch ammunition to destroy an inland cave using indirect fire, and concluded that under the circumstances shore artillery and aircraft should be used for the destruction of such targets. "Naval gunfire," he concluded, "should be permitted to concentrate on targets visible from the ships, so that they can take advantage of the inherently greater accuracy of direct fire." [62] Other naval officers were even less optimistic about the efficiency of naval guns against distant caves. One, a destroyer commander, reported that after going ashore when the fighting was finished he was convinced that 5-inch fire against caves was little better than harassing. Even where a direct hit was scored against the mouth of a cave he discovered little inside damage. He concluded that of the 16,000 rounds fired by his ship (*U.S.S. Picking*) during the entire operation, the half which had been used against caves was merely harassing rather than destructive in effect.

Perhaps the most serious problem raised in connection with the employment of supporting arms at Okinawa was that of coordination of naval gunfire, aerial support, and artillery. The size of the operation, the large number of support ships, artillery pieces, and planes, plus the fact that both guns and aircraft from all three services were being employed concurrently along the same front, all served to complicate matters considerably. Nevertheless there was a surprisingly small amount of friction between the various supporting arms considering the inherent difficulties involved.

One reason for the comparative lack of confusion was that at least in the upper echelons responsibility for the allocation of targets among the different types of supporting arms rested in one section—artillery. On the highest echelon, the Tenth Army artillery section assumed the functions of a support coordination agency. At the outset the naval gunfire support officer attached to this section plus the army's artillery officer and his intelligence and operations sections were embarked on Turner's flagship. Until the actual landing of the heavy pieces the chief job of the army's artillery officer was to determine what targets should be attacked by particular ships and to assign priorities to them. As the heavy guns were gradually landed the program of naval bombardment was integrated with that of the land-based artillery. Then on April 18 the artillery section moved ashore and operated in the vicinity of Buckner's command post. The naval gunfire officer, however, remained aboard the flagship to continue coordination and maintain representation and liaison for the artillery section. The latter was informed twice daily by despatch of the availability of support ships. In addition a twelve-hour summary in outline form was forwarded, giving all information on naval gunfire available at that time.[63]

The same general division of responsibility took place on corps and divisional levels, with the respective artillery officers of each echelon retaining paramount authority in questions involving allocation of targets and coordination of fires between air, artillery, and naval gunfire. Each corps and division artillery headquarters maintained a target information center covering all targets within their respective zones of action. All target discoveries and all destruction reports were funnelled through these centers, and they therefore became the basic sources of information concerning all likely targets whether assigned to ships, aircraft, or artillery. In the marine divisions these centers were located near the fire direction center of each artillery regiment. Also located at the division command post were the shore fire-control party and the air liaison party, with a direct wire connecting this post and the artillery center. In this way some congestion was avoided in the artillery and at the same time all three supporting arms were in constant contact.

In the lower echelons coordination of fires was somewhat more cumbersome. Naval liaison officers wanting ships' fire on a particular target had to clear their requests with the regimental liaison officers who in turn had to consult the artillery liaison officer of the direct support battalion as well as higher authorities. This complicated network through which requests for naval gunfire or air strikes had to pass often caused undue delay or a negative reply to the request.⁶⁴

Whenever marine and army units were fighting alongside each other, some effort toward liaison was made at least on the divisional level. The First Marine Division consistently exchanged liaison officers with whatever army division was operating on its left flank, and direct telephone communication was established between the fire direction centers of both organizations.

Generally speaking, in spite of some criticisms by regimental and battalion commanders, coordination among fires worked successfully according to most of the reports from troop echelons. For example on three different occasions planes from the old battleship *New York* spotted artillery fire from the Eleventh Marines (cannoneers for the First Marine Division) into targets which could not be hit by naval gunfire. On another occasion fire from the Eleventh Marines upon an enemy machine gun position was even directed from the conning tower of the cruiser *Tuscaloosa*.⁶⁵ These of course were variations from the standard procedure, but the fact that they were employed indicates a degree of flexibility which the bare picture of the routine of coordination fails to reveal.

The only major criticism of the coordination of support weapons is that throughout the operation there was a tendency for naval gunfire to assume more responsibility than should have been allocated to it. Even naval officers admitted that missions were too frequently assigned to ships which could have been better accomplished by field artillery. Del Valle concluded as a result of his observations that "considering the limitation of ammunition and life of a gun tube in naval artillery, it is believed that excessive use of naval gunfire was made in this operation. After field artillery is ashore, naval gunfire should be used as reinforcing only on missions so deep or so situated that artillery cannot reach them as effectively. . . ." *⁶⁶ Also there was some "theft of targets" by some vessels resulting in an indiscriminate use of naval fire. In several instances while artillery aerial observers were still making registrations on check points, a support ship proceeded to open up on the points being checked or would dispatch a navy

---

* Major General Shepherd, commanding the Sixth Marine Division on Okinawa, takes issue with this statement. He maintains: "You can never have too much fire support. Naval gunfire was employed most effectively throughout the campaign by the Sixth Marine Division in close as well as deep support." Lemuel C. Shepherd, Jr., ltr to P. A. Crowl, 23 Nov. 1949, Princeton University Library.

spotting plane to the same area. This of course meant unnecessary duplication of effort, interference with the artillery in the execution of its proper mission and general confusion and waste of ammunition.[67]

As could be expected of an operation of the length of Okinawa, artillery played a more vital role than was usual in most Pacific operations. In all, the American forces had at their disposal thirty-three battalions of corps and divisional artillery, making a total of 396 pieces ranging from 8-inch to 75-millimeter howitzers. The largest single display of artillery preparation in the entire Pacific War occurred on April 19 just prior to the first grand push against the Shuri defense line. Twenty-seven battalions (324 pieces) fired steadily for forty minutes into the enemy's lines while the infantry prepared to jump off. A total of 19,000 shells was expended in this brief time.[68]

Army and Marine Corps battalions were employed interchangeably as the situated warranted. No better demonstration of practical cooperation between the two services can be cited. Within a week after the landing, five battalions of Marine Corps 155-millimeter howitzers and guns were assigned to the XXIV Corps to support army operations on the southern line. Working alongside army 8-inch howitzers, they were under command of an army officer. During most of the May and June fighting, the 105-millimeter and 155-millimeter howitzers of the 27th Infantry Division were under the operational control of the Third Amphibious Corps.[69] During most of April the artillery battalions of the First Marine Division, being unemployed, were distributed among the three army divisions which were fighting in the south. In all the welter of controversy that developed during and since the war between these two services the fact is often overlooked that in most instances they worked together smoothly when called upon to do so. Okinawa was in every way a model of interservice cooperation. Artillery support was only one of many examples.

Liaison between infantry and artillery was consistently better than it was with either air or naval support ships. Troop units could ordinarily get quicker action on their requests for artillery support than they could from either pilots or naval gunners. One reason was that some of the links in the chain of command were eliminated. Such was the case in the zone of action of the First Marine Division. After May 7 one army and two marine howitzer battalions were assigned by the Third Corps to support this division. No clearance from corps was required on requests for fire. These originated with regimental commanders and after being approved by the division's artillery officer went directly to the headquarters of the most convenient artillery battalion. To the rear of these three battalions was stationed another group of three 155-millimeter gun battalions which had the job of general support of the entire Third Corps area. Either division could request fire from this group also without clearing through corps. Throughout its operations on the southern line the First Division could always rely on at least three and often many more battalions in addition to its own organic artillery. Furthermore most units of both Third Corps and XXIV Corps artillery were available on call, as well as the guns and howitzers of Sixth Marine Division and 96th Infantry Division on either flank.

Marine infantrymen were not accustomed to such bounty, but they were glad to get it. Massed fires of four or five battalions, as the First Division's commander happily reported, were "a common occurrence." On one occasion when the division was attacking the town of Makabe it had a total of twenty-two battalions ranging from 75-millimeter to 8-inch howitzers under its control.[70] At another time, one regiment of the Sixth Marine Division had twenty-one battalions firing at once.[71]

The only serious handicap to effective artillery support came as a result of materiel shortage. Neither marine division had enough observation planes or enough transportation for its guns and howitzers. Although both pilots and observers were experienced and turned in excellent jobs in spite of heavy antiaircraft fire, there simply were not enough planes to do the work properly. It was generally impossible to keep more than one plane on station with one on call at Yontan Field, whereas ideally two or even three planes should have been on station during the daylight hours.[72]

The shortage of proper vehicles for moving pieces was even more serious. Marine corps artillery regiments had few tractors available and had to depend largely on wheeled vehicles. They were even short of these, since only seventy-five per cent of the total allowed by the tables of organization had been shipped to Okinawa. During the torrential rains in the last week of May nothing on wheels could move through the mud. Had it not been for the liberality of neighboring army units who loaned the marines their heavy tractors, the First Division would have been virtually immobilized.[73]

As in the case of the other supporting arms, the most distinguishing feature of aerial support of ground troops on Okinawa was its tremendous size. More bombs and napalm tanks were dropped, and more rockets and machine guns were fired by aircraft than in any previous campaign in which marines had taken part. Here, too, marine pilots got the chance to exercise one specialty for which they had been especially trained—the close support of ground troops. In the Solomons and Philippines marine air groups had conclusively demonstrated their unmistakable talents along this line. Now at Okinawa for the first time on any grand scale since Bougainville they could at last perform one of the most important functions for which they had been trained—bombing and strafing in close support of their fellow marines on the ground. This is not to say that the job of close support was a Marine Corps monopoly. Navy and army planes flew many missions of this sort. Nor was there any sharp division of labor between aircraft of the three services, nor should there have been. Whatever plane or group of planes was the most available was assigned to the mission at hand without regard to the identification of the ground unit concerned. In general, ground troops of both services preferred land-based planes to those from the carriers, but they made no fine distinctions between army and marine aircraft. If an infantry commander, no matter what his uniform, wanted a cave sealed up or an artillery piece knocked out, he was grateful to get either a marine "Corsair" (F-4U) or an army "Thunderbolt" (P-47). Here was merely another case of practical working unity between the services.

In view of the great number of planes employed it is not surprising that the system of control of air strikes should have been more complex and more centralized than was customary in Pacific operations. For the first six weeks of the operation, overall control of air operations in the area, including combat air patrol (against enemy planes), antisubmarine patrol, and the myriad other duties assigned to aircraft, was vested in a naval air support control unit located on the headquarters ship *Eldorado*. But the job of supervising aircraft in direct support of the two corps of ground troops was delegated to two subordinate control units stationed on different ships. Finally by the end of the first ten days of fighting, control of troop support missions was delegated to two shore-based landing force air support control units assigned respectively to the Third and the XXIV Corps. These were predominantly marine units. They were in turn subordinate to the Air Support Command of the Landing Force, who maintained close liaison with Headquarters, Tenth Army, and with the tactical air components.[74]

Operating with the Third Amphibious Corps throughout the operation was Landing Force Air Support Control Unit One, commanded by a marine officer and consisting mostly of Marine Corps personnel. This group went ashore on April 6 and by April 10 had assumed control of all air support for this corps. Although there was comparatively little action at first, activity picked up considerably as the Sixth Marine Division advanced up the Motobu Peninsula; and during the later phase of the operation, after the two marine divisions had been transferred to the southern line, calls for air strikes came in a steady stream.[75]

The unit itself was located immediately adjacent to corps headquarters and connected directly by land wire to all major troop units and also by land wire to the corps target information center. The latter connection enabled it to keep in constant communication with artillery and naval gunfire. In all cases, of course, the artillery officer either at corps or Tenth Army target information centers had the final word on questions concerning coordination between the three supporting arms.

On the other end of the scale, requests for air strikes might originate from the battalion air liaison officer who would make his plea, whenever possible, over tactical wire to the regimental air liaison officer who would in turn relay it to the control unit by radio. Division headquarters monitored the assigned frequency and could veto any battalion or regimental request it disapproved.[76]

This was a complex procedure, although doubtless necessary to avoid duplication of fire and the general confusion which would have resulted if all the many battalions and regiments along the southern front had enjoyed greater autonomy. Excessive delay in answering requests for fire which might have resulted from this procedure was partly avoided by planning in advance what the daily targets for air should be. In fact, only a fairly small percentage of all aerial sorties flown in support of ground troops came as a result of air liaison party requests. During the entire campaign, a total of 1,388 missions of this type were flown, and of these only 507, or thirty-seven per cent, were dispatched on the request of lower echelon air liaison parties. The rest were chosen by advanced planning on the basis of estimates of what the next day's needs would be.[77]

The chief defect in the execution of ground support missions by aircraft was, as usual, delay. Although as the operation progressed execution of missions improved considerably, the commander of both marine divisions as well as their subordinate officers repeated the ancient complaint that pilots were too frequently not on time, and that it took too long to get an answer to requests for air strikes.[78] At least one regimental commander again complained because his air liaison parties were not permitted to control air strikes close to front lines by direct communications with the pilot concerned. He added that his battalion commanders "at the present time are very dubious of air strikes close to our lines unless Air Liaison Teams are in direct radio communication with the flight leader." [79]

This last criticism is not altogether justified. It is true that on Okinawa close air support was less flexible than it had been in the Philippines, especially on Luzon. There, army units had used marine planes more or less in the manner of organic artillery. A battalion commander could request aerial bombardment on a particular target and expect to receive it in a matter of minutes. His air liaison officer would be in direct radio communication with the pilot and would personally coach him into the target. This was largely possible and feasible because the tactical situation of the First Cavalry Division in their dash for Manila was fluid. That is, they were moving rapidly forward, and were relatively isolated from other troops. Air support, if it were to be delivered at all, had to be provided quickly, and there was no serious danger of planes misplacing their bombs on adjacent units.

On Okinawa the tactical situation was much different, at least after the fighting had begun along the southern front. As Colonel Vernon E. Megee USMC, who commanded the corps landing force air support control unit, later remarked, "to have permitted each battalion air liaison party to control striking aircraft on a corps front of only ten miles, when many simultaneous air strikes were being run, would obviously have led only to pandemonium and grave hazard for all those concerned. On the other hand, where conditions approximated those in the Philippines, i.e. battalion or regimental actions in an uncrowded area, actual control of aircraft was frequently delegated to the air liaison party." [80]

The air arm in its various roles played a significant part in the Okinawa operation, in particular as a supporting arm to the ground troops. Although carrier-based planes were sometimes sent on close support missions, the primary responsibility for this job fell on the Tenth Army's "tactical air force." This organization was commanded by Major General Francis P. Mulcahy USMC for most of the operation and consisted chiefly of marine and army fighter planes. By the end of May a total of 270 Corsairs and 80 army Thunderbolts were operating out of fields at Yontan, Kadena, and on Ie Shima; and this number was increased by the addition of several army fighter and bomber squadrons before the campaign was over.

Since the Marine Corps had done more than any other service in the Pacific to develop a doctrine of close air support, command of this mixed organization was logically given to a marine officer, and the command staff was set up with the headquarters of the Second Marine Air Wing as a nucleus. The first two groups of fighter planes to operate out of Yontan and Kadena Fields were marine-flown, and throughout the operation marine aircraft predominated.

Every type of job was assigned to these planes. They knocked out Japanese planes over Okinawa, were sent on radar picket duty to intercept oncoming enemy aircraft, bombed enemy aircraft and shipping on ground and water, and flew close support missions for the infantry. They dropped some 400,000 pounds of food, medical supplies, and ammunition to front line troops which could not be reached by normal means of transportation. Finally they evacuated wounded marines and soldiers when the heavy rains made the roads of southern Okinawa impassable to ambulance trucks and tractors. In all, the planes of the tactical air force flew 30,403 sorties.[81]

By April 7 the first marine fighter units were ashore at Yontan Field and flying morning and dusk patrols, but in the initial stages of the operation there was little occasion for marine troops to call for close support. But as the Sixth Marine Division pushed against the Motobu Peninsula, enemy resistance stiffened, and air was called on to destroy gun emplacements and observation posts and to bomb troop concentrations. Napalm was used extensively and successfully to burn off camouflage and reveal targets which would otherwise have remained concealed. Fortified caves came under air attack, and it was discovered that the most successful method of dealing with them was rocket fire.[82]

Of course the greatest call for help from the sky came from all troop units as they pitted themselves against the solid wall of Japanese fortifications in the south. Where artillery and naval gunfire failed to penetrate, airpower more than once dealt the death blow.

In the area of the XXIV Corps alone a total of 817 strike missions were flown, making an average of twelve daily during the actual combat period. On one day forty-three missions were flown. The largest single strike occurred on April 19 in support of a coordinated attack against the Shuri line. A total of 139 planes armed chiefly with 1,000 and 2,000 pound bombs flew in this mission.[83] Only in the area of the Sixth Marine Division was air support of limited usefulness. Rainy weather made it impractical during much of the battle for Naha. During most of the battles for Oroku Peninsula the fighting was at such close quarters that air strikes were not feasible except just before the morning jump offs.[84] However, all the other divisions were enthusiastic in their praise of close support, as well they might be.[85]

The planes employed in these operations had to put up with severe handicaps, some avoidable and others not. The first hazard for pilots to overcome was their own maps. These were miserable for northern Okinawa, and close bombing and strafing was made even more haphazard by the fact that frequently the troop air liaison parties and the pilots they were directing had different maps of the same area. This situation was improved considerably in the later part of the campaign, but there were still too many cartographic inaccuracies. Poor radio procedure and occasional bad radio discipline also had serious consequences. On more than one occasion it resulted in the bombing of friendly troops.

Rain and low ceilings tended to curtail operations, especially between May 19 and June 5. On many occasions during this period strikes were called, and when the flight was over the designated target area the weather had closed in so much that pilots had to drop their bombs on secondary targets or at random over enemy territory. However in one instance the Japanese relied too heavily on low ceilings to protect their troop movements from aerial attack. On May 27 the First Marine Division called for an air strike at a time when the weather was so bad that no planes were on station, but two groups immediately took to the air, discovered the enemy and strafed and rocketed at will, a performance which prompted del Valle to dispatch the message: "Our congratulations and thanks for prompt response this afternoon when Nips were caut [sic] on roads with kimonos down." [86]

Sometimes however, to mix the metaphor, the shoe was on the other foot. Japanese efforts to frustrate their aerial attackers were ingenious if not overwhelmingly successful. When American ground troops marked targets for aircraft with white phosphorous the enemy frequently confused the situation by scattering puffs of white smoke over the general landscape in the area. Also Japanese antiaircraft fire, though not great in size, was cleverly employed. Gunners usually held fire until after the planes had passed over the target and were pulling out of their run which gave them a free shot without danger of strafing from the plane's own guns, which could train only forward. This was a good tactic, presuming of course that the Japanese gunner had survived the run itself.

But the results of enemy antiaircraft action were not impressive. Casualties to American flight personnel of the tactical air force for the entire operation numbered only ninety-nine. Against this is the figure of 602 enemy planes, with probably over 1,000 personnel, reported shot down by the same force. And of course the damage inflicted to enemy troops and material by American aircraft cannot be estimated except that the results were "highly satisfactory." [87] They should have been, considering the amount of explosives and incendiaries dropped and fired. In the eighty-two days that it took to secure the island, 1,904 direct support missions were flown; there were 17,361 individual plane sorties; 7,144 tons of bombs were dropped, 1,573 belly tanks of napalm (165 gallons each); 49,641 rockets (5-inch)fired from planes; and 9,300,000 rounds of fifty-caliber ammunition.[88]

In addition, air support planes flew many so-called "housekeeping" missions. They delivered supplies and ammunition to isolated troops. They evacuated casualties. They sprayed American lines with DDT. Occasionally they went on courier missions, acted as observer and spotter planes, flew photo-reconnaissance sorties, and dropped propaganda leaflets behind enemy lines. Of these missions, the most important was the first. In the heavy rains of late May and early June ordinary transportation in some areas became practically impossible. This was especially true for the marine divisions which had insufficient transport anyway, not having been allotted the full amount prescribed by the tables of organization. According to del Valle, air supply drop was "the determining factor in the Division's rapid advance on Shuri Castle." Over 581 loads of supplies, totalling nearly 400,000 pounds, were dropped by parachute to this Division alone in this critical stage.[89]

Sometimes, as against Shuri Castle, all three supporting arms were used simultaneously, and this was found to be highly successful.

Procedures used on previous operations whereby ships and artillery were compelled to cease fire during an aerial strike were almost totally abandoned. It was found that properly briefed pilots could safely operate in an area where shells were falling.[90] Most of the naval support ships followed the practice of continuing fire while planes were over a target.[91] No casualties to aircraft from naval fire resulted, and of course it was of considerable advantage to the ground troops to have this much added fire.

LOGISTICS

Logistical plans for the invasion of the Ryukyus were perforce more complex than they had been in previous Pacific landings, and again largely because of the magnitude of the campaign. For the first phase a total of almost 183,000 personnel and 746,850 measurement tons of cargo had to be loaded into 433 assault transports and landing ships by eight different subordinate embarkation authorities at eleven different ports extending some 6,000 miles from Seattle to Leyte. Many of these harbors, especially those in the forward areas, had inadequate facilities for pier-side loading. Many of the vessels employed had to be partially loaded at one port before proceeding elsewhere to pick up complete loads. Responsibility for loading these ships was often imposed on commands who would not do the unloading. Equipment and supplies for the XXIV Corps arrived at Leyte too late to sail, and quick substitutions had to be made. Finally there was considerable overlapping both in the planning and execution of loadings for Iwo Jima and Okinawa. These were only some of the problems which beset high-echelon planners, transport quartermasters, and ship captains in their effort to meet the tremendous logistical problem posed by the Okinawa operation.

The joint expeditionary force for the campaign was composed of approximately 1,400 ships and landing craft of all types. This fact, coupled with the long distances involved, created logistics difficulties of greater magnitude than any heretofore encountered in the Pacific theater. The various units of the force were assembled and staged at Ulithi, Guadalcanal, Russell Islands, Espiritu Santo, Nouméa, Saipan, and Leyte. Combat loading teams consisting of one marine or army officer, one navy officer, and appropriate enlisted ratings were dispatched first to Leyte and the Guadalcanal-Russells area where the XXIV and Third Corps respectively were being loaded. The Second Marine Division making up the troops of the demonstration group was similarly loaded out at Saipan, and the 27th Infantry Division, the floating reserve, at Espiritu.[92]

The results were not always satisfactory. Logistics officers in the Marine Corps complained that too often ships' characteristics data as furnished were incorrect, and no characteristics were available for some ships. For this reason at least two ships assigned to the First Division were long delayed in loading. Another vessel assigned to the same division had taken both between-decks areas of number three hatch for ships' materiel, which was a serious loss to the embarked troops.

The First Division logistics officer also complained that the paper work required by Fleet Marine Force, Pacific, was much too detailed and complicated for the average line officer to complete. Since there was insufficient time for trained transport quartermaster personnel to do this work, troop transport quartermasters became confused and made many errors. Forms were repetitious and redundant, and too many of them served no purpose except to delay execution of loading plans.

The plans for loading tank landing ships went somewhat astray because of faulty information received from higher headquarters. It had originally been decided that only six of these ships assigned to the First Division would carry tank landing craft on board. Actually the division was assigned eleven tank landing ships carrying tank landing craft, which of course reduced available space by about 15,000 square feet. The tactical plan of employing tank landing ships was changed just prior to loading. No representative of the tank landing ship flotilla was available during planning, and proper planning was consequently impossible. Many tank landing ship captains were (perhaps naturally) convinced that their ships should not carry fuel or ammunition. Navy ammunition in some cases was not stowed topside according to plan and in many instances had to be restowed in order to load vehicles topside. Ships' captains received confusing orders. For example, one ship left Banika for Pavuvu (both in the Russells) and was next heard of in Tulagi.[93]

From the Sixth Marine Division's commanding general came other complaints. According to General Shepherd, the primary difficulties encountered during the preparatory period "resulted from unavoidable reasons incident to the distance of the division from its supply agencies." The problem which caused the greatest concern was the uncertainty as to dates of arrival of many items of equipment and supplies, and this concern became acute as the date of embarkation approached. For example, seven 105-millimeter howitzers were due from San Francisco on February 7. They failed to arrive on schedule, so the marines had to arrange a last-minute deal to draw them from army sources. The relations of the marine supply service of Fleet Marine Force, Pacific, to the several combat and service commands in the area were excessively cumbersome. For the Sixth Division, the Fourth Marine Service and Supply Battalion located on Guadalcanal was designated to be the chief supply agency. Actually this battalion was a transfer rather than a stocking agency, and the division in fact had to draw its supplies from a base depot located on the Russell Islands. This depot was in turn directly subordinate to the Second Marine Field Service Command. All this made for excessive red tape, delay and general confusion, and matters were not simplified by the addition of still another senior supply echelon, the South Pacific Echelon of Fleet Marine Force, Pacific.

The root of the difficulty, according to the Sixth Division's commanding general, was the recent change in the concept of operation of the Marine Corps, by which administration of divisions was theoretically divorced from corps headquarters and assigned to Fleet Marine Force, Pacific. "Supply and administration," as he put it, "cannot, in practice, be separated from command. Continuity of administration of corps and its divisions throughout the rehabilitation and planning phases is essential." [94]

Other difficulties arose because of failure of coordination between navy and marine staffs. The First Marine Division logistics section found this to be particularly the case. The navy staff with which it should have maintained the closest sort of cooperation working out loading details, boat allocation plans, boat assignment tables, and debarkation schedules remained ashore within proximity of the division's headquarters for only three days. Thereafter they returned to their ships, which were continually under way from one place to another in the Russell Islands. A great deal of confusion, delay, and misunderstanding resulted.[95]

Navy transport commanders were equally frank in criticizing the embarkation of troops and materiel from the Guadalcanal-Russells area. Not only were some ships' characteristics not up-to-date, but some ships arrived late in the loading area. Paper loading plans, with inadequate, outdated, and in some cases no characteristics at all, had to be tentative. According to established doctrine, the final loading plans should have been approved by both ship's captain and troop commander. In some cases complete loading plans had to be made after the ship was alongside waiting to take a load.

Finally, in the opinion of one transport group commander (assigned to carry the First Marine Division), "it can be fairly stated that these ships were not combat-loaded. It is true that cargo was landed according to priority. However, the 60 per cent combat load as expressed in Transport Doctrine was greatly exceeded. All ships were, in the opinion of the squadron transport quartermaster, commercial loaded, according to a definite priority . . . *but not combat-loaded.*" [96] The reason was a shortage of ships plus confusion in their actual loading. Luckily the errors and deficiencies were to make no material difference since there would be ample time to straighten out the confusion after the beachhead at Okinawa had been so easily established. But this was an unexpected piece of good fortune.

Primary responsibility for unloading supplies rested on the division shore parties, which were in turn subordinate to corps and Tenth Army shore party commanders. These battalions with their attached units each consisted of 208 officers and 4,465 men and included a navy beach party, a joint assault signal company (less shore fire-control and air liaison sections), three platoons of military police, parts of two naval construction battalions, and a detachment from the division's motor transport battalion, plus replacement drafts. Personnel of the pioneer battalion were used primarily to control the movement of cargo in the beach area, to improve and construct roads for getting cargo to the dump areas, and to operate barge-mounted cranes at the reef transfer points. Military police controlled the movement of traffic on the beach and in the supply dumps and later handled prisoners of war and captured or refugee civilians. The joint assault signal companies established communication by wire and radio laterally along the beach between the several supply dumps and the beach command post, and by radio and visual signals from shore to the control boats offshore. The navy beach parties which were set up to parallel shore party echelons provided radio and visual communications between the shore and ship, set up beach evacuation stations to supplement those of the pioneer battalions, and controlled the movement of boats from parent ships to the transfer line at the reef. Naval construction battalions assisted by marine personnel from replacement drafts provided the manpower to unload cargo from ships into small boats.[97]

This was on the whole an efficient organization, and in general its record throughout the Okinawa operation was excellent. But one unexpected factor temporarily interfered with the scheduled plans for unloading supplies and equipment on the beaches. This was the unexpectedly rapid advance of the troops inland, which resulted in a rapid depletion of unloading vehicles on the shore. As the First and Sixth Marine Divisions pushed quickly east and north they took with them almost all their vehicles, which left a severe shortage on the beach, and at a time when the stress on unloading was at a maximum.

This was only slightly less true in the area of the XXIV Corps.[98] The truth is that neither marine division ever had enough motor transportation either to supply itself adequately or to move its artillery. An allotment of motor vehicles and prime movers which might have been sufficient to the normal small island type of fighting to which marines were accustomed was insufficient for a long operation such as Okinawa. Had it not been for army generosity and for air supply drop and waterborne supply into the Naha area, both divisions would have suffered extremely serious materiel shortages in the southern phase of the fighting.

Moreover, certain other miscarriages in unloading plans took place. It had been provided that on the day of the initial landing, barge-mounted cranes should be dispatched to the reef line as soon as possible to assist the transfer of supplies and equipment from small boats. Many of these were late in arriving, and priority cargo had to be transferred by hand. By 1800 of the landing day, only six of the twelve transfer barges had arrived in the sector of the First Marine Division. Two had been lost in transit, and the full transfer line was not established until two days after the landings.[99]

Navy coxswains contributed to the already existing confusion by "an almost fierce determination to be first ashore with their individual boats, regardless of the orderly assignment to unloading points." [100] Much unwanted cargo was sent in by transports during the first few days of the operation in evident haste to clear their holds. Tons of material for barbed-wire entanglements, many boat loads only half or even less than half full, arrived with priority tickets when the beach was calling for 155-millimeter ammunition. The crane barges on the beaches of the First Division broke down frequently and caused considerable congestion at the reef's edge. On several evenings operating cranes were secured by the beach authorities while boats were still pouring into the transfer area.

In spite of these defects, unloading at least in the area of the two marine divisions was reasonably expeditious. Shore parties suffered from inadequate personnel, but on the whole performed their jobs efficiently in spite of back-breaking and nerve-wracking hours of labor during the first few days.[101] As at Iwo, the "hot cargo" system of unloading was employed. An initial load of approximately 1,000 pounds was in each amphibian tractor with the early waves and was thrown out on the beach for use in the initial phase of the action. As usual the marine divisions did not use pallets extensively, except for such items as barbed wire and pickets. Their argument was that pallets were heavy, difficult to handle, used an excessive amount of shipping space, and broke easily.[102]

Some concept of the comparative size of the unloading job at Okinawa can be derived from a table showing the amounts of cargo by assault and first echelon garrison types which were unloaded in all the Central Pacific campaigns from the Gilberts through Okinawa: [103]

Operation	Total Ships	Personnel	Measurement Tons	Short Tons
Gilberts	63	34,214	148,782	58,376
Marshalls	122	85,201	293,792	146,949
Marianas	210	141,519	437,653	201,256
Palau	109	55,887	199,963	92,920
Iwo Jima	174	86,516	280,447	119,078
Okinawa Gunto	458	193,852	824,567	312,795

In other words, in the mere quantity of tons of supplies and equipment unloaded, Okinawa represents almost twice that for the entire Marianas and almost three times that for Iwo Jima. If magnitude were the sole criterion, the logistics program would have to be judged an unqualified success. Errors in execution somewhat marred the picture, but none was important enough to delay victory for any considerable length of time.

GROUND TACTICS

In the end it was neither naval guns nor aircraft, nor heavy artillery nor shore parties that wrested the island from the enemy. The ultimate weapon here was the infantryman working with his supporting tanks.

The tank-infantry team on Okinawa reached the apex of its development for the entire Pacific War. As General Shepherd concluded, "If any one supporting arm can be singled out as having contributed more than any others during the progress of the campaign, the tank would certainly be selected. Okinawa represents an accurate foretaste of what is to be expected in the Jap homeland. Our enemy, an inveterate digger, contrives to place himself so deep in the earth that neither artillery nor bombs can visit the full force of their destructive effort upon him. A powerful direct fire weapon, of great accuracy and well protected, is required. The medium [Sherman] tank fills this requirement admirably." [104] Even more convincing testimony is found in a dispatch of General Ushijima issued shortly before his death: "The enemy's power lies in its tanks. It has become obvious that our general battle against the American Forces is a battle against their . . . tanks." [105]

In the two marine divisions tanks fought at all times as *infantry* tanks and functioned as a major direct-fire close support weapon. At no time in the Third Corps did tanks operate beyond the observation and cover of infantry. In other words, "panzer" tactics so common in the European War were avoided by the marines, and for good reason.

The nature of the terrain and foliage and the antitank tactics employed by the enemy precluded panzer attacks. On the occasions when army tank units attempted to act independently of their supporting infantry, they met with disaster.[106]

In general there were two types of uses to which the tank-infantry team could be put. Tanks, artillery, rockets, and mortars might lay down a heavy neutralization fire, and then the infantry, preceded by tanks, would move forward and seize the area under fire. This type of attack, however successful, could be used only to secure ground which was relatively lightly defended. Against areas containing heavy underground fortification it usually succeeded only in temporary neutralization. Often the infantry would move forward only to find itself in possession of an area which was swept by enemy fire shortly after supporting neutralization ceased. No easy movement was then possible, either forward or backward. They usually found the ground untenable and had to withdraw with heavy losses.

A second method, used especially in southern Okinawa, was far more successful against heavily defended areas. It consisted of preparatory close-range destruction of caves, bunkers, and tomb emplacements by tanks which were in turn covered by fire teams prior to a general tank-infantry advance. Tanks and flamethrowing tanks ranged out to positions up to 800 yards beyond the marines' front lines, systematically destroying positions on forward and reverse slopes by point-blank 75-millimeter fire into caves and by flame attacks. In addition tanks could destroy enemy direct fire positions on forward slopes for an additional 1,500 yards to the front beyond the farthest point of their advance. In order to give the enemy no opportunity to reorganize, two relays of tanks were used to permit rearming while maintaining a continuous attack. Once destruction was reported complete, infantry troops would then advance their lines to the 500 yard point achieved by the tanks, often with comparatively few losses. It was a slow procedure and could not be employed for all sorts of terrain. But against the Shuri line and the defenses to the southward it was the only feasible way of ferreting out the enemy.[107]

While the tanks were thus paving the way for the infantry advance, the latter in turn stood by to protect their own protectors. The first great hazard to tanks was mine fields, of which the Japanese had laid down many. These were by and large effectively dealt with by tank-engineer teams, and comparatively few tank casualties came from this source.[108]

Another source of danger was the Japanese tank-hunter team which employed a variety of techniques of destruction, the most spectacular being a suicide run against an American tank by a Japanese soldier carrying a satchel charge. Close infantry coverage was essential to counteract this sort of tactic, and it is interesting to note that in one marine division (the First) not a single tank was destroyed or even stopped by tank hunters.

Aside from their primary use, tanks were put to other employments. In the early phases of the operation when the First Marine Division had little active fighting, armored patrols of platoon strength with infantry fire teams riding on tanks were used in general mopping up and patrol operations. The Sixth Division also employed tank-infantry reconnaissance units very successfully during the initial attack across Okinawa from the landing beaches, and on its advance to the north.[109]

Tank dozers were very valuable in filling in bomb craters, ditches and canals and in the removal of road blocks.[110] Armored amphibians were used as auxiliary tanks on occasion by the Sixth Marine Division. Due to the fact that during the last phase of the operation the division held a flank position along the coast, armored amphibians were given direct support missions and functioned from seaward somewhat in the same manner as tanks, in spite of their light armor.[111]

But the most successful weapon employed on Okinawa in conjunction with tank-infantry tactics was the newly developed tank-mounted flamethrower. As General Buckner put it, in the last analysis the best method of attacking Japanese fortified caves was the "blowtorch and corkscrew" method.[112] The blowtorch was the flamethrower; the corkscrew was demolitions.

Marines in earlier operations had used small flamethrowers mounted on amphibian tractors and in light tanks, but on Okinawa as on Iwo Jima a far more efficient weapon was employed. This was a high-powered flamethrower mounted in the 75-millimeter gun of a Sherman. Marines knew them by the less formal title of "Zippos," after the popular wartime cigarette lighter.[113]

The flamethrower on this tank operated under high pressure. Tank capacity was 300 gallons and effective range was from 80 to 100 yards, using a fuel of mixed napalm and gasoline. Fifty-five of these fiery monsters were organized into the 713th Tank Battalion (Army), which was in turn distributed among the various divisions.[114] Elements up to company size were assigned to each of the marine divisions. In general they were used principally and most effectively against rocky crags, reverse ridges and against towns. Flame proved to be the most and at times the only effective weapon against these targets.

Cooperation between army and marine units in this connection deserves comment as another example of the excellent coordination between these two services on Okinawa. The point is perhaps made best by the report of the commanding officer of the armored flamethrower company (army) which was attached to the First Marine Tank

Battalion: "Tactics developed by us for use of flamethrowers fit in very nicely with the way the First Marine Tank Battalion had trained their officers and men. Cooperation of the First Marine Tank Battalion has been excellent. Both officers and men of this company can ask for no better cooperation than they got. We did in turn our utmost to keep a maximum number of vehicles operative and fulfilled every mission requested of us. There has never been a time when rivalry between Army and Marine units has been anything but friendly." [115]

In general these remarks typify relations between the services during the Okinawa campaign, and there were no serious "incidents" such as occurred on Saipan to mar the picture of cooperation. Army artillery supported marine infantry and vice versa; marine and army planes were used interchangeably and operated under the same tactical command; on the southern line each contiguous infantry unit was mutually supporting and interdependent. And of course the navy's participation was vital to both throughout. To those who would dwell upon disunity among the services and emphasize the areas of friction among men and units wearing different uniforms of the United States, Okinawa stands as indisputable proof that joint operations were successful. The mere fact that American fighting men were under separate organizational control was no necessary deterrent to military efficiency and coordinated effort.

4. Conclusion

Perhaps this, in the end, is the most useful lesson which students of amphibious operations could derive from Okinawa. At least this was the opinion of Major General Frank D. Merrill USA, who accompanied General Joseph W. Stilwell USA to Okinawa when the latter took over command of the Tenth Army. He wrote, "to my mind, the importance of Okinawa and the Tenth Army has been largely overlooked since the implications of the unique organization have been ignored in the present day clamor for 'unification.' In the Tenth Army there was genuine unification. No one cared what type of a uniform a man wore; no one bothered about where credit or publicity would be focused; all hands turned to and did their individual best to accomplish assigned missions, and it worked without a hitch, entirely oblivious of the fact that in a few years what was achieved voluntarily was to be wrecked by petty jealousies in peace." [116]

Such splendid cooperation boded well for the projected operations against Japan proper, where all six marine divisions were planned to be committed alongside several times that number of army divisions. The first of these proposed invasions was scheduled to take place in the late autumn of 1945. A three-pronged assault against the island of

Kyushu was to be made by three separate corps of the Sixth United States Army under General Walter Krueger USA. One of these was the Fifth Marine Amphibious Corps made up of the Second, Third, and Fifth Marine Divisions. The other two scheduled for Kyushu were the XI Army Corps (43rd, 1st Cavalry, and Americal Divisions) and the I Corps (25th, 33rd, and 41st Infantry Divisions). The second phase of the projected Japanese invasion, the campaign against Honshu, was to be carried out in the early spring of 1946. For this phase the Third Marine Amphibious Corps, including the First, Fourth, and Sixth Marine Divisions, along with nine army infantry divisions and two armored divisions of the Eighth and Tenth United States Armies were to assault the Tokyo plain of eastern Honshu.[117]

The capture of Okinawa contributed much to ending the war. With the development of airfields on Okinawa, Army, Navy, and Marine Corps bombers and fighters were brought within easy range of the China coast, Korea, Shikoku, Kyushu, and Honshu and were able to bring Japanese shipping in these waters to a virtual standstill. The night before the war ended the first flight of B-29's took off from Okinawa to bomb industrial targets on northern Honshu. Other bombers were poised for the take-off when word of the surrender came. Along the shore feverish preparations were in progress for the large naval task force which was expected to be mounted out of Okinawa for Japan.[118]

Okinawa had been purchased at a high cost. Total American battle casualties were over 49,000 of which about 12,500 were killed or missing. Thirty-six American ships were sunk; 368 were damaged, many beyond repair. Plane losses came to 763.

The enemy, of course, suffered far more heavily. An estimated 110,000 Japanese were killed and about 7,400 taken prisoner. Almost 7,800 planes, many of them of the kamikaze corps, were knocked down by American fighters and antiaircraft fire.[119] But the greatest blow which the Japanese suffered cannot be measured in terms of either manpower or materiel lost during the operation. Far more important was the fact that they had surrendered to the American forces a large land base from which aerial and naval power and later invading troops could easily be dispatched against the homeland and its adjacent waters.

CHAPTER XII

AMPHIBIOUS PROGRESS, 1941-1945

WITH the seizure of Okinawa, the drive across the Central Pacific reached the doorstep of Japan. As the Joint Chiefs of Staff had long hoped, an invasion of the home islands was not necessary. Iwo Jima and Okinawa had conclusively shown the Japanese that regardless of terrain, they could defend neither beaches nor inshore strong points against American assault. Submarines and the recapture of the Philippines by Southwest Pacific forces and by the Pacific Fleet had severed Japan's life line to the Netherlands East Indies and Southeast Asia, and bases in the Marianas, the Nanpo Shoto, and the Ryukyus were servicing the ships and planes needed to strangle the home islands of Japan and to destroy their industrial potential.

Okinawa, in other words, ended the assault phase of the Pacific War and introduced the siege phase. American naval and air power made Japan's cities untenable and her commerce impossible. Only those Americans anxious to deploy large land armies insisted that immediate invasion was necessary, and it is now evident that Japan would have surrendered without the ordeal of atomic bombs, although American intelligence was unaware of this fact in August 1945.[1] Yet it may reasonably be maintained that American military and political leadership erred in not recognizing, after Okinawa, that the siege phase of the Pacific War had arrived and that only patience and continued air-sea attacks were required for final victory. In other words, the atomic bombs were dropped to save lives of the men who were scheduled to begin the invasion of Kyushu in November 1945, when the invasion itself was unnecessary.

Thus, having defeated the Japanese navy and air force, it was not necessary for America to come fully to grips with the Japanese army. This possibility was recognized by the Joint Staff Planners, the Joint Strategic Survey Committee, and the Joint Chiefs of Staff early in 1943 when studying the feasibility of opening up the Central Pacific front, and their foresight was admirable. The Central Pacific drive destroyed Japanese strength in the critical strategic zone and denied the enemy bases from which he could deploy his remaining air-sea power to halt it.

The strategy of the Central Pacific offensive was to secure the path to Japan by seizing key bases, neutralizing surrounding enemy positions, and pressing forward without first clearing out by-passed zones.

It was a classic application of the principles of economy of force, of mobility, and of concentration. Carrier air backed by surface strength provided the mobility to isolate and prepare distant targets, and marines supplied a large part of the brawn required to take them.

At least by the close of 1943 the Joint Chiefs of Staff recognized that the quickest way to defeat Japan was to seize bases in the Central Pacific from which Japanese sea and air power could be engaged decisively, her industry bombed, and her overseas commerce strangulated. Without detracting from the tremendous value of the assistance rendered by the successive campaigns in the Southwest Pacific Area, the fact remains that the Central Pacific drive was recognized by top strategic planners to be paramount and was in fact the more decisive in the final defeat of Japan.

In this theater the Marine Corps provided the greater part of the fighting troops. But this was not the Corps' major contribution to victory in the Pacific. The Central Pacific drive could not conceivably have been undertaken had it not been clear by the end of 1943 that the American amphibious doctrine developed largely by the Marine Corps and Navy was sound. In the Central Pacific, American troops were compelled to assault strongly fortified islands from the sea. There was no possibility of effecting surprise landings against undefended or lightly held beaches, as was the case in most of the operations conducted in MacArthur's theater. In the Central Pacific the amphibious assault was the key to sucess. Fortunately American forces had on hand a systematic body of tactical principles which enabled them to make such assaults. The capture of Tarawa, in spite of defects in execution, conclusively demonstrated that American amphibious doctrine was valid, that even the strongest island fortress could be seized. The subsequent application and improvement of amphibious assault tactics and techniques coupled with the tremendous expansion of American carrier-based air power and submarine strength were the three most significant factors bringing about defeat of the Japanese.

The extent of this amphibious improvement becomes immediately apparent on comparing the Marines' first two major amphibious operations in the Pacific with their last. To veterans who remembered the lean days of Guadalcanal and Tarawa, the magnitude and the precision of the invasion of Okinawa were amazing. By contrast, those early landings appeared puny and amateurish.

Yet the contrast between early amphibious operations and the near perfection that marked the landing on Okinawa is not an accurate or just measure of amphibious progress between the beginning and the close of the Pacific War. It is a distortion in the sense that it exaggerates the shortcomings of American amphibious doctrine at the outset of the conflict. A closer examination of these first operations shows that the chief shortcomings were not in doctrine, but rather in the means to put existing doctrine into effect. The near disaster at Guadalcanal sprang primarily from the early departure of naval support and supply ships which in turn was predicated on the inability or presumed inability of the fleet elements operating in those waters to control the sea and air. The failure to gain full impact of assault at Betio was largely because there were not enough amphibian tractors on hand to carry all the assault troops across the offshore reef.

At the war's beginning, United States forces had at their disposal a body of tactical principles forming a basic amphibious doctrine which the test of warfare proved to be sound. This doctrine was first set forth by the Marine Corps in 1934 and officially accepted by the Navy in 1938. An examination of these first statements of tactical principles for employment in amphibious war reveals that for the most part they stood up well and, with slight modifications, were as valid throughout the war as when written.

This is not to say that the war in the Pacific taught no new amphibious lessons. Such a proposition would be absurd on the face of it, and the foregoing chapters of this volume should be sufficient to disprove it completely. But the modifications wrought between 1942 and 1945 in the art of amphibious warfare did not seriously affect underlying principles. Those modifications sprang from two main causes. The first was production. Quantities of new amphibious equipment permitted tremendous enlargement of the scope of operations as well as a wide variety of methods for overcoming many of the difficulties inherent in landing seaborne troops on hostile shores. The second cause was the refinement of certain techniques which had already been conceived before the war but which needed the experience of combat itself to achieve any degree of perfection.

The part played by the introduction of new types of amphibious equipment in modifying the nature of amphibious operations can perhaps best be understood by examining refinements in the ship-to-shore movement. The basic pattern remained unchanged. By at least 1941 it had been clearly demonstrated that the most feasible method of landing assault troops was to embark them in unbroken tactical units aboard specially equipped transports and cargo vessels with their essential combat supplies and equipment stowed to permit rapid unloading to meet the tactical situation ashore. Once at the target area, transports anchored offshore and disembarked their troops and supplies in landing craft the construction of which permitted carrying small troop units intact to the beach or close to the shore line. At a designated time these approached a line-of-departure parallel to and seaward of the landing beaches, marked by control vessels. After the completion of the preassault naval and air bombardment the troop-laden craft on signal deployed tactically and ran for the beach.

The only significant changes made in this original concept stemmed from technological innovations—the introduction of new amphibious gadgets. Standard landing craft such as the various models of Higgins boats were incapable of negotiating the offshore reefs which were so common in the Pacific. The answer lay in the amphibian tractor, a vehicle which had originally been intended chiefly for logistical employment but which was to become one of the most important tactical weapons of the Pacific War. Tarawa illustrated both the utility of these vehicles and the folly of not having them on hand in large numbers. Never again in the Pacific War were assault troops to be handicapped by serious shortages of this vital piece of equipment. Later the same machine was armored and armed with guns or howitzers and employed to lead the first waves of troops into the shore.

Also important was the amphibian truck, the Dukw, which made its first appearance in the Pacific at Kwajalein. This was exclusively a United States Army contribution and its value as a carrier of supplies and equipment, especially artillery and ammunition, was repeatedly shown.

New inventions and improvisations on old inventions in the field of larger landing craft had a signal effect on the potency and effectiveness of the amphibious assault technique. Of these vessels, probably the most important was the tank landing ship, the work horse of the amphibious fleet. These vessels, originally of British design, were first intended to beach and to land tanks to support assault troops. In the Pacific, and especially in the Central Pacific, they frequently could not be put to this use because hydrographic conditions prevented reaching the shore. But they were ideal for lifting amphibian tractors and Dukws which could be easily disembarked into the water through the huge bow doors. Thus the tank landing ship became an assault transport. Beginning with the Marianas campaign and throughout the rest of the Pacific War, because of lessons learned earlier in the Marshalls, the assault troops of the first landing waves were transferred to these vessels at the staging area, and tank landing ships regularly moved into the combat zone ready to deliver into the water their litters of amphibian vehicles loaded with foot troops and artillery. Tank landing ships were put to other uses as well. Some were modified and equipped to become repair ships or offshore radar stations, others were made into hospital wards. In the main, however, tank landing ships carried and serviced amphibian vehicles, and tanks were lifted to the target by the larger dock landing ships.

Another type of large landing craft also originally of British design underwent an even more radical metamorphosis in the Pacific. This was the infantry landing craft equipped with ramps on either side of the bow for the rapid debarkation of troops at or close to the beach. Again the presence of reefs throughout the Central Pacific precluded their extensive employment in this manner. Hence many were converted to gunboats, rocket boats, and mortar boats. The first appearance of these converted craft was in the New Britain campaign, and thereafter it became standard procedure for these vessels to precede the first wave of troops close to shore to deliver a last-minute area bombardment.

These are only examples. Other vessels such as medium landing ships and tank landing craft with modifications and mutations were introduced to enhance the power and flexibility of the ship-to-shore movement and to expedite landing supplies and equipment for the combat troops.

Other examples of technological improvements occur in the field of communications. The period just before and during the ship-to-shore movement is the one in which effective control by responsible command authorities over the scattered units under them is the hardest to maintain. This is the juncture when exact timing among all elements of the assault is at once the most necessary and the most difficult to obtain. Such control and timing, to be flexible, demands reliable communications. The confusion resulting from the breakdown of communications aboard the attack force flagship at Tarawa was ample proof of the dangerous consequence of interrupted control. That no serious breakdown was repeated in the Pacific War was due largely to the introduction of the specially designed amphibious headquarters ship with extensive new types of communications equipment. Two of these made their first appearance in the Marshalls, and the type became standard in subsequent amphibious campaigns. Another communications lesson driven home at Tarawa was the need for better-equipped control craft at the line-of-departure, to serve as the nerve center of the assault ashore. Contact between ship and shore was also made more regular and efficient by various improvements in existing types of radios, by the introduction of lighter weight sets more adaptable to amphibious landings, and by progress in methods of waterproofing against the inevitable hazards of seaborne transportation.

Just as these and other technological developments changed the face of amphibious operations without altering underlying doctrines, so did refinements of technique give those operations a new appearance. Important examples of better techniques include the improved coordination of supporting arms, the evolution of close air support, and the perfection of naval gunfire support.

Coordination among all elements of the amphibious force and especially among the supporting arms of air, artillery, and naval gunfire was considerably improved throughout the war by the adoption of new techniques as well as by technological advance. Again as a result of communications failures at Tarawa, the joint assault signal company was born. Within this organization were pooled communications personnel from naval fire support ships, air liaison parties, and marine and army shore parties. This permitted uniform training in communications techniques and procedures, helped to eliminate unnecessary congestion of radio circuits, and brought about economies in the employment of skilled manpower. Also, Tarawa showed that greater tank-infantry-demolition coordination was mandatory, and brought again into focus the need for underwater demolition teams.

At Iwo Jima there appeared for the first time the fire support control center ashore as well as afloat. To this agency was assigned the duty of coordinating requests for and allocating fire missions of the three main supporting arms of air, naval gunfire, and artillery. This was simply an extension of the centralized coordination exercised from the amphibious flagship during the early phases of the operation. It was a formalization of procedures which had been worked out on an *ad hoc* basis in previous operations. It provided one of the best wartime examples of control by cooperation. Separate service branches and arms were effectively coordinated without resort to command authority. Later at Okinawa final authority for the allocation of supporting fires rested with the artillery representative at the support control center, but in practice arbitrary authority was rarely exercised. As at Iwo, decisions were ordinarily reached by consultation and compromise to the end that the greater effectiveness and economy in the employment of all three arms were achieved.

In the employment of close air support for ground troops progress was disappointingly slow. This was a specialty for which the marines claimed to be peculiarly suited and one which their doctrine had espoused before the war commenced. Yet not until late in the war were the means available for marine aviation to put its own close support doctrine into execution. Marine planes in the South Pacific were kept too busy flying combat air patrol and bombing missions to provide much in the way of close support. In the Central Pacific, until late in 1944, marine pilots and planes were largely used to keep by-passed islands neutralized.

Marine officers from the commandant down had repeatedly recommended the assignment of escort carriers for the exclusive use of marine aviators. Only thus, they maintained, could their ground troops be guaranteed uninterrupted and efficient close air support during the assault phase of their amphibious operations. Not until the very end of the war, and then too late for active employment, did the navy designate escort carriers for the sole use of marine aviation.

One reason why marine infantry commanders were so anxious to be supported by their own planes was that they felt the navy's system of controlling close air strikes was too inflexible. Complaints about the excessive rigidity of the control system and needless delays in the execution of close support missions were particularly strong during the Marianas campaign, where close overall control was exercised by navy officers with headquarters aboard ship out of immediate contact with the ground situation.

Within the Marine Corps itself, two techniques for controlling air strikes were worked out, each designed to meet a particular tactical situation. In the Philippines, where marine planes were used to support army troops, a highly flexible system of control was employed. Various links in the chain of command were eliminated and pilots were typically coached into their targets by air liaison personnel located at the front lines. In the given situation this system was both speedy and efficient, but it was possible only because marine pilots were supporting no more than one division at a time and the ground troops were making rapid movement forward.

On Okinawa, where for most of the operation four divisions were fighting abreast on a relatively static front, such decentralization of control over air strikes was infeasible. Only by fairly close control through a central agency over requests for and execution of close support missions could the danger of planes assigned to one unit dropping their bombs within the lines of other adjacent units be avoided or could proper coordination of air support with artillery and naval gunfire be achieved.

The system of control finally evolved by the end of the war attempted to incorporate both the flexibility demonstrated in the Philippines and the excellent coordination set up on Okinawa. Higher echelon authorities monitored requests from lower troop units for close air support. Silence of intermediate and higher commands was interpreted as consent. Moreover, once approval of an air strike was granted and wherever the tactical situation permitted, on-the-spot direction of the strike was delegated to front-line tactical air parties. Thus flexibility could be obtained without sacrifice to the safety of ground troops or without interference with the overall tactical direction of all components of the ground force.

Nowhere in the history of amphibious warfare in World War II was progress more rapid or decisive than in the field of naval gunfire support. Here again advances were made not so much as a result of technological improvements in naval guns or shells but rather because of refinements of established techniques coupled with the assimilation of lessons learned through experience and a rigorous program of training.

At least by the close of the Saipan invasion, where the fast battleships of Spruance's Fifth Fleet failed to make any serious dent in the island's defenses, it was apparent that one of the prime requisites for naval bombardment was specialized training of shipboard personnel in the duties of spotting and delivering fire on shore targets. That this had long been recognized by the Marine Corps is shown by the establishment of the first gunnery range at Bloodsworth Island, Maryland, by the organization of a naval gunnery program under the Fifth Amphibious Corps at Kahoolawe Island, Hawaii, and by a similar program set up by the Third Amphibious Corps in the Solomons. Before June 1944, all the old battleships of the Pacific Fleet, many of them survivors of Pearl Harbor, as well as numerous cruisers and destroyers had gone through one or more of these courses and had gained valuable training in the peculiar problems of naval gunfire support ashore. This, together with experience gained in repeated attacks against one island after another, brought into being a powerful team of naval vessels whose primary function was recognized to be shore bombardment and whose skill in the performance of that function was, on the whole, magnificent.

Two important lessons gradually emerged from this experience. The first was that area fire was useful for neutralization in the preassault phase on the morning of the landing, but ineffective in knocking out enemy gun installations and well-constructed defenses, and that for naval gunfire to perform its chief mission it was essential that ships deliver prolonged deliberate destructive pinpoint fire against known or suspected difficult targets. This meant moving in close to the beaches even with vessels as heavy as battleships. Admiral Conolly's performance in the Marshalls, which was later emulated by other fire support commanders, firmly established this principle of close deliberate destructive fire. A second and corollary lesson was that a prolonged period of preliminary naval gunfire was essential if exorbitant casualties to landing troops were to be avoided. Success in preparatory gunfire could not be measured in terms merely of the weight of ammunition expended. Careful deliberate pinpoint fire from short ranges was mandatory, and this took time.

Early in the war any such program would have involved excessive risks to valuable naval ships from enemy air and submarine activity. But with the successive defeats administered to the Japanese fleet in the Solomons and in the Battles of the Philippine Sea and Leyte Gulf much of that danger was removed. To be sure, at Iwo considerations of grand strategy induced Spruance and Turner to restrict the preliminary bombardment of that island to considerably fewer days than what marine commanders thought necessary. Whatever the wisdom of their decision in respect to the big picture, there can be no doubt that the troops ashore suffered because of it and that the final seizure of that fortress was delayed to a point which was seriously detrimental to the marine units and dangerous to the fleet components in the area. At Okinawa no such economy of ships and ammunition was observed. Seven full days were allotted to naval bombardment before the day the first troops were put ashore on the main island in the Ryukyus. This was in spite of the known danger from enemy kamikaze planes, which in fact later did take a frightful toll from American shipping. Clearly by the end of the war it was recognized that in the absence of compelling reasons to the contrary, an extensive period of prelanding naval bombardment was one of the vital keys to amphibious success.

Adoption of such measures meant the sacrifice of tactical and to a certain extent even strategical surprise. When large naval task forces accompanied by minesweepers, underwater demolition teams, and all the other paraphernalia of the naval amphibious support force hove into view of an island target well in advance of the landing troops, there could be no doubt in the minds of the enemy commanders where the next blow was to fall. A small measure of deception could still be maintained by diversionary threats against beaches other than those chosen for the landing, but except on the larger islands these could have little effect on defensive tactics.

Thus the lesson gained from the experience of naval bombardment in the Pacific War must be read with care. Success depended upon deliberation, and deliberation took time. This inevitably gave the enemy ample warning of the attackers' intentions and the element of surprise was lost. Whether such tactics would be feasible in amphibious operations against a well-defended continental land mass is doubtful. Where the enemy has powerful forces distributed over an extensive area and a system of land communications capable of massing these forces rapidly in any desired spot, advanced warning of the location of the key beaches which the attackers intend to strike might well prove disastrous to assault. It is not difficult to imagine, for example, what would have happened to the attack forces at the Normandy beaches in June 1944 if a large naval task force had moved in several days before the initial landing was to be made, if it had commenced to shell the selected beaches, and if the Germans had correctly estimated the situation.

The only condition under which prolonged preliminary naval bombardment can be safely employed in an amphibious operation is when the target area can be completely or almost completely localized. In every instance after Guadalcanal this was possible because of the growing power of the United States Pacific Fleet. Where it is not possible, then surprise is essential to the success of amphibious operations, and prolonged bombardment must be sacrificed. But on the other hand, an enemy holding an extensive coast line can not be powerful at every point of the periphery, and thus is open to deception.

The foregoing discussion treats only the more important World War II advances in amphibious techniques and materiel. In the face of these advances it is the more remarkable that the ideas and concepts upon which they rested remained basically unchanged. The amphibious doctrine developed in the 1930's and given material substance in the 1940's was proved sound by the test of war.

Since the close of the war much of the thinking on questions of amphibious doctrine and techniques has been retrospective in nature. After any successful war there is a tendency on the part of military minds on the winning side to learn the lessons of the past too well, to rely on former solutions to solve future problems, and to relax into the comfortable illusion that past successes spell future victories. There is a danger that such will be the case with the American doctrine of amphibious warfare. The theories and techniques which worked so well by the close of World War II might easily become crystallized into dogma and from dogma into holy writ.

There is another and perhaps more serious danger evident in some military circles today. That is the belief that large scale amphibious operations are obsolete. This stems in part from a conviction that the atomic bomb has made it too hazardous to concentrate into small areas the massive naval task forces necessary for launching amphibious landings comparable to those of World War II. It also arises from the theory that airborne operations offer a practical and economical substitute for landing troops on hostile shores.

Both of these attitudes are unfortunate in about equal measure. Amphibious warfare did not reach ultimate perfection in 1945. Nor is it likely within the foreseeable future that the United States and her allies can hope to avoid amphibious operations in the event of a major war.

The Marine Corps, which both by tradition and law has a special interest in the evolution of the art of amphibious warfare, is not bemused either by the theory that such operations are obsolete or that there is no room for improvement on established doctrine and techniques. After the end of World War II the Corps began again to experiment with novel devices and ideas to improve on old techniques. The most spectacular of these is the helicopter intended to lift assault troops from shipboard to points beyond strong enemy beach installations. The helicopter, in short, may supplant the amphibious tractor. Another larger model of the helicopter has been tested for use in landing artillery, in gunfire spotting, in evacuation of casualties, and in ammunition resupply.[2]

Whatever the outcome of these and kindred experiments, the spirit in which they are being conducted is reassuring to those who concern themselves with the military security of the United States and the United Nations. If the world again erupts in total war, bases essential to the effective employment of air and sea power must be seized regardless of the opposition encountered, and beachheads on large land masses will probably have to be wrested from hostile powers. To accomplish these ends the best possible amphibious doctrine will be essential. If the past record of the Marine Corps is any indication of future performance, the world can be reasonably confident that such a doctrine will be provided.

REFERENCES

Glossary of Abbreviations

IAC	First Amphibious Corps
IIIAC	Third Amphibious Corps
VAC	Fifth Amphibious Corps
AFSC	Armed Forces Staff College
AGF	Army Ground Forces
Amphib Recon Bn	Amphibious Reconnaissance Battalion
Amph Track	Amphibian Tractor
Amph Truck	Amphibian Truck
Arm'd AmphTrack	Armored Amphibian Tractor
ANSC	Army-Navy Staff College
Bn	Battalion
CG	Commanding General
CinCLant	Commander in Chief Atlantic Fleet
CinCPac	Commander in Chief Pacific Fleet
CinCPOA	Commander in Chief Pacific Ocean Areas
CinCSWPA	Commander in Chief Southwest Pacific Area
CMC	Commandant Marine Corps
CNO	Chief of Naval Operations
CO	Commanding Officer
Com	Commander
ComAirForPac	Commander Air Force Pacific Fleet
ComAirSoPac	Commander Aircraft South Pacific Area
ComCenPacFor	Commander Central Pacific Force
ComCortCarPac	Commander Escort Carriers, Pacific Fleet
Com5thFlt	Commander Fifth Fleet
ComPhibForsPac	Commander Amphibious Forces Pacific Fleet
ComPhibForSoPac	Commander Amphibious Forces South Pacific Area
ComSoPac	Commander South Pacific Area
CominCh	Commander in Chief United States Fleet
ComTransDivsSoPacFor	Commander Transport Divisions, South Pacific Force
ComTransLant	Commander Transports Atlantic Fleet
C/S USA	Chief of Staff, United States Army
Def	Defense
Eng	Engineer
ExpTrps	Expeditionary Troops
5th Flt	Fifth Fleet
Flex	Fleet Landing Exercise
Flot	Flotilla
FMF	Fleet Marine Force
FMFPac	Fleet Marine Force Pacific
F.T.P.	Fleet Training Publication
Guad I–V	First Marine Division Guadalcanal action report, issued in five separate sections
Hq USMC	Historical Division, Headquarters United States Marine Corps
InfDiv	Infantry Division
Inf	Used with a number, as 165thInf, means the 165th Infantry Regiment reinforced
JASCO	Joint Assault Signal Company
JCS	Joint Chiefs of Staff
JICPOA	Joint Intelligence Center Pacific Ocean Areas
LCI	Landing Craft Infantry

LVT	Landing Vehicle Tracked
MAG	Marine Air Group
MarBrig	Marine Brigade
MarDiv	Marine Division
Mars	Used with a number as 1stMars, means the First Marine Regiment reinforced
MCS	Marine Corps Schools
Med	Medical
Nat'l Arch	National Archives
NOB	Naval Operating Base
NGF	Naval Gunfire
ONI	Office of Naval Intelligence
ONRL	Office of Naval Records and Library
PacFlt	Pacific Fleet
Para	Parachute
PhibsLant	Amphibious Force Atlantic Fleet
PhibFor	Amphibious Force
PhibGrp	Amphibious Group
Pion	Pioneer
POA	Pacific Ocean Areas
ProvFAGrp	Provisional Field Artillery Group
ProvMarBrig	Provisional Marine Brigade
PUL	Marine Corps History Project Manuscripts in Princeton University Library
Raid	Raider
RCT	Regimental Combat Team
RS MCS	Records Section, Marine Corps Schools
3dFlt	Third Fleet
TAF	Tactical Air Force
Trans Div	Transport Division
Trans Grp	Transport Group
TQM	Transport Quartermaster
UDT	Underwater Demolition Team
USAFCenPac	United States Army Forces in the Central Pacific Area
USAFPOA	United States Army Forces in Pacific Ocean Areas
USAFISPA	United States Army Forces in the South Pacific Area
USSBS(P)	United States Strategic Bombing Survey (Pacific)
VMF	Marine Fighter Squadron
WPD	War Plans Division, Office of Chief of Naval Operations

CHAPTER I

1. As quoted by Robert E. Sherwood, *Roosevelt and Hopkins: An Intimate History* (New York, 1948), 783–784.
2. Kent R. Greenfield, Robert R. Palmer, and Bell I. Wiley, *The Organization of Ground Combat Troops* (vol in U.S. Army in World War II, Washington, 1947), 85.
3. Alexander A. Vandegrift, "The Marine Corps in 1948"; James D. Hittle, "Sea Power and a National General Staff," *U.S. Naval Institute Proceedings*, Feb 1948, Oct 1949, 135–143, 1091–1103. Holland M. Smith, "Amphibious Tactics," *Marine Corps Gazette*, Jun 1945–Mar 1947.
4. Hittle, "Jomini and Amphibious Thought," *Marine Corps Gazette*, May 1946, 35–38. Antoine H. Jomini, *Précis de l'art de la guerre*, IIe partie (Paris, 1838), 138–145, 297–339.
5. Alexander Kiralfy, "Sea Power in the Eastern War," *Brassey's Naval Annual, 1942* (London, c1942), 150–160. Liddell Hart, *The Defence of Britain* (London, 1939), 130.
6. CMC, memo to CNO on the mission of the land, naval, and air forces, 19 Apr

1946, Hq USMC. Greenfield, et al., *Organization of Ground Combat Troops*, 101.
7. Dwight D. Eisenhower, "Harmony in the Armed Services," interview in *U.S. News and World Report*, 3 Feb 1950, 17.
8. John F. C. Fuller, *The Second World War, 1939-45* (London, 1948), 207.
9. Raymond A. Spruance to Jeter A. Isely, 17 Jan 1950, PUL. Bernard Brodie, *A Guide to Naval Strategy* (Princeton, 1944), 170-194.
10. CG 1stMarDiv, covering ltr Guad V, 1 Jul 1943, Hq USMC.
11. Sherwood, *Roosevelt and Hopkins*, 591.
12. Eisenhower, *Crusade in Europe* (New York, 1948), 220-265. Bernard L. Montgomery, *Normandy to the Baltic* (Boston, 1948), 1-72. Frederick Morgan, *Overture to Overlord* (New York, 1950). Historical Division, War Dept., *Omaha Beachhead*, and *Utah Beach to Cherbourg* (vols in American Forces in Action Series, Washington, c1945, 1947), 1-91, 1-75.
13. Eisenhower, "Harmony in the Armed Services," *U.S. News*, 3 Feb 1950, 17.
14. Louis Morton, "American and Allied Strategy in the Far East," *Military Review*, Dec 1949, 22-39.
15. CinCPac, Feb 1945 operations in POA, 27 Aug 1945, ONRL. Vandegrift, "Amphibious Miracle of Our Time," *New York Times*, 6 Aug 1944, section VI (magazine), 38.
16. Eisenhower, "Harmony in the Armed Services," *U.S. News*, 3 Feb 1950, 17.
17. Roy E. Appleman, James M. Burns, Russell A. Gugeler, and John Stevens, *Okinawa, the Last Battle* (vol in U.S. Army in World War II, Washington, 1948), 496.
18. Clyde H. Metcalf, *A History of the United States Marine Corps* (New York, 1939), *passim*.

CHAPTER II

1. Sir Roger Keyes, *The Naval Memoirs of the Admiral of the Fleet, Sir Roger Keyes* (New York, 1934); *Amphibious Warfare and Combined Operations* (New York, 1943). Sir Charles E. Callwell, *The Dardanelles* (Boston, 1919). Julian S. Corbett, *Naval Operations*, vols II and III (London, 1921). Thomas G. Frothingham, *The Naval History of the World War*, vol II (Cambridge, 1925). William D. Puleston, *The Dardanelles Campaign* (Annapolis, 1927), 1-56.
2. Keyes, *Combined Operations*, 53.
3. Puleston, *Dardanelles*, 168.
4. CMC, annual rpt, in *Annual Report of the Navy Department* for the years given, 1916.
5. Cited by Dion Williams to whom the remark was made, in *U.S. Naval Institute Proceedings*, Apr 1922, 597-598.
6. Williams, "The Naval Advanced Base," lecture before U.S. Naval War College, 26 Jul 1912 (Washington, 1912).
7. CMC, annual rpt, 1903. Williams, "Advanced Base." Holland M. Smith and Percy Finch, *Coral and Brass* (New York, 1949), 19.
8. CMC, annual rpts, 1910, 1911, 1918, 1919, 1920. Williams, "Advanced Base."
9. CMC, annual rpt, 1912.
10. CMC, annual rpt, 1914.
11. Williams, "Advanced Base."
12. Corroborated in H. M. Smith, "Amphibious Tactics," *Marine Corps Gazette*, Jul 1946, 47.
13. CMC, annual rpt, 1920.
14. Earl H. Ellis, "Naval Bases: Their Location, Resources, and Security," RS MCS. Place and date of this lecture are unknown, but internal evidence indicates that it was written before the mandated islands were turned over to Japan.
15. Ellis, Operations Plan 712 H, "Advanced Base Operations in Micronesia," RS MCS.
16. Rufus H. Lane, "The Mission and Doctrine of the Marine Corps," *Marine Corps Gazette*, Mar 1923, 1-13.
17. John A. Lejeune, "The United States Marine Corps," *Marine Corps Gazette*, Dec 1923, 243-254; "The United States Marine Corps" and "The Marine Corps," *U.S. Naval Institute Proceedings*, Oct 1925, Oct 1926, 1858-1870, 1961-1969; *The United States Marine Corps* (Washington, 1925).
18. Eli K. Cole, "Joint Overseas Operations," *U.S. Naval Institute Proceedings*, Nov 1929, 928.
19. "Army-Navy Joint Action," cited in Cole, "Joint Overseas Operations," *U.S. Naval Institute Proceedings*, Nov 1929, 927-937.
20. Smith, *Coral and Brass*, 57.
21. CMC, annual rpts, 1924-1932.
22. CMC, annual rpts, 1921, 1925.
23. CMC, annual rpts, 1921, 1922, 1924, 1925.
24. W. L. Redles, "The Corps Expeditionary Force, United States Fleet, and the Winter Maneuvers, 1924, at Culebra, P. R., Problem No. 4," Hq USMC. CMC, annual rpts, 1922, 1924.
25. Redles, "Corps Expeditionary Force," 43-44, 65-66.
26. CMC, annual rpt, 1924.
27. CMC, memo to CNO, mission of land, naval and air forces, 19 Apr 1946, Hq USMC.
28. Frederick L. Wieseman, "Proper Design and Employment of a Marine Corps Tank for Landing Operations," lecture at MCS, Mar 1949, RS MCS.

H. M. Smith, "Amphibious Tactics," *Marine Corps Gazette*, Aug 1946, 43.
29. CMC, annual rpts, 1925, 1926, 1932. H. M. Smith, "Amphibious Tactics," *Marine Corps Gazette*, Aug 1946, 44.
30. CMC, annual rpts, 1916, 1922, 1931.
31. CMC, annual rpts, 1922–1929.
32. Clayton C. Jerome, "Close Air Support in Landing Operations," lecture at Naval Air Training Command, 24 Mar 1948, 1–2, U.S. Naval Air Station, Pensacola, Fla.
33. John H. Russell, correspondence in Hq USMC; and "The Birth of the Fleet Marine Force," *U.S. Naval Institute Proceedings*, Jan 1946, 49–51. WPD, ltr to CNO, 23 Aug 1933; CNO, ltr to CominCh, 25 Aug 1933; CominCh, ltr to CNO, 2 Sep 1933; CNO, ltr to CMC, 12 Sep 1933, Hq USMC.
34. CMC, annual rpt, 1934.
35. Anthony A. Francis, typescript dated 1945, RS MCS, 46. Authors' italics.
36. *Landing Force Manual*, U.S. Navy, 1920, 1927.
37. Joint Board of the Army and Navy, *Joint Overseas Expeditions*, 12 Jan 1933.
38. MCS conference on *Tentative Manual for Landing Operations*, 9 Jan 1934, RS MCS.
39. MCS conference, 9 Jan 1934, RS MCS.
40. WD FM #31–5, *Landing Operations on Hostile Shores*, 2 Jun 1941.
41. *Tentative Landing Manual*, par 1–34.
42. *Tent. Man.*, pars 2–301, 2–303.
43. *Tent. Man.*, pars 2–314, 2–315, 2–317, 2–321, 2–323, 3–20.
44. *Tent. Man.*, pars 2–401, 2–404, 2–407 through 418, 2–424 through 426.
45. *Tent. Man.*, par 2–403.
46. *Tent. Man.*, pars 2–100 through 105, 2–109 through 113.
47. *Tent. Man.*, pars 2–407, 2–408, 2–1000, 2–1002, 2–210, 2–602.
48. *Tent. Man.*, pars 5–900, 5–901, 5–903, 5–907, 5–909, 5–910.

CHAPTER III

1. CMC, annual rpt, 1936.
2. Joint MCS-Naval War College problems are in RS MCS.
3. CO Special Service Squadron, Flex 1 rpt, 4 Apr 1935, Nat'l Arch. H. M. Smith, "Amphibious Tactics," *Marine Corps Gazette*, Sep 1946, 43–44. Benjamin W. Gally, "A History of U.S. Fleet Landing Exercises," mimeograph, Sep 1939, 2–4, Hq USMC.
4. David L. Nutter, "Gunfire Support in Fleet Landing Exercises," mimeograph, Sep 1939, Hq USMC. CG FMF, Flex 1 rpt, Feb 1935; Ass't Chief Observer, *Arkansas*, Flex 1 NGF rpt, 5 Mar 1935; CO Special Service Squadron, Flex 1 rpt, 4 Apr 1935, Nat'l Arch.
5. Aerial Spotting Officer, Air Officer and Observer, Communications Officer, MAG 1, Flex 1 rpts, 2 and 4 Mar 1935, Nat'l Arch.
6. CO BtryA 10thMars, Flex 1 rpt, landing and embarkation of 155-mm guns using artillery lighters; FMF Engr Officer, Flex 1 rpt, 22 Mar 1935; CG FMF, rpt, comments on ramp equipment, 30 Mar 1935, Nat'l Arch.
7. For a general account of Flex 2 see H. M. Smith, "Amphibious Tactics," *Marine Corps Gazette*, Sep 1946, 43–47; and Gally, "Fleet Landing Exercises," 4–6, Hq USMC; U.S. Army Observer, Flex 2 rpt, 15 Mar 1936, Nat'l Arch.
8. Nutter, "Gunfire Support," Hq USMC. Commander Training Squadron, Flex 2 rpt, 11 May 1936, Nat'l Arch.
9. CO MAG 1, Flex 2 rpt, 13 Mar 1936, Nat'l Arch.
10. CO VMF 9, Flex 2 rpt, 3 Mar 1936, Nat'l Arch.
11. Operations Officer 2dBn5thMars, Flex 2 rpt, 11 Feb 1936, Nat'l Arch. William P. T. Hill, "The Characteristics of Coral Formations of the Pacific Islands," RS MCS.
12. Maj. Jesse L. Perkins USMC, ltr to CO 1stMarBrig, 20 Feb 1936, Nat'l Arch.
13. U.S. Army Observer, Flex 2 rpt, Nat'l Arch.
14. Hard S. Fassett, ltr to CO 1stMarBrig, 27 Feb 1936, Nat'l Arch.
15. U.S. Army Observer, Flex 2 rpt, Nat'l Arch.
16. H. M. Smith, "Amphibious Tactics," *Marine Corps Gazette*, Sep 1946, 43–47. Gally, "Fleet Landing Exercises," Hq USMC. CG FMF, Flex 3 rpt, Nat'l Arch.
17. CG 1stMarBrig, Flex 3 rpt, 28 Feb 1937, Nat'l Arch.
18. Hq 4thArmy, Flex 3 rpt, Nat'l Arch. Lt. Col. Thomas E. Watson USMC, rpt on assistance by Marine Corps instructors in training army units for Flex 3, 4 Mar 1937, Nat'l Arch.
19. CO 5thMars, Flex 3 rpt, 26 Feb 1937, Nat'l Arch.
20. Nutter, "Gunfire Support," Hq USMC. CG FMF, Flex 3 rpt, Nat'l Arch.
21. Hq 4thArmy, Flex 3 rpt, Nat'l Arch.
22. CG FMF, CO Force Aircraft FMF, 2dMarBrig Air Officer, Operations Officers 1st and 2nd MAGs Flex 3 rpts, 2 and 5 Mar, 24 and 25 Feb 1937, Nat'l Arch.
23. Communications Officer, 2dMarBrig, Flex 3 rpt, Nat'l Arch.
24. Watson, rpt on USMC instruction of army units, Flex 3; Hq 4thArmy, Flex 3 rpt, Nat'l Arch.
25. CG FMF, Flex 3 rpt, Nat'l Arch.
26. CG 1stMarBrig, Flex 3 rpt, 28 Feb 1937, Nat'l Arch.
27. CG 1stMarBrig, Flex 3 critique, 19 Feb 1937, Nat'l Arch.

28. H. M. Smith, "Amphibious Tactics," *Marine Corps Gazette*, Sep, Oct, 1946, 43–46, 41–55. CMC, annual rpts, 1938–1941. Gally, "Fleet Landing Exercises," 8–10, Hq USMC. CNO, ltr to CominCh, 1 Dec 1939, Nat'l Arch.
29. CG 1stMarBrig, Flex 4 rpt, 12 Mar 1938, Nat'l Arch. USMC Observer, Flex 4 rpt, 15 Mar 1938, Nat'l Arch.
30. CG 1stMarBrig, Flex 6 rpt, 29 Apr 1940, Nat'l Arch.
31. CG 1stMarBrig, Flex 4 rpt, 12 Mar 1938; Personnel Officer, 1stMarBrig, Flex 4 rpt, 17 Mar 1938, Nat'l Arch.
32. CG 1stMarBrig, Flex 4 and 5 rpts, 12 Mar 1938, 1 Apr 1939; CinCLant, Flex 6 rpt, 13 Jun 1940; CNO, ltr to Commandant, N.Y. Navy Yard, 28 Jan 1939, Nat'l Arch.
33. Artillery Officer 1stMarDiv, Flex 7 NGF rpt, 28 Feb 1941, Nat'l Arch.
34. MCS, "An Evaluation of Air Operations Affecting the U.S. Marine Corps in World War II," 31 Dec 1945, RS MCS.
35. C. Jerome, "Close Air Support in Landing Operations," lecture at Naval Air Training Command, U.S. Naval Air Station, Pensacola, Fla.
36. CO MAG 1, Flex 5 rpt, Nat'l Arch.
37. MCS. *Marine Corps Aviation, General* (Washington, 1940), 49.
38. CG 1stMarBrig, Flex 6 rpt, 29 Apr 1940, Nat'l Arch.
39. CinCLant, despatch to CNO, 3 Feb 1941; CG 1stMarDiv, ltr to CinCLant, 6 Mar 1941; ComTransLant, ltr to CinCLant, ship-to-shore training, 10 Mar 1943, Nat'l Arch.
40. CinCLant, Flex 7 rpt, 15 Mar 1941, Nat'l Arch.
41. CG 1stMarDiv, Flex 7 rpt, 6 Mar 1941, Nat'l Arch.
42. Artillery Officer 1stMarDiv, Flex 7 rpt, 6 Mar 1941, Nat'l Arch.
43. CinCLant, Flex 7 rpt, 15 Mar 1941, Nat'l Arch. Donald M. Weller to Philip A. Crowl, 7 Apr 1949, PUL.
44. H. M. Smith, *Coral and Brass*, 80–81.
45. H. M. Smith, "Amphibious Tactics," *Marine Corps Gazette*, Oct 1946, 54. USMC Table of Organization, 28 Mar 1941, Hq USMC.
46. Rpt of Conference aboard *Alcor*, NOB Norfolk, 15 Jan 1942, Hq USMC.
47. H. M. Smith, "Amphibious Tactics," *Marine Corps Gazette*, Oct 1946, 41–55.
48. CG Caribbean Force, 1st Joint Training Force Exercise rpt, 28 Aug 1941, Nat'l Arch.
49. CO 5thMars, 1st Joint Training Force Exercise rpt, 9 Sep 1941.
50. CG PhibsLant, 1st Joint Training Force Exercise rpt, 9 Sep 1941, Nat'l Arch.
51. CO 5thMars, CO 2ndBn7thMars, CO Shore Party 7thMars, 1st Joint Training Force Exercise rpts, 22 Aug 1941, Nat'l Arch.
52. CG PhibsLant, 1st Joint Training Force Exercise rpt, 9 Sep 1941, Nat'l Arch.
53. CO 1stBn5thMars, 1st Joint Training Force Exercise rpt, 23 Aug 1941, Nat'l Arch.
54. CG PhibsLant, ltr to Commander Naval Attack Force, 31 Dec 1941; CG PhibsLant, Lynhaven Roads Exercise Rpt, 10 Feb 1942, Nat'l Arch.
55. MCS Naval Gunfire Section, table, "Major Activities of the Amphibious Corps Atlantic Fleet, May 1941–July 1942," RS MCS.
56. Ely J. Kahn, Jr. and Henry McLemore, *Fighting Divisions* (Washington, 1945), 1–2, 5–6, 13–14, 17–19.
57. Higgins Industries, *The Eureka News Bulletin*, Jan 1942. H. M. Smith, *Coral and Brass*, 90–96. Correspondence between Victor H. Krulak (Smith's boat officer) and Andrew J. Higgins, in Krulak's possession.
58. Marine Corps Equipment Board, Minutes of Meeting, 24 Apr 1941, MC Equipt Bd, Quantico. H. M. Smith, *Coral and Brass*, 91. Higgins, ltr to Thomas Holcomb, 27 Aug 1942, copy in Krulak's files.
59. MC Eqpt Bd, Minutes, 10 Jan, 22 Mar, 19 Apr 1938, 26 Oct 1939, 7 Nov 1940, MC Eqpt Bd, Quantico. Sec Nav, Continuing Board for the Development of Landing Vehicle Tracked, "History of Landing Vehicle Tracked," 1 Dec 1945, ONRL.
60. Ernest E. Linsert, ltrs to Donald Roebling, 28 Sep 1940, 3 Nov 1941; Linsert, ltrs to W. E. Anderson, 18 Oct 1941, and to Alfred H. Noble, 24 Nov 1941; Anderson, ltr to Linsert 15 Dec 1941, MC Eqpt Bd.
61. Sec Nav, Continuing Board, "History of Landing Vehicle Tracked," 1 Dec 1945, ONRL.
62. Robert D. Heinl, Jr., "Naval Gunfire Training in the Pacific," *Marine Corps Gazette*, Jun 1948, 10–15. D. M. Weller, ltr to P. A. Crowl, 7 Apr 1949, PUL.

CHAPTER IV

1. William H. Hobbes, *The Fortress Islands of the Pacific* (Ann Arbor, Mich., 1945).
2. Herbert Rosinski, "The Strategy of Japan," *Brassey's Naval Annual, 1946*, 99–113. Samuel E. Morison, *The Rising Sun in the Pacific* (vol III, History of United States Naval Operations in World War II, Boston, 1948), 184–208, 223–254.
3. Robert D. Heinl, Jr, *The Defense of Wake* (vol in the official history of the U.S. Marine Corps in World War II, Washington, 1947). Morison, *Rising Sun*

in the Pacific, 223–254. Robert Sherrod, "History of Marine Corps Aviation in World War II" (MS in preparation for publication, Hq USMC), pt II.
4. Hanson W. Baldwin, "The Fourth Marines at Corregidor," *Marine Corps Gazette,* Nov 1946–Feb 1947.
5. Morison, *Rising Sun in the Pacific,* 389–398.
6. Morison, *Coral Sea, Midway and Submarine Actions* (vol IV, History of United States Naval Operations in World War II, Boston, 1949), 3–64.
7. Heinl, *Marines at Midway* (vol in the official history of the U.S. Marine Corps in World War II, Washington, 1948), 20.
8. Sherrod, "USMC Aviation," pt VII, Hq USMC.
9. Morison, *Coral Sea and Midway,* 69–159. Heinl, *Marines at Midway.* The Joint Army-Navy Assessment Committee, *Japanese Naval and Merchant Shipping Losses During World War II by All Causes* (Washington, 1947), 1–2, 29–32. Wesley F. Craven, James L. Cate, eds, *The Army Air Forces in World War II,* vol I (Chicago, 1948), 451–462; vol IV (Chicago, 1950), 63, 89–98, 106–162, 242, 261, 265, 281–310, 319.
10. Morison, *Rising Sun in the Pacific,* 271–380.
11. Edmund G. Love, "The Gilberts-Marshalls Campaign" (MS first draft of vol in U.S. Army in World War II, PUL), ch 1, p 7. Grace S. Person, ltr with encls to J. A. Isely, 1 May 1950, PUL.
12. "The Organization and Functions of the Joint Chiefs of Staff" (lecture at AFSC, 20 Feb 1947), RS MCS. Craven and Cate, eds, *Army Air Forces in World War II,* vol IV, "Foreword." G. S. Person, ltr with encls to J. A. Isely, 1 May 1950, PUL.
13. ComInCh, airmailgram to U.S. Fleet, 13 Jun 1943, Hq USMC. Ernest J. King, ltr to J. A. Isely, 31 Mar 1950, PUL.
14. "Organization for Joint Operations"; "The Mission and Responsibilities of a Theater Commander"; "Organization for Joint Overseas Operations"; "Command Responsibilities in a Joint Operation"; "Responsibilities of a Theater Commander" (all lectures delivered at AFSC, 20 Feb, 7 and 18 Apr 1947), RS MCS.
15. "JCS and Theater Organization," "JCS Directives to CinCPOA and CinCSWPA," *Basic Reading for Members of Joint Operations Review Board, ANSC,* RS MCS. Morison, *Coral Sea and Midway,* 250.
16. ComInCh, basic plan for establishing a South Pacific Amphibious Force, 29 Apr 1942; CG 1stMarDiv, covering ltr Guad V, to CMC, 1 Jul 1943, Hq USMC. Morison, *Coral Sea and Midway,* 246–

251. John L. Zimmerman, *The Guadalcanal Campaign* (vol in official history of the U.S. Marine Corps in World War II, Washington, 1949), 4. John Miller. Jr., *Guadalcanal, The First Offensive* (vol in U.S. Army in World War II, Washington, 1949), 9.
17. Morison, *Coral Sea and Midway,* 259–260. Miller, *Guadalcanal,* 15. Zimmerman, *Guadalcanal,* 6–7.
18. Alan Villiers, *The Coral Sea* (New York, 1949), 2, 7.
19. Brief of despatch from CinCSWPA, 3 Aug 1942; CinCSWPA and ComSoPac, despatch to C/S USA, ComInCh, and CinCPac, 8 Jul 1942 in ComSoPac "War Diary," 9 Jul 1942, ONRL. G. S. Person, ltr with encls to J. A. Isely, 1 May 1950, PUL.
20. CMC, memo to ComInCh on boundary between SoPac and SWPA, 15 Aug 1942; Ass't C/S (War Plans) for Hq ComInCh, 1st endorsement on a memo to himself on limitations in training of 25thInfDiv, from CNO, 28 Nov 1942, Hq USMC. CinCPac, ltr to ComInCh on future employment of PacFlt carriers, 2 Sep 1942, ONRL.
21. Zimmerman, *Guadalcanal,* 5–6. Miller, *Guadalcanal,* 7–10. ONI *Daily,* Apr–Jul 1942, Hq USMC.
22. ComInCh, despatch to CinCPac and CinCSWPA, 25 Jun 1942, ONRL. Miller, *Guadalcanal,* 14–16.
23. ComInCh, despatch to CinCPac, 2 Jul 1942, in ComSoPac, "War Diary," 2 Jul 1942, ONRL.
24. Craven and Cate, *Army Air Forces in World War II,* vol I, footnote 5 to ch 13, p 722.
25. King, *U.S. Navy at War* (Washington, 1946), 49. E. J. King, ltr to J. A. Isely (with encl), 30 Mar 1950, PUL.
26. William F. Halsey, Jr. and J. Bryan III, *Admiral Halsey's Story* (New York, 1947), 114–115, 125–129.

CHAPTER V

1. John Hersey, *Into the Valley* (New York, 1944), 3–124. Herbert L. Merillat, *The Island* (Boston, 1944), 20–27.
2. ComSoPac, transcript of recordgraph describing his duties, 22 Jan 1943; see also ComSoPac, "War Diary," Jun–Oct 1942, ONRL.
3. Miller, *Guadalcanal,* 24. CinCPac, ltr to ComSoPac on instructions as to duties, 12 May 1942, Hq USMC.
4. ComInCh, memo to C/S USA on garrison forces for the Solomons area, 15 Jul 1942, ONRL.
5. ComInCh, memo to C/S USA on 8 Jul 1942 despatch from CinCSWPA and ComSoPac, 10 Jul 1942, ONRL.
6. Miller, *Guadalcanal,* 26–27, 32. Craven and Cate, eds., *The Army Air Forces in*

World War II, Vol. IV (Chicago, 1950), 37–60.
7. Morison, *Coral Sea and Midway*, 270–271.
8. Zimmerman, *Guadalcanal*, 11.
9. Miller, *Guadalcanal*, 40–50.
10. Miller, *Guadalcanal*, 31–33, 81, 83–87. Halsey, "Responsibilities of a Theater Commander," lecture at AFSC, 7 Apr 1947, RS MCS.
11. As quoted in Miller, *Guadalcanal*, 85.
12. CO Motor Torpedo Boat Flotilla One, Solomons rpt, 7 Mar 1943; ComPhibForSoPac, Operation Order A19-42, 5 Oct 1942, in his "War Diary," 5 Oct 1942; ComSoPac, "War Diary," Aug 1942, ONRL. CG 1stMarDiv annex N (intelligence) to Guad V, Hq USMC.
13. Miller, *Guadalcanal*, 81.
14. CG 1stMarDiv, rpt on movement of 1stMarDiv, 26 Jul 1942, Hq USMC.
15. Merrill B. Twining, "Guadalcanal, the Commander and his Staff," lecture at MCS, RS MCS. Transcript of interview between CG 1stMarDiv and CMC, 1 Feb 1943, Hq USMC.
16. CG 1stMarDiv, basic doc and annex E (intelligence) to Guad I, Hq USMC. Twining, "Guadalcanal," RS MCS.
17. CG 1stMarDiv, annexes J (Administration Order 1A-42) and L (logistics) to Guad I; annex Z (logistics) to Guad V, Hq USMC. Pedro del Valle, "Marine Artillery on Guadalcanal," *Marine Corps Gazette*, Nov 1943, 10. Twining, "Guadalcanal," RS MCS.
18. Unfinished, unsigned, undated MS in Hq USMC, "Draft History . . . Overseas Mission of the First Marine Division, Fleet Marine Force."
19. Twining, "Guadalcanal," RS MCS. CG 1stMarDiv, covering ltr, Guad V; annex E (intelligence) to Guad I, Hq USMC. Leo B. Shinn, "Amphibious Reconnaissance," and William F. Coleman, "Amphibious Reconnaissance Patrols," *Marine Corps Gazette*, Apr and Dec 1945, 50–51, 22–25. Fletcher Pratt, *The Marines' War* (New York, 1948), 11.
20. E. F. Kumpe, ltr to John Miller, 16 Aug 1948, copy in PUL. CG 1stMarDiv, basic docs and annexes E, G, and F (all intelligence) to Guads I, II, and III respectively, Hq USMC. ComAirSoPac, "War Diary," Jun–Aug 1942, ONRL. Craven and Cate, eds., *Army Air Forces in World War II*, vol IV, 25–30.
21. CG 1stMarDiv, Annex F (Operation Order 7-42) to Guad I, Hq USMC. Twining, "Guadalcanal," RS MCS. Zimmerman, *Guadalcanal*, 42–43. Miller, *Guadalcanal*, 53, 235, 290–305.
22. Eric A. Feldt, *The Coast Watchers* (New York, 1946). "Draft History . . . First Marine Division"; CG 1stMarDiv, annexes D (Operation Order 6-42), E (intelligence), O (Communications) to Guad I, Hq USMC. ComPhibForSoPac, rpt on communications difficulties during Guadalcanal-Tulagi operations, 16 Aug 1942, ONRL.
23. Twining, "Guadalcanal," RS MCS.
24. CG 1stMarDiv, annex L (logistics) to Guad I, Hq USMC.
25. Miller, *Guadalcanal*, 25–28. CG 1stMarDiv, Guads I and II, Hq USMC.
26. del Valle, "Marine Artillery on Guadalcanal," *Marine Corps Gazette*, Nov 1943, 9.
27. CO 3dDefBn, Guadalcanal rpt, 7 Mar 1943, Hq USMC.
28. Notes on Princeton conference on Guadalcanal, 12 Mar 1948, PUL.
29. Hq CominCh, "Battle Experience, Solomons Island Actions, August and September 1942," *Information Bulletin No. 2*. ch X, 10, ONRL.
30. CG 1stMarDiv, Guads I and II; "Draft History . . . First Marine Division," Hq USMC.
31. ComSoPac, Operation Plan 1-42, 16 Jul 1942, ONRL.
32. Morison, *Rising Sun in the Pacific*, 242–254; *Coral Sea and Midway*, 21–60; 251–253; *The Struggle for Guadalcanal* (vol V, History of United States Naval Operations in World War II, Boston, 1949), 27–28, 58, 106.
33. Twining, "Guadalcanal," RS MCS. ComSoPac, "War Diary," 2 Aug 1942, ONRL.
34. Pratt, *The Marines' War*, 14–15.
35. Twining, "Guadalcanal," RS MCS.
36. ComSoPac, ComPhibForSoPac, "War Diaries," Jul–Aug 1942, ONRL.
37. CG 1stMarDiv, Guads II and III, and covering ltr Guad V, Hq USMC.
38. CG 1stMarDiv, Guad IV, Hq USMC.
39. ComAirSoPac, Operation Plan 1-42, 25 Jul 1942, ONRL. Miller, *Guadalcanal*, 32–35. Morison, *Coral Sea*, 235–241. Craven and Cate, eds., *Army Air Forces in World War II*, Vol. IV, 3–60.
40. ComPhibForSoPac, Operation Plan A4-42, 31 Jul 1942, ONRL. CG 1stMarDiv, annex F (Operation Order 7-42), to Guad I; ComTransDivsSoPacFor, Guadalcanal-Tulagi rpt, 7–9 Aug 1942 action, 23 Sep 1942, Hq USMC.
41. Clifton B. Cates, " 'My First,' on Guadalcanal, 7 Aug.–22 Dec. 1942," MS in possession of its author (now CMC).
42. ComPhibForSoPac, Operation Plan A3-42, 30 Jul 1942, ONRL. CG 1stMarDiv, annexes D and F (Operation Orders 6-42 and 7-42), Guad I, Hq USMC.
43. CG 1stMarDiv, Guad II, Hq USMC.
44. CG 1stMarDiv, basic doc and annex G (intelligence) to Guad II; annex C (logistics) to Guad III, Hq USMC. USSBS(P), Naval Analysis Division, *The Allied*

Campaign Against Rabaul (Washington, 1946), 79. Miller, *Guadalcanal*, 73.
45. CG 1stMarDiv, annexes E (intelligence) and Q (1stMars rpt) to Guad I; basic doc and annex M (1stMars rpt) to Guad II; covering ltr Guad V, Hq USMC. Twining, "Guadalcanal," RS MCS.
46. CG 1stMarDiv, Guads I and II, Hq USMC.
47. CG 1stMarDiv, Guad II, Hq USMC.
48. CG 1stMarDiv, annex D (Ass'tDivComd'r's rpt) to Guad II, Hq USMC. Miller, *Guadalcanal*, 61–65.
49. CG 1stMarDiv, annex K (personnel) to Guad I, Hq USMC.
50. Executive Officer 1stMarParaBn, Gavutu-Tananbogo rpt, not dated; CG 1stMarDiv, annex D (Ass'tDivComdr's rpt) to Guad II; CO *Wasp*, encl B (Wasp Air Group Commander's rpt) to Guadalcanal-Tulagi rpt, 14 Aug 1942, Hq USMC. Zimmerman, *Guadalcanal*, 33–40. Harry Torgerson, "Jap-Blaster," James D. Horan and Gerald Frank, eds., *Out in the Boondocks* (New York, 1943), 160–170.
51. CG 1stMarDiv, Guad II; "Draft History . . . First Marine Division," Hq USMC.
52. CG 1stMarDiv, annex D (Ass'tDivComdr's rpt) to Guad II; CO 2dBn2-Mars, Gavutu-Tanambogo rpts, 18 and 26 Aug 1942, Hq USMC. Zimmerman, *Guadalcanal*, 39. Miller, *Guadalcanal*, 67.
53. Hq CominCh, "Battle Experience, Solomons Island Actions," *Information Bulletin No. 2*, ch X, p 10, ONRL.
54. CG 1stMarDiv, basic doc and annex D (Ass'tDivComdr's rpt) to Guad II; ComPhibForSoPac, encls A (Executive Officer 1stMarRaidBn, notes on Japanese defensive tactics), K (ComFireSupport-Grp Mike rpt), V (CO *Heywood* rpt) to Guadalcanal-Tulagi rpt on 7–9 Aug 1942 opns, 22 Feb 1943; CO *Henley*, Palm Island bombardment rpt, 13 Aug 1942, Hq USMC.
55. CO *Wasp*, encl B (*Wasp* Air Group Commander's rpt) to Guadalcanal-Tulagi rpt, 14 Aug 1942; CG 1stMarDiv, Guad II, Hq USMC. Hq CominCh, *Notes on Amphibious Warfare No. 2*, ch VI, pp 4–6 (quoting and commenting on what should be correctly cited as CG 1stMarDiv, ltr to ComPhibForSoPac on the problem of air-ground communications, carried as an encl to annex D [communications], to CG 1stMarDiv, Guad IV, Hq USMC).
56. CG 1stMarDiv, annexes K (aviation) and N (operations journal entry 7 Aug 1942) to Guad II, Hq USMC.
57. CG 1stMarDiv, Guad II and annex F (Operation Order 7–42) to Guad I; ComTransDivsSoPacFor, Guadalcanal-Tulagi rpt, 23 Sep 1943, Hq USMC. Zimmerman, *Guadalcanal*, 46–47.
58. CO *Hunter Liggett*, "War Diary," 7–9 Aug 1942. ONRL.
59. ComPhibForSoPac, encl U (ComTransDiv 8 rpt) to Guadalcanal-Tulagi rpt of 7–9 Aug 1942 operations, Hq USMC.
60. C/S (formerly operations officer) 1stMarDiv, transcript of interview with Quartermaster Hq USMC, 30 Jan 1943, Hq USMC.
61. Cates, "'My First'." CG 1stMarDiv, Guad II, and basic doc, annexes C (logistics) and E (operations journal, 12 Aug 1942) to Guad III; ComPhibForSoPac, encls and endorsements to Guadalcanal-Tulagi rpt of 7–9 Aug 1942 opns; ComTransGrp Xray, Guadalcanal-Tulagi rpt, 23 Sep 1942, Hq USMC. ComSoPac, "War Diary," Aug 1942; CO *Hunter Liggett*, "War Diary," 7–9 Aug 1942, ONRL.
62. ComSoPac, Operation Plan 1–42, 16 Jul 1942. ONRL. Zimmerman, *Guadalcanal*, 23. Morison, *Guadalcanal*, 27–28.
63. ComSoPac, despatch to CinCPac, 9 Aug 1942; CinCPac, despatch to ComSoPac, 11 Aug 1942, in ComSoPac, "War Diary," 9, 11 Aug 1942; Hq CominCh, "Battle Experience, Solomons Island Actions," *Information Bulletin No. 2*, chs X and XI, ONRL. CinCPac, 1st endorsements on ComSoPac, Guadalcanal-Tulagi rpts, 16 Aug, 17 Oct 1942, Hq USMC.
64. Morison, *Guadalcanal*, 17–64. ComPhibForSoPac, ltr to ComSoPac forwarding Commander Screening Group's Savo Island rpt, 6 Apr 1943, ONRL. ComPhibForSoPac, encls and endorsements to Guadalcanal-Tulagi rpt of 7–9 Aug 1942 opns, Hq USMC. ONI, "Solomon Islands Campaign: I, The Landing in the Solomons, 7–8 Aug 1942," and ". . . : II, The Battle of Savo Island, 9 Aug 1942," *Combat Narratives* (Washington, 1943).
65. USSBS(P), Naval Analysis Division, *Campaigns of the Pacific War* (Washington, 1946), 106–107; *Interrogations of Japanese Officials* (2 vols, Washington, 1946), I, 255–256; II, 361–362, 471–472.
66. Pratt, *The Marines' War*, 27–37. "Draft History . . . First Marine Division," Hq USMC.
67. *Newsweek*, 5 Oct 1942, 20.
68. CG 1stMarDiv, Guad III, Hq USMC.
69. Cates, "'My First'."
70. CG 1stMarDiv, annex G (artillery) to Guad III, Hq USMC.
71. CG 1stMarDiv, Guads I, II and III, Hq USMC.
72. CG 1stMarDiv, annex T (medical) to Guad V, Hq USMC.

73. CG 1stMarDiv, Guad III, Hq USMC.
74. CG 1stMarDiv, annexes C (logistics), E (operations journal), H (medical) and K (communications) to Guad III; annexes R (artillery) and Z (logistics) to Guad V; transcripts of interviews, CG 1stMarDiv with CMC, and CG and C/S 1stMarDiv with Quartermaster Hq USMC, 1 Feb and 30 Jan 1943, Hq USMC.
75. Zimmerman, *Guadalcanal*, 63–65.
76. Miller, *Guadalcanal*, 50, 95, 114, 135, 142, 155, 214. Zimmerman, *Guadalcanal*, 52.
77. Sherrod, "USMC Aviation," pt II, p 9, Hq USMC.
78. Cates, "'My First'." CG 1stMarDiv, Guad III, Hq USMC.
79. Sherrod, "USMC Aviation," pt II, pp 1–2, Hq USMC.
80. Sherrod, "USMC Aviation," pt II, p 2, Hq USMC.
81. Morison, *Guadalcanal*, 123–124.
82. Sherrod, "USMC Aviation," pt II, p 4, Hq USMC.
83. Zimmerman, *Guadalcanal*, p 58, footnote 9.
84. CG 1stMarDiv, Guads I and II, and covering ltr Guad II, 1 Jul 1943, Hq USMC.
85. Zimmerman, *Guadalcanal*, 101.
86. CG 1stMarDiv, Guads IV and V, Hq USMC. Twining, "Guadalcanal," RS MCS. Zimmerman, *Guadalcanal*, 77–79.
87. Patrol rpt 53 of 3dBn1stMars, 3 Nov 1942, encl to Cates, "'My First'."
88. Miller, *Guadalcanal*, 59–350. William H. Whyte, Jr., "Hyakutake Meets the Marines," *Marine Corps Gazette*, Jul-Aug 1045, 3–11, 33–42.
89. CG 1stMarDiv, basic doc and annexes E (artillery) and G (history of 1stMars) to Guad IV, Hq USMC.
90. CG 1stMarDiv, annex I (operations journal) to Guad IV, Hq USMC.
91. Sherrod, "USMC Aviation," pt II, p 6, Hq USMC.
92. Morison, *Guadalcanal*, 104–105. Sherrod, "USMC Aviation," pt III, pp 2–4. Morison, "The Conquest of Micronesia" (first draft of Vol. VII, History of United States Naval Operations in World War II, Office of Naval History) ch XI, p 94.
93. Sherrod, "USMC Aviation," pt I, pp 8–9. Pratt, *The Marines' War*, 49–55. USSBS(P), *Campaigns*, 110–172; *Rabaul*, 5–10.
94. Zimmerman's notes on interview with former intelligence officer, 1stMarDiv, 3 Jul 1947, Hq USMC.
95. Hersey, *Into the Valley*, 11.
96. CG 1stMarDiv, basic doc and annex E (artillery) to Guad IV; Executive Officer 1stMarParaBn, rpt on Edson's Ridge, 15 Oct 1942, Hq USMC. Twining, "Guadalcanal," RS MCS. P. del Valle, "Marine Artillery on Guadalcanal," *Marine Corps Gazette*, Nov 1943, 12–13. Miller, *Guadalcanal*, 110–119. Zimmerman, *Guadalcanal*, 84–91.
97. Pratt, "The Loss of the Wasp," *U.S. Naval Institute Proceedings*, Jul 1946, 909–915. ComPhibForSoPac, Operation Plan A9–42, 20 Aug 1942, in his "War Diary," 20 Aug 1942; "War Diary," Sep 1942, ONRL. Miller, *Guadalcanal*, 119–125. Zimmerman, *Guadalcanal*, 93.
98. Sherrod, "USMC Aviation," pt IV, pp 3–4.
99. CG 1stMarDiv, basic doc and annexes A (Operation Order 11–42), N (intelligence), Q (aviation), W (personnel), and Z (logistics) to Guad V, Hq USMC. Twining, "Guadalcanal," RS MCS.
100. Miller, *Guadalcanal*, 185–186. Sherrod, "USMC Aviation," pt III, pp 13–14, Hq USMC.
101. Morison, *Guadalcanal*, 182.
102. Craven and Cate, eds., *Army Air Forces in World War II*, vol IV, 151.
103. Morison, *Guadalcanal*, 178.
104. CG 1stMarDiv, annex I (translation of notebook of CO 29th Infantry Regt) to Guad V, Hq USMC.
105. Miller, *Guadalcanal*, 135–166. Zimmerman, *Guadalcanal*, 113–125. P. del Valle, "Marine Corps Artillery on Guadalcanal," *Marine Corps Gazette*, Feb 1944, 39–43. CG 1stMarDiv, basic doc and annex P (artillery) to Guad V, Hq USMC.
106. Morison, *Guadalcanal*, 199–219. Sherrod, "USMC Aviation," pt IV, pp 9–12, Hq USMC.
107. ComPhibForSoPac, "War Diary," Aug-Nov 1942, ONRL.
108. Miller, *Guadalcanal*, 81. ComPhibForSoPac, ltr to CO 2dMars, 24 Aug 1942, Hq USMC.
109. Zimmerman, *Guadalcanal*, 52–54.
110. ComPhibForSoPac, memo to ComSoPac on raider battalions, 29 Aug 1942, ONRL. CinCPac, despatch to ComInCh, 1 Sep 1942; CMC, memo to ComInCh, 2 Sep 1942; ComInCh, despatch to CinCPac, 3 Sep 1942; ComSoPac, despatch to CinCPac, 5 Sep 1942; CinCPac, despatch to ComInCh, 6 Sep 1942; ComInCh, despatch to CinCPac and CMC, 8 Sep 1942; CMC, despatch to CG Defense Force Samoa, 10 Sep 1942; CMC, memo to ComInCh, 12 Sep 1942; ComInCh, memo to CMC, 16 Sep 1942; CMC (acting), ltr to CG Amphibious Corps, Pacific Fleet, 22 Sep 1942; senior marine officer in War Plans, Hq ComInCh, memo to ComInCh, 6 Oct 1942, Hq USMC.
111. CinCPac, memo to ComInCh on additional raider battalions, 16 Jul 1942; CMC, ltr to CG Amphibious Corps Atlantic Fleet, 16 Jun 1942, Hq USMC.

112. Sherrod, "USMC Aviation," pt II, p 7.
113. As quoted in Miller, *Guadalcanal*, 358, see also 139–145.
114. Sherrod, "USMC Aviation," pts III–IV, Hq USMC. Halsey, *Admiral Halsey's Story*, 108–123.
115. CG 1stMarDiv, personal ltr to unknown addressee, 6 Dec 1942; see also Guad V, Hq USMC.
116. CinCSWPA and ComSoPac, despatch to C/S USA, CominCh, and CinCPac, 8 Jul 1942, in ComSoPac, "War Diary," 9 Jul 1942, ONRL.
117. Halsey, *Halsey's Story*, 136–138.
118. Morison, *Guadalcanal*, footnote 13, p 182, 183–187.
119. Zimmerman's notes on interview with former intelligence officer 1stMarDiv, 27 Jun, 1 and 2 Jul 1947; see also CG 1stMarDiv, annexes E, G, F, A, N (all intelligence) to Guads I–V respectively, Hq USMC.
120. Halsey, *Halsey's Story*, 117–119. Zimmerman, *Guadalcanal*, 128–130. Sherrod, "USMC Aviation," pt IV, pp 5–6.
121. Morison, *Guadalcanal*, 225–234. Sherrod, "USMC Aviation," pt IV, pp 14–16, Hq USMC. CG 1stMarDiv, basic doc and annex R (artillery) to Guad V, Hq USMC. P. del Valle, "Marine artillery on Guadalcanal," *Marine Corps Gazette*, Feb 1944, 39–43.
122. Sherrod, "USMC Aviation," pt IV, pp 17–18, Hq USMC.
123. Morison, *Guadalcanal*, 263. Halsey, *Halsey's Story*, 131.
124. Miller, *Guadalcanal*, 220–231. Sherrod, "USMC Aviation," pt V, pp 3–4, Hq USMC.
125. Zimmerman, *Guadalcanal*, 141–145. Halsey, *Halsey's Story*, 119. CO 2dMarRaidBn Guadalcanal rpt on 4 Nov–4 Dec 1942 opns, 20 Dec 1942, Hq USMC.
126. Cates, "'My First'."
127. CG 1stMarDiv, annex T (medical) to Guad V, Hq USMC.
128. Acting C/S USA, memo to CominCh on possible withdrawal of 1stMarDiv from Australia, 23 Jun 1943, ONRL.
129. Vandegrift, personal ltr to unknown addressee, 6 Dec 1942, Hq USMC.
130. Cates, "'My First'."
131. Com3dPhibFor, 1st endorsement to Commander Destroyer Division 44, Munda bombardment rpt, 3 Sep 1943, ONRL.
132. Miller, *Guadalcanal*, 349.
133. Zimmerman, *Guadalcanal*, 166–167.
134. Sherrod, "USMC Aviation," pt I, p 7, Hq USMC.
135. ComSoPac, "War Diary," Jan–Feb 1943, ONRL.
136. CominCh, ltr to C/S USA on SoPac-SWPA command relations, 6 Jan 1943, ONRL.
137. ComSoPac, despatch to CinCSWPA, 28 Nov 1942, in ComSoPac "War Diary," 28 Nov 1942; ComSoPac "War Diary," Jan–Feb 1943; CinCPac, ltr to CominCh on future operations in area of Solomon Sea, 8 Dec 1942, ONRL.
138. Craven and Cate, eds., *Army Air Forces in World War II*, vol. IV, esp. 63–200, 261, 264, 319. Hq SWPA, *Chronology of the War in the Southwest Pacific, 1941–1945* (Historical Division, Hq SWPA, date and place of publication unknown). William D. Leahy, *I Was There* (New York, 1950), 152–153. Historical Division, War Dept, *Papuan Campaign, The Buna-Sanananda Operation* (vol in Armed Forces in Action Series, Washington, 1944).
139. Intelligence section Hq ComSoPac, narrative on air aspects of the Munda operation, 15 Aug 1943, ONRL.
140. Com3dPhibFor, 1st endorsement to Commander Destroyer Division 44, Munda bombardment rpt, 3 Sep 1943, ONRL.
141. CMC (acting), order to CG FMF and CG Amphibious Corps Pacific Fleet organizing IAC, 19 Sep 1942, Hq USMC. ComSoPac, "War Diary," 16 Nov 1942; ComPhibForSoPac, "War Diary," 16 Nov 1942, ONRL.
142. Halsey, *Halsey's Story*, 161. Sherrod, "USMC Aviation," pt VI, p 9, Hq USMC.
143. John N. Rentz, *Bougainville and the Northern Solomons* (vol in the official history of the U.S. Marine Corps in World War II, Washington, 1948), 5–6. Halsey, *Halsey's Story*, 153–172.
144. Sherrod, "USMC Aviation," pt IV, p 13, pt VIII, pp 7, 14–15, pt X, pp 2–8.
145. Frank O. Hough, *The Island War* (Philadelphia, 1944), Sherrod, "USMC Aviation," pt IX, pp 5–7. Pratt, *The Marines' War*, 124–132.
146. H. M. Smith, "Amphibious Tactics"; John DeChant, "Devil Birds," *Marine Corps Gazette*, Feb and Apr 1947, 32, and 32–39.
147. Duncan S. Ballantine, Jr. *U.S. Naval Logistics in the Second World War* (Princeton, 1947), 54–59. Hough, *The Island War*, 100–103.
148. CG USAFISPA, memo to ComSoPac on conference with CinCSWPA at Port Moresby, 19 Sep 1943, Hq USMC.
149. Rentz, *Bougainville*, 7–23.
150. CinCPac, Oct and Nov 1943 operations in POA, 18 Jan and 28 Feb 1944, ONRL. CG IAC, encl K (IAC warning order 18–43) to section A, phase I, Bougainville rpt, 21 Mar 1944, Hq USMC.
151. CG IAC, encls G (8th New Zealand Brigade Group, Treasury Islands rpt) and N (IAC ltr of instructions to CO 8th New Zealand Brigade Group, 28 Sep

REFERENCES

151. 1943) to section A, phase I, Bougainville rpt, Hq USMC.
152. CG IAC, encl Q (CO 2dMarParaBn, Choiseul preliminary rpt) to section A, phase I, Bougainville rpt, Hq USMC.
153. CG IAC, phase I, Bougainville rpt; Com3dPhibFor, Bougainville rpt on 1–13 Nov 1943 operations, 3 Dec 1943, Hq USMC. CinCPac, Oct and Nov 1943 operations in POA, 18 Jan and 28 Feb 1944, ONRL.
154. David W. Stonecliffe, "Historical Study of the Initial Landing at Empress Augusta Bay . . . by the 3d Marine Division on 1 November 1943," RS MCS. Appendix on accumulation of intelligence in mimeographed first draft of Rentz, *Bougainville*, Hq USMC.
155. Stonecliffe, "Initial Landing at Empress Augusta Bay," RS MCS.
156. Com3dPhibFor, Bougainville rpt on 1–13 November operations, 3 Dec 1943, Hq USMC.
157. Com3dPhibFor, annex A (naval gunfire) to Operation Order A15–43, 18 Oct 1943, Hq USMC.
158. Hq USMC, *An Evaluation of Air Operations*, pt III, "Close Air Support at Bougainville," 26–31. Sherrod, "USMC Aviation," pt XI, pp 10–12, Hq USMC.
159. Rentz, *Bougainville*, 24–38.
160. CG IAC, Bougainville rpt, phases I, II, and III, Hq USMC.
161. Sherrod, "USMC Aviation," pt XI, pp 16–18.
162. USSBS(P), *Campaigns*, 152–157. Halsey, *Halsey's Story*, 180–184. Sherrod, "USMC Aviation," pt XI, pp 13–16. Craven and Cate, eds., *Army Air Forces in World War II*, vol IV, 245–280.
163. CG IAC, "War Diary," Dec 1943, Hq USMC.
164. Sherrod, "USMC Aviation," pt VIII, pp 4–5.
165. CominCh, memo to C/S USA on withdrawal of 1stMarDiv from SWPA, 14 Jun 1943; C/S (acting) USA, reply to CominCh, 23 Jun 1943, ONRL.
166. CG 1stMarDiv, ltr to CinCSWPA on rehabilitation of 1stMarDiv, 23 Dec 1942; personal ltr to CMC, 26 Dec 1942; excerpts from various ltrs and despatches on rehabilitation of 1stMarDiv all copied on CominCh stationery, 29 Nov 1942 to 1 Jan 1943, Hq USMC.
167. As quoted in Hough, *Island War*, 88.
168. CG 1stMarDiv, annexes A (intelligence) and C (logistics and supply) to Cape Gloucester rpt; Ass't Operations Officer Hq Sixth Army, memo to AGF Board SWPA on Cape Gloucester action, 4 Jan 1944, Hq USMC. G. D. Gayle, ltr to J. A. Isely, 24 May 1950, PUL.
169. Com7thPhibFor, Arawe rpt, no date, Hq USMC.
170. CG 1stMarDiv, annex D (amphibian tractors) to Cape Gloucester rpt, no date; liaison officer from Hq Sixth Army, Cape Gloucester rpt, 5 Jan 1944, Hq USMC.
171. CG 1stMarDiv, Cape Gloucester rpt; Com7thPhibFor, Cape Gloucester rpt, 3 Feb 1944, Hq USMC. Hough, *Island War*, 148–183.
172. Ass't operations officers, Sixth Army, Cape Gloucester rpts, 4 and 9 Jan 1944, Hq USMC.
173. Com3dPhibFor, Green Islands rpt, 24 Mar 1944, ONRL.
174. Historical Division, War Dept, *The Admiralties* (vol in American Forces in Action Series, Washington, 1916).
175. USSBS(P), *Rabaul*, 10–18. Craven and Cate, eds., *Army Air Forces in World War II*, vol IV, 194.
176. Com3dPhibFor, Emirau rpt, 7 Apr 1944, ONRL.

CHAPTER VI

1. Raymond A. Spruance, ltr to J. A. Isely, 14 Jan 1949, PUL. See also Morison, "Micronesia," ch I, Office of Naval History; and Craven and Cate, eds., *Army Air Forces in World War II*, vol IV, 260–261.
2. Love, "Gilberts-Marshalls" chs I–II, PUL. G. S. Person, ltr to J. A. Isely, with encls, 3 May 1949, PUL. Craven and Cate, eds., *Army Air Forces in World War II*, vol IV, 129–135, 193–196, 245.
3. ComAirForPacFlt, encl S to comments on operations of carrier task forces, 14 Apr 1943, ONRL.
4. Morison, "Micronesia," ch I, Office of Naval History.
5. Love, "Gilberts-Marshalls," ch I, p 12, PUL. Craven and Cate, eds., *Army Air Forces in World War II*, vol IV, passim.
6. Morison, "Micronesia," ch I, Office of Naval History. Love, "Gilberts-Marshalls," ch I, pp 10–12, PUL.
7. Love, "Gilberts-Marshalls," ch I, p 14, PUL.
8. Morison, "Micronesia," ch I, Office of Naval History. Love, "Gilberts-Marshalls," ch II, pp 11–14, PUL.
9. Address of R. A. Spruance to the Royal United Service Institution in London, Oct 1946, Walter Karig, Russell L. Harris, and Frank A. Manson, *Battle Report, The End of an Empire* (New York, 1948), 76–78.
10. CinCPac, outline plan for operations in POA to establish forces in a position to cause the surrender of Japan, 13 Jan 1944, RS MCS.
11. Morison, "Micronesia," ch I, Office of Naval History.
12. E. J. King, ltr to J. A. Isely (with encl), 30 Mar 1950, PUL.
13. Henry H. Arnold, *Global Mission*

(New York, 1949), 476–477. Craven and Cate, eds., *Army Air Forces in World War II*, vol IV, 550–554, 570–574.
14. C. D. Meany, ltr to J. A. Isely, 9 Sep 1949, PUL. Comment by R. A. Spruance on Morison, "Micronesia," ch I, ONRL.
15. ComCenPacFor, Operation Plan Cen 1–43; general instructions for the Gilberts operation to all flag officers CenPacFor; and preliminary Gilberts rpt 25 Oct, 29 Oct, and 10 Dec 1943; ComAirCenPacFor, "War Diary," Nov 1943; CinCPac, annex E (Gilberts) to rpt on Nov 1943 operations in POA, 28 Feb 1944, ONRL.
16. USSBS(P), *Campaigns*, 191–193. (See also *Interrogations*, vols I and II, especially naval interrogations numbers 30, 38, 43, 82, 96, and 108).
17. Sherrod, "USMC Aviation," pt 14, p 4, Hq USMC. See also, Craven and Cate, eds., *Army Air Forces in World War II*, vol IV, 258–260, 310.
18. CinCPac, Operation Plan 13–43, 5 Oct 1943; ComAirCenPacFor, "War Diary," Nov 1943, ONRL.
19. CG VAC, Gilberts rpt, 11 Jan 1944, RS MCS. Smith, *Coral and Brass*, 102–134.
20. CinCPac, Operation Plan 13–43, ONRL.
21. CG VAC, encl C (intelligence) to Gilberts rpt, RS MCS. H. M. Smith, *Coral and Brass*, 125–127.
22. CinCPac, 1st endorsement on ComCenPacFor. ltr to CominCh, 10 Dec 1943, ONRL.
23. CG VAC, encl A (Operation Plan 1–43) to Gilberts rpt, RS MCS.
24. CG 2dMarDiv, annex H (replacement plan) to Operation Order 14, 23 Oct 1943, RS MCS.
25. C/S 2dMarDiv, supplementary estimate of the Gilberts situation, 25 Oct 1943, Hq USMC.
26. Julian C. Smith's notes in James R. Stockman, *The Battle for Tarawa* (vol in the official history of the U.S. Marines in World War II, Washington, 1947), made in mid-June 1947, Hq USMC; CG VAC, encl A (Operation Plan 1–43) to Gilberts rpt, RS MCS.
27. Presley M. Rixey, ltr to J. A. Isely, 6 Sep 1949, PUL. CG 2dMarDiv, Operation Order 14, RS MCS. Stockman, *Tarawa*, 1–5. Pratt, *The Marines' War*, 140–159.
28. CG 2dMarDiv, appendix 1 to annex D (intelligence) to Operation Order 14, RS MCS. Stockman, *Tarawa*, 80.
29. CG VAC, encl C (intelligence) to Gilberts rpt, RS MCS. Commander Southern Attack Force, Tarawa rpt, 13 Dec 1943 ONRL.
30. Thomas J. Colley, "The Aerial Photo in Amphibious Intelligence," *Marine Corps Gazette*, Oct 1945, 32–35.
31. R. A. Spruance, comments on Morison, "Micronesia," ch I, Office of Naval History.
32. CG 2dMarDiv, annex F (landing craft allocation) to Operation Plan 14, 25 Oct 1943, RS MCS.
33. CG VAC, Gilberts rpt; CG 2dMarDiv, basic doc and annex L (rpts of battalion commanders, 2dPhibTracBn rpt) to Tarawa rpt, RS MCS. Notes on conferences of Harry W. Hill, J. C. Smith, and Jeter A. Isely, and J. C. Smith and J. A. Isely, 28–29 Oct 1948, PUL.
34. *New York Times*, 10 Jan 1944, p 4, col 6.
35. CominCh, memo for JCS on strategy in the Pacific (Gilberts-Marshalls operations) 20 Jul 1943, ONRL. R. A. Spruance, ltr to J. A. Isely, 3 Jul 1949; P. M. Rixey, ltr to J. A. Isely, 6 Sep 1949, PUL.
36. Stockman, *Tarawa*, 3–5, 68. C. D. Meany, ltr to J. A. Isely, 9 Sep 1949; notes on conferences of H. W. Hill, J. C. Smith, and J. A. Isely; G. D. Gayle, ltr with encl to J. A. Isely, 29 May 1950, PUL. See also CG VAC, encl D (CO Sumner, memo on tides at Betio) to encl F (special staff officers' rpts) and encl F to Tarawa rpt, RS MCS.
37. 2dMarDiv and JICPOA, *Study of Japanese Defenses of Betio Island (Tarawa Atoll)*, pt I, "Fortification and Weapons," p 4, 20 Dec 1943, Hq USMC.
38. C/S 2dMarDiv, estimate of the Gilberts situation, 5 Oct 1943; 2dMarDiv and JICPOA, *Study of Japanese Defenses Betio*, 3 parts, dated 20 Dec 1943 to 20 Jan 1944, Hq USMC. CG 2dMarDiv, annex D (intelligence) to Operation Order 14, 25 Oct 1943, RS MCS. CinCPac, annex E (Gilberts) to Nov 1943 operations in POA, 28 Feb 1944, ONRL.
39. ComCenPacFor, preliminary Gilberts rpt, 10 Dec 1943; Commander Carrier Forces CenPacFor, Gilberts rpt, 16 Dec 1943; CinCPac, annex E (Gilberts) to Nov 1943 operations in POA; ComAirCenPacFor, "War Diary," Nov 1943, ONRL.
40. ComCenPacFor, general instructions to all flag officers CenPacFor for Gilberts operation, 29 Oct 1943, ONRL.
41. ComPhibGrpTwo, Tarawa rpt, 13 Dec 1943, ONRL. Notes on conferences of H. W. Hill, J. C. Smith, and J. A. Isely, PUL.
42. Statement made by CMC in interview with CG 1stMarDiv, 1 Feb 1943, transcript in Hq USMC.
43. Com5thPhibFor, Operation Plan A2–43, 23 Oct 1943, in his "War Diary" for Dec 1943; CinCPac, annex E (Gilberts) to Nov 1943 operations in POA, ONRL. CG VAC, encl A (Operation Plan 1–43) to Gilberts rpt, RS MCS.
44. Duncan S. Ballantine, *U.S. Naval Lo-*

gistics in the Second World War (Princeton, 1947), 167–180. CinCPac, covering ltr for "Central Pacific advanced bases logistical supply policy," 20 Feb 1943; CinCPac, annex A (logistics plan for land-based forces and fleet logistic plan) to Operation Plan 13–43; CinCPac, master base development plan for Apamama, 7 Oct 1943, Hq USMC. CG VAC, annex A (supply) to encl A (Administrative Order 4–43) to Gilberts rpt, RS MCS.

45. Stockman, *Tarawa*, 39.
46. CG VAC, encls F (transports quartermaster's rpt) and G (VAC observer's rpt, Capt. R. F. Whitehead USN) to Gilberts rpt; CG 2dMarDiv, Tarawa rpt, 23 Dec 1943, RS MCS.
47. CG 2dMarDiv, basic doc and encls (regimental and battalion rpts) to Tarawa rpt, RS MCS. Notes on conferences of H. W. Hill, J. C. Smith, and J. A. Isely; G. D. Gayle, ltr with encl to J. A. Isely 29 May 1950, PUL.
48. Notes on conference of H. W. Hill, J. C. Smith, and J. A. Isely. PUL. CG VAC, Gilberts rpt, RS MCS. Commander Carrier Division 22, Tarawa rpt, 12 Dec 1943, ONRL. See also CG VAC, encl G (VAC Observer's Tarawa rpt) to Gilberts rpt, RS MCS.
49. CG VAC, Gilberts rpt, RS MCS.
50. CG 2dMarDiv, basic doc and encls (quotation from encl L, 2dTankBn rpt) to Tarawa rpt, RS MCS. See also comments of Arthur J. Rauchle, Frederick R. Smith, and Benjamin K. Weatherwax on Stockman, *Tarawa*, Hq USMC. Notes on conferences of H. W. Hill, J. C. Smith, and J. A. Isely. PUL.
51. Com5thPhibFor, annex A (general instructions to Operation Plan A2–43), ONRL.
52. William B. Oldfield, "Shore Fire Control Parties," and R. D. Heinl, Jr., "Naval Gunfire Training in the Pacific," *Marine Corps Gazette*, Nov 1945 and Jun 1948, 53–54, 10–15.
53. As quoted in Earl J. Wilson, Jim F. Lucas, Samuel Shaffer, and C. Peter Zurlinden, *Betio Beachhead* (New York, 1945), 32. Notes on conference of H. W. Hill, J. C. Smith, and J. A. Isely; G. D. Gayle, ltr with encl and ltr to J. A. Isely, 29 May and 27 Jul 1950, PUL.
54. CG VAC encls B (operations) and F (naval gunfire) to Gilberts rpt, RS MCS.
55. Historical Division, War Dept, *The Capture of Makin* (vol in American forces in action series, Washington, 1946), 41, 44, 76. Love, "Gilberts-Marshalls," ch IV, p 11, PUL.
56. CG VAC, encl B (operations) to Gilberts rpt, RS MCS.
57. Historical Division, War Department, *Makin*, 124, 132. Stockman, *Tarawa*, 59.

H. M. Smith, *Coral and Brass*, 125–129. Morison, "Micronesia," ch III, Office of Naval History.

58. CG VAC, encl H (VAC Reconnaissance Company "War Diary") to Gilberts rpt, RS MCS.
59. CinCPac, preliminary study of action rpts on the Gilberts operation, 31 Dec 1943, ONRL.
60. Stockman, *Tarawa*, 12–15. CinCPac, preliminary study of action rpts on the Gilberts operation; ComPhibGrpTwo, encl C (ComTransDiv 18 rpt) to Tarawa rpt, ONRL. CG 2dMarDiv, narrative account of Tarawa action, 6 Jan 1944, Hq USMC. Notes on conferences of H. W. Hill, J. C. Smith, and J. A. Isely, PUL.
61. CinCPac, annex E (Gilberts) to Nov 1943 operations in POA, ONRL. Morison, "Micronesia," ch IV, Office of Naval History.
62. ComPhibGrpTwo, Tarawa rpt, ONRL.
63. Com5thPhibFor, Operation Plan A2–43, 23 Oct 1943; ComPhibGrpTwo, basic doc and encls, especially encl E (Operation Order A104–43, revised, 4 Nov 1943) to Tarawa rpt, ONRL.
64. Stockman, *Tarawa*, 12–13.
65. CG VAC, Gilberts rpt, RS MCS. Pratt, *The Marines' War*, 151. Notes on conferences of H. W. Hill, J. C. Smith, and J. A. Isely, PUL.
66. Stockman, *Tarawa*, 12. CinCPac, annex E (Gilberts) to Nov 1943 operations in POA, ONRL. Thomas E. Watson's comments (enclosing statement of Kenneth J. Fagan) on Stockman, *Tarawa*, Hq USMC. Notes on conferences of H. W. Hill, J. C. Smith, and J. A. Isely, PUL.
67. ComPhibGrpTwo, Operation Order A104–43 (revised); Com5thPhibFor, Operation Plan A2–43, ONRL.
68. CinCPac, annex E (Gilberts) to Nov 1943 operations in POA, ONRL. Notes on conferences of H. W. Hill, J. C. Smith, and J. A. Isely, PUL.
69. ComPhibGrpTwo, Tarawa rpt, ONRL.
70. Stockman, *Tarawa*, 15–16. Notes on conferences of H. W. Hill, J. C. Smith, and J. A. Isely. PUL.
71. Com5thPhibFor, annex C (air support) to Operation Plan A2–43, ONRL.
72. ComPhibGrpTwo, Tarawa rpt, and encl E (Operation Order A104–43 revised) to "War Diary," Nov 1943; Com5thPhibFor, Operation Plan A2–43, 23 Oct 1943, ONRL.
73. CG 2dMarDiv, narrative account of Tarawa action, Hq USMC. ComPhibGrpTwo, Tarawa rpt, ONRL. Stockman, *Tarawa*, 13. Notes on conferences of H. W. Hill, J. C. Smith, and J. A. Isely, PUL.
74. CinCPac, preliminary studies of action

rpts on the Gilberts operation, 31 Dec 1943, ONRL.
75. CinCPac, 1st endorsement on ComCenPacFor rpt of 10 Dec 1943, ONRL.
76. As quoted in Stockman, *Tarawa*, 59.
77. CG VAC, Gilberts rpt, RS MCS. See also Sherrod, "USMC Aviation," pt XIV, Hq USMC.
78. ComPhibGrpTwo, Tarawa rpt, ONRL. CG VAC, encl G (corps observer's rpt, Brig. Gen. J. L. Underhill) to Gilberts rpt, RS MCS.
79. ComPhibGrpTwo, Tarawa rpt, ONRL. CG VAC, Gilberts rpt, RS MCS.
80. CG VAC, encl F (naval gunfire) to Gilberts rpt, RS MCS.
81. 2dMars naval gunfire officer, Tarawa rpt, 3 Nov 1943, filed with comments on Stockman, *Tarawa*, Hq USMC.
82. ComPhibGrpTwo, basic doc and encl A (naval gunfire rpt) to Tarawa rpt, ONRL.
83. Com5thPhibFor, encl A (general recommendations) to Gilberts rpt; Commander Gunfire Support Group, rpt of 17–22 Nov 1943 action, 25 Dec 1943; CinCPac, preliminary study of action rpts on the Gilberts operation, ONRL.
84. Commander Gunfire Support Group, rpt of 17–22 Nov 1943 action, ONRL.
85. Notes on conferences of H. W. Hill, J. C. Smith, and J. A. Isely, PUL. CG VAC, encl F (engineer rpt, pt II) to Gilberts rpt, RS MCS.
86. CG 2dMarDiv, encl L (1stBn10thMars rpt) to Tarawa rpt; CG VAC, encl F (engineer rpt, pt II) to Gilberts rpt, RS MCS. Presley M. Rixey, ltr to J. A. Isely, 6 Sep 1949, PUL.
87. ComPhibGrpTwo, Operation Order A104-43, ONRL.
88. CG VAC, encl F (naval gunfire) to Gilberts rpt, RS MCS.
89. CG VAC, annex A to encl B (operations) and encl F (engineer rpt, pt II) to Gilberts rpt, RS MCS. Com5thPhibFor, Marshalls rpt, 25 Feb 1944, ONRL. CG VAC basic doc and encl D (intelligence) to Marshalls rpt, 6 Mar 1944, RS MCS.
90. CG VAC basic doc and encls F (naval gunfire) and G (Underhill rpt) to Gilberts rpt, RS MCS. Notes on conferences of H. W. Hill, J. C. Smith, and J. A. Isely, PUL.
91. ComPhibGrpTwo, Tarawa rpt, ONRL.
92. Commander Gunfire Support Group, rpt of 17–22 Nov 1943 action, ONRL.
93. Stockman, *Tarawa*, 15–18. ComPhibGrpTwo, Tarawa rpt, ONRL. CG 2dMarDiv, encls A (2d Mars rpt), C (2dBn2dMars rpt), D (3dBn2dMars rpt), J (2dBn8thMars rpt), and L (battalion commanders misc rpts) to Tarawa rpt, RS MCS. Notes on conferences of H. W. Hill, J. C. Smith, and J. A. Isely, PUL.
94. A. A. Vandegrift, "Summary," to Wilson et al., *Betio Beachhead*, 158.
95. Morison, "Micronesia," ch IV, Office of Naval History.
96. As quoted in Stockman, *Tarawa*, 7.
97. CinCPac, preliminary study of action rpts on the Gilberts operation, ONRL. 2dMarDiv and JICPOA, *Study of Japanese Defenses of Betio*, pt II, "Communications and Power Plants," 1 Jun 1944, pt III, "Base Installations," 20 Jan 1944, Hq USMC.
98. Robert Sherrod, *Tarawa: the Story of a Battle* (New York, 1944), 108. Notes on conferences of H. W. Hill, J. C. Smith, and J. A. Isely, PUL.
99. Stockman, *Tarawa*, 15–16.
100. CG VAC, encl G (corps observer's rpt, Lt. Col. C. D. Roberts) to Gilberts rpt, RS MCS.
101. Stockman, *Tarawa*, 4, 15–17.
102. As quoted in Sherrod, *Tarawa*, 80.
103. Stockman, *Tarawa*, 16, 18, 28. CG 2dMarDiv, encls J (2dBn8thMars rpt), K (3dBn8thMars rpt), and encl L (2dBn8thMars and 3dBn8thMars rpts) to Tarawa rpt, RS MCS.
104. CG VAC, encl G (corps observer's rpt, Lt. Col. W. I. Jordan) to Gilberts rpt, RS MCS.
105. CG 2dMarDiv, encl L (3dBn2dMars rpt) to Tarawa rpt, RS MCS. Stockman, *Tarawa*, 17.
106. Stockman, *Tarawa*, 17–18. CG 2dMarDiv, encl L (misc rpts) to Tarawa rpt, RS MCS.
107. CG VAC, encl G (corps observer's rpt, Lt. Col. E. F. Carlson) to Gilberts rpt, RS MCS.
108. Stockman, *Tarawa*, 18–19, 21.
109. CG 2dMarDiv, encl L (3dBn2dMars rpt) to Tarawa rpt, RS MCS.
110. CG VAC, encl B (operations) to Gilberts rpt, RS MCS.
111. Notes on conferences of H. W. Hill, J. C. Smith, and J. A. Isely, PUL. Stockman, *Tarawa*, 24–29.
112. Stockman, *Tarawa*, 18–29. Notes on conferences of H. W. Hill, J. C. Smith, and J. A. Isely, PUL.
113. CG VAC, encl G (Carlson rpt) to Gilberts rpt, RS MCS.
114. Presley M. Rixey and Wendell H. Best, "Artillery at Tarawa," *Marine Corps Gazette*, Nov 1944, 32–34.
115. CG 2dMarDiv, encl L (3dBn2dMars rpt) to Tarawa rpt, RS MCS.
116. CG VAC, encl G (Carlson rpt) to Gilberts rpt, RS MCS.
117. Stockman, *Tarawa*, 29–40.
118. 2dMarDiv and JICPOA, *Study of Japanese Defenses of Betio*, pt I, 4–5.
119. CG 2dMarDiv, encl L (1stBn6thMars rpt) to Tarawa rpt, RS MCS.
120. As quoted in Stockman, *Tarawa*, 51.

Notes on conferences of H. W. Hill, J. C. Smith, and J. A. Isely, PUL.
121. Stockman, *Tarawa*, 56–60.
122. CG VAC, encl F (naval gunfire) to Gilberts rpt, RS MCS. ComPhibGrpTwo, Tarawa rpt, ONRL.
123. ComPhibGrpTwo, Tarawa rpt, ONRL. CG VAC, encl F (naval gunfire) to Gilberts rpt, RS MCS.
124. As quoted by Sherrod, *Tarawa*, 98.
125. CG 2dMarDiv, narrative account of the Tarawa action, RS MCS. CG VAC, basic doc and encl D (logistics) to Gilberts rpt, RS MCS.
126. CinCPac, preliminary study of action rpts on the Gilberts operation; ComPhibGrpTwo, Tarawa rpt, ONRL.
127. CG VAC, encl G (Carlson rpt) to Gilberts rpt, RS MCS.
128. Stockman, *Tarawa*, 18–19. CG 2dMarDiv, encl L (2dPhibTracBn rpt) to Tarawa rpt, RS MCS. Notes on conferences of H. W. Hill, J. C. Smith, and J. A. Isely, PUL.
129. CG VAC, basic doc and encl D (logistics) to Gilberts rpt, RS MCS.
130. CG 2dMarDiv, Tarawa rpt, RS MCS. G. D. Gayle, ltr with encl to J. A. Isely, 29 May 1950, PUL.
131. Robert D. Heinl, Jr., "Minority Report on (J)ASCO" *Marine Corps Gazette*, Jul 1947, 22–32.

CHAPTER VII

1. As quoted by John Bishop, "The Battle of the Drains," *Saturday Evening Post*, 3 Jun 1944, 102.
2. *New York Times*, 24 Feb 1944, p 4.
3. CinCPac, basic doc and pt I of outline plan for operations in POA, 13 Jan 1944, RS MCS.
4. CinCPac, Operation Plans 16–43 and 1–44, 14 Dec 1943 and 5 Jan 1944, ONRL. CG VAC, Marshalls rpt, 6 Mar 1944, RS MCS.
5. Raymond A. Spruance, ltr to J. A. Isely, 14 Jan 1949; Chester W. Nimitz to J. A. Isely, 18 Jan 1949, PUL.
6. CG VAC, encl D (intelligence) to Marshalls rpt, RS MCS. See also Com5thPhibFor, encl B (intelligence) to Operation Plan A6–43, 3 Jan 1944, ONRL. CG VAC, encl G (intelligence) to Operation Plan 1–44, RS MCS.
7. CG VAC, encl D (intelligence) to Marshalls rpt, RS MCS.
8. CinCPac, annex B (Eniwetok) to Feb 1944 operations in POA, 3 Jun 1944, RS MCS.
9. ComCenPacFor, Operation Plan Cen 1–44, 6 Jan 1944; and Marshalls rpt, 1 Mar 1944, ONRL.
10. Com5thPhibFor, Marshalls rpt, 25 Feb 1944; ComPhibGrpThree, Roi-Namur rpt, 23 Feb 1944; CG VAC, encls C (operations), D (intelligence), and H (communications) to Marshalls rpt, RS MCS.
11. CG VAC, basic doc and encls C (operations), D (intelligence), G (Corps Liaison Team 4 rpt), and I (VAC Reconnaissance Company "War Diary") to Marshalls rpt, RS MCS. ComPhibGrpTwo, Majuro rpt, 15 Feb 1944, ONRL.
12. CG VAC, Marshalls rpt, RS MCS.
13. Morison, "Micronesia," ch VI, Office of Naval History.
14. CG VAC, encls C (operations) and D (intelligence) to Marshalls rpt; CG 4thMarDiv, encl J (comments on questionnaire) to Roi-Namur rpt, 17 Mar 1944, RS MCS.
15. CG VAC, basic doc and encls B (civil affairs) and H (communications) to Marshalls rpt, RS MCS.
16. Morison, "Micronesia," ch VI, Office of Naval History.
17. Com5thPhibFor, Operation Plan A6–43, ONRL.
18. *Time*, 31 Jan and 7 Feb 1944, 28, 19.
19. CinCPac, Feb 1944 operations in POA; Com5thPhibFor, Marshalls rpt, ONRL. Harry Schmidt, ltr to J. A. Isely, 1 Aug 1949, PUL.
20. Com5thPhibFor, Marshalls rpt, ONRL. CG VAC, basic doc and encl D (intelligence) to Marshalls rpt, RS MCS.
21. Com5thPhibFor, Operation Plan A6–43, ONRL. CG 4thMarDiv, Roi-Namur rpt; CG VAC, encl D (intelligence) to Marshalls rpt, RS MCS.
22. CG VAC, encl D (intelligence) to Marshalls rpt, RS MCS.
23. As quoted in Morison, "Micronesia," ch X, Office of Naval History. Charles H. Corlett, ltr to J. A. Isely, 1 Oct 1949, PUL.
24. CG VAC, Marshalls rpt, RS MCS.
25. CG 4thMarDiv, encl J (comments on questionnaire) to Roi-Namur rpt (see also basic doc of this rpt); CG VAC, basic doc and encl F (logistics) to Marshalls rpt, RS MCS. Love, "Gilberts-Marshalls," chs X and XI, PUL.
26. John C. Chapin, "The Fourth Marine Division in World War II" (multilithed, Hq USMC, 1945), 1–2.
27. CG 4thMarDiv, basic doc and encl E (24thMars rpt) to Roi-Namur rpt, RS MCS.
28. CG 4thMarDiv, encl J (comments on questionnaire) to Roi-Namur rpt, RS MCS.
29. CG VAC, encl F (logistics) to Marshalls rpt, RS MCS. Richard L. Conolly, ltr to J. A. Isely, 31 Aug 1949, PUL.
30. ComPhibGrpThree, Roi-Namur rpt, 23 Feb 1944, ONRL. Samuel E. Morison, ltr to J. A. Isely, 16 Mar 1950; R. L. Conolly, ltr to J. A. Isely, 31 Aug 1949, PUL.

31. CG 4thMarDiv, encl E (24thMars rpt) to Roi-Namur rpt, ONRL.
32. CG 4thMarDiv, basic doc and encl C (Ivan Landing Group rpt) to Roi-Namur rpt, RS MCS.
33. CG VAC, app A (17 Jan 1944 estimate of the situation) to encl D (intelligence), and encl D to Marshalls rpt, RS MCS. USSBS(P), *Campaigns*, 193–195; *The Reduction of Truk* (Washington, 1947), 9–10. See also Com5thPhibFor, encl B (intelligence) to Operation Plan A6-43, ONRL; and CG VAC, encl G (intelligence) to Operation Plan 1-44, RS MCS.
34. Robert Trumbull, *New York Times*, 2 Feb 1944, p 1, col 7.
35. CinCPac, annex A (Majuro and Kwajalein) to Feb 1944 operations in POA; ComCenPacFor, Operation Plan Cen 1-44, and Marshalls rpt, ONRL.
36. CinCPac, Feb 1944 operations in POA; ComCenPacFor, Marshalls rpt; Com5thPhibFor, Operation Plan A6-43, and encls C (ComPhibGrpOne, Attack Order A1-44), E (naval gunfire and air support), and F (Commander Support Aircraft rpt) to Marshalls rpt; Commander Fast Carrier Task Force, Marshalls rpt, 6 Mar 1944; Commander Carrier Group One, Marshalls rpt, 1 Mar 1944; Commander Carrier Group Two, Marshalls rpt, 25 Feb 1944; ComPhibGrpThree, Operation Order A157-44, 8 Jan 1944, and Roi-Namur rpt, ONRL. CG VAC, basic doc and encls A (Operation Plan 1-44) and H (special staff officers' rpts) to Marshalls rpt; CG 4thMarDiv, Roi-Namur rpt, RS MCS.
37. ComPhibGrpTwo, Majuro rpt, 15 Feb 1944, ONRL. CG VAC, basic doc and encls C (operations), D (intelligence), G (Corps Liaison Team 4 rpt), and I (VAC Reconnaissance Company "War Diary") to Marshalls rpt, RS MCS. H. W. Hill, ltr to J. A. Isely, 15 Jun 1949, PUL.
38. Com5thPhibFor, encl E (naval gunfire, air and artillery support) to Marshalls rpt; ComPhibGrpThree, Roi-Namur rpt, ONRL. CG 4thMarDiv, basic doc and encl G (10thMars rpt) to Roi-Namur rpt, RS MCS. Love, "Gilberts-Marshalls," chs X–XII, PUL.
39. CG 4thMarDiv, basic doc and encl A (narrative of operations) to Roi-Namur rpt, RS MCS.
40. CG VAC, encl H (communications) to Marshalls rpt; CG 4thMarDiv, encl D (23dMars rpt) to Roi-Namur rpt, RS MCS. Samuel E. Morison, ltr to J. A. Isely, 16 Mar 1950, PUL.
41. CG 4thMarDiv, Roi-Namur rpt, RS MCS. R. L. Conolly, ltr to J. A. Isely, 31 Aug 1949, PUL.
42. CG 4thMarDiv, basic doc and encls A (narrative of operations) and D (23dMars rpt) to Roi-Namur rpt, RS MCS.
43. William G. Wendell, "The Marshalls Islands Operations" (mimeographed, Hq USMC, 1945), 24. Notes on a discussion of this monograph between Wendell and Col. Homer L. Litzenberg, Jr., USMC dated 10 Jul 1945, PUL.
44. CG VAC, encl A (communications rpt) to encl H (special staff officers' rpts) to Marshalls rpt, RS MCS.
45. CG 4thMarDiv, basic doc and encl D (23dMars rpt) to Roi-Namur rpt, RS MCS.
46. Robert D. Heinl, Jr., "The Marshalls Campaign," (MS first draft of vol in the official history of the U.S. Marine Corps in World War II, Hq USMC), ch II, PUL.
47. ComPhibGrpThree, Roi-Namur rpt; CG 4thMarDiv, encl C (Ass't Div Com'dr's rpt) to Roi-Namur rpt, RS MCS.
48. CG 4thMarDiv, basic doc and encls C (Ass't Div Com'dr's rpt), E (24thMars rpt), F (25thMars rpt), and G (14thMars rpt) to Roi-Namur rpt; CG VAC, 1st endorsement to CG 4thMarDiv, Roi-Namur rpt, 28 Mar 1944, RS MCS.
49. Com5thPhibFor, encl H (employment of amphibian tractors and Dukws by the 7th Division) to Marshalls rpt, ONRL. CG VAC, encl C (operations) to Marshalls rpt, RS MCS. Morison, "Micronesia," ch XI, Office of Naval History. Love, "Gilberts-Marshalls," ch XII, PUL.
50. CinCPac, annex A (Majuro and Kwajalein) to Feb 1944 operations in POA, ONRL.
51. CinCPac, Feb 1944 operations in POA; ComCenPacFor, Marshalls rpt; Com5thPhibFor, Operation Plan A6-43, and encls C (ComPhibGrpOne, Attack Order A1-44), E (naval gunfire and air support), and F (Commander Support Aircraft rpt) to Marshalls rpt; Commander Fast Carrier Task Force, Marshalls rpt; Commander Carrier Group One, Marshalls rpt; Commander Carrier Group Two, Marshalls rpt; ComPhibGrpThree, Operation Order A157-44, 8 Jan 1944, and Roi-Namur rpt, ONRL. CG VAC, basic doc and encls A (Operation Plan 1-44) and H (special staff of officers' rpts) to Marshalls rpt; CG 4thMarDiv, encl E (24thMars rpt) to Roi-Namur rpt, RS MCS.
52. Morris Markey, *New York Times*, 8 Feb 1944, p 3, col 6.
53. CG VAC, Marshalls rpt, RS MCS. Com5thPhibFor, Marshalls rpt, ONRL.
54. CG VAC, app A (17 Jan 1944 estimate of the situation) to encl D (intelligence), encls D and H (engineering) to Marshalls rpt, RS MCS.
55. CG 4thMarDiv, encls D (23dMars rpt) and E (24thMars rpt) to Roi-Namur rpt, RS MCS. R. L. Conolly, ltr to J. A. Isely, 31 Aug 1949, PUL.

56. CG 4thMarDiv, encls D (23dMars rpt) and E (24thMars rpt) to Roi-Namur rpt, RS MCS. Harry Schmidt, ltr to J. A. Isely, 1 Aug 1949; Francis H. Brink, ltrs to J. A. Isely, 14 and 25 Jul 1949, PUL.
57. CG 4thMarDiv, encl E (24thMars rpt) to Roi-Namur rpt, RS MCS.
58. Love, "Gilberts-Marshalls," chs XII–XIV, PUL. Samuel L. A. Marshall, *Island Victory* (New York, 1945), *passim*. H. M. Smith, *Coral and Brass*, 141–151. C. H. Corlett, ltr to J. A. Isely, 1 Oct 1949, PUL.
59. CG VAC, encl C (operations, especially encl D to this encl, observations and recommendations) and encls D (intelligence) and H (engineering) to Marshalls rpt, RS MCS.
60. Marshall, *Island Victory*, *passim*. Love, "Gilberts-Marshalls," ch XIV; C. H. Corlett, ltr to J. A. Isely, 1 Oct 1949, PUL. Com5thPhibFor, Marshalls rpt, ONRL. CG VAC, basic doc and all encls, especially C (operations), D (intelligence), and H (engineering) to Marshalls rpt, RS MCS.
61. Love, "Gilberts-Marshalls," chs XII–XIV, PUL.
62. Com5thPhibFor, encl D (operations of control, shore and beach parties) to Marshalls rpt, ONRL. CG VAC, basic doc and encl F (logistics) to Marshalls rpt, RS MCS.
63. Love, "Gilberts-Marshalls," chs XII–XVII; Robert R. Smith, ltr to J. A. Isely, Jun 1949, PUL.
64. As quoted in Hq CominCh, "Amphibious Operations, the Marshalls Islands January–February 1944," (multilithed, Washington, 1944), ch IX, pp 6–7.
65. CG VAC, basic doc and app A (17 Jan 1944 estimate of the situation) to encl D (intelligence) to Marshalls rpt, RS MCS.
66. CG VAC, encl H (special staff officers' rpts, see Ass't Corps Surgeon's rpt) to Marshalls rpt, RS MCS.
67. CG VAC, encl H (Ass't Corps Surgeon's rpt) to Marshalls rpt, RS MCS.
68. Robert Trumbull, *New York Times*, 9 Feb 1944, p 1, col 5. CinCPac, annex B (Eniwetok) to rpt of Feb 1944 operations in POA, ONRL.
69. R. A. Spruance, ltr to J. A. Isely, 14 Jan 1949, PUL.
70. H. M. Smith, *Coral and Brass*, 149. R. A. Spruance, ltr to J. A. Isely, 14 Jan 1949, PUL.
71. H. W. Hill, ltr to J. A. Isely, 15 Jun 1949, PUL. ComPhibGrpTwo, Eniwetok rpt, 7 Mar 1944, ONRL.
72. CG Tactical Group One, VAC, Eniwetok rpt, 10 Mar 1944, RS MCS.
73. CinCPac, annex B (Eniwetok) to Feb 1944 operations in POA, ONRL. USSBS(P), *Campaigns*, 194–195.
74. ComPhibGrpTwo, encl A (narrative) to Eniwetok rpt, ONRL. CG Tactical Group One, VAC, encls D (VAC Reconnaissance Company rpt) and E (Company D 4thTankBn rpt) to Eniwetok rpt, RS MCS. H. W. Hill, ltr to J. A. Isely, 15 Jun 1949, PUL.
75. James R. Stockman, *The Sixth Marine Division* (multilith, Hq USMC, 1946), 3.
76. CG Tactical Group One, VAC, encl B (Kwajalein and Eniwetok special rpt) to Eniwetok rpt, RS MCS.
77. ComPhibGrpTwo, encls A (narrative) and B (unloading) to Eniwetok rpt, ONRL. CG Tactical Group One, VAC, encls A (narrative) and B (special rpt) and special encls (two rpts of 708th Army Amphibian Tank Bn, being a 1st endorsement to CG VAC) to Eniwetok rpt, RS MCS.
78. ComPhibGrpTwo, Eniwetok rpt; CinCPac, annex B (Eniwetok) to Feb 1944 operations in POA, ONRL, CG Tactical Group One, VAC, Eniwetok rpt; Arthur H. Weinberger, "The Capture of Engebi Island"; Ernest R. West, "The Capture of Eniwetok Atoll"; and Elmer A. Wrenn, "The Seizure of Eniwetok Atoll," monographs in senior course MCS, RS MCS.
79. Perry Finch, *New York Times*, 25 Feb 1944, p 4, col 7.
80. CinCPac, annex B (Eniwetok) to Feb 1944 operations in POA, ONRL. H. W. Hill, ltr to J. A. Isely, 15 Jun 1949, PUL.
81. CinCPac, annex B (Eniwetok) to Feb 1944 operations in POA, ONRL. Love, "Gilberts-Marshalls," ch XVII p 49, citing a rpt of the 106th Infantry which gives the total enemy dead on Eniwetok Islet as 1,097; H. W. Hill, ltr to J. A. Isely, 10 Jan 1949, PUL.
82. Love, "Gilberts-Marshalls," ch XVII, PUL. ComPhibGrpTwo, Eniwetok rpt, ONRL. CG Tactical Group I, VAC, Eniwetok rpt, RS MCS.
83. CG Tactical Group One, VAC, encl B (special rpt) to Eniwetok rpt, RS MCS.
84. ComPhibGrpTwo, Eniwetok rpt, ONRL. CG Tactical Group One, VAC, Eniwetok rpt, RS MCS.
85. CG VAC, Marshalls rpt, RS MCS.
86. R. A. Spruance, ltr to J. A. Isely, 14 Jan 1949, PUL.
87. USSBS(P), *Truk*, 10–31.
88. Morison, "Micronesia," ch XII, Office of Naval History. Joint Army-Navy Assessment Committee, *Japanese Naval and Merchant Shipping Losses*, 9–10, 52–54.
89. *The Asiatic Review*, Oct 1944, 429.
90. Craven and Cate, eds., *Army Air Forces in World War II*, vol IV, 549–574 (quotations from pp 550 and 572).
91. Craven and Cate, eds., *Army Air Forces in World War II*, vol IV, 575–670.
92. CinCPac, outline plan for operations in POA, 13 Jan 1944, RS MCS.

93. George McMillan, *The Old Breed, a History of the First Marine Division in World War II* (Washington, 1949), 228-270.
94. Walter Lippmann, *New York Herald-Tribune*, 22 Feb 1944, 21.

CHAPTER VIII

1. USSBS(P), Interrogation 308, 10 Nov 1945, copy in Historical Division, War Dept.
2. USSBS(P), *Interrogations*, I, 177; II, 331, 356, 384, 423, 424, 426.
3. CG ExpTrps, encl D (intelligence) to Marianas rpt, 2 Oct 1944, Hq USMC.
4. James R. Stockman, "The Battle for Saipan," *Campaign for the Marianas* (U.S. Marine Corps Monograph, Washington, 1946), 5-6.
5. Stockman, "The Tinian Fight," *Campaign for the Marianas*, 2.
6. ONI Bulletin 99, "Strategic Study of Guam," 1 Feb 1944; JICPOA Bulletin 7-44, "Marianas," 25 Jan 1944, ONRL. Kenneth E. Martin, "The Capture of Orote Peninsula," monograph for MCS senior course, 2-4, RS MCS. Phillips D. Carleton, "The Guam Operation," *Campaign for the Marianas*, 3.
7. Fletcher Pratt, *Fleet Against Japan* (New York, 1943), 136.
8. CinCPac, pt I, outline plan for operations in POA, 13 Jan 1944, ONRL.
9. CinCPac, pt II E, outline plan for operations in POA, 13 Jan 1944, ONRL.
10. Henry H. Arnold, *Global Mission* (New York, 1949), 476-480, 536.
11. CinCPac, pts I, II E, and II F, outline plan for operations in POA, 13 Jan 1944, ONRL.
12. CG VAC, Saipan rpt, 12 Aug 1944, RS MCS.
13. CinCPac, campaign plan for Guam, pt I, 3 Jun 1944, ONRL.
14. CG 2dMarDiv, addendum 1 (27 May 1944 estimate of enemy situation) to app 1 (1 May 1944 estimate of enemy situation) and app 1 all to annex E (intelligence) to Operation Order 18, 1 May 1944; Intelligence Officer VAC, special study of enemy troop strength in the southern Marianas, 9 May 1944, RS MCS.
15. CG VAC, Saipan rpt, RS MCS.
16. CG 4thMarDiv, Operation Plan 4-44, 6 May 1944, RS MCS.
17. CG 2dMarDiv, Operation Order 18, RS MCS.
18. Stockman, "Battle for Saipan," *Campaign for the Marianas*, 2. CG VAC, Operation Plan 3-44, 1 May 1944; CG 2dMarDiv, Operation Order 18, RS MCS.
19. CG VAC, annex K (special landing instructions) to Operation Plan 3-44; CG 4thMarDiv, app 1 (special landing instructions) to annex I (landing diagram) to Operation Plan 4-44, 6 May 1944, RS MCS.
20. CG VAC, annexes C (naval gunfire support) and F (artillery) to Operation Plan 3-44; CG 2dMarDiv, annex D (aviation) to Operation Order 18, RS MCS.
21. CG 4thMarDiv, Saipan rpt, 2 Sep 1944, RS MCS. CG 27thInfDiv, operations combat rpt in Saipan rpt, Historical Division, War Dept.
22. CG VAC, Saipan rpt, RS MCS.
23. Hq CominCh, "Amphibious Operations, Invasion of the Marianas, June to August 1944" (multilith, Washington, 1944), ch IV, p 19.
24. The best accounts of the battle for Saipan are the following: Carl Hoffman, "Saipan" (MS in preparation for publication in the official history of the U.S. Marine Corps in World War II, Hq USMC); Stockman, "The Battle for Saipan" *Campaign for the Marianas*; Love, *The 27th Infantry Division in World War II*, (Washington, 1949) 112-519; Love, "The Battle for Saipan," MS in Historical Division, Dept of the Army.
25. USSBS(P), Naval Analysis Division, *Campaigns*, 213-215.
26. CG VAC, basic doc and encls E (operations rpt) and F (supply rpt) to Saipan rpt; CG 2dMarDiv, Saipan rpt, 11 Sep 1944; CG 4thMarDiv, annex H (23dMars rpt) to Saipan rpt, RS MCS.
27. CG 2dMarDiv, Saipan rpt, RS MCS.
28. U.S. Army Observer, Saipan rpt to CG VAC, 12 Jul 1944, Hq USMC.
29. CG 4thMarDiv, annex H (23dMars rpt) to Saipan rpt; CG 2dMarDiv, Saipan rpt, RS MCS. U.S. Army Observer, Saipan rpt to CG Army Ground Forces, 11 Jul 1944, Hq USMC.
30. CG 4thMarDiv, annex H (23dMars rpt) to Saipan rpt, RS MCS. CG USAFPOA, "Information from Combat Observers' Reports, Saipan Operation," 2 Aug 1944, RS MCS.
31. CG VAC, enclosures E (operations periodic rpt) and F (supply) to Saipan rpt, RS MCS.
32. Hq CominCh, "Invasion of the Marianas," ch V, p 7.
33. CG VAC, encl I (3) (naval gunfire support) to Saipan rpt; Donald E. Weller, "Introduction to Naval Gunfire Support," lecture at MCS, 1947; CG 4thMarDiv, annex E (special comments) to Saipan rpt, RS MCS.
34. CG 4thMarDiv, annex C (operations) to Saipan rpt, RS MCS.
35. CG VAC, encl I (3) (naval gunfire support) to Saipan rpt, RS MCS.
36. Board to reexamine functions of the U.S. Marine Corps, "An Evaluation of Air Operations Affecting the U.S. Marine Corps in World War II," pt III, p 59, 31 Dec 1945, RS MCS.

37. D. E. Weller, chart of changes in shore fire-control parties, no date, RS MCS. CG VAC, encl I (3) (naval gunfire support) to Saipan rpt; CG 4thMarDiv, annexes C (operations) and F (14thMars rpt) to Saipan rpt, RS MCS.
38. Hq CominCh, "Invasion of the Marianas," ch III p 3. CG VAC, encl I (3) (naval gunfire support) to Saipan rpt, RS MCS.
39. CG ExpTrps, encl G (naval gunfire support) to Saipan rpt, RS MCS.
40. CG 4thMarDiv, annex I (24thMars rpt) to Saipan rpt; CG 2dMarDiv, Saipan rpt, RS MCS.
41. CG VAC, encl I (3) (naval gunfire support) to Saipan rpt; CG 4thMarDiv, annex C (operations) to Saipan rpt; CG ExpTrps, encl G (naval gunfire support) to Saipan rpt, RS MCS.
42. CG 4thMarDiv, annexes C (operations) and I (24thMars rpt) to Saipan rpt, RS MCS.
43. CG 4thMarDiv, annex H (23dMars rpt) to Saipan rpt, RS MCS. Hq CominCh, "Invasion of the Marianas," ch II, p 7.
44. USMC, Tables of Organization, "The Marine Division," 5 May 1944. CG 4thMarDiv, annex C (operations) to Saipan rpt, RS MCS.
45. CG 2dMarDiv, Saipan rpt, RS MCS.
46. CG VAC, Saipan rpt, RS MCS.
47. CG 2dMarDiv, Saipan rpt, RS MCS.
48. Hoffman, "Saipan," 121.
49. CG 4thMarDiv, annexes H (23dMars rpt) and J (25thMars rpt) to Saipan rpt, RS MCS.
50. CG 2dMarDiv, Saipan rpt, RS MCS.
51. Hoffman, "Saipan," 125.
52. Howard J. Rice, "Tactical Employment of Armored Amphibians," lecture at Command and General Staff School, Fort Leavenworth, Kansas.
53. CG VAC, basic doc and encls C (personnel), and D (intelligence) to Saipan rpt, RS MCS.
54. CG ExpTrps, enclosure C (operations) to Saipan rpt, RS MCS.
55. CG 2dMarDiv, Saipan rpt; CG VAC, encl F (personnel) to Saipan rpt, RS MCS.
56. USMC Tables of Organization, "The Marine Division," 5 May 1944, Hq USMC. War Dept, "Table of Organization and Equipment, 6–10," 26 Feb 1944, Historical Division, Dept. of the Army.
57. CG VAC, encl F (personnel) to Saipan rpt, RS MCS.
58. War Dept, "Table of Organization and Equipment, 7–17," 26 Feb 1944, Historical Division, Dept. of the Army USMC, "Table of Organization, F-1," 27 Mar 1944, Hq USMC.
59. Notes on interview between P. A. Crowl and Gordon D. Gayle and Carl W. Hoffman, Mar 1950, PUL.
60. War Dept, "Table of Organization, 7-17," Historical Division, Dept. of the Army.
61. Operations Officer 27thInfDiv, ltr to Maj. Gen. Orland Ward USA, 2 Feb 1950, Historical Division, Dept. of the Army.
62. CG XIV Corps, Field Order 1, 16 Jan 1943, app C to Miller, *Guadalcanal*.
63. Appleman, et al., *Okinawa*, 208.
64. CG 27thInfDiv, Intelligence Journal, 21 Jun 1944, Historical Division, Dept. of the Army.
65. CG 27thInfDiv, Operations Journal, 21 Jun, 1944, Historical Division, Dept. of the Army.
66. CG 27thInfDiv, Operations Journal, 22 Jun 1944, Historical Division, Dept. of the Army.
67. CG VAC, encl E (operations) to Saipan rpt, and special rpt to Commander Joint Expeditionary Force, "Events leading to the Relief from command of Major General Ralph Smith USA," 27 Jun 1944, RS MCS. CG VAC, Operation Order 10–44, 22 Jun 1944, RS MCS. Love, *27th Infantry Division*, 187–189, 194–195.
68. CG VAC, Operation Order 10–44, RS MCS. CG 27thInfDiv, Field Order 46, 22 Jun 1944, Historical Division, War Dept.
69. CG VAC, encl E (operations) to Saipan rpt, RS MCS. CO 105thInf, Saipan rpt, 22 Jun 1944, Historical Division, War Dept.
70. U.S. Army Observer, Saipan rpt to CG Army Ground Forces, Hq USMC.
71. CO 106thInf and CO 165thInf, Saipan rpts, 14 Jul 1944, Historical Division, Dept. of the Army.
72. H. M. Smith, *Coral and Brass*, 171–173.
73. Maj. Gen. Sanderford Jarman USA, memo dated 23 Jun 1944, enclosed in ltr to CG USAFPOA, 30 Jun 1944, Hq USMC.
74. CG FMFPac, encl B (statement of Maj. Gen. George W. Griner USA) to abbreviated text of "Proceedings of a board of officers . . . to inquire into the relief of Major General Ralph C. Smith USA," 29 Aug 1944, Hq USMC.
75. CG VAC, special action rpt of 27thInfDiv, 29 Nov 1944. RS MCS.
76. Maj. Gen. Sanderford Jarman USA, ltr to CG USAFPOA, 30 Jun 1944, Hq USMC.
77. CG VAC, special action rpt of 27thInfDiv, RS MCS.
78. Love, *27th Infantry Division*, Ch. XLVII.
79. CG USAFCenPac, exhibit ZZ (Certificate of Maj. Gen. George W. Griner USA) to "Proceedings of a board of officers . . . to inquire into the relief of Major General Ralph C. Smith USA," 12 Jul 1944, Hq USMC.
80. CG 27thInfDiv, operations periodic

rpt, 7 Jul 1944, Historical Division, Dept. of the Army.
81. CG VAC, ltr to CG 27thInfDiv, 15 Jul 1944, Historical Division, Dept. of the Army.
82. Com5thFlt, rpt of Japanese counterattack at Saipan on 7 Jul 1944, 19 Jul 1944, Hq USMC.
83. Love, the *27th Infantry Division*, Chs. XXXIX–XL.
84. CG 4thMarDiv, annexes H (23dMars rpt) and I (24thMars rpt) to Saipan rpt, RS MCS.
85. CG ExpTrps, encl D (intelligence) to Saipan rpt, RS MCS.
86. CG VAC, Tinian rpt, 12 Aug 1944, RS MCS.
87. CG VAC, Tinian rpt, RS MCS.
88. CG 2dMarDiv, Tinian rpt, 11 Sept 1944; CG 4thMarDiv, annex B (intelligence) to Tinian rpt, 25 Sep 1944; CG VAC, basic doc and app A (reconnaissance of beach White 1) to encl D (intelligence), encl D and annex A (record of events) to encl L (1) (amphibious reconnaissance battalion rpt) to Tinian rpt, RS MCS. ComPhibGrpTwo Tinian rpt, 24 Aug 1944, ONRL.
89. CG VAC, Tinian rpt, RS MCS.
90. CG VAC, encl D (intelligence) to Tinian rpt; CG 4thMarDiv, basic doc and annex B (intelligence) to Tinian rpt, RS MCS.
91. CG 4thMarDiv, Tinian rpt, RS MCS.
92. CG VAC, Operation Plan 30–44, 13 Jul 1944, and encl D (intelligence) to Tinian rpt, RS MCS.
93. CG VAC, encl D (intelligence) to Tinian rpt, RS MCS.
94. ComPhibGrpTwo, Tinian rpt, ONRL. CG VAC, Tinian rpt, RS MCS.
95. CG VAC, basic doc and encl E (operations) to Tinian rpt, RS MCS.
96. CG 4thMarDiv, Tinian rpt, RS MCS.
97. CG VAC, encl E (operations) to Tinian rpt; CG 4thMarDiv, Tinian rpt; CG 2dMarDiv, Tinian rpt, RS MCS.
98. CG VAC, basic doc and encl E (operations) to Tinian rpt; CG 4thMarDiv, Tinian rpt; CG 2dMarDiv, Tinian rpt, RS MCS.
99. CG VAC, encl E (operations) to Tinian rpt; CG 4thMarDiv, Tinian rpt; CG 2dMarDiv, Tinian rpt, RS MCS.
100. ComPhibGrpTwo, Tinian rpt, ONRL.
101. CG VAC, basic doc and encl D (intelligence) to Tinian rpt, RS MCS.
102. CG VAC, encl I (3) (naval gunfire) to Tinian rpt; CG VAC, annex C (naval gunfire) to Operation Plan 30–44; CG 4thMarDiv, annex C (operations) to Tinian rpt, RS MCS; ComPhibGrpTwo, encl A (naval gunfire) to Tinian rpt, ONRL.
103. ComPhibGrpTwo, encl A (naval gunfire) to Tinian rpt; CG VAC, Tinian rpt, RS MCS.
104. CG VAC, encl I (3) (naval gunfire) to Tinian rpt, RS MCS.
105. CG 4thMarDiv, annex C (operations) to Tinian rpt, RS MCS.
106. CG VAC, encl I (3) (naval gunfire) to Tinian rpt; ComPhibGrpTwo, encl A (naval gunfire) to Tinian rpt, RS MCS.
107. ComPhibGrpTwo, encl A (naval gunfire) to Tinian rpt; CG ExpTrps, encl G (special staff officers' rpts) to Marianas rpt; CG VAC, encl I (3) (naval gunfire) to Tinian rpt; CG 4thMarDiv, annex C (operations) to Tinian rpt, RS MCS.
108. CG 4thMarDiv, encl C (operations) to Tinian rpt, RS MCS.
109. ComPhibGrpTwo, Tinian rpt, RS MCS.
110. ComPhibGrpTwo, Tinian rpt; CG 2ndMarDiv, Tinian rpt; CG VAC, encl I (2) (air support) to Tinian rpt; CG 4thMarDiv, annex C (operations) to Tinian rpt, RS MCS.
111. CG 4thMarDiv, app A (revised equipment for air liaison parties) to annex H (23dMars rpt) to Tinian rpt, RS MCS.
112. CG 4thMarDiv, basic doc and annexes C (operations) and I (24thMars rpt) to Tinian rpt, RS MCS.
113. CG 4thMarDiv, annex E (special comments and recommendations) to Tinian rpt, RS MCS.
114. CG 2dMarDiv, Tinian rpt; CG 4thMarDiv, basic doc and annex I (24thMars rpt) to Tinian rpt, RS MCS.
115. ComPhibGrpTwo, Tinian rpt; CG VAC, encl I (2) (air support) to Tinian rpt, RS MCS. Harry W. Hill, ltr to J. A. Isely, 15 Jun 1949, PUL.
116. ComPhibGrpTwo, Tinian rpt; CG VAC, encl I (1) (XXIV Corps artillery rpt) to Tinian rpt, RS MCS.
117. CG VAC, basic doc and encl E (operations) to Tinian rpt, RS MCS.
118. CG 4thMarDiv, basic doc and annex C (operations) to Tinian rpt, RS MCS.
119. CG VAC, encl J (1) (transport quartermaster's rpt) to Tinian rpt, RS MCS.
120. CG VAC Tinian rpt, RS MCS.
121. CG VAC, encl F (supply) to Tinian rpt, RS MCS.
122. CG 4thMarDiv, Tinian rpt; ComPhibGrpTwo, encl B (portable ramps for amphibian tractors) to Tinian rpt, RS MCS.
123. ComPhibGrpTwo, encl B (portable ramps for amphibian tractors) to Tinian rpt; CG VAC, encl J (2) (engineer and shore party rpt) to Tinian rpt, RS MCS.
124. CG 4thMarDiv, app A (revised equipment for air liaison parties) to annex H (23dMars rpt), and annex G (25thMars rpt) to Tinian rpt; CG VAC, encl J (2) (engineer and shore party rpt) to Tinian rpt, RS MCS.

125. CG 4thMarDiv, annex G (25thMars rpt) to Tinian rpt; CG VAC, encl J (2) (engineer and shore party rpt) to Tinian rpt, RS MCS.
126. ComPhibGrpTwo, Tinian rpt, RS MCS.
127. CG VAC, encl F (supply) to Tinian rpt, RS MCS.
128. CG 4thMarDiv, basic doc and annex I (24thMars rpt) to Tinian rpt; ComPhibGrpTwo, Tinian rpt, RS MCS.
129. CG 2dMarDiv, Tinian rpt; CG 4thMarDiv, Tinian rpt, RS MCS.
130. CG 4thMarDiv, basic doc and annexes C (operations), K (4thTankBn rpt) and I (24thMars rpt) to Tinian rpt, RS MCS.
131. CG 4thMarDiv, annex B (intelligence) to Tinian rpt, RS MCS.
132. CG 4thMarDiv, basic doc and annex E (special comments and recommendations) to Tinian rpt, RS MCS.
133. Operations Officer 3dMarDiv, annex B (operations) to Guam rpt, 19 Aug 1944; CG IIIAC, encl A (planning) to Guam rpt, 3 Sep 1944; ComPhibGrpThree, Guam rpt, RS MCS.
134. CG IIIAC, Guam rpt; ComPhibGrpThree, Guam rpt, RS MCS. Historical Division, War Dept, *Guam, Operations of the 77th Division* (vol in American forces in action series, Washington, 1946), 10.
135. CG ExpTrps, encl D (Guam) to encl C (operations) to Marianas rpt, RS MCS.
136. CG IIIAC, Guam rpt, RS MCS. CG ExpTrps, encl D (Guam) to encl C (operations) to Marianas rpt, RS MCS.
137. CG ExpTrps, encl D (Guam) to encl C (operations) to Marianas rpt, RS MCS.
138. CG IIIAC, encl B (operations) to Guam rpt; Operations Officer 3dMarDiv, Guam rpt; CG ExpTrps, encl D (Guam) to encl C (operations) and encl D (intelligence) to Marianas rpt; CO 19thMars, Guam rpt, 17 Aug 1944, RS MCS.
139. Operations Officer 3dMarDiv, Guam rpt, RS MCS.
140. Account of action is drawn from the following sources: CG ExpTrps, encls D (Guam) and G (operations journal) to encl C (operations), and encl D (intelligence) to Marianas rpt; CG IIIAC, encls A (planning) and B (operations) to Guam rpt; CG 1stProvMarBrig, Guam rpt, 19 Aug 1944; Kenneth E. Martin, "The Capture of Orote Peninsula," MCS monograph senior course; CO 3dMars, Guam rpt, 16 Aug 1944, RS MCS. Phillips D. Carleton, "The Guam Operation," *Campaign for the Marianas*. Robert E. Cushman, Jr., "The Fight at Fonte," *Marine Corps Gazette*, Apr 1947, 10–16. Historical Division, War Dept, *Guam*.
141. Holland Smith, CG ExpTrps, gives the following figures:

	Killed	Wounded	Missing	Total
3rdMarDiv	620	2,294	65	3,609
77thInfDiv	405	1,744	51	2,200
1stProvMarBrig	191	704	20	915
CorpsArty	4	12	0	16
CorpsTrps	69	264	12	345
	1,289	5,018	148	7,085

CG ExpTrps, encl G (medical) to Marianas rpt, RS MCS.
142. Historical Division, War Dept, *Guam*, 133–134. CG ExpTrps, encl D (intelligence) to Marianas rpt; ComPhibGrpThree, annex B (intelligence) to Operation Plan A162–44, RS MCS.
143. CG 1stProvMarBrig, Guam rpt, RS MCS.
144. CG ExpTrps, encl G (special staff officers' rpts) to Marianas rpt, RS MCS.
145. CG IIIAC, encl G (naval gunfire) to Guam rpt; ComPhibGrpThree, encl B (naval gunfire) to Guam rpt, RS MCS.
146. CG ExpTrps, encl G (special staff officers' rpts) to Marianas rpt; ComPhibGrpThree, encl B (naval gunfire) to Guam rpt, RS MCS.
147. CG IIIAC, encl G (naval gunfire) to Guam rpt; CG ExpTrps, encl G (special staff officers' rpts) to Marianas rpt; CO 3dMars, Guam rpt, RS, MCS.
148. Operations Officer 3dMarDiv, annex C (naval gunfire) to Guam rpt; CG 1stProvMarBrig, Guam rpt, RS MCS.
149. CG IIIAC, app B (medical) to encl C (intelligence) to Guam rpt, RS MCS.
150. Hq CominCh, "Invasion of the Marianas," ch III, pp 13–14.
151. CG ExpTrps, encl G (special staff officers' rpts) to Marianas rpt; Operations Officer 3dMarDiv, annex D (air support) to Guam rpt; CG 1stProvMarBrig, Guam rpt, RS MCS.
152. Operations Officer 3dMarDiv, annex D (air support) to Guam rpt; CO 19thMars and CO 3dMars, Guam rpts, RS MCS.
153. Hq CominCh, "Invasion of the Marianas," ch II, p 7.
154. CG 1stProvMarBrig, Guam rpt, RS MCS.
155. Carleton, "Guam," *Campaign for the Marianas*, 44. CG 1stProvMarBrig, Guam rpt; CO 14thDefBn, Guam rpt, 18 Aug 1944; Operations Officer 3dMarDiv, annex B (operations) to Guam rpt, RS MCS.
156. Hq CominCh, "Invasion of the Marianas," ch IV, pp 12, 19. CO 3dAmphTrackBn, Guam rpt, 16 Aug 1944; Operations Officer 3dMarDiv, annex B (operations) to Guam rpt, RS MCS.
157. ComPhibGrpThree, Guam rpt, RS MCS.
158. Hq CominCh, "Invasion of the Marianas," ch V, pp 9, 15–16. ComPhib-

GrpThree, Guam rpt; CG ExpTrps, Marianas rpt, RS MCS.
159. ComPhibGrpThree, Guam rpt; CG 1stProvMarBrig, Guam rpt, RS MCS. Historical Division, War Dept, *Guam*, 55.
160. CG IIIAC, encl K (engineer-shore party rpt) to Guam rpt; Operations Officer 3rdMarDiv, annex E (logistics) to Guam rpt, RS MCS.
161. CO 12thMars, Guam rpt, RS MCS.
162. CG IIIAC, encl C (intelligence) to Guam rpt; CG 1stProvMarBrig, Guam rpt, RS MCS.
163. CG IIIAC, encl C (intelligence) to Guam rpt, RS MCS.
164. CG IIIAC, encl C (intelligence) to Guam rpt, RS MCS.
165. CG IIIAC, Guam rpt, RS MCS.
166. Arnold, *Global Mission*, 540. George C. Marshall, "Biennial Report of the Chief of Staff to the Secretary of War, July 1, 1943 to June 30, 1945," *United States News* (extra number), 10 Oct 1945. USSBS(P), Military Analysis Division, *Air Campaigns of the Pacific War* (Washington, July 1946) 46–52. USSBS(P) *Summary Report, Pacific War* (Washington, 1946) 16–17.

CHAPTER IX

1. Ernest J. King, *U.S. Navy at War, Second Official Report Covering Combat Operations March 1, 1944 to March 1, 1945*, 15–16. Robert R. Smith, "Approach to the Philippines" (MS vol in U.S. Army in World War II, Historical Division, War Dept), *passim*.
2. Chester W. Nimitz, ltr to P. A. Crowl, 5 Oct 1949, PUL.
3. CinCPac-CinCPOA, joint staff studies for Palau, 20 March, 18 May, 3 Jun, 14 Jun 1944, ONRL.
4. CinCPac-CinCPOA, Operations in the Pacific Ocean Areas, Sep 1944, p 38, ONRL. CG IIIAC, encl A (planning) to Palau rpt, 24 Oct 1944, RS MCS.
5. CG ExpTrps3dFlt, Palau rpt, 12 Oct 1944, RS MCS.
6. Halsey, *Halsey's Story*, 199–201.
7. Oliver P. Smith, ltr to J. A. Isely, 7 Mar 1950, PUL.
8. CG 1stMarDiv, Palau rpt, 13 Sep 1944, RS MCS.
9. Kimber H. Boyer, "Formation and Employment of an Armored Amphibian Battalion," monograph at MCS senior course, 1946–47, RS MCS.
10. CG 1stMarDiv, Palau rpt, RS MCS. McMillan, *The Old Breed*, ch XVI.
11. CinCPac-CinCPOA, Sep 1944 Operations in POA, par 60, ONRL. CG 1stMarDiv, annex B (intelligence) to Palau rpt, RS MCS.
12. CG IIIAC, encl C (intelligence) to Palau rpt, RS MCS.
13. Oliver P. Smith, ltr to J. A. Isely, 7 Mar 1950, PUL.
14. CG ExpTrps3dFlt, app 10 (intelligence) to Palau rpt, RS MCS. CG IIIAC, encl C (intelligence) to Palau rpt, RS MCS.
15. CG IIIAC, encl C (intelligence) to Palau rpt, RS MCS.
16. Edwin A. Law, "The Palau Operation, Historical Tactical Study," monograph in MCS senior course 1946–47, RS MCS.
17. McMillan, *The Old Breed*, 269.
18. CinCPac-CinCPOA, Sep 1944 Operations in POA, par 72. George H. Fort, ltr to P. A. Crowl, 15 Mar 1950, PUL.
19. CinCPac-CinCPOA, Sep 1944 Operations in POA, par 74, ONRL.
20. CG 1stMarDiv, annex C (logistics) to Palau rpt, RS MCS.
21. CG 1stMarDiv, annex J (tanks) to Palau rpt, RS MCS.
22. CG IIIAC, annex I (engineer) to Palau rpt, RS MCS.
23. O. P. Smith, ltr to J. A. Isely, 7 Mar 1950, PUL.
24. Law, "The Palau Operation"; Jens C. Aggerback, "RCT 321 in Peleliu, Historical Tactical Study," monograph in MCS senior course, 1946–47, RS MCS. Gordon D. Gayle, ltr to P. A. Crowl, 9 Mar 1950, PUL.
25. Pratt, *Marines' War*, 341. O. P. Smith, ltr to J. A. Isely, 7 Mar 1950, PUL. Frank Hough, "The Palaus" (MS of vol in the official history of the U.S. Marine Corps in World War II, Hq USMC), II-25. McMillan, *The Old Breed*, 262–263.
26. G. D. Gayle, ltr to P. A. Crowl, 9 Mar 1950, PUL.
27. CG IIIAC, encl B (operations) to Palau rpt; CG 1stMarDiv, Palau rpt, RS MCS. Hough "The Palaus," II-24.
28. CinCPac-CinCPOA, Sep 1944 Operations in POA, pars 140–142, ONRL.
29. Hough, "The Palaus," VI-3.
30. CinCPac-CinCPOA, Sep 1944 Operations in POA, pars 77–83, ONRL.
31. CG IIIAC, encl F (air support) to Palau rpt, RS MCS.
32. CG IIIAC, encl G (naval gunfire) to Palau rpt, RS MCS.
33. Donald M. Weller, ltr to P. A. Crowl, 22 Mar 1950, PUL. Jesse B. Oldendorf, ltr to Clayton C. Jerome, 25 Mar 1950, Hq USMC.
34. CG IIIAC, encl G (naval gunfire) to Palau rpt; CG 1stMarDiv, annex B (intelligence) to Palau rpt, RS MCS.
35. CG 1stMarDiv, annex K (naval gunfire) to Palau rpt, RS MCS.
36. D. M. Weller, "Introduction to Naval Gunfire Support," lecture in senior course, MCS, 1947, RS MCS. Ira E. McMillian, The Development of Naval Gunfire Support of Amphibious Operations, *U.S. Naval Institute Proceedings*, Jan 1948, 1–2. George H. Fort, ltrs to P.

REFERENCES

A. Crowl and Kenneth W. Condit, 15 Mar and 20 Feb 1950, PUL.
37. CinCPac-CinCPOA, Operations in POA, Sep 1944, pars 140–151, ONRL.
38. K. H. Boyer, "Formation and Employment of an Armored Amphibian Battalion," RS MCS.
39. CG 1stMarDiv, annex J (tanks) to Palau rpt, RS MCS.
40. Hough, "The Palaus," III-30 to III-37. CG 1stMarDiv, Palau rpt, RS MCS.
41. CG 1stMarDiv, Palau rpt, RS MCS. Hough, "The Palaus," III-38 to III-47.
42. The following brief narrative of infantry fighting on Peleliu is derived from the following sources: CG IIIAC encl B (operations) to Palau rpt; CG 1stMarDiv, Palau rpt, RS MCS. Hough, "The Palaus," chs IV–VI. McMillan, *The Old Breed*, chs XVIII–XX. For operations of the 81st Infantry Division, see Smith, "Approach to the Philippines"; and *The 81st Infantry Wildcat Division in World War II* (Washington, 1948), ch XVII.
43. CinCPac-CinCPOA, Sep 1944 Operations in POA, par 182, ONRL.
44. O. P. Smith, ltr to J. A. Isely, 7 Mar 1950, PUL.
45. CinCPac-CinCPOA, Sep 1944 Operations in POA, pars 244–265, ONRL.
46. CG 1stMarDiv, Palau rpt, RS MCS.
47. CG 1stMarDiv, Palau rpt, RS MCS.
48. G. D. Gayle, ltr to P. A. Crowl, 9 Mar 1950, PUL.
49. CG IIIAC, encl C (intelligence) to Palau rpt; CG 1stMarDiv, annex B (intelligence) to Palau rpt; J. C. Aggerback, "RCT 321 in Peleliu," par 3, RS MCS.
50. CG 1stMarDiv, annexes A (infantry) and I (engineer) to Palau rpt, RS MCS.
51. CG 1stMarDiv, annex H (artillery) to Palau rpt, RS MCS.
52. Hough, "The Palaus," IV-81 to IV-82, VI-11 to VI-12.
53. CG 1stMarDiv, annex C (logistics) to Palau rpt, RS MCS.
54. CinCPac-CinCPOA, Sep 1944 Operations in POA, pars 206–210, ONRL. CG IIIAC, encl D (supply) to Palau rpt; CG Garrison Air Force, Western Carolines, War Diary, 4–7 Oct 1944, RS MCS.
55. CG IIIAC, encl K (shore party operations) to Palau rpt, RS MCS.
56. CG 1stMarDiv, annexes C (logistics) and I (engineer) to Palau rpt, RS MCS.
57. CG 1stMarDiv, annex G (personnel) to Palau rpt, RS MCS.
58. ComPhibGrpFive, Palau rpt, 16 Oct 1944, RS MCS.
59. CG IIIAC, encl G (naval gunfire) to Palau rpt, RS MCS.
60. CG 1stMarDiv, annex K (naval gunfire) to Palau rpt, RS MCS.
61. CG IIIAC, encl G (naval gunfire) to Palau rpt, RS MCS.
62. CG IIIAC, encl B (operations) to Palau rpt, RS MCS.
63. Louis E. Woods, Marine Corps Aviation—an integral part of an outstanding air-ground team—the Marine Corps, rpt to CMC, 20 Apr 1946, Hq USMC.
64. CinCPac-CinCPOA, Sep 1944 Operations in POA, par 196, ONRL.
65. CinCPac-CinCPOA, Sep 1944 Operations in POA, par 214, ONRL.
66. CG Garrison Air Force, Western Carolines, War Diary, 24 Sep and Oct 1944, RS MCS.
67. CG IIIAC, encl F (air support) to Palau rpt, RS MCS.
68. CG 1stMarDiv, annex L (air support) to Palau rpt, RS MCS.
69. CG Garrison Air Force, Western Carolines, War Diary May–Oct 1944, quote from 9 Oct 1944, RS MCS.
70. CG Garrison Air Force, Western Carolines, War Diary, 28 Sep 1944, RS MCS. CinCPac-CinCPOA, Sep 1944 Operations in POA, pars 219–223, ONRL. Lewis W. Walt, "The Closer the Better," *Marine Corps Gazette*, Sep 1946, 37.
71. Walt, "The Closer the Better," *Marine Corps Gazette*, Sep 1946, 38–39. CG Garrison Air Forces, Western Carolines, War Diary 30 Sep and Oct 1944, RS MCS.
72. Keith B. McCutcheon, "Close Support Aviation," mimeograph in Hq USMC.
73. C. Van Woodward, *The Battle for Leyte Gulf* (New York, 1947). James A. Field, Jr., *The Japanese at Leyte Gulf; The Shō Operation* (Princeton, 1947).
74. USMC Intelligence Section, Division of Aviation, "Marine Dive Bombers in the Philippines," 5 May 1945, pp 3,5,9, Hq USMC.
75. McCutcheon, "Air Support Techniques," *Marine Corps Gazette*, Apr 1946, 24.
76. USMC Intelligence Section, Division of Aviation, "Marine Fighter Squadrons in the Philippines, February, April 1945," July, 1945, Hq USMC, *passim*, quote on p 4. G. A. Gayle, encl 1 (memo by Clayton C. Jerome) to ltr to P. A. Crowl, 9 Mar 1950.
77. Louis E. Woods, encls C (commendation by Lt. Gen. Eichelberger), D (commendation of MAG 24 by Gen. Walter Kreuger), and E (commendation of MAG 32 by Kreuger) to rpt on Marine Corps Aviation, 20 Apr 1946, Hq USMC.
78. Halsey, *Halsey's Story*, 195.
79. USSBS(P), *Interrogations*, vol II, p 523.
80. Jesse B. Oldendorf, ltr to Clayton C. Jerome, 25 March 1950, PUL.
81. Craven and Cate, eds, MS of "The Army Air Forces in World War II," vol IV, ch X, pp 74–75, Historical Division, War Dept.
82. O. P. Smith, ltr to J. A. Isely, 7 Mar 1950, PUL. Authority for the number

of Japanese who surrendered on the northern islands is Maj. Gen. Ford O. Rogers who received the surrender.

CHAPTER X

1. Com5thFlt, Iwo rpt, 14 Jun 1945, ONRL.
2. George C. Marshall, "Biennial Report of the Chief of Staff of the U.S. Army to the Secretary of War," *The United States News* (extra number) 10 Oct 1945, 80.
3. Appleman, et al., *Okinawa*, 1–7. CinCPac, Feb 1945 operations in POA, 27 Aug 1945; Com5thFlt, Iwo rpt, 14 Jun 1945; ComPhibGrpOne, Iwo rpt, 12 Apr 1945, ONRL. CG FMFPac, Iwo rpt, 1 Apr 1945; CG VAC, basic doc and app 3 (operations) to annex B (general staff sections rpts) to Iwo rpt, 13 May 1945, RS MCS.
4. CinCPac, Operation Plan 77–44, 25 Nov 1944, ONRL.
5. CinCPac, Feb 1945 operation in POA, ONRL.
6. As quoted in *New York Times*, 16 Mar 1945, p 12, col 2.
7. CG FMFPac, encl C (intelligence) to Iwo rpt, RS MCS. CMC, memo to ComInCh, 25 May 1944, Hq USMC. CMC, memo to CinCPac, 2 Apr 1944; CG FMFPac, Special Order 2–44. 23 Aug 1944; CMC, memo to CG FMFPac, 31 Aug 1944, ONRL.
8. Robert Sherrod, *On To Westward* (New York, 1945), 259.
9. ComPhibForsPac, Iwo rpt, 19 May 1945, ONRL.
10. CG FMFPac, basic doc and #2 (naval gunfire rpt) to encl F (joint supporting arms rpt) to Iwo rpt; CG VAC, basic doc and app 2 (naval gunfire) to annex C (special staff sections rpts) to Iwo rpt, RS MCS.
11. Craven and Cate, eds, *Army Air Forces in World War II*, vol IV, 281–310, 549–574, 671–693. G. D. Gayle, ltr with encl to J. A. Isely, 14 Jan 1950, PUL. Joint Army-Navy Assessment Committee, *Japanese Naval and Merchant Shipping Losses During World War II by All Causes*, 12–22, 61–82.
12. CG FMFPac, encl C (intelligence) to Iwo rpt, RS MCS. Notes on conference at Princeton on Iwo Jima, 17 Dec 1949, PUL. William H. P. Blandy, ltr to J. A. Isely, 5 Dec 1949; John S. Letcher, ltr to J. A. Isely, 21 Nov 1949, PUL.
13. CG FMFPac, basic doc and #2 (naval gunfire rpt) to encl F (supporting arms rpt) to Iwo rpt; CG VAC, basic doc and app 2 (naval gunfire rpt) to annex C (special staff sections rpts) to Iwo rpt, RS MCS. Notes on conference at Princeton on Iwo Jima, PUL.
14. CG FMFPac, encl E (comments and recommendations) to encl B (operations) to Iwo rpt, RS MCS.
15. CG FMFPac, app A (state of enemy defenses, 13 Feb 1945) to encl C (intelligence) to Iwo rpt, RS MCS.
16. Harry Schmidt, ltr to J. A. Isely, 11 Dec 1949, PUL.
17. CG VAC, Iwo rpt, RS MCS.
18. CinCPac, Feb 1945 opns in POA, ONRL.
19. CG FMFPac, #2 (naval gunfire) to encl F (joint supporting arms rpt) to Iwo rpt, RS MCS.
20. Kenyth A. Damke, "Was the Mission of the pre-D-day Bombardment accomplished at Iwo Jima?" monograph in MCS, senior course, RS MCS.
21. Com5thFlt, Operation Plan 13–44, ONRL. R. A. Spruance, ltr to J. A. Isely, 8 Jan 1950, PUL.
22. CG FMFPac, #2 (naval gunfire) to encl F (joint supporting arms rpt) to Iwo rpt; CG VAC, app 2 (naval gunfire) to annex C (special staff sections' rpts) to Iwo rpt, RS MCS. William W. Rogers, ltr to J. A. Isely, 26 Dec 1949, PUL.
23. CG FMFPac, #2 (naval gunfire) to encl F (joint supporting arms rpt) to Iwo rpt, RS MCS. Donald M. Weller, ltr to J. A. Isely, 26 Jan 1950, PUL.
24. CinCPac, Feb 1945 operations in POA; Com5thFlt, Iwo rpt; ComPhibForsPac, Iwo rpt; ComPhibGrpOne, Iwo rpt, ONRL. CG FMFPac, Iwo rpt; CG VAC, basic doc and app 2 (naval gunfire support) to annex C (special staff sections rpts) to Iwo rpt, RS MCS.
25. H. M. Smith, *Coral and Brass*, 246–247.
26. CinCPac, Feb 1945 operations in POA, ONRL. Appleman, et al., *Okinawa*, 63–67, 253–255.
27. Com5thFlt, Operation Plan 13–44, ONRL.
28. Com5thFlt, Iwo rpt, ONRL. CG FMFPac, encl B (operations) to Iwo rpt, RS MCS.
29. H. M. Smith, *Coral and Brass*, 247.
30. Com5thFlt, Iwo rpt, ONRL. King, *U.S. Navy at War, 1941–1945*, 131–132. USSBS(P) Naval Analysis Division, *Interrogations*, vol I, 118–121. R. A. Spruance, ltrs to J. A. Isely, 8 Jan, 3 and 27 Feb 1950; W. H. P. Blandy, ltr to J. A. Isely, 5 Dec 1949; D. M. Weller, ltr to J. A. Isely, 26 Jan 1950; J. S. Letcher, ltr to J. A. Isely, 21 Nov 1949, PUL.
31. USSBS(P), Naval Analysis Division, *Interrogations*, vol I, 23–24; *Campaigns*, 320–321, 324–328.
32. CG VAC, Iwo rpt, RS MCS.
33. CinCPac, Feb 1945 operations in POA, ONRL.
34. ComPhibForsPac, Iwo rpt; ComPhibGrpOne, Iwo rpt, 22 Feb 1945; ComPhibGrpEleven, Iwo rpt, 10 Mar 1945; ComPhibGrpTwo, Iwo rpt, 2 Apr 1945, ONRL. CG FMFPac, basic doc, app 4 (supply rpt) to annex B (general staff

sections rpts), and app 7 (TQM rpt) to annex C (special staff sections rpts) to Iwo rpt; CG 3dMarDiv, Iwo rpt, 30 Apr 1945, RS MCS. H. M. Smith, *Coral and Brass*, 267–268. W. H. P. Blandy, ltr to J. A. Isely, 5 Dec 1949. PUL.
35. H. M. Smith, *Coral and Brass*, 248–249.
36. *New York Times*, 8 Mar 1945, p 12, col 6. CG VAC, app 8 (medical rpt) to annex C (special staff sections rpts) to Iwo rpt; CG 5thMarDiv, encls A (logistics concept) and B (concept of supply beyond O-1) to annex D (supply) to Iwo rpt, 28 Apr 1945, RS MCS.
37. CG FMFPac, #6 (TQM rpt) to encl G (special staff officers rpts) to Iwo rpt, RS MCS. Hq CominCh, "Capture of Iwo Jima," ch I, p 5. King, *U.S. Navy at War*, 129.
38. CG VAC, basic doc and app 3 (operations rpt) to encl B (general staff sections rpts) to Iwo rpt; CG 3dMarDiv, Iwo rpt, RS MCS. Edward A. Craig, ltr to J. A. Isely, 17 Jan 1950; G. D. Gayle, ltr to J. A. Isely, 17 Nov 1949, PUL.
39. CG FMFPac, basic doc and encl D (operations narrative) to encl B (operations) to Iwo rpt; CG 3dMarDiv, Iwo rpt, RS MCS.
40. John C. Chapin, "The Fifth Marine Division in World War II" (multilithed, Hq USMC, Washington, 1945), 1–5. CG VAC, app 3 (operations rpt) to annex B (general staff sections rpt) to Iwo rpt; CG 5thMarDiv, annexes A (personnel rpt) and Q (26thMars rpt) to Iwo rpt, RS MCS.
41. CG VAC, Iwo rpt; CG 3dMarDiv, Operation Plan 1–45, 22 Jan 1945; CG 4thMarDiv, Operation Plan 49–44 (preferred), 26 Dec 1945; CG 5thMarDiv, Operation Plan 2–44 (preferred), 31 Dec 1945, RS MCS.
42. Hq CominCh, "Capture of Iwo Jima," ch VII, pp 1–2. CG FMFPac, basic doc and encl C (training, embarkation, and movement) to encl B (operations rpt) to Iwo rpt; CG VAC, basic doc, app 3 (operations rpt) to annex B (general staff sections rpts), and app 6 (amphibious vehicles rpt) to annex C (special staff sections rpts) to Iwo rpt; CG 4thMarDiv, basic doc and annex D (logistics rpt) to Iwo rpt; CG 5thMarDiv, Iwo rpt, RS MCS.
43. CG 5thMarDiv, annexes E (TQM rpt) and R (27thMars rpt) to Iwo rpt; CG 4thMarDiv, annex G (2dBn 23dMars rpt) to annex F (23dMars rpt) to Iwo rpt, RS MCS.
44. CG VAC, app 3 (operations rpt) to annex B (general staff sections rpts) to Iwo rpt; CG 4thMarDiv, Iwo rpt, RS MCS.
45. CG FMFPac, encl C (intelligence rpt) to Iwo rpt; CG VAC, app 2 (intelligence rpt) to annex B (general staff sections rpts) and app 5 (engineering rpt) to annex C (special staff sections rpts) to Iwo rpt; CG 4thMarDiv, annex B (intelligence rpt) to Iwo rpt, RS MCS. H. W. Hill, ltr to J. A. Isely, 13 Jan 1950, PUL.
46. CG 3dMarDiv, Iwo rpt; CG 4thMarDiv, Iwo rpt; CG 5thMarDiv, annex I (artillery rpt) to Iwo rpt, RS MCS.
47. CG 5thMarDiv, encl B (intelligence rpt) to annex R (27thMars rpt) to Iwo rpt; CG VAC, app 2 (intelligence) to annex B (general staff sections rpts) to Iwo rpt, RS MCS.
48. CG FMFPac, app C (intelligence periodic rpts, *viz.* rpt 17, 6–7 Mar 1945) to encl C (intelligence) and encl C to Iwo rpt, RS MCS.
49. CG 4thMarDiv, annex B (intelligence rpt) to Iwo rpt; CG 5thMarDiv, annex L (5th TankBn rpt) to Iwo rpt, RS MCS.
50. CG VAC, app 3 (operations rpt) to annex B (general staff sections rpts) to Iwo rpt, RS MCS.
51. CG 4thMarDiv, apps 7 (2dBn 25thMars rpt) and 8 (3dBn 25thMars rpt) to annex H (25thMars rpt) to Iwo rpt, RS MCS.
52. CG 4thMarDiv, app 8 (3dBn 25thMars rpt) to annex H (25thMars rpt) to Iwo rpt, RS MCS.
53. CG VAC, app 3 (operations rpt) to annex B (general staff sections rpts) to Iwo rpt, RS MCS.
54. CG FMFPac, encl E (comments and recommendations) to encl B (operations) and encl C (intelligence) to Iwo rpt, RS MCS. E. A. Craig, ltr to J. A. Isely, 17 Jan 1950, PUL.
55. CG VAC, basic doc and app 3 (operations rpt) to annex B (general staff sections rpts) to Iwo rpt, RS MCS.
56. CG 5thMarDiv, basic doc and annex L (5thTankBn rpt) to Iwo rpt; CG FMFPac, encl D (logistics rpt) to Iwo rpt; CG 3dMarDiv, Iwo rpt; CG 4thMarDiv, Iwo rpt, RS MCS. E. A. Craig, ltr to J. A. Isely, 17 Jan 1950, PUL.
57. CG 5thMarDiv, basic doc, annexes A (personnel rpt), J (5thEngBn rpt), and app 4 (2dBn 26thMars rpt) to annex Q (26thMars rpt) to Iwo rpt, RS MCS.
58. CG FMFPac, encl F (personnel rpt) to Marianas rpt; CG 3dMarDiv, basic doc, encl A (1stBn 9thMars rpt) to encl C (9thMars rpt), encl B (2dBn 3dMars rpt) to encl E (3dMars rpt), encl F (12thMars rpt), encl C (3dMedBn rpt) to encl G (service troops rpt), encl H (3dTankBn rpt), encl I (3dEngBn rpt), encl J (3dPionBn rpt) to Iwo rpt; CG FMFPac, #1 (artillery rpt) to encl G (special staff officers rpts) to Iwo rpt, RS MCS.
59. CG 4thMarDiv, basic doc and annex A (personnel rpt), annex F (23dMars rpt) and annex E (communications rpt) to annex F, annex H (3dBn 24thMars rpt)

60. CG 4thMarDiv, basic doc and annex D (logistics) to Iwo rpt; CG VAC, Iwo rpt; CG 3dMarDiv, Iwo rpt, RS MCS.
61. CG FMFPac, #6 (TQM rpt) to encl G (special staff sections rpts) to Iwo rpt; CG VAC, app 7 (TQM rpts) to annex C (special staff sections rpts) to Iwo rpt, RS MCS. W. W. Rogers, ltr to J. A. Isely, 26 Dec 1949, PUL.
62. CG FMFPac, annex A (supply and resupply plan) to encl A (Administration Order 1–44) and encl D (logistics rpt) to Iwo rpt; CG VAC, app 4 (supply rpt) to annex B (general staff sections rpts) to Iwo rpt; CG 3dMarDiv, basic doc and encl G (service troops rpt) to Iwo rpt, RS MCS.
63. Hq ComInCh, "Capture of Iwo Jima," ch I, p 5, and ch 7, p 1. CG FFMPac, encl A (shipping by types) to #6 (TQM rpt) to encl G (special staff sections rpts) to Iwo rpt; CG 4thMarDiv, Iwo rpt; CG VAC, 1st endorsement to 4thMarDiv rpt, 24 May 1945, RS MCS.
64. CG FMFPac, encl B (operations) to Iwo rpt; CG 3dMarDiv, Iwo rpt; CG 4thMarDiv, basic doc and annex C (operations rpt) to Iwo rpt; CG 5thMarDiv, basic doc and annex C (operations rpt) to Iwo rpt, RS MCS. ComPhibForsPac, Iwo rpt; ComPhibGrpTwo, Iwo rpt, ONRL.
65. CG FMFPac, Iwo rpt, RS MCS.
66. CG FMFPac, app C (intelligence periodic rpts) to encl C (intelligence rpt) to Iwo rpt, RS MCS.
67. ComPhibGrpOne, 1st endorsement on ComPhibGrpEleven, Iwo rpt, 12 Apr 1945; ComPhibGrpEleven, Iwo rpt, ONRL. CG 5thMarDiv, app 4 (daylight and dark table) to annex B (intelligence) to Operation Plan 2–44, 31 Dec 1945; CG VAC, app 2 (naval gunfire rpt) to annex C (special staff sections rpts) to Iwo rpt, RS MCS.
68. ComPhibForsPac, annex H (naval gunfire) to Operation Plan A25–44, and Iwo rpt; ComPhibGrpOne, basic doc, encls C (naval gunfire rpt) and D (air support rpt) to Iwo rpt; ComPhibGrpEleven Iwo rpt, ONRL. CG VAC, app 2 (naval gunfire rpt) to annex C (special staff sections rpts) to Iwo rpt; D. M. Weller, "Introduction to Naval Gunfire Support," lecture in MCS senior course, 1947, RS MCS.
69. ComPhibForsPac, Iwo rpt; ComPhibGrpOne, basic doc and encl C (naval gunfire rpt) to Iwo rpt; ComPhibGrpEleven, Iwo rpt; Com Underwater Demolition Teams PacFlt, Iwo rpt, ONRL. CG FMFPac, basic doc and #2 (naval gunfire rpt) to encl F (joint supporting arms rpt) to Iwo rpt; CG VAC, app 2 (naval gunfire rpt) to annex C (special staff sections rpts) to Iwo rpt, RS MCS.
70. As quoted in the *New York Times*, 3 Mar 1945, p 5, col 3. H. M. Smith, *Coral and Brass*, 255. D. M. Weller, ltr to J. A. Isely, 26 Jan 1950, PUL.
71. Warren Moscow, *New York Times*, 18 Feb 1945, p 4, col 1.
72. ComPhibGrpEleven, Iwo rpt, ONRL.
73. Com5thFlt, Iwo rpt; Commander First Carrier Task Force, PacFlt, Iwo rpt, 13 Mar 1945; ComCortCarPac, Iwo rpt, 21 Apr 1945; ComPhibForsPac, Iwo rpt, ONRL. CG VAC, app 3 (air support rpt) to annex C (special staff sections rpts) to Iwo rpt, RS MCS.
74. CinCPac, Feb 1945 operations in POA; ComPhibForsPac, Iwo rpt; ComPhibGrpOne, basic doc and encl D (air support rpt) to Iwo rpt; ComCortCarPac, Iwo rpt, ONRL. CG VAC, app 3 (air support rpt) to annex C (special staff sections rpts) to Iwo rpt, RS MCS.
75. ComPhibGrpOne, encl D (air support rpt) to Iwo rpt, ONRL.
76. CG VAC, encl A (notes) to #2 (VAC liaison team with 4thMarDiv rpt) to app 9 (VAC liaison rpts) to annex C (special staff sections rpts) to Iwo rpt. RS MCS.
77. CG 4thMarDiv, Iwo rpt; CG VAC, Iwo rpt and 1st endorsement to 4thMarDiv rpt, to CMC 24 May 1945, RS MCS. W. H. P. Blandy, ltr to J. A. Isely, 5 Dec 1949; J. S. Letcher, ltr to J. A. Isely, 21 Nov 1949, PUL.
78. Damke, "Pre-D-Day Bombardment Iwo Jima"; CG FMFPac, app A (state of enemy defenses, 13 Feb 1945) to encl C (intelligence rpt) and encls C and F (joint supporting arms rpt) to Iwo rpt; CG VAC, apps 2 (intelligence) and 3 (operations) to annex B (general staff sections rpts) and apps 2 (naval gunfire) and 3 (air support) to annex C (special staff sections rpts) to Iwo rpt, RS MCS.
79. ComPhibForsPac, Iwo rpt; ComPhibGrpOne, Iwo rpt; ComPhibGrpEleven, Iwo rpt, ONRL. W. H. P. Blandy, ltr to J. A. Isely, 5 Dec 1949, PUL.
80. R. A. Spruance, ltr to J. A. Isely, 3 Feb 1950; E. A. Craig, ltr to J. A. Isely, 17 Jan 1950; J. S. Letcher, ltr to J. A. Isely, 21 Nov 1949, PUL.
81. As quoted by the *New York Times*, 26 Feb 1945, p 4, col 4.
82. CG FMFPac, app C (intelligence periodic rpts) to encl C (intelligence) to Iwo rpt; CG VAC, app 3 (operations) to annex B (general staff sections rpts) and encl C (special action rpt) to app 4

(supply) to annex B (general staff sections rpts) and app 2 (naval gunfire) to annex C (special staff sections rpts) to Iwo rpt, RS MCS.
83. ComPhibForsPac, Iwo rpt, and annexes H (naval gunfire) and I (air support) to Operation Plan A25–44; ComPhibGrp-Two, basic doc, sect D (ship-to-shore) and part IV (support arms) to section D to Iwo rpt; ComLCIFlotTwenty-one, Iwo rpt, 2 Mar 1945, ONRL. CG FMFPac, encl F (operations periodic rpts) to encl B (operations) and encl F (joint supporting arms rpt) to Iwo rpt; CG VAC, basic doc, app 3 (operations) to annex B (general staff sections rpts), and apps 2 (naval gunfire), 3 (air support) and 6 (amphibious vehicles) to annex C (special staff sections rpts) to Iwo rpt; CG 4thMarDiv, basic doc and annexes C (operations) and M (2dArm'dAmphTrackBn rpt) to Iwo rpt; CG 5thMarDiv, basic doc, and annexes G (air support) and H (naval gunfire) to Iwo rpt, RS MCS.
84. CG 4thMarDiv, annexes M (2dArm'dAmphTrackBn rpt), N (5thAmphTrackBn rpt) and O (10thAmphTrackBn rpt) to Iwo rpt; CG 5thMarDiv, annex M (amphibious vehicles rpt) and encl C (supply) to annex R (27thMars rpt) to Iwo rpt, RS MCS.
85. Allen R. Matthews, *The Assault* (New York, 1947), 39.
86. CG VAC, app 10 (shore party rpt) to annex C (special staff sections rpts) to Iwo rpt; CG 4thMarDiv, app 2 (2dBn 14thMars rpt) to annex I (artillery rpt) to Iwo rpt, RS MCS.
87. CG FMFPac, encl F (operations periodic rpts) to encl B (operations) to Iwo rpt; CG VAC, basic doc and app 6 (amphibious vehicles rpt) to annex C (special staff sections rpts) to Iwo rpt; CG 4thMarDiv, annex M (2dArm'dTrackBn rpt) to Iwo rpt, RS MCS.
88. CG FMFPac, encl D (operations narrative) to encl B (operations) to Iwo rpt; CG 4thMarDiv, annex J (4thTankBn rpt) to Iwo rpt; CG 5thMarDiv, encl A (logistics concept) to annex D (supply), annexes L (tanks) and R (27thMars rpt) to Iwo rpt, RS MCS. W. W. Rogers, ltr to J. A. Isely, 26 Dec 1949, PUL.
89. CG VAC, app 10 (shore party) to annex C (special staff sections rpts) to Iwo rpt; CG 4thMarDiv, annexes M (2dArm'dAmphBn rpt), N (5thAmphBn rpt) and O (10thAmphBn rpt) to Iwo rpt, RS MCS. D. M. Weller, ltr to J. A. Isely, 26 Jan 1950, PUL.
90. CG VAC, app 2 (naval gunfire rpt) to annex C (special staff sections rpts) to Iwo rpt, RS MCS.
91. CG 5thMarDiv, annexes M (1stBn 28thMars rpt) and N (2dBn 28thMars rpt) to annex S (28thMars rpt) and annex S to Iwo rpt, RS MCS.
92. CG 5thMarDiv, basic doc and annex R (27thMars rpt) to Iwo rpt, RS MCS.
93. CG FMFPac, encl D (operations narrative) to encl B (operations). CG VAC, app 2 (naval gunfire) to annex C (special staff sections rpts) to Iwo rpt; CG 4thMarDiv, basic doc and annex B (intelligence) to Iwo rpt, RS MCS.
94. *Time*, 5 Mar 1945, p 27, cols 1–2.
95. CG 4thMarDiv, annex F (23dMars rpt) to Iwo rpt, RS MCS.
96. CG 4thMarDiv, basic doc, apps 7 (2dBn 25thMars rpt) and (3dBn 25thMars rpt) to annex H (25thMars rpt) and annex H to Iwo rpt, RS MCS.
97. CG FMFPac, basic doc, encls D (operations narrative) and F (periodic rpts) to encl B (operations), app C (intelligence periodic rpts) to encl C (intelligence), and encl E (personnel) to Iwo rpt; CG VAC, basic doc and app 3 (operations) to annex B (general staff sections rpts) to Iwo rpt; CG 4thMarDiv, basic doc, apps 5 (476th AmphTruckCo rpt) and 6 (4thAmphTruckCo rpt) to annex I (artillery rpt) and annex I to Iwo rpt; CG 5thMarDiv, basic doc and annex I (artillery rpt) to Iwo rpt; John S. Oldfield, "Artillery Landing Under Fire, Iwo Jima," study in MCS senior course, RS MCS.
98. CG FMFPac, encl E (personnel) to Iwo rpt; CG VAC, Iwo rpt; CG 4thMarDiv, basic doc and annexes F (1stBn 23dMars rpt) G (2dBn 23dMars rpt) and H (3dBn 23dMars rpt) to annex F (23dMars rpt) and annexes F, G (24thMars rpt), apps 6 (1stBn 25thMars rpt), 7 (2dBn 25thMars rpt) and 8 (3dBn 25thMars rpt) to annex H (25thMars rpt) and annex H to Iwo rpt, RS MCS.
99. CG FMFPac, encl F (periodic rpts) to encl B (operations) to Iwo rpt, RS MCS.
100. CG FMFPac, app C (periodic rpts) to encl C (intelligence) and encl C to Iwo rpt, RS MCS.
101. CinCPac, Feb 1945 operations in POA, ONRL.
102. CG FMFPac, app C (periodical rpts) to encl C (intelligence) to Iwo rpt; CG VAC, app 2 (intelligence) to annex B (general staff sections rpts) to Iwo rpt, RS MCS.
103. H. M. Smith, *Coral and Brass*, 256. CG VAC, basic doc, apps 2 (intelligence) and 3 (operations) to annex B (general staff sections rpts) and annex B to Iwo rpt; CG 3dMarDiv, encl C (3dBn 21stMars rpt) to encl D (21stMars rpt) to Iwo rpt, RS MCS.
104. Miller, *Guadalcanal*, 249. CG 5thMarDiv, annex O (3dBn 28thMars rpt) to annex S (28thMars rpt) to Iwo rpt, RS MCS.
105. CG FMFPac, encl C (intelligence) to

Iwo rpt; CG VAC, encl G (2dBomb Disposal Co rpt) to app 5 (engineer rpt) to annex C (special staff sections rpts) to Iwo rpt; CG 4thMarDiv, annexes J (4thTankBn rpt) and K (4thEngBn rpt) to Iwo rpt; CG 5thMarDiv, annexes J (engineer rpt) and K (ordnance rpt) to Iwo rpt; CG 3dMarDiv, basic doc, encl C (9thMars rpt) encl C (3dBn 21stMars rpt) to encl D (21stMars rpt), encls H (3dTankBn rpt), I (3dEngBn rpt) and J (3dPioneerBn rpt) to Iwo rpt, RS MCS.
106. CG FMFPac, encl E (comments and recommendations) to encl B (operations) and encl C (intelligence) to Iwo rpt; CG VAC, basic doc, apps 2 (intelligence) and 3 (operations) to annex B (general staff sections rpts), apps 2 (naval gunfire) and 5 (engineer rpt) to Iwo rpt; CG 4thMarDiv, annex B (intelligence) to Iwo rpt; CG 5thMarDiv, annex Q (26thMars rpt) to Iwo rpt; CG 3dMarDiv, basic doc, encls A (intelligence), C (9thMars rpt), D (21stMars rpt) and I (3dEngBn rpt) to Iwo rpt, RS MCS.
107. H. M. Smith, *Coral and Brass*, 269. As quoted by Robert Trumbull and Robert Sherrod, *New York Times,* 10 Mar 1945, p 7, col 1, and *Life,* 5 Mar 1945, p 41, col 1.
108. CG FMFPac, encl E (comments and recommendations) to encl B (operations) and encl C (intelligence) to Iwo rpt; CG VAC, app 3 (operations) to annex B (general staff sections rpts), app 4 (artillery) to annex C (special staff sections rpts) to Iwo rpt; CG 4thMarDiv, annexes B (intelligence) and I (artillery) to Iwo rpt; CG 5thMarDiv, annexes I (artillery) and Q (26thMars rpt) to Iwo rpt; CG 3dMarDiv, basic doc and encl F (12thMars rpt) to Iwo rpt, RS MCS.
109. CG FMFPac, app C (periodic rpts) to encl C (intelligence) to Iwo rpt, RS MCS.
110. CG FMFPac, encl C (intelligence) to Iwo rpt, RS MCS.
111. Matthews, *The Assault,* 48.
112. H. M. Smith, *Coral and Brass,* 261–262. *U.S.S. Eldorado,* War Diary, 23 Feb 1945, ONRL. Harry B. Liversedge, ltr to J. A. Isely, 10 Jan 1950, PUL.
113. CG 5thMarDiv, annex S (28thMars rpt) to Iwo rpt, RS MCS.
114. John Lardner, "D-Day, Iwo Jima," *New Yorker,* 17 Mar 1945, p 48, col 1. *Newsweek,* 26 Feb 1945, p 28, cols 1–2. CG FMFPac, Iwo rpt; CG VAC, Iwo rpt, RS MCS.
115. CG VAC, app 3 (operations) to annex B (general staff sections rpts) to Iwo rpt, RS MCS.
116. CG 4thMarDiv, Iwo rpt; CG 5thMarDiv, Iwo rpt; CG 3dMarDiv, basic doc and encl F (12thMars rpt) to Iwo rpt, RS MCS. James D. Hittle, ltr to J. A. Isely, 28 Nov 1949, PUL.
117. CG FMFPac, encl F (periodic rpts) to encl B (operations), #1 (artillery) to encl G (special staff officers rpts) to Iwo rpt; CG VAC, app 3 (operations) to annex B (general staff sections rpts), app 4 (artillery) to annex C (special staff sections rpts) to Iwo rpt; CG 4thMarDiv, Iwo rpt; CG 5thMarDiv, basic doc and app 4 (4thBn 13thMars rpt) to annex I (14thMars rpt) to Iwo rpt; CG 3dMarDiv, basic doc, encls A (1stBn 9thMars rpt), B (2dBn 9thMars rpt) and C (3dBn 9thMars rpt) to encl C (9thMars rpt) and encl C, encls A (1stBn 21stMars rpt), B (2dBn 21stMars rpt) and C (3dBn 21stMars rpt) to encl D (21stMars rpt) to Iwo rpt; George B. Thomas, "[Third] Division Artillery at Iwo Jima," study in MCS senior course, RS MCS. Notes on conference at Princeton on Iwo Jima, PUL.
118. CG 3dMarDiv, Iwo rpt, RS MCS.
119. CG VAC, basic doc, app 3 (operations) to annex B (general staff sections rpts), and app 10 (shore party rpt) to annex C (special staff sections rpts) to Iwo rpt; CG 4thMarDiv, Iwo rpt; CG 5thMarDiv, Iwo rpt, RS MCS.
120. CG 3dMarDiv, basic doc, encls A (1stBn 9thMars rpt), B (2dBn 9thMars rpt), and C (3dBn 9thMars rpt) to encl C (9thMars rpt) and encl C, encls A (1stBn 21stMars rpt), B (2dBn 21stMars rpt), and C (3dBn 21stMars rpt) to encl D (21stMars rpt) and encls D, F (12thMars rpt) and H (3dTank Bn rpt) to Iwo rpt; Howard J. Turton, "A Division PreDawn Attack—A Study of Offensive Tactics," study in MCS senior course, RS MCS. Robert D. Heinl, Jr., "Dark Horse on Iwo," *Marine Corps Gazette,* Aug 1945, 3–7, 58–60. Howard N. Kenyon, ltr to J. A. Isely, 9 Feb 1950, PUL.
121. Raymond Henri, James G. Lucas, David K. Dempsey, W. Keyes Beech, and Alvin M. Josephy, Jr., *The U.S. Marines on Iwo Jima* (New York, 1945) 123–145.
122. CG 4thMarDiv, basic doc, annex C (operations), annexes F (1stBn 23dMars rpt), G (2dBn 23dMars rpt), and H (3dBn 23dMars rpt), to annex F (23dMars rpt), annexes F (1stBn 24thMars rpt), G (2dBn 24thMars rpt) and H (3dBn 24thMars rpt) to annex G (24thMars rpt), annex G, apps 6 (1stBn 25thMars rpt), 7 (2dBn 25thMars rpt), 8 (3dBn 25thMars rpt) to annex H (25thMars rpt), annexes H, I (artillery) and J (4thTankBn rpt) to Iwo rpt; CG FMFPac, app C (periodic rpts) to encl C (intelligence) to Iwo rpt, RS MCS.
123. CG 5thMarDiv, basic doc, annexes I (artillery) and L (tanks), apps 3 (1stBn

26thMars rpt), 4 (2dBn 26thMars rpt), 5 (3dBn 26thMars rpt) to annex Q (26thMars rpt), annex Q, encls E (1stBn 27thMars rpt), F (2dBn 27thMars rpt), and G (3dBn 27thMars rpt) to annex R (27thMars rpt), annexes R and S (28thMars rpt) to Iwo rpt, RS MCS.

124. Notes on conference at Princeton on Iwo Jima, PUL.

125. CG FMFPac, encls B (operations) and C (intelligence) to Iwo rpt; CG VAC, basic doc, and apps 2 (intelligence) and 3 (operations) to annex B (general staff sections rpts) to Iwo rpt; CG 4thMarDiv, basic doc, annexes F (23dMars rpt), G (24thMars rpt), H (25thMars rpt), I (artillery), and J (4thTankBn rpt) to Iwo rpt; CG 5thMarDiv, basic doc, and annexes I (artillery), L (tanks), Q (26thMars rpt), R (27thMars rpt) and S (28thMars rpt), to Iwo rpt; CG 3dMarDiv, basic doc, encls C (9thMars rpt), D (21stMars rpt), F (12thMars rpt) and H (3dTankBn rpt) to Iwo rpt, RS MCS. Keller E. Rockey, ltr to J. A. Isely, 17 Feb 1950; Leland S. Swindler, ltr with encl to J. A. Isely, 28 Nov 1949; H. W. Hill, ltr to J. A. Isely, 13 Jan 1950, PUL.

126. CG VAC, app 10 (shore party) to annex C (special staff sections rpts) to Iwo rpt, RS MCS.

127. CG FMFPac, encl D (capture, occupation and defense of Iwo) to encl B (operations) to Iwo rpt; CG 5thMarDiv, Iwo rpt; CG 3dMarDiv, basic doc and encl C (3dBn 9thMars rpt) to encl C (9thMars rpt) to Iwo rpt, RS MCS.

128. As quoted in *Newsweek*, 2 Apr 1945, p 36, cols 2–3. H. M. Smith, *Coral and Brass*, 255.

129. Office of Public Information, *Navy Department Communiques 301 to 600, and Pacific Fleet Communiques, March 6, 1943, to May 24, 1943* (Washington, 1945), CinCPOA communique #300, 16 Mar 1945, 370.

130. Hq CominCh, "Capture of Iwo Jima," ch II, pp 3–4, ch III, pp 1–3. CG FMFPac, #4 (signal) to encl G (special staff officers rpts) to Iwo rpt; CG VAC, app 2 (naval gunfire) to annex C (special staff sections rpts) to Iwo rpt; CG 4thMarDiv, annexes E (signal) and L (JASCO rpt) to Iwo rpt; CG 5thMarDiv annexes H (naval gunfire) and O (signal) to Iwo rpt; CG 3dMarDiv, basic doc, encl A (JASCO rpt) to encls K (HqBn rpt) to Iwo rpt, RS MCS.

131. CG VAC, app 1 (signal) to annex C (special staff sections rpts) to Iwo rpt, RS MCS.

132. Hq CominCh, "Capture of Iwo Jima," ch III, pp 4–5. CinCPac, Feb 1945 operations in POA, ONRL. CG FMFPac, encl F (joint supporting arms rpt) to Iwo rpt; CG VAC, app 4 (artillery rpt) to annex C (special staff sections rpts) to Iwo rpt, RS MCS. Vernon E. Megee, ltr to J. A. Isely, 10 Feb 1950, PUL.

133. CG 3dMarDiv, Iwo rpt RS MCS.

134. CG VAC, encl A (liaison officers notes) to #2 (liaison team #2 rpt) to app 9 (liaison officers rpts) to Iwo rpt, RS MCS.

135. CG FMFPac, encl C (intelligence) and #1 (artillery) to encl G (special staff officers rpts) to Iwo rpt; CG VAC, basic doc, apps 2 (intelligence) and 3 (operations) to annex B (general staff sections rpts), and apps 3 (air support), 4 (artillery) and 5 (engineer) to annex C (special staff sections rpts) to Iwo rpt, RS MCS.

136. CG 4thMarDiv, annex F (23dMars rpt) to Iwo rpt, RS MCS.

137. CG VAC, 1st endorsement on 4thMarDiv, Iwo rpt, 24 May 1945, RS MCS.

138. ComCruDivFive, Iwo rpt, 14 Mar 1945, ONRL.

139. Hq CominCh, "Capture of Iwo Jima," ch I, pp 1–4. CG VAC, basic doc and app 3 (air support) to annex C (special staff sections rpts) to Iwo rpt, CG 3dMarDiv, Iwo rpt, RS MCS. R. A. Spruance, ltrs to J. A. Isely, 8 Jan, 3 and 27 Feb 1950, PUL.

140. CinCPac, Feb 1945 operations in POA; ComCortCarPac, Iwo rpt, ONRL. CG VAC app 3 (air support) to annex C (special staff sections rpts) to Iwo rpt; CG FMFPac, #1 (air support) to encl F (joint supporting arms rpt) to Iwo rpt, RS MCS.

141. V. E. Megee, ltr to J. A. Isely, 10 Feb 1950, PUL.

142. CinCPac, 1st endorsement to CMC, memo on marine aviation in the Pacific, no date; Hq CominCh, "Invasion of the Marianas," ch II, p 7; CG FMFPac, memo on assumption of air support functions, 12 Oct 1944; CinCPac, memo on type command of air support control units, 21 Oct 1944, ONRL. K. E. Rockey, ltr to J. A. Isely, 17 Feb 1950; G. D. Gayle, ltrs with encls, to J. A. Isely, 23 Dec 1949 and 28 Feb 1950, PUL. Sherrod, "USMC Aviation," pt XX, Hq USMC.

143. Memos on squadron designation of marine units for carrier duty: Capt. W. M. Beakley, to C/S CominCh, 9 Oct 1944; C/S CominCh to CominCh, 10 Oct 1944, RAdm. M. F. Schoeffel to CominCh and C/S CominCh, 19 and 25 Oct 1944, ONRL. Memos on decommissioning four marine bombing squadrons: Beakley to C/S CominCh, 7 Nov 1944; Deputy CominCh-CNO to CominCh, 7 Nov 1944; CominCh to Deputy CominCh-CNO and CMC, 8 Nov 1944, ONRL.

144. CG VAC, app 3 (air support) to annex C (special staff sections rpts) to Iwo rpt; CG 4thMarDiv, annex C (operations) and annex C (operations) to annex F (23dMars rpt) to Iwo rpt, RS MCS.

145. CG 5thMarDiv, annexes M (1stBn 28thMars rpt), N (2ndBn 28thMars rpt) and O (3dBn 28thMars rpt) to annex S (28thMars rpt) to Iwo rpt, RS MCS.
146. CinCPac, Feb 1945 operations in POA; ComPhibForsPac, sect E (air) to pt V of Iwo rpt, ONRL. CG VAC, app 3 (air support) to annex C (special staff sections rpts) and annex F (landing force air support control unit rpt) to Iwo rpt; CG 4thMarDiv, annex C (operations) to Iwo rpt, RS MCS.
147. CG 3dMarDiv, Iwo rpt, RS MCS.
148. ComPhibForsPac, sect E (air) to pt V, Iwo rpt, ONRL. CG VAC, app 3 (air support) to annex C (special staff sections rpts) and annex F (landing force air support control unit rpt) to Iwo rpt, RS MCS. CG 4thMarDiv, annex C (operations) to Iwo rpt; CG 5thMarDiv, pt IV-3 (operations) to annex Q (26thMars rpt), app F (air support) to encl G (3dBn 27thMars rpt) to annex R (27thMars rpt), and annex F (air support) to annex M (1stBn 28thMars rpt) to annex S (28thMars rpt) to Iwo rpt; CG 3dMarDiv, basic doc and encls C (9thMars rpt) and D (21stMars rpt) to Iwo rpt, RS MCS.
149. CG 4thMarDiv, annexes C (operations) and F (23dMars rpt) to Iwo rpt; CG 5thMarDiv, app 1 (air strike control procedure) to annex G (air support), and annex F (air support) to annex N (2dBn 28thMars rpt) to annex S (28thMars rpt) to Iwo rpt, RS MCS.
150. V. E. Megee, ltr to J. A. Isely, 10 Feb 1950, PUL.
151. CG VAC, app 3 (air support) to annex C (special staff sections rpts) to Iwo rpt, RS MCS.
152. CinCPac, Feb 1945 operations in POA, ONRL. CG FMFPac, app C (periodic rpts) to encl C (intelligence) to Iwo rpt; CG VAC, basic doc, and app 3 (air support) to annex C (special staff sections rpts) to Iwo rpt; CG 4thMarDiv, annex C (operations) to Iwo rpt; CG 3dMarDiv, Iwo rpt, RS MCS.
153. ComCortCarPac, Iwo rpt, ONRL. CG VAC, app 3 (air support) to annex C (special staff sections rpts); Avery R. Kier, "Air Operations in Support of Iwo Jima," study in MCS senior course, RS MCS.
154. ComPhibForsPac, sect E (air), pt V of Iwo rpt; ComPhibGrpTwo, pt V of Iwo rpt, ONRL. CG VAC, app 3 (operations) to annex B (general staff sections rpts), app 3 (air support) to annex C (special staff sections rpts), and annex F (landing force air support control unit rpt) to Iwo rpt; CG 4thMarDiv, annex C (operations) to Iwo rpt; CG 5thMarDiv, basic doc, and app 1 (air strike control procedure) to annex G (air support) to Iwo rpt; MCS, "Evaluation of Air Operations," pt III, RS MCS.
155. ComPhibForsPac, sect C, pt V of Iwo rpt, ONRL. CG VAC, app 2 (naval gunfire) to annex C (special staff sections rpt) to Iwo rpt; CG 3dMarDiv, basic doc and encl C (9thMars rpt) to Iwo rpt, RS MCS.
156. CinCPac, Feb 1945 operations in POA; ComPhibForsPac, pt III and sect C, pt V of Iwo rpt; ComPhibGrpTwo, sects A (gunboat fire) and B (rocket fire) to pt IV of Iwo rpt; ComCortCarPac, Iwo rpt; ComLCIFlotTwenty-one, Iwo rpt, 2 Mar 1945, ONRL. CG FMFPac, encl F (periodical rpts) to encl B (operations) to Iwo rpt; CG VAC, app 2 (naval gunfire) to annex C (special staff sections rpts) to Iwo rpt; CG 4thMarDiv, basic doc and annexes C (operations), F (23dMars rpt) and M (2dArm'd-AmphBn rpt) to Iwo rpt; CG 5thMarDiv, basic doc, annex H (naval gunfire), and annex G (naval gunfire) to annex S (28thMars rpt) to Iwo rpt; CG 3dMarDiv, basic doc and encls C (9thMars rpt) and D (21stMars rpt) to Iwo rpt, RS MCS.
157. ComCruDivFive, Iwo rpt, ONRL. E. A. Craig, ltr to J. A. Isely, 17 Jan 1950, PUL.
158. CG FMFPac, #1 (artillery) to encl G (special staff officers rpt) to Iwo rpt; CG 3dMarDiv, Iwo rpt, RS MCS. H. Schmidt, ltr to J. A. Isely, 11 Dec 1949, PUL.
159. ComCortCarPac, Iwo rpt; CG FMFPac, #1 (artillery) to encl G (special staff officers rpts) to Iwo rpt; CG VAC, app 3 (operations) to annex B (general staff sections rpts) and app 4 (artillery) to annex C (special staff sections rpts) to Iwo rpt; CG 4thMarDiv, annexes C (operations), I (artillery) and N (5thAmphBn rpt) to Iwo rpt; CG 5thMarDiv, basic doc, app 1 (air observer's rpt) to annex C (operations), annexes I (artillery) and R (27thMars rpt), and app 4 (covering ltr to 2ndBn 26thMars rpt) to annex Q (26thMars rpt) to Iwo rpt; CG 3dMarDiv, basic doc and annex F (12thMars rpt) to Iwo rpt, RS MCS. K. E. Rockey, ltr to J. A. Isely, 17 Feb 1950, PUL.
160. CG FMFPac, app C (periodical rpts) to encl C (intelligence) to Iwo rpt; CG VAC, app 3 (operations) to annex B (general staff sections rpts) and encl A (Co B AmphibReconBn rpt) to app 13 (Hq Commandant's rpt) to annex C (special staff sections rpts) to Iwo rpt; CG 5thMarDiv, annex I (artillery), and encl F (2ndBn 27thMars rpt) to annex R (27thMars rpt) to Iwo rpt, RS MCS. W. W. Rogers, ltr to J. A. Isely, 26 Dec 1949; notes on conference at Princeton on Iwo Jima, PUL.
161. CG 5thMarDiv basic doc, annex I (artillery) and encl G (3dBn 27thMars rpt) to annex R (27thMars rpt) to Iwo rpt, RS MCS.

REFERENCES 621

162. CG FMFPac, encl B (operations), and #1 (artillery) to encl G (special staff officers rpts) to Iwo rpt; CG VAC, app 4 (supply) to annex C (special staff sections rpts) to Iwo rpt; CG 4thMarDiv, annex C (operations) to annex F (23dMars rpt), and annex I (artillery) to Iwo rpt; CG 5thMarDiv, annex I (artillery) and annex H (artillery) to annex S (28thMars rpt) to Iwo rpt; CG 3dMarDiv, basic doc and encl F (12thMars rpt) to Iwo rpt, RS MCS.
163. CG 3dMarDiv, encl C (9thMars rpt) to Iwo rpt, RS MCS.
164. CG FMFPac, #1 (artillery) to encl G (special staff officers rpts) to Iwo rpt; CG 4thMarDiv, annexes N (5thAmphBn rpts) and O (10thAmphBn rpt) to Iwo rpt; CG 5thMarDiv annex M (amphibian vehicles) to Iwo rpt; CG 3dMarDiv, encl C (3dBn 12thMars rpt) to encl F (12thMars rpt) to Iwo rpt, RS MCS.
165. CG FMFPac, encl B (operations) to Iwo rpt, RS MCS. As quoted in the *New York Times*, 26 Feb 1945, p 1, col 6.
166. CG VAC, app 3 (operations) to annex B (general staff sections rpts) and encl A (8th Field Depot special rpt) to app 10 (shore party rpt) to annex C (special staff sections rpts) to Iwo rpt; CG 4thMarDiv, annex G (2ndBn 23dMars rpt) to annex F (23dMars rpt) and annex H (25thMars rpt) to Iwo rpt; CG 5thMarDiv, basic doc, and annex C (operations) to annex O (3dBn 28thMars rpt) to annex S (28thMars rpt) to Iwo rpt, RS MCS.
167. CG FMFPac, encl C (intelligence) to Iwo rpt; CG 4thMarDiv, annexes C (operations) and G (2dBn 23dMars rpt) to annex F (23dMars rpt), annex G (24thMars rpt), app 3 (operations) to annex H (25thMars rpt), and annex C (operations) to annex K (4th EngBn rpt) to Iwo rpt; CG 5thMarDiv, basic doc, annexes D (supply), J (engineer), and L (tanks), app C (general) to encl G (3dBn 27thMars rpt) to annex R (23dMars rpt), and annexes C (operations) and N (2dBn 28thMars rpt) to annex S (28thMars rpt) to Iwo rpt, RS MCS.
168. CG VAC, app 3 (operations) to annex B (general staff sections rpts) to Iwo rpt; CG 4thMarDiv, annex G (24thMars rpt) to Iwo rpt; CG 5thMarDiv, annex C (operations) to annex S (28thMars rpt), annex C (operations) to annex N (2ndBn 28thMars rpt) to annex S (28thMars rpt), and annex C (operations) to annex O (3dBn 28thMars rpt) to annex S (28thMars rpt) to Iwo rpt, RS MCS.
169. CG 5thMarDiv, Iwo rpt, RS MCS.
170. CG 5thMarDiv, encl F (2ndBn 27thMars rpt) to annex R (27thMars rpt) to Iwo rpt; CG VAC, app 3 (operations) to annex B (general staff sections rpts) to Iwo rpt; CG 4thMarDiv, annex C (operations) to annex F (23dMars rpt) and annex F to Iwo rpt, RS MCS. Notes on conference at Princeton on Iwo Jima; G. D. Gayle, ltr to J. A. Isely, 24 Jul 1950, PUL.
171. CG FMFPac, encl B (operations) to Iwo rpt; CG VAC, app 3 (operations) to annex B (general staff sections rpts) to Iwo rpt; CG 4thMarDiv, annex C (operations) to annex F (23dMars rpt), annex F and annex G (24thMars rpt) to Iwo rpt; CG 5thMarDiv, app 4 (covering ltr, 2ndBn 26thMars rpt) to annex Q (26thMars rpt), annex Q, app A (ordnance) to encl C (supply), encl E (1stBn 27thMars rpt), app C (general) to encl G (3dBn 27thMars rpt) all to annex R (27thMars rpt), annex C (operations) to annex S (28thMars rpt) and annex C (operations) to annex N (2ndBn 28thMars rpt) to annex S to Iwo rpt; CG 3dMarDiv, Iwo rpt, RS MCS.
172. CG VAC, app 3 (operations) to annex B (general staff sections rpts) to Iwo rpt; CG 4thMarDiv, annexes C (operations) and F (23dMars rpt) and annex C (operations) to annex F to Iwo rpt; CG 5thMarDiv, basic doc, encl F (2dBn 27thMars rpt) to annex R (27thMars rpt), annex R, annex C (operations) to annex O (3dBn 28thMars rpt) to annex S (28thMars rpt), and annex C (operations) to annex S to Iwo rpt; CG 3dMarDiv, Iwo rpt, RS MCS.
173. CG FMFPac, #1 (artillery) to encl G (special staff officers rpts) to Iwo rpt; CG 4thMarDiv, annex C (operations) to annex F (23dMars rpt) and annex H (25thMars rpt) to Iwo rpt, RS MCS.
174. CG FMFPac, encl F (periodical rpts) to encl B (operations) to Iwo rpt; CG VAC, basic doc, app 3 (operations) to annex B (general staff sections rpts), and app 10 (shore party rpt) to annex C (special staff sections rpts) to Iwo rpt; CG 4thMarDiv, basic doc, annex C (operations) to annex F (23dMars rpt), and annexes C (9thMars rpt), F, and J (4thPionBn rpt) to Iwo rpt; CG 5thMarDiv, basic doc, annexes L (5thTankBn rpt), Q (26thMars rpt), app 3 (1stBn 26thMars rpt) to annex Q, annex R (27thMars rpt), encl E (1stBn 27thMars rpt) to annex R, annex C (operations) to annex O (3dBn 28thMars rpt) to annex S (28thMars rpt) and annex C (operations) to annex S to Iwo rpt; CG 3dMarDiv, basic doc, encls B (2ndBn 9thMars rpt) and C (3dBn 9thMars rpt) to encl C (9thMars rpt), and encl H (3dTankBn rpt) to Iwo rpt, RS MCS. H. M. Smith, *Coral and Brass* 269–270.
175. CG 3dMarDiv, encl B (2ndBn 21stMars rpt) to encl C (9thMars rpt) to Iwo rpt, RS MCS.
176. CG FMFPac, #1 (artillery) to encl G (special staff officers rpts) to Iwo rpt, RS

MCS. Editorial, *New York Times*, 25 Feb 1945, p 8 E, cols 2-3.
177. As quoted by Robert Trumbull, *New York Times*, 25 Feb 1945, p 28, col 2; and by William Hipple, *Newsweek*, 12 Mar 1945, p 35, col 3.
178. CG 5thMarDiv, Iwo rpt, RS MCS.
179. CG VAC, app 10 (shore party rpt) to annex C (special staff sections rpts) to Iwo rpt, RS MCS.
180. Hq CominCh, "The Capture of Iwo Jima," ch VII, pp 1-2. CG VAC, app 10 (shore party rpt) to annex C (special staff sections rpts) to Iwo rpt, RS MCS.
181. Hq CominCh, "The Capture of Iwo Jima," chs VI-VII. ComPhibForsPac, Iwo rpt; ComPhibGrpTwo, Iwo rpt, ONRL. CG FMFPac, encl F (periodical rpts) to encl B (operations), and #6 (TQM rpt) to encl G (special staff officers rpts) to Iwo rpt; CG VAC, app 7 (TQM rpt) and 10 (shore party rpt) to annex C (special staff sections rpts) to Iwo rpt; CG 4thMarDiv, Iwo rpt; CG 5thMarDiv, encl A (green beach rpt) to encl B (2nd shore party rpt) to annex F (shore party rpt) to Iwo rpt, RS MCS.
182. Hq CominCh, "The Capture of Iwo Jima," chs V-VII. ComPhibForsPac, Iwo rpt, ONRL. CG VAC, basic doc, app 1 (signal rpt) 6 (LVT rpt), and 10 (shore party rpt) to annex C (special staff sections rpt) to Iwo rpt; CG 3dMarDiv, basic doc, encl C (3dBn 9thMars rpt) to encl C (9thMars rpt), and encl B (2ndBn 12th-Mars rpt) to encl F (12thMars rpt) to Iwo rpt, RS MCS.
183. Hq CominCh, "The Capture of Iwo Jima," chs V-VII. ComPhibGrpTwo, Iwo rpt, ONRL. CG VAC, basic doc, app 4 (supply) to annex B (general staff sections rpts), and apps 7 (TQM rpt) and 10 (shore party rpt) to Iwo rpt; CG 4thMarDiv, basic doc, and app 1 (division shore party rpt) to annex D (logistics) to Iwo rpt; CG 5thMarDiv, basic doc, and annexes D (supply) and F (shore party rpt) to Iwo rpt; CG 3dMarDiv, basic doc and encl J (3dPionBn rpt) to Iwo rpt, RS MCS. Notes on conference at Princeton on Iwo Jima, PUL.
184. CG 5thMarDiv, basic doc, annex D (supply), and encl B (red beach #2 rpt) to encl A (1st Shore Party Bn rpt) to encl F (5th Shore Party Bn rpt) to Iwo rpt; CG 4thMarDiv, Iwo rpt, RS MCS. H. W. Hill, ltr to J. A. Isely, 13 Jan 1950, PUL.
185. CG VAC, app 4 (supply) to annex B (general staff sections rpts) to Iwo rpt, RS MCS.
186. CG FMFPac, encl D (logistics) to Iwo rpt; CG VAC, app 6 (LVT rpt) to annex C (special staff sections rpts); CG 4thMarDiv, basic doc and annex D (logistics) to Iwo rpt; CG 5thMarDiv, basic doc, encl A (logistics concept) to annex D (supply), annex D, encl B (red beach #2 rpt) to encl A (1st Shore Party Bn rpt) to annex F (5th Shore Party rpt), annex F, encl C (supply) to annex R (27thMars rpt) and annex R to Iwo rpt, RS MCS.
187. Hq CominCh, "The Capture of Iwo Jima," chs V-VII. ComPhibGrpTwo, Iwo rpt, ONRL. CG VAC, basic doc, app 6 (LVT rpt) to annex C (special staff sections rpts) to Iwo rpt; CG 4thMarDiv, basic doc, annex D (logistics), and apps 5 (476th Amph Truck Co rpt) and 6 (4th Amph Truck Co rpt) to Iwo rpt; CG 5thMarDiv, basic doc, and annexes D (supply), M (amphibious vehicles), and W (5thPionBn rpt) to Iwo rpt, RS MCS.
188. L. S. Swindler, ltr with encl to J. A. Isely, 26 Nov 1949, PUL. CG VAC, apps 4 (artillery rpt), 6 (LVT rpt), 7 (TQM rpt), and 10 (shore party rpt) to annex C (special staff sections rpts) to Iwo rpt; CG 4thMarDiv, app 3 (QM rpt) to annex D (logistics rpt) and app 3 (operations rpt) to annex I (artillery rpt) to Iwo rpt; CG 5thMarDiv, annexes D (supply rpt), E (TQM rpt), K (ordnance rpt), and R (27thMars rpt) to Iwo rpt; CG 3dMarDiv, basic doc, encls A (1stBn 9th-Mars rpt) and C (3dBn 9thMars rpt) to encl C (9thMars rpt), and encl J (3dPionBn rpt) to Iwo rpt, RS MCS.
189. Hq CominCh, "The Capture of Iwo Jima," ch VII, p 2.
190. ComPhibForsPac, Iwo rpt; ComPhibGrpTwo, Iwo rpt, ONRL. CG VAC, app 3 (operations) to annex B (general staff sections rpts) and app 6 (LVT rpt) to annex C (special staff sections rpts) to Iwo rpt; CG 4thMarDiv, basic doc, app 5 (476thAmphTruckCo rpt) and 6 (4thAmphTruckCo rpt) to annex I (artillery), annexes N (5thAmphTrackBn rpt) and O (10thAmphTrackBn rpt) to Iwo rpt; CG 5thMarDiv, basic doc and annex M (amphibious vehicles rpt) to Iwo rpt; CG 3dMarDiv, Iwo rpt, RS MCS.
191. CG 4thMarDiv, annex N (5thAmphTrackBn rpt) and O (10thAmphTrackBn rpt) to Iwo rpt; CG 5thMarDiv, annex F (5th Shore Party rpt) to Iwo rpt, RS MCS.
192. CG 4thMarDiv, Iwo rpt, RS MCS.
193. Hq CominCh, "The Capture of Iwo Jima," ch VII. ComPhibForsPac, Iwo rpt, ComPhibGrpTwo, Iwo rpt, ONRL. CG VAC, basic doc, and apps 4 (artillery), 6 (LVT rpt) and 10 (shore party rpt) to annex C (special staff sections rpts) to Iwo rpt; CG 4thMarDiv, basic doc, app 1 (division shore party rpt) to annex D (logistics), app 5 (476thAmphTruck Co rpt) to annex I (artillery rpt), and annexes H (5thAmphTrackBn rpt)

and O (10thAmphTrackBn rpt) to Iwo rpt; CG 5thMarDiv, basic doc and annexes F (5th Shore Party rpt), I (artillery rpt) and M (amphibious vehicles rpt) to Iwo rpt, RS MCS.

194. Hq ComInCh, "The Capture of Iwo Jima," ch I, p 5, and chs V-VII. ComUDTsPhibForsPac, Iwo rpt, 13 May 1945; CG 4thMarDiv, basic doc, app 1 (division shore party rpt) to annex D (logistics) and annex D to Iwo rpt; CG 5thMarDiv, basic doc, annexes F (5th Shore Party rpt), I (artillery) and R (27thMars rpt) to Iwo rpt, RS MCS.

195. L. S. Swindler, ltr to J. A. Isely, 26 Nov 1949, PUL. CG FMFPac, encl D (logistics) to Iwo rpt; CG VAC, app 10 (shore party rpt) to annex C (special staff sections rpts) to Iwo rpt; CG 4thMarDiv, app 1 (shore party rpt) to annex D (logistics) to Iwo rpt; CG 3dMarDiv, basic doc and encl J (3dPionBn rpt) to Iwo rpt, RS MCS.

196. CG VAC, app 10 (shore party) to annex C (special staff sections rpts) to Iwo rpt; Edmund M. Williams, "Logistics . . . Iwo Jima Operation," study in MSC senior course, RS MCS.

197. CG FMFPac, encl D (logistics) and #1 (artillery) to encl G (special staff officers rpts) to Iwo rpt; CG VAC, app 4 (supply) to annex B (general staff sections rpts) and apps 4 (artillery) and 10 (shore party rpt) to annex C (special staff sections rpts) to Iwo rpt; CG 4thMarDiv, annex D (logistics), app 2 (2ndBn 14thMars rpt) to annex I (14thMars rpt) and annex J (4thTankBn rpt) to Iwo rpt; CG 5thMarDiv, annexes D (supply), O (signal) and Q (26thMars rpt) to Iwo rpt; CG 3dMarDiv, basic doc, encl D (21stMars rpt), encl B (2ndBn 12thMars rpt) to encl F (12thMars rpt) and encl F to Iwo rpt, RS MCS.

198. CG FMFPac, encl D (logistics) to Iwo rpt; CG VAC, app 3 (operations) and 4 (supply) to annex B (general staff sections rpts) to Iwo rpt; CG 4thMarDiv, basic doc, annexes D (logistics), and H (25thMars rpt) to Iwo rpt; CG 5thMarDiv, annex D (supply), encl F (2ndBn 27thMars rpt) to annex R (27thMars rpt), annex C (supply) to encl F to annex R. and annex D (supply) to annex S (28thMars rpt) to Iwo rpt; CG 3dMarDiv, basic doc encl D (21stMars rpt) and encl D (4thBn 12thMars rpt) to encl F (12thMars rpt) to Iwo rpt, RS MCS.

199. CG VAC, app 4 (supply) to annex B (general staff sections rpts), and app 8 (medical) to annex C (special staff sections rpts) to Iwo rpt, RS MCS.

200. Walker Y. Brooks, "Engineers on Iwo"; and James D. Hittle, "Crazy Quilt of Iwo," *Marine Corps Gazette*, Oct 1945, 48–51, and Mar 1946, 21–23. CG VAC, app 5 (engineer) to annex C (special staff sections rpts) to Iwo rpt; CG 4thMarDiv, annex K (4thEngBn rpt) to Iwo rpt; CG 5thMarDiv, annex J (5thEngBn rpt) to Iwo rpt; CG 3dMarDiv, basic doc, and encl I (3dEngBn rpt) to Iwo rpt, RS MCS. K. E. Rockey, ltr to J. A. Isely, 17 Feb 1950, PUL.

201. CG VAC, app 10 (shore party rpt) to annex C (special staff sections rpts) to Iwo rpt, RS MCS.

202. CG 3dMarDiv, encl C (3dBn 3dMars rpt) to encl E (3dMars rpt) to Iwo rpt, RS MCS.

203. H. M. Smith, ltr to J. A. Isely, 16 Sep 1949; W. W. Rogers, ltr to J. A. Isely, 26 Dec 1949; H. Schmidt, ltr to J. A. Isely, 11 Dec 1949, PUL.

204. CG FMFPac, encls B (operations) and E (personnel) to Iwo rpt; CG VAC, apps 1 (personnel) and 3 (operation) to annex B (general staff sections rpts) to Iwo rpt; CG 4thMarDiv, basic doc and annex A (administration) to Iwo rpt; CG 5thMarDiv, basic doc, annex A (administration) and annex N (2ndBn 28thMars rpt) to annex S (28thMars rpt) to Iwo rpt; CG 3dMarDiv, Iwo rpt, RS MCS. Morehouse, *Iwo Jima*, app D (casualties).

205. CG 4thMarDiv, annex C (operations) to annex G (24thMars rpt) to Iwo rpt, RS MCS.

206. CG FMFPac, #5 (surgeon's rpt) to encl G (special staff officers rpts) to Iwo rpt; CG VAC, app 8 (medical) to annex C (special staff sections rpts) to Iwo rpt; CG 4thMarDiv, app 2 (surgeon's rpt) to annex D (logistics) to Iwo rpt; CG 5thMarDiv, annex N (surgeon's rpt) to Iwo rpt; CG 3dMarDiv, basic doc and encl C (surgeon's rpt) to Iwo rpt, RS MCS.

207. CG VAC, app 3 (operations) to annex B (general staff sections rpts) to Iwo rpt, RS MCS.

208. Attached reply, J. A. Isely, ltr to G. D. Gayle, 12 Jun 1950, PUL. Hq ComInCh, "Capture of Iwo Jima," ch VI, pp 9–10. CG VAC, app 8 (medical) to annex C (special staff sections rpts) to Iwo rpt, RS MCS. Morehouse, *Iwo Jima*, app F (use of Iwo airfields). H. M. Smith, *Coral and Brass*, 241.

209. CinCPac, Feb 1945 operations in POA, ONRL. Bureau of Yards and Docks, *Building the Navy's Bases in World War II*, vol II (Washington, 1947), 337–373. USSBS(P), *Air Campaigns of the Pacific War*, 50–54; *Final Report Covering Air-Raid Protection and Allied Subjects in Japan* (Washington, 1947), 200, exhibit A-3. CG VAC, app 3 (air officer rpt) to annex C (special staff sections rpt) to Iwo rpt, RS MCS.

210. As quoted by Morehouse, *Iwo Jima*,

app E (R. Adm. R. Ichimaru, ltr to President Roosevelt).

CHAPTER XI

1. Francis L. Hawks, ed., *Narrative of the Expedition to the China Seas and Japan . . . Under the Command of Commander M. C. Perry, United States Navy* (New York, 1856), 175-176.
2. Hawks, ed, *Expedition to the China Seas and Japan*, 180.
3. CinCPac-CinCPOA Bulletin 161-44, 15 Nov 1944, ONRL. Appleman, et al., *Okinawa*, 7-14.
4. King, *U.S. Navy at War, 1941-1945*, 175. CG 1stMarDiv, Okinawa rpt, 10 Jul 1945, RS MCS.
5. R. A. Spruance, ltr to P. A. Crowl, 6 Jan 1950, PUL.
6. Hq CominCh, "Amphibious Operations, Capture of Okinawa" (Washington, 1945), Ch I, p 18.
7. CG 1stMarDiv, Iwo rpt, RS MCS.
8. Hq CominCh, "Capture of Okinawa," ch I, pp 20-22.
9. Appleman, et al., *Okinawa*, 51-63. Hq CominCh, "Capture of Okinawa," ch I, pp 58-59.
10. Appleman, et al., *Okinawa*, 69-74. CG 1stMarDiv, Iwo rpt; CG 6thMarDiv, Okinawa rpt, 30 Jan 1945, RS MCS. James R. Stockman, *The First Marine Division on Okinawa* (U.S. Marine Corps Monograph, Washington, 1946), 2. Stockman, *The Sixth Marine Division* (Hq USMC, no date), 5.
11. USSBS(P), *Interrogations*, vol I, 60-61.
12. Hq CominCh, "Capture of Okinawa," ch I, p 11. See also CG 2ndMarDiv, Okinawa rpt, 21 May 1945, RS MCS. Richard W. Johnston, *Follow Me: The Story of the Second Marine Division in World War II* (New York, 1948), 262.
13. CG 1stMarDiv, Okinawa rpt, RS MCS. Stockman, *First Marine Division on Okinawa*, 2-4.
14. CG 6thMarDiv, Okinawa rpt, RS MCS.
15. Appleman, et al., *Okinawa*, 74-79.
16. USSBS(P), *Campaigns* (Washington, 1946), 327-328.
17. Appleman, et al., *Okinawa*, 91-96.
18. CG 1stMarDiv, Okinawa rpt, RS MCS.
19. CG 1stMarDiv, Okinawa rpt, RS MCS.
20. Appleman, et al., *Okinawa*, 113-129, 132-137.
21. CG 6thMarDiv, Okinawa rpt, RS MCS; and Stockman, *Sixth Marine Division*, 6-8.
22. Appleman, et al., *Okinawa*, 149-183.
23. Appleman, et al., *Okinawa*, 184-208.
24. CG 1stMarDiv, Okinawa rpt, RS MCS. Appleman, et al., *Okinawa*, 265-267.
25. Appleman, et al., *Okinawa*, 264-302.
26. CG 1stMarDiv, Okinawa rpt, RS MCS.
27. CG 6thMarDiv, Okinawa rpt, RS MCS.
28. Appleman, et al., *Okinawa*, 311-312.
29. CG 6thMarDiv, Okinawa rpt, RS MCS. Stockman, *Sixth Marine Division*, 6-12.
30. CG 1stMarDiv, Okinawa rpt, RS MCS. Stockman, *First Marine Division on Okinawa*, 20-32.
31. Appleman, et al., *Okinawa*, 332-359.
32. Hq Tenth Army, prisoner of war interrogation rpt, Col. Hiromichi Yahara, 6 Aug 1945, Historical Division, Dept of the Army.
33. Appleman, et al., *Okinawa*, 360-372, 377-382. CG 6thMarDiv, Okinawa rpt; CG 1stMarDiv, Okinawa rpt, RS MCS.
34. Pedro A. del Valle, ltr to P. A. Crowl, 22 Nov 1949, PUL. Appleman, et al., *Okinawa*, 388-392.
35. CG 6thMarDiv, Okinawa rpt, RS MCS.
36. Appleman, et al., *Okinawa*, 425-450.
37. CG 1stMarDiv, Okinawa rpt, RS MCS.
38. Horace Knapp, ltr to P. A. Crowl, 8 Oct 1949; Pedro A. del Valle, ltr to P. A. Crowl, 22 Nov 1949, PUL.
39. CG 1stMarDiv, Okinawa rpt, RS MCS.
40. As quoted in CG 1stMarDiv, Okinawa rpt, RS MCS.
41. Hq CominCh, "Capture of Okinawa," ch I, p 18.
42. Appleman, et al., *Okinawa*, 92-93.
43. As quoted by D. M. Weller, "Introduction to Naval Gunfire Support," lecture at MCS senior course, 1947, RS MCS.
44. Hq CominCh, "Capture of Okinawa," ch IV, pp 1, 9-10.
45. CG 1stMarDiv, Okinawa rpt, RS MCS.
46. CG IIIAC, app 1 (composition of military govt detachment "A") to annex A (military govt) to Operation Plan 1-45, 16 Jan 1945, RS MCS. Hq CominCh, "Capture of Okinawa," ch I, p 18. Appleman, et al., *Okinawa*, 91.
47. CG IIIAC, app 1 (composition of military govt detachment "A") to annex A (military govt) to Operation Plan 1-45, RS MCS.
48. Hq CominCh, "Capture of Okinawa," ch II, p 10.
49. Hq CominCh, "Capture of Okinawa," ch I, pp 15, 32; ch II, pp 21, 39. W. H. P. Blandy, ltr to K. W. Condit, 14 Dec 1949, PUL.
50. Appleman, et al., *Okinawa*, 57.
51. Hq CominCh, "Capture of Okinawa," ch II, p 24.
52. CG 1stMarDiv, Okinawa rpt; CG 6thMarDiv, Okinawa rpt, RS MCS.
53. Deyo was relieved by Rear Admiral Allen E. Smith USN on 4 May 1945. Hq CNO, "Capture of Okinawa," ch I, pp 22-23.
54. Hq CominCh, "Capture of Okinawa," 1-2 to 1-3. USSBS(P) *Campaigns*, 331-338.
55. Hq CominCh, "Capture of Okinawa," ch II, p 26.
56. CG 1stMarDiv, Okinawa rpt, RS MCS.
57. CG 6thMarDiv, Okinawa rpt, RS MCS.

REFERENCES

58. Hq CominCh, "Capture of Okinawa," ch II, pp 49–50.
59. CG 1stMarDiv, Okinawa rpt, RS MCS.
60. Hq CominCh, "Capture of Okinawa," ch II, pp 41, 44.
61. CG 6thMarDiv, Okinawa rpt, RS MCS.
62. Hq CominCh, "Capture of Okinawa," ch II, p 42.
63. Hq CominCh, "Capture of Okinawa," ch II, pp 30–31, 43.
64. CG 1stMarDiv, Okinawa rpt, RS MCS. CG 6thMarDiv, basic doc and annex A (4thMars rpt) to Okinawa rpt, RS MCS.
65. CG 1stMarDiv, artillery and naval gunfire annexes to Okinawa rpt, RS MCS. In this rpt annexes and enclosures were not designated by number or letter. Regimental rpts were not attached.
66. CG 1stMarDiv, artillery annex to Okinawa rpt, RS MCS.
67. CO IIIAC Artillery, encl A (2nd Prov FAGrp rpt) to Okinawa rpt, 25 Jul 1945, RS MCS.
68. Appleman, et al., *Okinawa*, 194.
69. CO IIIAC Artillery, Okinawa rpt, RS MCS.
70. CG 1stMarDiv, artillery annex to Okinawa rpt, RS MCS.
71. CG 6thMarDiv, annex A (4thMars rpt) to Okinawa rpt, RS MCS.
72. CG 1stMarDiv, artillery annex to Okinawa rpt; CG 6thMarDiv, Okinawa rpt, RS MCS.
73. CG 1stMarDiv, artillery annex to Okinawa rpt, RS MCS.
74. Hq CominCh, "Capture of Okinawa," ch III, pp 27–28. Comments of Vernon E. Megee, enclosed in Merwin H. Silverthorn, ltr to K. W. Condit, 21 Nov 1949, PUL.
75. CO, Landing Force Air Support Control Unit One, Okinawa rpt, 22 Jul 1945, RS MCS.
76. CG 1stMarDiv, air support annex to Okinawa rpt, RS MCS.
77. Hq CominCh, "Capture of Okinawa," ch III, p 28.
78. CG 1stMarDiv, air support annex to Okinawa rpt; CG 6thMarDiv, Okinawa rpt, RS MCS.
79. CG 6thMarDiv, annex A (4thMars rpt) to Okinawa rpt, RS MCS.
80. Comments of V. E. Megee, enclosed in M. H. Silverthorn, ltr to K. W. Condit, 21 Nov 1949, PUL.
81. Mulcahy was relieved by Maj. Gen. Louis E. Woods USMC on 11 June 1945. CG TAF 10thArmy, Okinawa rpt, 12 Jul 1945, RS MCS.
82. CG 1stMarDiv, Okinawa rpt; CG 6thMarDiv, Okinawa rpt, RS MCS.
83. Maj. Gen. L. E. Woods USMC, encl D (air support for XXIV Corps) to special rpt on Marine Corps Aviation 1 Jun 1946, RS MCS.
84. CG 6thMarDiv, annexes A (4thMars rpt) and B (22ndMars rpt) to Okinawa rpt, RS MCS.
85. Maj. Gen. L. E. Woods USMC, encls B (air support for 1stMarDiv), D (air support for XXIV Corps), E (7thInfDiv air support rpt), F (27thInfDiv air support rpt) and H (96thInfDiv air support rpt) to special rpt on Marine Corps Aviation, RS MCS.
86. CO Landing Force Air Support Control Unit One, Okinawa rpt, RS MCS.
87. CO Landing Force Air Support Control Unit One, Okinawa rpt, RS MCS.
88. USSBS(P), A Report for the Naval Analysis Division, 37.
89. CG 1stMarDiv, air support annex to Iwo rpt, RS MCS.
90. CG 1stMarDiv, air support annex to Iwo rpt; Maj. Gen. L. E. Woods USMC, encl H (96thInfDiv air support rpt) to special rpt on Marine Corps Aviation.
91. Hq CominCh, "Capture of Okinawa," ch III, pp 35–36.
92. Hq CominCh, "Capture of Okinawa, ch VII, pp 19–20.
93. CG 1stMarDiv, Okinawa rpt, RS MCS.
94. CG 1stMarDiv, Okinawa rpt, RS MCS. Hq CominCh, "Capture of Okinawa," ch VI, p 14.
95. CG 1stMarDiv, Okinawa rpt, RS MCS.
96. Hq CominCh, "Capture of Okinawa," ch VII, p 32.
97. CG 1stMarDiv, Okinawa rpt; CG 6thMarDiv, Okinawa rpt, RS MCS.
98. Hq CominCh, "Capture of Okinawa," ch VI, pp 10–12.
99. CG 1stMarDiv, Okinawa rpt, RS MCS.
100. Hq CominCh, "Capture of Okinawa," ch VII, p 55.
101. CG 1stMarDiv, Okinawa rpt; CG 6thMarDiv, basic doc and annex A (4thMars rpt) to Okinawa rpt, RS MCS.
102. CG 6thMarDiv, Okinawa rpt, RS MCS.
103. Hq CominCh, "Capture of Okinawa," ch VII, p 46.
104. CG 6thMarDiv, Okinawa rpt, RS MCS.
105. Quoted in CG 1stMarDiv, tank annex to Okinawa rpt, RS MCS.
106. CG 1stMarDiv, tank annex to Okinawa rpt; CG 6thMarDiv, Okinawa rpt, RS MCS.
107. CG 1stMarDiv, tank annex to Okinawa rpt, RS MCS.
108. CG 1stMarDiv, engineer annex to Okinawa rpt, RS MCS.
109. Lemuel C. Shepherd Jr, ltr to P. A. Crowl, 23 Nov 1949, PUL.
110. CG 1stMarDiv, tank annex to Okinawa rpt, RS MCS.
111. CG 6thMarDiv, Okinawa rpt, RS MCS.
112. Appleman, et al., *Okinawa*, 256.
113. CG 6thMarDiv, annex A (4thMars rpt) to Okinawa rpt, RS MCS.
114. Appleman, et al., *Okinawa*, 257.
115. Quoted in CG 1stMarDiv, tank annex to Okinawa rpt, RS MCS.

116. Frank D. Merrill, ltr to K. W. Condit, 30 Nov 1949, PUL.
117. Marshall, *Biennial Report of the Chief of Staff, U.S. Army to the Secretary of War, 1943-1945* (Washington, 1945), 84-85.
118. King, *U.S. Navy at War*, 19.
119. Appleman, et al., *Okinawa*, 473-474.

CHAPTER XII

1. William D. Leahy, *I Was There* (New York, 1950), 257-442. Henry L. Stimson and Mc George Bundy, *On Active Service in Peace and War* (New York, 1948), 612-633.
2. Washington *Evening Star*, 15 Jun 1950, pp. 1, 3.

INDEX

Abe, Vice Admiral Hiroaki, 160
Admiralty Islands, 74, 88, 189, 307
advance base force, 25
aerial photography, 125, 429, 504-5; *see also* photographic reconnaissance
aerial reconnaissance, 178, 185, 256, 354-5
aerial spotting, 53, 71; *see also*, spotters
Afetna Point, 316-17, 320, 322
Agingan Point, 320, 330, 331
aircraft, 96, 120, 134
aircraft carriers, 90-3, 135, 181, 290, 384
Air Liaison Party, 362
air support, 40, 53, 58, 78, 125-6, 137, 224, 230-1, 248*ff*., 289, 301, 329*ff*., 362-3, 385, 418-21, 422*ff*., 471-2, 501*ff*., 508-11, 557-70, 585-6
Air Support Command, 565
Alaska, 199
Alexandria, 18
Aleutian Islands, 194, 198-9, 202, 258
Alifan Ridge, 377
alligators, Roebling, 69, 188
Amey, Lieutenant Colonel Herbert R., 239
Amiangal Mountain, 408
amphibian tractors, 68, 173, 179, 188, 208, 210-11, 221, 224, 228, 235, 237, 240, 250-2, 262, 265, 268-9, 273-8, 317-19, 328, 336, 368, 395, 409, 454, 462, 479, 521-4, 527
amphibious assault, 3*ff*., 78, 124, 173, 181, 188, 191, 192, 200, 201, 223, 251*ff*., 320, 444, 478, 530, 554, 539
Amphibious Corps, 67, 70
amphibious equipment, 192, 582-4
amphibious fighting, broad concepts of, 4
Amphibious Support Force, 464, 465, 554
Amphibious Training Staff, 62
Anderson, Captain Carl E., 517
Angaur, 392-3, 402, 406, 408, 410, 418, 429-31
Anglo-American Chiefs of Staff, 304
Antares, 51
Anzacs, 18-20; Anzac region, 83, 87, 97
Anzio, 67
Aola, 158-9, 162
Apamama, 203, 204, 215, 216, 220*ff*.
Appalachian, 257, 260
Apra Harbor, 25, 312, 377
Arawe, 186
Arkansas, 54, 70
Army-Navy Joint Action Board, 28

Army units, United States: Fifth Air Force, 167, 183; Seventh Air Force, 437, 438; Thirteenth Air Force, 183, 306; Twentieth Air Force, 390, 391; 708th Amphibian Tank Battalion, 296; Sixth Army, 186, 427, 579; Eighth Army, 579; Tenth Army, 534, 536, 546, 550, 553, 556, 561, 565-7, 578-9; I Army Corps, 579; X Army Corps, 427; XI Army Corps, 579; XIV Army Corps, 164, 183, 306, 318, 326, 334, 359, 364, 535, 538, 541, 544, 563-5, 568, 570, 571, 574; 11th Bombardment Group, 118; 1st Cavalry Division, 186, 426, 579; 112th Cavalry Division, 186; American Division, 150, 156, 159, 164, 579; 1st Infantry Division, 62-3, 66, 67; 3rd Infantry Division, 62, 67; 6th Infantry Division, 426; 7th Infantry Division, 16, 63, 67, 254, 258, 260, 264-5, 276, 284-7, 290, 301, 308, 535, 536, 538, 541, 544, 546, 559; 9th Infantry Division, 62, 66, 67, 70; 25th Infantry Division, 164, 579; 27th Infantry Division, 203, 255, 296, 301, 308, 315, 317, 319, 322-3, 327, 330, 335, 339, 340-9, 354, 364, 371, 373, 535, 543, 544, 563, 571; 33rd Infantry Division, 579; 41st Infantry Division, 427, 428, 579; 43rd Infantry Division, 170, 579; 77th Infantry Division, 308, 316, 373, 374, 377, 378, 390, 535, 541-4, 547, 548; 81st Infantry Division, 393, 400, 401, 408, 410, 411, 414, 429, 431, 535; 96th Infantry Division, 16, 535, 536, 541, 546, 550, 564; 1341st Engineer Battalion, 367; 1st Expeditionary Brigade, 52; 7th Field Artillery, 56; 67th Fighter Squadron, 134, 137; 11th Heavy Bombardment Group, 105; 17th Infantry Regiment, 289; 18th Infantry Regiment, 56; 29th Infantry Regiment, 151; 32nd Infantry Regiment, 284; 30th Infantry Regiment, 52; 105th Infantry Regiment, 322, 328, 342, 343, 347-50; 106th Infantry Regiment, 254-5, 258, 272, 296, 299, 301, 322, 323, 342, 348; 147th Infantry Regiment, 500; 148th Infantry Regiment, 172; 164th Infantry Regiment, 150, 151, 156, 157; 165th Infantry Regiment, 221, 222, 323, 328, 342, 345; 182nd Infantry Regiment, 159, 160; 184th Infantry Regiment, 284; 321st Infantry Regiment, 406, 408, 410;

INDEX

Army Units (*Continued*)
106th Regimental Combat Team, 298;
165th Regimental Combat Team, 322;
75th Signal Company, 286; 713th Tank Battalion, 577
Arnold, General Henry H., 81, 84, 196, 304, 306, 314
artillery, 340, 364, 365, 385, 413*ff.*, 482, 501*ff.*, 513, 557-70
artillery lighters, 47, 51
Asiga Bay, 352, 356, 359
Aslito Airfield, 311, 317-19, 322, 333
assault squads, 456
Astoria, 130
Attu, 67, 80, 199, 264
Aukland, 108-9, 157
Australia, 80, 89, 103, 104, 111, 112, 129, 163, 185, 197
Australia, H.M.A.S., 129-30
Avenger torpedo planes, 418
aviation, 32, 50, 53-4, 58-9, 117, 135-6, 171

B-29, 390
Babelthuap, 392, 393, 400, 416
Bairiki, 246, 247, 248, 249
Baker Island, 193
Baldwin, Hanson, 131, 253
banzai, 248
Barbey, Rear Admiral Daniel E., 167
Barrett, Major General Charles D., 175
Bataan Peninsula, 74, 78, 161
Bay Head, 57
bazooka, 413, 457, 482, 515
beachhead, 42
"beetle," the, 20
Betio, 204-8, 210, 212-15, 217-18, 220, 222, 224-5, 228-37, 242-5, 247-51, 254, 262, 268, 274, 281-5, 288, 301
Biak Island, 307, 392
Birmingham, 560
Bismarck Archipelago, 99, 168, 182, 190, 194, 200
Bismarck Sea, Battle of, 167
Blandy, Rear Admiral William H. P., 436, 446, 449, 464-7, 470, 473-4, 502, 505, 530, 554
Bloodsworth Island, 71
Bloody Ridge, Battle of, 143
Boat Rig A, 47, 51
Borgen Bay, 188
Borgen-Warner Corporation, 69
Bougainville, 168, 174-9, 181-3, 185, 198, 200-1, 220
Brewster fighters, 82
Brisbane, 185
British New Guinea, 79
Browning Automatic Rifle, 341
Bruce, General Andrew D., 535, 543

Buckner, Lieutenant General Simon Bolivar Jr., 532, 534, 542, 550, 559-60, 577
Buin, 136
Buka, 136
Buka-Bonis, 178
Buna-Gona, 167
Bunker Hill, 182
Bureau of Ships, 57, 64, 68-9
Burma Road, 194
Butaritari Islet, 221-2
Butler, Brigadier General Smedley D., 29

Cabras Island, 376
Cairo Conference, 304-5, 314
Calhoun, 59
Callaghan, Rear Admiral Daniel J., 117
Callahan, Rear Admiral Daniel J., 160
Cambria, 361, 363
camouflage, 140, 467, 469, 505, 522
Camp Pendleton, 267, 452
Canberra, H.M.A.S., 130
Cape Esperance, 164-5, 372
Cape Esperance, Battle of, 147-8
Cape Gloucester, 67, 185-6, 188-9
Cape Torokina, 178
Carden, Vice-Admiral Sir Sackville, 17
Carlson, Lieutenant Colonel Evans F., 154, 162, 241, 243-6, 250
Caroline Islands, 25-6, 97, 107, 194, 199, 291-2, 303, 305, 314
Casablanca Conference, 67, 193-4
Cates, Major General Clifton B., 121, 354, 452, 458, 460-61, 472, 480-81, 490, 492-3, 495, 498, 522, 524
Cavite naval base, 78
Celebes Sea, 194, 199, 253, 304
Central Visayas, 427
Charan Kanoa, 316-7, 331, 337, 366
Chateau Thierry, 59
Chengtu, 312
Chicago, 130, 142
China, 29, 78, 194, 198, 314, 533
Choiseul, 177-8
Christie amphibian tank, 69
Christie, J. Walter, 31
Chungking, 314
Churchill, Prime Minister Winston, 17, 21, 72, 84
Cincinnati, 70
close air support, *see* air support
clothing, 525
Cole, Brigadier General Eli K., 28, 30-31
Colorado, 559
combat loading, 43, 326*ff.*
Combined Chiefs of Staff, 194, 197, 314
command relations, 37, 83*ff.*, 153*ff.*, 342*ff.*, 380
Commander Support Aircraft, 334, 361
communications, 219, 224, 228, 239, 242,

INDEX

249, 252, 257, 274, 275, 284, 334, 363, 394, 402, 424, 503, 509, 516, 519, 521, 573, 584-5
Conical Hill, 546-8
Conolly, Rear Admiral Richard L., 260, 268-9, 272, 274, 281-2, 316, 318-19, 371-2, 379-82, 384, 390, 587
Coral Sea, 80, 83, 87-9, 90
Corlett, Major General Charles H., 265-6
Corregidor, 74, 78-9, 190
Corsair (F-4U), 171, 418, 420, 422, 428, 565, 567
Craig, Colonel Edward A., 490
Crowe, Major Henry P., 238-41, 244-6, 249
Crutchley, Rear Admiral Victor A. C., 115, 117, 129
Culebra, 22-3, 30-31, 46, 56-7, 61
Cunningham, Commander Winfield S., 76

Dampier Straits, 167, 175, 183, 185-6, 188
Dardanelles, 5
Dardanelles-Gallipoli campaign, 17-21
Darwin, Charles, 260
DDT, 569
Death Valley, 323, 345, 348
del Valle, Colonel Pedro A., 121, 126, 159, 538, 540, 559, 562, 569-70
demolitions, 335, 339, 358, 413, 457, 482, 488, 514, 577
demolition squads, 288, 296, 319, 329, 411, 415, 456, 467-9, 474, 478, 525, 543, 556
Devereux, Major James P. S., 76-8
Dewey, Commodore George, 22
Deyo, Rear Admiral Morton L., 554, 557
discipline, 127, 296, 337
dogs, war, 162-3
Doolittle, Lieutenant Colonel James H., 79
Douglas dive bombers, 134
Duke University, 513
Dukws, 16-17, 262, 265, 277, 294, 302, 328, 364, 366-8, 388, 413, 454, 462, 482, 517-18, 521-4, 583
Durgin, Rear Admiral Calvin T., 471, 506
Dutch New Guinea, 7, 97

East China Sea, 533
Edson, Lieutenant Colonel Merritt A., 65, 120, 143-5, 205, 246
Edson's Ridge, 143, 145
Efate, 105, 179-80, 217, 220
Eisenhower, General Dwight D., 6, 9-10
Ellice Islands, 88, 193
Ellis, Major Earl H., 25-7, 233
Embick, Lieutenant General Stanley G., 305
Emmet, Captain Robert M., 60
Emirau, 190
Empress Augusta Bay, 175, 177-8, 181-2, 189
Empress Augusta Bay, Battle of, 201
Engebi, 293-4, 296-300

engineers, 132, 143, 398-9, 485, 504, 516, 525-7
Eniwetok, 27, 193, 211, 251, 271, 277, 291-4, 296-302, 308, 312, 319, 333, 373
Enterprise, 106, 115, 141, 145, 152, 159-61, 506
Erskine, Major General Graves B., 453, 458, 461, 492-9, 509, 511, 513
Espiritu Santo, 93, 108, 118, 131, 134, 143, 149, 154, 159-60
Essex, 182, 230
"Eureka," 68
Expeditionary Force, 29-30, 33

Fabius San Hilo Point, 360
Farallon de Pajaros, 310
Field Officers' School, *see* Quantico
Fifth Fleet, 202, 224, 292, 331, 445, 587
Fiji Islands, 105-6, 111, 114
fire control, 39, 66, 219, 232, 252, 332, 361, 416, 476, 502, 511
fire discipline, 266
Fire Support Coordination Center, 502-7
First Joint Training Force, 62, 69-70
Fitch, Rear Admiral Aubrey W., 158
flamethrowers, 173, 181, 218, 245, 247, 252, 267, 288, 296-7, 335, 339, 358, 370, 409, 411, 413, 456, 457, 482, 488, 514, 578
flamethrowing tanks, 458, 500, 516, 576
Fleet Base Defense Force, *see* Fleet Marine Force
fleet landing exercises, 46, 64: 2nd, 48; 3rd, 52-5; 4th, 56; 6th, 57; 7th, 59, 63
Fleet Marine Force, 33-35, 37, 54, 63, 67, 85-6, 435, 461, 571
Fleet Training Publication 36, 63, 167
Fletcher, Vice Admiral Frank Jack, 106-9, 115-16, 117, 128-9, 141
Florida Islands, 124, 163
Formosa, 304, 306, 533
Forrestal, James V., 103, 210, 488, 514
Fort, Rear Admiral George H., 309, 393, 415
Fort Bragg, 67, 70
Fort Devens, 63
Freeport, 57
Fukodome, Vice Admiral Shigeru, 430
Fuller, Major General John F. C., 6
Furumiya, Colonel Masajiro, 151

Gallipoli Peninsula, 5, 20-1, 27, 220
Garand (M-1 rifle), 456
Garapan, 317, 320, 330, 333
Garguan Point, 355
Gasmata, 186
Gavutu-Tananbogo, 119-20, 122-5, 145, 222
Geiger, Major General Roy S., 59, 134, 146, 149, 158, 183, 315, 371-3, 380, 385, 390, 394, 402, 411, 535, 550-1

Ghormley, Vice Admiral Robert L., 87, 103-9, 114, 116-7, 128-9, 147, 153, 155-7
Gilbert Islands, 74, 88, 118, 182, 192-252
Gilliam, Major William M., 381
Goto, Rear Admiral Aritomo, 148
Grahm, Colonel Chester B., 499
grenades, 339
Green Islands, 189
Griner, Major General George W., 323, 342, 347, 349
ground tactics, 575-8
Grumman fighters, 76, 134, 136-7
Guadalcanal, 7, 9, 12, 66-7, 69, 72-3, 93, 98, 101, 103-104, 106-14, 119-184, 188, 199, 208, 217-8, 222, 372, 582
Guardfish, 178
Guam, 25, 45, 74, 79, 190, 310-12, 315-6, 319, 329-30, 371-91, 434

Halcomb, Lieutenant General Thomas, 507
Hall, Colonel Elmer E., 206, 243-4, 246
Halmaheras, 253
Halsey, Vice Admiral William F., 156-9, 161, 165-6, 168, 170, 182, 190, 255, 305, 393, 401, 423-4, 426, 430, 434, 445
Hamilton, General Sir Ian, 18
Hansell, Brigadier General Haywood S. Jr., 306
Harding, President Warren G., 29
Harmon, Major General Millard F., 104, 108, 156
Harry Lee, 59-60
Hart, Liddell, 5
Hawkins, Lieutenant William D., 236-7
Hays, Major Lawrence C. Jr., 245
Helicopters, 589
Hellcats, 418
Henderson Field, 134-7, 139-43, 145-50, 153, 156, 158-62, 164-6, 183
Henderson Field, Battle for, 151-2, 159
Hermle, Brigadier General Leo D., 244-5, 248
Hester, Major General John H., 170
"H-hour," 223
Hiei, 160
Higgins, Andrew J., 57, 68
Higgins boats, 64, 366, 583
Hill, Rear Admiral Harry W., 204, 208, 216, 224-5, 228-30, 232, 234, 258, 271, 292, 294, 296, 298-9, 302, 333, 354, 363, 436, 462, 468, 478, 517, 519, 524, 530
Hiroshima, 391
Hodge, Major General John R., 393
Holcomb, Lieutenant General Thomas, 90, 154-5
Holland, Major F. L. G., 212
Hollandia, 7, 307, 392
Holmes, Colonel Maurice G., 206, 246

Homma, Lieutenant General Masakaru, 79
Hong Kong, 194
Honshu, 12, 433
Hoover, Rear Admiral John H., 202, 214-5, 257, 270
Hornet, 79, 145, 150, 152
Howard, Colonel Samuel L., 78-9
howitzers, 34, 61, 112, 114, 121, 144, 151, 414, 482
Hunt, Major General LeRoy P., 121, 536
Hunter Liggett, 59, 114
Huon Peninsula, 167
Hyakutake, Lieutenant General Harukichi, 139-40, 149, 164

Ichiki, Colonel Kiyono, 140-1,
Ichiki Detachment, 139-40, 142, 162
Idaho, 470
Ie Shima, 542-3, 567
Independence, 182
infiltration, 333, 483, 497
Inoguchi, Captain Rikibei, 536
intelligence, 110-11, 122, 125, 138, 143, 157, 179, 185, 207-8, 293, 337-8, 351, 359, 429, 438, 444, 454, 473, 478, 483, 497, 505, 548, 552-5, 580
Iron Bottom Sound, 105, 131-2, 148-50, 158, 164
Isely Field, 333, 347, 361-2
Ishimi Ridge, 547
Itoman, 540
Iwo Jima, 11, 181, 211, 251, 312, 390, 432-530

Jaluit, 193, 256
Japanese Army Units: 7th Army, 164; 14th Army, 79; 17th Army, 139; 32nd Army, 539; 38th Division, 139, 161-2; 52nd Division, 270; 50th Regiment, 355; 1st Sea Borne Mobile Brigade, 293; (see also Sendai Division, Kawaguchi Brigade, Ichiki Detachment)
Japanese First Air Fleet, 304
Jarman, Major General Sanderford, 323-4, 346-8
jeeps, 140
Jerome, Colonel Clayton C., 428
Joint Army-Navy Assessment Committee, 81
Joint Board, 35, 85
Joint Chiefs of Staff, 84-6, 89, 94-5 97, 99, 101, 104-6, 150, 165, 190, 193-4, 196-8. 200, 252, 254-5, 292, 304-6, 315, 394, 430, 433-4, 441, 580-1
Joint Intelligence Center, 207, 213, 454, 552
Joint Staff Planners, 194, 196-7, 305-6, 580
Joint Strategical Survey Committee, 194, 305
Jomini, Antoine Henri, 4

Jones, Major William K., 247, 249
Jordan, Colonel Walter I., 239-40, 245, 498

Kadena Field, 567
Kagman Peninsula, 323, 343, 348
Kahoolawe, 318
Kakazu Ridge, 540-1, 543-4
Kaluf, Major John, 69
kamikaze tactics, 184, 449-50, 507, 536, 555, 558, 579, 588
Kavieng, 190, 255, 306, 309, 315
Kawaguchi, Major General Kiyotake, 141
Kawaguchi Brigade, 139, 142-5, 162
Keise Shima, 15, 535, 556
Kenney, Major General George C., 81, 167, 182, 186, 305
Kenyon, Colonel Howard N., 492
Kerama Retto, 15, 535, 555-8
Keyes, Commodore Roger, 20
Kido, Marquis Koichi, 310
King, Rear Admiral Ernest J., 59, 69, 71, 84, 86-9, 92, 94-5, 97, 99, 104-5, 110, 114, 116, 153, 156-7, 166, 193-4, 197, 199-200, 211, 253, 305, 314, 508
Kingman, Rear Admiral Howard F., 233-4
Kinkaid, Rear Admiral Thomas C., 152, 160, 423-4
Kiralfy, Alexander, 5
Kirishima, 161
Kiska, 67, 80, 199, 265
Kolombangara Island, 170
Koreans, 483, 487, 533
Koro Island, 114-17, 128, 136
Kossol Passage, 414
Kreuger, Lieutenant General Walter, 185, 189, 578
Kukum, 133
Kuribayashi, Lieutenant General Tadamichi, 468, 474, 484-8, 498-501, 530, 551
Kuriles Islands, 198-9
Kusaie, 294
Kwajalein Atoll, 67, 192-3, 198, 211, 251, 253-309, 334, 339
Kyle, Major Wood B., 240, 245
Kyushu, 12, 534, 579

Lake Susupe, 311, 322, 337
Lamustrek Group, 26
landing craft, 47, 57-8, 173-4, 180, 210, *see also* amphibious equipment
Lane, Brigadier General Rufus H., 27
Lanigan, Colonel John R., 481
LCI's, 173
LCM's, 68, 174
LCT's, 174
LCVP's, 174
League of Nations, 24, 73, 260
Leahy, Admiral William D., 84
Lee, Rear Admiral Willis A., 152, 161

Lejeune, John A., Major General Commandant, 28
Lemnos, 18
Letcher, Colonel John S., 502-4, 512
Lew Ch'ew, 531, 532; *see also* Okinawa
Lexington, 32
Leyte Gulf, Battle for, 77, 423-4, 426, 430-1, 442, 445, 587
Leyte Island, 7, 67, 394, 423-4, 427, 570
Liberators, 419
Linsert, Major Ernest E., 69
Liscome Bay, 205, 222
Little, 59
Liversedge, Colonel Harry B., 172, 480, 488
logistics, 43, 51, 66, 85-6, 88, 96-7, 108, 116, 127, 167, 173, 177, 179-80, 185, 191, 201, 216-7, 248ff., 253, 266, 327ff., 365-9, 387-9, 413ff., 428, 454, 480, 517-29, 570-5
LSD's 173
LSM's, 15-16, 173
LST's, 15-16, 173
Lunga airfield, 122
Lunga Point, 121, 127, 140, 158, 162
Lunga River, 101, 113, 132-3, 140
Luzon Island, 7, 306, 426-7, 433
LVT's, 16, 31, 69

MacArthur, General Douglas, 7, 9, 70, 84-5, 87, 88-9, 90-7, 103, 104-5, 118, 155, 157, 163, 165-8, 175, 182, 183, 185, 189-90, 194, 196-200, 253, 304-8, 315, 392-431, 533
McCain, Rear Admiral John, 105, 107, 108, 113, 115, 118, 158
McCawley, 59, 63, 114, 126, 129
McGovern, Captain John B., 250
McLeod, Lieutenant Colonel Kenneth F., 248
Magicienne Bay, 311, 317, 338
Mahan, Captain Alfred T., 22, 74, 96
Majuro, 193, 254, 255, 258, 271, 272, 296, 308
Makin Atoll, 203-5, 215, 216, 220ff.
Malaita, 118
Malaya, 197
Maloelap, 193, 254, 256
Manchuria, 199, 533
Manila, 426
Manila Bay, 22, 79
Manley, 57
Mantell, Lieutenant Colonel L. K., 290
Marcus, 76
Mariana Islands, 25, 88, 200, 211, 251, 252, 292, 294, 303-9, 310-91, 432, 510
"Marianas Turkey Shoot," 184
Marine Corps Equipment Board, 68-9
Marine Corps Schools, 35, 36, 45, 59; *see also*, Quantico
Marine Corps Units: First Air Group, 48, 53, 56, 60; Second Air Group, 53; Air Group 11, 419, 420; Air Group 12, 427,

Marine Corps Units (*Continued*)
428; Air Group 14, 427; Air Group 23, 134; Air Group 24, 422, 423, 426; Air Group 25, 149; Air Group 32, 426, 428; First Air Wing, 134, 149; Second Air Wing, 567; First Amphibious Corps, 168, 175, 179, 306; Third Amphibious Corps, 306-7, 315, 316, 371, 383, 389, 393, 394, 417, 435, 534, 544, 550, 552, 553, 563, 565, 571, 579, 587; Fifth Amphibious Corps, 202, 204, 221, 237-8, 252, 258, 260, 265, 280, 294, 315, 329, 335, 344, 352, 354, 359, 417, 432, 435, 501, 579; Amphibious Reconnaissance Battalion, 352; First Brigade, 48, 53, 56, 58, 59, 60; Second Brigade, 52; Second Defense Battalion, 206; Third Defense Battalion, 115, 121, 133; First Division, 16, 60, 62, 63, 67, 70, 89, 90, 103, 109, 110, 114, 117, 127, 131, 138, 157, 163, 168, 185, 188, 189, 307-8, 393-414, 429, 431, 535-8, 544-50, 559, 562, 563, 569, 571-9; Second Division, 62-3, 114, 159, 163, 164, 168, 191, 198, 203-5, 208-19, 222, 233, 248, 308, 315, 317-24, 333, 336, 337, 340, 349, 354, 356-8, 366, 535, 536, 571, 579; Third Division, 168, 174, 176, 179, 307, 308, 312, 315, 372-8, 382, 383, 432, 451-3, 459, 460, 462, 485, 490, 491-8, 516, 526, 528, 579; Fourth Division, 254, 258, 260-8, 274, 285-7, 308, 315-23, 336, 339-77, 432, 451-3, 460-3, 472, 480-1, 489-99, 521, 528, 542, 579; Fifth Division, 432, 451-3, 458, 463, 480-1, 488-500, 505, 521, 579; Sixth Division, 16, 190, 372, 535-8, 541-2, 546-9, 558, 559, 564, 568, 571-3, 577, 579; Fighter Squadron 114, 421; First Joint Assault Signal Company, 361; Third Joint Assault Signal Company, 383; First Marines, 66, 110-11, 113-14, 121, 126, 399, 400, 408, 411; Second Marines, 114, 119, 120, 124, 130, 154, 163, 205, 239-42; Third Marines, 385; Fourth Marines, 79, 190, 538, 547, 549; Fifth Marines, 46, 48-9, 53, 56, 61, 65, 110-11, 114, 121, 123, 127, 141, 144, 400, 406, 411, 418; Sixth Marines, 163, 203, 246, 247, 248, 320, 335; Seventh Marines, 151, 155, 156, 399, 400, 407; Eighth Marines, 159, 163, 205, 238, 239, 243-8, 320, 335, 336; Ninth Marines, 374, 376, 385, 491-2, 499, 500; Tenth Marines, 46, 48, 56, 318, 348, 369; Eleventh Marines, 61, 66, 114, 121, 189, 562; Fourteenth Marines, 318, 348; Twenty-first Marines, 374, 376, 452, 492, 493, 497, 500; Twenty-second Marines, 254, 258, 296-301, 374, 377, 542, 547; Twenty-third Marines, 266, 280, 282, 320, 490; Twenty-fourth Marines, 267, 276, 281, 282, 283, 356, 369, 481, 498; Twenty-fifth Marines, 267, 269, 274, 320, 348, 350; Twenty-sixth Marines, 480; Twenty-eighth Marines, 480, 481, 488; Twenty-ninth Marines, 542, 547; First Parachute Battalion, 57, 66, 114, 120, 124, 143; Second Parachute Battalion, 177; First Pioneer Battalion, 415; Fifth Pioneer Battalion, 500; First Provisional Marine Brigade, 315, 372, 374, 377; First Raider Battalion, 66, 114, 120, 124, 143, 151, 172; Second Raider Battalion, 154, 162; Third Regimental Combat Team, 376; Sixth Regimental Combat Team, 246, 322-3; Seventh Regimental Combat Team, 407; Twenty-third Regimental Combat Team, 327, 329, 337; Twenty-fifth Regimental Combat Team, 336, 356; First Tank Battalion, 577-8; Second Tank Battalion, 219

Marpi Point, 316
Marshall, General George C., 3, 84, 87, 88-9, 94, 97, 103-5, 166, 305, 432
Marshall, Colonel St. Julien R., 280
Marshall Islands, 16-17, 25, 26, 76, 192, 193, 197, 198, 201-4, 211, 216, 251, 252, 253-309, 330
Martyr, Colonel Cyril W., 206
Maryland, 143-5, 216, 224, 225, 228, 229, 241
Matanikau River, 133, 145, 148, 150, 164, 176
Maui, 318
Meade, Brigadier General James J., 55, 161
"Meat Grinder," 498
Megee, Colonel Vernon E., 502-4, 510, 567
Melbourne, 168, 185
Merrill, Rear Admiral Aaron S., 181, 182
Merrill, Major General Frank D., 578
Midway Island, 73, 74, 79-82, 83, 87-9, 197, 308
Mili, 193, 256
Millington, Lieutenant Colonel William A., 507
Minami Village, 498-9
Mindanao, 194, 197, 427
Mindoro Island, 426
mines, 171, 200, 208, 213, 263, 369, 412, 484, 549, 555, 556
Mitchell, Major General Ralph J., 178
Mitscher, Vice Admiral Marc A., 318, 319, 380, 384, 534, 552, 558
Montgomery, Rear Admiral Alfred E., 182, 201, 225
Moore, Brigadier General James T., 419
Morison, Samuel Eliot, 116, 225
mortars, 122, 124, 144, 164, 485
Moses, Brigadier General Emile P., 68
Motobu Peninsula, 558, 559
Motoyama, 466
Motoyama Airfield Number One, 439, 452, 454, 478

INDEX

Motoyama Airfield Number Two, 472, 492
Motoyama Plateau, 474, 489-99, 504, 513
Motoyama Village, 494, 499
Mount Austen, 140, 176
Mount Barrigada, 378
Mount Lasso, 311, 354, 357, 362, 365
Mount McKinley, 415, 416, 419
Mount Santa Rosa, 312
Mount Tapotchau, 311, 317, 319, 323, 338
Mount Tenjo, 312, 376, 377
Mount Tipo Pale, 317, 323
Mudge, Major General Verne D., 426, 427
Mudros, 18
Mueller, Major General Paul, 411
Mulcahy, Major General Francis P., 567
Munda, 136, 159, 168, 170, 172, 175, 182
Murray, Lieutenant Colonel Raymond L., 246

Nafutan Point, 322, 343, 347
Naha, 548
Nakagusuku Wan (Bay), 532
Namur, 283, 369, *see also* Roi
Nanpo Shoto (group), 26, 312, 434, 437, 445, 449, 483
Nansei Shoto, 532, 534
napalm bomb, 299, 363-4, 422, 471, 506, 510, 568
Nauru Island, 197-8, 203
Nautilus, 222-3
naval gunfire, 38, 53, 57, 65, 125, 186, 223, 225-35, 246-7, 248ff., 262, 268, 271-2, 277, 284, 293, 296, 298-9, 301, 318, 329ff., 359-61, 373, 380, 384, 402-3, 416ff., 438, 440, 442-3, 446, 464ff., 476, 480, 501ff., 511-12, 534, 540, 557-70, 586-7
Naval Gunfire Liaison Officers' Schools, 70
Ndeni, 93-4, 99, 105, 107-8, 110, 114, 118-9, 124, 130, 153-8
Negano, Fleet Admiral Osami, 165
Negro troops, 500
Netherlands East Indies, 74, 197, 199, 306, 310
Nevada, 469-70
New Britain, 74, 88, 92-3, 99, 182, 185-6, 189
New Caledonia, 80, 93, 105-6, 157, 172
New Georgia Island, 136, 168, 170-3, 248
New Guinea, 74, 88, 92-4, 99, 131, 166, 167, 196-7, 199-200, 253, 307, 392
New Hebrides, 80, 93, 179, 217
New Ireland, 74, 255
Newport, Rhode Island, 22
New River, 22, 61, 63, 65, 70
New York, 470, 559, 562
New Zealand, 80, 108, 110-12, 170, 174, 177, 189, 198, 212, 233
Ngesebus, 421
Nicaragua, 6, 29, 33
night landings, 56-7

Nimitz, Admiral Chester W., 11, 84-5, 87, 89, 92, 94-7, 105-8, 114, 116, 128-9, 150, 153, 156-7, 161, 165, 182, 194, 196-200, 202-4, 207, 215, 224-5, 230, 251-7, 260, 262, 270, 290-3, 298, 303-8, 312, 315, 330, 373, 392, 394, 424, 430, 434-5, 440-2, 449, 455, 462, 473, 483, 501, 508
Noemfoor Island, 307, 392
Normandy, 6, 10, 67, 70
North Africa, 70, 104
North Carolina, 106, 145, 161
North China, 533
Nouméa, 106, 150, 157-8
Noyes, Rear Admiral Leigh, 115

Oahu Island, 32-3
O'Brien, 145
Ogata, Colonel, 355
Ohmae, Captain Toshikazu, 164
Oka, Colonel Akinosuka, 151-2
Okinawa, 8, 11-12, 14-17, 67, 154, 181, 190, 211, 342, 428, 433-5, 444-5, 531-79, 581
Oldendorf, Rear Admiral Jesse B., 402-3, 431
Open Door Policy, 25
"Operation Shoestring," 98
Oran, 67
Oruku Peninsula, 549
Orote Peninsula, 376-7, 379, 382, 386
Owen Stanley Mountains, 139

P-38, 159
P-47, 361-2, 371
P-51, 511
PBY, 105
Pacific Ocean Areas Mobile Air Force, 105
Palau Islands, 25, 45, 98, 190, 211, 251, 304, 306-7, 309, 392-431
Palermo, 67
Palm Islet, 125
Panama, 30
Panama Canal, 86
Papuan Peninsula, 87-8, 90, 92-3, 99, 139, 167
paratroopers, 7
Parris Island, 67, 70
Parry Islet, 293-4, 298-301
Patch, Major General Alexander M., 150, 163-4, 342
patrols, 138-9
Pavuvu Island, 308, 395
Pearl Harbor, 25, 72, 74, 77, 106, 110, 115-17, 138, 202-3, 371, 373
Peleliu, 67, 188, 392-422, 428-31, 451
Pelelle Harbor, 25
Pelew Islands, 26 (*see* Palau Islands)
Pennsylvania, 216
perimeter defense, 146, 174, 176, 188, 317, 348, 376

Perry, Commodore Matthew C., 531
Phelps, 275
Philadelphia, 70
Philippine Islands, 7, 25, 78, 88, 93, 97, 177, 181, 194, 198, 199, 254, 309, 392-431, 433, 466, 580, 586
Philippine Sea, Battle of, 184, 322, 328, 333, 338, 373, 587
Phoenix Islands, 88, 193
photographic reconnaissance, 192, 206-8, 261, 354-5, 396, 552-3
pioneers, 66, 112, 127, 132, 143, 367, 414, 452, 520, 526, see also shore parties
Piti Navy Yard, 376
preparatory fires, see naval gunfire
Princeton, 182
Ponape, 294
Port Moresby, 79-80, 89, 111, 139, 166-7
Postal service, 488
Puerto Rico, 56
Purple Heart Ridge, 323
Pursuit, 250

Quantico, Virginia, 22, 24, 29, 32, 34-5, 56, 67-70
Quincy, 70, 130

Rabaul, 80, 88, 90, 92-7, 99, 105, 107, 116, 119, 128, 142, 152, 158-9, 165-6, 168, 170, 175-6, 179, 181-5, 189-90, 194, 199, 201, 218, 220, 225, 306, 309, 315
radar, 76, 129, 133, 142, 148, 165, 171, 177, 224, 233, 532, 558, 567, 583
radio, 54, 67, 179, 241-2, 271, 275, 284, 333, 363, 369, 385, 510-11, 516, 566, 568
radiojeep, 426
Red Bank, 57
red tape, 571-2
Reifsnider, Rear Admiral Lawrence F., 382
Rekata Bay, 150
reorganization, 61
Rice Anchorage, 172
Richardson, Lieutenant General Robert C., 265
rifle squads, 341
Rixey, Lieutenant Colonel Presley M., 206, 241, 244-5, 248
Rockey, Major General Keller E., 452, 480, 481, 492-3, 495, 497-500, 515, 522
Rockey Mount, 257-8, 284
Roebline, Donald, 69, see also "Alligators"
Rogers, Colonel William W., 441
Rodgers, Rear Admiral Bertram J., 465
Roi (Roi-Namur), 258, 260, 263-4, 268-9, 271-3, 275-7, 280, 282, 284-8, 290, 302
Ronson portable flamethrower, 515
Roosevelt, President Franklin D., 72, 84-5, 150, 161
Royal Australian Navy, 107

Royal Marines, 17
Rupertus, Major General William H., 120, 122, 124, 188-9, 396, 401, 408, 410, 420
Russell, Major General, 34
Russell Islands, 148, 165, 168, 308
Russia, 198-9
Ruud, Major Robert H., 238-9, 245-6
Ryan, Major Michael P., 242, 245, 247, 249
Ryukyu Archipelago, 26, 450, 532, 536, 539, 544, 570

St. George Channel, 99, 105
St. Matthias Islands, 190
Saipan, 45, 67, 310-51, 360, 365-7, 369, 373, 434, 436
Saito, General, 338
Salazar, Lieutenant Colonel Chester J., 206, 250
Samar, 427
Samoa, 105, 110
San Clemente Island, 46, 52, 268
San Juan, 152
Sansapoor, 307
Santa Cruz, 93-5
Santa Cruz Islands, Battle of, 152, 159
Saratoga, 32, 106, 115, 142, 145, 161, 182, 450, 506
Savannah, 70
Savo Island, Battle of, 77, 118, 129-31, 134, 150, 154-5
Schmidt, Major General Harry, 267-9, 274-5, 281-2, 348-9, 354-5, 358, 360, 432, 435-6, 439, 441-3, 449-50, 453-4, 457-8, 463, 470, 481, 489, 492, 495, 499, 501-2, 504-5, 526, 528-30
Schoettel, Major John F., 240
Scott, Rear Admiral Norman, 147, 160
Seabees, 60, 398-9, 452, 520
Seeadler Harbor, 307
Sendai Division (Japanese), 139, 147, 150-2, 156, 159, 162
Seventh Fleet, 423-4
Seventh Amphibious Force, 167
Shepherd, Major General Lemuel C. Jr., 374, 383, 538, 549, 571, 575
Sherman, Rear Admiral Frederick C., 182-3, 201
Sherrod, Robert, 184, 201, 238, 481
Sherwood, Robert, 9
Shibasaki, Rear Admiral Meichi, 236, 243
ship-to-shore movement, 41, 54, 335ff., 368, 386, 478, 557, 584
Sho-Go operation, 423, 430
shore party units, 64, 66, 128, 179, 185, 520, 522, 525, 573; see also pioneers
Shortlands, 142-3
Shoup, David M., 205-6, 210, 236, 238, 240-6, 248, 250
Shuri, 543, 546-7

INDEX

Shuri Castle, 540, 548, 570
Siberia, 199
Sicily, 67, 70
Singapore, 304
"Sleepless Lagoon," 149
Small, Rear Admiral Ernest G., 270
Smith, Rear Admiral Allan E., 505-6, 512
Smith, Major General Holland M., 22, 29, 59-60, 62-3, 65, 153, 193, 202-3, 205, 207, 210, 215-17, 220-1, 230, 243, 249, 254, 255, 257, 258, 261-2, 264, 266, 275, 278, 284, 288, 291-2, 302, 315-6, 318, 320, 322-3, 327-8, 330, 337-40, 342, 344, 345, 347, 349-50, 352, 354, 360, 371-2, 385, 435-6, 439, 441, 443, 446, 450, 453, 457, 464, 488-9, 507-8, 528, 530
Smith, Major General Julian C., 204-8, 210, 212, 216-8, 220, 228, 230, 233, 236, 238, 241-8, 250, 262, 393-4
Smith, Brigadier General Oliver P., 406
Smith, Major General Ralph C., 203, 323, 339, 342-7
smoke screen, 77
Solomon Islands, 57, 74, 79, 80, 83, 86-9, 92-4, 96-9, 101, 103-5, 107-11, 113-4, 116, 118-9, 122, 128, 131, 134-6, 138, 141-2, 152, 154-5, 157, 159, 162, 165-6, 168, 170-5, 177, 181, 183-4, 190, 201, 204, 308, 398
Solomons, Battle of the Eastern, 142
Solomon Sea, 80, 90-2, 97, 182, 185
South China Sea, 199
South Dakota, 152, 161
South Pacific Area, 87-8, 92-3, 108, 114, 128, 153, 157, 168, 305, 392
Southwest Pacific Area, 87-9, 92, 94-5, 112, 129, 163, 167, 185, 194, 253, 580
Special Service Squadron, 46
"spider webs," 485
spotting, 50
Spruance, Admiral Raymond A., 106-7, 115, 153, 193, 200, 202-3, 211, 214-5, 220, 255, 257, 260-2, 269-70, 291-2, 294, 316, 318, 329, 331, 345, 349, 354, 372-3, 401, 432, 435-6, 440, 442-6, 448-50, 466, 474, 534, 554, 587
Stanley Mountains, 167
star shells, 302, 333, 382, 416
Stilwell, General Joseph W., 578
Strategic Air Force, 534
strategy, 303
submarines, 303, 580
Sugar Loaf Hill, 546-8
suicide boats, 535
Sulva Bay, 20
Sunharon Bay, 352
supplies, 133-4; *see also* logistics
Suribachi, 439, 452, 455, 469, 475-6, 480-1, 485, 488*ff*., 513, 516, 528
"Suribachi Screamer," 497

Sutherland, Major General Richard K., 305-6
Swindler, Colonel Leland S., 525

tactical by-passing, 285
Tanambogo, 57
Tanapag, 311
Tanapag Harbor, 320, 367
tank dozers, 577
tank lighters, 55, 57, 60, 64, 188
tanks, 55, 61, 68, 124, 141, 146, 173, 181, 238, 242, 247-8, 252, 297, 299, 349, 370, 398, 456, 461-2, 484-5, 488, 516, 540, 575-7; *see also* flamethrowing tanks
Tarawa, 11, 67, 83, 191-252, 262, 288, 302, 330, 581, 584
Task Force 58, 318, 445-8, 471, 475, 507
Tassafaronga, Battle of, 158, 162
Tassafaronga Point, 149, 150
Tawi-Tawi, 304
Taylor, Rear Admiral Montgomery, 31
Tenaru River, 132, 151
Tenaru River, Battle of, 140-1, 165
Tennessee, 331, 470
Tentative Manual for Landing Operations, 36-44, 46, 51, 52, 64
tetryol charges, 556
Texas, 58, 470
Third Fleet, 424, 426, 434
Thunderbolt (P-47), 565, 567
Tinian Harbor, 356
Tinian Island, 67, 310-11, 315, 317-9, 329, 351-71, 432, 434, 436, 510
Tinian Town, 358-60
Tiyan Field, 378
Tojo, 310
Tokyo, 79, 390, 443, 445, 447-8
Tokyo Express, 136, 148, 159
Tongatabu, 105
Torokina Point, 180, 183
Training, 46, 453-64; *see also* **Marine Corps Schools**
Treasury Islands, 177
"Troop Barge A," 31
Truk, 45, 97, 107, 116, 119, 147, 159, 193, 199, 201, 252-3, 270, 292, 294, 303-4, 306-9, 315
Tulagi, 7, 80, 93-5, 98-9, 101, 103-12, 114, 119-24, 127, 131-3, 135, 146, 153-5, 222
Turkey, 17, 19
Turnage, Major General Allen H., 179, 374, 383
Turner, Rear Admiral Richmond Kelley, 107-9, 112-17, 124, 126, 128-30, 145, 149-50, 153-8, 160, 163, 168, 175, 202-3, 215-6, 229, 255, 257-8, 262, 263, 265-6, 284, 292, 301, 316, 318-9, 327-8, 330-1, 345, 354, 371-2, 393, 435-6, 440-4, 446, 462, 474, 486, 510, 523, 528, 530, 553, 554, 561, 587

Ulithi Atoll, 410, 429, 431, 447, 466, 555
Umurbrogol Mountains, 407-9, 411, 414, 421
Underhill, Brigadier General James L., 267, 269, 272, 275
Underwater swimmers, 469; *see also* demolition squads
United Nations, 590
Ushijima, Lieutenant General Mitsuru, 539-40, 544, 546, 548, 550-1, 575
Ushi Point, 355, 362, 368

Vandegrift, Major General Alexander A., 4, 9, 11, 109-10, 114-17, 119-22, 124, 126, 129, 131-3, 135-7, 139, 141, 143, 145-6, 148-51, 153-9, 162-3, 165, 172, 176-81, 183, 235, 507
Vella Lavella, 168, 170, 174-5, 177, 182
Versailles, Treaty of, 24
Vicksburg, 470
Vincennes, 130
Vitiaz Strait, 167-8, 175
Vogel, Major General Clayton B., 62-3, 170, 175
Vogelkop Peninsula, 307, 392

Wainwright, Major General Jonathan, 79
Wake Island, 74-9, 133, 197-8, 270, 291, 294
Wallace, Colonel William J., 134
Washington, 161
Washington Conference of 1921–22, 10

Wasp, 106, 114, 145
Watson, Major General Thomas J., 52, 292-3, 296, 298, 301, 337
Wavell, General Sir Archibald, 83
"weasles," 515, 521-3
Weller, Major Donald M., 71, 441, 502-3, 512
Wellington, 168, 203, 205
Wensinger, Colonel Walter W., 481
Western Island Attack Group (Navy), 535
Wilkinson, Rear Admiral Theodore S., 168, 175, 177
Wilkinson, Vice Admiral Thomas F., 393
Williams, Major Dion, 23
Williams, Major Robert H., 120
Willson, Vice Admiral Russell, 305
Withers, Colonel Hartnoll J., 491
Whaling, Colonel William J., 138
Wharton, 59-60
Wornham, Colonel Thomas A., 480
Wotje, 193, 254, 256

X-ray Provisional Amphibious Corps, 393-4

Yamamota, Admiral Isoroku, 80, 152
Yap, 308, 402
Yontan Field, 538, 567-8
Yubari, 77

Zamboanga, 428
Zero, 76, 82, 136-7, 171